University Centre
Barnsley

Telephone: 01226 216 884

This book is to be returned on or before the last
date stamped below. Thank you!

YEAH YEAH YEAH

The Story of Modern Pop

BOB STANLEY

faber and faber

First published in 2013
by Faber and Faber Limited
Bloomsbury House
74–77 Great Russell Street
London WC1B 3DA

Typeset by Ian Bahrami
Printed in the UK by CPI Group (UK) Ltd, Croydon CR0 4YY

A CIP record for this book
is available from the British Library

ISBN 978–0–571–28197–8

2 4 6 8 10 9 7 5 3 1

For Tessa

CONTENTS

INTRODUCTION

I remember reading about a kid, twelve or thirteen years old, who used to spend Saturday mornings lurking in the Vintage Record Centre on Roman Way in North London. He would watch the old Teds and the young rockabillies, the dandified fifties revivalists and the single middle-aged men walk through the door, thumb through the racks, and all ask for the same record: 'Do you have "Cast Iron Arm" by Peanuts Wilson?' The answer was always no. The kid was in awe of this record. It must, he figured, be the best record ever made. What could it sound like? Who was Peanuts Wilson? Why was the arm made of cast iron? This would have been in the mid-seventies and there was no way he could find out the answers to these questions, or even get to hear the record because it was so rare, and so in demand. He dreamed about it, tried to imagine how it might sound: harder than 'Hound Dog', sharper than 'Summertime Blues'. For this kid, in its magical elusiveness, 'Cast Iron Arm' embodied the wonder of pop music.

In the twenty-first century anyone can type the name Peanuts Wilson into YouTube or Spotify or iTunes and hear 'Cast Iron Arm', with its honking sax, comic interludes and thunking backbeat. The same goes for the rarest British hard-rock album, *Growers of Mushroom* by Leaf Hound. Or 'Carry Me Home', a still unreleased Beach Boys outtake from their *Holland* album. This wasn't possible in the pre-digital age, when information was passed around pop fans via music papers and radio shows, fanzines, cassettes and word of mouth – analogue technology, airwaves, printing presses, everything in perpetual motion. Before the arrival of Napster in 2000, the gateway for iTunes, it had been this way for the best part of five decades: this was the modern pop era.

There have been many great music books written since 2000, on genres, micro-genres, single albums, even single songs. But there hasn't, as far as I'm aware, been a book on the whole of modern pop's development, none to explain when and why things happened, the connections, the splinters, what has been lost or forgotten along the way.

My intention with *Yeah Yeah Yeah* is to give the reader a feel for pop's development as it happened, by drawing a straight line – with the odd wiggle and personal diversion – from the birth of the seven-inch single to the decline of pop music as a palpable, physical thing in the nineties. Chronologically, I will explore how each new era brought with it new icons and iconoclasts, the arrival and excitement of hot sounds, and how, when they began to cool off, several different styles developed and myriad subgenres were created.

From the fifties to the nineties, pop was personal and private. You could live in its wider world but also shape it to your own ends by amassing a collection of vinyl, making tapes of singles in the order you wanted to hear them, then passing on the secret to fellow travellers. I had exercise books in which I'd write down the new Top 20 every Tuesday: at 12.45 we'd have the radio on at school, and friends huddled together to find out whether the heroic Altered Images had dislodged the dreadful Dave Stewart and Barbara Gaskin from the top of the chart. It was a religion. I didn't feel the need to go to church.

My first published work was in a fanzine called *Pop Avalanche* in 1986. I sent a copy to the *New Musical Express* and they sent me off to review a Johnny Cash show in Peterborough. Since 1990, I've been fortunate enough to see the pop world from both sides, as a fan, a writer, and also as a member of a pop group: I was twenty-five when Saint Etienne started, and we had the remarkable good fortune to appear on *Top of the Pops*, on the cover of the *NME* and on stage around the world. For the last dozen years I have written for *The Times* and the *Guardian*, which has given me the opportunity to interview stars and – equally important to me – to shine some light on records, singers, writers and producers who I thought were undeservedly obscure.

This book picks up the threads that connect doo wop, via Philly soul, to house music, or – possibly less obviously – ones that link Johnny Duncan's 'Last Train to San Fernando' to the Buzzcocks' 'Boredom' to the Prodigy's 'Everybody in the Place'. I want to give a sense of how the web was woven. Where does Frankie Lymon fit in? More to the point, in a world where Nick Drake is considerably better known than Fairport Convention, how were both perceived at the time, and how did they affect pop's climate? Chronologically, I explore how the technology not only interacts with music, but helps to start the era (the portable record player), then kill it (the compact disc as Trojan horse), and how modern pop was built up by communication, the distribution of information, the secret world of music papers and fanzines, late-night or illegal radio broadcasts, and stolen moments on TV shows.

I wanted to write this book because there is no such guide. I wanted to argue that the separation of rock and pop is false, and that disco and large swathes of black and electronic music have been virtually ignored by traditional pop histories. This situation has changed considerably since Saint Etienne formed in 1990, though rockism still exists, and snobbery is still rife. At the other extreme, some purists don't think of albums as pop at all, but I'm not going to be a seven-inch fascist – albums were an essential part of modern pop's development.

What exactly is pop? For me, it includes rock, R&B, soul, hip hop, house, techno, metal and country. If you make records, singles and albums, and if you go on TV or on tour to promote them, you're in the pop business. If you sing a cappella folk songs in a pub in Whitby, you're not. Pop needs an audience that the artist doesn't know personally – it has to be transferable. Most basically, anything that gets into the charts is pop, be it Buddy Holly, Black Sabbath or Bucks Fizz. So, Laurie Anderson's 'O Superman' is pop music (UK no. 2 in 1981), as is Waldo de los Ríos's 'Mozart No. 40' (UK no. 5 '71), and the Marcels' 'Blue Moon' (UK and US no. 1 '61). The charts are vital social history. It is much harder to recover the menacing impact of 'Be-Bop-a-Lula' or future shock of 'I Feel Love' without hearing them alongside contemporary hits: the former shared a chart with Mel Tormé's 'Mountain Greenery' and Ted Heath's 'The Faithful Hussar'; the latter entered the chart sandwiched between Alessi's 'Oh Lori' and the Muppets' 'Halfway down the Stairs'. Context is everything.

What creates great pop? Tension, opposition, progress and fear of progress. I love the tensions between the industry and the underground, between artifice and authenticity, between the adventurers and the curators, between rock and pop, between dumb and clever, between boys and girls. A permanent state of flux informed the modern pop era and taking sides is part of the fun. Some saw punk, for instance, as a way of rewriting the rules completely, as the Futurists had done in art, while others read 1977 as a return to roots, the excitement of first-wave rock 'n' roll revisited. Both sides had a strong case. On the one hand you had Malcolm McLaren's Debord-quoting art-school insurrection; on the other you had the Clash and Joe Strummer's 'cut the crap' ideology. In pop, the conservative can be seen as cool. But pop music isn't there to be contained. It isn't school – it only has unwritten rules, and they're all there to be broken. The energy and insight of pop comes from juggling its contradictions rather than purging them. Queen may have proudly printed 'no synthesizers' on their first few album covers, suggesting they were all rock, no artifice, but when they changed their minds in 1980 for 'Another One Bites the Dust' it gave them an international number one, and became an early source for hip-hop samples; pop moved forward and everyone was happy.

So is modern pop just chart music? Well, partly, as the magic of the charts is that they can be perfect time capsules, and can cover all pop genres with no favouring the hip or the entitled, the homebodies or the voyagers. Yet the charts did not always reflect emerging movements. Instead, the new music would percolate, inspire and – eventually – burst into the chart at a later date: the UK's chart stats don't bear out the influence of the Velvet Underground (one UK Top 10 hit for Lou Reed), or Marvin Gaye's *What's Going On* (none of the four singles from it even reached the Top 50), or the Smiths (none of their singles went any higher than number ten). It may seem contradictory to write about the hitless Johnny Burnette Trio or the Stooges or Minor Threat or Juan Atkins in this book, but they emerged in the modern pop era and their influence on it, and the music of the future, is undeniable. Outliers get absorbed into the mainstream. Pop is a decades-long love affair. Opposites attract.

When did the modern pop era start? In 1952, as I will soon explain. The end point is more complicated; the start of the digital age is much blurrier, and the tail-off is gradual. I'm using the end of vinyl as pop's main format as a line in the sand. When Culture Beat's 'Mr Vain' reached number one in the UK in 1993, it was the first chart-topper since Lita Roza's '(How Much Is) That Doggie in the Window' in 1953 not to have been issued on a seven-inch single; soon after 'Mr Vain' came the first number one not available on vinyl at all, only CD and cassette – Celine Dion's 'Think Twice' in February '95.

This book is not meant to be an encyclopedia; I believe in the myth and legend of pop as much as anyone who grew up on *TOTP*, the *NME* and *Smash Hits*, the histories and half-truths about Gene Vincent, Arthur Lee, David Bowie or Agnetha Fältskog that made it so constantly thrilling. I love the flash and glory of pop's superstars, whether it's the Beatles hurtling down the platform at Marylebone station to avoid screaming fans, or a quick glimpse of Kylie's knickers on stage.

I love the underdog equally – Lou Christie and his almost forgotten falsetto that made Frankie Valli sound like Johnny Cash – and the bit-part players, the backroom staff, the hack writers, and the ham-radio nerds who end up as engineers: Joe Meek, Giorgio Moroder, Rodney Jerkins, studio-bound characters like Derrick May, Martin Hannett and Holland/Dozier/Holland. And John Carter, the soft-spoken Brummie songwriter who could switch from Eurovision entries (Mary Hopkin's 'Knock, Knock Who's There', UK no. 2 '70), to garage bubblegum (the Music Explosion's 'Little Bit of Soul', US no. 2 '67), and then write the all-time summer anthem in First Class's 'Beach Baby'. Some say it's just ersatz Beach Boys. Not me. I think it is the work of a committed pop fan, wanting to give something back, trying to amplify his love of the Beach Boys.

There are so many connections which can be lost in the fractured, static nature of the digital age; without record labels to give us the names of writers and producers to study, without record shops or fanzines to filter endless information, we are less likely to find the obvious connections that run through modern pop. Listening to Amy Winehouse's 'Tears Dry on Their Own' on iTunes we wouldn't know that she samples Marvin Gaye and Tammi Terrell's 'Ain't No Mountain High Enough'. Or that this song was written by Motown staffers Nick Ashford and Valerie Simpson, who went on to write Chaka Khan's 'I'm Every Woman' and their own hit 'Solid' (US no. 12, UK no. 3 '84) but had previously worked for New York's Scepter/Wand labels, where they wrote for ex-beauty queen and early soul pioneer Maxine Brown. Or that Scepter/Wand initially made its money from girl group the Shirelles, whose first major hit was 'Will You Love Me Tomorrow' (US no. 1, UK no. 3 '60), and who were also favourites of Amy Winehouse. We have to know where music has come from in order to understand where it's at and where it could be heading. This book is a framework, and hopefully it will lead you to discover plenty of new favourites and new inspirations.

PROLOGUE

Britain and America were two very different worlds in the early fifties, with two very different pop cultures. 1945 had been the year in which the twentieth century had truly become the American century: the USA was the only country to emerge from the war stronger than it had been in 1939, with the Depression a distant memory, and the Marshall Plan had enabled it to enrich and rebuild future allies (Germany, Japan, Turkey), while cocking a snook at potential rivals (Great Britain). American and British cultures had thrillingly intersected – and clashed – during the war, when ordinary Britons were both dazzled by handsome GIs stationed in London, Newport, Southampton and Suffolk, and also appalled by the fact of segregation. Pre-war there had been little cultural overlap; post-war, the countries separated again, but that brief encounter played on their memories.

Bombed-out Britain, at the turn of the fifties, looked to America for inspiration, and to Hollywood and Broadway for entertainment. It would have found a fair amount of dirt on the edges of American popular culture after the war: big-circulation magazines packaged prostitution, rape and violence as entertainment in short stories on the Wild West, which Hollywood then mined for its cowboy movies; film noir, a yet-to-be-christened genre, was equally charged, crime-ridden and rich in sin. After all, one and all had just been at war and seen some very terrible things.*

But mainstream American popular music was quite dissimilar. Post-war and pre-rock 'n' roll, it conformed to a Macy's Thanksgiving Day

---

* One infamous post-war reaction to peacetime was the 1947 biker riot in Hollister, California, where ex-soldiers hopped up on speed were looking for the kinds of excitement and camaraderie they had found in the war. Amphetamines had been standard issue in the US army – this would later have grave consequences for modern pop's first superstar, Elvis Presley.

Parade aesthetic, which British writers and performers aspired to mimic. Prior to the war the pop charts in *Billboard*, America's trade magazine for the music industry, had been very urban and very white, and – on the surface – nothing much had changed by the early fifties.

Britain, on the other hand, was a musical backwater – variety shows, summer seasons in seaside resorts, state-run radio, virtually no TV – and it had none of the pop pretensions which would see it rise in the sixties. It sucked up everything America provided, with little knowledge of the upheavals that were affecting 'the home of modern popular music'.

To try and understand the beginnings of the modern pop era better, we have to dig back a little and explore the major changes that had occurred in American popular music in the forties. During the war there had been two strikes in America – both for an increase in royalties – which had significant long-term consequences. The first, by the American Society of Composers, Authors and Publishers (ASCAP) in 1941, blocked any of the organisation's songs from being played on the radio, a gift to rival set-up BMI (Broadcast Music Incorporated). ASCAP was home to established songwriters like Irving Berlin, Cole Porter, Johnny Mercer and Sammy Cahn, ones who could both read and write music. BMI looked to the future, away from sheet music, and its copyrights were largely of jazz, blues and country music, which ASCAP had effectively boycotted. Jazz pianist Bobby Troup wrote 'Daddy',* a number one in 1941 for big-band leader Sammy Kaye which Kaye would likely never have recorded if ASCAP hadn't been on strike. It was also possible to record ancient, out-of-copyright music: in January '41 *Time* magazine reported how 'the airwaves gave off strange sounds last week. Ray Noble's magnificent band was reduced to rendering a super-syncopated version of "Camptown Races", followed by "Liebestraum" in rumba time.' Another surreal result of the ban was a string of foreign songs – also beyond ASCAP copyright – reaching the chart: Jimmy Dorsey's 'Amapola', Artie Shaw's 'Frenesi' and Glenn

---

* Bobby Troup later wrote 'Route 66', associated with both Nat King Cole and the Rolling Stones, and produced Julie London's exquisite 'Cry Me a River' (US no. 9 '56, UK no. 22 '57). London was so impressed with his work that she married Troup in 1961.

Miller's 'Song of the Volga Boatmen' were all US number ones in 1941. These were new flavours and ingredients for American pop music which would continue to inform it long after the strike ended: major hits of 1950, for instance, included Anton Karas's 'Harry Lime Theme' from the Vienna-set movie *The Third Man*, Vaughn Monroe's hushed, eerie and exotic 'Bamboo', and the Weavers' version of Leadbelly's folk-blues song 'Goodnight Irene'.

As if the ASCAP ban hadn't shaken up the American music industry enough, a 1942 strike by the US musicians' union led to a ban on all recording. Live performances were still allowed, but no new records could be made. Record companies quickly realised that the strike didn't apply to singers, just musicians, so they put together vocal groups who sang a cappella backing behind stars such as the Tommy Dorsey band's Frank Sinatra. Singers remained in the public eye, while musicians were reduced to making a living from public performances. In the swing era – the big-band years from 1935 to 1945 – the singers had usually taken second billing to the band leaders; when the musicians' union finally negotiated settlements with the record companies, they found that the popularity of the bands had been largely eclipsed by their vocalists.*

The decline of the big band had an even more dramatic effect on American radio, where 'disc jockeys' – a term first used as an insult by *Variety* magazine in 1941 – began to replace live on-air music. This was down to simple economics (a live band cost a lot more to employ than one man with a stack of records) and also the rise of small local

---

* Les Baxter was a fascinating exception. He had been tenor-sax player with Artie Shaw and vocal arranger for Mel Tormé's Mel-Tones, before he put together a small band in 1947 with novel instrumentation – 'a cello, a French horn, a theremin, a rhythm section and a twelve-voice choir' – for Harry Revel's ten-inch album *Music out of the Moon*. 'It was a little weird,' he confessed. 'I didn't know what popular records were. I wanted to be innovative.' He then split his career into adventurous self-composed albums like *Ritual of the Savage* (1951) and pleasant but straightforward arrangements for singles which resulted in US number-one hits – Nat King Cole's 'Too Young' (1951), his own 'Unchained Melody' (1955) and 'Poor People of Paris' (1956), none of which he wrote. The one record which jumped the fence was Martin Denny's 'Quiet Village' (US no. 4 '59), a Baxter-written Tiki-influenced instrumental which became the touchstone for the 'exotica' revival in the nineties.

stations after the war. The biggest influence in this shift from live music to records was a man called Martin Block. At WNEW in New York, Block had started a programme in 1935 called *Make Believe Ballroom*, entirely made up of his record collection. On air, he would read out facts about each record from *Billboard* and *Variety* – before Block, radio announcers had only read out the titles in stern newsreader voices.* He also ad-libbed commercials to four million listeners, which began to earn WNEW a lot of revenue. Block's airplay alone could create a hit record.† He syndicated his show nationwide in 1948, the year in which the transistor was invented, making the portable transistor radio possible and taking music out of the house and onto the street.

By the late forties the popularity of Block's show had sparked a whole industry – radio advertising – exemplified by the jingle. America was almost unique in seeing radio, from its inception in the twenties, as a purely commercial enterprise rather than as a government tool. As catchy jingles became more prevalent, the records played between them began to sound similarly perky – Teresa Brewer's 'Music Music Music', the first US number one of the fifties, could have worked just as well if it had been used as a Lucky Strike jingle. In other words, the jingles drove radio; records were largely there to fill the space in between.‡

* Block had borrowed both the name and concept of *Make Believe Ballroom* from a DJ called Al Jervis on KFWB in Hollywood, where Block had been an assistant.
† An appearance on TV had far less impact. In the late forties TV shows were in their infancy; they were basically flat reproductions of radio shows, and did little to help sell records – compare staid clips of Kay Starr singing 'Wheel of Fortune' on TV in 1952 to the gorgeous, Technicolor musical scenes from *Singin' in the Rain* the same year. What's more, having your own TV variety show effectively meant you became a host, and were no longer a pop star. Dinah Shore discovered this in 1950; Cliff Richard, Cilla Black and Glen Campbell would later. The impact of TV would change dramatically in the late fifties and it would take a Briton, Jack Good, to draw its full pop potential.
‡ Another reason for the change in the way pop music sounded was the decline of Broadway. It had been a solid provider of hit songs since the twenties, but took a steep drop in popularity in the early fifties. This must have seemed unlikely in 1950, when the new season brought Rodgers and Hammerstein's *The King and I* ('Getting to Know You', 'Shall We Dance'), Frank Loesser's *Guys and Dolls* ('If I Were a Bell', 'A Bushel and a Peck') and Irving Berlin's *Call Me Madam* ('You're Just in Love'), giving us a fresh clutch of standards. In 1951, though, all the new

Most countries in Europe saw radio as a means of broadcasting educational material or propaganda, and the BBC's three channels – the Home Service (which started in 1939), the Light Programme (1945) and the Third Programme (1946) – had a monopoly in Britain; pop music barely existed. Among the few music shows on the Light Programme in 1952 was *Those Were the Days*: Harry Davidson's Orchestra played old-time dance music, and the live studio audience were invited to do the Boston two-step, the palais glide and the empress tango; the show had all the excitement of a warm cup of squash next to Martin Block's Coke float and root beer. The more free-spirited Jack Jackson presented *Record Roundup*, which ran from 1948 to 1977; he would punctuate records with clips he had pre-recorded onto tape, which made him the first British DJ to mix sound, speech and comedy.*

An alternative was provided by Radio Luxembourg. It was the duchy's national station, set up in 1929; unlike the BBC it was a commercial enterprise, and so it aimed to maximise its listenership and, in turn, its advertising revenue. From 1934 it started a regular schedule of English-language radio transmissions to Britain and Ireland from eight-fifteen in the mornings until midnight on Sundays, and at various times during the rest of the week. Programmes were recorded in London and flown out to be broadcast from Luxembourg. The station came into its own after the war – from autumn 1948, on Sunday nights when the BBC restricted itself to religious and heavyweight topics, Luxembourg played the Top 20 songs on the 'hit parade', based on sheet-music sales, beginning a British tradition that continues to this day.†

Broadway shows lost money. What happened? Possibly the cold war helped to foster a bunker mentality, with people happier staying at home with their new televisions, wireless radios and gramophones. What's more, those radios would no longer have had live broadcasts by big bands playing the current Broadway hits, as they had done for the last twenty-odd years, and so a vital strand of publicity for shows was lost. The next big hit – 1954's *The Pajama Game* – was quickly made into a film before the trail went cold.

* When BBC Radio 1 started in 1967, Jackson was still around, and was referred to by Kenny Everett as 'the daddy of all disc jockeys'.

† The very first Top 20 countdown signature tune, pre-dating *Pick of the Pops*' 'At the Sign of the Swinging Cymbal' (Brian Fahey) and *Top of the Pops*' 'Whole

At the turn of the fifties there was still food rationing in Britain, and very little money for any kind of reconstruction. Everywhere there were bomb sites, physical reminders of terrible trauma. 1951 saw the Festival of Britain open on London's semi-derelict South Bank, an exhibition of design, architecture and technology notable for its vivid colour, its modernism and its newness. After the festival closed, Britain was desperate to build on its success and spirit.

In November '52 EMI launched the first 45s, and pop's truest format – the firewood for future youth clubs, mobile discos and furtive fumbles at teenage parties – was born.* The forty-five-revolutions-per-minute single was pressed on vinyl rather than the fragile, brittle shellac which had been used for 78s, the main recorded-music format for more than thirty years. Vinyl, boasted the sleeves of the earliest EMI singles, was 'unbreakable' – it was lighter than shellac, too, and its microgrooves gave a much clearer, louder sound than 78s. Vinyl was also more portable, and hence more sociable. Twelve-inch vinyl albums, around since the late forties, were initially for adults:† the

---

Lotta Love' (CCS), was 'Doodletown Fifers' by the Sauter-Finegan Band on Radio Luxembourg.

* Britain was one step removed from America, the birthplace of vinyl – the 33 rpm, twelve-inch long-playing record and the 45 rpm, seven-inch single. This meant Britain didn't have to worry about the fraught and complex process that had gone into creating these formats: Columbia had first produced the LP in 1948 and RCA the seven-inch single in '49 – both also made the machines on which the discs were played and, for some time, they refused to compromise and were at each other's throats trying to win the 'battle of the speeds'. Columbia called the 45 'unorthodox'; RCA's David Sarnoff countered, 'I challenge . . . anybody in the world to demonstrate that a seven-inch 33⅓ record can produce the same kind of quality that a seven-inch 45 rpm record can and does produce'. *New York Times* critic Howard Taubman, writing in 1950, conceded that Sarnoff was right, but that the LP was better for 'sheer listening comfort and continuity of performances'. The LP, initially, was perfect for classical music, and the 45 for pop.

† 33 rpm records were designed for longer music – expressly, classical symphonies – and hence had one kind of cultural value embedded. 'Albums', up to this point, had meant leaved or boxed collections of several 78s, like a stamp or photo album. So a 33 rpm long-player (or LP) was actually a replacement for the album, a whole that had previously been necessarily but awkwardly divided up on several shellac 78s, each side of which had a maximum playing time of roughly five minutes. The terminology remained, with 'LP' and 'album' interchangeable.

cheaper, handier, less precious seven-inch would become the property of the teenager. EMI tentatively issued classical-only 45s at first,
but they quickly realised the three- or four-minute playing time was
much better suited to pop. EMI was the parent company to four pop
labels – HMV, Columbia, Parlophone and MGM – and in January '53
they issued, respectively, Eddie Fisher's 'I'm Yours', Ray Martin's 'Blue
Tango', Humphrey Lyttelton's 'Out of the Galleon' and Judy Garland
and Mickey Rooney's 'A Couple of Swells' as their opening shots; by
the end of 1953 EMI had issued close to three hundred 45 rpm titles,
and the raw materials for a revolution were in place.

Locking down seven-inch singles as a youth format, the portable
Dansette record player was registered as a trademark in October 1952.
Prior to this, record players were literally pieces of furniture, oak or
mahogany, heavy and expensive; the radiogram, with its combined
gramophone and wireless, was the size of a fridge. Until the fifties, electrical goods were classed as either 'white' (washing machines, fridges)
or 'brown' (televisions, radios, gramophones). The Dansette was manufactured at a factory on Old Street in London's East End; reflecting the
primary colours of the Festival of Britain, it came in vivid red, blue,
green, cream or pink leatherette. As the fifties progressed, the owner
of the Dansette company, Samuel Margolin, was sharp enough to listen to teenagers, and he designed exactly what they wanted. He added
an auto-changer, which meant singles could be stacked in a pile; Elvis
would automatically be followed by Pat Boone or Duane Eddy, lined up
and ready to be dropped automatically onto the turntable. The Dansette
was party perfect.

America provided another building block of the modern pop world.
The first magazine for teenagers, *Seventeen*,* had been launched in 1944;
though it was primarily aimed at girls and featured little on music, it
was a start. In Britain, the only magazine to feature pop in 1952 was

---

* *Seventeen*'s first editorial set out the terms for a youthquake: 'You're going to
have to run this show – so the sooner you start thinking about it, the better. In a
world that is changing as quickly and profoundly as ours is, we hope to provide a
clearing house for your ideas.' Those ideas took a good few years to filter through,
but it was a launchpad. The magazine still exists today.

Picturegoer, which – as the name suggests – was primarily about movies. The record reviews were sniffy about anything beyond Sinatra. Actress Janette Scott's 'Teen Page' revealed she was 'a bit of a disc fiend', though she had no time for 'criers and the arm-flappers and the rest . . . I know I'll raise a bit of a storm here but I'm not really wild about Frankie Laine and Johnnie Ray.'

Unlike Janette Scott, though, much of Britain was pop hungry, and in need of refreshment.

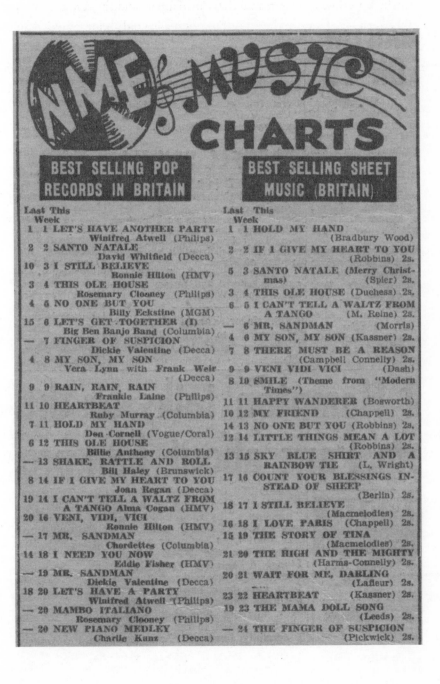

NME MUSIC CHARTS

BEST SELLING POP RECORDS IN BRITAIN

Last Week	This Week	
1	1	LET'S HAVE ANOTHER PARTY — Winifred Atwell (Philips)
2	2	SANTO NATALE — David Whitfield (Decca)
10	3	I STILL BELIEVE — Ronnie Hilton (HMV)
3	4	THIS OLE HOUSE — Rosemary Clooney (Philips)
4	5	NO ONE BUT YOU — Billy Eckstine (MGM)
15	6	LET'S GET TOGETHER (I) — Big Ben Banjo Band (Columbia)
—	7	FINGER OF SUSPICION — Dickie Valentine (Decca)
4	8	MY SON, MY SON — Vera Lynn with Frank Weir (Decca)
9	9	RAIN, RAIN, RAIN — Frankie Laine (Philips)
11	10	HEARTBEAT — Ruby Murray (Columbia)
7	11	HOLD MY HAND — Don Cornell (Vogue/Coral)
6	12	THIS OLE HOUSE — Billie Anthony (Columbia)
—	13	SHAKE, RATTLE AND ROLL — Bill Haley (Brunswick)
8	14	IF I GIVE MY HEART TO YOU — Joan Regan (Decca)
19	14	I CAN'T TELL A WALTZ FROM A TANGO — Alma Cogan (HMV)
20	16	VENI, VIDI, VICI — Ronnie Hilton (HMV)
—	17	MR. SANDMAN — Chordettes (Columbia)
14	18	I NEED YOU NOW — Eddie Fisher (HMV)
—	19	MR. SANDMAN — Dickie Valentine (Decca)
18	20	LET'S HAVE A PARTY — Winifred Atwell (Philips)
—	20	MAMBO ITALIANO — Rosemary Clooney (Philips)
—	20	NEW PIANO MEDLEY — Charlie Kunz (Decca)

BEST SELLING SHEET MUSIC (BRITAIN)

Last Week	This Week	
1	1	HOLD MY HAND (Bradbury Wood)
2	2	IF I GIVE MY HEART TO YOU (Robbins) 2s.
5	3	SANTO NATALE (Merry Christmas) (Spier) 2s.
3	4	THIS OLE HOUSE (Duchess) 2s.
6	5	I CAN'T TELL A WALTZ FROM A TANGO (M. Reine) 2s.
—	6	MR. SANDMAN (Morris)
4	6	MY SON, MY SON (Kassner) 2s.
7	8	THERE MUST BE A REASON (Campbell Connelly) 2s.
9	9	VENI VIDI VICI (Dash)
8	10	SMILE (Theme from "Modern Times")
11	11	HAPPY WANDERER (Bosworth)
10	12	MY FRIEND (Chappell) 2s.
14	13	NO ONE BUT YOU (Robbins) 2s.
12	14	LITTLE THINGS MEAN A LOT (Robbins) 2s.
13	15	SKY BLUE SHIRT AND A RAINBOW TIE (L. Wright)
17	16	COUNT YOUR BLESSINGS INSTEAD OF SHEEP (Berlin) 2s.
18	17	I STILL BELIEVE (Macmelodies) 2s.
16	18	I LOVE PARIS (Chappell) 2s.
15	19	THE STORY OF TINA (Macmelodies) 2s.
21	20	THE HIGH AND THE MIGHTY (Harms-Connelly) 2s.
20	21	WAIT FOR ME, DARLING (Lafleur) 2s.
23	22	HEARTBEAT (Kassner) 2s.
19	23	THE MAMA DOLL SONG (Leeds) 2s.
—	24	THE FINGER OF SUSPICION (Pickwick) 2s.

FEET UP: THE FIRST BRITISH HIT PARADE

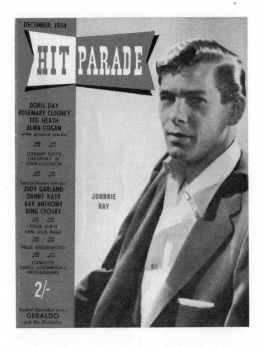

For Britain, the modern pop era began in 1952. Not only was it the year the first seven-inch singles were released, and the nation's most significant and longest-running music paper – the *New Musical Express* – was first published, but on November 14th the *NME* printed the first singles chart.* All three creations would become cornerstones of the pop world until their simultaneous decline in the nineties, as the digital era got into its stride. The singles chart in particular – or the 'hit parade' as it was called in the fifties, borrowing American terminology – had a special appeal to the British sensibility.

It meant competition, excitement in league-table form, pop music

* It was the idea of the *NME*'s Percy Dickins, who compiled it himself by obtaining sales figures from twenty record shops around the country. Initially, the chart was a Top 12, expanding to a Top 20 in 1955.

as a sport. It would pit Frankie Laine against Johnnie Ray, Blur against Oasis, Brits against Yanks, Decca against EMI; it would become fuel for a nation obsessed with train numbers and cricket statistics. The charts dictated what you heard on the radio, what you saw on TV, how high your heroes' stock had risen. For over four decades they would be a national fixture in Britain, like the FA Cup, like Christmas.

The barely documented years between 1945 and 1954 are pop's Dark Ages, invisible and obscure. If it's remembered at all, it's as a period of stagnation, a stop-gap between the swing era and the rock era, full of identikit balladeers, stars of their day who have all but vanished from collective memory. Tony Brent? Billie Anthony? Would anyone remember Eddie Fisher if he hadn't married so well and so often? Or Ruby Murray if her name hadn't become rhyming slang for the national dish? It's a period I find oddly attractive because of its persistent obscurity. Though the songs are largely forgotten, the first UK chart contained a mix of genres (country, ballads, instrumentals, film themes, exotic novelties, poster-boy pop) which would recur throughout the following decades. For Justin Timberlake, there was Johnnie Ray; for 'My Heart Will Go On', the theme from *High Noon*; for 'The Ketchup Song', see 'Cowpuncher's Cantata'.

All of these singles were released on shellac 78s – only Mario Lanza's 'Because You're Mine' was available in the shops on a seven-inch in November 1952, as EMI had just issued it as one of their very first 45 rpm singles. It is also notable how US-dominated the chart was, with only Vera Lynn, Max Bygraves and band leader Ray Martin from Britain.

Britain's inferiority complex was tangible, even when it tried to promote itself. The sleevenotes to Tony Brent's *Off Stage* album claimed he was 'above the local, in the international class; he is one of the few British vocalists who come within hailing distance of Sinatra or Cole'. Eddie Calvert, who scored a solitary US Top 10 hit in 1954, had similarly humble words printed on the back cover of *The Man with the Golden Trumpet*: 'At one time, not very long ago, the idea of a British musician making a record that would sell hundreds of thousands in the United States, the home of modern popular music, was in the nature of a fantasy.'

In 1952 Britain had little self-confidence, then, and no reason to believe it could compete with the likes of pert, blonde, virginal Doris Day, square-jawed cowboy Frankie Laine, Italian operatic import Mario Lanza or Bing Crosby, king of the crooners, and now twenty-odd years at the top. America was a country of conspicuous wealth and immaculately turned out stars of stage and screen; pockmarked Britain was still awaiting redevelopment seven years after the end of the war. Hollywood in 1952 meant Ava Gardner and Gregory Peck in *The Snows of Kilimanjaro*, and Gary Cooper as the ultimate good guy in *High Noon*; Gene Barry stirred up fears of unimaginable disaster in *The Atomic City*; Gene Kelly's *Singin' in the Rain* was the year's hit musical. Britain, meanwhile, had Michael Redgrave starring in an adaptation of Oscar Wilde's *The Importance of Being Earnest* – a great story and a fine movie, but really . . . The only hint of local danger came from bad girl Diana Dors, who starred as a thieving teenage seductress in *The Last Page*. There was no suggestion whatsoever of an imminent, and remarkable, convergence of British and American pop culture.

That was all yet to come. Let's try to picture pop music at the dawn of vinyl, in the days before rock 'n' roll, and see what we can learn from the very first hit parade. Though it was a Top 12, three positions were tied, and so the first chart featured fifteen singles.

1 Al Martino, 'Here in My Heart' (Capitol CL 13779)

The war had caused massive upheaval for the big bands that had dominated popular music in the thirties and forties. They had been decimated on three fronts: by individuals who had been called up and sometimes lost in service; by jazz's leftfield move into bop, which was hard to dance to (tempos were often too fast or too slow) and consequently had less mass appeal than swing; and by financial constraints. The fall in cinema attendances hurt, too – in the thirties and forties many bands had played in theatres before a movie, which had effectively subsidised their performance. The rise of television after the war put paid to this. There were fewer venues, and consequently less money, available – out of necessity bands became smaller, or simply split. By

1950 the better-known singers, rather than touring the country and playing theatres with a big band as they had done, now played in exclusive clubs; radio and TV presence aside, they became almost invisible to the general public.

The new breed of solo singer who benefited in the post-war, pre-rock era included the voluble Italian American Al Martino. 'Here in My Heart' was his very first single, released in America on a tiny Philadelphia label called BBS. He'd been a bricklayer and was injured at Iwo Jima in the war, but his dream was to emulate family friend Mario Lanza. He got his break in 1952, when he came first on Arthur Godfrey's *Talent Scouts*, singing Perry Como's 'If', a US number one from the previous year. 'Here in My Heart' went to number one in the States in June '52, he was quickly signed by Capitol, and it was issued in the UK on a 78, where it would spend nine weeks at number one – to date, only five singles have spent more weeks at the top.

You'd have expected Martino's career to be sustained, but his management contract was bought out by the mafia and he fled to Britain, where he headlined the London Palladium and had regular hits for the next couple of years (including the epically tortured 'Rachel', no. 10 '53). But the London Palladium wasn't Madison Square Garden. He returned to the US in 1960, scored a few more hits ('I Love You Because', US no. 3 '63) and later starred in *The Godfather*. He did OK, but nothing was on the same scale as 'Here in My Heart'.

Al Martino's instant fame was unusual and – coming via TV – something quite new. His British light-opera counterpart was David Whitfield. Aside from his navy years, Whitfield had never made it out of Hull, where he worked in the concrete business before obtaining a deal with Decca. His blubbing, rubbery voice would ordinarily have been thought laughable, a disgrace to opera and pop alike, but instead he became the best-selling British star of the era.

How did this happen? Whitfield looked like a grandfather while still in his mid-twenties. He was from one of Britain's dullest cities and had cement in his fingernails but, in pop, none of this mattered. What did matter was that Whitfield had entered the first *Opportunity Knocks* talent show on Radio Luxembourg, and won, which made him the godfather of an ignoble pop strand.* He was Britain's first Pop Idol, the original *X Factor* champion, and wasn't off the charts for four years, scoring two number ones and nine more Top 10 hits between 1953 and '57 by squashing Richard Tauber, religion and readymix sincerity into singles like 'The Book', 'Bridge of Sighs' and 'My September Love'. In 1954 his 'Cara Mia' was number one for ten weeks. The week it hit the top, food rationing finally ended. Little else could explain a rash national leap into the arms of 'Cara Mia' and its feeble Italianate promise: over-cooked spaghetti bolognese washed down with milky coffee. After so many battleship-grey years, this must have seemed exotic.† 'At home they used to say I was better than Tauber,' Whitfield said. 'Now the kids tear my clothes. I don't mind really. It comes off income tax, for a start.'

2 Jo Stafford, 'You Belong to Me' (Columbia DB 3152)

If the war had any positive effect on pop it was to create a desire to stretch beyond Anglo-American music hall and the big-band set-up. The British working classes had been sent to far-flung parts of the world and, while they may have had no desire to return to Burma, it meant they had come home with tales of mischief and freshness. This was reflected in a bunch of hits that had a foreign intrigue: 'Istanbul', 'West of Zanzibar', 'Cara Mia', 'Granada', 'Poor People of Paris'. They made no concessions to ethnic accuracy – Rosemary Clooney's 'Mambo Italiano' spoofed them neatly – but they scratched an itch we hadn't had before.

Best of the lot was 'You Belong to Me' by Jo Stafford, a gorgeous travelogue-cum-love song floating on a jetstream of marimbas. 'Fly

---

* *Opportunity Knocks* started as a radio show in 1949, moved to ITV in 1956 and stayed on the air until 1978. Listeners and viewers phoned in to vote for their favourite performer, who could be a comedian, a magician or a singing dog – the format survives as *Britain's Got Talent*. The show was referenced by George Harrison on the BBC TV show *Blackpool Night Out*, as the Beatles premiered 'Yesterday': 'For Paul McCartney of Liverpool, opportunity knocks!'
† Mantovani's atmospheric arrangement on 'Cara Mia', I should add, is something else. Genuinely celestial. If anyone with a degree of subtlety was singing, it would be quite a record.

the ocean in a silver plane, see the jungle when it's wet with rain.' The performance was cool, and worked a treat if you found restraint sexier than blatant emotionality. Her delivery was languid yet precise, and her pitching was perfect, but there was steel in her seduction: 'Send me photographs and souvenirs but just remember, when a dream appears, you belong to me.' You didn't mess with Jo.

She could have been singing to a high-flying executive – or maybe a representative of the newly formed United Nations – at the dawn of the jet age. Or her lover could have been a soldier. The music of 1952 was the music of the generation who had been in the war, and if some craved more of the same excitement and exotica, plenty craved calm, reserve and culture that hinted more than it blared. The later idea that modern pop was all about the spreading around of forbidden knowledge didn't really count in the decade after the war ended, when there was pretty good reason for people not to be sharing the things they'd learnt in the Pacific or in Europe.

3 Nat King Cole, 'Somewhere along the Way' (Capitol CL 13774)

In the pre-rock fifties, for the first time, pop records were produced rather than just recorded. The prime concern of recording engineers had always been to replicate a live recording as closely as possible; 1950 brought the first hit records that faded out (Teresa Brewer's 'Music Music Music', Bing Crosby's 'Mule Train', Frankie Laine's 'Cry of the Wild Goose'). This was a technique which had been used in films to cut between scenes and on lengthy jazz recordings that were split over two sides of a disc, but never had it been done just because it sounded good. The same year had produced Patti Page's 'Tennessee Waltz', on which 'the Singing Rage' was double-tracked, harmonising with herself. It was released on Mercury, whose head of A&R Mitch Miller was in favour of using the studio and its capabilities as an instrument in itself. Miller had been experimenting with overdubbing since 1948, but 'Tennessee Waltz' was an entirely new sound to most listeners and sold seven million copies. Guitarist Les Paul had previously double-tracked his playing on record; with his wife Mary Ford he went to town with overdubbing, both on their voices and his guitar, to create a string of atomic-age hits in the early fifties: 'How High the Moon', 'Mockingbird Hill', 'Vaya con Dios'.

'Somewhere along the Way' features an arrangement by Capitol Records' Nelson Riddle that plucks, sweeps and mourns beneath the despair of the singer. It's autumnal, and has moments of both stridency (the severity of the intro) and intimacy – at times it almost disappears completely. It's a full and remarkable production.

Nat King Cole had been a respected jazz pianist before switching to orchestrated ballads in the late forties, cutting a long string of records that were purpose-built to couch and caress his extraordinary voice. Whereas David Whitfield was keen for you to know that he was straining every sinew to get his point across, Cole had the knack of sounding as if he was ad-libbing songs as he went along. There is a richness to 'Somewhere along the Way', and his restraint is similar to Jo Stafford's, but Cole was rarely a seducer. Usually, he was to be found in the near distance, there to accompany the wooing of other couples ('When I Fall in Love', 'Let There Be Love') or to tell stories of other unfortunates and outsiders ('Ballerina', 'Nature Boy'), but he was at his most effective when he had lost in love, was resigned and melancholy. This was where his silvered but weary voice excelled: 'Pretend' (UK and US no. 2 '53), 'Smile' (US no. 10, UK no. 2 '54), 'A Blossom Fell' (US no. 2, UK no. 3 '55); ultimately, there was 'Stardust'.

'Somewhere along the Way' has the same sense of unforgettable loss as 'Stardust', the definitive Cole ballad from his 1957 album *Love Is the Thing*. Cole runs his fingers lightly down the keys, echoing the line 'I used to walk with you, along the avenue,' and in his delivery you hear the deep-blue sounds of Roy Orbison and Scott Walker to come. At one point the brushed drums and Riddle's understanding strings leave him alone at the piano, briefly, to sing, 'I should forget, but with the loneliness of night I start remembering . . . everything.' And in that last 'everything' there's despair, possibly lust, a whole relationship wrapped inside three syllables. There is also more than a suggestion of soul. As much as David Whitfield and Al Martino look backwards, right back to Caruso, 'Somewhere along the Way' looks forward, to Marvin Gaye, to Luther Vandross, to R. Kelly.

4 Bing Crosby, 'The Isle of Innisfree' (Brunswick 04900)

Bing Crosby had been the king of the singers since the late twenties, the man who'd made an art form out of crooning. On the American charts, he had accumulated 341 hits between 1931 and the release of 'The Isle of Innisfree' in 1952, yet this single didn't chart there at all and he would only have one more US Top 10 hit – 'True Love', a duet with Grace Kelly (UK no. 4, US no. 3 '56). Crosby had been the single biggest singing influence in pop before 1952, thanks to the advent of electronic recording, which had allowed his warm, gentle voice to be preserved on 78.

As Crosby approached fifty, a crop of younger singers were set to usurp their elder. There was the buttery Don Cornell ('Hold My Hand', UK no. 1, US no. 3 '54), the philandering Eddie Fisher ('Outside of Heaven' and 'I'm Walking Behind You', both UK no. 1 in '53), Al Martino's more mellow counterpart Dean Martin and, smoothest and most successful of all, Perry Como. Como had started out with the Ted Weems band in the early forties. He was a seventh son of a seventh son from Pennsylvania, and you couldn't make up how clean and good he was. Aged eleven he was helping out in the local barber shop to supplement the family income; by sixteen he had his own shop and sang to his customers. The barber of civility. By 1943 Como had a solo contract with RCA and was made for life, selling sixty million records in his own unhurried way, only quitting in the eighties. 'Magic Moments', 'Wanted', 'Idle Gossip', 'Catch a Falling Star' – his voice was downy and comforting, never excitable or exciting. He communicated security and a short back and sides, and he summed up the early fifties' friendly persuasion but also its lack of thrills, of any raw emotion. A 1956 poll claimed Como as America's ideal husband, but he was no one's ideal lover.

'The Isle of Innisfree' was a peculiar song. Irish ballads had been hits since the dawn of recorded music, there to provide a constant comfort, memories of the old world; they would remain an irregular chart presence right through to hits like the Fureys' 'When You Were Sweet Sixteen' (UK no. 14 '81). Verdant fields, village greens, tall oak trees

– their vision was defiantly non-urban. Bing had periodically recorded songs of old Ireland – 'Tobermory Bay', 'Danny Boy' and 'Galway Bay', the last of which had been number one in the UK sheet-music charts for twenty-two weeks in 1948 – and 'The Isle of Innisfree' similarly brims with nostalgia and the trauma of separation.

The catch is that Innisfree doesn't actually exist – William Butler Yeats created the utopian, fictional Lake Isle of Innisfree in an 1888 poem, and the song's author, Dick Farrelly, borrowed its imagery. So when Bing Crosby is singing from the heart of a city in which he can 'scarcely feel its wonder or its laughter', he is Billy Fisher, dreaming of Ambrosia, or Richard Brautigan's detective C. Card, adrift in his own Babylon. He isn't escaping into the fog of the past, but into an imaginary wonderland. Modern pop would likewise follow him into new utopian ports of pleasure: Brian Wilson created Surf City, with two girls for every boy; in 1967 the Who's dreamscape was Armenia City in the Sky ('If you're troubled and you can't relax, close your eyes and think of this'); Martha and the Muffins' Echo Beach was a new-wave escape route from the nine-to-five ('my job is very boring – I'm an office clerk'); Lipps Inc found disco nirvana in Funkytown (US no. 1, UK no. 2 '80); while Guns n' Roses' Paradise City – 'where the grass is green and the girls are pretty' – sounded remarkably like Innisfree.

'Soon I'm back to stern reality.' Bing's reverie – like any dream, like the greatest night of your life – couldn't last forever. Reality in 1952 meant couples working things out after the inevitable infidelities of separation, families trying to patch themselves together after the horrors of war, at home and abroad. When Crosby sang about Innisfree offering 'a peace no other land could know', he may even have been singing about death itself.

5 Guy Mitchell, 'Feet Up' (Columbia DB 3151)

Another way through the post-war malaise was to celebrate the family – mums, dads and kids, just the way it used to be. There was a remarkable number of songs about babies in the decade after the war: Rosemary Clooney's 'Where Will the Dimple Be' (UK no. 6 '55), Alma Cogan's

'Twenty Tiny Fingers' (UK no. 17 '55), and this raucous singalong. On 'Feet Up', Guy Mitchell wasn't shy in sharing his wayward past – 'I've been known to gamble, take a little drink . . . but now my rootin' tootin' days are done. Gotta be the man that he thinks I am, 'cos I love my son!' He dangled the poor kid in the air to 'pat him on the po-po', while bragging that he 'knew a lot of women' in his dog days; he also claimed 'my girl Rosie ain't that kind', leaving you to ponder the kind of floozies he'd been spending time with.

In 1952 everybody in Britain secretly wanted to be American. You only had to hear a Guy Mitchell record to know what America was like, and it's telling that he carried on having major hit singles in the UK after his star waned at home ('Feet Up' reached number two here but only number fourteen in the States). Mitchell was a man who always wore his hat at a jaunty angle, the kind of fella who would say '*Sure!*' to pretty much anything. Though he usually painted himself as Jack the Lad, his songs were like Southern cooking, collard greens and biscuits, and everything loaded with sugar because the sun has got his hat on and life's a beach: 'Pretty Little Black Eyed Susie' (no. 2 '53), 'She Wears Red Feathers' (no. 1 '53), 'Cloud Lucky Seven' (no. 2 '54) – they oozed bonhomie. 'Feet Up' featured swanee whistles and a laughing solo. It was hard to believe there was a war on in Korea.

'Feet Up' was written by a man who could stake a claim to be the king of pre-rock, Bob Merrill. Legend has it that his first attempt at songwriting was rejected by a publisher as too complex, so he went home and wrote, 'If I knew you were comin' I'd have baked a cake, howdja do, howdja doo, howdja doo.' It became a US number one for Eileen Barton in 1950.

By 1953 Bob Merrill was the best-selling composer in the world, the heir to Hoagy Carmichael, Cole Porter and Sammy Cahn, with million-sellers like 'Feet Up', '(How Much Is) That Doggie in the Window', 'Mambo Italiano' and 'Where Will the Dimple Be', all composed on a toy xylophone. The other perceived enemy of the Great American Songbook was A&R man Mitch Miller, by now at Columbia Records and Merrill's number-one fan, who coerced his artists – Jo Stafford, Rosemary Clooney, Guy Mitchell, Patti Page – into singing these family-friendly novelties.

The rise of the solo singer and the growing significance of record sales over sheet music in the early fifties had enabled record-label executives like Miller to wrest control of the music industry from the old publishing firms. Effectively he became the first pop manager, cultivating the careers of his charges and picking their singles; Miller's approach would be a foundation stone of the new vinyl-based music industry. Frank Sinatra, with his career at rock bottom, had been convinced to cut 'Mama Will Bark' with a pack of dogs in 1953; in 1954 he bought his way out of his Columbia contract rather than stay under Miller's thumb. A few years later, with Sinatra in his Capitol-era pomp, the two met in a hotel lobby. As Miller extended his hand, Sinatra snapped, 'Fuck you, keep walking.'

6 Rosemary Clooney, 'Half as Much' (Columbia DB 3129)

Of the female stars of the early fifties – too prim and preened to be called girls – Kay Starr, Doris Day, Patti Page and Rosemary Clooney were dominant. Once in a while they broke rank and caused a raised eyebrow – Jo Stafford sang 'Make Love to Me' in 1954 and got a BBC ban for her troubles – but largely they were as much a post-war comfort blanket as the men. Doris sang sweet, Patti sang country, Kay sang 'Comes Along a Love' (UK no. 1 '53), a fabulous proto-rocker with a walking bassline. Part Native American, she had a strong dark look, like the older sister of a girl you fancied, and was clearly someone who wouldn't stand for wallflowers at her house party. Rosemary Clooney, likewise, set herself up as more than a little saucy on 'Come On a My House', the biggest record of 1951, co-written by Armenian American novelist William Saroyan. Mitch Miller helmed it, backing Clooney with a manic, distorted harpsichord. 'I'm gonna give you Easter egg,' she sang, licking her lips. 'I'm gonna give you everything.'

'Half as Much' was a ballad written by country's premier songwriter, Hank Williams, who would collapse and die on New Year's Day 1953. That he never scored a bigger hit than 'Jambalaya' (US no. 20 '52) was down to the segregation of the American chart. Before submitting record sales, *Billboard* magazine would ask shops to divide them into pop, hillbilly (later country and western) and race (later rhythm and blues, or R&B). This made it almost impossible for music on the outside of white, urban pop to break into the charts. Hank Williams's 'Jambalaya' spent fourteen weeks at number one in the country chart, so presumably sufficient retailers considered it big enough to count as a pop record and filed its sales as such. This musical apartheid would eventually be corrected with the introduction of the Top 100 (soon renamed the Hot Hundred) in 1955, which counted all record sales towards the pop chart. The American singles chart, however, was further complicated by its combination of record sales, jukebox plays, radio plays and – at least in the fifties – sheet-music sales. It lacked the clarity of the British pop chart, which was, and would remain, purely sales based.

Was Rosie buttering us up to become a nation of country-music fans? Despite the fact that the UK isn't meant to 'get' country and western, 'Half as Much' would be followed into the chart by her cover of 'Jambalaya', the Midwestern swing of Bonnie Lou's 'Tennessee Wig Walk' (no. 4 '53) and Ruby Wright's 'Bimbo' (no. 7 '54), neither of which registered in the States at all (though Bonnie Lou had a number-six hit on the country-and-western chart).

=7 Frankie Laine, 'High Noon' (Columbia DB 3113)

Westerns were another reason for the unlikely incursions of country music into the UK charts. 'High Noon' was the theme to a film in which sheriff Gary Cooper is 'torn between love and duty'. Though Tex Ritter sang it on the soundtrack, Frankie Laine had the hit – he was already the foremost purveyor of this kind of dark epic. With a choral caravan of courage behind him he sings, over a lazy clip-clop beat that could be a death march, 'I do not know what fate awaits me . . . I must face a man who hates me, or lie a craven coward in my grave.'

What darkness there was in the music of 1952 came almost entirely from this square-jawed, geometric man with a letter-box mouth. Frankie Laine had won a marathon dance contest in 1932 and smashed the world record, going for 145 consecutive days. Everything he did was on this scale. His songs were pure Hollywood, set under swirling, swollen skies in bleak dustbowl settings: 'Cool Water', 'Where the Winds Blow', 'The Cry of the Wild Goose'. Laine was pop's Gregory Peck, a tortured stoic, a lion with a thorn in his toe, not any old loser in love but a man who'd had his heart physically ripped out by Jezebel. On 'Blowin' Wild' (UK no. 2 '55) he was tormented to the brink of insanity by his woman after, improbably, they'd struck oil in their back garden; Laine roars his pain over a backing of doodlebug brass and a howling, near-atonal chorus. His biggest hits, though, were less apocalyptic – 'Answer Me' and 'I Believe' were safe, ship-steadying ballads that smelt of church and stayed at number one for months in '53 and '54.*

=7 Vera Lynn, 'Forget Me Not' (Decca F 9985)

The forces' sweetheart of World War Two had three songs on the first British hit parade. She had barely registered a record sale since the end of the war, but Korea brought her back into the chart. 1952 had seen the Battle of White Horse, the Battle of Old Baldy and the Battle of Triangle Hill, all of which sounded like Frankie Laine hits in waiting. In November '52 president elect Dwight Eisenhower flew to Korea to kick-start ceasefire negotiations, UN fighting all but stopped, and the war would finally end the following July.

'Forget Me Not' was Vera Lynn's third hit of the year, and was incredibly, impressively dirge-like – its melody recalled 'The Last Post' and, though it started with a sprig of flighty strings, like something from *I Dream of Jeannie*, the tempo soon dropped like a stone; Vera sounded distant, echoing, a ghost of Christmas future; eventually the song simply faded away, with the haunted vocals of the Johnson Singers (one of whom wrote the song) trailing behind her, walking slowly into the distance and the darkness. Joe Meek would have been doing his national service in 1952, as an RAF radar technician, and he'd have been listening to the thunder of 'High Noon' and the desolation of 'Forget Me

---

* Laine was a rock-era prototype – the bruised, sensitive, big man. His movie-screen mannerisms crop up periodically, notably on Roy Orbison's 'Running Scared' (US no. 1, UK no. 9 '60), P. J. Proby's 'I Can't Make It Alone' (UK no. 37 '66) and Chris Isaak's 'Wicked Game' (US no. 6, UK no. 10 '90).

Not'; almost a decade later he would be recycling and renewing their impact on John Leyton's 'Johnny Remember Me'.

=8 Doris Day and Frankie Laine, 'Sugarbush' (Columbia DB 3123)

The summer of 1954 brought Britain's first pop-music magazine aimed at teenagers, a proto-*Smash Hits* called *Hit Parade*, with posters, news, gossip and reviews, and its first cover star was Doris Day. Up to this point, pop fans had to make do with the weightier music papers, the *NME* and *Melody Maker*, both of which were effectively specialist newspapers, or the odd article in *Picturegoer* and *Picture Show*, but they had never had a magazine of their own. The first *Hit Parade* featured Frankie Laine's life story in strip cartoon, the whole month's listings for Radio Luxembourg (Sunday June 27th: 7.30 *Guy Mitchell Sings for You*; 9.15 *The Alka Seltzer Show* – details to be announced; 11.00 *Top Twenty*), a Johnnie Ray feature ('I want to marry a British girl') and 'Hit Parade's June Pin-Up', Doris Day, who was celebrating her current number-one hit, 'Secret Love'.

The only comparable US magazine was the similarly titled *Hit Parader*, which paid far less attention to detail and was almost entirely made up of lyrics to the current hits. In October '54 the *NME* expanded its hit parade from a Top 12 to a Top 20; the following month the *Daily Mirror* ran a readers' poll to celebrate 'the fabulous world of the gramophone record'. A hundred thousand voters picked Ronnie Hilton as best newcomer, and Winifred Atwell as best instrumentalist; they played in front of seven thousand people at the *Daily Mirror* Disc Festival. Up to this point singers and bands had performed at summer seasons, pantomimes and Royal Variety Performances – strictly adult territory. The *Mirror* was clearly aiming at teenagers and, for Christmas 1954, it published *Discland*, a hardback book and Britain's first pop annual: 'Today the spinning disc is the number-one force in show business. The names of recording stars are as familiar around the house as salt, mustard or vinegar. The stars come right into your homes.'

Back in 1952 Doris Day had been singing the flirtatious 'Sugarbush', a record that – had the chart existed – would have been a hit a few weeks earlier for Eve Boswell, a British-based, Hungarian-born singer. Boswell was a classically trained pianist who also played the saxophone and the clarinet, had mastered tap dancing and the odd ballet step, and would record an album (*Sugar and Spice*, 1956) that featured songs in nine different languages. In Blackpool, she once appeared on stage by jumping through a paper hoop while juggling. Somehow – maybe unsurprisingly – she always gave the impression of having ladders in her tights; her only hit would turn out to be the daffy 'Pickin' a Chicken' (UK no. 9 '55).

Doris Day, on the other hand, cut duets with Frankie Laine and Johnnie Ray, starred in a Hitchcock film with James Stewart, co-starred in further movies with Rock Hudson and James Garner, became a gay icon for her role in *Calamity Jane*, set up the Doris Day Animal League in the seventies (which introduced the annual Spay Day USA), and had a son, Terry, who went on to produce the Byrds and would have been a victim of the Manson family if he had been at home one night in 1969.

While Doris got to smooch Rock Hudson, earn an Academy Award nomination and receive the Presidential Medal of Freedom, the enchanting Eve got to do a summer season in Southport with 'TV's Mad Magician' Tommy Cooper. This was the state of Britain in the early fifties – strictly end of the pier.

=8 Ray Martin, 'Blue Tango' (Columbia DB 3051)

> So-called light music has its own values . . . it acts as a series of vials, often charmingly shaped and coloured, for the distillations of memory. The first few bars of it remove the stopper; we find ourselves re-living, not remembering but magically re-living, some exact moments of our past.
>
> J. B. Priestley

The other major difference between post-war Britain and post-war America was the empire, or rather the end of the empire. Previously, the British working classes had had the option of escaping from their back-to-back terraces via the colonial office, to Canada, India, Africa; you could make your way, reinvent your life. In 1947 India became independent, and suddenly there were fewer places to visit. Our playground would have to be on our doorstep.

This may explain the popularity of instrumentals, the other major pre-rock trend. For one thing, they were, like songs about kids and burgeoning happy families, a way of avoiding mentioning the war – this made them safe choices for BBC radio. Also, they covered much of the ground that Jo Stafford's silver plane flew over, foreign climes which were now out of the reach of many Britons: Norrie Paramor's 'April in Portugal', Winifred Atwell's 'Poor People of Paris', Frank Chacksfield's 'In Old Lisbon', Lou Busch's 'Zambezi' and Mantovani's 1953 number one, 'Moulin Rouge'.

The orchestrated instrumentals were called 'light music', a melodic, digestible, atmospheric style that sat between pop and classical, and after which the BBC's Light Programme had been named in 1945. British band leader Ray Martin was your tour guide on 'Swedish Rhapsody' (UK no. 4 '53), a piece of music that was fifty years old and genuinely Swedish, but was chirpy in the extreme, much like his 'Blue Tango' with its accordion, skipping strings and light South American pitter-patter beat.

Other instrumentals on the chart – Cyril Stapleton's 'Blue Star', Leroy Anderson's 'Forgotten Dreams', Les Baxter's 'Unchained Melody' – worked as balm, lullabies for wrecked communities. They tucked a nation into bed while the new world was constructed outside their window. The record that epitomised early-fifties Britain was German in origin – Eddie Calvert's 'Oh Mein Papa', which spent nine weeks at number one in early 1954. Redolent of bottle-green paint and utility furniture, I imagine it on the Light Programme's morning show *Housewives' Choice*, mirroring a yearning for romantic ballroom clinches (maybe with Calvert himself, the Man with the Golden Trumpet and the Brylcreemed hair), a yearning for something, anything, to aid escape from austerity Britain. It has an otherworldliness – which its village-hall organ aggressively attempts to ground – that stems from Calvert's rather wayward blowing; not exactly jazz but still straying into dreamy, lonesome bullfighter territory. Certainly, it is quite an abstruse take on a tribute to a dead father.*

---

* Eddie Fisher's vocal cover version was an American number one in 1954. It was both more cloying than Calvert's recording and comically damning with faint praise: 'Oh my papa, so funny . . . in his way.'

Instrumentals were for the mass of grown-ups who had experienced quite enough heart-quickening action between 1939 and 1945. For many kids, though, the war had been a constant adventure – they may not have been economically independent, but it had left them a private world of bomb sites, dens built in half-destroyed houses which, for adults, were no-go areas. Their older brothers, though, had gone off to war, and returned as adults with shared experiences, creating an unbridgeable generational divide between them and their siblings.

Those who had experienced the awful realities of armed conflict understood 'Oh Mein Papa' and 'Blue Tango'; those who hadn't shunned this adult music. It would occasionally resurface, like a buried childhood memory, even decades later, suggesting there was something in the British psyche that needed these soothing, atmospheric instrumentals – the Shadows' 'Wonderful Land', Fleetwood Mac's 'Albatross', 808 State's 'Pacific State'. Their moment of dominance, though, was long gone. Listening to Mantovani's 'Moulin Rouge' is to realise that something significant was lost as well as gained in the rock 'n' roll era.

9 Vera Lynn, 'The Homing Waltz' (Decca F 9959)

At her 1940s peak, Vera Lynn's main rivals had been the rumbustious Gracie Fields and the sweet, much younger Ann Shelton, wartime heroines whose careers turned to charity work in peacetime, or at least until there was another conflict to rouse the British blood – Shelton scored a UK number one with the grinning, khaki-clad 'Lay Down Your Arms' in 1956, just as the Suez crisis threatened to become a full-blown war. By the early fifties, though, there were several other British girls waiting to steal Vera and Ann's glory.

American stars had the lip gloss, the nylons and the best suits, the accoutrements of class and style. Post-war Britain was another story. Big ball gowns, bigger and fruitier than everyone else's, that was Alma Cogan's shtick. She wasn't especially pretty, and got through by smiling a lot and playing up the cute catch in her voice. She scored hits with chirpy, brass-driven material like 'Never Do a Tango with an Eskimo' (no. 6 '56) and 'Dreamboat' (no. 1 '55) – on which she serenades her lover as if he was an Airedale puppy – but she could also take American R&B hits like LaVern Baker's 'Tweedle Dee' and Fats Domino's 'I'm in Love Again' and present them to a music-hall crowd at the Golders Green Hippodrome without anyone getting alarmed. That was new and brave and, decades later, people still admired her for it.*

Lita Roza was notably more glamorous, with her boyish haircut and catlike grace. She was a Scouser, her dad was a Spanish docker, and she'd risen to prominence singing with the Ted Heath band. When she went solo in 1952, Lita cut albums like *Listening in the After-hours* and *Love Is the Answer*, titles that spelt out her name. Her best songs – 'Allentown Jail', 'Hey There', 'Leave Me Alone' – had a mink and smoke-ringed atmosphere that perfectly conjured up the make-do-and-mend glamour of fifties Soho, all cool seduction with hints of illegality. You heard none of this in the voice of Ruby Murray, the breakthrough star of 1955. Genuinely, she seemed like a naif, an Irish colleen whispering 'Softly, Softly', a number one, like a stuttering schoolgirl. Britain quickly took to her fluttering eyelashes; at one point in the spring of '55 she had five singles in the Top 20,† and was something of a (very quiet) pop explosion. But blushing cheeks could only take her so far. Ill-advised duets with Norman Wisdom were not the way forward. The public had already tired of her by 1956, after which she hit the bottle and sank from view.

Accessibility was often the key to a British pop star's success. Unlike America, British singers in the early fifties still hoofed around the country playing on variety bills. If Frank Sinatra wasn't around, then you'd have to make do with 'the British Frank Sinatra', another former singer with the Ted Heath band called Dickie Valentine. Of the wave of pre-rock

---

* Alma Cogan died of cancer in 1965, by which time she had become London's most famous party hostess, carousing with Sammy Davis Jr and the Beatles alike. When Gordon Burn wrote a novel about Britain in the fifties and sixties, he called it *Alma Cogan*, fictionalising her life and imagining she was still alive, looking back at her career.
† Ruby Murray could've been bigger than the Beatles . . . wait a minute, she was! No other act in the vinyl era managed to have as many singles simultaneously in the Top 20.

singers who made the British bobby-soxers shriek and sigh, Orson Welles lookalike Valentine was the most interesting. On stage, he would begin his set in a mellow mood – with sleepy ballads like 'All the Time and Everywhere' (UK no. 9 '53) – then he'd crank it up and sing like Johnnie Ray one minute, Mario Lanza the next, Edward G. Robinson for pudding. It was a weird act, but it made him extremely popular. 'I'm a Jekyll and Hyde, you see,' he explained. 'As Dickie Valentine I feel shy and handcuffed. It's when I'm imitating others, when I'm not myself, that I can throw myself about the stage.' You can almost hear Morrissey in that quote. If Dickie had emerged three years later, he might have made more interesting records. As it was, he only cut a handful – 'Finger of Suspicion' was the best, all waxed-moustache charm, a three-minute chat-up line, and it made number one in December '54. Unable to shift with the rock 'n' roll era, by 1971 he was reduced to haring around the country from one small nightclub to another. It was four in the morning, Dave and Ansell Collins's 'Double Barrel' was number one, and he was doing 90 mph when he crashed and died on a single-lane bridge at Glangrwyney, Wales. He was forty-one.

=10 Vera Lynn, 'Auf Wiederseh'n' (Decca F 9927)

Vera's first hit of the year had been a much more rousing effort than the forlorn 'Forget Me Not'. By November it was dropping off the chart, but 'Auf Wiederseh'n' would turn out to be the biggest seller of 1952. It was also a number-one single in America; Vera was the first British act to achieve this feat. The song's romantic take on World War Two was shameless – it even references 'We'll Meet Again' – but it was mostly notable for its singalong qualities. In case you missed the point of it, there was a massed choir of soldiers almost drowning out the lead vocal. Join in and sing. Follow the leader.

It had a reactionary streak that would remain strong in modern pop. The friction between conservatism on one hand (the deliberately dumb) and art school on the other (pop with pretensions of greatness) caused a crucial tension that would fire glam's internal battles, would set up Texan garage punk's blurting aggression as a counterpoint to

psychedelia's cosmic quest, and would play the basic, joyous noise of
UK rave off against the perceived 'intelligence' of drum and bass.

What would fans of 'Auf Wiederseh'n' have heard in its simple chant
in 1952? They would have considered it a solid song, one you could
directly relate to, with real history behind it. In America, country music
served a similar purpose; later, metal would become a similarly solid,
conservative pop strand. You weren't taking a risk with this music; you
weren't backing anything that could be here and gone in a flash, or
something that could overly embarrass you if a friend pulled it off your
shelf two years later. There was no fear of looking silly among your peers
if you supported it.

At the same time, 'Auf Wiederseh'n' sounds older than anything else
on the first chart. This was the sound of a closing-time pub singalong, or
family get-togethers around the piano in the parlour, decades-old habits. By the early fifties people were dumping their pianos on the street
– there were so many second-hand ones on the market, you couldn't sell
them – and replacing them with radios, gramophones and televisions.
The fact that the *NME* singles chart existed at all meant that songs like
'Auf Wiederseh'n' were on the wane.

=10 Mario Lanza, 'Because You're Mine' (HMV DA 2017)

'Because You're Mine' was the first-ever hit single as we know it, an
actual piece of seven-inch vinyl. As a slice of light opera it shamed
British pretenders like David Whitfield and Lee Lawrence, and even
Al Martino – all of them sound puny alongside the lung power of bon
viveur Mario Lanza.

His meteoric career was decidedly modern. Lanza was an astonishing
tenor who studied with conductor Leonard Bernstein before making his
stage debut aged twenty-one in 1942 – the *New York Times* reckoned,
very early on, that he had 'few equals among tenors of the day in terms
of quality, warmth and power'. After serving in the war, his career took
off and by 1947 his voice was reducing people to tears at the Hollywood
Bowl. Louis Mayer was in the crowd, and convinced Lanza that he
could be a film star. He was right: in 1950 Lanza starred in *The Toast*

of New Orleans, singing 'Be My Love', which became a million-seller; a year later he was the only possible candidate for the lead in *The Great Caruso*, which played fast and loose with Caruso's life story and made a pop song – 'The Loveliest Night of the Year' – out of 'Sobre las Olas'. Opera critics were horrified. Lanza's love of food and drink began to bloat him. 'Because You're Mine' became his last million-seller, and by the time of his death in 1959 he was both ignored by opera critics and regarded by pop fans as a has-been. The perils of getting caught up in the machinery would run through the modern pop story – Lanza's rise and fall would find echoes in the lives of Marc Bolan and Kurt Cobain.

As modern pop grew up, it would subtly attempt to reintroduce elements that had been cast aside in rock 'n' roll's birthing. If we can say that the Shadows were subtly bringing the influence of Mantovani back into the chart, then it's safe to say Elvis was channelling Mario Lanza on 'It's Now or Never' (UK and US no. 1 '60) and, most obviously, at the climax of 'Surrender' (UK and US no. 1 '61). Elvis was trying to recapture the intangible magic of the music he had grown up with; in turn, the sixties beat era would be a twenty-something's recap of their Elvis moment, reigniting the thrill they had felt when they first heard 'Heartbreak Hotel' as young teenagers. T. Rextasy would reference Beatlemania – and the process continued. This was one of modern pop's magical properties: by participating, you could be more than just a consumer – you were helping to create pop history. There came a point where you realised you were a scholar with access to a personal, hand-built library rather than a rotten pupil who had been bunking off school to buy seven-inch singles.

11 Max Bygraves, 'Cowpuncher's Cantata' (HMV B 10250)

Along with his Mario Lanza albums, Elvis Presley's record collection included the soundtrack to *The Pajama Game*, televangelist Jack Van Impe's *Marked for Death: Can America Survive?* and Max Bygraves's *Singalongachristmas*. This was more likely to be because Elvis used to buy every new Christmas album each year than for any strong feelings he had for the music of Max Bygraves. 'Cowpuncher's Cantata' was a medley of recent country-flavoured songs which, while its humour was fairly lame, at least signified the nascent presence of what the *Daily Mirror* called 'commercial folk music' in Britain.

By 1955 a noticeable breeze would be catching Britain's weather vane. There was a strong thread of country music, something approximating Americana, nudging to the fore in the British singles charts. Slim Whitman, a yodeller who meant little outside of specialist markets in the US, scored the year's biggest hit, 'Rose Marie' – eleven weeks at number one – which was lyrically as racked as Frankie Laine and sonically quite windswept: 'Of all the queens who ever lived, I'd choose you to rule me, my Rose Marie.' It sounded like it was recorded in a ghost town, with clanking pianola and tumbleweed vocal.

Tennessee Ernie Ford's 'Sixteen Tons' followed 'Rose Marie' to number one a few months later, a deeply atmospheric piece which featured little more than Ford's earth-shaking baritone, his menacing finger-clicking and some sparse, strange woodwind accompaniment: 'I was born one morning, it was drizzling rain,' he sang, his voice sliding into subsonics on the last word. Jimmy Young's 'The Man from Laramie', another 1955 number one, was similarly minimal, albeit Omo-washed and starched, a cowboy song all the way from the barren prairies of Wiltshire. Yet it indicated a desire for something different, something a little more gritty than 'Blue Tango' or 'Feet Up'. The British public may not have known what it wanted, but it was just about to get it.

12 Johnnie Ray, 'Walking My Baby Back Home' (Columbia DB 3060)

Aside from Frankie Laine and Slim Whitman, two other pre-rock American figures suggested pop's possible futures. Roy Hamilton was a little more subtle than Frankie Laine; he was also one of the few black singers outside of jazz to impact on pre-rock. He never bothered the British charts but, more than any of his contemporaries, his US hits laid some kind of blueprint for the next two decades. Hamilton had studied commercial art, had operatic and classical voice training, then became a

heavyweight Golden Gloves boxer, a combination that lent him a sonorous authority, with just a hint of real danger.

His material was strong red meat: he hit the R&B Top 10 with 'Ebb
Tide', 'Hurt', 'If I Loved You' and 'You'll Never Walk Alone' (all 1954),
before reaching number six in the pop chart with 'Unchained Melody'
(1955). No one else has sung 'I've hungered for your touch' as affectingly. Roy Hamilton brought gospel into pop, and dug the earliest foundations for soul.

Almost uniquely, he could appear on the US pop charts while still
playing at the Apollo in Harlem; he'd have become a major star but
he caught tuberculosis in '56 and was forced into semi-retirement.
Emotive, rocking hits came intermittently to show what might have
been ('Don't Let Go', no. 13 '58; 'You Can Have Her', no. 12 '61),
but he never fully recovered. In 1969 he attempted another comeback,
recording 'Dark End of the Street' in Memphis, while Elvis Presley –
cutting 'Suspicious Minds' in the adjoining studio – watched on with
due respect. Hamilton died of a stroke just a few weeks later.

Arguably the most significant modern pop forebear was Johnnie Ray,
who was raised in rural Oregon, where an accident at a Boy Scout jamboree had left him deaf in his right ear. Unlike pretty much all his contemporaries, he was inspired by black singers like Roy Hamilton, LaVern
Baker and Ivory Joe Hunter. At the turn of the fifties, in Detroit's Flame
Showbar, Ray mixed up pre-rock and R&B and created a sensation.

Several things marked Ray out as something quite new. For a start
he cut a less than manly figure, more emaciated even than the forties
Sinatra, and looked in urgent need of a nap as well as a square meal. He
also looked uncomfortable on stage, clenching his fists and wiping his
sweaty palms on his suit trousers, and – and this was a first – women
unashamedly wanted to mother him and smother him. Then there was
his hearing aid. Using these props he'd wind himself up with windmill
arm movements until, climactically, he broke out in tears. 'I don't have a
voice,' he explained to the *Daily Mirror*, 'I got a style.' Johnnie Ray was
not easy listening, and he wasn't about to win any ideal husband poll.

The perception of Ray was also complicated because he had hits
on the R&B chart, which was almost unknown for a white singer in

the early fifties. He would mess about with black recordings like the Drifters' 'Such a Night', adding his own oohs, mmms and slow intakes of breath to up the ante. 'When we kissed . . . I had to fall in love'; if Chuck Jones's leering wolf was a record, this would be it. 'Such a Night' went all the way to number one in the UK (it only made nineteen in the US), between the spectacularly chaste pairing of Doris Day and David Whitfield; that alone goes some way to explaining Ray's pre-rock impact.

As a record of how audiences – Britain's first teen screamers – reacted to Ray's stage act, there was the 1954 *Live at the London Palladium* album. They sighed and gasped as if they were watching a saucy circus act. They screamed for 'Such a Night', which he reprised, and reprised again. And he did this until you can hear girls shout '*Johnnie!!*', at which point modern pop came alive.*

A mid-fifties British TV documentary called *Fan Fever* interviewed Dickie Valentine, Alma Cogan and Dennis Lotis, focusing on the new fad for screaming at stars on stage. Lotis, smoking a pipe, recalled with no small displeasure how one inflamed girl managed to grab and remove one of his shoes. The Johnnie Ray Fan Club of Great Britain were interviewed – all of them were girls. Some were content to collect Ray's records; others knitted their own jumpers emblazoned with their idol's name. One had a piece of clothing, a sacred shred ripped from his

---

* America had already encountered teen screams as far back as October 12th 1944, when thirty-five thousand girls, many wearing bobby sox and bow ties, caused a near riot outside the Paramount in New York because they couldn't get in to see Frank Sinatra. It became known as the Columbus Day Riot. Sinatra was already twenty-nine; to many of his fans he would have seemed like a father figure, even if he did make them feel all churned up inside. But he was a phenomenon, and the bobby soxers who swooned for him also wet themselves and threw their bras at him. Sinatra was a pointer to the future for youth culture, a harbinger, though the Columbus Day Riot was something of an anomaly. While it was commonplace for Hollywood stars to get mauled and screamed at, no pop star would receive remotely similar treatment until Eddie Fisher (much more gently) at the turn of the fifties. Sinatra's career was in decline by this point; after attempting suicide, he starred in *From Here to Eternity* in '53, then worked with Nelson Riddle on 'Young at Heart' in '54, and successfully recast himself as a purely adult artist just as rock 'n' roll hit the mainstream. His fans grew up with him.

body. Another particularly tough-looking girl had primitively carved Ray's name on her arm – you hoped for her sake it wasn't a real tattoo. A studio panel furrowed its brow and passed judgement. A grizzled American psychiatrist gave his opinion. They agreed unanimously – it was a passing craze.

FLIP, FLOP AND FLY: BILL HALEY AND JUMP BLUES

One summer night in 1954 a train travelling from Southend-on-Sea to London came to a sudden halt when someone pulled the emergency cord. But there was no emergency. No one was ill, there was no real reason for it. After a moment's ominous silence came the sound of smashing glass as lightbulbs got busted, plunging carriages into darkness. When the trashed train pulled into Barking, police arrested a bunch of youths in Edwardian suits.

Teddy boys and Teddy girls pre-date rock 'n' roll. Theirs was the first public display of fidgeting, the first tangible proof that Britain's younger generation was restless and wanted meatier entertainment than the gruel they were being offered. Their parents had been too caught up in staying alive; they'd had enough excitement.

The first generation of Teds had their own dances – the creep, the stroll – and danced to the more rhythmically forceful big bands, the ones with a touch of burlesque, like the Kirchins and Ken Mackintosh. Music was part of their identity, as were the coffee bars that had sprung up like bright formica flowers on most high streets since the Festival of Britain. They had no adult supervision beyond the owners, who knew they could get a brick through their window if they interfered with this teenage business. Jukeboxes sat in the corner, restlessly waiting for the new rhythm.

In 1955 Bill Haley and his Comets released 'Rock around the Clock', and it was the sound the Teds had been waiting for. It was the first record to have – all in one place – a lyric about all-night partying, a thrilling guitar solo and a rock-solid beat, with its drums way up in the mix. What's more, its success was on an international scale, and this is why it crossed a generational threshold, ushering in the rock 'n' roll era.

The beauty of rock 'n' roll was not just its newness but its gleeful awareness of its newness, wiping out the repression of the post-war decade. It wasn't as if the old guard didn't put up a fight, but once the door was opened, once 'Rock around the Clock' hit number one in Britain and America in 1955, the heart of pop beat differently. At least fifty per cent of the genre's biggest hits could conceivably be filed under novelty: Buddy Holly's hiccup, Little Richard's shrieks, Elvis's pelvic thrusts, gimmicks all over, go ape crazy – everything was now permissible as long as it created the most stupidly, gloriously distorted noise.

Whether the sounds were created by genuine madmen or were manufactured mayhem was irrelevant; the rock 'n' roll aesthetic was anti-boredom. Suddenly, noise and overexcitement became values rather than marks of low quality. It was here and gone in a flash – hardly more than two years between initial explosion and self-parody. When later generations coined the term 'rock 'n' roll lifestyle' for leather-jacket-wearing, TV-smashing, Jack Daniels-swilling, smacked-out oblivion, they did the innovators a bad disservice: first-wave rock 'n' roll was fast-moving, fun, disposable and defiantly youthful, no time for cliché. There is more rock 'n' roll in the three minutes of passionate dishevelment in Barbara Pitman's 'I Need a Man' than the combined catalogues of Aerosmith and Mötley Crüe.

The codes that have riddled modern pop since the rock 'n' roll explosion – rock versus pop, underground versus Top 40 – were some way off in the mid-fifties. Almost nobody aside from radio DJs was collecting records or filling in catalogue numbers. Ideologues weren't yet squabbling over Ricky Nelson or Buddy Holly or Johnny Burnette's place in the rock pantheon because nobody was talking about a rock pantheon.

In the twenty-first century Bill Haley is rarely included in any critic's list of prime movers, which is sad and a little ridiculous. Whichever way you slice it, he was at the front of the queue. Haley invented rock 'n' roll. No one had blended country and R&B before Haley wrote and recorded 'Rock the Joint';* no one hit the *Billboard* Top 20 with something that could be safely labelled rock 'n' roll before 'Crazy Man Crazy'; and no one scored a rocking number one before 'Rock around the Clock' turned the music world upside down.

* * *

Teds had been searching for their own musical identity, and it was clear that minor variations on the big-band music their parents had danced to were unsatisfactory. Equally clearly, the opening sequence of 1955 movie *Blackboard Jungle* was just what they needed: juvenile delinquents take over a school and symbolically smash a teacher's collection of jazz 78s into little pieces, to the soundtrack of 'Rock around the Clock'.

In America, a potential musical revolution had been flagged as far back as 1951, when Leo Fender sold his first electric bass guitar, and early adopters – like Shifty Henry of Louis Jordan's Tympany Five and the Lionel Hampton band's Roy Johnson – began to change the dynamics of R&B and jazz. But in 1955 Britain, the metallic backbeat of 'Rock around the Clock', the walking bassline and the perceptible change in volume would have seemed to have come from nowhere, a total shock to the system; it unleashed a whirlwind of media attention as cinema seats were slashed by Teds across Britain.

The film's progressive and controversial take on racial integration was

---

* Though Haley claimed the writing credit, it was based on Jimmy Preston and the Prestonians' 1949 boogie-woogie record of the same title. Country had been influenced by black musicians for decades, and there was a strain known as 'country boogie' in the late forties: the Delmore Brothers' 'Hillbilly Boogie' (1945), Jack Guthrie's 'Oakie Boogie' (1947), Arthur 'Guitar' Smith's 'Guitar Boogie' (1948), Tennessee Ernie Ford's 'Shotgun Boogie' (1950). The only other strong claim to the first cohesive R&B/country blend is Hardrock Gunter's 'Birmingham Bounce' (1950), a country-boogie single that mentioned rockin' – and was in turn derived from black ragtime pianist Charles 'Cow Cow' Davenport's 1929 single 'Mama Don't Allow No Easy Riders Here' – though it still sounds like a hillbilly record. Haley's 'Rock the Joint' was the first to effectively rip an R&B single and make it feel comfortable in the hands of a country band.

enough to get *Blackboard Jungle* widely banned in the States, and the Eisenhower administration kept it from being shown at the Venice Film Festival. 'Rock around the Clock' and *Blackboard Jungle*'s two-pronged assault effectively compacted white teenage self-assertion and black political justice; on one side an adolescent matter, on the other very much not. This coming together, symbolised in Haley's single, was a very big deal – for the times and for modern pop.* It transformed a raucous hit record and a pop moment into something teenagers of the fifties could look back on later with more than just nostalgia, something all young people could take retrospective pride in. By the first week of July 1955 government edicts counted for nothing – 'Rock around the Clock' was America's number-one single.

The main source material for 'Rock around the Clock' was jump blues, which had been around since the mid-forties. Jump blues had utilised the big-band swing sound that had dominated the thirties and forties, stripped back the number of musicians, placed the saxophone at the front of the brass section, replaced croons with harsher blues vocals and shifted the guitar to the rhythm section. With all hands to the rhythm pump, the music literally began to jump. The lyrics were frequently filthy and a whole lot of fun.

Arkansas-born Louis Jordan was the king of jump blues. He had been the one star name who – if you wanted a severely edited pop history – provided a smooth transition between the swing and rock 'n' roll eras. With the Tympany Five, he had laced his scaled-down swing sound with a blue comedian's shtick and ribald titles ('You Run Your Mouth and I'll Run My Business', 'I Like 'Em Fat Like That', 'That Chick's

---

* Racism in the music industry was a given before rock 'n' roll. When RCA came to release DeFord Bailey's version of 'John Henry' in 1928, they had a problem – it was a folk instrumental played on the harmonica, but Bailey was black. It ended up being released separately in both RCA's race and hillbilly series. Never the twain would meet, apparently. Hindsight's a fine thing but it's hard to understand how RCA in Britain released nine EPs of vintage blues under the banner of the RCA Victor Race series in 1965 – that's after the Rolling Stones' cover of Willie Dixon's 'Little Red Rooster' had been number one, Sonny Boy Williamson and John Lee Hooker had toured Britain, playing to largely white crowds, and Millie's 'My Boy Lollipop' had been the UK's first major ska hit.

Too Young to Fry'). Fast-talking tales of gals in fox furs and zoot-suited brothers were propelled by boogie-woogie piano* and saucy sax solos. A 1941 engagement at Chicago's Capitol Lounge, supporting the Mills Brothers, had proved to be his breakthrough; Jordan's records were then issued in Decca's Sepia series (which was meant to appeal to both black and white audiences): 'What's the Use of Gettin' Sober (When You're Gonna Get Drunk Again)' was his first number one on the race chart in '42; 'Is You Is or Is You Ain't Ma Baby' was a pop number one, and a million-seller, in '44. In Jordan's wake came Roy Brown ('Good Rocking Tonight'), Big Joe Turner ('Shake, Rattle and Roll'), Wynonie Harris ('Bloodshot Eyes'), Stick McGhee ('Drinkin' Wine Spo-Dee-o-Dee') – stepping it up, amplifying and emphasising the beat until someone at *Billboard* magazine† decided it wasn't plain blues any more, it was rhythm and blues, and the moniker stuck: the 'race' chart was renamed the R&B chart in 1947.

A DJ in Cleveland called Alan Freed had been using another term, 'rock 'n' roll', since he started his *Moondog* radio show in 1951: 'OK, kids, let's rock and roll with the rhythm and blues!' he'd shout, beating out the time on a phone book.‡ Freed's hold over Cleveland youth became clear when he put on the Moondog Coronation Ball in March 1952: more than twenty thousand turned up for a bill that included R&B vocal acts the Dominoes, featuring the dynamic tenor of Clyde McPhatter, and the Orioles, along with the lesser known Tiny Grimes, Rockin' Highlanders, Danny Cobb and Varetta Dillard. In the event,

---

* Boogie-woogie had been a major step up for blues in the late thirties, more urban, less country, reflecting the migration of black Southern workers to cities like Chicago. The rolling, rhythmic piano that pushed it along was as basic and direct as the name, which, like rock 'n' roll, was a euphemism for sex.

† It was Jerry Wexler of *Billboard* magazine who coined it as a marketing term in 1948, as 'race music' had become an embarrassing name even to the white music industry. Louis Jordan has the cosmic claim of eighteen R&B chart number ones, a figure only bettered by Aretha Franklin and Stevie Wonder.

‡ As the rise of television forced non-network radio stations to go for a more distinctive, specialised sound in order to keep their audience, it led to the rise of other hip DJs around the country in 1953 and '54 who were white but happy to play black music to a mixed audience: Dewey Phillips (Memphis), Art Laboe (Los Angeles), Bob 'Wolfman Jack' Smith (Shreveport).

only Paul 'Hucklebuck' Williams got to play before the police broke it up, as kids smashed their way into the basketball stadium. One act or none, it qualifies as the first-ever rock concert. The audience, for the record, was almost entirely black.

Soon enough, by concentrating on ballads with a beat, hollering over them on the radio and almost willing the music to sound younger, Freed's *Moondog* show began to stretch out into the suburbs of the north-east – the white neighbourhoods. Two years later he moved to New York, to radio station WINS, and there he introduced millions of white teens to the new music. The *New York Times* reckoned he 'jumped into radio like a stripper into Swan Lake'.*

Bill Haley was a pro musician with a keen ear. He had started recording back in the mid-forties as the Rambling Yodeller and was already thirty by the time 'Rock around the Clock' hit number one and there was no turning back. In 1952, around the time the *Moondog* show was keeping Cleveland's cops occupied, he began to loosen his cowboy image, changed his band's name from the Saddlemen to the Comets, and incorporated R&B into their set. First off, they covered Jackie Brenston's 'Rocket 88' – Haley added an intro with a car starting up because he understood pop well, and reasoned that no song couldn't be improved by the sound of a car revving out of your radio. It became a hit in the north-eastern states.†

* No one will counter Freed's claim to coining the term 'rock 'n' roll'; claims on the first rock 'n' roll single, though, are almost entirely subjective. Revisionists have given a big shout for Jackie Brenston's 'Rocket 88', a 1951 Sun Studios recording that featured a sax solo, a boogie-woogie piano intro later pinched note-for-note on Little Richard's 'Good Golly Miss Molly', distorted electric guitar, a leering vocal and a suitably teenage lyric (cars, no more or less). It was a great record, and topped the rhythm and blues chart for five weeks. The ingredients were pretty much ready for the chef, then, but Brenston's 'Rocket 88' was all murk, rich with the fug of a speakeasy. It hardly sounded young at all. It was *proto*-rock 'n' roll, but it wasn't any more rock 'n' roll than the Ames Brothers' irresistible, nonsensical, beat-backed, guitar-driven 'Rag Mop', a US number one in 1950.

† Different regions of the US had local charts, which could be based on record sales but were more often compiled by radio stations, combining airplay and sales. The vastness of America meant that records could be purely regional

Haley later told *Melody Maker* that 'the real turning point for me came with a record called "Icy Heart". This song broke into the country charts, and I was on the road to Nashville promoting that song and with an introduction to get me onto the Grand Ole Opry. Then suddenly I had a call [from his manager]. Somebody had started to play the other side, which was a fast boogie thing, "Rock the Joint", and it was selling to blacks and to white teenagers. So he said, get back here, take off the cowboy hat and those boots and get yourself a tuxedo. You're going into the northern club circuit. It happened just like that, literally.'

On a roll, Haley picked up the title 'Crazy Man Crazy' from teenage jive speak and crossed over from huckster showman to the big time, writing himself a US number-twelve hit in 1953; in some cities it was a number one, and it soon sold one hundred thousand copies. 'We were booked into jazz clubs often, because there was no precedent for us. There was no rock 'n' roll then. So, with a number-one hit on the chart in Chicago in 1953, we found ourselves booked on a double bill with Dizzy Gillespie. The club owner hated us and he threw us out on the street.'*

He may have been travelling without a guide, a true innovator, but Haley was never a pin-up and his voice was reedy, short on sustain, almost asthmatic. He was partially blind and tried to cover his bad eye with a plastered-down kiss curl. The Comets were a perfectly good, driving little C&W dance band that upped the ante by acting like a circus menagerie on stage – bassist Marshall Lyttle defied physics by twirling his double bass above his head. This way, you didn't notice the receding hairlines or the crow's feet. But what took them out of the backwoods and into history was their unintentional adherence to one of

---

phenomena. Tommy James and the Shondells' 'Hanky Panky', for instance, was picked up by a Pittsburgh DJ in 1966 three years after it was recorded, and the record was re-pressed locally, becoming a Pittsburgh number one before it eventually broke nationally. Los Angeles band the Merry-Go-Round had two LA number ones in 1967 but neither even reached the national Top 20.

* This tale reveals the widening gap between a music for white teenagers and club-based jazz – still very much a black, adult music. As the music the Comets were playing had no obvious name, Haley toyed with idea of calling it 'crazy' music. Luckily Alan Freed came up with a rather better name for it soon after.

pop's primary unwritten laws – they were in the right place at the right time. Bill Haley did it all when it really mattered.

A cover of Big Joe Turner's 'Shake, Rattle and Roll' in 1954 took him into the US Top 10 and, incredibly, to number four in the UK. Hearing it alongside the three records above it in the British charts – Dickie Valentine's brilliantined 'Finger of Suspicion', pub pianist Winifred Atwell's 'Let's Have Another Party', the Chordettes' antique nursery rhyme 'Mr Sandman' – 'Shake, Rattle and Roll' must have sounded like a bomb had gone off at the school gates.*

The clincher for Haley's career came when his manager Dave Myers nailed 'Rock around the Clock' – a song he'd co-written that had been on the B-side of 'Thirteen Women' in '54 – to *Blackboard Jungle*'s opening credits. It duly became, eighteen months after it was recorded, the first international teen anthem.

It wasn't that rock, or even rock 'n' roll, hadn't been mentioned in lyrics before 'Rock around the Clock': possibly first out of the blocks was Wild Bill Moore's 'We're Gonna Rock, We're Gonna Roll' (1947);† Gunter Lee Carr's 'We're Gonna Rock' (1950) was more basic and brutal, pounded out on a loosely tuned piano. While both implied high jinks, neither was a clarion call.

The link between the old and new worlds was producer Milt Gabler, who had helped Louis Jordan's move from the race chart to the mainstream pop chart, producing and co-writing his million-selling 'Choo Choo Ch'Boogie' in 1946. Gabler rushed the arrangement of 'Rock around the Clock', as it was only a B-side, to spend more time on the top side, 'Thirteen Women'. This left a clattering, drum-heavy mix. It sounded like jump blues, only with someone dismantling scaffolding in the studio.

* It is received wisdom that Haley's version is bowdlerised, deleting the black slang from Turner's take, making it acceptable to picket-fence America and privet-hedge Britain. Yes, he lost 'I can look at you 'til you ain't no child no more', which probably sounded faintly uncomfortable then and sounds a whole lot worse now. More importantly, Haley kept in 'I'm like a one-eyed cat peeping in a seafood store', which remains the most sexually graphic and grubby line on a Top 5 single to this day.
† Moore later played the joyous sax break on Marvin Gaye's 'Mercy Mercy Me'.

There are a few intros in the pop canon that can give you an adrenalin shot within a second – literally – of them starting up, intros that are guaranteed to cause a sharp intake of breath and a dash to the dancefloor. The hard, silver chord that opens 'A Hard Day's Night' is one; there's also the oddly dolorous but huge sound that launches T. Rex's 'Metal Guru', the barely controlled bagpipe glee of the Crystals' 'Da Doo Ron Ron', the cascade of Pepsi bubbles on Cyndi Lauper's 'Girls Just Wanna Have Fun'. Right at the beginning there was the sharp double snare hit, followed by 'One two three o'clock, four o'clock rock . . .'

The two solos in 'Rock around the Clock' paint a remarkable contrast. The first, an unfeasibly fast-picked guitar line, is a total blast, like a double-speed *Tom and Jerry* party piece – not violent but exciting enough to make you laugh out loud. The second solo, a unison brass line, was straight out of Glenn Miller, the forties biplane sound of 'In the Mood' with the merest sprinkling of modernity.

Ten years of county fairs and working as a local DJ, working like a dog, had sharpened Haley's sensibilities; no question, he'd hit on an instantly identifiable sound, and he milked it. In 1957 he had seven more UK hits, five of them Top 10, which all adhered to the same tempo, the same greased-down backbeat: 'See You Later, Alligator', 'Rock-a-Beatin' Boogie', 'The Saints Rock 'n' Roll', 'Rockin' through the Rye', 'Rip It Up'. There was even a film called *Rock around the Clock*. Having played his hand so well, the firestarter decided to tour Britain in early '57. Moondog's coronation may have brought twenty thousand out to party and break free from ballad hell in Cleveland, but Bill Haley's first tour of Britain was like the second coming. Thousands met him and the Comets, the saviours of modern youth, when they docked at Southampton. They were expecting a sun god, they wanted to anoint the man who had delivered us from Vera Lynn. Instead, they got pop's own Wizard of Oz. Bill Haley was no deity, he was an uncle.

Even this may not have been too tragic. But he wasn't your cool Uncle Bill, the one who'd play you his stash of Wynonie Harris 78s and give you a sneaky can of beer when your mum wasn't about – the one who made you feel like part of a secret society, a cut above the meatheads at school. No, this was the Uncle Bill who was a bit too loud and sweaty at a wedding party, dark rings under his sleeves, making bitter, off-colour jokes about his ex-wife.

Having obeyed one of modern pop's primary rules with his sense of timing, Bill Haley messed up on another: keep the mystery caged. The kids had fun at his shows, made the most of it, but the sense of anti-climax was palpable. Haley had one more hit after his UK tour, then disappeared from the charts.

By 1967, when he toured again, the Comets were a museum piece. 'We're going through the same period that Sinatra and Armstrong went through,' he told the *NME*. 'You're up, you're down, and if you were good in the first place, you make it back. We'll be there.' The Vegas engagements never came; instead he was seen almost as a novelty figure, Fatty Arbuckle with a guitar, consigned to cabaret until his lonely death in 1981. His heyday was brief but, truthfully, without Bill Haley the rest of this book could not have been written.

A MESS OF BLUES: ELVIS PRESLEY

In the early seventies Elvis Presley's record label, RCA, released an album of unreleased outtakes called *A Legendary Performer*: when it outsold his new album of maudlin country ballads, the singer must have felt he had begun to lose the battle with his own myth. Trapped inside Graceland, the Memphis mansion that was half home, half prison, the humble country boy who had done more than anyone to invent teen culture grew overweight and suffered severe depression; to the outside world, though, he was still the ultimate superstar, the invincible King of Rock 'n' Roll. Eighteen months before he died, Elvis told his producer Felton Jarvis, 'I'm so tired of being Elvis Presley.'

No one has had the pop-culture impact of Elvis Presley. Adults didn't get him at all. He invented himself, a true modernist, drawing on the best of everything that surrounded him and making it new. He rose faster, fell further, had the most glorious comeback, and died young, alone in his palace. Elvis Presley was a deity and a comic monstrosity. He was tender, thuggish, generous, narcissistic, charming, sensitive, self-destructive and paranoid. Sam Phillips, the producer at Sun Records who first recorded the boy wonder in 1954, remembered Elvis, even at the outset, as having 'the greatest inferiority complex of any person, black or white, that I had worked with. He was a total loner. He kind of felt locked out.' His music was also sweet, brutal, lonely, ecstatic. And for this Elvis has been loved more fiercely than any pop star since.

Some argue that rock 'n' roll would have happened without Elvis, and they may be right, but that doesn't mean it would have taken over, not at all. Bill Haley had arrived at his sound by trial and error, mixing graft, a keen ear for what the customer wanted and a willingness to dabble in R&B's black arts. It took him ten years to find the right sound. Elvis Presley walked into Sun Studios, Memphis, one day in summer 1954, and did it in a heartbeat.

He was pure instinct. What's more, he was so precisely what post-war youth had been waiting for: sex incarnate – 'I got so many women I don't know which way to jump.' With 'Heartbreak Hotel', his national breakout hit (US no. 1, UK no. 2 '56), America suddenly discovered it had hormones that Haley, Eddie Fisher and Perry Como – perfect husband or not – were never going to stir. For the rest of the world, living in desperate times, he was just what they wanted – the consummate American. The low, heavy lids, the curling lip, the pelvis. Best of all, adults thought him crude, vulgar, animalistic. At a stroke, Elvis Presley created the generation gap.

The mid-fifties American cultural landscape was dry tinder for Elvis. He had a rapport with his generation that nobody – not Glenn Miller, Frank Sinatra or anyone – had had before. Early TV appearances show him to be amused and impressed by his own power over the teenage audience. On an *Ed Sullivan* performance, filmed from the waist up in a panicked attempt to contain him, he sends himself up by hiccuping a line on 'Don't Be Cruel' ('at least please a-te-le-phone-ahh!'), and closes by pulling an outrageous Valentino pose that drowns out the last few lines of the song with ear-shredding screams. He took Rodgers and Hart's 'Blue Moon' (UK no. 9 '56) and gave it an eerie falsetto reading, already sounding like his own ghost, thoroughly spooking America in 1956. There was none of the artifice of the torch-singing balladeer:

on Jerry Leiber and Mike Stoller's 'Love Me' he throbbed, groaned and choked with such visceral physicality it prompted interviewer Hy Gardner to ask him, 'What about the rumour that you once shot your mother?'

True, Bill Haley had done the groundwork, jump-starting the hillbilly sound by borrowing heavily from R&B. Crucially, Elvis didn't just get out his library card – he accentuated the rough edges, the danger of R&B, turned it from a nudge-nudge sound for streetwise black folk into something that threatened the social fabric of the USA. 'Hound Dog', his first out-and-out rocker, was a song written by Leiber and Stoller for R&B singer Big Mama Thornton. Her version breathes fire, no question, but lurches like a drunken bloodhound alongside Elvis's cover: so intense and beautiful, he turned it into two minutes of sustained viciousness and sheer malicious glee.

It seemed like Elvis came from nowhere, and that was pretty much the case. He was a country boy, born in Tupelo, Mississippi, a town of fewer than ten thousand inhabitants. He loved to sing in church, played a little guitar, and called people 'sir' and 'ma'am'. His folks moved to Memphis when he was thirteen and developing an interest in clothes – he started to wear his hair long and greased back, a waterfall pompadour in the style of a truck driver. At the same time he bought his clothes at black stores, hung out in the black-music heartland of Beale Street, and loved the blues sounds he heard. Cutting a record for his mother at Sam Phillips's Sun Studio, he told an inquisitive receptionist, 'I don't sing like nobody.' She was impressed enough to pass Presley's name on to Phillips, who teamed him up with local boys Scotty Moore and Bill Black. Together they cut an old Arthur Crudup blues song called 'That's All Right' in 1954. The sound was hillbilly but it rocked hard. They followed it with another five singles on Sun, all blending country tunes ('Blue Moon of Kentucky', 'I Don't Care if the Sun Don't Shine') with R&B ('Mystery Train', 'Good Rocking Tonight') as if it was the most natural thing in the world. On stage at the Louisiana Hayride Elvis gyrated, wore a pink shirt and peg slacks. He looked raw, sounded rawer, and girls melted.

The person behind the curling lip, the real Elvis, remains nothing as remotely straightforward as the image. The fact he survived his stillborn twin brother, Jesse Garon, may conceivably have led to feelings of guilt and incompleteness from the beginning. It could also explain the strong ties Elvis had to his mother (who almost died giving birth) and his pack of surrogate brothers – the Memphis Mafia – who lived with him at Graceland even after he married. When his mother died aged forty-two, just as Elvis was set to do a stint in the army that he was convinced would destroy his career, the sense of isolation only grew.

One of his Memphis sidekicks was Jerry Schilling, who was just twelve years old when he met Elvis, playing football, in 1954. By 1965 Schilling was in his hero's employ, at a time when Elvis had been eclipsed by the Beatles and Bob Dylan and was rapidly becoming an anachronism who churned out irrelevant, vapid movies. His post-army career had begun most promisingly in 1960 with *Elvis Is Back!*, arguably his best album: during the sessions he covered light opera ('It's Now or Never'), superior teen pop ('The Girl of My Best Friend'), Johnnie Ray (the camp, flirtatious 'Such a Night') and dirty blues ('Reconsider Baby' and 'A Mess of Blues', a number-two single in the UK), an outrageously broad range for anyone but a master craftsman. Then in 1961 the mediocre *GI Blues* became a huge cinema hit, the crass pre-school novelty 'Wooden Heart' an international number one, and suddenly Elvis was living in Tinseltown. 'He wanted to grow like any of us,' said Schilling, 'but the machinery wasn't built that way.' Trapped by his manager Colonel Tom Parker into a Hollywood contract that required three movies a year, there was barely time to sing enough songs for the soundtracks, let alone anything worthwhile; by 1965, the year of *Rubber Soul* and 'Like a Rolling Stone', the erstwhile King Rocker was singing 'Do the Clam' and 'Petunia the Gardener's Daughter'. No wonder he was looking for a way out.

That option arrived in the unlikely guise of a hairdresser called Larry Geller. 'We were just good old boys,' said Schilling of the Memphis Mafia. 'We talked about girls, football, but Elvis was a real thinker. Larry gave him an outlet. He could explore his spiritual side.' Soon Geller and Elvis were investigating 'numerology, astrology, Indian philosophy. Most of the guys didn't want to read a book. They gave Larry a rough time.'

One day in 1966, staring at clouds, Elvis became overcome with emotion – a cloud had begun looking like Joseph Stalin, then mutated into Jesus. How could he carry on making those dumb movies, he asked Geller, after seeing the face of God? When the story got back to Colonel Parker, he told Elvis to get off his religious kick; a hurt Elvis snarled back, 'My life is not a kick.' The Colonel's response was to oust Geller from the Presley camp and force his singer to perform the demeaning 'Yoga Is as Yoga Does' in his next movie.

The obvious way out of the Colonel's grasp wasn't an option. While girls fell at his feet, Elvis was unlucky in love. During his army duty he thought he had found the real thing with a young teenager called Priscilla Beaulieu but, just as he promised himself to her, he met the actress Ann-Margret on the set of *Viva Las Vegas* in 1964 and, according to many, discovered what true love was all about. They even discussed marriage.*

And yet Elvis and Priscilla married in '67, then divorced in '72. Biographer Paul Simpson calls this the 'golden age of Elvisness' – it included his first (and only significant) refusal to bow to the Colonel's demands, when he concocted the electrifying 1968 'comeback special' with TV producer Steve Binder rather than sing a bunch of corny Christmas songs, as well as his return to Memphis to record such classics as 'In the Ghetto' (US no. 3, UK no. 2 '69) and 'Suspicious Minds' (US no. 1, UK no. 2 '69). The divorce, though, seemed to be a tipping point. He began to immerse himself in autobiographical ballads ('Always on My Mind', 'Separate Ways') and self-pity. At one of his Vegas shows that year, the spotlight fell on Ann-Margret in the audience. 'Leave the light on her, man,' mumbled Elvis, 'I just want to look at her.'

While the songs of these twilight years are often dismissed as schmaltz, they are just as much a part of the real Elvis as 'Jailhouse Rock' or 'Hound Dog'. Elvis's taste in music extended way beyond the R&B/hillbilly fusion that made his name; his record collection at Graceland stretched from Eddy Arnold and Judy Garland to the Animals, Otis

---

* Elvis wanted the Colonel to manage Ann-Margret – he had very positive feelings for her career, too. When the Colonel explained that his time would then be split fifty–fifty between them, Elvis thought it wasn't such a good idea after all.

Redding and Max Bygraves. His admiration for both hillbilly singer Cowboy Copas and opera's biggest pop star Mario Lanza informed his ability to switch from an ethereal falsetto on 'Blue Moon' to Neapolitan tenor on 'It's Now or Never' and intense country soul on 'Long Black Limousine'. Asked to name his favourite singers he usually plumped for Frank Sinatra, Roy Orbison or Roy Hamilton, yet gospel remained his music of choice and often brought out his best performances – the fire he poured into mid-seventies renditions of Hamilton's 'Hurt' and 'Unchained Melody' was normally reserved for numbers like 'How Great Thou Art' and the show-stopping 'American Trilogy' (US no. 66, UK no. 8 '72). Thankfully, late-period recordings like Roger Whittaker's nautical ballad 'The Last Farewell' were an aberration – his taste in songs was usually as solid as his taste in interior decoration was dubious.

As the possibility of touring outside the States was continually thwarted by Colonel Parker (an illegal immigrant, as Elvis discovered very late in his career), his frequent Vegas shows became punctuated by weird monologues,* karate exhibitions and comedy. Once he rode on stage on the back of Mafia member Lamar Fike, with a toy monkey attached to his neck, and sang an X-rated version of 'Love Me Tender'. It laid bare to the public the medication abuse that insiders had known about for years. After the *Aloha from Hawaii* show, his last real success, broadcast live by satellite to more than a billion people, a combination of pain pills, liquid Demerol and heavy-duty depressants caused an interaction that led to throat and lung congestion, and so to further medication. During his next Las Vegas engagement he saw six physicians as well as his two regular doctors. Their motives were questionable. One gave him a course of acupuncture that involved syringes.

'I lost my friend early due to creative disappointment,' said Jerry Schilling. His Memphis Mafia colleague Red West once asked, 'How do you protect a man from himself?' Elvis, surrounded by kowtowing

---

* Most were about his divorce, occasionally they were about the hotel staff in Las Vegas, and once he had a go at Bill Cosby, who had just left the room to go to the toilet: 'Where's Bill . . . where's Cosby? After that buildup the SOB left? The hell with him! I won't pay him. No, he gets ten grand, whether he wants it or not. He can stick it up his nose.'

buddies, was not good at taking criticism or interference; all the inner circle could do was hope for the best and fear the worst.

The wonder was not when he died, but the fact that Elvis could die at all. Only the deaths of John Lennon and Princess Diana have caused such shock and bewilderment since. In the 1981 documentary *This Is Elvis*, his later performances are almost physically painful to watch, the only explanation for why he is performing in public rather than lying in a hospital bed being that his manager, his doctors, his record company, his fans and anyone else who had seen his bloated face, heard him slurring on stage, couldn't entertain the idea of Elvis ever dying. As you hear him struggle through 'Are You Lonesome Tonight' ('I was', he mumbles on the intro, 'and I am') it seems that Elvis Presley was the only person in the world who was aware of his mortality.

PUT YOUR CAT CLOTHES ON:
SUN RECORDS AND ROCKABILLY

At the same time as he hijacked and twisted R&B, Elvis Presley destroyed country. He wore eye shadow the first time he played Nashville's Grand Ole Opry and came off stage to be told: 'We don't use nigger music.' Pretty soon the bigots had no choice in the matter: within a couple of years every country boy wanted to sing just like Elvis, and rockabilly – the rocked-up, itchy hillbilly sound – had laid waste to the niceties of Nashville country.

The musicians came from white farming families, picking up on the rhythmic country blues of their black neighbours, specifically Big Bill Broonzy and Leadbelly, whose 'Pick a Bale of Cotton' was effectively a rockabilly blueprint. Country music didn't use drums, so rockabilly musicians would slap the double bass to get a rhythm going. This was the sound of white people losing their taboos, making music with a beat they could dance to. Maybe they had no job but they still wanted to dress up. They wanted to look sharp and they wanted to party.

Rockabilly was entirely about rhythm. Vocals echoed and doubled up, guitars played one note, the double bass twanged, everything bang on the beat, until the whole thing rattled and shook violently, the musical equivalent of a racing jalopy on the verge of breaking up into pieces. The production created not just the record but often the song – it's hard to imagine Elvis Presley's 'Baby Let's Play House' existing without its strategic, rhythmic, bottom-of-the-well echo. Rockabilly sounded primal, greasy, and had the most pared-back subject matter of any pop genre: the constituent parts were clothes (Bill Beach's 'Peg Pants', Carl Perkins's 'Blue Suede Shoes', Dwight Pullen's 'Sunglasses after Dark'), cars (Curtis Gordon's 'Draggin'', Sammy Masters's 'Pink Cadillac', Hoyt Stevens's '55 Chevy') and teenage girls (Johnny Carroll's 'Wild Wild Women', Sonee West's 'Rock-Ola Ruby', Skeets McDonald's 'Heart Breakin' Mama'). Sonny Fisher's 'Pink and Black' combined the lot within its opening couplet: 'I got a pink Cadillac, pink and black shoes, a high-school baby rockin' to the blues.'

Even the lyrics were designed to aid the bone-rattling rhythm on songs like Wanda Jackson's 'Tongue Tied' and Buck Griffin's daffy 'Stutterin' Papa'. Beyond this, rockabilly just loved to celebrate its own existence: Glenn Reeves's 'Rockin' Country Style', Hoyt Scoggins's 'Tennessee Rock' and Thumper Jones's 'Rock It', which sounds very much like it was made by a man in dungarees. Did the older generation all despise the new sound, and all want to stick to their bluegrass and cowboy laments? Not according to Jimmy Murphy ('Granpaw's a Cat'), Mac Curtis ('Grandaddy's Rockin'') or Marvin Rainwater ('You Oughta See Grandma Rock').

Chief architect of rockabilly was Sam Phillips and his Sun record label. He was born in Alabama in 1923. By 1952 he was cutting demos and masters for local blues singers (Howlin' Wolf, B. B. King, Rufus Thomas, Bobby Bland, Junior Parker) in his small studio, and licensing them on to majors. Cutting out the middle man, he formed Sun in '53, and then in July 1954 he released a single by Elvis Presley.

Phillips was shrewd. He knew he was selling a percentage of his up-tempo boogie singles to white kids, but he knew none of them could relate to Junior Parker the way they could to a white teenager – someone who was one of them.

This was the point at which music previously regarded as outside of pop – unformed, too wild – suddenly flooded in: now there was control, calculation and intelligence behind it, not Elvis's perhaps (though he was excruciatingly modest – and a man channelling Mario Lanza and Big Mama Thornton had more grasp of the situation than he let on), but certainly that of wily Sam Phillips, savvy medicine-show salesman and genuine modernist biblical prophet. There was a vast whirling sandstorm outside the Sun studio; Sam Phillips not only recognised this when no one else seemed to, but he managed to control the storm and consciously direct it through his door.

'That's All Right' – Sun Records no. 209, credited to Elvis Presley, Scotty and Bill – was debuted by Dewey Phillips (no relation), Memphis's most influential disc jockey, one night in July 1954. Elvis hid in a cinema, telling his parents to listen in. Forty-seven listeners phoned the radio station, demanding to hear it again. It was played seven times that night, and sold seven thousand copies in Memphis in the first week alone. Five Presley singles later, at the end of 1955 Sun sold Elvis's contract and all the masters to RCA for $35,000.

Art and commerce, sacred and secular; having found the formula for mixing rocking blues and hillbilly – rockabilly – Sam Phillips rarely recorded another black singer. There were plenty of country hybrids and nutcases brought out of the woodwork by Elvis's success – so, he rightly figured, why look any further?*

Let's take a look at the assortment of characters Sam Phillips spent his time on from 1955 onwards. If Elvis was considered dangerous, then Jerry Lee Lewis was outright terrifying. He wore custard-yellow suits with black piping and had a sneer that spelt out sex and dirt and a regal arrogance. He was a mean, mean man. 'We're going to hell,' he'd cry. 'Fire and brimstone. The fire never dies, the burning never dies, the

---

* Among Sun's second-stringers were some real finds: Charlie Rich was brooding and scored a hit with the echoing, handclap-led 'Lonely Weekends' (US no. 22 '60); Roy Orbison cut the uptempo 'Ooby Dooby' before finding his range later on; Billy Lee Riley sang 'Red Hot', which truly was; Malcolm Yelvington was held back by a name better suited to a stockbroker; Charlie Feathers hiccupped passionately.

fire never quenches for the weeping, wailing, gnashing of teeth. Yessir, going to hell. The Bible tells us so.' He was nicknamed the Killer, largely for what he did to his poor piano, his golden curls of hair flying as he sweated, battered and molested the poor thing.

The piano on his first hit, 'Whole Lotta Shakin' Goin' On' (US no. 3, UK no. 6 '57), sounded like it could break through the floorboards; it made a roaring, echoing noise like ominous approaching clouds. The storm broke on 'Great Balls of Fire', a ludicrous, lascivious single that mixed camp, sex and intimations of eternal suffering for such sin: 'You broke my will, but what a thrill!'

But a bigger storm was round the corner. Entering Britain in 1958, after hitting number one with 'Great Balls of Fire', he made the mistake of bringing his child bride, thirteen-year-old Myra Gail. Confronted by the press, she said she was fifteen because she thought it would sound better. Jerry Lee's fans howled him off stage and the tour was cancelled after two shows. Here was an early example of the conservative strand in modern pop, of teenagers thinking they understood right from wrong, good from bad, cool from uncool. Quite possibly they were right on this occasion, and Jerry Lee did deserve derision for his obvious indiscretion, but there would be many future occasions where this teen conservatism was a lot more complex and problematic for the modern pop narrative.

Anyway, teenage Britain's reaction to Jerry Lee and Myra Gail's marriage killed the Killer, artistically and commercially. Nowadays he'd hire a lawyer, falsify Myra's passport, do *something*, but this was 1958. After one more classic bopper, 'High School Confidential' (US no. 21, UK no. 12 '58), his records lost their lick of hellfire. By the late sixties he'd regrouped as a singer of country weepies, and scored a whole new run of hits on the country chart. This didn't matter. On stage, he was only in demand for the music he had made in the six months when he ruled the world: for that brief flash, that shortest of hit runs, rockers still adore him. 'There's only been four of us,' he'd proclaim, 'Al Jolson, Jimmie Rodgers, Hank Williams, and Jerry Lee Lewis. That's your only goddam four stylists that ever lived.'

Lantern-jawed Carl Perkins's version of 'Blue Suede Shoes' sold one and a half million copies on Sun in 1956; it topped the *Billboard* pop, country and R&B charts simultaneously. For a few months, then, Carl had it all, yet he was humble and horribly shy: 'When you're a country boy just a month from the plough, and suddenly you're a star with money in your pocket, cars, women, big cities, crowds, the change is just too fast. You're the same person inside, but you're a star outside, so you don't know how to act. You're embarrassed about the way you talk, the way you eat, the way you look.' On tour he got homesick. In another age he could have been a bedsit figure, an alt-country hero, natural student fodder: 'I think the happiest time in my life was when I was a little boy in the country in the summer. Then I thought time was standing still and the world was mine.' He could have been a proto-Neil Young. But he was too country for that, and instead wrote a beautiful self-deprecating thing called 'Everybody's Trying to Be My Baby': 'Well they took some honey from a tree, dressed it up and they called it me.'

Johnny Cash was the Man in Black. He had a wood-carved face and a look of resolute danger; when he sang his voice could go deeper than a coal mine. He was all granite and grit, a real man – even Jerry Lee seemed rather childish and squeaky by comparison. His first major hit was 'I Walk the Line' (US no. 17 '56), possessive and paranoiac, sat over a boom-chicka-boom rhythm track he would employ for the next forty years; it sounded like a train running along the railroad, carrying restless Johnny out of Tennessee, to everywhere and nowhere. On 'Folsom Prison Blues' he 'shot a man in Reno just to watch him die'.

Cash stuck closer to country than any of his stablemates, yet eschewed rhinestones. He was big on causes, cutting whole albums dedicated to the working man, to his homeland (1965's *From Sea to Shining Sea*) and to the American Indian, while also enshrining his outlaw status by getting busted for drugs several times in the mid-sixties; he started a forest fire that destroyed half a national park; he slept in a cave and had a religious awakening; most famously, he played shows in prisons. No one doubted that he was a free spirit.

And, in spite of all this kudos, if you asked anyone to name more than four songs by him they'd struggle: 'I Walk the Line', 'Ring of Fire',

'A Boy Named Sue'. That was pretty much it. Still, the music was almost beside the point. If you squinted, he looked like an American eagle; he could even look, with his furrowed brow and soulful eyes, like the pioneering spirit of his entire country, and he was quite happy not to dispel this image. In this respect, he was more of a myth than anyone else in this book.

Outside of Sun there were dozens of independent labels cutting rockabilly, hundreds of acts, all trying to get a slice of Elvis's cake. One of the best was Wanda Jackson, the Queen of Rockabilly. She wore fringe dresses, high heels and long earrings, and with her dark hair, dark eyes and porcelain skin she looked like a sexy Snow White. She dated Elvis, and he convinced her that she could switch from straight country to something with a bigger beat. He was right; Wanda could growl. Her biggest hit in the US was 'Let's Have a Party' (no. 37 '60) but her most incendiary was 'Fujiyama Mama', a beautifully mannered shuffler with Wanda wrecking her throat on lines like 'I've been to Nagasaki, Hiroshima too. The same I did to them, baby, I can do to you.' It was a major hit in Japan, which says something for their sense of humour.

Johnny Burnette was a lightweight and welterweight boxer who fought his way to a Memphis City Golden Gloves championship. His brother Dorsey was a Southern pro champ, and they met guitarist Paul Burlison at an amateur boxing tournament in Memphis in 1949. So nobody was about to argue the case when they moved to New York and called their band, with stark efficiency, the Rock 'n' Roll Trio – one listen to 'Train Kept a Rollin'' and you knew they may as well have been the *only* rock 'n' roll trio. It was one sustained howl of sexual obsession and torment, basic and impossibly loud. Flick-knife shrieks and a fuzzed-up, deep two-note guitar line pushed it into territory beyond mere aggro – it was a genuinely frightening record. The intensity extended into the Trio's everyday world; they fought as if they were constantly in the ring and split after just three singles. Johnny ('Dreamin'', US no. 11, UK no. 5 '60; 'You're Sixteen', US no. 8, UK no. 3 '61) and Dorsey ('Tall Oak Tree', US no. 23 '60) both went on to tame but successful solo careers. Both, not surprisingly, died young.

Their sound was all blood and guts and, for rocking country blues, they truly had no equals.*

By the time Johnny and Dorsey were enjoying hit singles, Nashville had regrouped, after resigning itself to the fact it had lost its youth audience, and many of its younger players, to rock 'n' roll. Under the aegis of guitarist Chet Atkins, it created the MOR Nashville sound, which was later dubbed 'countrypolitan'. This was a very smooth version of country, which we'll return to later; it incorporated straight pop, dropped the

---

* The Rock 'n' Roll Trio's recordings were among the most fetishised 45s when rockabilly became the first modern pop scene to get a serious revival in Britain, starting in the mid-seventies. Rockabilly's cycle of exclusivity, commerciality and eventual dispersal makes for an interesting case study. When kids whose dads were original Teds began turning up at school in home-made drapes around 1974, a new, younger set of rockabilly fans emerged. They began to dig deeper than the obvious rock 'n' roll heroes, back to Sun rockabilly acts like Sonny Burgess, Warren Smith and Charlie Feathers. As original singles were already costing up to £100, demand was filled by bootleggers in the Netherlands. Rights to the originals could still be picked up at bargain prices, as no one in America seemed especially interested. Independent English record companies like Charly (who bought the complete Sun recordings, except Elvis) and Chiswick started to reissue compilations of obscure rockabilly legally in Britain; RCA and CBS soon cashed in on the recordings they owned. As for the 'cat clothes' look, a shop called Flip opened branches in the King's Road, Covent Garden and the East End in 1978 selling open-necked shirts, box jackets and peg trousers which arrived in packing crates from the States. Many hadn't seen the light of day since the fifties. As the scene boomed, Rock a Cha opened in Kensington Market in 1980 selling cheap repro and customised fifties gear, and a new wave of British rockabilly acts appeared: the Stargazers, the Polecats, the Shakin' Pyramids. The original fans in this exclusive scene – with its own music, fashion, language – felt betrayed as the media pounced on rockabilly as the latest passing trend, and America's Stray Cats started to score Top 10 hits in 1981. A London Weekend Television programme called *20th Century Box* captured the feelings of rockabilly fans, one of whom thought it was 'all getting commercialised. We want it to be our own little thing, 'cos otherwise all the clothes go, all the records go, and they all go to saps. We're like our own little family, know what I mean?' Other fans found that the answer was to diversify into subgenres, or to move back in time to other related musics – hillbilly bop, swing, strollers, jivers, Cajun, black forties R&B – and to start getting deeper into the scene. The word 'research' cropped up. Two rockabillies were reaching back to the look and sound of crooners from the forties: 'It's like a Rolls-Royce. When something's good,' one of them reasoned, 'it's good. It's there forever.'

steel guitars, lacked any sense of danger, and made stars of Jim Reeves, Dottie West and Don Gibson. When asked to define the Nashville sound, Chet Atkins reached into his pocket, shook the loose change, and said, 'That's what it is. It's the sound of money.'

TEENAGE WILDLIFE: ROCK 'N' ROLL

I MET GENE VINCENT!
BY JUSTIN BUCKLEY
Teen Regional Reporter

A local radio station had a contest to win an interview with Gene Vincent . . . when he was expected to come and visit our town for a personal appearance. Being a fan of his, I was eager to try my luck at winning. The rules of the contest were to say in 25 words or less, "why I would like to interview Gene." What a contest!

> The obscenity and vulgarity of the rock 'n' roll music is obviously a means by which the white man and his children can be driven to the level of the nigger.
>
> Anonymous man, from the documentary *This Is Elvis*

Showbiz did not like rock 'n' roll. Liberace called Elvis 'dangerous'. Frank Sinatra went further, claiming rock 'n' roll was the work of 'cretinous goons . . . it manages to be the martial music of every side-burned delinquent on the face of the earth'. Still, this didn't stop Tin Pan Alley trying to hijack and reinvent the new sound while it continued to bathe the world in a pale late-forties glow. Within weeks of 'Rock around the Clock' breaking the ice, white vocal acts like the Crew Cuts ('Earth Angel') and Jimmy Parkinson ('The Great Pretender') had top-ten hits with sweetened covers of Alan Freed-sanctioned records. Guy Mitchell was reborn in drapes and hit number one in the UK in 1957 with a song called 'Rock-a-Billy' (which was nothing of the sort). Kay Starr, in an attempt to narrow the generation gap with 'Rock and Roll Waltz' – a transatlantic number one in '56 – only enhanced it exponentially.

Independent labels, especially in the South, flourished as New York's Tin Pan Alley tried to keep its hands clean. For old-time record labels, publishers and entertainers, rock 'n' roll was simply a passing fad to be treated with the same gravitas as the mambo craze which hit in early 1955 (Rosemary Clooney had scored the biggest hit – a UK number one – with 'Mambo Italiano').

The singer who took most of the flack for this grubby business was Pat Boone, a devout Christian in his twenties who tamed some of the wildest rock 'n' roll hits – 'Ain't That a Shame', 'Long Tall Sally' and 'Tutti Frutti' – for a more mainstream, largely white, audience. It worked. Boone became a huge star and was soon able to switch from neutered R&B to pre-rock ballads and softer covers (the Flamingos' 'I'll Be Home'). On his better ballads ('Friendly Persuasion', 'Love Letters in the Sand') Boone could be almost as effective as the crooning Elvis of 'Loving You' and 'Love Me Tender'; he was seen in the media as the good-guy sheriff to Elvis's Captain Black throughout 1956 and '57, and a genuine equal.

As a rocker Boone was horribly out of his depth, but the melliflu-ous 'please wait for me' leading into the sweet octave change on 'I'll Be Home' (US no. 4, UK no. 1 '56) anticipates Roy Orbison, and has a square-jawed, unbreakable sound that could well indicate incarceration for the wrong reasons: soldier, prisoner of war, or someone similar to Henry Fonda's tragic character in *The Wrong Man*.

Still, he was so clean-scrubbed it was nauseating: he refused to give Shirley Jones a screen kiss because she was married in real life, and point-blank refused a role alongside Marilyn Monroe, possibly because she was too blonde and curvy. It was hard not to cackle when, in the eighties, *Hustler* magazine claimed to have a photo of a young Boone exposing his genitals through a hole in a cardboard box.

Boone was some way short of an innovator, and 1956 brought an abundance of them. So let's move on, further south, and take a look at

Little Richard Penniman. What is our initial reaction to this strange-looking man? He could be a pimp with his pencil-thin moustache and red velvet suit, or a transvestite with his caked make-up. Listen to him sing and he could be a voodoo practitioner, possessed, bawling out nonsense: 'Awop-bop-aloobop alop-bam-boom!' After Pat Boone's scrawny version, Little Richard's 'Tutti Frutti' is like an electric shock – it knocks you back physically.

And, thanks to Alan Freed and other brave souls like the Specialty label, the spontaneity and *cri de cœur* of Little Richard's originals – the needling, throat-shredding 'Lucille'; 'Jenny Jenny', on which he literally screams until he runs out of breath – overcame the showbiz enemy, made the Top 10, and a T-junction was reached; pop turned left. Rock 'n' roll had won. It was as significant as Dada taking over the art world. All manner of outsiders and maniacs now blew in; every week seemed to usher in a major new talent. And the freakiest freak of them all was Little Richard.

'I am the beautiful Little Richard from way down in Macon, Georgia. You know Otis Redding is from there, and James Brown's from there . . . I was the best-looking one so I left there first. Prettiest thing in the kitchen, yes sir!'

Richard's raw noise – pounding piano, driving rock rhythm, insane shrieks, unavoidably sexual lyrics – wasn't easy to hum or whistle. It was hard to listen to more than a couple of his singles in succession without getting the jitters. There were virtually no tunes (check the Everly Brothers' 1960 cover of his 'Lucille', on which their voices merge in a monotone biplane drone); it was all energy. This makes his breakthrough and vast success all the more incredible: in Britain he had seven hits in 1957 alone. And then, in 1959, with a diva's sense of drama, he threw it all away, chucked his jewellery into a river and declared he'd been playing the devil's music. He turned to preaching and returned to Georgia. Of course, he staged the occasional comeback, but the momentum was gone and he never scored another major hit. He still thought he was the greatest, but he was gracious in decline.

'When I came out they wasn't playing no black artists on no Top 40 stations, I was the first to get played on the Top 40 stations – but it took people like Elvis and Pat Boone, Gene Vincent to open the door for this kind of music, and I thank God for Elvis Presley. I thank the Lord for sending Elvis to open that door so I could walk down the road, you understand?'

Like Little Richard, St Louis-born Chuck Berry's chart career predated Elvis's, first scoring with 'Maybellene' in 1955, an R&B/rockabilly hybrid that went as high as number five in the US. He had the look of a card sharp blessed with luck, a brown-eyed handsome man with a cherry-red Gibson and a major thing for cars and girls that he syphoned into super-detailed lyrics. He became the chief correspondent for young America. Some think he was the most significant figure in all rock 'n' roll; certainly, he was an A-grade innovator.

His presentation of the rock 'n' roll experience, as lived by real-life teenagers, was so exact and vivid that it's quite likely Berry mapped it out and then real life followed his plot. 'Hail, hail rock 'n' roll, deliver me from the days of old.' The odd thing was that Berry was already in his mid-twenties when he cut 'Maybellene'. He was always the first to admit that his inspirations came from the days of old – lyrical sauce from Louis Jordan and guitar licks from T-Bone Walker – but he honed them into motorvating marvels, without any of the forties murk that clouded his antecedents' work. These songs were bright, shiny, very fast and super-modern; they sounded like the tail fins on Cadillacs. He also wrote some of the best guitar lines ever recorded. Though he had a tendency to use the same R&B riff as a chassis ('Johnny B. Goode', 'Carol', 'Back in the USA'), his best singles are among the most joyous in all pop. The lyrics were exclusively about dancing, driving, sex and rock, the consumer society, and all delivered with the machine-gun vocal rhythm of an auctioneer: 'Sweet Little Sixteen', 'School Day', 'Too Much Monkey Business', 'Rock and Roll Music', 'Roll Over Beethoven', 'Nadine', 'You Never Can Tell', each one a beautiful two-minute youth-culture libretto.

Yet no matter how accurate, original, sharp and funny his songs, the man was hard to love: 'The dollar dictates what music is written' was his mantra. He would duck-walk across the stage in a strange, crouched shuffle, and seemed disdainful of his audience. He was the least charming of the original rockers, rude and incredibly tight-fisted. Publicising his biography on British TV in the eighties, he was asked if he could play his signature tune, 'Johnny B. Goode'. 'No,' he said. 'For second-class money you get a second-class song,' and he played 'Memphis, Tennessee' instead.

Had it not been for cover versions of some of his songs by the Beatles, the Rolling Stones and the Kinks, Berry might have slipped into obscurity after doing a four-year jail term for driving an underage girl over state lines to work at his St Louis nightclub. Instead, he re-emerged in 1963 to a hero's welcome; 'No Particular Place to Go', with the lyrical motif of a girl trapped in his car, gave him a number three in 1964, his biggest-ever British hit.* The cat had landed on his feet again.

Bo Diddley was Berry's labelmate at Chicago's Chess Records. If Berry had the lyrics down pat, Bo had the beat. Take his onomatopoeic name for a start – it was so good, he used it in a dozen different song titles: 'Bo Diddley', 'Diddley Daddy', 'Bo Diddley Is a Lover', 'Bo's a Lumberjack'. He chopped up rock 'n' roll's square 4/4 rhythm into jagged pieces with his rectangular guitar, hired a maracas player called Jerome Green to add a counter-rhythm, and rarely bothered with chord changes. Bo claimed to have come across his patented beat while trying to play Gene Autry's '(I've Got Spurs That) Jingle Jangle Jingle', though it more closely recalled the rhumba rhythm of the Andrews Sisters' 1945 hit 'Rum and Coca Cola'.

Futuristic beat aside,† Bo was a stylist. He rode a scooter with his name emblazoned on the side, and hired female rhythm guitarists – first Peggy Jones, and later a beautiful woman known only as the Duchess

* Technically, Chuck Berry's 1972 novelty hit 'My Ding-a-Ling' was his highest-charting record, a UK and US number one, but it seems almost cruel to mention it.
† Among the future hits to feature or adapt the Bo Diddley rhythm were Elvis Presley's 'His Latest Flame', Them's 'Mystic Eyes', the Who's 'Magic Bus', the Stooges' '1969', David Bowie's 'Panic in Detroit', George Michael's 'Faith' and the Smiths' 'How Soon Is Now'. That's not including covers of Bo's songs, which made up a good percentage of repertoires on the British R&B circuit in 1963 and '64: 'Mona', 'Pretty Thing', 'Road Runner', 'I'm a Man', 'Who Do You Love' and 'You Can't Judge a Book by the Cover'.

– who provided a luminous visual foil to his solid frame as well as future inspiration to Suzi Quatro and Joan Jett. The only thing he couldn't do was score major hits – 'Say Man' (US no. 20 '60) was his only Top 20 hit in Britain or America.

Going further back than any other classic rocker was the round, kind-faced Fats Domino. His first R&B number one, 'The Fat Man', had been as far back as 1950, but his easy style and soupy New Orleans beat sat alongside the emerging rock sound quite perfectly. He was a master entertainer, and not flamboyant in any way. Nothing ever changed. He just sat at his piano and let the good times roll: 'Blueberry Hill' (US no. 2, UK no. 6 '56), 'I'm Walkin'' (US no. 4, UK no. 19 '57), 'Be My Guest' (US no. 8, UK no. 11 '59), all impossible to dislike and all served from the same stewpot. The last of his twenty British hits, 1961's 'Let the Four Winds Blow', was recorded at his sixtieth recording session, and featured almost the exact same line-up of musicians as 'The Fat Man'.

As Hurricane Katrina destroyed his home town in 2005, Fats was initially believed to have drowned. When he was spotted on the roof of his house a few days later, there was an international sigh of relief.

Gene Vincent first emerged when he won a local Search for a Star contest specifically trying to find the new Elvis Presley. His weaselly looks, mop of oil-black hair and manic smile were hardly a match for Presley's godlike charisma, but his music was on another plane, unhinged, like a freeform rockabilly.

A poor Virginian, he acquired his first guitar aged twelve. In 1955, after joining the navy, he had an accident while riding his brand-new Triumph motorcycle and ended up in the naval hospital with a severely smashed left leg. Doctors recommended amputation; Vincent settled for a steel brace which left him with a permanent limp.

In September 1955 Vincent, leg still in plaster, saw Hank Snow's All Star Jamboree in Norfolk, Virginia, featuring Cowboy Copas, the Louvin Brothers and the King of Western Bop from Tupelo, Elvis Presley. Almost immediately afterwards, Vincent wrote 'Be-Bop-a-Lula' – based on comic-strip character Little Lulu – while stuck in the hospital. Assembling a hard-bitten band called the Blue Caps, they cut 'Be-Bop-a-Lula' (US no. 7, UK no. 16 '56) for Capitol and sold half a million copies. Everything was in the delivery: a vocal born from Vincent's bedridden frustration, Cliff Gallup's piercing trebly guitar lines that walked the line of atonal, and the impromptu shrieks of drummer Dickie Harrell, so perfectly timed that any other take would fall short of perfection. The gibberish, the echo, the twin promise of sex and violence, 'Be-Bop-a-Lula' had the lot.

Miraculously, Vincent and the Blue Caps held it together long enough to cut a string of breakneck rocking classics. They were all aggro, trouble, you'd cross the street to avoid them. Check the titles: 'Race with the Devil', 'Wild Cat', 'High Blood Pressure', 'Who Slapped John'. When the wheels came off the wagon, Vincent was brought over to Britain in 1960 by impresario Jack Good. The shy, polite country gentleman who addressed him as 'sir' was no use to Good. He revised Vincent's image, dressed him from head to toe in black leather and placed a heavy silver chain around his neck. Pretty soon he racked up more hits, less brutal but still good, solid rock 'n' roll: 'She She Little Sheila', 'My Heart', 'Pistol Packin' Mama'. He toured the country with Eddie Cochran and, driving between shows, they crashed at Chippenham in Wiltshire. Cochran was killed. Vincent survived, only to enter an alcoholic tailspin which resulted in his death from a perforated ulcer in 1971. It was a rotten waste of talent. Aside from a few stinging folk-rock sides for Challenge in 1966,* he hadn't made a good record in years.

Though he was one of his closest friends, Oklahoman Eddie Cochran didn't appear to carry any of Vincent's self-destructive baggage. He started as straight country, was a noted guitarist rather than a singer, and his first hit was with a middling teen ballad called 'Sittin' in the Balcony' (US no. 18 '57). It became clear that he was capable of a whole lot more when he sang 'Twenty Flight Rock' in the Jayne Mansfield

---

* Though surprisingly obscure, cuts like 'Love Is a Bird' and 'Born to Be a Rolling Stone' brought out something in Vincent's voice, which by 1966 was not dissimilar to that of the Byrds' Gene Clark, and suggested there could have been a country/folk-rock future for him. 'Bird Doggin'' on the other hand was as fierce as his pioneering 45s, raw garage-rock simplicity. These sessions were collected on an album called *Gene Vincent* that only appeared in Britain in '66, and have been scattered across compilations since.

movie *The Girl Can't Help It*. The poster for this tremendous rock 'n' roll sexploitation flick screamed: 'It's got the HEAT! and the BEAT! for your happiest time!' Fats Domino, the Platters, Gene Vincent and Little Richard also appeared, though ultimately it was jazz singer Julie London who stole the show and made her career with a spectral, sensual performance of 'Cry Me a River'.

More than anyone, Eddie Cochran was the stereotypical rocker: the perfect greased ducktail, the square shoulders, fists like hams and a permanent look of street-smart confidence. Listen to the lyrics, though, and he was a sheep in wolf's clothing. Unlike Chuck Berry he *was* a teenager, and understood the frustrations that Berry skipped over in his search for the promised land. Mostly, these were parental and financial: on 'Somethin' Else' (UK no. 22 '59) he works real hard, saves his dough and gets both car and girl. Moral: yes, it's that simple. Moody parents capable of grounding Eddie, not so easily swayed by his cheeky charm and golden quiff, cloud the horizon on 'Summertime Blues' (US no. 8, UK no. 18 '58) and 'C'mon Everybody' (US no. 35, UK no. 6 '59). Weedier yet, in 'Twenty Flight Rock' he's too tired to rock with his baby, because he's had to climb the stairs thanks to a broken elevator. This was the romance of the American Dream with added naturalism. Cochran developed a semi-spoken, semi-sung style that made it seem like he was sharing a conversation with the teenage world.

'Weekend', 'Teenage Heaven' and 'Jeannie Jeannie Jeannie' are fairground rock 'n' roll in a matchbox: tough vocals, a driving sound, some kind of earthquake. Drive-ins and sock hops were Cochran's habitat and, even if his pockets were empty, he'd always got the wherewithal to pull. This was nowhere more evident than on his posthumous UK number one, 'Three Steps to Heaven': check the directness and confidence of both song and delivery. The almost Spanish guitar line sets up Eddie the matador to give us 'the formula for heaven'. Women clearly fall at his feet (see Step 2), so, while I don't doubt his sincerity, Eddie's formula wasn't much use to a cauliflower-eared, bandy-legged kid from Croydon. I assume, looking back, that he *did* know the formula, but why would he tell all and let other kids cut in on his action?

If it's sad to think of what Eddie Cochran could have achieved if he'd lived past twenty-one, then Buddy Holly's loss is truly tragic.

Buddy Holly was very important to Britain, and almost single-handedly responsible for what came later. He was a new kind of hero, and packed an indecent amount into his twenty-two years on earth. For a start, he didn't look remotely like a pop star, lacked any of the Hollywood gloss or outright weirdness of his contemporaries. Frankly, he looked like a geek. In spite of this he was defiant and narcissistic – he wouldn't have been content with the small beer of the localised rocka-billy scene; he wanted to be a pop star and played up his bespectacled, scrawny look to get what he wanted. He even married the pretty Puerto Rican receptionist at Coral Records.

Holly had been born Charles Hardin Holley in Lubbock, a small Texas town that only wanted him to play straight-down-the-line coun-try – a couple of dispiriting singles on Decca remain as proof. But by 1957, teaming up with drummer Jerry Allison and bassist Joe Maudlin as the Crickets, and working with producer Norman Petty, Holly quickly learnt his way around a studio; Coral in New York signed him on the strength of a demo. The vim of the homely three-piece on 'That'll Be the Day', 'Oh, Boy!', 'Rave On' and 'Maybe Baby' encouraged shy, bespectacled, skinny-limbed kids everywhere and gave them hope.*

He was a good businessman, too. Records came out by the Crickets *and* Buddy Holly, giving him double the hit tally of his contemporar-ies – ten major UK hits in less than eighteen months. It all seemed too good to be true. On a British tour, producer Joe Meek rushed backstage to see Holly – his experiments in the occult had led him to believe the singer would die on August 3rd 1958. The day came and went and Holly lived, but exactly six months later he was killed in a plane crash.

Non-Hollywood looks aside, Holly affected the UK in four ways: as a singer, composer, guitarist and producer. His group, the Crickets, was entirely self-contained. He was just starting to move into an orches-trated sound ('True Love Ways', 'It Doesn't Matter Anymore' – a post-humous UK number one) when he died. Where he'd have gone next is

---

* It's hard to imagine bespectacled Hank Marvin, for one, having the nerve to take the stage without Holly's precedent.

anyone's guess, but the British beat scene would have been very different without him.

Few of the classic rock figures who survived the late-fifties rock 'n' roll carnage sustained themselves artistically through the sixties. The exceptions were Phil and Don, Kentucky's Everly Brothers. They may have looked the very image of Southern hoodlums but they had the voices of harmonising bluebirds, so close in timbre it was almost impossible to tell them apart.

In 1957, after the obligatory country debut single, they hooked up with writers Felice and Boudleaux Bryant. Boudleaux had already been responsible for Frankie Laine's best UK number one, a cackling, bullying, hilarious country lurcher called 'Hey Joe' in '53. The Bryants had light and humour and sly winks in their best uptempo songs ('Bye Bye Love', 'Wake Up Little Susie', 'Bird Dog'), which the Everlys revved up with hard-hitting acoustic rhythms. They could also turn around and write the most molten, ancient-sounding ballads, decades of country, folk and old-world influences distilled into two and a half magical minutes. The story goes that Felice was working as an elevator operator in a Milwaukee hotel. One day the lift doors opened and Boudleaux stepped in. She knew him at once – she had seen his face in a dream when she was eight years old and knew he was her future husband. Given this back story, 'All I Have to Do Is Dream' and 'Devoted to You' (both 1958), hymnal and heavenly, two of rock 'n' roll's greatest love songs, seem like true miracles.

The Bryants and Everlys continued to turn out pristine bopping pop ('(Till) I Kissed You', 'Problems', 'When Will I Be Loved') right up to 1960 – rock 'n' roll's *annus miserabilis* – when they suddenly seemed to stand alone: Chuck Berry had been sent to prison for an indiscretion with a minor; Buddy Holly and Eddie Cochran had died; Little Richard had found God; and Elvis had returned from the army, not to deliver us from 'Living Doll', but to sing Neapolitan light opera. When the Everlys' contract with independent label Cadence was up in 1960, Warner Brothers pounced on the last rockers in town.

The brothers got a million dollars for a ten-year contract, pop's biggest-ever deal at that point. Their first single for the label, like a car with a flashy registration plate, had a catalogue number of WB1. The initial run was pressed on gold vinyl. Confidence was not misplaced. The record was 'Cathy's Clown' and it was a transatlantic number one, staying at the top in Britain for nine weeks.

It's an overfamiliar tune, but if you're listening to 'Cathy's Clown' rather than just hearing it on the radio, it is quite extraordinary: the metallic drum roll following the condemned man on the chorus morphs into the bar-room rinky-tink of the verse as Don Everly drowns his sorrows, even slurring his delivery. This was the first time Don had had the time and facilities to truly *produce* an Everlys record. Even pop's first master producers, Phil Spector and Joe Meek, were learning their craft in 1960, and here was one of the most bankable pop stars in the world stealing a march. An early pop aesthete, his arrangement for 'Cathy's Clown' was inspired by André Kostelanetz's *Grand Canyon Suite*. Warners also saw the Everlys as potential film stars, real actors. They had the looks, and hadn't blotted their copybook by ogling Jayne Mansfield in a rock 'n' roll cash-in movie. A number-one hit, Hollywood calling, what could go wrong?

Their first mistake was relocating from Nashville to LA. The Kentucky boys fully embraced the California lifestyle, which was fine while they were riding high but not so good to them after they failed a screen test. Next, they recorded an old Bing Crosby song called 'Temptation'. The crazed arrangement – *yeah yeah yeah*s battering against a wall of wailing banshees and twelve massed guitars, a vision of eternal torment in two minutes fourteen seconds – came to Don in a dream. The trouble was that their manager and publisher Wesley Rose hated it. He had no financial control over the song and didn't give a hoot for Don's producer ambitions if they weren't going to earn him money. The Everlys wouldn't back down and 'Temptation' finally became a single in summer '61, spending a month at number one in the UK. Rose, slighted, quit as their manager and prevented the brothers from using any of the writers he published. That included not only Felice and Boudleaux Bryant, but also the Everlys themselves. Then they got drafted, and spent six months in the marines.

Cut adrift, musically and geographically, they still had to produce two albums a year for Warner Brothers. Without access to their touchstone writers the brothers panicked and recorded novelties like 'The Sheik of Araby' and country standards. They lost ground fast. Back in civvies, as fast as they could they hooked up with a new breed of sophisticated east-coast writers – Gerry Goffin and Carole King in particular – and crafted the beautiful 'Crying in the Rain', which at least put them back in the Top 10 in 1962. A few months later the Beatles arrived and all resistance was futile.

Behind the scenes, Don Everly had been in turmoil. Years later, a cache of his dark, unreleased work from 1962 and '63 was revealed. One song, the bleak beyond belief 'Nancy's Minuet', was inspired by Henry Mancini's 'Experiment in Terror'. 'I was trying to get harpsichord sounds into my music. We were young, we were in Hollywood on our own, it was terrible actually. Divorces . . . I was drugged out by then. It was a bitter time for me.'

They recorded a Gerry Goffin/Jack Keller song called 'Little Hollywood Girl' – a cautionary tale with cute girly backing vocals that would have been at home on a Cliff Richard single – and shelved it. A few weeks later Don worked up a new arrangement with abrasive piano and an atmosphere of circling menace. In this version, the poppet that Goffin and Keller envisaged has been used and used up by the movie industry. Don Everly recasts the song as if it's the ravaged climax of *Mulholland Drive*. Months later, on a tour of Britain, he attempted suicide – brother Phil completed a forty-date tour on his own. They regrouped, abandoned the sonic experiments, and Don channelled his anger into songs like the hard-drinking 'Price of Love', which took them back to number one in Britain in 1965.

Almost alone among their contemporaries, the Everlys took on and embraced the British beat invasion that had threatened to destroy their career. Violent folk-rocker 'Leave My Girl Alone' and the deeply bereft 'It's All Over' are highlights from their baroque mid-sixties period. By 1968 they had reconnected with their country boyhood on an album, *Roots*, a lightly psychedelicised trip back to Nashville which won them plaudits and was in the vanguard of new country, but brought no sales. They finally ran out of steam in 1970, splitting, then intermittently re-forming. In the whole fourteen-year period from 'Bye Bye Love' to

1970 single 'Yves', they hardly ever cut a bad record and are maybe the most underrated act of their era.

These were the leading lights of rock 'n' roll. Outside of the heavyweights were hundreds of beautiful one-off singles, and acts who came and went leaving a permanent footprint or two. There was Larry Williams, who had an ice-cream bouffant and wrote character sketches, aural cartoon strips about girls like Bony Moronie ('as skinny as a stick of macaroni'), Dizzy Miss Lizzy and Short Fat Fannie. Williams was groomed by producer Robert 'Bumps' Blackwell as Little Richard's successor, and his records had similarly raw vocals, piano-driven intensity and the same sense of dumb, sexy fun. Fast on his feet as well as on vinyl, Williams turned out to be the hustler that Little Richard had only appeared to be. He was a pimp and a drug dealer, and allegedly once pulled a gun on Richard over a debt. There's gratitude for you.

Jack Scott was a pussycat, even though he looked like he'd walked out of a thirties gangster movie. He was the archetypal rock 'n' roll singer, raised in Detroit on hillbilly music with local blues and gospel bubbling into his laconic style. Like Williams, he wrote vignettes for rocking outcasts like the jailbird 'Leroy', gals with names like 'Geraldine' and 'Midgie' ('the strangest girl in the land'), and sang them in a gruff, rangy baritone. They were simple, hard and repetitive. 'Goodbye Baby' (US no. 8 '58) was allegedly the first record Elvis would look for on a jukebox and consisted of little more than the title sung over and over with an ever-growing, keening sense of loss. Best of all was the cocksure 'The Way I Walk' (US no. 35, UK no. 30 '59), which had a zen-like minimalism ('The way I walk's just the way I walk, the way I talk's just the way I talk').

First of the teen-dream pin-up boys who would hog the charts in the early sixties, filling the void left by otherwise occupied or deceased rockers, was Ricky Nelson, who had a light and shoulder-shrugging vocal style that often suggested he was waiting for a bus, slightly bored. He was lucky enough to have guitarist James Burton's work all over his early hits ('Stood Up', 'My Bucket's Got a Hole in It', 'Believe What You Say' – all Top 5 in the US). Burton's efforts were always surprisingly high in the mix, which was a good thing. In mid-'58 Ricky recorded a ballad without Burton's fierceness, 'Poor Little Fool', and it was his first US number one. From this point on he steadily lost energy, even if some of his later hits (especially 'Never Be Anyone Else but You', a UK number three) were quite lovely.

The month that 'Poor Little Fool' spent at the top of the chart can be seen as a turning point, the beginning of the end of the rock 'n' roll era; it was just two and a half years since 'Rock around the Clock' had started the stampede.

The first US number one of 1958 had been the Silhouettes' 'Get a Job', which captured the magic of the era almost perfectly: big noise, angry parents, nonsense syllables, snare drums like upturned dust-bins, unrefined joy. Who were the Silhouettes? What was their follow-up? Who cares? The relentless run of one-off hits on tiny new labels like Clock (Dave 'Baby' Cortez's 'The Happy Organ'), Josie (Bobby Freeman's 'Do You Wanna Dance') and Ember ('Get a Job') was the very heart of rock 'n' roll. There was 'Sea Cruise', Frankie Ford's impression of an ocean liner about to hit an iceberg; Ronnie Self's raucous, demented tribute to 'Bop-a-Lena' – 'man, I dig that freak juvenile!'; Dale Hawkins's futuristic, rhythmic masterpiece 'Susie Q' (which also benefited from James Burton's ferocious guitar-playing); and the Monotones' neanderthal 'Book of Love' (US no. 5 '58), which featured nothing but muffled harmonies, a wildly off-key bassman and a frantic beat on a cardboard box. No grace, no streamlining, just pure fun.* The first wave of rock 'n' roll had absolutely no rules about who sang, how they sang, how they were recorded or how the record was distributed. It was anarchy, the boulder in the middle of the lake, and nothing was quite the same, or quite as new, or quite as free, ever again.

* Like a touchstone for the whole era, 'Book of Love' has been referenced in various songs since, including Don McLean's 'American Pie'. I might be wrong, but the bassman's voice could also be the model for the Muppets' Fozzie Bear.

FIFTEEN MILES FROM
MIDDLESBROUGH: SKIFFLE

Father Geoffrey Beaumont rehearsing his "Jazz Mass" with a local Skiffle Group

If the geographical origins of American rock 'n' roll are rich and varied, with New York, Cleveland, New Orleans and Memphis all in with a shout as birthplace, British rock 'n' roll can be narrowed down, quite definitively, to the London suburb of Cranford. More specifically, to a pub called the White Hart on Bath Road, and to a corrugated-iron hut around the side.

Skiffle – 'folk songs sung to a jazz beat', according to the Reverend Brian Bird's 1958 book on the subject – feels so distant from a twenty-first-century understanding of pop that it can be hard to see where it fits in, or why it was significant. The closest American comparison would be rockabilly – both scenes picked up on Leadbelly's 'Pick a Bale of Cotton' for inspiration – but, in a nutshell, it caused a commotion in the mid-fifties because it was fast and loud, it was a racket and, as Rev.

Bird pointed out, most significantly it was 'homemade, "do-it-yourself" music, within the reach of all of limited means and no more than average ability'. In 1955 almost everything broadcast by the BBC smelt of delicacy and refinement, prettiness and propriety; up against home-grown Carusos like David Whitfield, skiffle was an exciting noise. And it was exciting purely *because* it was a noise.

So it was the original DIY music, cut-and-paste, no qualifications necessary; amid the combination of washboard percussion, broom-handle bass, kazoos and nasal shrieks you can hear the first footsteps on a path that led to Joe Meek, to punk and to jungle. This urgency and sense of constructing something out of nothing – and doing it right now! – was fundamental to the progression of British pop. Some of Lonnie Donegan's hits may sound like scrunched-up tinfoil, but the airplay that 'Rock Island Line' received on the BBC in 1955 inspired John Lennon, Paul McCartney and Jimmy Page to pick up guitars for the first time; it's one of the unlikelier facts of history that a song about illegally transporting pig iron is British pop's fountainhead.

So how did a Leadbelly song get onto BBC radio and cause a revolution? Skiffle emanated from the trad-jazz revival – Dixieland stuff, with no homegrown embellishment – which had been picking up speed in Britain since the mid-forties, helmed by the popular and likeable BBC Light Programme regular Humphrey Lyttelton.* Over in Cranford was Ken Colyer, an irascible New Orleans jazz obsessive. By 1949 he'd found some like-minded souls and formed a group; they hired the hut next to the White Hart, a stone's throw from Heathrow. Naming themselves after one of the Thames's more obscure tributaries, the Crane River Jazz Band were confident enough to charge people to enter their hut and watch as they played a primitive set with two guitars, a double

---

* Lyttelton deserves at least a footnote in this book for his constant gentle presence, even though he was a jazzer through and through. On VE Day 1945 he was inadvertently recorded by the BBC playing his trumpet while sitting in a wheelbarrow – the recording is still in their archive. His 'Out of the Galleon' was one of the first four seven-inch singles released in Britain; his 'Bad Penny Blues' was Joe Meek's first hit single in 1956; he part-owned the 100 Club on Oxford Street, home to the firestarting Punk Rock Festival in September '76; and he played on and arranged 'Life in a Glasshouse' for Radiohead's *Amnesiac* album in 2001.

bass, a washboard for rhythm and a modified kazoo with a horn stuck into the end.* The repertoire was very similar to the sounds that would soon inspire rockabilly in the States, a country-blues mix of Leadbelly, Big Bill Broonzy, Lonnie Johnson, Sonny Terry and Brownie McGhee numbers, though – significantly – there were no original songs. It was ultra-basic and the crowds loved it; by mid-1950 they had a residency in a West End cellar bar. Somewhere along the line the Cranes came up with the name 'skiffle' – a New Orleans term for house parties organised to pay the rent – to describe what they were doing.

Melody Maker, the jazz weekly, hated Colyer's band. He was a purist, a grouchy extremist who thought Louis Armstrong had sold out when he brought a saxophone into his band. His conservatism accidentally beat a new path. What he did with skiffle was to revive a music that was so old it seemed radically new; in this way, he is a forefather to Morrissey – who took early-sixties, pre-Beatles pop culture to shape the Smiths' image and lyrics – and the indie revolution. What seemed like exotic distance to Ken Colyer seemed very real to people still living in two-up two-downs, in ramshackle Victorian structures with galley kitchens and outdoor toilets. The washboard, the mop, the bucket – these were everyday items in working-class fifties Britain. Transforming them into musical instruments with a few nails and a few screws caught the imagination of kids like a home-made Meccano set.

Tony 'Lonnie' Donegan was an accomplished jazz guitarist with an interest in blues. Nothing if not resourceful, he had discovered a source of blues and folk music in the library of the American Embassy. Donegan was a regular visitor and diligently listened to everything they had – he even pinched a couple of rare 78s, including 'a record that Muddy Waters had made when he was a farm worker in Mississippi. I

---

* The original New Orleans term for skiffle bands was 'spasm bands', who – unable to afford brass instruments or banjos – played whatever instruments came to hand. One of the earliest documented spasm bands played in Doc Malney's Minstrel Show, and its members' bizarre names anticipate the DIY punk acts of the late seventies: Stale Bread (zither), Cajun (harmonica), Slew-Foot Pete (guitar, made from a cigar box), Whisky (string bass, made from a half-barrel) and Warm Gravy (banjo, constructed from a cheese box).

borrowed it and never took it back. I told them that I'd lost it and paid a fine, quite happily of course.' Donegan was an opportunist as well as an enthusiast.

When the Crane River Jazz Band split in '52, Ken Colyer joined the navy and went AWOL in New Orleans.* On his return to England, after a stint in a Louisiana jail, the rebel Colyer was met at Waterloo station as a conquering hero by the fast-rising Chris Barber Band, who now included the pilfering Lonnie Donegan on banjo; Colyer joined them immediately. Their skiffle interludes got the crowds more excited than anything in Barber's main set, but pretty soon sparks flew between uptight Ken and wily Lonnie. Colyer was the enthusiast, the idealist and natural leader, but Donegan had the hunger for fame and fortune. Colyer issued an ultimatum, lost it and quit the band.

The Chris Barber Band had already cut 'Rock Island Line' as an album track with Donegan in 1954. It started as a spoken-word thing, a folk story about getting one up on the customs man who thinks the narrator has livestock on his train; the premise couldn't be less promising, but the record gets gradually faster, and 'Rock Island Line' ends up mildly demented. Unexpectedly, it picked up one BBC radio play, which led to a torrent of requests, repeat plays and a single release on Decca in late '55, when it reached number eight; for teenage Britain, it was the most influential British record of the decade. Photos of Liverpool skiffle band the Quarrymen at the Woolton church fete are testament (Donegan's 'Gamblin' Man' was number one on the day Lennon and McCartney met in 1957). 'Rock Island Line' was the point at which British pop – 'I fooled you! I fooled you! I got *pig iron*! I got *pig iron*!' – audibly gained momentum.

When British teens realised that they could make it onto the radio by mastering a broomstick and a kazoo, the revolution commenced. Every town suddenly had a skiffle band – the Vikings

---

* He spent his time mixing with his heroes, such as Lawrence Marrero, Joe Watkins and Alcide 'Slow Drag' Pavageau. Letters home were written up in the newly respectful *Melody Maker*. The local police were less impressed and advised him to play with white musicians. Colyer did no such thing. This was enough to get his visa rescinded and have him thrown in jail.

from Birmingham, the Dominoes in Leigh, Lancashire, and the Lea Valley Skiffle Group from Hackney Wick, an area which probably dealt with industrial by-products far more gruesome than pig iron. Grandchildren of the Industrial Revolution, they all had the right to sing through their noses.

For a good twelve months skiffle ruled, with 'Rock Island Line' (US no. 8 '56) and Chas McDevitt and Nancy Whiskey's 'Freight Train' (UK no. 5, US no. 40 '57) even hitting the American charts. Generally, the rougher and louder it was, the better. Johnny Duncan's brace of 1957 hits 'Last Train to San Fernando' (UK no. 2) and 'Footprints in the Snow' (UK no. 27) stand out, and Jimmy Miller and the Barbecues' rabid 'Sizzling Hot' is a raucous match for any lost rockabilly classic. Lonnie Donegan, his dander up, produced a pair of the most primitive British number ones ever in 'Cumberland Gap' and 'Gamblin' Man' (both 1957). The latter is a two-chord thrash, entirely unmoored from melody, with a one-note guitar solo, that works its way to self-obliteration, coming close to white noise by the three-minute mark. Here are other pointers to British pop's future: you can hear the drone and repetition of Status Quo and, with a markedly similar DIY drive, the Fall.

Why was skiffle's sudden decline in 1958 as rapid as its rise three years earlier? Largely it was down to the limited number of songs that punters demanded to hear – there were no British skiffle compositions, there was no way forward. Almost no British teenagers would have thought to write their own songs as – aside from Tommy Steele, who operated in a quite different area – there were no role models. Harder to understand, in retrospect, is why no one dared to cover contemporaneous rock 'n' roll songs. So everybody's skiffle set included the same Leadbelly tunes and a breakneck 'Don't You Rock Me Daddy-O'; skiffle's lack of ambition and fear of tampering with its folk tradition gave it a built-in sell-by date. Copies of the Reverend Brian Bird's *Skiffle: The Story of Folk-song with a Jazz Beat* gathered dust. The music was swept away like outdoor toilets and back-to-back houses.

As it turned out, Lonnie Donegan had real staying power, and racked up twenty-nine Top 40 hits, only fading from the view with the advent of Beatlemania in late '62; he worked hard, but he was always a man with a hand on his wallet, and while Chris Barber dug deeper, bringing blues and jazz musicians over to Britain for the first time and helping to birth the first truly international movement in British pop, Donegan abandoned skiffle in 1958 for music hall ('Does Your Chewing Gum Lose Its Flavour', UK no. 3, US no. 5 '61), folk ('Tom Dooley', UK no. 3 '58; 'Battle of New Orleans', UK no. 2 '59) and comedy. He scored his biggest-ever hit, 'My Old Man's a Dustman', in 1960, a year of bloody awful records, of which shameless Lonnie's number one was possibly the worst.

ROCK WITH THE CAVEMEN:
BRITISH ROCK 'N' ROLL

If skiffle was shed-grown and organic, British rock 'n' roll started off as the most genetically modified music of the fifties. When 'Rock around the Clock' reached number one, the publishing companies on Denmark Street and pro musicians, mainly jazzers, tripped over themselves to get some shillings from the new fad. In America, new independent record labels took chances and hoovered up untrained, unsigned acts from street corners; in Britain, the Victor Silvester band bought three dozen pairs of blue suede shoes from Freeman Hardy Willis and tried vainly to adapt Bill Haley for the ballrooms of Bognor and Barnstaple.* Commitment was non-existent. Don Lusher's 'Rock and Roll', released on Decca in

---

* Silvester's contribution was 'Society Rock', a doomed attempt to blend blue rinse and Brylcreem. Other band leaders did show some understanding of the music, notably Ted Heath, who recorded Ella Mae Morse songs with Lita Roza.

1955, was theoretically the first UK rock single, but when you took it home and stuck it on the Dansette you only heard big-band swing with a lightly oiled drum track; it had nothing at all to do with Chuck Berry. The big Tin Pan Alley story of '55 wasn't Bill Haley, it was Ruby Murray.

The old guard cut covers of American songs as they always had, thus nipped-and-tucked Denmark Street versions of Fats Domino's 'Ain't That a Shame' (the Southlanders), the Drifters' 'Honey Love' (Dennis Lotis) and Little Richard's 'Tutti Frutti' (the Four Jones Boys, who thoughtfully added an extra verse about ice cream) came and went while Britain was largely oblivious to the originals. Almost all were dire. Exceptions came from the reliable Alma Cogan ('Why Do Fools Fall in Love' and Fats Domino's 'I'm in Love Again') and Frankie Vaughan (Boyd Bennett's 'My Boy Flat Top').* And then there was Jimmy Young.

An odd reversal of the Pat Boone phenomenon, Young sounded godawful on ballads ('Unchained Melody', UK no. 1 '55) and starchy on country and western ('The Man from Laramie', 'Wayward Wind'). 'Chain Gang', though, a number-nine hit from early 1956, was just plain weird. The backing – caterwauling brass, whipcrack snare, moaning convicts – sounds like it was recorded in a quarry, and Young's vocal is drenched in reverb. On first listen I assumed it was an Anglo take on the 'Heartbreak Hotel' vocal production. Then I realised, with a jolt, that 'Chain Gang' predates Elvis's British debut by months. If this wasn't odd enough, at the song's climax it trips out into proto-dub, Young's voice echoing in a void of tape delay and lonesome stand-up bass, oblique, dissolving.

Still, one great, largely forgotten single didn't make a scene. Anthony Newley summed up the strangeness of the early British rock 'n' roll performers. He had played the Artful Dodger in David Lean's *Oliver Twist*

---

* Vaughan is an intriguing character, hard to pin down as anything more specific than pure showbiz – his nickname, after all, was Mr Versatility. He may have been built for the Palladium but he always gave a hysterical edge to his covers of American hits – notably Jim Lowe's 'Green Door' (UK no. 2 '56) and Gene McDaniels's 'Tower of Strength' (UK no. 1 '61) – that made him hard to ignore. Later in the sixties he covered Jimmy Radcliffe's big-city soul ballad 'There Goes the Forgotten Man' and the Beatles' 'Wait', and didn't disgrace himself on either.

in 1948, then appeared in the mid-fifties radio comedy series *Floggit's* before doing his national service. Drawing on this experience, Newley was chosen to star in 1959's *Idle on Parade*, in which he played a rocker in the army; it was slightly snarky, a kind of *Carry On Elvis*, but two songs in the film became hits – the title track (number thirteen) and the ballad 'I've Waited So Long' (number three) – and so Newley became a bona fide pop star. That the songs were parodies didn't seem to bother anyone.*

While London's music-publishing world couldn't see rock 'n' roll as a genuine breakthrough, there was a clutch of younger hucksters who certainly could. The whole rock scene was condensed into a few coffee bars in Soho, notably the 2i's on Old Compton Street, yards away from the hive of musical-instrument shops on Charing Cross Road and publishers on Denmark Street. Larry Parnes was the most significant new face in town, a shrewd manager in his late twenties who collected autographs at the London Palladium. His first charge was Tommy Steele, né Hicks, a blond moptop with an endless grin who came from the docks of Bermondsey. Steele had been a merchant seaman, travelling the world with his acoustic guitar and picking up a bunch of rock 'n' roll numbers en route which virtually no one in Britain knew – and certainly nobody else was playing live. On his return he found himself a gig at the 2i's, where he pricked up the ears of publicity man John Kennedy and the excitable Parnes: 'The first time I saw Tommy, the moment he hit the stage in his jeans, it was electrifying, the same as with Johnnie Ray.'

Steele's first single, the frantic frolic 'Rock with the Caveman' (UK no. 13 '56), was written by musical writer Lionel Bart and hard-living actor Mike Pratt, who would provide him with a string of hits plus the material for a brace of film soundtracks, *The Tommy Steele Story*

---

* Newley's hit run included covers of American rock 'n' roll (Lloyd Price's 'Personality', no. 6 '59), Italian ballads ('If She Should Come to You', no. 4 '60), jazzy wise-ass versions of folk songs ('Strawberry Fair', no. 3 '60; 'Pop Goes the Weasel', no. 12 '61), and the gloopiest teen pop (Frankie Avalon's 'Why', no. 1 '60). He tried his hand at pretty much everything, married Joan Collins, moved to Hollywood and eventually became a respected writer, responsible for Nina Simone's 'Feelin' Good', the lyrics to the *Goldfinger* theme and the soundtrack to *Willie Wonka*. And Newley owed it all to a couple of clunky rock parodies.

and *The Duke Wore Jeans*. This was an impressively fast rise to the top, but with only Jimmy Young and the skifflers to contend with, and no American rockers playing in Britain until 1957, it had been a pretty simple move from playing to fifty people at the 2i's to main attraction at the Roxy. Most of Steele's ensuing singles – 'Elevator Rock', 'Shiralee', 'Butterfingers' – were charming and naive, endearingly amateurish, with odd smudges of echo and strangely slurred vocals, as if the new American sound had been passed to Bermondsey by Chinese whispers. He was groundbreaking, Britain's first rocker, but Tommy Steele is still better remembered for the dozens of pantos and musicals he starred in after renouncing rock 'n' roll in 1959. 'When Tommy Steele steps on to a theatre stage,' said *Picture Post* in 1957, 'it is like killing day at some fantastic piggery. The act itself is simple enough. It's ninety per cent youthful exuberance. There is not a trace of sex, real or implied.'

More significant in the long term than Denmark Street's attempts to cash in on a passing trend, or Tommy Steele's cute movies, was the London label. This was an offshoot of Decca which licensed American recordings from independent American labels for UK release, and was the closest British fans could get to the American rock 'n' roll experience. In 1956 London issued the first British singles by Fats Domino, Little Richard and Carl Perkins; a year later Ricky Nelson and Jerry Lee Lewis joined the roster, and in 1958 they released a staggering 242 singles, from the ubiquitous (Eddie Cochran's 'Summertime Blues') to the more esoteric ('Daddy Lolo' by Ganim's Asia Minors). The silver-on-black label was a reliable source, a trusted friend when there was precious little information in the press or on the radio about the new sound, and it was quickly fetishised by British rock 'n' roll fans.

Singles on London served to emphasise the clear distinction between the sound of Britain's homegrown rock 'n' roll and its US counterpart. Raw sexuality was largely replaced by the embarrassment of hard-up jazzers and red-faced politeness. The major exception to the rule was Billy Fury; if Elvis was all about sex and immortality, then Billy Fury's appeal was sex and death. As a child he'd contracted rheumatic fever – he wasn't expected to live past sixteen. His fans knew this, and Fury played on it; his greatest songs were huge and tragic, orchestrated burlesques of kitchen-sink, monochrome Britain. Halfway to Paradise, nothing ever quite fulfilled.

Having scored with Tommy Steele, Larry Parnes had begun to build a management stable of artists with widescreen names: Marty Wilde, Duffy Power, Vince Eager, Dickie Pride and Billy Fury. Most were from London and hung out at the 2i's, but Fury – once Ron Wycherley – was a teenage tugboat worker from the Dingle in Liverpool. This hillside area, thick with terraced slums, had already been singled out as gang central in the 1958 Frankie Vaughan vehicle *Dangerous Youth*. A year later Wycherley, with cheeks freshly scarred by cigarettes in a gang fight, auditioned for Parnes backstage at a Marty Wilde show in Birkenhead; as if it were a scene from a Judy Garland film, he was instantly given support billing on the rest of the tour.

From 1959 until the rise of the Beatles in 1963, Fury would be one of a triumvirate of British boys who were permanent fixtures in the Top 10. Adam Faith (né Terry Nelhams) certainly looked the part when he first appeared with a blond fringe and a beatnik jumper. He resembled a moody French student, though his gargled and spluttered delivery on breakthrough hit 'What Do You Want' (UK no. 1 '59) was less Acton's Antoine Doinel than an over-caffeinated Buddy Holly. His singles were usually very short, well under two minutes long, and stuck closely to the blueprint of 'What Do You Want', which in turn had leant heavily on Holly's swansong 'It Doesn't Matter Anymore'. They were all froth and bubbles, guitar and drums pushed aside in favour of John Barry's playful pizzicato arrangements, and they were hard to dislike. Alone of the original British rockers, he later took Merseybeat head-on when his career started to flag, hiring the Roulettes as a backing group and coming up with a tremendous second run of hits in '63 and '64 ('The First Time', no. 5 '63; 'We Are in Love', no. 11 '64) that included his only American Top 40 entry, a raucous screamer called 'It's Alright'.

Cheshunt's Cliff Richard was the biggest star at the 2i's after Tommy Steele. His Anglo-Indian complexion and pink jacket gave him an exotic air, and he practised his moody look well. Cliff's first few singles were written by his guitarist Ian Samwell and they were all impressive, low-slung rockers, especially 'Move It' (no. 2 '58) and 'Dynamite' (no.

16 '59). 'Latin and calypso got nothin' on real country music that just drives along,' he sang, giving the impression that he not only had an ethnographic grasp on where it came from but also knew rock 'n' roll was here to stay. In spite of this, he soon settled down into a harmless easy-rock sound typified by Lionel Bart's decidedly non-driving country song 'Living Doll', his first number one in 1959. Cliff quickly stopped sneering, ditched the pink jacket, and four decades of hits gently followed.

Billy Fury, however, looked and sounded exactly as a pop star should: he had fine bone structure, a tremulous voice and a real sense of mystery. On stage he wore gold lamé suits, like Merseyside's very own Elvis – he could have passed for an American. Unusually, he also wrote his own songs, slowies about how much he missed his numerous exes ('Margo', 'Colette') and rockers about how much he'd love to see them suffer ('Gonna Type a Letter', 'Don't Knock upon My Door'); this way he had as many male fans as female, something neither Adam nor Cliff could manage. He also wrote every song on his Anglo-rockabilly album *The Sound of Fury* (1960) – no other UK debut would be entirely self-written until Pink Floyd's *Piper at the Gates of Dawn* seven years later – which earned him plenty of respect among fellow musicians. John Lennon was once caught asking for his autograph.

Fury's first few singles sold well enough, hovering just inside the Top 20, but when he devoted more time to ballads everything clicked: his seventh hit, 'Wond'rous Place' (no. 25 '60), was sparse and thick with atmosphere, the vocal all echoed sighs and whispers. It was the most sensual record yet in British pop: 'I found a place full of charms, a magic world in my baby's arms, a soft embrace like satin and lace.' He rarely cut rockers after this waymark.

'Halfway to Paradise', his biggest hit (UK no. 4 '61), was opulently arranged by Ivor Raymonde, with an intro like a triple-speed Beethoven's Fifth cushioned by booming tympani. It could have been about an ex or, possibly, the heartbreaking barrier between star and fan. The biggest-sounding Fury single of all was 'I'm Lost Without You' (no. 14 '65), which had wailing choirs and a vortex of strings that sounded like World War Three in a minor key – and still it had room for moments of awful fragility. It was Fury's best record, but by then time and fashion were shoving him aside. Never one for the spotlight – a foible which made him even more alluring to his loyal fanbase – he went into semi-retirement in 1967, living on a farm, tending injured animals. Occasionally he'd sneak out, and he had a fine cameo as Stormy Tempest in David Puttnam's 1973 take on fifties Britain *That'll Be the Day*. Beyond that lay the twilight of cabaret and an early death, aged forty-one, in 1983.

A highlight of his live set in the sixties had been a mawkish thing called 'Nobody's Child': Billy sang, 'Sometimes I get so lonesome I wish that I could die,' and three thousand girls screamed back, 'DON'T DIE BILLY!' An exhibitionist on stage, Billy Fury was fidgety and nervous off it: 'People thought I was a real moody sod. This has all got to do with shyness and paranoia. I had a thick Liverpool accent and I was really shy about opening my mouth. I didn't think I'd be understood and I thought it'd be easier if I didn't say anything.' The shy extrovert with the perfect quiff, Billy Fury was the blueprint for the British pop star.

Though he only had one minor hit ('Jet Black Machine', UK no. 15 '60), Vince Taylor should not go unrecognised. For pure image, he blew even Billy Fury off stage. If much of British rock 'n' roll was close to theatre, it made sense that a bloke from Hounslow who pretended to be from Hollywood, and was managed by Joe Barbera of the Hanna-Barbera cartoon empire, could become one of its minor legends.

Taylor was a proper showman, and far too wild to succeed in fifties Britain. On stage he would stand in darkness, and all you could see was the glint of his swinging bike chain. Then the lights would go up and he was covered head to toe in black leather. His best remembered song is 'Brand New Cadillac', later covered by the Clash, but his image and myth count for plenty more. He found fame in France in 1961, stayed there, took too much LSD, and by 1965 had rechristened himself Mateus – white-robed, he walked along the banks of the Seine proclaiming to his few remaining followers that he was the son of God.

Like Billy Fury, he endlessly intrigued the young David Bowie. The legend of long-lost Vince, a forgotten link in the chain, would resurface a little while later in the guise of Ziggy Stardust.

The best record of the entire scene was no obscurity, though. Johnny Kidd and the Pirates are remembered for little else, and they never scored another Top 20 hit, but 'Shakin' All Over' was a masterpiece. It had a teasing guitar line,* a menacing panther of a bassline, and Johnny with his eye patch and nervous vocal defined the British sexual experience – total fear: 'When you move in right up close to me, that's when I get the shakes all over me.' Deservedly it was a number one in 1960, the highlight of a tainted pop year.

Vince and Billy and Johnny had the looks, the moves and the sounds, but still they looked to America to shape them. Arguably the most significant character in this chapter, largely written out of history, is the avuncular Bert Weedon. In the forties he had been a guitarist for Ted Heath, much in demand as a session man in the fifties, and was playing in Cyril Stapleton's big band when he first heard 'Rock around the Clock'. Unlike any of his contemporaries, Weedon was thrilled by the guitar-playing. While he carried on as Britain's premier session guitarist – backing Frank Sinatra, Judy Garland and Tony Bennett when they came to town – he was evangelical about guitar-playing and wanted others to join in the fun. He wrote a book called *Play in a Day* in 1957: it was the acknowledged starting point for Joe Brown – who played guitar on *The Sound of Fury* in 1960 – as well as an acknowledged primer for Paul McCartney, George Harrison, Peter Green, Jimmy Page, Pete Townshend, Eric Clapton, Tony Iommi and Brian May, the full flower of British rock to come. Without Weedon's generous guidance, Britain might have remained a pop backwater. He was the key enabler.

In the north-east, bespectacled Brian Rankin and his best friend Bruce Welch practised every day, as per Bert's instructions. They came down to London for a talent contest in 1958, stayed overnight at King's Cross station, and the following day made their way to the 2i's. They never went home. Brian changed his name to Hank Marvin, and promptly

---

* The guitarist was Joe Moretti, a session man who deserves a mention here – he also played on Vince Taylor's 'Brand New Cadillac' and contributed the high hook line on Tom Jones's 'It's Not Unusual'. Mick Ronson would later pay homage to Moretti by mimicking his guitar lines on David Bowie's 1973 tribute to his sixties youth, 'Pin Ups'.

became the teenage guitar hero Bert Weedon – already approaching forty – could never be.

Writer Paul Morley has said that the Shadows have always been a disappointment to him as their name implies a darkness which doesn't really tally with Hank Marvin's grin. I think the name is perfect; they have remained in the background, a rarely mentioned influence on British pop that is nevertheless always there, just out of sight. The Shadows were not only the most successful group of the era, they were also the very first to have a distinctly Anglo sound. Initially they were made up of the star players at the 2i's, and were corralled to back Cliff Richard on his first British tour. Then, after a couple of flop vocal singles, they stepped out with the moody instrumental 'Apache',* a number one in 1960. Cliff played an alluring hand drum on the intro, Tony Meehan alternated a steady rock beat with a catlike grace on the cymbals, while Hank Marvin played the melody slow and low. It was deeply atmospheric. Crucially, this was no copy but the sound of an imagined America, refracted through British eyes – the impact of Westerns and crime movies on underfed post-war kids mixing with the exoticism of rock 'n' roll's armoury; Hank played a Fender Stratocaster,† Jet Harris had the first electric bass guitar in Britain. Jet was bottle-blond, heavy-lidded and intense, and drummer Tony Meehan was a schoolkid, but

---

* 'Apache' was first recorded by Bert Weedon. Its composer, Jerry Lordan – who went on to provide the Shadows with 'Wonderful Land' and 'Atlantis' – was unimpressed by Weedon's slow, slightly jazzy arrangement, and passed it on to Hank Marvin during a tour, suggesting that if the Shadows recorded it quickly they could beat Weedon's version into the shops. Though chart positions don't do his legacy justice – he only scored one Top 10 hit with 'Guitar Boogie Shuffle' in 1959 – Bert would belatedly have his day in the sun when 22 Golden Guitar Greats gave him a surprise number-one album in 1976.
† Hank Marvin: 'Cliff bought me a red Stratocaster in 1959, and it played such a huge part in the development of my style. We loved James Burton's sound on the Ricky Nelson records, and we knew he played a Fender. Also, Buddy Holly had this outrageous-looking guitar on the cover of The Chirping Crickets. There was an import ban on American guitars then, so we got the brochure and found out Buddy Holly's guitar was a Stratocaster. And because it was the most expensive one, we assumed that's what James Burton played. It was just stunning, even to look at.'

it was Hank who schoolboys wanted to copy, miming to a string of perfectly titled Top 5 singles ('Apache', 'FBI', 'Man of Mystery', 'The Frightened City', 'Kon-Tiki') with a tennis racket in front of the bedroom mirror.

It's impossible to overstate the Shadows' importance. Each new single was an event, and they scored five further number ones in the wake of 'Apache'. Brian May taped 'Foot Tapper' (their last number one, in March '63) off the radio and learnt to play it before the record was in the shops. Pete Townshend later called them 'a living myth . . . frozen in my mind as one of the greatest passions of my life'. The Beatles' first composition, recorded in Hamburg, was an instrumental called 'Cry for a Shadow'. Every kid in Britain wanted to be in the Shadows.

Their best single was 'Wonderful Land', which spent eight weeks at number one in early '62. It was probably written as a hymn to America, its glamour, its colour and its endless skies.* But what I hear in 'Wonderful Land' is a British dream of the future, the primary-coloured optimism of post-war Britain, people moving to the new towns ringing London, the space and light in the bright open spaces of Crawley and Stevenage (or the modernist sweep down to the water in reconstructed Plymouth, the Gerry Anderson-like underpass and flyover in Croydon). There is also a definite melancholy to the song, in the melody and the string arrangement's huge sense of promise, and its awareness that the promise is too huge to ever be truly fulfilled. Just months ahead of the Beatles' annexation of British pop, condemning everyone in this chapter to instant museum status,† 'Wonderful Land' sounds vast, blue-skied, and still so sad.

---

* The reality of America in 1962 was certainly glamorous, but possibly not in the way the wide-eyed Shads would have imagined: during its stay at number one, the American president, John F. Kennedy, spent the night with the closest thing to American royalty, Marilyn Monroe.
† Cliff Richard was the sole survivor of the Beatles revolution. After aping the Mersey beat with a brace of ace singles – 'Don't Talk to Him' (no. 2 late '63) and 'I'm the Lonely One' (no. 8 early '64 – note the precipitous drop in chart position) – Cliff dug deep into ballad territory, where the Beatles couldn't touch him. It wasn't until 1972 that he finally released a flop, 'A Brand New Song' failing to reach the Top 50. But he'd be back.

WHISPERING BELLS: DOO WOP

NOLAN STRONG ┇ DIABLOS

Ever-loved, Everlasting Hits

♦ "THE WIND" ♦ "MIND OVER MATTER"
♦ "YOU ARE" ♦ "ADIOS, MY DESERT LOVE"
♦ "DADDY ROCKIN' STRONG" ♦ "VILLAGE OF LOVE"
MANY OTHERS—PLUS

FORTUNE of HITS

L P No. 8010   VOLUME 1 and VOLUME 2   L P No. 8012
AT LAST! The Sensational New Album

Exclusively On

ⓕRTUNE

LP No. 8015 "MIND OVER MATTER"

While Britain struggled to find its own rock 'n' roll voice in the fifties, America already had several, and they all called out from different cities: in Memphis and Nashville there was rockabilly; New Orleans had its own swampy, lolloping R&B; and New York had the street-corner symphonies that would wind up being tagged, onomatopoeically, as doo wop.

Doo wop lived within and outside of rock 'n' roll. Singing on street corners wasn't new to pop; it was part of an urban folk tradition. Even Perry Como had learnt how to sing harmony in a barber shop. But the style that became known as doo wop* was the first to incorporate

---

* The term wasn't in common usage until the seventies, and its origins are disputed. It's safe to say that 'doo wop', 'boo wop' and 'doo wah' are vocal approximations of a horn section, but the nonsense syllables 'doo wop' first appeared on a modern pop single in 1954 – 'Never' by Los Angeles group Carlyle Dundee and the Dundees; the first hit with a prominent 'doo wop' backing was the Turbans' 'When You Dance' (US no. 33 '55) a year later. The late New York DJ Gus Gossert is credited with first using 'doo wop' as a descriptive term for group-harmony music in the late sixties, but Gossert, maybe out of modesty, claimed it was already being used in California.

singers as musicians – if you loved rock 'n' roll but couldn't afford a stand-up bass, you found yourself a baritone to do the trick; chances are you couldn't afford a saxophone either, so you would pick out a resonant tenor. Decades later, the human beatbox would continue the tradition for kids without the wherewithal to buy a Roland TR-909.

In some ways doo wop is the purest pop form: reliant on the flexibility of the human voice, it is infinitely adaptable. Its essence is simplicity. Doo wop is passionate and joyous, naive too, and has a sensuality missing from other rock 'n' roll subgenres (almost all aggressively sexual) which would have a lasting influence on pop.

Doo wop can veer from the ethereal, like Nolan Strong and the Diablos' 'The Wind' with its endless melancholy and deathless romance, a blissed-out purgatory, to the barely human sound of the Chips' 'Rubber Biscuit' (or 'r-r-r-r-rubber biscuit' as the chief Chip would have it), something like an aural Harpo Marx skit. At its best you can hear automobiles, subway trains and church bells in the harmonies. The voices reverberated around alleys and subways, hallways and staircases, even school gyms, anywhere its perpetrators could find an echo to lift the sound from the ground, closer to the stars. The acme of doo wop, the Five Satins' 'In the Still of the Nite', was recorded in a church basement. It contains the beautiful noise, the essence of a city, that Neil Diamond later referenced; to my ears it condenses the entire fabric of New York inside three minutes, and has a saturated saxophone break that sounds like it echoes from one end of the Holland tunnel to the other.

Doo wop had its roots in the thirties. The Ink Spots were a vocal group who scored several international hits ('Whispering Grass', 'Do I Worry', 'If I Didn't Care', 'Don't Get around Much Anymore') which set a secular template, with Bill Kenny's high tenor lead at its heart, and the novelty of Hoppy Jones's basso profundo, which would often drift into a lengthy spoken section. They were widely imitated – Elvis copped their style on 'Are You Lonesome Tonight' – and they even made it to Hollywood, appearing in a movie called *Pardon My Sarong*.

As well as the secular Ink Spots and Mills Brothers, doo wop also had sacred roots, which lay in two different kinds of vocal group – jubilee (multi-voice harmony lead) and quartet (solo lead with harmony back-ing). Post-war, a bunch of groups emerged who were influenced by both sacred and secular strands, notably the Orioles. If R&B was earthy, then the Orioles were all air: led by the light and clear voice of Sonny Til, they sounded sophisticated, they made girls scream rather unreligiously, and this helped them to cross over from the R&B charts to the US Top 20 with 'It's Too Soon to Know' (1948) and 'Crying in the Chapel' (1953).

The Orioles were from Baltimore, and took their name from the Maryland state bird. In their wake, partly as a tribute and partly hoping lightning would strike twice, came a vast number of 'bird' groups: the Larks ('My Reverie'), the Crows ('Gee'), the Penguins ('Earth Angel'), the Flamingos ('I Only Have Eyes for You'), the Robins ('Smokey Joe's Cafe'). As with later genres which largely thrived on one-shot, one-hit wonders – girl groups, garage punk, disco, rave – anonymity was built in, and almost seemed prized, as if the groups were just happy to be part of an ongoing scene.

The classic story of a doo-wop act was that a gang of kids would be dragged off the street to record two songs in a shack of a studio. Their 'manager' – a local businessman with little feel for the music – then pressed a single which, nineteen times out of twenty, sold locally and maybe made him a few bucks. Typical were the Five Sharps, from the Jamaica housing project in Queens, New York. They recorded a maud-lin version of 'Stormy Weather' as their sole single.* Tenor Bobby Ward remembers they were paid in hot dogs and soda pop, and sales were so bad they had to buy their own copies.

Every so often, one of these singles would catch fire. The manager got richer, the group received assurances and, when they turned twenty-one, they realised they'd been turned over. Songwriting credits were falsified,

---

* Extremely rare and only issued on 78, a copy of 'Stormy Weather' was discov-ered and sold at an auction in 1977 for $3,866. This, the only extant copy of the record, is now in a bank vault. Its owners listen to it once every five years. Doo-wop collectors are a fierce breed. Bob Hite, of blues-rockers Canned Heat, used to buy spare copies of any rare record he owned just to smash them and make his copy rarer.

publishing royalties never materialised. None flew higher or fell harder than Frankie Lymon and the Teenagers.

Their influence extends well beyond the range of their recorded legacy. It's hard to imagine the Jackson Five without the Teenagers; the entire sixties girl-group genre is based on their sound. Lymon was born in Washington Heights in 1942. In 1956 he sold two million copies of 'Why Do Fools Fall in Love'. The answer to the song's question is simple – because we're alive. And few records make you feel more alive than 'Why Do Fools Fall in Love'.

It starts as a conventional doo-wop single: the bassman sets the beat, and later on there's a cacophonous sax break. But in between it's entirely Lymon's song, fresh and exuberant and unbelievably youthful. It was only the second rock 'n' roll record to reach number one in Britain. The combination of almost feminine high tenor and bubbling bass was instant fun; anyone could get in on the act and, within a year, there were over seventy groups in the States who featured a black male lead on the edge of puberty.

Unfortunately, the group were hustled by George Goldner, one of the era's toughest wheeler-dealers but also an inveterate gambler. To give him his due, he was also a fan who understood pop instinctively, and did more to unite black and white in early-fifties America than almost anyone. Originally he was a mambo teacher with a string of dancehalls across New York. Increasing interest from black New Yorkers in the mambo led him to start an R&B label, Rama, in 1953. Pretty soon he realised that black vocal groups could cross over to a white audience if they steered a little closer to pop and a little further away from the church. The Crows' basic but beautiful 'Gee' ('My my, oh gee. Oh gosh, oh gee. How I love my girl!') gave him a million-seller, a number-fourteen hit in 1954, appealing to white kids who were just starting to switch their radio dials from Martin Block's *Make Believe Ballroom* to Alan Freed's *Moondog* show. Sales in New York alone were strong enough to give Goldner low national-chart placings for the Cleftones, the Regents, the Channels; beyond that he scored further Top 20 hits with the Chantels ('Maybe', US no. 15 '58), Little Anthony and the Imperials ('Tears on My Pillow', US no. 4 '58) and the Flamingos ('I

Only Have Eyes for You', US no. 11 '59). Frankie Lymon and the Teenagers earned him his first international hit.

Lymon was working in grocery stores by the time he was ten and smoking reefers before he started grade school. He was no doe-eyed innocent. Once the single was a huge hit, Goldner tried to prise him away from the Teenagers, presumably to double his money-making potential, and unfortunately he succeeded – torpid 45s followed, recorded in the UK while he was on tour. Lymon's and his erstwhile schoolmates' careers quickly withered on the vine.

On February 28th 1968 Frankie Lymon's body was discovered on the bathroom floor of his grandmother's apartment. Three times married, an international star earning $5,000 a week at the age of thirteen, he was dead from a heroin overdose at twenty-six. His last disc, 'I'm Sorry', was released posthumously.

Given the naivety, the yearning for serenity in the centre of the city, and its childish love of nonsense syllables, it isn't surprising that collectors have obsessed over doo wop for so long.* Its romantic nature – like the love it celebrates, it can never die – is inherent in the music. For this reason, it was also the first form of modern pop to undergo a revival; this was the very first sign that modern pop could feed on its own past. Beyond this, it could get nostalgic.

The rock 'n' roll explosion had been a narrowing as well as a revelation, as it had dismissed out of hand much of what had gone before, baulking at the sight of Frankie Laine or Mantovani appearing on the same hit parade as Carl Perkins or Frankie Lymon. Part of the unfolding story of modern pop would be that rock 'n' roll grew up, and over the years it would struggle to reintroduce elements that had been cast aside in the process of its social and commercial breakthrough.

The second generation of doo-wop acts were a clear early signal of this doubt and re-evaluation. The revival came almost entirely from the north-east, where white European immigration had been greatest and the vocal tradition ran deepest. Eschewing the lewder, R&B side of doo wop

---

* Doo-wop fans and nascent record archivists first gathered in Irving 'Slim' Rose's Times Square record shop in Manhattan at the turn of the sixties.

(the Checkers' 'I Wasn't Thinkin', I Was Drinkin", or the Toppers' 'Baby Let Me Bang Your Box'), they focused on rosiness and reveries. Mostly the new groups were Italian, but Spaniards, Poles and Puerto Ricans rode doo wop's second wave too, using a purity of tone that Smokey Robinson would later make into an art form but which had been beyond the ability of many of the earlier, rougher groups.* The Elegants' 'Little Star' (US no. 1 '58), the Mystics' 'Hushabye' (US no. 20 '59), the Crests' 'Sixteen Candles' (US no. 2 '59), the Skyliners' 'Since I Don't Have You' (US no. 12 '59) and the Capris' 'There's a Moon Out Tonight' (US no. 3 '61) are musical wedding cakes, beautifully constructed, very sweet and very poignant, and – though slightly out of sync with the world even when they came out – have become default signifiers of fifties America.

Unlike first-generation doo wop, the new wave existed in something of a bubble, a self-perpetuating, cyclical sound with a solid fanbase – for a while, enthusiasts formed new acts to keep the sound alive. The revival peaked in 1961 with a glut of huge doo-wop hits; the rock 'n' roll era was effectively over in America, and this was its last gasp. The Marcels' delicious proto-gabber 'Blue Moon' was an odd throwback and a transatlantic number one. There were two more cosmic US number ones in Gene Chandler's 'Duke of Earl' and Maurice Williams and the Zodiacs' 'Stay', both of which pointed to a way forward with early soul stylings, evidenced by a new freedom in the lead vocal. But it is against modern pop's nature for a genre to consciously sustain itself; eventually it will spoil. When Little Caesar and the Romans scored a telltale US Top 10 hit in 1961 with 'Those Oldies but Goodies (Remind Me of You)', it was the sound of people in mourning for doo wop, trying to revive its corpse.† All that remained was to move on.

---

* A rare example of primitive second-wave doo wop is the Metallics' 'Need Your Love', a west-coast production which featured the imploring falsetto of J. D. 'Wimpy' Wright. Wright was already thirty but the other Metallics were teenagers, barely competent, and the production is all wool and wail. And yet, the single has an intangible magic that can bring tears to my eyes every time I hear it.
† A few flop sequels later, Little Caesar and the Romans released a self-referencing single called 'Memories of Those Oldies but Goodies', a sentimental echo of a hit which was already an echo of 'In the Still of the Nite'.

1960: IT WILL STAND

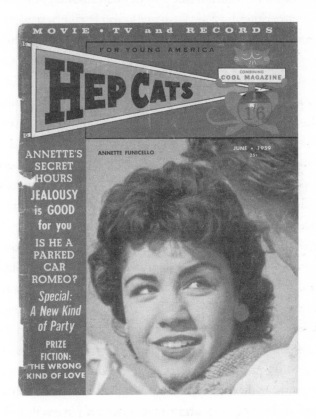

With rock 'n' roll, three gulfs had temporarily vanished: the gulf between black and white, the gulf between child and grown-up, and the gulf between the US and the UK. This shouldn't be forgotten, but it often is. What happened at the tail end of the fifties would set up how the memorialisation of this amazing event, its replay in the sixties, seventies and eighties – in *American Graffiti*, or *Happy Days*, or a Levi's ad, or even among hardcore record collectors – would often be at the expense of the feel of the fact.

1960 was a hiatus in modern pop. To kids who had grown up with the shrill call to arms of 'Good Golly Miss Molly' or 'Rave On', turning on the radio and hearing the lightweight pleasures of Frankie Avalon's 'Why' (US no. 1 '60), or Cliff Richard's 'Voice in the Wilderness' (UK no. 2 '60), it might have seemed the moment to move on to different interests: American students like Minnesota's Robert Zimmerman had their intellect tickled by folk; in Britain, mods and beatniks eschewed pop for various kinds of jazz. In their callow way, these bright kids turned to musics that seemed more overtly clever, less trivial, apparently less disposable than pop. In one way they were right – their intellect was going to be needed to take modern pop out of its post-rock 'n' roll slough. In another way, they were wrong: pop was going to be the vessel – not folk, not jazz – for the transformation. Besides, there were a number of stronger characters, occupying Top 20 space, who weren't about to be trampled underfoot by the new vogue for pre-rock forms. They would not idly stand by and watch the rebuilding of walls between age and race. They had the Showmen's 'It Will Stand' as their 'We Shall Overcome', possibly the first song to give modern pop – or rock 'n' roll, at least – the stature of a religion: 'Some folks don't understand it, that's why they don't demand it. They're out trying to ruin. Forgive them for they know not what they're doin'.'

Let's take a look at the baddies in this part of the story. By 1959 chart-friendly rock 'n' roll had become formulaic enough for two American promoters to try and invent the perfect pin-up by sending out a questionnaire to three thousand girls. Joe Mulhall and Paul Neff remain a footnote as their computer-printout pop star, a fifteen-year-old Italian American weightlifter called Johnny Restivo, only had one minor hit ('The Shape I'm In', US no. 80 '59). Over the years others would try and improve on Mulhall and Neff's piece of social engineering, with varying degrees of success.

This new pop process – the streamlining of fifties rock 'n' roll, tailoring it to teenage girls and blending its more parent-friendly aspects with pre-rock smoothness – had begun with the rise of Paul Anka in 1957. He was an Italian American pin-up with the trappings of a rock 'n' roll singer, exactly the kind of kid Mulhall and Neff would have been looking for when they dug up Restivo, and he cut a string of huge hits in the late fifties: 'Diana' (UK and US no. 1) was the biggest-selling single of

1957, and he followed it with 'I Love You Baby' (UK no. 3 '57), 'You Are My Destiny' (US no. 7, UK no. 6 '58), 'All of a Sudden My Heart Sings' (US no. 15, UK no. 10 '58), 'Lonely Boy' (US no. 1, UK no. 3 '59) and 'Put Your Head on My Shoulder' (US no. 2, UK no. 7 '59), and outsold Elvis in most of Europe. Some of his records – like the comically unhinged 'Crazy Love' – sounded more like a John Waters rewrite of the fifties than the genuine article.

Tame and slick, smarmily good-looking and clearly more in thrall to the Rat Pack than Fats Domino, Paul Anka became the prototype for a bunch of coiffed identikit idols who, by 1960, had filled the vacuum left by rock 'n' roll's sudden decline: there was Frankie Avalon ('Venus') and Bobby Rydell ('Swingin' School') in the States, Mark Wynter ('Venus in Blue Jeans') and Craig Douglas ('Pretty Blue Eyes') in Britain, all well groomed and milky, enjoyable enough but not especially exciting. Modern pop would see their like recurring whenever times got tough and inspiration was low.

How had rock 'n' roll dipped so fast? It's standard practice to say that rock 'n' roll's decline began with Buddy Holly's death, and the contemporaneous disappearance from the scene of Chuck Berry, Jerry Lee Lewis, Eddie Cochran, Little Richard and Elvis. In fact, it had been in decline since mid-1958, when Ricky Nelson's 'Poor Little Fool' ushered in the rock-ballad era: the only new rockers to first appear in '58 were Bobby Darin, the American equivalent to Anthony Newley, who switched from rock 'n' roll ('Queen of the Hop', 'Dream Lover') to Rat Packery within a year; Jack Scott, who history has largely forgotten; and Duane Eddy, an instrumentalist.

The curtain fell on the rock 'n' roll era – as it would with other glorious pop eras to come* – in a rather embarrassing wave of novelty records: the Champs' 'Tequila' and Sheb Wooley's 'Purple People Eater' – both US number ones in '58 – had a slight whiff of self-parody, even if they were hard not to love. Johnny Preston's 'Running Bear',† the Hollywood

---

* Merseybeat: the Fourmost's 'A Little Lovin''; punk: 'Jilted John' by Jilted John; new pop: Culture Club's 'The War Song'; rave: Shaft's 'Roobarb and Custard'; Britpop: Space and Catatonia's 'The Ballad of Tom Jones'.
† Preston was one of the few new names of 1960, and he was a very strange

Argyles' 'Alley Oop' and Larry Verne's 'Mr Custer' were all history lessons delivered comic-book style, and were all US number ones in 1960. On records like Steve Lawrence's 'Footsteps' (US no. 7, UK no. 9), the archetypal 1960 hit, the production almost sounds sarcastic: the male back-ups go 'well-uh well-uh', the girls sing through their noses like eight-year-olds, and Steve himself has a giveaway high-society tone to his voice that somehow sneaked past ABC-Paramount's youth experts.

By 1960, then, with so many of pop's independently minded practitioners out of the picture and few new names to keep up the pace, the music industry re-established its grip and attempted to reverse the very real progress of the fifties. Beach movies provided hit singles for the well-groomed Frankie Avalon and curvy ex-Mouseketeer Annette Funicello, the drive-in set's Fred and Ginger. Symbolically, Bobby Rydell covered Dean Martin's 'Volare' and took it to number two in the US charts, Bobby Darin did the same in Britain with Hoagy Carmichael's 'Lazy River', and Elvis took a thirty-year-old country song – 'Are You Lonesome Tonight' – to number one in both countries.

And yet not all of 1960 was bad. On the distaff side, Brenda Lee broke through with 'Sweet Nothin's', and Connie Francis wrung out her hanky on 'Mama' (US no. 8, UK no. 2) and 'My Heart Has a Mind of Its Own' (US no. 1, UK no. 3) as country and western began to make its post-rock 'n' roll presence felt. A trio of talented singers emerged, all direct descendants of the Orioles' Sonny Til: Hoagy Lands, who worked closely with Brill Building writer Bert Berns,* and deserved but never scored a hit; Jimmy Jones, who had two monsters with the rickety 'Handy Man' (US no. 2, UK no. 3 '60) and 'Good Timin'' (US no. 3, UK no. 1 '60)

---

cove. 'Running Bear' was written by the Big Bopper, who had died the year before. He followed it with the nursery beat 'Cradle of Love' (US no. 7, UK no. 2) and a freakish cover of Shirley and Lee's R&B hit 'Feel So Fine' before disappearing in 1961.
* Considering Bert Berns's magic touch – he wrote 'Twist and Shout', Them's 'Here Comes the Night', the Exciters' 'Tell Him', Solomon Burke's 'Cry to Me', the McCoys' 'Hang On Sloopy', Tami Lynn's 'I'm Gonna Run Away from You' – this is extraordinarily unlucky. Berns's 'It's Gonna Be Morning' is perfect for the swooping range of Lands, who turns it into a lament for the mid-sixties passing of New York as pop's capital city.

but faded fast;* and Dee Clark, screwed up and intense, who usually saved his best, inhumanly high notes for the last thirty seconds of hits like the sweetly harrowing 'Raindrops', a US number two in 1961.

Though the major beneficiaries of 1960's hiatus were the smooth teen idols, floating in and around the makeweights were some new, more durable names: Roy Orbison ('Only the Lonely', US no. 2, UK no. 1), Dion ('Lonely Teenager', US no. 12), and a year later Gene Pitney ('Town Without Pity', US no. 13, UK no. 32) and Del Shannon ('Runaway', US and UK no. 1). They were men, not boys; they walked alone, self-sufficient with their songwriting and instrumentation, and in this they were unwitting pointers to the future. All of them seemed to live harder, hurt harder, than the Anka-ites and their music was solidly emotive. Let's take a closer look.

Gene Pitney wrote upbeat hits for others – Bobby Vee's 'Rubber Ball' (UK no. 4, US no. 6 '61), Ricky Nelson's 'Hello Mary Lou' (UK no. 2, US no. 9 '61), the Crystals' 'He's a Rebel' (UK no. 19, US no.1 '62) – but picked other writers' songs for himself that tended to see his composure gradually crumble inside three minutes, whether through love's intensity ('Twenty-four Hours from Tulsa', UK no. 5, US no. 17 '63) or through despair ('I'm Gonna Be Strong', UK no. 2, US no. 9 '64); most extreme of all was 1968's 'Billy You're My Friend', a traumatic love triangle that sounded like it was being sung with Gene inside a straitjacket.

Dion had previously been the leader of doo-wop act the Belmonts. He may have seemed all Little Italy machismo but, 'The Wanderer' aside, he was all too easily ground under the heel of some Bronx minx. There was 'Runaround Sue', 'Sandy' and – cruellest of all – 'Little Diane' ('Bad girls like you are a disgrace'). His smile suggested he was in on a secret you couldn't understand. It turned out he was – Dion was heroin-addicted long before the travails of Lou Reed, Marianne Faithfull or anyone from Elastica or Alice in Chains became public knowledge. At the time it was seen as shameful, unmentionable, and

---

* Like most of the hit-makers of this era, he continued to make records for many years after his star had dimmed. One stand-out was the cheeky soul smoocher 'Ain't Nothin' Wrong Makin' Love the First Night' in 1975, which sounded like a more honest update of the boastful 'Handy Man'.

his sudden disappearance from the charts in 1964 after a run of twelve US Top 20 hits seemed inexplicable. He regrouped, discovered a love of folk and blues and, with Columbia producer John Hammond helming the sessions, cut the best records of his career: 'Tomorrow Won't Bring the Rain', 'Wonder Where I'm Bound', 'My Girl the Month of May'. Eventually, in 1968, he returned to the charts, clean and sober, with a harp-plucking peace anthem called 'Abraham, Martin and John' (US no. 4); its B-side, 'Daddy Rollin' (in Your Arms)', was something else again, a lupine howl that made heroin sound both desirable and deathly.

Roy Orbison was no one's idea of a pin-up, so he hid behind his shades (many assumed he was blind), dressed in black, stood elegant and dignified. The Big O had a heartbreaking, almost operatic baritone that even Elvis struggled to match. The most intense Orbison single of all was 'It's Over', a British number one at the height of Beatlemania in 1964 (opening line: 'Your baby doesn't love you any more'). It could be Roy talking to himself as he contemplates taking his life ('you won't be seeing rainbows any more') or, worse, the world turning in on the singer, mocking his dreams, his belief in true love; the brief pause before the climactic cry of the title will make your heart drop into your stomach. All these hits pre-dated real tragedy in Orbison's life – his wife died in a bike crash in 1966, his sons were killed in a fire that destroyed his home in 1969 – which unsurprisingly curtailed his run of hits.* He soldiered on, though, barely changing his style, and when he was rightly deified in the late eighties his comeback hit 'You Got It' (UK no. 3, US no. 9 '88) sounded just like his records had in 1960. With typical ill fortune, he died just weeks after 'You Got It' had made him a star all over again.

'Runaway', Del Shannon's debut single, was the biggest hit in the US and the UK in summer 1961. It was, and remains, the ultimate fairground

* Orbison was of huge significance in Britain and parts of the Commonwealth, where he continued to score hits right through the sixties: 'Ride Away' went to number one in Canada in '65, while the masochistic – even by Orbison's stand-ards – 'Crawling Back' made number two in '66; the same year saw 'It's Too Soon to Know' at number three in the UK; Australia remained especially loyal, sending 1969's superficially chirpy 'Penny Arcade' (don't be fooled, it's about addicted gamblers – 'roll up and spend your last dime!') to number one.

anthem, the 45 you'd most expect to turn up on a Wurlitzer jukebox in a forgotten suburban caff. 'Runaway' was all energy and mystery, from the dense, almost discordant opening guitar chords, through its falsetto hook ('wah-wah-wonder') to the eerie, space-organ solo. The lyric was beyond melancholy, filled with dread and paranoia; the runaway girl may not even be alive. It was the kind of record you could build a career on, and Del Shannon didn't disappoint. The existential angst of 'Runaway' became a template that he was still using at the far end of the decade on the ghostlike 'Colorado Rain'. He couldn't write any other way – the fear and the demons in Shannon's music echoed the mind of its maker.

In the beginning he was Charles Westover and he was from Battle Creek, Michigan. Two events shaped his future: when he bought his first electric guitar he practised in the bathroom, amp perched on the toilet lid, and discovered he liked the rumbling acoustics; a little later he asked a girl called Karen to the high-school prom, but she dumped him for another guy; young Charles was so cut up that he would still talk about this years later. He was drafted in the fifties, married Shirley, got a job in a carpet store and renamed himself Del Shannon in honour of a local wrestler. By night he played rock 'n' roll covers in the Big Little Show Band at Battle Creek's Hi-Lo Club.

Stuck in Battle Creek, Shannon was already in his mid-twenties when a college kid from Kalamazoo called Max Crook joined the band. Crook brought with him a home-made, three-legged proto-synth that he called a 'musitron'. Straight away, the two of them began writing great songs. One was called 'Runaway', the lyric penned by Shannon on the sly while working at the carpet store. Released on New York's tiny Big Top label, it exploded in the spring of 1961 and became an international number one. In the anodyne Ankoid era, the intense, square-jawed Shannon cut a heroic figure, and he was swiftly elevated to the level of Orbison, Dion and Pitney.

Invigorated by stardom, he followed 'Runaway' with two fabulously nasty rockers. 'Hats Off to Larry' (US no. 5, UK no. 6 '61) again featured a Max Crook solo, but this was a spiteful riposte to an ex who has been ditched by her new beau. 'So Long Baby' was possibly the most relentless, tuneless Top 10 hit of the early sixties, fuelled entirely by bitterness: 'I've got news for you, I was untrue too!' Crook had left to make a solo single (the deathless 'Twistin' Ghost'), and so his musitron was replaced on 'So Long Baby' by what sounded like a giant electronic kazoo. While his profile dipped in the States, Del's hits in Europe continued unabated. 1962's loopy 'Swiss Maid' (Question: Will the yodelling, pig-tailed lass ever find true love? Answer: No.) reached number two in the UK but failed to even make the Hot Hundred; 'Little Town Flirt' was big enough in Britain to have been a prime influence on Merseybeat (imagine the Searchers singing it); 'Cry Myself to Sleep' was later revisited by Elton John as 'Crocodile Rock'.

In spite of all these hits, all this success, Shannon – like the Big O – was riddled with insecurities. Musically this manifested itself in some lame soundalike sequels ('Two Kinds of Teardrops' followed the tightly perfect 'Little Town Flirt', but was too jolly by half) or songs that clearly aped his contemporaries: 'Sue's Gonna Be Mine' is basically a Four Seasons composite; Dion would surely have sued had Shannon's 'Mary Jane' sold in quantity. These singles came in an eighteen-month barren patch which coincided with the first beat boom – he may well have been the first act to chart with a Lennon/McCartney song ('From Me to You', no. 77) in the US, but Del Shannon still felt the chill wind from the Mersey in '63 and '64 like pretty much every other American act. He sought solace in whisky.

And that might have been the end of his career had he not remembered why 'Runaway' was so original and successful, and rediscovered his groove with 'Keep Searchin'' (US no. 9, UK no. 3) at the end of '64. 'Gotta find a place to hide with my baby by my side' – the lyric was even bleaker, the sound more deeply shadowed than 'Runaway', newly toughened by the Brit beat influence. The cry of the fugitive, a possible abductor with his (underage?) girl who's 'been hurt so much, they treat her mean and cruel', 'Keep Searchin'' ends with a desperate, beautiful falsetto wail of release.

From this point until the end of the decade, Shannon's recordings rarely stumbled. 'Keep Searchin'' had an even more paranoiac sequel in 'Stranger in Town', where a private detective, or maybe a hitman, was thrown into the equation. On 'Break Up' in 1965 he was so racked and tortured that he couldn't even convey his fears in words, silently resigning himself to losing his girl, the misery completely internalised. The single was a flop ('Stranger in Town' turned out to be his last UK hit) and Del was devastated. He took boxes of the single and threw them tearfully into a Michigan river.*

'That's the Way Love Is', a forgotten single from late '63, put the Del Shannon story in a nutshell. It started up like a conventional love song, with girly back-ups straight off a Steve Lawrence session. Then he started to remember his misery, and by the end of the song he was shaking, smashing things, putting his fist through doors, and still the pain wouldn't go away.

There was one last hurrah before Shannon's semi-retirement in 1969. 'Colorado Rain' formed a neat circle in its tale of a runaway hippie girl who flitted into the singer's life via a sinister piano motif, only to leave again just as unexpectedly as the rain, as ever, pours down. His suicide in 1991, just as he was set to reignite his career in the Traveling Wilburys, seems to have stymied reassessment. But Del Shannon, king of pain, was truly one of pop's heavyweight champs.

Looking at the 1960 charts through the prism of Del Shannon, Dion and Roy Orbison is ultimately misleading, though. They were very much exceptions. For every 'Only the Lonely' on the UK chart, there was Anthony Newley's 'Strawberry Fair', Shirley Bassey's 'As Long as He Needs Me' and the Kaye Sisters' 'Paper Roses', a multitude of pre-rock throwbacks.

It's best to think of 1960 as a pause for breath. Unlikely green shoots were springing up in Hamburg, which nobody but a bunch of drunken sailors would have been aware of. More immediately, there was a revolution happening in the offices and studios on New York's Broadway.

---

* The intensity and hardness of mid-sixties singles like 'Break Up' and the tinnitus-inducing 'Move It On Over' betrayed a Rolling Stones influence. Coincidentally, Shannon was a heavy hero to their producer/manager, Andrew Loog Oldham, and the two got together for the *Home and Away* album in '67. A record of full baroque beauty, it was shelved at the time, probably because none of its accompanying singles was a hit. Oldham pulled every Spectorian stunt from the box; songs like 'Cut and Come Again' and 'He Cheated' recast Del as a black orchid for the flower generation.

WALK WITH ME IN PARADISE GARDEN: PHIL SPECTOR AND JOE MEEK

While the no-man's-land of 1960 had made stars of Frankie Avalon and Bobby Vee, wipe-clean fifties faces who would inform future revivals like *Grease*, it had also allowed for a second, slower and less vaunted, wave of modern pop. Pop's deceleration led to a dark, post-rock 'n' roll sound, one which would became a fertile nursery for a pair of innovators who began experimenting in earnest, a pair who would give modern pop renewed vigour.

If rock 'n' roll's initial blithe cacophony (1955–58) had liberated teenagers, then the period immediately after (1958–61), like the final scene of *The Graduate*, saw doubt and fear and a sense of agoraphobia creeping in. These were new and very real teenage emotions, and they needed an artistic outlet, away from the increasingly adult (Darin's 'Mack the Knife', US and UK no. 1 '59) and plain silly (Brian Hyland's 'Itsy Bitsy Teenie Weenie Yellow Polka Dot Bikini', US no. 1, UK no. 8 '60) records dominating the chart. The Aquatones' 'You', a minor American hit from the tail end of '58, had articulated this still, small need for calm. It was a 6/8 ballad that owed little to classic rock 'n' roll beyond its heavy backbeat. The backing track was a mush of repetitive piano, thrummed acoustic guitars and dense, soupy bass. It sounded like the musicians were three rooms away. Over this, a keening female vocal, high and pure yet oddly emotionless, echoing in a well of loneliness, gave the record a hypnotic, womblike quality.

The single's eerie qualities would be exaggerated further by the Teddy Bears' 'To Know Him Is to Love Him' (US no. 1, UK no. 2 '58) a few months later; the vocal was softer but still pure, soothing, almost maternal, and the lyric sat halfway between a love song and a eulogy.* Again the backing track had a half-speed, sludgy drum sound, everything was soft and heavy at the same time, creating a mantra-like feel. It was remarkable, and after it hit number one in America in late '58 this sound was soon replicated: Ritchie Valens' 'Donna', Donnie Owens' 'Need You', Rosie and the Originals' 'Angel Baby', all great, all big hits. There was even a Hawaiian variation, Santo and Johnny's 'Sleep Walk', which was another US number one. We can safely assume that David Lynch bought these records.

By '61 the soft-heavy sound had been perfected and peaked with the skeletal, delicately terrifying 'Tragedy' by the Fleetwoods (US no. 10 '61) and the Paris Sisters' 'I Love How You Love Me' (US no. 5 '61). Priscilla Paris had one of the sexiest female voices in all pop. 'I love how your eyes close whenever you're near me,' she sang, in a super-suggestive whisper that, placed over the dense, muffled rock-a-bye backing, simultaneously suggested an eager sexuality and a return to the comfort of the cradle. This and the Teddy Bears' sole hit were both the work of a young, five-foot-nothing New Yorker called Phil Spector, who was slowly mixing the ingredients for a vast, regal pop that would peak with the Ronettes' 'Baby I Love You' and the Righteous Brothers' 'You've Lost That Lovin' Feelin'' three years later.

In a separate but related proto-goth move, newly liberated teens – as well as yearning for sex and childhood – developed a taste for 'death discs' around 1960/61,† possibly prompted by the early demise of Buddy

---

* The title was taken from an inscription on Spector's father's tombstone, 'To know him was to love him'.
† The most extreme 1960 example came from the pen of Burt Bacharach: Paul Hampton narrates the astonishing 'Two Hour Honeymoon', which opens with

Holly, Ritchie Valens and Eddie Cochran. In the States, Mark Dinning's 'Teen Angel' (girlfriend dies on a railroad track) and Ray Peterson's 'Tell Laura I Love Her' (boyfriend dies in a stock-car race) were huge hits, but the 'death disc' monster was John Leyton's 'Johnny Remember Me', the most thrilling, feverish pop record Britain had yet produced – the drums galloped and the skies darkened as Leyton's echo-choked voice mourned the girl he 'loved and lost a year ago'. In a year that also gave us Elvis Presley's 'Wooden Heart' and Acker Bilk's 'Stranger on the Shore', it was a lightning bolt, and with a primetime TV slot* it couldn't miss, giving its producer Joe Meek a number one that summer.

Joe Meek was Britain's first record producer.† Before he started working as a studio engineer in 1955, the UK's pop records were made by sticking a microphone in the middle of the room and placing singers and musicians strategically around it. Meek was the first to challenge this orthodoxy, the first to argue that records didn't need to directly mimic a live performance, that they could sound more exciting – and more commercial – with a little mechanical manipulation. As an engineer, the Merrie Melodies bow-and-arrow effect ('p-*doiiiiing*') he added to Gary Miller's 1955 single 'Robin Hood' (UK no. 10) was his first showcase; Anne Shelton's 'Lay Down Your Arms' (UK no. 1 '56) featured a shaken

---

screeching tyres and ends with an ungodly atonal burst of brass. Death discs survived the beat boom: two of the biggest hits – Twinkle's 'Terry' (UK no. 4) and the Shangri-Las' 'Leader of the Pack' (US no. 1, UK no. 11) – came at the end of '64, while the Buoys' cannibal drama 'Timothy' (US no. 17) was a hit as late as 1971. Tom Jones's 'Delilah' (US no. 15, UK no. 2 '68), Tony Christie's 'I Did What I Did for Maria' (UK no. 2 '71) and R. Dean Taylor's 'Indiana Wants Me' (US no. 5 '70, UK no. 2 '71) put a new twist on the genre, romanticising murder through wounded male pride.

* Leyton played a pop star called Johnny St Cyr in an episode of department-store soap *Harpers West One*. It was a neat twist that Meek's studio, where they rush-recorded a song for the fictional St Cyr, was next door to a real furniture shop called Harpers of Holloway. The shop's name is still just about visible on the wall.

† He could be described as the first record producer in the world. In the pre-rock era, there had been two significant names who could challenge this: Les Paul, through his wild guitar effects and close-miked vocals on his duets with Mary Ford, and Mitch Miller, who had double-tracked Patti Page and backed Rosemary Clooney with a distorted harpsichord. But Meek was the first to manipulate every element of the track, imagining the record as a complete production.

tray of gravel to mimic marching feet; on 'Poor People of Paris' (UK no. 1 '56) he added a musical saw to jolly along Winifred Atwell's ragtime pub piano. Clearly, he had commercial clout. The first record Meek produced on his own was Humphrey Lyttelton's straight jazz instrumental 'Bad Penny Blues' (UK no. 19 '56), on which he exaggerated the low notes on the piano to make it danceable, got the brushed drums to fizz, and gave Lyttelton his only hit – the Beatles later pinched its feel wholesale for 'Lady Madonna'.

Meek was in love with the future (space travel, satellites), Americana (teen idols and cowboys) and the world beyond – ghosts, death, deceased lovers returning as guardian angels. He sought to replicate these obsessions via overdubbing, compression, sound separation and distortion. With his *I Hear a New World* album (1960) and the Tornados' transatlantic number one 'Telstar' (1962) Meek's mind was connected directly to the machinery.

Along with being tone deaf, incapable of playing an instrument, and possessing a vicious temper that wasn't helped by his daily diet of steak, coffee and pep pills, Meek was also gay, which gave him deep-seated, lifelong issues. Pop music was as much of an escape route for him as boxing would have been to a kid in Bethnal Green. As an 'indoors' child in rural Gloucestershire, Meek had rigged up speakers in the local orchards and played pre-rock 78s to entertain the cherry pickers. His bedroom overflowed with soldering irons and gadgetry. He worked at a radar station during his national service in the early fifties and, soon after, found himself at IBC and Lansdowne studios in London. A high proportion of the best British fifties records – Johnny Duncan's 'Last Train to San Fernando', Lonnie Donegan's 'Cumberland Gap' (no. 1 '57) – had seen Meek's hand on the controls. Yet once he became a fully fledged independent producer in 1960 things got serious.

After falling out with just about everyone he'd ever worked with, Meek set up his own RGM studio above a leather-goods shop at 301 Holloway Road, the main road north out of London. Vocals were recorded in the toilet, string sections stood on the stairs, and it should have been a joke. Instead, two of the best records he ever made appeared almost straight away: Mike Berry's 'Tribute to Buddy Holly', and 'Johnny Remember Me', both in '61. They were written by Reading-born Geoff Goddard, who shared Meek's interest in the occult, and were garish and cinematic, bunching together the Wild West, plane crashes, war-comic heroes and *Wuthering Heights* heroines.

Dozens of RGM productions were released in quick succession, not always great, though they all shared the trademarks of speeded-up vocals, sound effects, angelic backing vocals, massed strings and a hint of clammy, illicit trysts. The classic RGM single was so sonically compressed it sounded like an orchestra had been squeezed into a wardrobe.

Meek was heavily inspired by another thread of the immediate post-rock 'n' roll era, the instrumental, which had provided a rare safe haven for tougher sounds: Duane Eddy's echo-drenched growling guitar ('Rebel Rouser', 'Because They're Young', 'Peter Gunn'), the Shadows' idealised evocations of the foreign ('Apache', 'FBI', 'Kon-Tiki') and Johnny and the Hurricanes' wasps'-nest-like organ ('Red River Rock', 'Beatnik Fly', 'Rockin' Goose') had all regularly made the UK Top 20 from 1958 to 1962. The Outlaws, Saints, Tornados and Moontrekkers were Meek's instrumental response, and the latter's 'Night of the Vampire' – with creaking coffin, deranged-cat keyboard and a frighteningly realistic female scream* – created a rare masterpiece on pop's *Carry On/Hammer House of Horror* interface.

The exact difference between British and American modern pop can be found by comparing Meek's and Spector's productions. Meek sped things up, worked at a frenetic pace, as if it was the best way to keep warm in his cramped North London flat. Spector's sound was panoramic, as big as Meek's but warmer, more luxurious; it used the finest ingredients, the greatest singers and musicians from New York and California, while Meek's seemed gaudy, straight out of Woolworths. Value for money – it's the British disease. Meek could turn out three singles in a week, but Spector took time, expensive LA studio time, perfecting his sound. Songwriter Jeff Barry remembered working on

---

* The woman's scream at the end of 'Night of the Vampire' was actually Meek's voice, possibly sped up, possibly not.

Spector's 1963 Christmas album as a physical and mental endurance test: 'I stood there for days and days and days, just playing shakers.'

Both had traumatic childhoods, simultaneously bullied and cosseted by their families; both were convinced other people were out to steal their ideas (Meek apparently received a call from Spector, just the once, and slammed the receiver down so hard it shattered). Both were out to gain revenge on the world, were ungracious while at the top, and crashed and burned when the world turned and they fell from favour.

* * *

The gulfs between age and race and between Britain and America had been bridged by rock 'n' roll. There was another gulf to be bridged, but this didn't really manifest itself until the early sixties. Commerce versus art: it was a fifties cliché that the arts were a fancy affair, highbrow for longhairs, worthy, important and a bit dull, and that the products of commerce were the obvious, stupid opposite. But a feeling was gathering that modern pop was suddenly, and quite unexpectedly, delivering something that art – as defined in the fifties – no longer understood. While there were plenty of wheeler-dealers trying to push their own Johnny Restivo or Vince Eager into teenage girls' hearts, it was apparent to some commentators that the likes of Roy Orbison, Dion, Del Shannon, Joe Meek and Phil Spector were operating on a different level, one closer to Richard Hamilton than Cliff Richard.

'I get a little angry when people say it's bad music,' Spector told Tom Wolfe during an interview for *Esquire* magazine. 'This music has a spontaneity that doesn't exist in any other kind of music, and it's what is here now. It has limited chord changes, and people are always saying the words are banal and why doesn't anybody write lyrics like Cole Porter any more, but we don't have any presidents like Lincoln any more, either. You know? It's pop blues. I feel it's very American. It's what people respond to today. It's not just the kids. I hear cab drivers, everybody, listening to it.'

Spector condensed pop to romance and sex, crushes and break-ups, love and pride. For many people who bought his records, he gave the subject matter the backdrop it deserved; this was the stuff of life itself. The sound was all-consuming, left no room for anything else in your head, and tore at your heart with tympani and an exuberant rush of noise: it was labelled the Wall of Sound.* In contrast to this barrage, the key to the directness of Spectorsound was lyrical simplicity. Take any random line from the Ronettes' 'Be My Baby' – 'I'll make you happy, baby, just wait and see' – and it's a crush in a heartbeat. Spector's best writers were Ellie Greenwich and Jeff Barry, a couple from Brooklyn who also happened to be very much in love when they wrote the Crystals' 'Da Doo Ron Ron' and 'Then He Kissed Me', Bob B. Soxx and the Blue Jeans' 'Not Too Young to Get Married' and Darlene Love's 'Wait Til My Bobby Gets Home'. And as Spector was very much in love with the Ronettes' Veronica Bennett, he saved their very best songs – 'Be My Baby' (US no. 2, UK no. 4 '63) and 'Baby I Love You' (US no. 24, UK no. 11 '64) – so that he could hear the words come out of her mouth and into his ears.

   Those Ronettes chart stats show that no matter how futuristic their sounds were, how big and progressive and damn near perfect, Meek and Spector, like so many others, staggered and faltered after the Beatles broke. Meek had a beat-era number one with the Honeycombs' 'Have I the Right', a foot-stomping hormonal howl ('Grrrrrr, *come right back*, I just can't bear it') that showed he could manufacture what he disparagingly called 'matchbox music' any time he wanted. Spector's last dance was altogether more tormented. By late '64 the Beatles and Motown were the now sounds, leaving even a single as lush and romantic and tearfully timeless as the Ronettes' 'Walking in the Rain' stranded outside the Top 20. Suddenly his sound seemed too teenage. He turned to Barry Mann and Cynthia Weil, New York's most furrowed and thoughtful songwriting team, for something a little more mature. They delivered 'You've Lost that Lovin' Feelin''.

* The term 'wall of sound' had first appeared in an 1884 *New York Times* piece describing Richard Wagner's redesigned Nibelungen Theater in Bayreuth in Germany, which – for the first time – placed the orchestra in a pit, creating an invisible 'wall of sound'. Closer to the Spector era, it had also been used to describe Stan Kenton's fifties band.

There is a staggering force in its opening line: 'You never close your eyes any more when I kiss your lips' is a dreadful inversion of the whispered promise of 'I Love How You Love Me', the Paris Sisters hit Barry Mann had written and Spector had produced four years previously. It chronicles the imminent death of a love affair in such a deeply wounded way that it's a blessed relief to know the song wasn't autobiographical. Spector 'borrowed' blue-eyed soul boys the Righteous Brothers, who weren't used to anything as slow and brooding. Spector arranged the session 'like he was going to invade Moscow', according to guitarist Barney Kessel. 'Musically, it was terribly simple, but the way he'd recorded and miked it, they'd diffuse it so that you couldn't pick out any one instrument.' The Aquatones' 'You', the spooked one-off hit from '58 that predicted this sound, had been almost a sketch of a song; now this sound had mutated into a dam-busting thing of extraordinary size and power. The vocals are angry, accusing, pleading; by the end all the flash and noise is reduced to one solitary bassline, before a final crescendo – 'bring back that lovin' feelin'' – and a fade into depthless introspection. It was Spector's masterpiece and made number one in both Britain (despite Cilla Black's cover version climbing as high as number two) and America.

After the Honeycombs' initial promise dissipated with a weak follow-up ('Is It Because', which barely charted), Joe Meek kept producing music at a prodigious rate but could hardly get a record released; his dogged independence was becoming a curse. Towards the end he was recording some of the most mentally damaged music to gain release on a major British label. Hear the eerie, empty winterscape of the Honeycombs' 'Eyes' (1965) or the feedback squall of the Syndicats' 'Crawdaddy Simone' (1965) and the Buzz's 'You're Holding Me Down' (1966) to hear the true sound of paranoia and encroaching insanity. Also in '66, Spector was crushed by the failure of Ike and Tina Turner's titanic 'River Deep – Mountain High', which took lyrical naivety (teddy bears, puppy dogs, pies) to a new extreme, twinning it with the most ferociously sexual vocal he ever recorded. It reached number 3 in the UK but fell away after a few dismal weeks in the bottom quarter of the *Billboard* Hot Hundred. Spent, he retired at twenty-five. Despite working in later years with the solo Beatles, the Ramones, even Celine Dion, he never recovered that march-on-Moscow bravado, and wallowed in his eccentricities for decades before his fondness for firearms ended with the death of an actress called Lana Clarkson.

Meek's twilight was far briefer; since shooting his landlady and then himself in 1967, his legacy has lived on in recording studios around the world via the equipment named after him, effects boxes he had invented and kept secret some four decades earlier. Meek and Spector were the first to really understand and engineer the power of the 45, the first to forge a new pop music from the white heat of technology. Unlike almost all of their contemporaries, they realised that great pop is, at its heart, about great-sounding records. Meek and Spector weren't trying to deal with reality, they were trying to improve on it.

THE TROUBLE WITH BOYS: THE BRILL BUILDING AND GIRL GROUPS

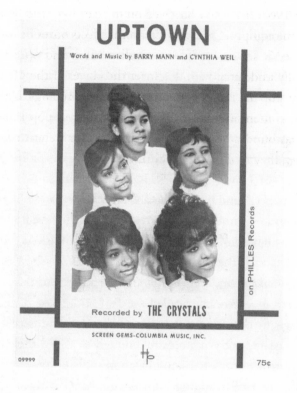

In 1962 the American record industry collected $161 million from the 210 million singles it sold. The major labels like Columbia and Mercury – after initially leaving rock 'n' roll to small independents like Sun – were now employing teenage A&R staff, having finally figured that no one understood the kids better than the kids themselves. Twenty-nine-year-old Don Kirshner, his Aldon publishing company and his Dimension record label were at the heart of this boom. Kirshner's nickname was 'the man with the golden ears'. He used a team of two dozen songwriters – who included Carole King, Barry Mann and Neil Sedaka, and none of whom were over twenty-five – working in a warren of cubicles, fitted with nothing more than a desk and a piano, in a nondescript building at 1650 Broadway. They redefined modern pop by taking rock 'n' roll uptown – they added Latin-influenced percussion, and string arrangements, and created little symphonies for the kids. Effortlessly, and on an industrial scale, they could turn out a song of the calibre of 'Will You Love Me Tomorrow', 'Up on the Roof', 'Da Doo Ron Ron', 'Be My Baby', 'Breaking Up Is Hard to Do' or 'The Locomotion' every week. Though the sounds emanated from several buildings in close proximity, the one most associated with this writer/production set-up was the Brill Building – after all, it had a catchier name than 1650 Broadway, and it soon became shorthand for the sound of early-sixties New York.

Broadway, the Great White Way, was already the heart of the entertainment industry when the original songwriting hothouse – the Brill Building, at 1619 – was built in 1931. It was a handsome art-deco creation of white brick and bronze, named after a company of haberdashers who owned the ground floor. Above them, on the first floor, had been the Paradise nightclub; the upper floors housed publishers,* agents, promoters, pluggers – the seamier end of showbiz. These interdependent businesses would meet, and they would sell songs, cut deals, make and break records in a restaurant called the Turf at the base of the building. The Turf was fitted with twenty phone booths for industry types working their way up, not yet successful enough to afford their own space, who had to make do with a standing-room-only office.

By 1962 the Brill Building housed 165 different music companies. Those with less money to splash on looking flash, like Don Kirshner, settled for cheaper accommodation on the stretch between 49th and 53rd Streets: the Brill Building sound also emanated from 1674, 1697 and Aldon's home at 1650. Writer Toni Wine ('A Groovy Kind of Love', 'Black Pearl', 'Knock Three Times') was just fourteen when she first started working for Aldon: 'You'd walk in and there was just music in every elevator, in the lobby, everywhere you walked.'

---

* Southern, Mills and Famous-Paramount were the earliest publishers to move into the Brill, beginning the trend during the Depression, when the building had few other takers.

The Brill Building and its neighbours had a quick-witted jangle – in the heart of the city they could adapt to and negotiate New York's multicultural street life. What also gave these buildings their special flavour, their feel for speed and a rapid turnover of hit songs, was what economists would call vertical integration. The old pre-rock school, the ASCAP-affiliated writers, had relied on sheet music to make a living, but the modern pop generation, plenty of whom couldn't read music, made the most of Broadway's all-inclusive set-up to deliver fast product: you could write a song, find a publisher to buy it, someone to arrange it and musicians to cut it (Allegro Studios were in the basement of 1650) for a total of around $60. The whole process could be completed in a day. Then you took your acetate to a record company and, if you'd done a good job, they signed it up. It was a division of labour, and specialisation for optimum impact. A lot of chaff was created, but no one has yet come up with a better, more reliable way of creating classic modern pop. In the little more than half a decade that made up the Brill Building era, the artists – that is, the writers, producers and arrangers – could write freely about the pains and pressures of growing up without the need to publicly front the agonies and ecstasies of their music.

Hits came out of the Brill Building through sheer hard work: writing to deadlines, rewriting, rearranging, sweat and toil. Unlike rock 'n' roll's Southern wildmen, Brill Building staffers weren't known for their carnal threat, heavy boozing or opulent jewellery. They went to the office, wore ties, wrote hits. To early rock 'n' roll aesthetes like Nik Cohn this was tantamount to cheating – he snarkily labelled it 'highschool'. The manufacturing of this music – which was no different from the creation of a standard like 'It Never Entered My Mind' (written by Rodgers and Hart, arranged by Nelson Riddle, sung by Frank Sinatra) – also added to the snob feeling among students and beatniks, which led them to ignore modern pop entirely in the early sixties and lean instead towards Dixieland (or 'trad') jazz in Britain and folk in America. Bob Dylan, in one of his more spiteful and less acute moments, ridiculed Brill Building songs as 'You love me, I love you, ooby dooby doo'.

Jerry Leiber and Mike Stoller were the godfathers of this new, post-rock 'n' roll writer/producer pop* and their best songs alone – rib-ald, self-produced with comic theatricality – were a solid defence against Dylan's low blows. Leiber and Stoller were east-coast Jewish wise guys with a taste for blues and boogie woogie who had met when both of their families relocated to California in the late forties. They were also pop snobs of the highest order,† finding the music of their forebears and contemporary white America to be sappy and sexless. Early on they had written lurid jump-blues pieces with titles like 'Fast Women and Sloe Gin', but broke through with Big Mama Thornton's 'Hound Dog', an R&B number one in 1952. They initially frowned on rock 'n' roll, but weren't complaining when 'Hound Dog' was covered by Elvis in '56 and made them wealthy. They quickly relocated to the heart of the new music, New York, and got themselves an office in the Brill Building in 1957. Once inside, they found a regular route into the Top 10 via a vocal group called the Coasters. Carl Gardner's perpetually pop-eyed lead vocals ('Take out the papers and the trash, or you don't get no spending cash!') were countered by the booming, shrugging bass of Bobby Nunn ('Why's everybody always picking on me?') on 'Searchin'' (US no. 3, UK no. 30 '57), 'Yakety Yak' (US no. 1, UK no. 12 '58), 'Charlie Brown' (US no. 2, UK no. 6 '59) and 'Poison Ivy' (US no. 7, UK no. 15 '59): each condensed teen-culture mainstays (nagging parents, elusive girls, class clowns) into a two-minute playlet, complete with breakneck rhythm and yakety sax. Leiber and Stoller also gave a first break to a young displaced west-coaster called Phil Spector. They let him work with them on former Drifter Ben E. King's first solo single, 'Spanish Harlem' (US no. 10 '60), an ode to a rose growing up through the cracks in a New York sidewalk.

It was their work for the Drifters – a vocal group of ever shifting membership – which would inspire younger New York's cub writers

---

* On the compilation *Elvis' Golden Records*, released in 1958, the sleevenotes called them 'the Gilbert and Sullivan of Rock and Roll'. Elsewhere, according to Stoller, 'we were called the Grandfathers of Rock 'n' Roll. At the time, we were twenty-five.'

† 'I thought he was a terrible music snob,' said Leiber of Stoller, recalling their first meeting years later, 'and I think so did he.'

and lay the foundations for what became the *sound* of the Brill Building. Leiber and Stoller had already written the Drifters a slew of excellent, raucous R&B hits in the late fifties ('Fools Fall in Love', 'Ruby Baby', 'Drip Drop') before they dramatically broke new ground with their production of 'There Goes My Baby', a US number two in 1959, the first R&B record to incorporate strings. Even now, it sounds like two different records playing at the same time, different urban strains rubbing up against each other. Ben E. King's lead vocal is wayward, piercingly lonely. A booming Brazilian baion beat* guides him through this uncharted landscape. Undeniably weird, always one step from chaos, it nevertheless opened up a new world of pop possibilities: here, for one thing, are the roots of sweet soul. In the wake of 'There Goes My Baby' a blend of Latin rhythms, orchestral sweetness and tenement passions, very cosmopolitan and very New York, began to fill the void caused by rock 'n' roll's demise.

Modern pop is essentially urban, and city living is a matter of constant shifting of context, between neighbourhoods and between roles. Two or more seemingly incompatible styles working at once is the existential reality of urban life. The term 'authenticity', one which causes a constant tension throughout the story of modern pop, was popularised by existentialism, the *du jour* beatnik/student philosophy of the early sixties. Beatniks, jazz fans and readers of Kierkegaard and Sartre may have heard 'There Goes My Baby' in the context of a TV show like Dick Clark's *American Bandstand* and dismissed it as inauthentic, emotionally infantile, but right here was a blend of different musics and neighbourhoods (Spanish Harlem, Long Island, the Bronx, Broadway) that related to shape-shifting street life much more closely than the venerated, undiluted directness of Pete Seeger's folk or Chris Barber's jazz.

Modern pop thrives on curious combinations. The same year as 'There Goes My Baby' was released, the unlikely pairing of a polio-stricken blues shouter from Williamsburg called Doc Pomus and lean,

* As a kid in New York, Stoller hung out with a Puerto Rican girl, and was introduced to congas, timbales, guiros and cowbells played on brownstone stoops on summer nights. He first heard the baion rhythm on the soundtrack of the Silvana Mangano movie *Anna*, and quickly absorbed it into his songwriting.

handsome New York Conservatory student Mort Shuman struck gold
from within the Brill Building. As a singer, Pomus had been on the
club scene for years, a hero to Leiber and Stoller, but he was broke and
desperate when, in 1959, he teamed up with the pop-savvy Shuman,
eleven years his junior. They clicked quickly, turning out two atmospheric doo-wop hits in the same week – the Mystics' 'Hushabye' (a US
number twenty in '59, all heaven and tears and goodnight kisses, later
covered with spirit by the Beach Boys) and Dion and the Belmonts'
'Teenager in Love'. With this hit (a number five in the US, and a
number two in the UK for Marty Wilde), Pomus began to assimilate
his love of the blues into the Brill Building sound. His previous most
noted song had been a lived-in, helpless number for Ray Charles called
'Lonely Avenue'. Now, with the boy Shuman at his side, Pomus felt
twenty years younger, and confident of channelling adolescent confusion into hit songs: 'One day I feel so happy, next day I feel so sad . . .
Each night I ask the stars up above, why must I be a teenager in love?'

They followed it with something better still, another orchestrated
landmark 45 for the Drifters. 'Save the Last Dance for Me', a US
number one and UK number two, was a love song from Doc Pomus
to his young bride Willi, the bittersweet atmosphere emanating from
the fact that, watching her dance with his crutches at his side, he would
never be able to join her.

Mort Shuman's youth lent a notable innocence to the Brill sound that
the older Leiber and Stoller were too streetwise and cynical to pull off.
A trio of young couples who occupied 1650's cubicles at the turn of the
sixties would refine and define the style further still.

An introvert chemistry student with sad eyes, Gerry Goffin grew up
in the Jamaica district of Brooklyn with the dream of writing a musical. At Queens College in 1958 he had met Carole King – born Carole
Klein, 'a musician who wrote bad lyrics' – who instantly suggested they
write a song together. She'd heard a rumour that R&B duo Mickey and
Kitty were looking for something new, so they got to work: within a
week the couple were dating, and within a month Mickey and Kitty's
'The Kid Brother' was the first (if far from the greatest) 45 to bear the
Goffin/King writing credit.

King was friends with a talented, conceited classical student at Queens called Neil Sedaka. He had a publishing deal with Aldon, and took King to 1650 Broadway, where, impressed by her single 'Oh Neil' (a rather sarcastic retort to Sedaka's hit 'Oh Carol'), Don Kirshner signed her and Goffin. Soon the urbane, painfully cool Barry Mann, the socially conscious actress/dancer Cynthia Weil, bubbly Ellie Greenwich and cowboy-hat-wearing Jeff Barry all signed up to Aldon. Just as quickly, they paired off and married: Goffin/King, Mann/Weil and Greenwich/Barry then set about dominating the American and British charts.

Although they looked up to Leiber/Stoller and Pomus/Shuman, the new teams' spirit was closer to Cole Porter, Hoagy Carmichael and the Broadway tradition than it was to R&B acts like Ray Charles or Big Mama Thornton. Yet they had spent their teens soaking up Alan Freed, the Orioles, the new sounds of New York. What they wanted from their music was to convey their own experiences of the big city, how it felt to be young and in love, and to be alive in a time of American affluence and influence.

Working on a production line, the Brill Building/1650 teams could turn out real pulp. A TV star called James Darren was the beneficiary of some of Goffin and King's worst songs, including 'Goodbye Cruel World' (US no. 3, UK no. 28 '61), which struggles like a tethered elephant behind a circus-organ motif. They were most effective when regularly working with hungrier, less cleanly professional singers, ones around whom they could create beautiful constructions, brimming with lust, and focusing on that most mythical source material of modern pop, the Boy. Concurrent with the youth takeover of the Brill Building was the rise of the girl group.

Connie Francis and Brenda Lee had made records that wouldn't scare your parents; the girl groups of the early sixties didn't even consider what adults might think. They made records about and for a complete teenage world. The Shirelles from Passaic, New Jersey, were first on the scene in late 1960 with Goffin and King's first hit, 'Will You Love Me Tomorrow' (US no. 1, UK no. 3). In 1958 Addie, Doris, Shirley and Beverley had been heard singing 'I Met Him on a Sunday' by a Passaic High classmate called Mary Jane Greenberg; she told her mother, Florence, who just happened to run Scepter Records, and they were quickly signed up. The bravery of 'Will You Love Me Tomorrow', with its post-virginal lyric, was something new, and the Shirelles were soon followed by interchangeable acts of girls who had met in high school and were often pictured in their prom dresses. Often, they were looking not for a long-term music career, or a way of making it to Hollywood, but simply for something fun to do for a couple of years before they got married and had kids. This gave their singing and their records a sense of spontaneity and freshness: 'Goodbye Cruel World' may not get much airplay these days, but the Crystals' 'Then He Kissed Me' certainly does.

Some girl groups were named, with great modernity, after the man-made fibres (Orlons, Rayons) which were putting Lancashire's cotton mills out of business. Others (Angels, Crystals, Kittens, Sweet Things, Fawns) were decidedly feminine, while others thought of variations on the Bobbettes and Chantels, two fifties girl groups who only managed one sizeable hit each ('Mr Lee' and 'Maybe' respectively) but whose influence was immense on dozens of sixties girl groups: Ronettes, Shirelles, Jaynetts, Darnells, Parlettes, Bluebelles, Darlettes, Percells. Their anonymity now seems quite shocking: in 1963 *Record Mirror*'s Norman Jopling wrote an appreciation of the Shirelles, who by this point had scored sixteen Hot Hundred hits, and said 'information on the group is very slight. Only four pictures have ever been seen in this country.'

The prime influence on the girl-group vocal sound had been the non-distaff, ill-fated Frankie Lymon: almost without exception, girl groups cited 'Why Do Fools Fall in Love' as the first song they harmonised. Veronica Bennett of the Ronettes even got to go on a date with Frankie, a messy business which ended with him being physically thrown from her mum's sofa.

As the Beatles dominated the British charts in 1963, the girl-group sound peaked in the States: fifty-one per cent of the year's Top 20 hits were made up of female-vocal or mixed-vocal records, the majority of which were Brill Building songs, and the majority of *these* came from the offices of Don Kirshner's Aldon Music.

Though he wasn't yet thirty, Don Kirshner was a father figure to his writers, and an editor. 'I can take someone else's material and see what was wrong with it, rewrite it, fix up the story line,' he said in 1963. 'The material is the most important thing. More important than the artist is the song – the material and the proper interpretation. People buy feels, ideas, sounds.'

The archetypal Brill Building sound was Mann and Weil's 'On Broadway', originally recorded by the Cookies in '62 but buffed up and made into a classic with help from Leiber and Stoller as a 1963 Drifters single. Mann and Weil specialised in urban squalor and class struggles, first showing their hand with the Crystals' racially conscious 'Uptown' (US no. 13) in '62 and peaking with 'We've Got to Get Out of This Place' (UK no. 2, US no. 13 '65), Bronx grit transferred to the sooty desolation of County Durham by Eric Burdon and the Animals.* With 'On Broadway', Mann and Weil captured New York City in a bottle. The singer walks alone, shuffling, in spite of the bustle and speed all around him. There are mariachi horns, *Dragnet* police sirens, 'magic in the air' and a rhythm that could be a team of workmen cracking open concrete in the sticky summer heat.

The strings climb note by note at the end, like a camera pulling back to reveal the vastness of the city, mocking the singer's dreams, making them seem less and less attainable: 'the glitter rubs right off, and you're nowhere'. It could be the story of any of the countless writers whose names crop up on the credits of the lesser, non-hit Brill Building 45s† – Kornfeld, Gluck, Hunter, Powers; history does not record their

---

* Bruce Springsteen played an acoustic version of 'We've Got to Get Out of This Place' at the South by Southwest festival in 2012 and declared: 'That's every song I've ever written. That's all of them. I'm not kidding, either.'
† A non-charting record that has everything good and progressive about the Brill sound – dramatically urban, adventurous, and fervent – is 'The Drifter' by Ray Pollard, a former Ink Spot who had lost an arm in Korea. It was written by Bob Feldman, Jerry Goldstein and Richard Gottehrer, a team best known for the Angels' gum-chewing bad-girl hit 'My Boyfriend's Back' (US no. 1, UK no. 50 '63) and the McCoys' fabulous but artless frathouse anthem 'Hang on Sloopy' (US no. 1, UK no. 5 '65). But if you can get past the middle eight of 'The Drifter' without welling up, you're made of colder stuff than me.

attempts to survive Beatlemania, let alone their Laurel Canyon solo albums. In spite of Don Kirshner's paternalism, it was 'On Broadway''s implied sense of imminent failure that drove on the star writers. 'All we did was write songs,' Barry Mann said later. 'All we wanted to do was have hits. It had nothing to do with money, it just had to do with the drive we had. We were always trying to please Daddy, Donnie Kirshner. The word "happy" was never really part of our thinking.'

The music's creators could only appreciate their achievements years later. The hothouse environment, then as now, meant you were only as hot as your current chart position.* Even now, Carole King is disinclined to look at the Brill Building era with great fondness, preferring to concentrate on the slow-working balm of her seventies singer-songwriter work.

Which is a shame, because Goffin and King were the best of the lot, the most tortured (the Crystals' 'No One Ever Tells You'), the most deeply in love (the Cookies' 'I Never Dreamed'), the most sensual (Aretha Franklin's 'Natural Woman'). Goffin was moody, insecure, obsessed with his perceived inauthenticity: 'When I write, I don't consciously try to appeal to the kids, but I try not to exclude them. If the lyrics are too clever without having any soul, then they make a song sound insincere and phony and the kids recognize it right away.' They picked up on stories directly from their whistling babysitter, 'Little' Eva Boyd, unsettling stories about her roughhouse boyfriend, and penned the stark, sadomasochistic 'He Hit Me (and It Felt Like a Kiss)'; cut by the Crystals with an uncharacteristically minimal production from Phil Spector, it was far too cold and disturbing for radio and flopped (for having her dirty laundry aired so publicly, Little Eva was later rewarded with 'The Locomotion', a substantially bigger hit).

Later, the couple turned to their own damaged relationship for inspiration. Few pop records are more clangorous and uncomfortable than Judy Henske's 'Road to Nowhere', the lyrics – 'I've tried to hold on for

* The songwriters thought of their songs as having a shelf life of a few weeks. Nevertheless, it was more than two decades after the dissolution of the great Brill Building teams before a year went by without at least one of their songs charting on *Billboard*'s Hot Hundred.

as long as I can' – spat out like so much sour milk, over vicious, disso-
nant piano and jagged percussion. Especially desperate, the Righteous
Brothers' 'Just Once in My Life' (US no. 9 '65) includes the bawled line
'I can't give you the world, but I would crawl for you girl'.* Goffin and
King finally divorced in 1968.

When Don Kirshner opened the doors to Aldon Music's new, plush
premises at 711 Fifth Avenue in the spring of 1963, he must have felt
like the boss of New York pop. Kirshner had sold Aldon to Columbia
Pictures, made himself a million dollars and moved to a fancy address
adjacent to Tiffany's. The new offices, though, were gauchely decorated.
When they arrived to work, his writers were suddenly lacking inspiration; soon they stopped turning up completely. Panicking, Kirshner
installed cubicles reminiscent of their old 1650 Broadway hangout to
make them feel at home, but according to Cynthia Weil, 'They looked
like concentration camps. Like we were automatons who were supposed
to go in there and write.'

When Kirshner damaged the fragile ecosystem of Aldon by moving
off Broadway, the seeds were sown for the sound's downfall.† Goffin
and King wrote another twenty hits over the next twelve months, but
moving their family home from Brooklyn to West Orange, New Jersey
(again at Kirshner's behest), only distanced them further from the teen
scene they drew upon.

Gerry Goffin and Carole King were passengers in Aldon colleague
Russ Titelman's car on a summer night in 1964. They were all on

---

* The CD age revealed this line could be 'I'd work hard for you girl', but the AM
static of the sixties made it more intense.
† I was only born the year of the British Invasion, and yet it seems to me like
something wonderful was nipped in the bud in 1964. The Brill Building aesthetic
carried on in reduced circumstances after the Beatles stormed America, notably
with the Red Bird label (the Dixie Cups, Ad Libs and Shangri-Las), Bob Crewe
and Bob Gaudio's songs for the Four Seasons, and the later Phil Spector hits (the
Ronettes' 'Walking in the Rain' and '(The Best Part of) Breaking Up') – here
was proof that there were possibilities for further development. Older heads were
still learning and perfecting their specialised craft; new writers (Neil Diamond,
Al Kooper), producers (Bert Berns) and arrangers (Horace Ott, Arnold Goland)
were on hand to take pop higher, deeper, somewhere more intense. Instead,
Merseybeat, at heart a reductivist sound, killed this progression stone dead.

their way to see *A Hard Day's Night* open in Manhattan. But as they approached the Lincoln Tunnel, King begged Titelman to turn round and take them back home to West Orange. She was afraid that she would be watching the world they knew dissolve on the cinema screen, and she was scared.

PART TWO

NRM Chart Survey

A LOOK AT THE U.S. CHARTS

FAST rising U.S. hits include—"Don't Think Twice It's All Right"—Peter, Paul, And Mary; "Sugar Shack"—Jimmy Gilmer and Fireballs; "Tell The Truth"—Nancy Wilson; "Monkey Shine"— Bill Black; "Red Salis In The Sunset"—Fats Domino; "Elephant Walk"—Donald Jenkins; "Enamorado"—Keith Colley; "Deep Purple"—April Stevens and Nino Tempo.

Recent new releases include—"Baby Get It"—Jackie Wilson; "Everybody Go Home"—Eydie Gorme; "Crossfire"—Orions; "Childhood Sweethearts"—Bobby Rydell; "He Understands Me"—Teresa Brewer; "Thumb Pick Pete"—Jimmy Dean; "Welcome Home"—Shelley Faberes; "Waiting For A Train"—Walter Brennan; "Misty"—Lloyd Price; "Last Song I'm Ever Gonna Sing"—Sonny Curtis; "Little Liza Jane"—Nina Simone; "She's A Fool"—Lesley Gore; "Speed Ball"—Ray Stevens; "No Hiding Place"—Vaughn Meader; "As Far As I'm Concerned"—Glenn Campbell.

New L.P.'s include "T'aint No Big Thing But HE is Jimmy Reed", "One Fine Day"—Chiffons; "Twanging Up A Storm"—Duane Eddy; "I Wrote A Song"—Don Gibson; "Night Beat"—Sam Cooke; "John Lee Hooker On Campus"; "The Impressions"; and "I'm The Greatest"—Cassius Clay.

Latest U.S. craze—"Ghost" discs. First L.P.—"Strange Truths" containing such tracks as "He Could Not Be Photographed", "The Psychic Donkey" and "Poltergeist Activity". Not to be listened to after midnight, or in the dark, says the ad!

N.J.

BRITAIN'S TOP 50

COMPILED BY THE RECORD RETAILER

UP GO THE CRYSTALS

WELL, it's certainly a good week for movement. There's more fast-risers this week than for a long time. Biggest are the Crystals with their fabulous "Then He Kissed Me", from nowhere to 22. Others include "Do You Love Me", "If I Had A Hammer", "Applejack", "Wishing", "Searchin'", etc.

Lower down we get discs like Allan Sherman's "Hello Muddah, Hello Faddah", the U.S. No. 1 comedy hit coming up. "It's Love That Really Counts" say the Merseybeats, while the Shadows look all set to go higher with their "Shindig". Little Peggy looks like having her first big 'un here on her hands with "Hello Heartache", while the Fourmost put more loot into the hands of the Beatles with the Lennon-McCartney composition "Hello Little Girl", going quickly up.

And we've got an idea that Mr. Roy Orbison is going to go a lot higher with his "Blue Bayou"/"Mean Woman Blues" double-sider.

BRITAIN'S TOP LP's

1 PLEASE PLEASE ME
(1) The Beatles
(Parlophone)

2 MEET THE SEARCHERS
(3) The Searchers (Pye)

3 SHADOWS GREATEST HITS
(2) The Shadows
(Columbia)

4 STEPTOE & SON
(7) Harry H. Corbett & Wilfred Brambell (Pye)

5 KENNY BALL'S GOLDEN HITS
(6) Kenny Ball (Pye)

6 WEST SIDE STORY
(5) Sound Track (CBS)

7 CLIFF'S HIT ALBUM
(4) Cliff Richard (Columbia)

8 CONCERT SINATRA
(10) Frank Sinatra (Reprise)

9 REMINISCING
(8) Buddy Holly (Coral)

10 I'LL REMEMBER YOU
(9) Frank Ifield (Columbia)

11 HITSVILLE!
(12) Various Artistes (Pye)

12 BORN FREE
(—) Frank Ifield (Columbia)

13 BUDDY HOLLY STORY Vol. 1
(17) Buddy Holly (Coral)

14 THE BEST OF RADIO LUXEMBOURG
(19) Various Artistes (Pye)

15 BILLY
(13) Billy Fury (Decca)

16 SOUTH PACIFIC
(15) Sound Track
(RCA-Victor)

17 SUMMER HOLIDAY
(11) Cliff Richard & The Shadows (Columbia)

18 IT HAPPENED AT THE WORLD'S FAIR
(14) Elvis Presley
(RCA-Victor)

19 THIS IS MERSEY BEAT Vol. 1
(18) Various Artistes

20 THIS IS HANCOCK
(20) Tony Hancock (Pye)

BRITAIN'S TOP EP's

1 TWIST AND SHOUT
(1) The Beatles
(Parlophone)

2 HOW DO YOU DO IT?
(2) Gerry & The Pacemakers (Columbia)

3 AIN'T GONNA KISS YA
(—) The Searchers (Pye)

4 HITS FROM THE FILM SUMMER HOLIDAY
(6) Cliff Richard & The Shadows (Columbia)

5 FRANK IFIELD'S HITS
(3) Frank Ifield (Columbia)

6 THE BEATLES' HITS
(—) The Beatles
(Parlophone)

7 MORE OF FRANK IFIELD'S HITS
(5) Frank Ifield (Columbia)

8 LOS SHADOWS
(—) The Shadows
(Columbia)

9 DANCE ON WITH THE SHADOWS
(4) The Shadows
(Columbia)

10 JET AND TONY
(8) Jet Harris & Tony Meehan (Decca)

11 IN DREAMS
(9) Roy Orbison (London)

12 JUST ONE MORE CHANCE
(—) Frank Ifield (Columbia)

13 TORNADO ROCK
(7) The Tornados (Decca)

14 DECK OF CARDS
(14) Wink Martindale
(London)

15 HOLIDAY CARNIVAL
(11) Cliff Richard
(Columbia)

16 SHADOWS TO THE FORE
(19) The Shadows
(Columbia)

17 FACTS OF LIFE FROM STEPTOE & SON
(16) Wilfred Brambell & Harry H. Corbett (Pye)

18 ALL ALONE AM I
(13) Brenda Lee
(Brunswick)

19 C'MON EVERYBODY
(—) Eddie Cochran
(Liberty)

20 TAKE THESE CHAINS FROM MY HEART
(—) Ray Charles (HMV)

1	SHE LOVES YOU 1 (4) The Beatles (Parlophone)	28	HELLO MUDDAH! HELLO FADDAH! 49 (2) Allan Sherman (Warner Bros.)
2	IT'S ALL IN THE GAME 2 (5) Cliff Richard (Columbia)	29	SURF CITY 26 (6) Jan & Dean (Liberty)
3	BAD TO ME 3 (8) Billy J. Kramer with The Dakotas (Parlophone)	30	FRANKIE & JOHNNY 34 (3) Sam Cooke (RCA-Victor)
4	I WANT TO STAY HERE 7 (5) Steve Lawrence/ Eydie Gorme (CBS)	31	IT'S LOVE THAT REALLY COUNTS 44 (2) The Merseybeats (Fontana)
5	I'LL NEVER GET OVER YOU 4 (9) Johnny Kidd & The Pirates (HMV)	32	SHINDIG — (1) The Shadows (Columbia)
6	I'M TELLING YOU NOW 5 (7) Freddie & The Dreamers (Columbia)	33	HELLO HEARTACHE, GOODBYE LOVE 46 (2) Little Peggy March (RCA-Victor)
7	YOU DON'T HAVE TO BE A BABY TO CRY 6 (7) The Caravelles (Decca)	34	DA DOO RON RON 20 (14) The Crystals (London)
8	JUST LIKE EDDIE 9 (7) Heinz (Decca)	35	THE GOOD LIFE 31 (10) Tony Bennett (CBS)
9	APPLEJACK 16 (3) Jet Harris & Tony Meehan (Decca)	36	HELLO LITTLE GIRL 50 (2) The Fourmost (Parlophone)
10	WIPE OUT 8 (9) The Surfaris (London)	37	STILL 37 (4) Ken Dodd (Columbia)
11	THEME FROM "THE LEGION'S LAST PATROL" 10 (10) Ken Thorne & Orch. (HMV)	38	ONLY THE HEARTACHES 23 (8) Houston Wells (Parlophone)
12	DO YOU LOVE ME? 33 (2) Brian Poole & The Tremeloes (Decca)	39	SUKIYAKI 25 (13) Kyu Sakamoto (HMV)
13	WISHING 18 (3) Buddy Holly (Coral)	40	NO ONE 47 (2) Ray Charles (HMV)
14	DANCE ON 11 (6) Kathy Kirby (Decca)	41	BLUE BAYOU/MEAN WOMAN BLUES — (1) Roy Orbison (London)
15	STILL 13 (5) Karl Denver (Decca)		
16	IF I HAD A HAMMER 36 (2) Trini Lopez (Reprise)	42	ATLANTIS 25 (14) The Shadows (Columbia)
17	SWEETS FOR MY SWEET 12 (13) The Searchers (Pye)	43	DEVIL IN DISGUISE 30 (12) Elvis Presley (RCA-Victor)
18	WHISPERING 21 (4) The Bachelors (Decca)	44	YOU CAN NEVER STOP ME LOVING YOU 39 (14) Kenny Lynch (HMV)
19	IN SUMMER 14 (9) Billy Fury (Decca)	45	ACAPULCO 1922 28 (5) Kenny Ball & His Jazzmen (Pye)
20	CONFESSIN' 15 (13) Frank Ifield (Columbia)	46	TAKE THESE CHAINS FROM MY HEART 45 (19) Ray Charles (HMV)
21	COME ON 22 (9) The Rolling Stones (Decca)	47	WELCOME TO MY WORLD 29 (15) Jim Reeves (RCA-Victor)
22	THEN HE KISSED ME — (1) The Crystals (London)	48	BE MY GIRL 48 (4) The Dennisons (Decca)
23	TWO SILHOUETTES 27 (5) Del Shannon (London)	49	THE FIRST TIME — (1) Adam Faith
24	I WANNA STAY HERE 24 (5) Miki & Griff (Pye)	50	MEMPHIS TENNESSEE — (1) Dave Berry & The Cruisers (Decca)
25	TWIST AND SHOUT 17 (12) Brian Poole & The Tremeloes (Decca)		
26	SEARCHIN' 32 (4) The Hollies (Parlophone)		
27	THE CRUEL SEA 19 (11) The Dakotas (Parlophone)		

(First figure denotes position last week; figure in parentheses denotes weeks in chart)

ACT NATURALLY: THE BEATLES

In January 1964 the Beatles left London for Paris. Even at the height of Beatlemania, with the world at their feet, they acted like hormonally challenged schoolkids, badgering manager Brian Epstein to arrange a tête-à-tête with Brigitte Bardot. They had to make do with playing support to local blonde pin-up Sylvie Vartan instead – the last time they would play second fiddle to anyone – and would recall with forgetful bemusement how, strangely, the audience was largely made up of frothing boys.

The group were holed up in the George V Hotel. In a few days they had to write enough songs for the soundtrack of what became *A Hard Day's Night*, so they had a piano installed in their suite. On a solitary day off they were required to record German-language versions of their two biggest hits, 'She Loves You' and 'I Want to Hold Your Hand': with an hour to spare at the end of the session they knocked out a new Paul McCartney song, 'Can't Buy Me Love'. Ten days later, the residency completed, and with thirteen new songs in the bag, they left Paris to spend a day in London before leaving for New York, where 'I Want to Hold Your Hand' had just broken all records by climbing from seventy-three to one on the *Billboard* chart in just two weeks. It all happened that quickly, that simply.

John Lennon was then twenty-four, Paul McCartney twenty-one. Seven years earlier they had met at Woolton church fete in a leafy part of south Liverpool and quickly formed a skiffle group called the Quarrymen; three years later, now with guitarist George Harrison and playing as the Beatles, they were dressed in leathers, performing hard-edged rock 'n' roll at all-night shows in Hamburg strip clubs. By the tail end of 1962, with drummer Ringo Starr having just joined, their debut 45, the wobbly 'Love Me Do', with its slight air of seafaring rough-ness, nudged into the UK Top 20. The following Christmas they were the biggest pop act in Britain. A few weeks into 1964 and they were the biggest in the world: their appearance on *The Ed Sullivan Show* on February 9th 1964 was possibly the most significant cultural event in post-war America.* Their rise, the scale of it and their impact on society, was completely unprecedented.

The arc of their story, covering the sixties from their Hamburg gen-esis to a messy, litigious end, couldn't be improved by a scriptwriter. Even when they were rubbish – large swathes of their *Let It Be* swan-song, for instance – it suits the narrative. As does having their own cartoon series, commissioning artwork from Peter Blake and Richard Hamilton, hanging out with Jayne Mansfield at the Whisky a Go Go,

---

* By chance, Sullivan had been passing through Heathrow airport in late 1963 and saw the screaming fans waiting to greet the Beatles on their return from a Swedish TV appearance. They were entirely unknown in America but, having seen nothing like this pandemonium since Elvis's breakthrough in 1956, Sullivan negotiated three Sunday-night performances on his show for the following February.

smoking dope in the toilets at Buckingham Palace, Ringo's plan to open a chain of hairdressing salons when he retired. They are the gang to end all gangs, self-sufficient, witty and all-inclusive – everybody wanted in and, somehow, everybody could feel a personal attachment to them, could become part of the Beatle world. From any angle, they are the perfect pop group.

And in 1964 everyone loved them. Everyone, that is, except for the people they admired most – the writers on Broadway and the girl groups. In two ways, they killed the careers of their heroes. The first two Beatles albums had included a number of cover versions – two Shirelles songs ('Baby It's You', 'Boys') were on *Please Please Me*, as was Goffin and King's 'Chains', originally recorded by the Cookies – but *A Hard Day's Night* was fully self-written, something that was pretty much unprecedented in pop. By becoming entirely reliant on their own material (indeed, having enough spare hits that they could score number ones with cast-offs like Peter and Gordon's 'A World without Love' and Billy J. Kramer's 'Bad to Me') they negated the need for outside songwriters; the Brill Building soon felt the chill. Secondly, the British acts who broke through in the Beatles' wake would similarly record girl-group songs by the Shirelles (Manfred Mann's 'Sha La La'), the Cookies (Herman's Hermits' 'I'm into Something Good'), Mann and Weil (the Animals' 'We've Got to Get Out of This Place') and Goffin and King (the Rockin' Berries' 'He's in Town'). Without exception, the UK-produced cover version became the bigger hit – there was a worldwide appetite for all things English.

This was hardly the Beatles' fault. What they reintroduced to pop, and what the emotional machinery of the Brill Building lacked, was the blatant sex and racing-heart *noise* that pre-army Elvis had provided. There was a sense of excitement and futuristic energy you could feel everywhere, the sure knowledge that a line was being drawn in history. And, just as Elvis had in '56, they created a new generation gap. Pre-rock. Pre-Beatles. Overnight, the Brill Building's craft, sweat and toil was part of the past. The Beatles' unscripted naturalism turned the lights on, and Broadway's neon suddenly looked rather cheap.

* * *

If you had to explain the Beatles' impact to a stranger, you'd play them the soundtrack to *A Hard Day's Night*. The songs, conceived in a hotel room in a spare couple of weeks between up-ending the British class system and conquering America, were full of bite and speed. There was adventure, knowingness, love and abundant charm.

Every stage of the Beatles' career had a complementary drug: speed (their Hamburg and Merseybeat period), cannabis (the sleepy *Rubber Soul*), acid (*Revolver* and *Sgt Pepper*) and heroin (Lennon's crack-up on *The White Album*). With *A Hard Day's Night*, the drug was adrenalin. The world loved them, and the world was their plaything. Ringo had an expression, 'Be here now,' which they consistently adhered to. Listening to 'If I Fell', the Everly-styled ballad in the movie, Lennon and McCartney are simultaneously playing to and teasing their newly acquired female fans, sounding far too vulnerable for Hamburg-hardened hellraisers, yet entirely believable. In the hands of anyone else, 'If I Fell' (its message: yes, girls, we are available, and ever so fragile) would sound simpering, patronising – the Beatles make it sound like an act of generosity.

They could do this because they were pop fans, happy to raise the profiles of other artists, thrilled to be part of pop's big picture. They believed in some continuity in pop – through rock 'n' roll and the Brill Building and girl-group scenes to the nascent Motown – and when they first arrived in the States they were keen to spill the beans on their inspirations. George would gladly admit that Carl Perkins was his primary influence, lending a country-and-western flavour to 'I'll Cry Instead'; John puffed up the Tamla Motown stable, whose 'Hitch Hike' informed the tough 'When I Get Home'. From the vantage point of Britain, they had the distance to see pop's progress, its writers and musicians, legends and lost heroes, with a bird's-eye view; they wanted to share their knowledge with the American kids at the eye of the storm. This was quite new. They also knew what they didn't like, which was the homegrown, panto-playing Cliff Richard and the Shadows.*

---

* Some of this antipathy was probably nothing other than envy. The Harrison-penned instrumental 'Cry for a Shadow' showed their loathing of the Shadows couldn't have run too deep.

Between 'Move It' in 1958 and 'Please Please Me', the Beatles' break-through Top 10 hit, Cliff and his backing group had amassed twenty-nine Top 10 hits, including twelve number ones. They were modern pop, but they worked within older showbiz rules. They covered their working-class upbringing by speaking clearly with accent-free, class-free vowel sounds, slightly mid-Atlantic – Geordie Hank Marvin and Cheshunt-raised Cliff Richard had almost identical speaking voices, presumably copied from Hollywood. It wasn't received pronunciation, at any rate; RP was the acceptable accent of Macmillan-era Britain, the voice of the BBC, of the Establishment, and in this respect they were originals, paving the way for TV presenters and politicians to come. The Beatles, though, proudly wore their accents on their sleeves, and – unlike the Shadows, with paymaster Cliff – were entirely democratic. At first glance they even looked the same, like pop's own Maoist army. If anything, they played up their Scouseness (speaking through their noses, turning every question into a gag) to challenge the BBC norms: in 1963 this alone spelt anarchy.

The Beatles moved too fast to ever become establishment, no matter how ripe the praise in *The Times* or how many medals the Queen gave them. They gave the impression of being one step ahead of everyone, of being in on some cosmic pop secret. *A Hard Day's Night* itself starts with a chord (G eleventh suspended fourth) that seems to signal a fresh start, a call to arms – that was then and this is NOW; in December '64 they prefigured '65's penchant for feedback with the buzzing fly intro to 'I Feel Fine'; at the start of '67 came the entirely new sound (a Mellotron flute, it transpired) on the opening moments of 'Strawberry Fields Forever' that introduced the world to English pastoral psychedelia.

The secret was nothing more than their fandom. Lennon, McCartney and, to an extent, Harrison were cultural omnivores. 'I Should Have Known Better', with its wheezing harmonica, showed prescient lean-ings towards *The Freewheelin' Bob Dylan*, an album George had picked up during their Paris trip; the limpid minor-key melancholy of 'And I Love Her' recalls Georges Delerue's score for *Jules et Jim* (a film the art-loving, romantic McCartney would surely have taken his upmarket girlfriend Jane Asher to see). It's safe to say hard-working beat groups like Gerry and the Pacemakers, the Swinging Blue Jeans or even the Hollies would not have incorporated such un-pop, deviating influences into their next potential hit-parade smash. The Beatles, through their appetite for cultural newness and apparent fearlessness, seemed to speak a future language.

It's easy to take this all-encompassing sense of adventure for granted when you read the Beatles story for the umpteenth time. In 1962 Adam Faith's gently mid-brow appearance on BBC TV show *Face to Face* had caused a media sensation. They had expected a grunting dullard, a rock 'n' roll caveman – that was how modern pop was regarded outside of coffee bars and school playgrounds in 1962 – but instead got a softly-spoken charmer who had read *The Catcher in the Rye*. By 1966 pop had moved so far in the public estimation that it was the main event of British art, and that was, no question, down to the Beatles. This final push occurred in '66, when the Beatles – bruised by pyres of their product in the Deep South, battered by Imelda Marcos's police – gave up touring and spent more time using the studio as a source of adventure. Straight away, they turned out the kaleidoscopic *Revolver*. It would be disingenuous to claim that you can hear the epochal soundscape of 'She Said She Said' or 'Rain' in anything on *A Hard Day's Night*, yet two tracks epitomise the future Lennon and McCartney directions.

'You Can't Do That' has a serrated sound from its opening line: 'I've got something to say that might cause you pain.' The relentless cowbell and vicious guitar break make for an enjoyably sadistic experience that (again) looks towards the bristling aggression of the Kinks' opening brace of hits – 'You Really Got Me', 'All Day and All of the Night' – later in the year. Lennon could use this aggression to rock hard ('Everybody's Got Something to Hide Except Me and My Monkey') or to sound spiteful ('Run for Your Life'), but later he turned it on himself ('Yer Blues', 'Cold Turkey'). The flip side of his nasty streak was the reflective apology ('Jealous Guy'). Either way, the listener wins.

On 'Things We Said Today', the wide-eyed sweetness of McCartney's melody and his pillowy vocal explain why children think of him as the Clever Beatle, and why anyone with a low tolerance for sugar can't take him. Beautiful, tricksy but catchy tunes came so easily to him that – on

'Lady Madonna', or solo efforts like 'Wild Life' – it was sometimes clear he really wasn't trying very hard, which wound up detractors and fans alike. Still, the one-note riff on 'Things We Said Today', the pointed tambourine shake, the sudden swing from goo to grit ('Me, I'm just the lucky kind, love to hear you say that love is love'), all of this adds up to a song where not a second is wasted. They may not have had Phil Spector's legions of musicians at their disposal in 1964, but the Beatles knew how to fill every moment of a record with heart-tugs and hooks.

'I'll Be Back' closes *A Hard Day's Night* on a strangely downbeat note. A sense of home, whether spiritual ('There's a Place') or physical ('Penny Lane'), would run through the Beatles' catalogue; 'I'll Be Back' shows their fear of displacement and sense of loss as their lives were becoming irrevocably changed. It would be followed by the more celebrated 'In My Life', 'Strawberry Fields Forever' and 'Penny Lane', and later aberrations like 'Maggie Mae' and 'The One after 909', when the group revived Liverpool songs of their youth in a forlorn attempt to plot a course home and save their listing ship.* It also hints at insecurities that were screamed out the following year in 'Help!'. The lyric is self-defeating, resigned to its loneliness ('You know if you break my heart I'll go, but I'll be back again'), while the chords shift uncertainly. Throughout, its nasal harmonies are very English, steeped like a teabag in Merseyside melancholia. The Beatles may sometimes seem emotionally buttoned up alongside their peers the Beach Boys, but 'I'll Be Back' is confused, resigned, mature. Just a few months after 'I Want to Hold Your Hand', this was their goodbye to the initial heady rush of Beatlemania and it remains one of their most affecting and underrated songs.

To keep a lid on their insecurity and the madness around them, the Beatles had an extraordinarily small but tight team. Manager Brian Epstein had ditched their Hamburg leathers, put them in suits and got them on TV; Derek Taylor was their equally well-spoken, dashing press officer; Neil Aspinall began as their van driver and became their personal

---

* After they broke up, Paul McCartney put more back into his home town – funding the LIPA fame school, writing the *Liverpool Oratorio* – than the other Beatles.

assistant; Mal Evans was part bodyguard, part tour manager. And that was pretty much it. This made decision-making simple, and kept the group flexible. With Epstein's death in 1967, things quickly got out of control. The group's ambition – on the back of *Sgt Pepper*'s international acceptance as a work of art – extended way beyond creating another pop record in a Technicolor sleeve. They were now at the forefront of a cultural revolution and, with energy to burn, set out on an altruistic mission named Apple to help discover and nurture the next Beatles or Burroughs, Bresson or Brando. Alarmingly, it seemed that they were thinking, 'We're not so special, we've just had the breaks.'

First they opened a clothes shop, the Apple Boutique, in late '67; it closed within a year, laid waste by shoplifters. They started an electronics division of their corporation which, unfortunately, had no connection with the omnipresent twenty-first-century company of the same name. Simply, they were out of their depth and had naively opened the doors they had kept so tightly shut in their early years. Nobody was really in charge. People were walking out of the Apple premises with typewriters; Hell's Angels were sleeping on the office floor.

Apple had been launched in May '68, that most optimistic, revolutionary and chastening of months, and by the year's end both Starr and Harrison had tried to quit the group, then been begged to stay. The end came, surreally, with Phil Spector overdubbing a demo of a McCartney song called 'The Long and Winding Road' with his usual bells and whistles. It became their last single. McCartney hated it and sloped off. 'We're all talking about peace and love,' he told the *Evening Standard*, 'but really, we're not feeling peaceful at all.' With the Beatles' demise, the sixties, an entire era, came to a dead stop.

* * *

So why them? Why not Del Shannon or the Four Seasons or the Beach Boys? It seems like a daft question, but it's legitimate. The only answer is that the Beatles were, literally, miraculous. They seemed to have some force protecting them, steering them – of the thousands of photos taken, there are none where one of them has his eyes closed, or is gurning a little. Not one. A few years ago someone found a few snapshots they had taken of John Lennon in 1968. It was a grey, muggy English summer day, and he was doing the most nondescript thing in the world. He was at a ferry terminal on the Isle of Wight, on his way to see his aunt. The whole thing sounds like an Alan Bennett yarn. And yet Lennon still looked incredible. He looked like a Beatle.

One story sums up their magical quality. On June 30th 1968, at the height of Apple optimism, Paul McCartney and Derek Taylor were driving back to London from Saltaire, Yorkshire, where they had been recording the Black Dyke Mills Band on a song of Paul's called 'Thingummybob'. They were in Bedfordshire. Let's pick a village on the map and pay it a visit, said Beatle Paul. He found a village called Harrold, which they found quite hilarious, and turned off the A5. Harrold turned out to be a picture-perfect village, with a picture-perfect pub at its heart. The pub was closed, but when the villagers saw there was a Beatle at the door they opened it up. Soon the whole village was in the pub, listening to Paul McCartney on the pub piano playing the as-yet-unreleased 'Hey Jude'. Every Harrold resident danced and sang along, and the revelry went on until 3 a.m. It was beautiful, perfect, spontaneous and full of love. Harrold. You couldn't make it up.

When the Beatles story ended in 1970, they could get their individuality back, be themselves for the first time in their adult lives instead of being a Beatle. And the magic cloak of protection seemed to vanish immediately – John was now coarse and self-pitying, Paul uptight and catty, George sat cross-legged, smug behind his beard, and Ringo drank for England while singing maudlin country from his barstool. They had always tried to tell us, and we finally had to face the truth: they were only human.

NEEDLES AND PINS: THE BEAT BOOM

Do you ever get the feeling that some people on the pop scene could only happen now? Not years before or the day before – not even the day after – just conclusively and exclusively now?

Big New Beat magazine, 1963

NORMAN: They've gone potty out there. The place is surging with girls.

JOHN: Please sir, can I have one to surge with sir, please sir?

A Hard Day's Night, 1964

In the fifties British pop had been chained and bound. The most success-
ful acts were overly groomed boys with eyeliner who made girls go gooey.
If you rocked too hard – like Vince Taylor or Johnny Kidd – you might
have the odd hit but little media support, which meant no staying power.
Most boys spent their late teens cleaning boots and bogs in the army.
Things changed quite dramatically with the end of national service.

The last people to be enlisted for national service in the UK were
signed up in November 1960 and discharged in May 1963; the Beatles
began their residency in Hamburg's Kaiserkeller on October 4th 1960
and scored their first number-one single, 'From Me to You', in May
1963. Their national service was played out in Litherland, Bootle, the
Cavern and the whorehouses of Hamburg. It certainly beat boot camp
in Catterick or Deepcut, and it signalled a final liberation for Britain's
teenagers. The boys could make as much noise as possible, the girls had
something with dirt under its fingernails that they could scream at. The
Beatles effectively signalled the end of World War Two in Britain.

Without the army to keep boys in line and batter dreams of Fender
Stratocasters out of their heads, sales of guitars shot up in 1961. Initially,
the Shadows were the role models, and instrumental groups playing clean, streamlined beat proliferated. They had landscaped names,
informed by the Shadows' widescreen hits: Dakotas, Fentones, Eagles,
Planets.

In Liverpool things were different, largely because of the Cunard
Yanks, the men working on the transatlantic liners in the fifties who
had brought unimaginable treasures back to austerity Britain – cameras,
jukeboxes, sharp clothes and exotic records – from their trips to New
York. They had the money and the hardware and, once back in their
home town, set up their own bars and clubs with the spoils.

This is how the kids with guitars in Liverpool were introduced to
early soul, R&B and manic rockers that their contemporaries in Lincoln,
Luton or Leeds would have struggled to hear – modern pop was still
strictly rationed on BBC radio. And, as with the birth of skiffle, everything seemed to emanate from one tiny room, this time a dank cellar
on Mathew Street called the Cavern. Originally the Cavern was a jazz
club but moved into rock 'n' roll at the start of 1960 with a landmark

set by Rory Storm and the Hurricanes. The Beatles first played there in February '61 and, toughened up by Hamburg, they tore the place apart. Kids would sag off school in their lunch hours to get to the Cavern – their eardrums took such a battering they could barely hear the teacher as they sat through double geography in the afternoon. Girls would slip out of their school uniforms and put on sweaters embroidered with the Beatles' names. Frieda Kelly, secretary of the Beatles fan club, was a regular: 'You could never deny you'd been at the Cavern because of the smell on your clothes' – a mixture of wet ferry ropes, rotten fruit from the neighbouring warehouses and sweat that streamed down the walls. 'Some people say it was offensive, but it wasn't. I know it was a mixture of different, horrible things, but it was unique. No other club had that.'

By the summer of 1961 there were over four hundred groups on Merseyside playing sets that featured the same two dozen songs, including Richie Barrett's 'Some Other Guy', Barrett Strong's 'Money', Don and Dewey's 'Farmer John' and half a dozen Chuck Berry covers. There was even a weekly paper, Bill Harry's *Mersey Beat*, to keep the teens informed on who was playing at the Cavern, the Blue Angel or the Iron Door that week. Harry was a literate man, and likened the scene to turn-of-the-century New Orleans, the melting pot that had created jazz. Once the Beatles broke through at the start of '63, London's talent scouts were thrilled to find a raw, ready-made local scene that had been operating for years, while the rest of the UK was still hooked on the Shads. Everyone on the scene had a Beatle haircut; everyone got a deal. The Beatles' impact was so strong, the demand for Merseybeat so extremely high, that eight out of twelve number ones from May to December '63 were by Liverpool groups.*

The beat boom didn't just provide a spike in record sales – consumers wanted more, to feel closer to their idols, to understand what *Boyfriend* magazine called the new music's 'strange compelling something'. *Boyfriend* had originally been launched in 1959 and tended to stick to

* Five of the first six number ones from early '63 had been by Cliff Richard, the Shadows or ex-Shadows Jet Harris and Tony Meehan. After 'Summer Holiday' topped the chart in May, for the rest of the decade they could only manage two more number ones between them.

safe, sexless pop – Russ Conway, Johnny Mathis – but found new desires stirring in 1963. It launched a separate monthly paper called *Big New Beat*, 'the first authentic photo book about the northern raves', which was Beatle-heavy and explained how they ate egg and chips and relaxed in 'a night spot called the Blue Angel, meeting their friends. There they spin the night away with talk of pop and old times . . . "bored" is a dirty word to them.' By 1964 the chart-focused *Record Mirror* was selling seventy thousand copies a week, while the newly launched *Fabulous* – with colour pin-up posters – and the *New Musical Express* were on two hundred thousand each. The glossy, slightly more upmarket *Rave* began publication in late '63. By then, total sales of music magazines were close to a million a week.

ITV's London broadcaster Rediffusion started a show to reflect the beat boom's popularity. *Ready Steady Go!* went out early on Friday evenings with the memorable tagline 'The weekend starts here!' The Surfaris' 'Wipe Out' was its theme tune, and the presenters were the ruggedly square Keith Fordyce and the gawky, befringed Cathy McGowan, who had answered an ad for 'a typical teenager'. It was live, slightly ramshackle, hugely popular, and led the BBC to launch a rival show called *Top of the Pops* on New Year's Day 1964. The first number one on the first *Top of the Pops* was the Beatles' 'I Want to Hold Your Hand'. They were dictating national television.

Brian Epstein once explained to Gerry Marsden that the Beatles were like the neon lights of Piccadilly Circus, while Gerry's own Pacemakers were more like a lightbulb – and Epstein managed both acts. If the Beatles' variety, modernity and songwriting put them in a different league from the rest of the Merseybeat scene, there was still a lot of quality action once the main event split for London in late '63.

Resident beat group at the Iron Door were the Searchers, fronted by an ex-boxer with a squashed nose called Tony Jackson. In the beginning they played incredibly fast, and – Beatles aside – their first two albums were the best evocations of the Liverpool beat cellars. For their third single, 'Needles and Pins' (UK no. 1, US no. 13 '64), guitarist Mike Pender took over the vocals and played the song's chiming hook in octaves, mimicking the sound of a twelve-string guitar; later in the year he even managed to buy an actual Rickenbacker for their best single, 'When You Walk in the Room' (UK no. 3, US no. 35 '64). Pender singing lead caused friction, and Tony Jackson, feeling unwanted, quit the group – the first-ever instance of a modern pop group splitting over musical differences at their peak. Fidgety drummer Chris Curtis took the reins, and the Searchers turned out more beautiful, ringing, harmonic singles: 'Goodbye My Love' (UK no. 4 '65), 'He's Got No Love' (UK no. 12 '65). Their lyrics involved blushing, stammering, a general lack of masculinity, and their sound became progressively softer, folkier, more feminine. By the time they covered the Ronettes' 'Be My Baby' on their *Take Me for What I'm Worth* album in '65, wispily, delicately, they were in danger of evaporating completely. They had no confidence in their own songwriting – group compositions were almost always B-sides or album tracks* – which scuppered their career when pop turned to self-authored rock. Their jangle clearly inspired the Byrds, and in turn Big Star and Tom Petty, but by the end of the sixties Chris Curtis was working in an office.

Looking more Scouse than any of their contemporaries, and so justifying their ultra-generic name, the Merseybeats' sound was as bruised as the Searchers', but they made the reverse trip. Initially they were Latin-tinged, and aped the softer end of the Brill Building sound on their second single 'I Think of You' (no. 5 '64). When the Who's manager Kit Lambert took control a year later, they cranked up the sound and got tougher than just about anyone. 'I Love You, Yes I Do' (no. 22 '65) was second-generation Merseybeat, brutal, soulful and melancholy, and – after abbreviating their name to the Merseys – they peaked with the brassy sadomasochistic swing of 'Sorrow', a UK no. 4 in 1966.† Another name change, to the similarly blunt Liverpool Express, saw them score

---

* Chris Curtis's 'If I Could Find Someone' and the Pender/McNally-written 'Don't Hide It Away' are among their best songs and deserve more exposure.
† George Harrison 'quoted' 'Sorrow' on the tail of 'It's All Too Much'. The Beatles must have been nostalgic for their home town in '67 – they also released 'Penny Lane' and sang the chorus of 'She Loves You' on the fade of 'All You Need Is Love'. But, as the Shangri-Las could have told them, they could never go home any more.

a number-eleven hit in 1976 with 'You Are My Love', a luminous, McCartneyesque song with an analgesic production – it sounds like the singer is drifting in and out of consciousness.

The biggest sellers, though, were Brian Epstein's second-stringers Gerry and the Pacemakers and Billy J. Kramer. Both knocked out several number ones in '63 and early '64, smiled constantly and were very famous for eighteen months. Neither was equipped to survive a fad perversely determined by geography; both sounded mildewed by the end of '64. The Swinging Blue Jeans ('Hippy Hippy Shake', UK no. 2 '64, 'You're No Good', UK no. 3 '64) were superb but had no personality at all, and never made the Top 30 again; the Cryin' Shames cut Joe Meek's last masterpiece, 'Please Stay', but its sales were so locally concentrated that while it was a Liverpool number one, it only made twenty-six nationally. Groups that got away included the Big Three, who were notorious ruffians but did leave the world the fierce 'Cavern Stomp', and the Escorts, who were more subtle and soul-flecked, and were Beatle George's personal favourites. Maybe the archetypal Merseybeat hit was the Mojos' 'Everything's Alright' (no. 9 '64), two minutes of screaming and wig-shaking that barely extended beyond a juddering riff and raucous repetition of the title.

What Merseybeat groups did was to get kids into dancehalls, get them raving, and encourage more teenagers to pick up guitars both in Britain and America. Most significantly, they helped make it acceptable for previously purist art students to stray away from jazz and blues, to form guitar, bass and drums combos. And, in doing so, they made themselves instantly redundant.

* * *

Now, what does the pop scene look like this month? Hair is a little longer. And everything becomes a little more rhythmic and a little more bluesy.
Big Beat: The Mod Paper for Pop Fans, January 1964

The British R&B boom seemed to follow Merseybeat into the British charts within weeks – the Rolling Stones' first single, 'Come On', had debuted on the UK chart on July 25th 1963, the same week in which the Searchers' debut 'Sweets for My Sweet' climbed to number three, and a full month before 'She Loves You' was released. By the end of 1964, when the Rolling Stones' cover of Willie Dixon's 'Little Red Rooster' reached number one, R&B had entirely eclipsed Merseybeat. The only Liverpool act to score a number one in 1965 was the Beatles.*

The two scenes had been growing in tandem. While Liverpool had the docks, a unique source of inspiration, London had the Soho boho scene, the 100 Club, sundry jazz and blues hangouts and a significant record shop for obscure American imports called Dobell's. The musical inspiration for both scenes came from black post-war American music; both deified Chuck Berry and Bo Diddley.

The crucial difference between Merseybeat and British R&B was that the latter started out as an art-school hobby – these groups weren't setting out to become professionals.† Brian Epstein's stable – Gerry Marsden, Billy J. Kramer, Cilla Black – had a work ethic, just like Cliff Richard and the Shadows or Dickie Valentine. You may not have wanted to do panto in Stockton-on-Tees for a month, but it was work and you wouldn't turn it down. Going to art school was the British way of dropping out from mainstream society, and it fed and nurtured successive waves of pop – the very first had been trad jazz, then came the short-lived skiffle boom, and from these sprang R&B.

As trad jazz went overground and into the charts at the end of the fifties,‡

* I almost forgot Ken Dodd, who had the year's biggest seller with a ballad called 'Tears'. Even now, if you go into a junk shop anywhere in Britain, you will find a copy of 'Tears'. It sold a million copies in 1965, and it seems like every single one was given away – either that or everyone kept hold of it until their dying day.
† It was born from an art-school sensibility but I should point out that not all participants in the R&B boom were students – the Yardbirds' Paul Samwell-Smith was an electrical engineer by day, and Bill Wyman was a bookmaker.
‡ Trad was the musical choice of British beatniks, CND members and baggy-jumpered weekend dropouts, while their American equivalents were digging the milky folk of the Kingston Trio, Peter, Paul and Mary, and Brothers Four. Dylan blew away these prim acts, and R&B's takeover of trad-jazz followers meant Kenny Ball and Acker Bilk never troubled the chart after 1963 (OK, Acker had a fluke Top 5 hit with 'Aria' in '76). Peter, Paul and Mary did manage a post-British Invasion hit with 'I Dig Rock and Roll Music', a US number nine in 1967; their heavy irony was so late in the day it was hard to tell if they were actually serious.

Chris Barber had started peppering his band's set with rhythm and blues to keep things fresh: by 1957 they were playing Muddy Waters's 'Got My Mojo Working', Ma Rainey's 'See See Rider', John Lee Hooker's 'Boom Boom' and 'Baby Please Don't Go'. Barber brought Muddy Waters over to Britain, and he shocked the beatnik purists at St Pancras Town Hall by playing electric guitar. Some booed; the rest thought about copying him. Just as had been the case with skiffle, it was a pair of former Barber side-men – harmonica player Cyril Davis and guitarist Alexis Korner – who left their leader and stoked the fire he'd started. They formed a loose, Muddy Waters-inspired aggregation called Blues Incorporated in 1961, opened their own G Club in Ealing a year later and found a ready crowd.

Alexis Korner – like the US bluesmen he worshipped – played a cheap and cheerful Kay electric guitar.* The affable Korner and the pur-ist Davis were a little too old and a little too paunchy to take financial advantage of the excitable crowd on their doorstep, but they were gen-erous souls and encouraged the audience to join in. The inspiration of this combo is incalculable: among the enthusiasts willing to get up on stage with Blues Incorporated and summon up the spirit of Mississippi from the backroom of a pub in Middlesex were Mick Jagger, Charlie Watts, Keith Richards, Brian Jones, Ginger Baker, Steve Marriott, Long John Baldry and Paul Jones; those watching but, for the time being, a little too timid to join in included future Kinks, Yardbirds and Pretty Things. All of these people would have significant careers and Top 10 hits within a couple of years. The firestarters went largely unrewarded. Heavy drinker Davis died suddenly in January 1964, aged thirty-one, while Korner had to be content with knowing that he had almost single-handedly birthed the British blues boom.†

Happily, the trad-jazz boom led to a transatlantic Top 5 hit – 'Petite Fleur' in 1959 – for R&B's chief disseminator Chris Barber.
* Korner was featured on the cover of the 1963 UK Kays catalogue, and inspired Eric Clapton to choose a Kay when he bought his first electric guitar.
† Korner did manage chart success as a singer with a new brass-powered group called CCS – or Collective Consciousness Society – in the early seventies. Produced by Mickie Most and helmed by Donovan's arranger John Cameron, they scored two Top 10 hits in '71 ('Walkin'', 'Tap Turns On the Water') and cut the definitive *Top of the Pops* theme with their version of 'Whole Lotta Love'.

British R&B groups picked up on an assemblage of influences – the rocking Chuck Berry and Bo Diddley sat alongside more gutbucket blues by Muddy Waters, Sonny Boy Williamson and Howlin' Wolf in the repertoires of Birmingham's Moody Blues, Newcastle's Animals, Sheffield's Dave Berry and the Cruisers, and – fiercest of all – Belfast's Them. Their leader was singer Van Morrison, who had a ruddy, sponge-pudding face and a mop of red hair. He set up an R&B club at the Maritime Hotel in April '64; by early July they were in Decca's West Hampstead studio recording 'Gloria'. With its cat-slink organ and Morrison's stuttering, panting expectation, he convinces you – unlikely as it may seem – that Gloria Grahame is about to walk through the door and mop his fevered brow. It's a dirty, dirty record, and a nervous Decca relegated it to the flip side of 'Baby Please Don't Go' (UK no. 10 '64), which was scarcely less thrilling. Them were all about phras-ing and dynamics, breakdowns and rave-ups. They took Paul Simon's 'Richard Cory' and swapped his sneering tone about the poor little rich guy who blows his brains out for one of stunned, barely articu-late disbelief. Given a high-quality but classically constructed song like Bert Berns's 'Here Comes the Night' (UK no. 2, US no. 24 '65) they sounded constricted, as if they were playing in suits that were a size too small. Their best single, 'Mystic Eyes' (US no. 33 '65), was the polar opposite. It came in from nowhere, everything turned up, turned on, distortion everywhere – presumably it was a jam that had been edited down for radio, but straight away you were in the eye of the storm. Its hook, if that's what you'd call it, was a two-chord breakdown on which Morrison ad-libbed about children playing among the tombstones of an 'old graveyard'. The title was repeated like an incantation until the beat picked up once again, fiercer still, with an abrasive one-note organ line adding to the noise, before it quickly faded. All over inside two minutes forty. 'Mystic Eyes' remains one of the unlikeliest rackets ever to have reached the US Top 40.

It may feel like there's a complete disconnect between the elbows-on-keyboards murderous noise of 'Mystic Eyes' and the Caledonian folk-soul of Morrison's solo career, but there was a single thread joining them – it's a late Them single called 'Friday's Child', a forgotten piece of 1966 magic. As Morrison's lyric dipped a toe into the slipstream, into what Dave Marsh has called his 'literary air of mystery', it was evocative of some past and future Caledonian legend: 'From the north to the south, you walked all the way.' Of course, it could have just been autobiographical – this was a group sure enough of their own legend to write a single called 'The Story of Them': 'You built all of your castles in the sun, and I watched you knock them down, each and every one.' The lead guitar could easily be a mandolin – the record practically invents REM. Delicate and tough in equal measure, 'Friday's Child' was Morrison's farewell to the loudest, most fractious group since Johnny Burnette's Rock and Roll Trio.

If Them were at one extreme of the R&B spectrum, then the Zombies were at the other, five unceasingly polite Hertfordshire boys whose take on Bo Diddley's 'Road Runner' is best described as weedy. They were the least nasty, the least gritty and the least raucous R&B act in the country. If they struggled with the raw Delta materials, this soon became an irrelevance as they married Colin Blunstone's menthol voice, and his pure St Albans Grammar enunciation, to Rod Argent's jazzy electric piano and came up with something all of their own. The arrangement on 'She's Not There' (UK no. 12, US no. 2 '64), at a time when R&B screamers ruled, was coolly restrained; guitarist Paul Atkinson was virtually inaudible. Shortly afterwards the Zombies recorded a version of 'Summertime' and made it sound more like 'Greensleeves' than Gershwin. Clearly, Old England was in their marrow. They scored another pair of sizeable US hits ('Tell Her No', no. 6 '64, 'Time of the Season', no. 3 '69) but were ignored in their homeland. Their 1968 farewell album *Odessey and Oracle*, recorded after they'd agreed to split, was one of the floweriest, most summery and most fully realised of that or any year.

The Zombies' love of minor chords was echoed and amplified by Glasgow's Poets, who used passionately thrummed acoustics and ghostly high harmonies to forge their own brand of Pre-Raphaelite R&B. They released six singles and the only one that charted was 1964's 'Now We're Thru', which crossed paths with 'She's Not There', climbing the Top 50 as the latter dropped down in October '64. The floor-shaking bassline of the follow-up, 'That's the Way It's Gotta Be', was borrowed for the Spencer Davis Group's 'Keep On Runnin'', a number one in early '66. By this point the Poets had already suffered about eight line-up changes, and manager Andrew Oldham eventually lost patience with them, which was really too bad. Tight and pumping, their aptly named farewell single, 'Wooden Spoon', in '67 saw them blend dive-bombing guitars and a Motown-styled backing track. They lacked the breaks and basic industry support to secure hit singles – in the mid-sixties, being from Glasgow meant they were so remote from the London-based record companies they may as well have been from Iceland.*

The most inventive act to emerge from the R&B scene turned out to be from the isolated North London suburb of Muswell Hill. The Kinks' guitarist Dave Davies may have worn his hair like a romantic poet, but when he slashed his amp speaker with a razor blade he created the single most violent sound in modern pop to date. Received wisdom says it invented heavy metal, which is simplistic, and does 'You Really Got Me' a disservice. Of course, there was the riff to end all riffs, a two-note electric shock of sound, but the power of 'You Really Got Me' was also in Pete Quaife's propulsive bass, the Gregorian drone of *yeeeeah*s and singer Ray Davies's rising, orgasmic melody. Most importantly, it shifted key twice during each verse to maximise excitement – no song had ever been structured this way before. This was sex and violence in perfect harmony. 'It's just like chatting up a girl,' explained Ray Davies. 'It starts with an opening – *da-nana-da-na!* – where you make a good impression. Then when she gets bored you change the key.' Within four weeks of release, 'You Really Got Me' was number one in Britain, dis-lodging the Honeycombs' Joe Meek-produced 'Have I the Right'.

Everything about the Kinks seemed anxious or aggressive. Ray Davies had met Bradford schoolgirl Rasa Didzpetris at a gig in Sheffield in May; with a little help from another Bradford native, singer Kiki Dee, they stayed in touch and Ray wrote the follow-up to 'You Really Got Me' about her. Described as 'neurotic' by Burt Bacharach on BBC TV's *Juke Box Jury*, 'All Day and All of the Night' had a lyric that walked a line

---

* There were a few Icelandic beat groups, naturally enough, and the best were called Thor's Hammer (in the UK) or Hljómar (in Iceland), meaning 'Chords'.

between possessive and sex-crazed. The group's leap in confidence can be measured by comparing the coiled-up-tight intro to 'You Really Got Me' with the ecstatic release of the cymbal crash on the beginning of 'All Day and All of the Night'. What's more, amid sniggers, it sounded like Ray said 'Whoa, get 'em off!' just before Dave's scything guitar break. An incredibly hard record, it reached number two in the UK chart and number seven in the States. The Kinks were the rawest, the toughest and – with their sexual confusion and readiness to self-destruct – the most distinctly English of the British R&B groups. They wore kinky boots and carried riding crops. Dave Davies would go around London restaurants with the Searchers' Chris Curtis trying to pick up the ugliest waiters. During a show in Cardiff, drummer Mick Avory hit Dave Davies with a cymbal and nearly sliced his head off.* There was blood everywhere. 'The police really wanted to get Mick,' said Ray Davies. 'I said it was part of the stage act . . . I really thought it was the end.' To cap it all, during an American tour in '65, Ray punched a union official and they failed to play an important show in Sacramento – the promoter reported them to the American Federation of Musicians, and the Kinks were blacklisted from playing in America until the end of the sixties. They spent the rest of the decade in splendid isolation, exiled in Muswell Hill, and Ray Davies focused his songwriting on his immediate surroundings.

So big was the beat boom, and so quickly did the new sound conquer the States in '64, that no-hit wonders like Liverpool's Ian and the Zodiacs could have whole albums issued. This was an incredibly strange development which, to this day, no one can very convincingly explain. America was traumatised by Kennedy's assassination at the end of '63, lost faith in itself and latched onto something foreign, cute, exciting, different – possibly. Still, the British Invasion was unexpected and hard to process for either side. No one could have predicted it. And no one in Britain could have predicted who would end up as the UK's best sellers stateside.

---

* Interviewed in 2000, Dave Davies explained the contretemps: 'I looked at Mick and said, "Why don't you get your cock out and play the snare drum with it? It'll probably sound better."'

Beatles and Stones aside, the biggest acts to break America ended up being from outside Liverpool and outside R&B; they tended towards caricature, the grotesque even. Manchester's Freddie and the Dreamers ('I'm Telling You Now') and Herman's Hermits ('Mrs Brown You've Got a Lovely Daughter', 'I'm Henry the Eighth, I Am') had number ones between them by playing on a goofy image which palled within minutes back home, but amused the pre-teen US market enormously. This was England as an outpost of the EPCOT project. Herman, aka Peter Noone, sang music-hall songs with a flat Mancunian accent, and they scored eleven US Top 10 hits; he stopped short of wearing a beefeater's hat and singing 'Roll Out the Barrel', but he may as well have done. Peter and Gordon ('A World without Love', 'Lady Godiva') and Chad and Jeremy ('A Summer Song', 'Before and After') were Oxbridge-type duos who were both far bigger in the US than the UK and weren't too proud to come up with hokey titles like 'Sunday for Tea'. Their every syllable was perfectly pronounced and quite, quite precious; both, oddly, made a lot more sense three years after Anglo Fever abated, when the world was engulfed in 1967's wave of gentility.

Biggest of all the non-Mersey British invaders, briefly outselling even the Beatles, were the Dave Clark Five. They didn't do any Max Miller gags. They were nothing much to look at, either. Clark was a steely-eyed North London businessman, a Spurs fan who clearly thought of music as a career. He played very basic drums and didn't sing, but assembled a smartly dressed band around him. He also recorded the group himself, keeping ownership of everything, and this marked him out as slick and uniquely far-sighted. The Dave Clark Five's back story might be better suited to the *Financial Times* than the story of modern pop.

The catch was that their records weren't slick at all. They were blindingly primitive, powered by Clark's anti-jazz drums, relentless two-note saxophone and Mike Smith's raw bellowed vocals. Unlike the early-sixties Spurs team that Clark watched from the terraces, this was route-one stuff. After a few false starts, 'Glad All Over' took them to number one, knocking the Beatles' 'I Want to Hold Your Hand' off the top ('Has the Five Jive Crushed the Beatles' Beat?' asked the papers) at the start of '64. It was loud, hard, fast, and all about a relentless thump. The sequel, 'Bits and Pieces' (UK no. 2), was a one-chord bawler that was never going to be written up in *The Times*.* Then, having inched their way onto *The Ed Sullivan Show* immediately after the Beatles' three-week run ended in March '64, they quit Britain for lucrative America and – charisma bypass notwithstanding – became even bigger. In Britain they released two albums between 1964 and 1968; in the US they released twelve.

They may have been the most calculating, unlovable beat group ever, but they were also one of the strangest. For a start, in 1965 they made a phenomenally cynical movie (director John Boorman's first) called *Catch Us If You Can* in which they literally sold meat, encountered middle-aged swingers, smackheads and army brutality, and ended up in a derelict seaside hotel, their dreams all over: here was a prematurely Broken Britain in all its monochrome glory.

The DC5 never re-formed, never reissued their albums and effectively wrote themselves out of pop's narrative.† Clark bought up the rights to *Ready Steady Go!*, briefly issued a few videos in the mid-eighties, cutting unrelated DC5 clips into the footage even though they were rarely on the show, and has sat on the tapes ever since. He has been reclusive; one of his rare reported appearances was as one of half a dozen guests at Freddie Mercury's funeral, and there are rumours of botched plastic surgery. More tragically, singer Mike Smith had a fall at his house in Spain, lay undiscovered for several days and ended up paralysed. He died in 2008. Beyond this information, there's nothing. The squarest beat group of the lot turned out to be the era's greatest enigma.

---

* The Beatles' 'Not a Second Time' had been praised by *The Times*' William Mann for its use of an 'Aeolian cadence'. In 1980 John Lennon told *Playboy* that he had 'no idea what they are. They sound like exotic birds.'
† The KLF attempted to do this, publicly announcing their strategy, three decades later, but somehow the DC5's disappearance seems more complete.

WHO'S DRIVING YOUR PLANE?
THE ROLLING STONES

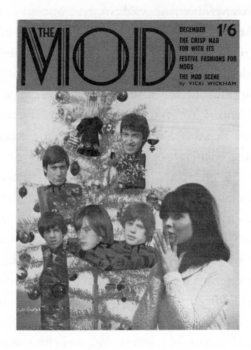

The unprecedented amount of positive energy created by the Beatles had to be earthed if it wasn't to burn out. In order for this to happen, it needed something to put its positivity in perspective, and that something was the Rolling Stones.

The Rolling Stones were seriously antisocial. They didn't smile. They didn't wear matching outfits. They were always rude about other groups, wore conspiratorial sarcastic grins, made snide asides at everybody else's expense. They refused to wave from the revolving stage of the London Palladium. They refused to put their name on their debut album cover, figuring the five threatening faces would be well known enough to sell it – if you didn't recognise them, you didn't count. They slouched, they sneered, they mumbled; they refused to explain anything.

Essentially, they refused to play the game. Even the Beatles and Elvis had played the pre-rock showbiz game up to a point, occasionally singing to a dog or smiling at the royal box. The Rolling Stones were all about anger, dissatisfaction, frustration and power, and they were loved or hated, really hated.

All of this darkness was harnessed and orchestrated by their manager and mentor, Andrew Oldham. Oldham was a tall, thin, sandy-haired nineteen-year-old who had given up on a singing career after stumbling through a version of 'Tell Laura I Love Her' at school. He got a job helping out on publicity for a singer called Mark Wynter ('Venus in Blue Jeans', UK no. 4 '62) and then, rather more interestingly, for the Beatles. He knew that the cosmic energy the Beatles had unleashed, that had been almost unanimously accepted by the Establishment, could also cause fires. He intended to find the lightning conductors and, one night in '63, he happened across the Rolling Stones at the Station Hotel in Richmond, Surrey.*

What he saw was a vision of the future, a totality of noise and image. Three worker Stones† were at the back – Wyman, Watts, Stewart – with the three star Stones – Jagger, Richards, Jones – at the front. They played amped-up Bo Diddley covers to a post-beatnik crowd, but the Stones were a cut above other Southern-based R&B acts like the Birds and the Pretty Things, due partly to Jones's and Richards's sharp dual guitar work but more so to their front man, the loose-lipped Mick Jagger, who had an animalistic androgyny.

Even though Oldham was younger than they were, and largely ignorant of the embryonic British R&B scene, he fell in love at first sight

---

* Oldham lived in Frognal, on an obscure railway route called the North London Line. Richmond was also on the line. He later admitted that if he'd had the hassle of changing trains, he might not have bothered going to see the Rolling Stones that night.

† No group had their name abbreviated before the Rolling Stones. This only tends to happen to rock acts, for the writer or fan to show an empathy with their art (see also Bowie, Dylan, Roxy). Straight pop groups – from the Trems to the Aloud – tend to get their names shortened as a nickname, in the same way as Paul 'Gazza' Gascoigne. I'm not quite sure of the exact difference, but I'm working on it.

and seized his chance. The Stones had been on the circuit, gaining a reputation but only financial crumbs, for a year. Oldham dazzled them, and told them he could get a record deal tomorrow. He'd learnt his spiel from the back row of the cinema, from watching Laurence Harvey in *Expresso Bongo* and Tony Curtis in *The Sweet Smell of Success*. He was calculated and succinct. For every kid who wants to take the Beatles home, he told them, there's another who doesn't want to share, who wants their own private group. He told them that they were it, that they were the chosen ones, and they fell into line immediately.

Up to this point, the Rolling Stones had been blues purist Brian Jones's group. Jones had a fine blond mop and a babyish face that looked as if it could break out in tears under the slightest strain. 'He was very clean,' remembered girlfriend Linda Lawrence. 'The other boys liked to make a lot of mess.' Maybe the Stones would have got somewhere helmed by Brian, without Andrew Oldham, but it's more likely they'd have been playing a fiftieth-anniversary show at the 100 Club to a few dozen nostalgic pensioners.

Once Oldham appeared and sussed out the potential, singer Mick Jagger and guitarist Keith Richards became the focus. On stage, Jagger was an incredible sight, wide-eyed, a human spinning top, with his unavoidably rude lips. Richards was a big-eared kid with a goofy grin, but within this underfed, gawky frame Oldham detected a sense of real menace. 'Whatever I decided people could be,' claimed Oldham, 'they became.' And he wanted the Stones to be the anti-Beatles.

He wasted little time, spoonfeeding a gullible press with headlines like 'Would you let your daughter go with a Rolling Stone?' Wearing their everyday clothes on stage was a showbiz no-no: Oldham took the casual nonchalance he'd seen in Richmond and multiplied it by ten, turned them into the ultimate bad boys. He also ditched the square-jawed Ian Stewart from photos; the silent sixth Stone would remain hidden from view, loyal to the band, until his death in 1985. With Oldham's blessing the Stones courted trouble and, eventually, they got it. In 1965 they were up in court after Bill Wyman had urinated against the wall of a Forest Gate garage: the petrol-pump attendant described him as 'a shaggy-haired monster wearing dark glasses'. Wyman's defence was a bladder complaint, but the group were all fined fifteen guineas; considering Elvis had been conscripted to get him off TV, the Stones initially got off lightly.

In the midst of all this ballyhoo they became exceptional, both as a group and as songwriters. As they channelled their snottiness away from blues snobbery and into the most relentless, abrasive sound Britain had yet produced they became, as Oldham knew they would, the most unavoidable force in pop outside of the Beatles.

Musically, their baby steps had been uncertain, though their progress up the charts was steady: 'Come On' made the Top 30 in late '63, 'I Wanna Be Your Man' was Top 20, 'Not Fade Away' went Top 5, and 'It's All Over Now' took them to number one in late summer '64. Their original songs at this point – all Jagger/Richards compositions – weren't worthy of consideration for A-sides, little more than half-formed, barely disguised rewrites of old blues and R&B numbers. Oldham tried their more promising early numbers out on other singers, and Gene Pitney took 'That Girl Belongs to Yesterday' into the UK Top 10. Some of their covers worked magic – Keith's cavernous, growling coda gives their take on 'It's All Over Now' the edge over the Valentinos' original – while others added nothing to pop's sense of progress. 'Little Red Rooster' remained no more than Southern blues played by a Thames-estuary tribute band, and its release as a single in late '64 was little more than roots one-upmanship (it was dislodged from number one in Britain by the Beatles' 'I Feel Fine', with its feedback buzz intro – no question at this stage who the modernists were).

In this way, they were the first group to mark themselves out as pop snobs, outsiders and proud of it, cutting themselves off from the squares and the straights with no intention of – as the Beatles initially had – working from within to smash the system. They also acted deliberately dumb. 'We're not Bob Dylan, y'know,' Jagger told the NME, by way of deciphering 'Nineteenth Nervous Breakdown' in 1966. 'It's not supposed to mean anything. It's just about a neurotic bird, that's all. I thought of the title first – it just sounded good.' Oldham kept promising a Stones movie; the title alone – Only Lovers Left Alive – was all the public had to go on. 'We're not gonna make Beatles movies,' snarled Jagger to a Melody Maker reporter. 'We're not comedians. I can't see, f'rinstance, Ringo with a gun in his hand, going to kill somebody. But I don't think you'd think it was very peculiar if you saw Brian do it.'

The youthful authority the Stones perceptively had – which even the Beatles lacked – resulted not from their knowledge of Muddy Waters B-sides but from their complete control of their image, sound and media angle from the start: Oldham produced the records and designed the sleeves, while Jagger and Richards made sure there would be no pantos, no synchronised head-shaking on stage, nothing predictable. It was very appealing.*

Their first single of 1965, 'The Last Time' was also their first self-penned single and the moment at which they fully justified their manager's hype. It was an incredible sound for a group from Kent. This was largely because it was recorded at one of the premier American studios (RCA in Los Angeles) and had assistance from one of the premier American arrangers (Phil Spector's henchman Jack Nitzsche), so there was light and space as well as a vortex created by the guitars, with Keith Richards's relentless spiralling hook sucking you in. From now on they were unstoppable: 'Satisfaction' (their manifesto, and first US number one), 'Get Off of My Cloud' (their most minimalist), 'Nineteenth Nervous Breakdown' (their most cutting) and, ultimately, in the glorious World Cup summer of '66, 'Paint It Black'. So intense that it never gets mentioned in round-ups of the subgenre, 'Paint It Black' is a death disc just as much as the Shangri-Las' 'Leader of the Pack' or 'Tell Laura I Love Her', the song that had marked the start and end of Andrew Oldham's singing career. Jagger's girlfriend is dead. We never learn why or how, but Brian Jones's sitar and Charlie Watts's drums mirror the throbbing, endless pain in the singer's head. Weird hums and an increasingly intense drone push Jagger's numbness to its limit, to the point of insanity. 'I want to see the sun blotted out from the sky.'

By this point they were the toast of London society and the *rive gauche*, the height of both fashion and debauchery, and making their very best,

---

* It's closer to the truth to say the Rolling Stones were middle-class kids slumming it, acting tough, and the Beatles – semi-detached suburban Lennon aside – were working-class rebels who had their wings clipped initially by Brian Epstein, and later by McCartney's commercial sensibilities.

misanthropic records. Still they didn't explain anything, barely had to speak, and in this way they built up a vast reserve of cool and kudos. Their blank expressions were a blank wall on which fans could write all kinds of rebellious slogans, from Maoist philosophy to 'teachers suck', while the Establishment could make them hate figures responsible for everything from rising drug use and teenage pregnancies to the ill manners of the gum-chewing girl behind the counter at Boots. Beyond this, their long hair and outsider status gave them the air of Byron, Blake or De Quincey; their girlfriends were the rudest, sexiest, poshest girls in town. So just who would break a butterfly on a wheel?

In 1967 came a drugs bust at Keith Richards's Redlands house. The press were leaked lurid details: Jagger's girlfriend was naked; a Mars bar was involved. This was a rearguard action against everything people thought the Stones stood for, their lawless joy, their youth. A week before the bust, the *News of the World* had fabricated a story about Jagger luring girls with drugs. The Establishment was primed, and this time they were sent down. This was swingeing London. In the witness box, Keith Richards – previously seen as a bit player to anyone but hardcore Stones fans – became a counterculture hero. Dressed like a cross between Beau Brummell and a highway robber, he told the prosecutor, 'We are not old men. We are not worried about petty morals.' He was sentenced to a year in Wormwood Scrubs. A *Times* editorial helped to get the verdict overturned, but the damage was done. Their next single, a beautiful, threatening, psychedelic kiss-off called 'We Love You', stalled well short of number one. Oldham and Jagger now bickered like a married couple and, soon after, divorced. Their messianic trip was over. 'You had no barometer', Oldham later explained, 'except Hitler or Jesus.'

Regrouping, the Stones got back to basics in '68, ditched the drug-addled Jones and Oldham, and lost their adventurous streak. Initially, they became darker, bluesier, and their new-found self-reliance imbued them with a confidence to cut some of their very best records: 'Jumpin' Jack Flash', 'Sympathy for the Devil', 'Gimme Shelter', 'You Can't Always Get What You Want'. By the early seventies, though, they had their own logo, official merchandise, even their own catchphrase: 'It's only rock 'n' roll!'

This was, literally, their get-out-of-jail card. To a large degree they became a different group in the seventies. Without Jones they never used a sitar, an ocarina or a tabla again. Without Oldham they gradually became a self-parody. The Stones of the mid-sixties had been an amazingly focused pop group; disobeying their mentor's number-one rule, they became predictable.

The Stones were the Bartlebys of modern pop, and could be seen either as refuseniks, street-fighting men or – forty years on – as libertarians, avatars of the new right. Whichever they really were, they weren't about to give the game away by letting you know. Through this, they were indirectly responsible for some of the worst aspects of modern pop – their nonchalance has been taken up by hundreds of bands in the last forty years, from the Doors onwards, to excuse lethargy, tedium, childishness; it's been a serial abuse of the term 'rock 'n' roll'.

Some people defined their basic worldview on whether they liked the Beatles or the Stones. Stones supporters thought the Beatles were cosy, white bread, establishment, lightweight; they considered themselves to be artistic adventurers, sympathisers with the underclass, rebellious outsiders, heavyweight. They thought the Beatles were Pop and the Stones were Rock. This was the first major fissure in modern pop, and it was soon to become a chasm.

THIS IS MY PRAYER: THE BIRTH OF SOUL

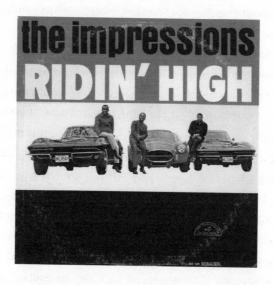

By 1963 R&B meant something quite different to Americans from what it did to the Rolling Stones. Their blues heroes belonged to an older generation. In the States, the Four Seasons' urban, razor-cut 'Sherry' topped the R&B chart at the end of '62, in spite of being pure New Jersey Italo doo wop – simply, it had a sound that black teenagers wanted just as much as white teenagers.* The Four Seasons as well as Chicago's Impressions, Detroit's Miracles, New York's Shirelles and Memphis's Booker T and the MGs were all creating something new on *Billboard*'s R&B chart, an urban post-rock 'n' roll stew with sass and class. The fact that Lesley Gore and the Four Seasons could rub shoulders with Ray Charles and Bobby 'Blue' Bland at the top of the R&B chart suggested

* From November 30th 1963 to January 23rd 1965 there was no *Billboard* R&B singles chart. No reason was given, but the prevailing wisdom was that the chart methodology was in question, as Caucasian acts were scoring big hits. However, *Cashbox*, *Billboard*'s main rival, continued to print R&B charts during 1964, and each of their number ones was by a black act.

something momentous was happening in still-segregated America.

Though 'soul' didn't emerge as a mass public name for the genre until Ben E. King's 1966 single 'What Is Soul', the music had entered the pop consciousness in 1957, on the day Sam Cooke left gospel and moved into secular music. It then developed, still nameless, in tandem with rock 'n' roll. Its constituent parts were contradictory and unstable, making it hard to pin down until Ben E. King nailed it. There had been explicit suggestions of something separate, a new expressive looseness in the vocal phrasing on some of the late-wave doo-wop hits of 1961: Shep and the Limelites' 'Daddy's Home' and the falsetto confessional 'My True Story' by the Jive Five were both American Top 3 hits that year, while the Impressions' elegant debut hit 'Gypsy Woman' made the Top 30. Gene Chandler suggested a further stretch when he followed 'Duke of Earl' (US no. 1, '61) with the tear-soaked wail of 'Rainbow' (US no. 47 '62). Then there was the gravel-voiced teen screamer 'Please Mr Postman' by the Marvelettes, another number one in 1961, and Solomon Burke's cover of the Faron Young and Patsy Cline oldie 'Just out of Reach' (no. 24 '61), produced by Jerry Wexler in New York for the Atlantic label. All of these records were definitely modern pop, and just as definitely not electric blues or speakeasy R&B; they were going back to elements of the church, even to country, to add a little more zing. The vocals had grit, spontaneity, and they felt personal. One man had this essence bottled.

There's a photograph of Sam Cooke standing, smiling, next to fellow R&B stars Jackie Wilson and LaVern Baker. Like most pictures of Cooke it has a slightly unreal quality: he looks like someone playing Sam Cooke in a movie. He seems too good to be true. Wilson has processed, piled-up hair and wears a safari suit; Baker looks almost mumsy. Next to them, Sam Cooke looks like he's been beamed in from the future.

He wasn't the first great stylist who had left the church to make girls weak at the knees: Sonny Til of the Orioles was the first post-war gospel pin-up, followed by the elastic, keening Clyde McPhatter, lead singer with Billy Ward and the Dominoes. Cooke, though, had a mix of gentility and gospel growl like nobody else; his singing was effortless and intense. He was the original quiet storm.

Sam Cooke was born in Clarksdale, Mississippi, in 1931. His family moved to Chicago in 1933 and, when he was nine, he joined his siblings in the Singing Children, who toured with their minister father. Of the seven kids, only Sam and his brother L.C. decided to pursue a musical career. Both were terribly handsome, and had charm to spare. In 1950, aged nineteen, Sam replaced tenor R. H. Harris as lead singer of the landmark gospel group the Soul Stirrers. Wherever he sang, the air was ripe with sexual excitement, yet he was boyish enough to carry it off without unsettling the conservatives. Everyone fell at his feet.

Leaving gospel in 1957 meant no way back and caused much disapproval in the pews. When his first single – 'Lovable' – did nothing, he must have wondered if he'd made the right decision. His second was 'You Send Me', and with it he had his answer. The candy-cane backing would have suited Johnny Mathis, but the vocal was clearly spontaneous, mellifluous in the extreme, gliding and besotted, dotted and darted with ad libs. It was very warm and very open, so easy and natural that it made Clyde McPhatter, Johnnie Ray and Elvis Presley seem like sweaty artisans. 'You Send Me' went to number one in the States and stayed there for three weeks, during which time Cooke not only became the premier pin-up for the black girls of the Bronx – the demographic he was primed for – but for the Jewish princesses in Brooklyn too.

Hit singles continued in a steady stream: the knowing 'Only Sixteen' (US no. 28, UK no. 23 '59), the self-deprecating 'Wonderful World' (US no. 12, UK no. 27 '60), 'Chain Gang' (US no. 2, UK no. 9 '60), 'Cupid' (US no. 17, UK no. 7 '61), 'Twistin' the Night Away' (US no. 9, UK no. 6 '62), 'Another Saturday Night' (US no. 10, UK no. 23 '63). Cooke was at a loss to explain his gift. 'When I do it, it just comes,' he once said. Still, there was always an undertow of rasp that let you know Sam may be cute but Sam meant business, and you might not trust him with your little sister. He could have made a tidy career criminal; as the leader of a pre-teen gang, he had convinced them to tear the slats off backyard fences, then sell them back to their previous owners as firewood. He was angel and devil, and his music contained the potent ambivalence of evangelist and repentant sinner.

Cooke was more than aware of his charms. Aged twenty-one he

had three pregnant girlfriends and shunned them all. To everyone else, though, he seemed golden, always one step ahead of the game. Having first laid the foundations of soul music, he then set up his own record company, SAR, and publishing arm, creating a musical nursery from which, among others, the Womack family sprang. This was all virtually unheard of for a black performer. He was the first person Cassius Clay called into the ring after he had defeated Sonny Liston, the singer for whom Aretha and Erma Franklin wore their best gowns just to watch him on television.

By 1962 there was a new intensity to Cooke's music, on the raw 'Bring It On Home to Me', even on 'Having a Party', which, as it declared 'the cokes are in the icebox, popcorn's on the table', had a strange air of melancholic desperation. That year the Kennedy administration had ordered the Interstate Commerce Commission (ICC) to issue a new desegregation order, allowing passengers to sit wherever they chose on the bus. 'White' and 'Colored' signs were then removed from bus terminals; lunch counters began serving people regardless of skin colour. In September a teenager called James Meredith won a lawsuit that allowed him admission to the University of Mississippi in September 1962; two people were killed in the ensuing riot but an armed guard made sure Meredith made it to college. The atmosphere in the South was tense, murderous, yet change was coming, and it affected American pop, especially black pop, considerably. The fierce heart-tug of 1963's 'That's Where It's At' reflected black pride, and black tribulations, but may have had less to do with the state of the nation than the slow unravelling of Sam Cooke's life: Barbara, his wife, was losing her mind over his drinking and womanising; and that summer their son, Vincent, drowned in the family swimming pool.

So Sam Cooke was a wild child, but he was generous, gullible, in some ways an innocent. He gave R&B singer Little Willie John $5,000 when he (falsely) claimed his mother had died. Then again, he'd go out clubbing, pick up girls, take them to motels. On December 11th 1964 he picked up the wrong girl, a prostitute who ran out with his clothes while Cooke was in the bathroom. Half naked and shouting, he scared the motel owner so much she shot him dead.

Posthumously, his career was still spotless – many people seemed to think his death was a cover-up, that there had to be more to it.* His last single was a double A-side of the relentless, hedonistic dancer 'Shake' ('Shake it like a bowl of soup!') and 'A Change Is Gonna Come', the song he wrote after hearing Bob Dylan's 'Blowin' in the Wind' and figuring he should really write something that reflected his life, his friends and families' lives, the lives of black Americans. 'I go to the movies and I go downtown, people there tell me don't hang around' – this was the America you didn't see on TV, everyday injustices you never heard about. It was an act of divination, shot through with hope and optimism; it's really too sad that it was Sam Cooke's epitaph.

If Sam Cooke was the voice, then Stax set the template for the sound of soul. Stax was set up by Memphis bank clerk Estelle Axton and her fiddle-playing brother Jim Stewart. The circumstances weren't promising. Memphis was a strictly segregated city in the late fifties when they bought up the derelict Capitol cinema on East McLemore. The popcorn stand out front was converted into a record shop called Satellite, which funded the studio. Estelle's son Packy had been rehearsing with a bunch of kids from Messick High School, including guitarist Steve Cropper and bassist Donald 'Duck' Dunn: calling themselves the Royal Spades, they experimented with country, R&B, rockabilly, practising until they became super-tight, and a backing group for any passing trade. Then they just hung around the shop and waited. One day in 1961 local DJ Rufus Thomas walked into the shop – his daughter Carla had something she'd written, a teenage poem called 'Gee Whiz', and he wanted her to record it. It was naive and irresistible, and when the Stax crew cut it 'Gee Whiz' became a Top 10 hit. Soon after, a dirty, brass-led, one-note Royal Spades instrumental called 'Last Night' – released under the name the Mar-Keys – made it as far as number two and Stax was off and running.

---

* In spite of exhaustive efforts by Sam Cooke's manager, Allen Klein, no alternative story of his death was ever uncovered, let alone proved. Cooke's widow Barbara started seeing his close friend and Valentinos guitarist Bobby Womack within days of the shooting. Womack began to liberally borrow clothes from the dead man's wardrobe, and the couple married barely ten weeks after Cooke's death, an event that biographer Peter Guralnick later described as the 'punchline of a dirty joke'.

The key that unlocked Stax's success was the Satellite record shop. It became a social club where black and white mixed and everyone heard the latest sounds as soon as they landed in the racks. Local kids like keyboard player Booker T. Jones and a grocery boy called David Porter were soon involved in studio sessions. Axton and Stewart worked in the shop by day, the studio by night and on weekends; once the hits began, some of the kids who frequented the shop became employees. Stewart had 'scarcely seen a black 'til I was grown. When I started I didn't know there was such a thing as Atlantic Records. I didn't know there was a Chess Records, or Imperial. I had no desire to start Stax Records, I had no dream of anything like that. I just wanted music. Just anything to be involved with music.'

Through a shared love of R&B and rock 'n' roll, the studio musicians had hit upon a new, gritty but streamlined sound that solidified by '63 into something distinctly Stax: triumphant horns, propellant vocals, plus Al Jackson and Duck Dunn's warm, compact rhythm section. Central to their tight groove was the cut-diamond, economical guitar-playing of Steve Cropper; it was clipped, clean and cool, the opposite of flash.

With two more hits in '62 – William Bell's gospel-influenced 'You Don't Miss Your Water' (US no. 95) and another house-band instrumental, the lean 'Green Onions' (US no. 3), credited to Booker T. and the MGs – Stax became the sound of Memphis, earning the right to hang a sign over the record shop that read 'Soulsville USA'. When musicians began to seek out the Stax sound, the studio ended up recording Sam and Dave, Otis Redding, Judy Clay, Eddie Floyd and Johnnie Taylor. Pretty soon, the sound became more important than the artist, a Southern equivalent to Spectorsound and the Brill Building.

The other label which defined the burgeoning sound of soul was New York's Atlantic Records. It had been set up as far back as 1947 to release R&B, jazz and blues for a largely black audience. There were three key figures behind Atlantic's success, and none of them was a singer: Ahmet Ertegun, an educated New Yorker and jazz lover who was the instigator; Jerry Wexler, a business reporter for *Billboard* who became a director in '53 and took Atlantic from the black districts of New York to the outside world; and Tom Dowd, an engineer whose scientific background involved a stint working on the Manhattan Project. Science and blind enthusiasm, sacred and secular, black and white, Atlantic embodied and extended all of soul's contradictions.

While Ertegun was the smooth businessman, immaculate in dress and manners, and Dowd was the diligent kid at the mixing desk, Wexler could be relied upon for cultural broadsides and grand pronouncements, and soon became the Matthew Arnold of pop. He had grounds, too. For a start, he was the man who, while working at *Billboard*, had coined the expression 'rhythm and blues', instantly granting what was previously called the race chart a little more respect. He also understood the mechanics: soul, he said, was 'a semantic fabrication. It was just a stage of the music, it evolved to a certain point.' But, when you got right down to it, 'it was rhythm and blues'. Ertegun, Dowd and Wexler. All three, like Leiber and Stoller, like Andrew Oldham, were very sure of themselves, their taste and their ideas on pop culture.

Ertegun, though, was first and foremost a money man. Before starting the label he spent a year hanging around a friend's record shop, getting a feel for what people were seeking out. One day in 1948 he was on the phone to a record distributor in New Orleans who was looking to buy five thousand copies of Stick McGhee's 'Drinkin' Wine Spo-Dee-o-Dee'. The original label, Ertegun discovered, had just gone bust. He tracked McGhee down that same day and re-recorded the song, selling six hundred thousand copies and financing Atlantic's studio recordings for the next few years.

Ertegun's first love was the blues, which is where Ray Charles came from. Initially, Charles was a pianist with a gift for mimicking his heroes Louis Jordan, Nat King Cole and Charles Brown. Occasionally he'd hint at what was to come with an arresting, untamed vocal – as on Leiber and Stoller's 'The Snow Is Falling' in '51 – but Atlantic pampered him until he struck gold. First he wrote 'I Got a Woman', an R&B number one in January '55 based on the Southern Tones' gospel record 'It Must Be Jesus', and later covered by Elvis Presley, the Beatles and Them. Then in '59 came 'What'd I Say', a call-and-response record of *yeah*s, *ooh*s and *ahh*s that lasted six minutes and was equal parts church revival and bordello dirt.* It sounded like nothing that had gone before. From this point until the mid-sixties Charles was cited as an influence by pretty much every aspiring musician, from Stevie Wonder to the Searchers: Brother Ray, the Genius, Soul Brother Number One. In no doubt of his ability, he became a dilettante, first cutting jazz instrumental albums, then toying with country on a cover of Hoagy Carmichael's 'Georgia on My Mind' (US no. 1 '60), a single that bled its torn loyalties – the South was home, but in 1960 it was also on the civil-rights frontline. Charles cut a whole album, *Modern Sounds in Country and Western*, in 1962. Blending country and soul was brave, but a delicate operation. By now he had left Atlantic after getting a large cheque from ABC-Paramount. Without Ertegun, Wexler and Dowd to question his judgement, Brother Ray went headfirst into the orchestrated countrypolitan sound and scored two of the biggest hits of his career ('I Can't Stop Loving You', 'You Don't Know Me', both US and UK Top 10) and a US number-one album. But the commercial success of this fusion diluted his artistic impulses – jazz, blues, even R&B were largely abandoned. By the mid-sixties he had repeated the country trick much too often (the sequel was called *Modern Sounds in Country and Western 2*), hurting his credibility with his rock-critic fanbase and fellow musicians so badly that he was barely spoken of by the end of the decade.

Barbara Lewis was maybe the most underrated Atlantic act, with a voice like polished jade on the half-fairground, half-boudoir shuffle 'Hello Stranger' (US no. 3 '62): you would die happy if, just the once, someone sang the song directly to you. Aretha Franklin, though, was their biggest signing in every sense. With a voice that wrecked microphones half a mile distant, she sang like a force of nature. Signed to Columbia by John Hammond – who perceived her as a successor to Billie Holiday – Aretha had released some fine, softly sung material, but, bringing her to Atlantic in '67, Ahmet Ertegun encouraged her to let rip, and the volume rarely dropped below eleven on any of her

---

* Stax's Jim Stewart was besotted with 'What'd I Say', it was his lodestone, which goes some way to explaining the direction his Stax productions took, away from country and rockabilly, focusing on R&B.

Atlantic singles from '67 onwards.* Even on 'I Say a Little Prayer' (UK
no. 4, US no. 10 '68) she sounds confined, straitjacketed, first at her
dressing table, then her work desk; compare it to Dionne Warwick's
lavender-dabbed rendition and you know in a trice whose love is the
more physical.

* * *

All across America there were equivalent, if less successful, versions of
Stax and Atlantic. More than any other modern pop genre, soul had
identifiable regional variations, usually with their own local imprint.
Generally, the further south you headed, the rawer, more gargled and
more guttural it became, while the north – especially Detroit – was
more about straight-ahead dancefloor action; simply, one was more
agrarian, one more industrial. Cincinatti had King, a bruiser of a label,
covering hardcore black music across the board with no particular interest in crossing over. Their lynchpin was James Brown, who never quite
reached number one but had more hit singles in America than anyone bar Elvis. Houston, Texas, was home to Duke (Bobby Bland) and
Backbeat (Carl Carlton); Nashville provided intense country soul on the
SSS International group of labels; New York had the Scepter and Wand
labels owned by Florence Greenberg, home to the stentorian Chuck
Jackson† and Tommy Hunt, both very adult, well groomed, manly singers. Wand was also home to Maxine Brown, a one-time beauty queen
with a smile that could make you buckle and bend, and she sang like
no gauche teenager: their records defined 'uptown' or 'big-city soul' –
mid-tempo, heavily orchestrated, fond of tympani and Latin flicks and
fancies.

As the genre tightened, became more immediately recognisable,
more consciously manufactured, Aretha Franklin became its figurehead.

---

* Aretha's Columbia recordings are often dismissed en masse, which is daft: her
1965 single 'Sweet Bitter Love', written by Van McCoy, is as intense and beautiful as anything she cut for Atlantic.
† Chuck Jackson was inadvertently the biggest influence on the Welsh singer Tom
Jones; it's a shame he didn't have the same talent for self-promotion.

Nicknamed Lady Soul, she was less about elegance than R.E.S.P.E.C.T. Her legend, which has survived some disastrous records,* tends to reduce all other female soul singers to the runner-up category: 'There are singers,' said Ray Charles, 'then there is Aretha. She towers above the rest. Others are good, but Aretha is great.' For my money there were several who had a little less lung power, but were more nuanced: Betty Harris, Bettye LaVette and Gladys Knight. With a crack in her voice that she used sparingly, exquisitely, and with her round cheeks and liquid eyes, Gladys Knight was a true Georgia peach, and many claim her bone-rattling take on 'I Heard It through the Grapevine', a US number two in late '67, is at least the equal of Marvin Gaye's hit a year hence. More than anyone, she presented soul as an adult format. Moving north in the early sixties she hooked up with Van McCoy,† a New York writer/producer of almost unwavering class and melodic strength: he gave Gladys her best material, from the stately, neo-classical string-bed of 'Giving Up' in '64 to the Sprite-lite disco 'Baby Don't Change Your Mind' thirteen years later. In between was a lengthy sojourn with Motown, who underused her talents horribly. By the mid-seventies, signed to Buddah, she was accessing Jim Weatherly's country-soul writing ('Midnight Train to Georgia', US no. 1 '73) and movie themes ('The Way We Were', UK no. 4 '74), a palette broad enough to make her the cross-border superstar

---

* Presumably in an attempt to score more sales with white fans, Atlantic fed Aretha inappropriate material like 'Bridge over Troubled Water' and 'Eleanor Rigby'. Like Ray Charles years before, her reputation suffered and the hits dried up. During the soul-obsessed mid-eighties she came back with an electro hit ('Who's Zoomin' Who') and a George Michael duet ('I Knew You Were Waiting for Me') which sold well but, again, hardly made the most of her extraordinary voice.

† McCoy's best known hits are Barbara Lewis's melty 'Baby I'm Yours' (US no. 11 '65), the Marvelettes' 'When You're Young and in Love' (UK no. 13 '67), Jackie Wilson's 'I Get the Sweetest Feeling' (US no. 34 '68, UK no. 9 '72) and, under his own name, the supernaturally cheerful 'The Hustle' (US no. 1, UK no. 3 '75). But among his list of chart flops are some of sophisticated soul's crowning moments: Aretha's 'Sweet Bitter Love', Esther Phillips's 'Some Things You Never Get Used To', Irma Thomas's 'It's Starting to Get to Me Now', Teri Thornton's 'Why Don't You Love Me', the Ad Libs' 'Giving Up', Judy Clay's 'Haven't Got What It Takes', the Sweet Things' 'You're My Loving Baby'. I can't recommend these records highly enough.

that Atlantic had dearly wanted Aretha Franklin to become. These days Gladys Knight runs a chain of chicken and waffle restaurants, and has taken to calling herself the Empress of Soul. I'm not going to argue.

Philadelphia had been a major player on the US charts since the demise of classic rock 'n' roll and the rise of teen-idol pop at the end of the fifties, largely because of a TV show called *American Bandstand*. Presented by Dick Clark, it offered a wholesome pop mix that kids wanted and parents couldn't object to. It also changed the rules of American television by being multiracial. The main beneficiary of the show was a local label called Cameo Parkway, and they had a real find in sixteen-year-old Dee Dee Sharp. Her 1962 single 'Mashed Potato Time' (US no. 2) was a direct steal from the Marvelettes' 'Please Mr Postman' but was irresistible, one of the finest girl-group 45s, all chorus and squealed anguish. She followed it with soundalikes ('Gravy', 'Ride', 'Do the Bird', all US Top 10 hits), before being given the bossa-soul 'Wild'* in '63; from this point on her records sold progressively less but got more beautiful. Performing 1965's 'I Really Love You', a ripe ballad with what sounds like a full symphony orchestra behind its depth-charge percussion, she sounds desperate, heavily lipglossed, sultry as hell. It was magical, but struggled to number seventy-eight in late '65 – Dee Dee had to make do with being both a has-been and a forerunner of the decade ahead.

Also from Philly, Barbara Mason had one of the laziest, most coquettish voices in all pop. Her biggest hit, a US number-five hit on the tiny Arctic label in 1965, was 'Yes I'm Ready', a faux-naive song with a wide-eyed, out-of-tune vocal by teenage Barbara: 'I don't even know how to love you, but I'm ready to learn.' She sang as if she had one finger in her mouth, making baby eyes at the poor sap who was about to fall hook, line and sinker. 'I don't even know how to hold your hand.' Who was she fooling? All her records were decidedly handmade, adding to their charm. In the seventies she made the tense, repetitive and breathy 'Give Me Your Love' with Curtis Mayfield; the eighties saw her

---

* The title wasn't misplaced. The Zombies recall Dee Dee being thrown off a tour bus out in the boondocks after she started yelling and waving a gun around.

nudging a little harder, scoring a club hit with a song about a bisexual boyfriend, 'Another Man' (UK no. 45 '84).

Chicago had been the home of urban blues in the forties and fifties, which subtly informed its soul in the sixties. The Dells, from Harvey, Illinois, deserve a mention here if only for their longevity. Formed in 1952, they were a presence on the Chicago scene all the way through R&B, doo wop and soul's mutations. Their songs usually built from a quiet group-harmony base, subtle, almost supper club, until the moment when their baritone Marvin Junior stepped in, and then all hell broke loose. On the churchy 'Stay in My Corner' (US no. 10 '68), the aerated skip of 'It's All Up to You' (no. 94 '72), or even on 'Love Is Blue', originally Luxembourg's 1967 Eurovision entry and the Dells' sole UK hit in 1969, he sounded like he'd been asked to encapsulate the sum of human suffering inside thirty seconds.* Curtis Mayfield, though, was the king of Chicago soul, and the best ambassador the genre ever had. While Atlantic loved to cut deals, invest heavily and duly accrue the riches, Mayfield was the people's champion. 'It's All Right', he sang, have a good time 'cos it's all right.

Leader of the Impressions, he had a sweet, high-registered voice, and his face beamed gentle inspiration. He radiated yearning on their first hit, 1961's castanet-heavy 'Gypsy Woman', a minimalist one-act soul tableau; he radiated devotional love on 1964's deathlessly pretty 'I'm So Proud' (US no. 14 '64). He radiated kindness and innocence, and the Impressions' run of sixties hits – 'I'm the One Who Loves You', 'Talking 'Bout My Baby', 'You Must Believe Me', 'Meeting Over Yonder' – is one of the most uplifting sequences in all pop. You can hear splashes of Mayfield in the Jimi Hendrix Experience – the title track of *Electric Ladyland* is more or less an Impressions pastiche, and even the glocken-spiel of 'I'm So Proud' makes a slight return on 'Little Wing'. In turn the Isley Brothers ('That Lady') and Prince ('If I Was Your Girlfriend') also borrowed Mayfield's beatified falsetto.

* One double-sided 45 of the floor-filling 'Make Sure' backed with a Vietnam lament called 'Does Anybody Know I'm Here' (with a particularly extreme inter-vention from Marvin Junior) is the best, most concise way into the Dells' enor-mous catalogue.

By the end of the sixties Mayfield had his own label, Curtom, he produced hits for others (Major Lance, Jan Bradley, the Winstons) and he dropped the veil, singing about black pride with no less benevolence. Chicago's urban blues may have been sonic fuel for the Rolling Stones' fire, but it also gave inspiration to Mayfield's inner-city cries. His song titles had often suggested civil rights ('People Get Ready', 'Keep On Pushing'), but by the end of the decade they spelled out slogans: 'This Is My Country', 'Choice of Colors' and 'We're a Winner' were all fine records, but I reckon he'd got to the nub of the issue with a more universal message on 'It's All Right' (US no. 4 '63) much earlier on: 'When you wake up early in the morning, feeling sad like so many of us do, hum a little soul. Make life your goal. And surely something's got to come to you.'

THE RAKE'S PROGRESS: BOB DYLAN

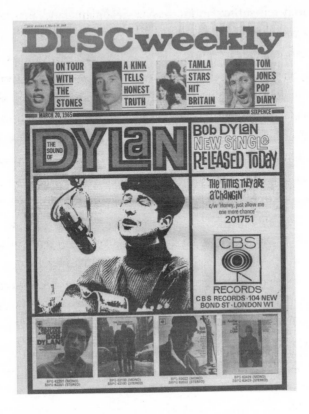

I was born very far from where I'm supposed to be. And so I'm
on my way home.
  Bob Dylan

Bob Dylan walks into a bar. He's just pre-fame, but on the brink. A
man he's never met before walks right up to him and starts giving him
a really hard time, starts making fun of him, imitating his voice, doing
everything to wind him up short of punching him in the face. And still
Dylan wins the fight, because instead of becoming angry or teary or
sneery, he refuses to let this man exist.

Before Dylan, all pop stars projected a persona to the outside world. Usually it was a professional competence, sometimes a little aloof (Sinatra), or cuddly (Como), but – even with the Beatles and the Stones – they let it be clear; you knew what they were about. Bob Dylan was closed, entirely self-sufficient. He was his own planet and, naturally, you desperately wanted to find a way to travel there.

Bob Dylan created, for good and ill, the modern rock star. On the debit side, he pioneered sunglasses after dark; along with the Stones he sealed the concept of snotty behaviour as a lifestyle, snarled at the conventional with his pack of giggling lickspittle dogs, and extended Brando's 'What have you got?' one-liner into a lifelong party of terse putdowns. Unlike the Stones, this came naturally to Dylan – he was sharp as a needle, and very funny with it. Instead of 'Look at that stupid girl,' he sang, 'Something is happening here but you don't know what it is.'

The positive, and most radical, impact of Dylan was gently disguised. He realised that self-education and self-transformation, the open quest for who or what you might be, could be a thrilling and rewarding challenge – and that following this pursuit in the public eye made it all the more rewarding. Yet this wasn't the legacy Dylan handed down to everyone. David Bowie understood it and so, to a lesser extent, did Bruce Springsteen. Unfortunately, others who were less quick-witted were happier copying the arid Dylan, borrowing the superficial stance of the outsider.

Dylan broke new ground in several other ways. He was the first figure in modern pop to have the burden of 'generational spokesman' to bear. He initially built this position by digging at the Masters of War, and predicting a Hard Rain on the acoustic records he cut during his Woody Guthrie phase, from 1962 to 1964. Poking fun at Tin Pan Alley, he associated himself with styles and moves that folk fans considered unmanufactured, then took the brunt of their anger when he formed a fearsome beat group in 1965. Also, he was the patron saint of non-singers. He sang in a voice that was entirely unfamiliar: needling, unsifted, but impossible to ignore. Most significantly, he wrote pop lyrics that were well beyond teenage fripperies, that had genuine wit. Dylan sounded deep. Gerry Goffin, writer of songs like 'Will You Love Me Tomorrow', 'Up on the Roof' and 'Some of Your Lovin'', lost his mind once he heard Dylan, deciding everything he'd ever written was shallow and worthless, trashing his old tapes and acetates, to the horror of his friends.

Dylan loved to mess with his myth, screw around with the minds of fans and critics. He gave the impression that he really did have the answer, even if no one was quite sure what the question was. His public image had a total lack of sentimentality, or sadness even, which made Dylan seem old and wise, cold and unbreakable. The more he obscured the truth, the more people dug for it. Eventually, he would wake each morning to find people rifling through his garbage, trying to find 'clues', trying to understand.

All of this adds up to a figure that was barely recognisable as pop at all, or only on the occasions when he fancied venturing into simple, melodic territory on a single like 'Lay Lady Lay' (US no. 7, UK no. 5 '69). Yet no one in this book is a greater shapeshifter, and virtually no one has had more impact on the shape of modern pop itself. So how could such a non-pop figure become so Pop?

Originally he was Robert Zimmerman from Hibbing, Minnesota, a mining town where 'it was so cold, you couldn't be a rebel'. Once he escaped his backwater town and made it to New York he found himself in one of the tightest scenes ever, the Greenwich Village folk revival, which was based around the coffee bars on Bleecker and MacDougal, and had evolved from the late-fifties beat-poetry scene in places like the Gaslight and Cafe Wha?. Greenwich Village had little to do with the America of Guy Mitchell, or even Buddy Holly: fights between Stalinists and Trotskyites were common. Yet it considered itself the soul of America. The Village folkies could take a talented, smart-aleck Jewish kid from the sticks and subsume him, make him part of their cause, use him to their own ends. Or so they thought.

The American folk scene had become bound and gagged after the Weavers' cover of Leadbelly's 'Goodnight Irene' was America's best-selling single of 1950, and it was still living with enforced conformism when Bob Dylan arrived in New York in 1961. The Weavers had been led by Pete Seeger, who was openly communist, and this, during the intense conformity of the McCarthy witch-hunt era, led to the belief that any other folk singer with an acoustic guitar might be a communist too. While skiffle boomed in Britain, the only safe way to play folk songs in the US was by frying them, tossing them and coating them in sugar: Harry Belafonte ('Banana Boat Song', US no. 5 '57), the Kingston Trio ('Tom Dooley', US no. 1 '58) and the Brothers Four ('Green Fields', US no. 2 '60) scored major hits, but it was a long, long way from Pete Seeger's American vision.

The Weavers had been dropped by Decca in '53, and Seeger quit the group after they did a cigarette ad. Still watched by the FBI, he holed up in Greenwich Village. To Seeger, and other Village bohos who soon gathered around him in the early sixties, the cause was crystal clear: America still had lynchings in the South, and Kennedy was taking the world to the brink of nuclear war. Siding with the left didn't necessarily mean siding with the Soviets, it meant not having a death wish, and the craziness in the country became a bounteous lyrical source. This concentration of like-minded liberals brought a large amount of self-righteousness and dogma, a self-inflicted conformism, into the new folk scene: when Phil Ochs cut an album called *All the News That's Fit to Sing* in 1964, you knew he wasn't going to include the football results.

Some of the Greenwich folkies gave the impression of a cause waiting to be lost (the sensitive but weak David Blue, who died when a wall collapsed on him when he was out jogging; Korean vet and helpless morphine addict Tim Hardin); others were pious and unlistenable (Peggy Seeger, the Village Akela). Phil Ochs was easily the most accessible, open, almost conservative in his patriotism. He was a singer with the bearing of a bear, the arms of a stevedore, an unflinching union man. He was also witty and pugnacious, and could write a beautiful melody. While he was the biggest draw on the scene, it's easy to imagine the hardliners frowning at his Kennedy tribute, 'That Was the President', and lines like 'systems, not men, are the enemy'. More worryingly yet, he had a quiff and loved Elvis.

Bob Dylan must have seemed much more Seeger's kind of people when he shuffled into town. He quickly learnt how to cover his tracks, reinvent himself, claiming that he 'never went to classes. Didn't have time.' Instead he had been reading Kerouac, Dylan Thomas, Woody Guthrie's *Bound for Glory*. The folk music he discovered – John Jacob Niles, Harry Belafonte, Odetta, the Clancy Brothers – reflected how Dylan felt about life, institutions, ideologies. It gave him a new way to live. Previously an Elvis fanatic, he swapped his electric guitar for an acoustic.

By the time Dylan arrived in '61 Greenwich Village was already something of a tourist trap; he looked out for singers who gave the impression of having a secret knowledge, something beyond the ability to play a few Leadbelly covers and knowing where to get the best espresso. He had ambition. He became a sponge, an actor even, and worked out some spiel about growing up in New Mexico, where he'd picked up songs from cowboys, other songs from Indians, real American roots stuff. He created this story after borrowing a bunch of rare, out-of-print folk albums from collector Paul Nelson, and learning obscure songs that weren't familiar on the Village circuit. Dylan aped Woody Guthrie's hobo look and, with his cute looks and youth – he was still only nineteen – made his way around the record companies. Vanguard was home to Joan Baez, the public face of Greenwich Village and a singer whose dark eyes radiated sincerity and understanding; they rejected him as 'too visceral'. John Hammond, an A&R man at Columbia who had signed Lena Horne, Billie Holiday, Count Basie and Miles Davis, was so confident in Dylan's ability and proclaimed it so loudly that even Mitch Miller – the Columbia-label boss who had signed Guy Mitchell and got Sinatra to bark like a dog – was convinced.

His first album in '62 didn't sell more than any other Village folkie tract. Dylan had picked the wrong songs and sounded uptight, but at least he'd borrowed Dave Van Ronk's arrangement of 'House of the Rising Sun', which would, gradually, cause pop's greatest coals-to-Newcastle moment.

He found himself a girlfriend, Suze Rotolo, who was good-looking enough to feature on the cover of his second album, 1963's *Freewheelin'*, as well as inspiring two of his best love songs ('Don't Think Twice, It's All Right', 'Tomorrow Is a Long Time'). Moreover, she worked for the

Congress of Racial Equality (CORE), and under her influence he wrote a bunch of songs that were politically charged, that sounded modern and ancient at the same time, the greatest songs in the civil-rights canon: 'With God on Our Side', 'Only a Pawn in Their Game', 'A Hard Rain's Gonna Fall'. Another was 'Blowin' in the Wind', which the biblically named Peter, Paul and Mary took all the way to number two on *Billboard*'s Hot Hundred in the wake of the Cuban missile crisis.

At this point Bob Dylan became a pop star. But he didn't honour pop, or pop radio. Most of his records were caught in one take, raw and unproduced, something that didn't change when he became a Top 20 regular after 'Like a Rolling Stone' (US no. 2, UK no. 4 '65) was released; his densest, longest and best recording was one that Dylan would have discarded altogether, moving straight on to the next song, if producer Bob Johnston hadn't rescued the tape and played it back to him a few days later.

Dylan was a receiver and, at his peak, he articulated what all of the Greenwich Village folkies wanted to say but couldn't. He wasn't only channelling Woody Guthrie, but Lenny Bruce, and Abraham Lincoln. In the wake of 'Blowin' in the Wind' and its attendant success he found himself sniped at as a sell-out by jealous contemporaries. They had initially giggled behind his back and thought him a political naif; suddenly he was on national TV, storming the charts and getting covers of his songs by everyone from Sam Cooke to Trini Lopez. Dylan had been the smart one, it transpired, and some of his Greenwich Village buddies, with their horizontal worldview, were pissed off. On top of this he dated Joan Baez, and they became the scene's celebrity couple, the spokespeople for disaffected youth. Given an award in late '63, Dylan declared that he no longer saw things as left and right, black and white, only up and down. He was no one's trained seal. To many he had become a shaman, but Dylan still thought himself an outsider and he wanted no part of this trip.

He first started to sidestep the folk scene with the apolitical *Another Side of Bob Dylan* in '64, but the trouble really began when he reverted to his rock 'n' roll roots on a 1965 single called 'Subterranean Homesick Blues'. When he plugged in at the '65 Newport Folk Festival, Pete Seeger tried to cut the electrical cables with an axe. If Dylan had come out as a secret Klansman, his folk fans couldn't have felt more wounded. Rock 'n' roll was for saps, unthinkers. What the hell was he playing at? Pop, that's what. The clues had been there all along: on his first album there's a 'Wake Up Little Susie' riff on 'Highway 61'; 'Mixed Up Confusion', a rattling, electric *Freewheelin'* outtake, was even released as a single in '63 but sank without trace.* He was a song-and-dance man. He was versatile. He wanted to let his corkscrew hair grow as wild as Little Richard's.

In the spotlight, finally letting the mask of unknowability slip, he was not a pretty sight. Like Elvis, Dylan coped with suffocating fame by constructing a gang around him. Instead of old high-school buddies, though, he chose hipsters, guys permanently wearing shades, sidekicks like Bob Neuwirth who were a manifestation of Dylan's worst characteristics. Dylan found that the best way to fight against the fear, envy and meanness of his erstwhile left-wing colleagues was to develop a scything misanthropy. In D. A. Pennebaker's *Don't Look Back* documentary, filmed on a UK tour in '65, he gets his kicks from attacking earnest Cambridge students, the clearly infatuated British folk singer Donovan and his soon-to-be ex Baez. One evening in 1966, in a limo cruising the New York streets, Phil Ochs suggested that Dylan's current single, 'Can You Please Crawl out Your Window', wasn't the best thing he'd ever done. The driver hit the brakes, the door flew open – 'Get outta the car, Ochs.' They didn't speak again for almost a decade.

By now people expected answers; they demanded them, fuelled by the weird mixture of love for the man and hatred for what he had done to the cause. Dylan spat right back in their faces: 'You've got a lot of nerve to say you are my friend.' And the music he made during this '65–66 period was extraordinary – thin wild mercury music, he called it. But his European shows with Canadian pickup group the Hawks†

---

* Dylan's earliest stagecraft had been learnt as part of teen idol Bobby Vee's backing group; the acoustic period was, effectively, a long interlude in his rock career.
† The Hawks were a tour-hardened outfit who had been the backing group for Canadian rocker Ronnie Hawkins. It doesn't take a huge leap of faith to get from Hawkins's best known single, 'Forty Days', a rock 'n' roll classic covered in the UK by Cliff Richard, to 'Subterranean Homesick Blues'.

were heckled by his old fans, who had no time for the hair-raising,
teeth-clenching rock 'n' roll Dylan was now dealing in.

Let's look at one single from this period, 1965's 'Like a Rolling Stone',
a contender for the best in the entire pop canon. Producer Tom Wilson
thinks Dylan had the Holy Ghost on his shoulder that day. It starts
with a gunshot snare, then bores deeper and deeper, somehow gains in
intensity – lyrically, vocally, physically – for a full six minutes. The story
is of a person (or a nation) falling hard, of ends and new beginnings, of
odd characters like the mystery tramp and Napoleon in rags – some of
whom may be Dylan himself. It's a once-in-a-lifetime recording. You are
transfixed and morbidly fascinated, as if you are a small child and Dylan
is explaining death to you for the first time. Outside of deep soul, it is
the most draining record in pop, the most physically demanding:

'I found myself writing this song, this story, this long piece of vomit,
twenty pages long and out of it I took "Like a Rolling Stone" and made
it as a single. And I'd never written anything like that before and it suddenly came to me that this is what I should do. Nobody had ever done
that before. I'm not saying it's *better* than anything else, I'm saying that I
think . . . I think "Like a Rolling Stone" is definitely the thing that I do.'

Dylan had peaked and he knew it. By now considered a cross between
Elvis Presley and Nostradamus, he had no direction home. After returning from a European tour, he had a mysterious bike smash in the summer of 1966 and disappeared for almost two years. When he re-emerged,
he looked totally different, sang in a new softer voice and came up with
lyrics like 'Oh me oh my, love that country pie.' Not surprisingly, people
thought this Dylan was an imposter – the real Bob Dylan, the prophet,
seer and sage, had been killed in that bike crash.

In some ways this comeback kid character is the closest Bob Dylan
ever got to dropping all the masks and revealing himself. He even called
his 1970 album *Self Portrait*, and on it he turned out to be a guy who
liked pie, country music, horses and his Canadian counterpart Gordon
Lightfoot. It also included a live version of 'Like a Rolling Stone' on
which he sang like Kermit the Frog. Critics called it 'shit'.* It was inter-

* This was the judgement of Greil Marcus in *Rolling Stone*. He was wrong. But

preted as an act of self-destruction – Dylan was desperate for someone else to be hailed as the new Dylan, to get the world off his shoulders.

Maybe his best album is 1970's *New Morning*. On the cover he has a slightly ratty, unkempt beard that suggests humility, openness; no more oversize polka dots and 'keep out' shades. He's looking directly at you, and he looks relaxed: if he was filling out a lonely-hearts ad he'd describe himself as 'comfortable in his own skin'. But there was no need for an ad. Dylan was now thoroughly domesticated, wife and kids and home on the range, recording the old American songbook the way it played in his head. Rabbits, roosters, automobiles, Dylan loved it all: he sounded as perky as Guy Mitchell had done on his folks' wireless back in Hibbing. 'So happy just to be alive underneath this sky of blue.'

There would be further peaks (*Blood on the Tracks*), troughs (*Hearts of Fire* and sundry cinema outings), and more unexpected leaps sideways (his misanthropic conversion to Christianity), but from the Dylan of *New Morning* you could draw a straight line to a point several decades on. By the twenty-first century he was relaxed enough to host a radio show, drawing up new road maps of America, his now smoky voice perfectly suited to late-night radio. He was aurally doodling, joining the dots between Jimmy Reed and the Honey Cone, Merle Haggard and Howlin' Wolf, Eddie Cochran, Prince Buster and the theme from *Top Cat*. This, it turned out, was what he was built for. It was a hard-won battle and he sounded all the better for it. 'I like email,' he'd say, 'but I miss the postman.' He almost sounded like fun.

Bob Dylan's back catalogue is like a library, with narrow, twisting corridors and deep oak shelves drawing you in: start leafing through the pages and you may never want to stop. His legacy is a lot of bad poetry, a lot of skinny guys in shades throwing 'fuck you' poses. It is also a sly cynicism. And it is also the lyrics of 'Strawberry Fields Forever', or Scott Walker's 'Montague Terrace in Blue', or the Fall's 'New Face in Hell'. Gerry Goffin may have lost his mind trying to get close to Dylan's muse, but in the process he wrote 'Goin' Back' for Dusty Springfield and the

---

maybe *A Self Portrait* would have been a more accurate title; he could have had plenty more in the attic.

Byrds' 'Wasn't Born to Follow', two philosophical songs you could build your life around; he may consider the sacrifice was worth it.

People were asking Bob Dylan the impossible, asking him to make sense of the world. That was beyond anybody. What is most remarkable about Dylan, and a task not far short, is that he helped America to make sense of itself.

AMERICA STRIKES BACK: THE BYRDS AND FOLK ROCK

Byrds International Fan Club

This is to certify that

Celia Edwards.

is a member in good standing

CHAPTER   CO-PRESIDENT

Jan 24, 1967
DATE   CO-PRESIDENT

The Beatles had been the first modern pop event that almost everyone in America could agree on. This had a lot to do with the fact that they were outsiders. Coming from England they couldn't aggravate prejudice; they were parachuted into a conflict without evident allegiances in either direction. As well as hooking *Ed Sullivan* viewers on first sight, they opened the door to a lot of other people – the pre-rock Vegas set, jazzers like Gary McFarland – who would have previously dismissed modern pop out of hand. Most significantly they converted folk singers, including Bob Dylan, and in this way they joined the finest minds and the lithest bodies in the country. Social revolt was imminent.

With very few exceptions, the old order had been swept aside in 1964; Bob Dylan gave American pop the strength to regroup, recover and rebuild after the hurricane of the British Invasion. Yet the first recording to reflect Dylan's popularity in the hit parade originated not in New York, or anywhere else in the States, but in Newcastle-upon-Tyne, England.

The Animals were a spotty R&B group* who picked up 'House of the Rising Sun' from Dylan's debut and turned it into a manic, organ-led rave-up. Singer Eric Burdon had a raw roar of a voice which often sounded too pleased with its own ability, but not in this instance. The tale of a New Orleans whorehouse went to number one just about everywhere in the summer of '64, and Dylan, plus dozens of other folkniks stateside, woke up to the possibilities of fusing folk with their new guilty pop pleasures, the Beatles and the Stones.

Los Angeles was about as far from Newcastle as Vladivostok, but the Animals' insurrectionary sound reached a bunch of country folksters who soon hitched onto the British beat bandwagon, calling themselves the Jet Set, then the Beefeaters and finally the Byrds. They were led by Jim McGuinn, who was so obsessed with aeroplanes and pilot lore that he later changed his name to Roger. McGuinn was completely taken with 'I Want to Hold Your Hand', and so convinced it would lead to a bright teenage future that he left the trad-folk Chad Mitchell Trio to go solo. At his first show, supporting country singer Hoyt Axton at LA's Troubadour club in early '64, he played nothing but Beatles songs. Nobody in the audience was particularly impressed, except for a lanky singer from Kansas, Gene Clark, who resembled a troubled bird of prey and had just left another established folk act, the New Christy Minstrels. He wondered if Jim would like to try songwriting with him. A few weeks later, round-faced cheeky boy David Crosby saw McGuinn and Clark at the Troubadour and leapt on stage to add a high, clear harmony. Crosby had already been attempting rocked-up takes on traditional songs with producer Jim Dickson; they added drummer Michael Clarke (who Crosby had seen playing bongos with proto-hippie Dino Valente) and bassist Chris Hillman (who had just finished making a bluegrass album with the Gosdin Brothers) to complete the group. They demo'd with Dickson, Lenny Bruce's mum got them their first paying gig (East Los Angeles College – they were paid $50), and Miles Davis heard about the commotion they caused and promptly told

---

* Eric Burdon refused to wear make-up on TV to cover his pimples, figuring that teenage viewers would be empathetic.

Columbia Records, who signed them in November '64. Their advance bought a drum kit for Clarke – he'd been playing on cardboard boxes, with a tambourine for a snare – and, crucially, a Rickenbacker twelve-string guitar for McGuinn. Columbia producer Terry Melcher, Doris Day's son, produced their debut 45, a cover of Dylan's 'Mr Tambourine Man'. Melcher's thinking was that Dylan couldn't sing, but he could write; using the Animals' 'House of the Rising Sun' as his guide, he rearranged Dylan's surreal lyric – cutting all but one verse – and, by placing McGuinn's twelve-string centre stage, he made the song 3D, a jingle-jangle morning of a record. 'All my senses have been stripped,' sang McGuinn, ready to go anywhere.

What is striking about the formation of the Byrds is how each member was absorbed by American music, each unique in its own way, and how this bore no relation to the existing pro musician set-up that had carried all modern pop, even rock 'n' roll, up to this point. They loved music and they wanted to see the rivers of their visions flow into one another. On the sleevenotes of their first album in summer '65, McGuinn said, 'Music is life.' Even Phil Spector and Joe Meek would have been a little more circumspect.

In the press, McGuinn wouldn't shut up about planes: 'I think the difference is in the mechanical sounds of our time. Like the sound of the airplane in the forties was a rrrrrooooooaaaaahhhhhhh sound and Sinatra and other people sang like that with those sort of overtones. Now we've got the krrrrriiiiissssshhhhhhhh jet sound, and the kids are singing up in there now.' Gene Clark, unfortunately, was terrified of flying, and quit after he wrote the Byrds' single 'Eight Miles High' (US no. 14, UK no. 24 '66), a woozy, hard, jazz-inflected evocation of jet lag in London, the release of which the group deemed important enough to warrant a press conference. Oddly, the public fell out of love with them right away, as soon as they tried to vary their jangle with jazz on the John Coltrane-influenced *5D* album (1966), and then with Moogs (*The Notorious Byrd Brothers*, early '68), and then with country (*Sweetheart of the Rodeo*, late '68). Beyond their stuttering commercial success, they were restless and fought like cats. Crosby, always looking like the cat that got the cream, was booted out in late '67. McGuinn still wore the goggles, but the magic then began to dissipate.

No matter. His noonday, church-chiming twelve-string had enabled the Byrds to turn songs about Welsh miners ('The Bells of Rhymney'), dead presidents ('He Was a Friend of Mine') and Hiroshima ('I Come and Stand at Every Door') into jet-age hymns. Smudged together with Clarke's rudimentary drums, Hillman's melodic, McCartney-esque basslines and their mountaintop harmonies, the Byrds' sound was a phenomenon, a drone, genuinely hair-raising and totally American. They may have borrowed the twelve-string ring and harmony chops of the Searchers but they took this brand of pop from the boxy, damp cellars of Liverpool into sun-kissed, spiritual, Californian territory.

The Animals and Dylan had left clues but the huge success of 'Mr Tambourine Man' – a US and UK number one in spring '65 – was the record that launched folk rock. Within weeks, west-coast kids like P. F. Sloan and former Spector sidekicks like Sonny and Cher ('I Got You Babe') joined in the fun and also scored number-one hits.* Over on the east coast, something less clearly indebted was cooking in hell's kitchen. The Lovin' Spoonful looked as if they'd turned up stoned at a jumble sale and hastily assembled what they took to be a beatnik Beatles look. All clashing spots and stripes, they were droll, human and a lot of fun. Folk, blues, jazz and rock 'n' roll were all thrown into their mixing bowl: 'We call it Good Time Music because we have a good time,' said singer John Sebastian. Even more than Dylan, the Spoonful were Americana, only with barely a hint of pretence or anger. Every song was coloured in with felt tips; they were like cartoons for grown-ups. Something as sad and beautiful as 'Didn't Want to Have to Do It' was like Linus walking away from the other *Peanuts* characters into the sunset, his blanket draped over his shoulder, while 'Did You Ever Have to Make Up Your

---

* P. F. Sloan's 'Eve of Destruction' was recorded by Barry McGuire, another former New Christy Minstrel who had sung 'Three Wheels on My Wagon', a favourite on BBC radio show *Junior Choice*. The shy Sloan later wrote hits for the Turtles ('You Baby', US no. 20 '66), Herman's Hermits ('A Must to Avoid', US no. 8, UK no. 6 '66) and the Grass Roots' 'Let's Live for Today' (US no. 8 '67). He was immortalised by Jimmy Webb's touching tribute 'P. F. Sloan' on his 1970 album *Words and Music*.

Mind' (US no. 2 '66) is one of pop's best agony-aunt songs, with shades of 'Summertime Blues' ('Better go home, son, and make up your mind') as well as visions of Droopy.

John Sebastian favoured steel-rim glasses and worn denim. He was born and raised in Greenwich Village, which made sense: his songs all sounded as if they were composed on a New York fire escape, five storeys up. In a coffee house he met and befriended Toronto-born Zally Yanovsky, an outsize spaniel of a man, with Joe Butler (drums and autoharp) and Steve Boone soon making up the band. In early '65 they debuted at the Night Owl cafe, sang mainly rock 'n' roll and sank like a stone. So they went away to lick their wounds and work on their sound until it was all Spoonful. They rehearsed in the basement of the Village's Hotel Albert, taking the freight elevator down with a laundry cart full of their gear. Their playing vibrated tiny flakes of century-old paint down from the ceiling, so they took to wearing hats to avoid looking as if they had chronic dandruff. Two months later, the Night Owl's owner was so impressed with their new, easy musicality that he gave them a residency. He also let loose a hundred balloons that read 'I love you, Lovin' Spoonful'.

Released in December '65, their debut single was equally warmhearted. It was a paean, an open love song to modern pop called 'Do You Believe in Magic', and it went like this: 'If you believe in magic, don't bother to choose if it's jug band music or rhythm and blues. Just go and listen, it'll start with a smile you won't wipe off your face, no matter how hard you try.' It also included a line that has forever summed up how musicians perceive the music industry: 'It's like trying to tell a stranger about rock 'n' roll.'

The chords were pinched from Martha and the Vandellas' 'Heatwave', which Sebastian thought was the most exciting record he'd ever heard. Play the chords twice as fast, he reckoned, and 'Do You Believe in Magic' would be twice as exciting. He was a sly fox, and he understood magic.

Very quickly, the Spoonful racked up a string of hits – all US Top 10: 'Do You Believe in Magic', 'You Didn't Have to Be So Nice', 'Daydream', 'Did You Ever Have to Make Up Your Mind', 'Summer in the City', 'Rain on the Roof', 'Nashville Cats'. Then Sebastian wrote 'Darling Be Home Soon', a fragile daisy chain of a song: 'I've been waiting since

I toddled for the great relief of having you to talk to.' It was beautiful enough to make you shudder. But it was not goofy in any way and, to Sebastian's horror, a disapproving Yanovsky gurned and clowned his way through a TV performance of it. Less than two years on from their first single and they were splintering. Worse soon followed: Yanovsky and Boone were caught holding drugs, and Yanovsky was threatened with deportation if he didn't identify his dealer – which he did. A *Rolling Stone* magazine-sanctioned boycott of the Spoonful followed. Yanovsky was sacked but the damage was done. In late '67 Sebastian wrote a sour, tired single called 'Money' aimed at the band's management, and they wisely split before things got cynical and boring.

The antithesis of the Lovin' Spoonful were Simon and Garfunkel, who, to the naked eye, looked as much fun as their undertaker name suggested. Originally, they were called Tom and Jerry – which made sense, as Art Garfunkel was long and feline, while Paul Simon was tiny. Simon had spent a while in London during the Soho folk boom, where he discovered 'Scarborough Fair', courtesy of guitarist Martin Carthy, and wrote 'Homeward Bound' while sitting, freezing, on a railway platform in Widnes. Arriving back in New York in 1965 with a sack full of new songs, Simon and Garfunkel quickly hit number one when 'The Sound of Silence' was given a ringing, post-Byrds electric backing, allegedly without their knowledge. If either of them minded, it didn't stop them riding the folk-rock wave: it was followed into the Top 20 in Britain and America by 'Homeward Bound' and 'I Am a Rock' in '66, both jingle-jangling for all they were worth.

They came across as horribly aloof and humourless, ostentatiously declaring their literary knowledge and college education in references like 'You read your Emily Dickinson and I my Robert Frost' ('The Dangling Conversation', US no. 25 '66). Simon was a stickler for grammar; when he wrote the first-day-of-spring anthem 'The 59th Street Bridge Song (Feelin' Groovy)', you knew that the dropped 'g' rankled and it was probably a record-company typo. Indeed, they would have been quite unbearable if Garfunkel hadn't sung like a choirboy Angel Clare, pining for Tess of the D'Urbervilles, and if Simon hadn't been the finest melody writer to emerge from Greenwich Village. His lyrics sounded smart and cryptic enough that people assumed 'Mrs Robinson' (US no. 1, UK no. 4 '68) was making complex Dylanesque comments about Anne Bancroft's character in *The Graduate* – in fact, Simon had no idea what the film was about when he wrote it. Still, 'Where have you gone, Joe DiMaggio? A nation turns its lonely eyes to you' certainly worked in a year when good men like Bobby Kennedy and Martin Luther King were taken out of the American narrative. By 1970, when Simon was introducing Andean pan-pipe music ('El Condor Pasa') and Latin jubilation ('Cecilia') to their sound, they had become a coffee-table phenomenon. It's one of pop's odder coincidences that in two of its most fallow years (1970 and 1986) Paul Simon has produced a multi-million seller. Almost no one would say he's their favourite songwriter, but 'Bridge over Troubled Water' and 'Graceland', firm family favourites, fun for mum and dad and all the kids, have probably soundtracked more car journeys than any Bob Dylan, Beach Boys or even Beatles album.

Outside of folk rock there were a few other breakthrough American acts in '65 and they, too, used an Anglo-beat template. Why was this? Beach Boys companion Van Dyke Parks has suggested it was the only way for musicians to 'wrest the trophy' back from the British invaders, as their girlfriends were all Beatle-crazy.

Gary Lewis and the Playboys were the lightest of the lightweight. They were discovered by Liberty Records' producer Snuff Garrett playing the annual Disneyland summer dance in 1964. He put them in his pocket, took them home, worked on a few Brill Building songs with them, and ended up with the biggest-selling American group of 1965.

Gary himself looked timid, even more like a mouse than Paul Simon, and was dwarfed by his drum kit – if you closed your eyes you could imagine him skittering across the skins, his tiny claws making a light, rhythmic sound not unlike Herman's Hermits. Their first hit, a US number one called 'This Diamond Ring' part written by Al Kooper, wore a lyric that bared the tortured soul of a cuckold. Billy Fury, flanked by fuzz guitar and wailing waifs, had cut it in late '64 as something that would run through your mind as you drove your car at speed towards Beachy Head; the Playboys' cover sounded like it was recorded on Fisher-Price toy instruments, with Lewis's pubescent rodent voice quadruple-tracked before it was even audible on AM radio. But he was cute, had Jerry Lewis for a dad, and – with 'Count Me In' (US no. 2 '65), 'Save Your Heart for Me' (US no. 2 '65) and 'She's Just My Style' (US no. 3 '65) – wasn't off American TV for three years. When things got lighter and sunnier in '67, Gary Lewis seemed positively prescient, and one single, 'Jill', was quite beautiful, a teenage love song on which it sounds as if his broken heart has literally claimed his life; by the end of the song, he can barely whisper the title.

Paul Revere and the Raiders were more like a pack of wolves. They hailed from the Pacific North West, an isolated area where classic rock 'n' roll had lived on longer than anywhere else in the US and spawned groups made of girders: the Sonics ('Psycho') and the Wailers ('Tall Cool One') were the most popular locally, while the Kingsmen ('Louie Louie') made the loudest noise nationally. Snare drums were broken on a daily basis, sore throats were a constant problem. These groups didn't want to take you on a trip aboard a magic swirling ship. They just wanted to dance and drink and screw.

The Raiders only broke bigger than their local rivals because they were pro, and unafraid to look dumb in order to make money, so they dressed like American revolutionary soldiers with tricorn hats, became favourites of post-Beatles teen mag *Tiger Beat* and got regular TV spots on ABC's *Where the Action Is*. 'Kids will be watching more than they'll be listening,' reasoned keyboard player Revere; Marshall McLuhan would have approved. Starting with 'Steppin' Out' (US no. 46 '65), they turned out a string of strutting hits with swollen-balls titles – 'Just Like Me' (US no. 11 '65), the Mann/Weil-penned 'Kicks' (US no. 4 '66) and 'Hungry' (US no. 6 '66), 'Him or Me – What's It Gonna Be' (US no. 5 '67) – that John Peel reckoned was as good as the Rolling Stones' sixties run. Singer Mark Lindsay, a Jagger soundalike, described his group as a 'bunch of white-bread kids doing their best to sound black'. So they were just doing a job, but they did it awfully well, and had racked up sixteen US Top 50 hits by the end of the sixties.

The Raiders' noise was the most commercially successful variant of garage punk. Unlike cramped and chilly mid-sixties Britain, America had a thriving economy and wide-open spaces, to be filled with highways dotted with Lincoln Continentals, tailfin-shaped diners that sold hamburgers the size of a house, and garages that had room for more than just a Vauxhall Viva. Middle-class high-school kids who had bugged their parents for a musical instrument after seeing the Beatles on *Ed Sullivan* could get together, practise in the garage and – with a rudimentary knowledge of three chords – become the local Stones or Kinks. The drummer probably played in a military band at school. The bassist, most likely, wanted to be the guitarist but wasn't assertive enough. Across the States, a whole generation of unprofessional kids picked up guitars and made the loudest noise they could. According to garage-punk historian Greg Shaw, in 1966 sixty-three per cent of American boys under twenty were in a group.

The garage-punk wave was driven by the British beat-boom invasion, and yet a record which pre-dated the Beatles' arrival and remains the ur-garage single was 'Louie Louie'. Richard Berry's three-chord R&B composition from 1956 is the tune which defines the sound: the Raiders cut it in '63, the Beach Boys, Otis Redding, the Kinks, the Sandpipers, Led Zeppelin, Motörhead, the Grateful Dead, the Fat Boys and Black Flag did it years later, but Oregon's Kingsmen, whose organ-led, bumbling bear-in-a-china-shop rendition hit number two in the US in December '63, led the charge. It's an anthem of noise, confusion and attitude over proficiency, the triumph of the amateur. Within weeks of the Kingsmen's hit came the British Invasion, stateside sales of musical instruments went through the roof, and every spare garage had the next Kingsmen learning to tune their guitars. 'Louie Louie' remained the blueprint. Its vocals were so slurred that the FBI ordered the song to be investigated, an honour only previously given to Elvis Presley's pelvic thrusts.

The garage-punk look was easy – straight hair in a fringe or a side parting, leather waistcoats and tight pants. The Beatles, after all, wore tight pants and had long hair, and even if their music was kinda cissy, the girls went nuts. So that was the look. If the drummer looked a bit like Brian Jones, so much the better.

The sound, though, was highly localised: Chicago had soul-influenced bands like the Outsiders and the Buckinghams; Californians like the Daily Flash and the Charlatans seemed to draw on the Old West; while in Texas there was nothing to explain the weird noises made by the Thirteenth Floor Elevators beyond spiked cactus juice. On 'You're Gonna Miss Me' (US no. 55 '66) singer Roky Erickson shrieked like a jungle primate in heat, while Tommy Hall played a mysterious instrument of his own devising which he called the 'electric jug'. This turned out to be a jug that he mumbled into – that was it. Their first album, with the telltale title *The Psychedelic Sounds of the Thirteenth Floor Elevators*, came out in late '66.

By this time, literally thousands of American bands had swamped the local gig circuit and started recording their own 45s, some for majors, others for parent-funded labels. It was crude, lewd and wildly exciting: the lustiest teenage fuzzbombs, like We the People's 'You Burn Me Up and Down', usually sold nothing, but once in a while something raw broke through – the Standells' 'Dirty Water' ('lovers, muggers and thieves – they're cool people!') reached number eleven in '66; Count Five rebuilt and supercharged the Yardbirds' 'I'm a Man' as 'Psychotic Reaction' (US no. 5 '66); and the Farfisa-driven squeaky sexual frustration of ? and the Mysterians' '96 Tears', entirely lovable because it was so basic, went all the way to number one.* Unprocessed, undomesticated and weird, this bastardised take on the beat boom became pop as surely as Simon and Garfunkel's abreactive poetry quotes.

Possibly the best of all the new post-Beatles American bands, though, were the Turtles. Their first hit was a folk-rock cover of Dylan's 'It Ain't Me Babe' (US no. 8 '65), but before this they had been a surf group (the Crossfires) and a coffee-house folk group (the Crosswind Singers). You could call them bandwagon jumpers, or you could say they were so enamoured of modern pop that they decided to embrace pretty much

---

* The marvel of garage punk is that it was barely acknowledged at the time and most bands, unlike ? and the Mysterians, never got beyond frat parties. Come the mid-seventies, when energy, zip and two-minute freak-outs were off the mainstream menu, garage punk was curated by Elektra producer and pop archaeologist Lenny Kaye on a double album called *Nuggets*. It hit a vein, and by the early eighties further digging led to the appearance of rare singles on compilations with names like *Pebbles, Psychedelic Unknowns* and *Back from the Grave*. Much of it was too basic, its obscurity warranted, but when it worked – the Litter's 'Action Woman', the Chob's 'We're Pretty Quick', the Jelly Bean Bandits' 'Generation' – it made all the years of scratching in the dirt worthwhile.

all of its many-faced, polydirectional moves from 1963 to 1969. They were a microcosm of the sixties, the archetypal pop group, and they outlived every trend they rode.

If they'd had the looks the Turtles would be remembered as one of the best groups of the decade. As it was, they looked like three Pillsbury dough boys, one in a bushy black fright wig, and their one potential pin-up was hidden behind the drum kit. As the Crossfires they had cut one of the densest, most frenetic surf records, 'Out of Control', but moved on when the British beat came to town. Singer Howard Kaylan: 'We used to go to bowling alleys and order tea with plenty of milk and tell them we were Gerry and the Pacemakers.'

Within months they had switched to folk. 'We were so young and so green – anything Dylan did was God.' They covered 'It Ain't Me Babe' à la Byrds, considered calling themselves the Tyrtles and settled on Turtles. It reached the US Top 10 and they were set. Only they switched, again, this time to euphoric harmony pop on 'You Baby' in '66, then tough garage punk for 'Outside Chance', and then doomy jazz raga for 'Grim Reaper of Love', one of the outright weirdest 45s of the sixties. Faltering commercially, they pulled out a plum with 'Happy Together', a love song so joyous that it's hard to avoid throwing your arms around the nearest human being every time it comes on the radio. Endless use in adverts cannot diminish its beauty. It reached number one in the summer of '67, and Tricia Nixon loved it so much she convinced her dad to let them play the White House. Even Elvis himself had to ask nicely before they'd let him in – the Turtles just sniggered their way past security. They were probably stoned. What a gas!

Some may see more worth in the catalogues of the Doors or the Grateful Dead, but the Turtles encompassed the American sixties – hip, square and freak – and they split, on cue, in 1969 with a baroque ballad called 'Lady-O', written by their one-time groupie Judee Sill. In their own grown-up fanboy way, they were as perfect as the Beatles. Their photos just needed a little more touching up.

UP THE LADDER TO THE ROOF:
TAMLA MOTOWN

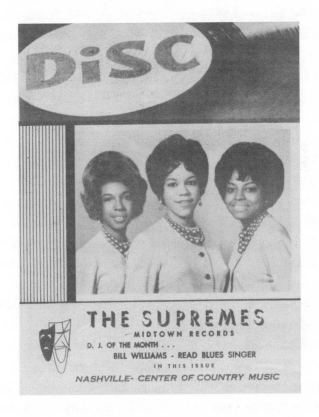

Detroit's Tamla Motown label gives us an insight into how the world might have been had the Beatles never happened in America.

Motown's writing and production set-up echoed and amplified the Brill Building model. Just as they praised their New York heroes, the Beatles never failed to mention the likes of Motown acts Smokey Robinson and Mary Wells in their early interviews, and covered songs by the Miracles ('You Really Got a Hold on Me') and the Marvelettes ('Please Mr Postman') on their second album. Motown spoke to the Beatles in a way that other American soul labels like Atlantic didn't – like the Brill Building's output, it cut across barriers. Motown was clean, bristling, highly dramatic, and had melodies that sat neatly between the Beatles and the Beach Boys on your radio: the sound of young America. Its roster was obscenely rich in talent, and lurking unseen in the backroom was a rhythm section that was just about the best pop has ever seen; even now, while Stax and Atlantic may get aficionados on their feet, the Motown sound's whipcrack snare and liquid bass will always guarantee a jam-packed dancefloor whether it's heard in Los Angeles, London, Lisbon or Lvov.

While the sage businessman Ahmet Ertegun wore a Mona Lisa smile and kept an enigmatic air of silence, Motown boss Berry Gordy was a loud-mouthed go-getter of the old school, a scrapper and one-time flyweight champion who wanted to be – and got to be – the biggest black entrepreneur in the world. Atlantic had been set up to service an existing, but small and constrained, market; Gordy wanted to invent a sound and create a market. He did this by constant hustling, trying over and over to get the best records on the market. If something worked, he would put out a subtle variant a few weeks later – following the Four Tops' 'I Can't Help Myself' (US no. 1 '65) with the three-per-cent-different sequel 'It's the Same Old Song' (US no. 5 '65) was Gordy's tongue-in-cheek acknowledgement of his savvy. He made Motown, but eventually he turned out to be its chief flaw.

By 1966 Motown was being run from eight houses on opposite sides of Detroit's West Grand Boulevard, and millionaire Berry Gordy was rumoured to be running with the mafia. But back in the mid-fifties he had been small-time, running a jazz record store and eating at Gladys's down-home restaurant in Detroit. In his spare time he wrote a few songs. One of these, 'Reet Petite', clicked for ex-Billy Ward and the Dominoes' lead Jackie Wilson, whom Gordy had met on the fight circuit in the late forties: it reached number sixty-two in 1957, going as high as number six in the UK in early '58, and the same team's 'Lonely Teardrops' was a US number-seven hit a year later. Wilson defined melisma. His ecstatic vocal acrobatics were designed to take on Gordy's pugilistic musical experiments, shuffling one minute ('look about, look about, look about . . .'), jabbing the next ('ooh! *ah!* ooh! *ah!*'). But the writer was fast learning the pitfalls of the music business. His jazz shop closed, a victim of the shift in taste towards modern pop, and he claimed not to have prospered from the Wilson hits: 'You can go broke with hits if someone else is producing them.' Within months, out of a small timber-frame house in Detroit, much like the fume-choked ones that line the road from JFK to Manhattan, he would inaugurate the Tamla and Motown labels.

Early Motown singles, from 1958 through to 1960, sound like they were built of wattle and daub. Straight gospel sat alongside blues and the occasional sax-led rocker. Singers had names like Henry Lumpkin. Searching for satori, Gordy covered a lot of ground early on – proto-surf, novelty songs about purple monsters, answer songs to Brill Building hits. Some were plain daft ('I Out-Duked the Duke' by Little Otis, with its confused concept of the English gentry), but there were a bunch of great 45s that tend to get forgotten as they don't really sound like Motown records: the Supremes' downright filthy 'Buttered Popcorn', Little Iva's 'Continental Strut', which sounds like a coffee percolator in orbit, and Mary Wells's first hit, the gritty 'Bye Bye Baby'. It hardly smelt like a flawless hit factory. Yet Gordy built Motown one piece at a time, and it barely cost him a dime.

The real beauty of Motown was its serendipity. The Jackie Wilson hits may have been the main reason musicians initially beat a path to 2648 West Grand Boulevard – or Hitsville USA, as Gordy boldly renamed the house – but it seemed that everyone who knocked on the door was a conduit to fame and fortune. Eddie Holland was a shy student and Jackie Wilson fan who suffered from stage fright and, after just one minor hit with 'Jamie' (US no. 30 '62), decided to try his hand at songwriting instead: at the time of writing he is the thirteenth most successful songwriter in UK chart history. Marvin Gaye was hired as a session drummer and initially saw his singing career, if he saw one at all, as a Nat King Cole imitator. Freddie Gorman was the local postman and Georgia Dobbins was a schoolgirl who had an idea for a song; together they knocked out 'Please Mr Postman' in the Motown shack one afternoon in 1961, and created the label's first US number one.

In 1960 Motown had been struggling to pay the electricity bill; in 1963 it released ten singles that reached the US Top 10, and another eight that made the Top 20. One of these went all the way to number one, and it was the most anarchic. Cut live at the Regal Theatre in Chicago, Little Stevie Wonder's 'Fingertips' is an instrumental that stops halfway through. Stevie finishes the song, then restarts it as an entirely new line-up of musicians are taking the stage. 'What key? What key?' shouts the baffled bassist, as they have all of six seconds to rediscover the groove. It's a rare exercise in rock 'n' roll improv and one of the most exciting records ever made. Its trip to the top was aided by Motown's marketing team, who leaked an unsubstantiated rumour that twelve-year-old Stevie was Ray Charles's illegitimate son.

'Fingertips' was also the least typical Motown number one. By 1963 Earl Van Dyke had put together a crack studio team modelled on the auto-industry assembly lines that most Detroit musicians would end up on if they didn't get the breaks. Van Dyke's team played like Brazil: confident, colourful, joyous, champions of the world. Meanwhile, Berry Gordy had pieced together his most formidable writing team – shy Eddie Holland, his brother Brian and Lamont Dozier. Their earliest Motown hits were church-inspired: the Miracles' call-and-response, one-chord dancer 'Mickey's Monkey' (US no. 8 '63); Marvin Gaye's 'Can I Get a Witness' (US no. 22 '63); the untethered vocals – 'Go ahead girl!' – on Martha and the Vandellas' 'Heatwave' (US no. 4 '63). Their reputation, though, is very pop, and that's because they wrote every major hit by the Supremes, a trio from the dirt-poor Brewster Projects fronted by Diana Ross, who had the most radio-friendly voice of the whole roster. No matter how muted or quiet the radio may be in a cafe or taxi, Ross's voice cuts through like a laser. It's uncanny. It also explains how the Supremes amassed eleven US number ones in the sixties, more than anyone except the Beatles. Ross's voice aside, it probably helped that she was dating Gordy – writers and producers worked that little bit harder on a Supremes 45, and it paid off for everybody.

In 1964 Motown became all-conquering. The Supremes had their first hit, 'Where Did Our Love Go', which pared the Motown sound down to its axles, nuts and bolts. It was so minimal that the tune barely existed, just a mantra of misery. The Marvelettes were offered it first and hated it; the Supremes did too but, coming off of several flops, weren't given the option by Berry Gordy. As skeletal as Kraftwerk, 'Where Did

Our Love Go' was a US number one and UK number three, and nobody whined about not liking it any more.

Gordy was the factory owner and, with business booming, he was ruthless. He snapped up acts from other Detroit labels Golden World (San Remo Strings) and Ric-Tic (Edwin Starr), putting the rival companies out of business. He wanted no credits for musicians on his artwork; he wanted everything clean and streamlined. It was all about Motown as a stamp of quality – like General Motors. If you bought a new car, Gordy figured, you wouldn't need to know who fitted the carburettor. The acts worked incredibly hard: in 1966, at Blinstrubb's nightclub in Boston, an underweight Diana Ross blacked out on stage. Obedience to Motown was expected. The husky Mary Wells had a number one with 'My Guy' in '64, decided she could stay at the top without the label's help, was signed by 20th Century Records, and her career died a death – Gordy, she suspected, had friends in high places. Mary Wilson knew better – the sexiest Supreme wore a ring to show she was 'engaged to Motown'.

One group Gordy had signed to his short-lived Jazz Workshop subsidiary turned out to be the most emotionally charged and floor-friendly of all. The Four Tops weren't pin-ups, and they were a few years older than their labelmates, but sonically they were the pinnacle of Motown.

Holland/Dozier/Holland laced their more simplistic lyrics with emotional landmines, lines that could make you catch your breath and twist your heart. The Four Tops' first hit, 'Baby I Need Your Loving' (US no. 11 '64), is littered with them: Levi Stubbs starts the song with the title, gently, not unlike Sam Cooke, and yes, it's a sad song, a lonely song, but the catch is that each verse has an unexpected extra line, a ninth bar that sneaks in just as you're expecting the chorus: ''cos I-I-I'm *so* lonely,' he coos first time; ''cos lately I've been losing sleep', the next time; and by the third verse the song is all dark shadows and empty hallways. Stubbs cries out how the emptiness, the loneliness inside him 'makes me feel half alive', and then the wave of building tension, almost unbearable, finally breaks on the chorus, this time without the addition of the ninth bar. From this first hit, the Four Tops projected need and devotion and the pain of love better than almost anyone, and HDH provided them with similarly clever, emotive, beautiful material until 1968: 'Ask the

Lonely', 'I Can't Help Myself', 'It's the Same Old Song', 'Reach Out I'll Be There', 'Standing in the Shadows of Love', 'Seven Rooms of Gloom', every one a heartbreaker.

So why did Motown get a critical cold shoulder? There are several reasons. Firstly, it didn't operate in a regional bubble, firming up the values of its own local community – adult black consumers – which is how a lot of (usually white) purists, from Alan Lomax to Peter Guralnick, like their black music. Nik Cohn called the Supremes 'Uncle Tom'. Motown followed pop trends aggressively, and its sidelining of jazz, blues and Atlantic-style soul was a genuine sadness for fans of that sound. 'When we were in Detroit,' Eric Burdon told *Crawdaddy* magazine in '66, 'I caused a bit of a disturbance there because I said on the radio I didn't like Motown, I thought it was whitened Negro music, it had taken the wildness and corralled it . . . Motown is just too pretty for me. Some of their artists are good, obviously, but I don't like it.' Still, on a purely musical level, one listen to Martha and the Vandellas' metallurgically galvanised cry of pain 'Nowhere to Run' (US no. 8 '65), or the fever of 'Heatwave' ('Sometimes I stare in space, tears all over my face'), should have at least raised the hairs on Burdon's neck.

Secondly, Gordy miscalculated by grooming his artists for Vegas, thinking that was where careers and cash would hold up the longest, and here his detractors are on firmer ground. The best aspects of Motown weren't sustained, they were sacrificed for time and money spent on deportment classes, and its critics were right to be wary. Besides, Gordy's prediction was wrong – the turn of the seventies marked the end of the Copa crowd, the Rat Pack clearly belonged to a previous generation, and they had no real successors.

Thirdly, there are the excruciating interviews, as bland and vacant as anything Disney could muster, in which one Supreme will explain that they don't go steady but 'sometimes when we're home in Detroit we double or triple date'. Paul Anka couldn't have sounded more gormless. It's notable that Atlantic and Stax stars were rarely interviewed – they knew to keep the mystery caged. Still waters run deep, and Motown was a babbling brook.

Yet even in the twenty-first century you will hear more of Tamla Motown's singles on the radio than those of any other record label. Why is this? For a start, it had taken Don Kirshner's 1650 Broadway model and supercharged it. There were so many competing writers* and such an abundance of great music produced every week that unissued recordings continue to emerge to this day – entire CDs' worth of material by the Marvelettes, Vandellas, Marvin Gaye, and astonishing songs by lesser known but equally worthwhile names like Chris Clark ('I Just Wanna Be Loving You'), Barbara McNair ('Baby a Go-Go'), Brenda Holloway ('Lonely Boy'), Kim Weston ('Absent Minded Lover'). These songs all sound like Top 10 hits, prime Hitsville USA material, and they just sat there gathering dust, waiting for an archivist to dig them out four decades later. It's safe to say the label's quality-control operative, Billie Jean Brown, was overstretched: Martha and the Vandellas' 'Jimmy Mack',† one of Motown's touchstone singles, was left on the shelf for over two years before Berry Gordy discovered it while rifling through unissued tapes in 1966 and, unsurprisingly, blew a gasket.

So Motown was too productive for its own good. Its hothouse environment is how I think most great pop music emerges. It couldn't last. We'll soon discover how some of its key names became disgruntled, tired of clocking in and clocking out, wanting to stretch out beyond two minutes forty and work away from the gaze of time-and-motion man Berry Gordy. Of course, most people don't think about any of this when they hear 'You Can't Hurry Love'. Motown is shorthand for goodtime party music, memories of simpler times when pop was there to make young America dance, not to challenge its audience. In this respect, nobody did it better.

* Even the writers on a song as familiar as Jimmy Ruffin's 'What Becomes of the Brokenhearted' – William Weatherspoon, Paul Riser and James Dean – remain obscure as they were surrounded by so many more successful colleagues.
† The song was conceived by Eddie Holland after he attended an awards meeting in 1963. Ronnie Mack, who had written the Chiffons' 'He's So Fine', had died that year, just weeks after the record hit number one. His mother was collecting an award on his behalf, telling the crowd how sad she felt that they would never hear another Ronnie Mack song. Holland was deeply affected, went home, sat at his piano and wrote 'Ronnie Mack, when are you coming back?' A few hours later he had a hit song that was partly a tribute to the dead songwriter, but also seemed to tease American soldiers in Vietnam, as their girls back home were 'trying hard to be true'.

1966: THE LONDON LOOK

I'm terribly pleased to be working-class because it's the most swinging thing to be now, a tremendous status symbol really. People are always asking, with a sort of envious reverence, 'Do you really live in a council house?'
  Margaret Forster, author of *Georgy Girl*, 1966

Elvis Presley is the greatest cultural force in the twentieth century.
  Leonard Bernstein, 1966

People who develop a love affair with pop music usually do so aged ten or eleven, maybe twelve at a push. At least, that is the oldest you can be and still fall in love with any guitar, any bass drum, soak up the whole of the Top 20 and love it all without question. Some people, for this reason, will have a favourite year – say 1960, 1975, 1985, 1997 – that is objectively a bad year for pop; it may seem to them that pop had evolved to reach the point of perfection (in the guise of 'Are You Lonesome Tonight' or 'I'm Not in Love' or 'A Different Corner' or 'Bitter Sweet Symphony'), and that that single year produced the records against which all else in the future has to be measured.

1966 is different. It was the first time that modern pop music had been seen as culturally and artistically significant. Anyone looking at any random Top 20 from 1966 will be able to pick out half a dozen singles that are stone, ten-out-of-ten, copper-bottomed classics. Brand-new, forward-looking, everyone pulling their weight. It was the year Leonard Bernstein theorised pop with a US TV documentary called *Inside Pop: The Rock Revolution.* He said he was 'fascinated by this strange and compelling scene called pop music . . . It's completely of, by, and for the kids. And by kids I mean anyone from eight years old to twenty-five . . . It raises lots of questions, but right now, for openers, here are the two that concern me most. One: why do adults resent it so, and two: why do I like it?' 1966 was the year it all came together.

One clue that something magical was happening was, perversely, Phil Spector's retirement. The man who had done more than anyone to progress the sonic impact of pop, to turn the studio into an instrument, and to elevate the teenage experience into an art form, could see no new avenues for the wall of sound after 'River Deep – Mountain High'. The Beach Boys' Brian Wilson had once been just a Spector disciple, belittled by his teacher's callous rejection of 'Don't Worry Baby', which he had written as a hymn to the Ronettes. Now he used everything he'd learnt from Spector and created the *Pet Sounds* album, more subtle, more moving than anything either had cut before. Pop had caught up with Spector and, if he couldn't be at the top of the tree, he would rather quit.*

Pop music was now treated as a genuine art form – by *The Times* in

---

* He was back in the studio three years later, quieter, possibly wiser, and recorded the Checkmates' largely unheralded but exquisite 'Black Pearl'. Within a year he was working with the Beatles.

England, by Tom Wolfe in *Esquire*. All other contemporary art – cinema, poetry, painting – seemed to coalesce around it. In Liverpool, one of the Mersey poets, Roger McGough, got into pop with the Scaffold ('Thank U Very Much', UK no. 4 '67); a few others started a group called, with an arched eyebrow, the Liverpool Scene. In New York, Andy Warhol gave his patronage to the Velvet Underground. In cinema, soundtrack writer John Barry became a bona fide pop star; not only did he score the James Bond films – 'million dollar Mickey Mouse music', as he called it – but he also married teenage model and actress Jane Birkin, who herself would have a number-one single in 1969; it was hard to imagine Dimitri Tiomkin doing anything as flash. Talking about his Cadogan Square flat, Barry nailed the new scene: 'I put on a suit and walk in one direction, throw on some blue jeans and walk in another, into Chelsea. I've got the best of both worlds.'

And maybe when John Barry gave that interview, David Bailey was on his way round to the flat to shoot Jane Birkin (though Barry would have been wise to stay in, given the photographer's reputation). Bailey was the thinly disguised subject of *Blow Up*, Italian director Michelangelo Antonioni's sexy movie based around the London art scene that included a live performance by the Yardbirds. The lead character was played by David Hemmings, an actor who would soon release an album of his own, with instrumental backing by the Byrds. And so it went on. Everything joined up.

London was the centre of the new order and the Rolling Stones were its embodiment, the ultimate dandy pop stars for louche aristocrats to be seen with. They would be seen at Old Etonian art dealer Robert Fraser's gallery – 'Groovy Bob' already numbered Paul McCartney among his circle of friends. Claes Oldenburg remembered: 'The role of the Rolling Stones was to be the bad kids on the block, early punks if you like, and the Beatles were the good guys. They played their roles very well. They came to the openings, and Mick Jagger said awfully nasty things to everybody and Paul McCartney was very nice, charming.' The Stones had already satirised the slumming debutante in 'Play with Fire', the flip side of 'The Last Time' in '65. Now, with Marianne Faithfull on his arm (who may have grown up in a terraced house in Reading, but had a cut-glass voice and an Austrian baroness for a mother), Mick Jagger was the highest-profile example of a suddenly classless society. Rich folks had patronised pop before, with Jackie Kennedy seen twisting at the Peppermint Lounge in 1962, but this time the gatecrashers were running the party. Everything was pop. Everyone – Michael Caine, Peter Blake, Truman Capote, Princess Margaret – was a pop star.

Leonard Bernstein realised, quite quickly, that this extended beyond party guest lists and the extent of your credit on Carnaby Street. This was an important movement, said Bernstein, socially and musically:

> I think this music has something terribly important to tell us adults, and I think we would be wise not to behave like ostriches about it.

Throughout pop in 1966, there was a sense of friendly competition, as if everyone was willing this golden moment to continue. Previous modern pop eras had felt fleeting – no matter how thrilling they may have been, there was no sense of progress from one Little Richard record to the next.* Now everyone felt obliged to better their previous record, and everyone *else's* previous record.

On the Four Tops' 'Reach Out I'll Be There' (US and UK no. 1), the drums send out signals to the distant damsel in distress, the woodwinds pine in empathy, and then Levi Stubbs rides in on a white horse, reaching down to pull the girl from the swamp. 1966 was the year John Lennon made his crack about the Beatles being bigger than Jesus – here was a Tamla Motown record that was a viable secular crutch, something to truly give you succour when the rain came down. Soul had many screamers who over-emoted, but Levi Stubbs wasn't one of them. Usually Four Tops songs found him standing in the shadows on a lonely street, but on 'Reach Out' he got to be a hero for once. It was followed at number one by the Beach Boys' 'Good Vibrations'; in a way, they are the ultimate number ones. Both records condense so much, deftly mixing so many genres and new sounds inside three minutes, that you can only marvel at how it must have felt to hear them on the radio for the first time.

* Buddy Holly bucks this trend.

For a sense of progression, take a look at some runs of singles from late '65 through '66: the Beatles' 'We Can Work It Out', 'Paperback Writer' and 'Eleanor Rigby'; the Beach Boys' 'Barbara Ann', 'Sloop John B', 'God Only Knows' and 'Good Vibrations'; the Kinks' 'Till the End of the Day', 'Dedicated Follower of Fashion', 'Sunny Afternoon' and 'Dead End Street'. This is also how the Rolling Stones ended up with the formless cacophony of 'Have You Seen Your Mother, Baby';* it was a relative failure, but you had to try, you had to.

> There is a new song, too complex to get all of first time round. It could come only out of the ferment that characterises today's pop music scene. Brian Wilson, leader of the famous Beach Boys, and one of today's most important pop musicians, sings his own 'Surf's Up'. Poetic, beautiful even in its obscurity. It is a symbol of the change many musicians see in our future . . . Serious and silly, sweet and grandiose.

A friend of mine's earliest memory is of his father coming home from work with a 45, telling the family to gather in the front room because he had something very important to play them. It was 'Good Vibrations'. Aside from its brief appearance on *Inside Pop*, the outside world wouldn't get to hear 'Surf's Up' until its official release in 1971, but it didn't seem to matter at the time, when there was so much you could draw from 'Good Vibrations', modern pop's first multi-movement single, the first suggestion that it was bursting out of its skin and its ideas and ambitions couldn't be contained on a seven-inch single. Little did anyone know this would be the last time Brian Wilson and the group's bellicose cheerleader Mike Love would gain commercial joy from their combative relationship. Brian had his classical leanings, and Mike was a jock with a roving eye for Southern girls 'who keep their boyfriends warm at night'; Love came up with the chorus hook, and Brian's disparate elements fell into place – it was a UK and US number one in October '66, and felt like the future.

A quick dissection of 'Good Vibrations': the opening keyboard sound

---

* This single, which broke their run of UK number ones by only reaching number five, also had a startling promo film shot by Peter Whitehead in which the Stones applied make-up and dressed as middle-aged women. It's still jaw-dropping to watch – no one broadcast it at the time.

always feels to me like sunlight through a kitchen window first thing in the morning, the death-ray theremin of the chorus sounds like *Star Trek* (first screened in 1966), and when I hear the harpsichord section there's a girl in a white dress sat on my lap in the back of an old jalopy. 'Good Vibrations' can make synaesthetes out of all of us. On top of all that, it's a pretty faultless love song. Right here, friends, we have the pinnacle of sixties pop.

> And it's not only the Beatles who make these inventions. For instance there's a group known as the Left Banke that has a tune called 'Pretty Ballerina'. This tune is built, not in the usual major or minor scale, but in a combination of the Lydian and Mixolydian modes – imagine that! Comes out with a sort of Turkish or Greek sound. Rather unusual, wouldn't you say?

Over in New York, a classically trained keyboard player called Michael Brown had been paying close attention to the emergence of the Zombies. 'She's Not There' was a far bigger hit in the States than it was in the UK, and Brown was inspired. He formed a band called the Left Banke and roped in his dad, the arranger Harry Lookofsky, to oversee their first single. The other players were rudimentary, so Lookofsky focused on Brown's harpsichord and the string quartet; 'Walk Away Renee' (US no. 5) was the first bona fide baroque pop hit at the end of '65.

Anglophiles to a man, the Left Banke neatly invented a sound which was soft but insistently sad. Like the Zombies' Colin Blunstone, their singer Steve Martin could belt them out if he wanted to but preferred the delicate touch, as witnessed on their second hit, 'Pretty Ballerina' (US no. 16 '66). Titles like 'Dark Is the Bark', 'Barterers and Their Wives' and 'Ivy, Ivy' gave away their lyrical inclinations. In a 1972 letter to a fan, guitarist Rick Brand claimed their lyrics 'were written as rather self consciously [*sic*] beautiful musical whimsy, as you find in the later 18th century romantic music, pre-Beethoven'.

For a while in '66 harpsichords and string quartets chimed with the charts – the Rolling Stones cut 'Lady Jane', the Kinks' *Face to Face* album featured 'Too Much on My Mind' and 'Two Sisters', and the Beatles melded Purcell baroque with the soundtrack to *Fahrenheit*

451 for 'Eleanor Rigby'. Possibly this was down to pop stars moving out of transit vans and into limos, away from package-tour shows in Accrington and Aylesbury, becoming society players and gaining a taste for the high life. But just as likely it was born from the excitable search for newness; no record before or since the Beach Boys' *Pet Sounds* has used the bass harmonica as a lead instrument. In 1966 things were moving so fast that each Beatles single seemed like a new era, and studio experimentation was a must. Bring on the clavichord, they cried.

The apogee of this arcane sonic adventure was the Beatles' *Sgt Pepper's Lonely Hearts Club Band* in the spring of '67, which mixed everyday lyrics with music hall and Edwardiana, creating lysergically enhanced parlour music. But as we'll see, just months later the Technicolor dreamcoats were put away, and replaced by soiled denims.

> Our pop generation reaches and spreads itself, grasping at the unattainable . . . The straining tenderness of those high, untrained young voices . . . Now of course, whereas I may call that straining after falsetto dreams of glory, you may call it nothing but a breakdown in gender, that same androgynous phenomenon of the pop scene that produces boys with long hair and ruffled shirts. And you may be right.

That the British Invasion swept away a whole strain of pop is largely true – the careers of Dion, the Everly Brothers, Billy Fury and the Shirelles, for instance, were put on ice in spite of the consistently strong singles they released through the mid-sixties, while the Brill Building style of hit-making was replaced by the autonomous band. Yet there are clear examples of groups, still capable of growth, who were unaffected. The Beach Boys were largely self-managed, and Detroit's Tamla Motown supplanted New York's Brill Building. Then there were the Four Seasons, a bunch of square-looking Jersey boys whose singer Frankie Valli had the most unearthly falsetto.* Some records may sound like New York

---

* From 'Ronnie' (US no. 6 '64) until the gently psychedelic, non-charting 'Saturday's Father' in 1968, the label credit on their singles read 'The Four Seasons featuring the "sound" of Frankie Valli', suggesting that the notes he emitted weren't all from his mouth, that they were somehow manufactured, or that Valli really wasn't of this planet.

– the Five Satins' 'In the Still of the Nite', the Drifters' 'On Broadway', Blondie's 'Union City Blue' – but the intro to the Four Seasons' 'Walk Like a Man' (US no. 1, UK no. 12 '63) is the only one I can think of that sounds like the Empire State Building being constructed.

Frankie Valli couldn't have been more old-school New York Italian if he'd been a method actor. He cut his first single in 1953, a year before Elvis even made it to a studio. He joined the Four Lovers in '56, who mutated into the Four Seasons in '61. Fame was worked at, sweated for. 'We were out there. People think we were an overnight success, but when we weren't singing we were filling in to feed families. I was a young kid working in a bowling alley, setting up pins. Also I was a hairdresser, construction worker, florist, I drove trucks. Whatever I had to do.'

After an aspiring singer and actor called Joe Pesci introduced Bob Gaudio to the group, they had themselves a songwriter. When producer Bob Crewe heard Valli's skyscraping voice in 1962, he decided he had to work with them: suddenly it all clicked, and they scored three US number ones on the bounce with 'Sherry', 'Big Girls Don't Cry' and 'Walk Like a Man'. Ex-Four Lover Charlie Calello returned to score their urban dramas, and Crewe and Gaudio became a writing machine, the former seeing sound in pictures, drawing clouds and waterfalls on Calello's orchestral notation. Between them they fashioned what Crewe called a 'fist of sound', a harder counterpart to Brian Wilson and Phil Spector's west-coast teen symphonies. The stories were usually of hair-shirted anguish ('Big Man in Town', 'Dawn Go Away', 'Bye Bye Baby') or denial, often on some dumb point of macho principle ('Big Girls Don't Cry', 'Silence Is Golden', 'Rag Doll') – with Joe Pesci as a connection it isn't a stretch to say these records anticipated the Scorsese-era acting boom.

By 1966 they should have been throwbacks, as lost as Dion and the Belmonts, but Crewe and Calello were tremendously inventive arrangers, and 1966 was open to all comers. They reached the US Top 20 with a song called 'Opus 17' that had the most chromatic key changes of any hit single.* The Four Seasons had sidestepped the British Invasion, and

* It starts in the key of F# and modulates five times before concluding in the key of B.

attuned and realigned their sound in late '65 with the Motown fuzz of 'Let's Hang On' (US no. 3, UK no. 4), following it with the blue-eyed soul of 'Working My Way Back to You' (US no. 9, UK no. 50 '66), 'Opus 17' (US no. 13 '66) and – best of all – 'I've Got You under My Skin' (US no. 9, UK no. 12 '66); Bernstein would have heard echoes of Schumann. They took Cole Porter's song and rendered it contemporary, with tubular bells, a scuffed Palm Springs pavement beat and an expansive, romantic intro that matched Brian Wilson's majestic opening for 'California Girls'.

'The idea came from a date we played in Florida,' said Valli. 'Sinatra was appearing and we were invited. Just amazing. I couldn't believe. So, three or four in the morning the phone rings. Bob Gaudio. Can it wait, I say? No . . . I got an idea for a song – it's "I've Got You under My Skin". *What?* The song we just heard Sinatra do? How can you make it better? Trust me, he says, I've got the whole thing in my head. And that's how it came out. Almost symphonic. Beautiful.'

Even Frankie Valli didn't have the screamiest voice of '66. That belonged to a Polish Italian from Pittsburgh called Lou Christie. I've never quite worked out how serious Christie is. His run of hits started at the same time as the Four Seasons' and, working with a gypsy songwriter twice his age called Twyla Herbert and a squeaky girl group called the Tammys, they made a batch of 45s that sounded like the Valli boys in a garden shed. There was something oddly knowing about Christie's hits – 'The Gypsy Cried', 'Two Faces Have I' and 'Lightnin' Strikes' (US no. 1, UK no. 11 '66). Maybe it was Herbert's input, written with the same distance of years that had made Chuck Berry's teen-lifestyle hits seem so vivid, almost super-realist. On 'Lightnin' Strikes', Christie starts pleading gruffly, unconvincingly ('Believe it or not, you're in my heart all the time'), then the music switches to a chocolate-box backing on the bridge, and Christie does his most gallant Bing Crosby croon ('There's a chapel in the pines . . .' – really!). Will she swallow this hokum? Surely not, as Christie's Mr Hyde starts to emerge on the punky pre-chorus ('When I see lips waiting to be kissed, I can't stop myself . . .') and explodes out of his skin, shrieking his lust on the falsetto chorus – '*Liiiiightniiiiing striiiiking agaiiiiin!*' Game over. Christie had a major hit every few years, a dozen Hot Hundred entries spread over as many years, and scored a big bubblegum hit in '69 with 'I'm Gonna Make You Mine' (US no. 10, UK no. 2). After this he was a *Playgirl* centrefold, cut a Polish Italian take on 'What's Going On' in 1971 with the panoramic *Paint America Love* album, gave up pop to become a truck driver for a year after it flopped, and married Miss Great Britain. He's probably worth a book of his own.

> Many of the lyrics in their oblique allusions and way-out metaphors are beginning to sound like real poems.

The influence of Dylan had been fully absorbed into the mainstream by 1966. On 'Semi-Detached Suburban Mr James' (UK no. 2), Manfred Mann told a wedding story from the point of view of a jilted lover, a tale familiar from Eddie Fisher's 'Outside of Heaven' (UK no. 1 '53) now grafted onto Dylan's ire: 'I can see you in the morning time – washing day, weather's fine – hanging things upon the line, as your life slips away.' Backed by Beach Boys harmonies (the Manfreds were the most bandwagon-happy of all the British beat groups), singer Mike D'Abo transported 'Ballad of a Thin Man' from the Lower East Side to Dorking: 'So you think you will be happy buttering the toast for your semi-detached suburban Mr Most?' Bob Lind combined Dylanesque imagery ('softly in the distance, through the canyons of your mind') with a dreamy cloudscape arrangement, courtesy of Jack Nitzsche, on the divine 'Elusive Butterfly' (US and UK no. 5). And at Motown, the motormouth delivery of 'Subterranean Homesick Blues' informed Stevie Wonder's 'Uptight' (US no. 3, UK no. 16), while Levi Stubbs's 'Reach Out I'll Be There' leaned on the cadences of Dylan's 'Queen Jane Approximately', a track from *Blonde on Blonde* which must have been in the shops for all of a month when the Four Tops went in to cut their masterpiece. You couldn't keep still.

> There's a good deal I don't like, and wouldn't dream of defending. I don't like volume for its own sake . . . This music can be coarse, faddish . . . It's mostly trash, but that good five per cent is so exciting and vital and, may I say, significant that it claims the attention of every thinking person.

There's little doubt the Troggs would have been among Bernstein's ninety-five per cent. 'Wild Thing' (UK no. 2, US no. 1) showed there was still room for primitivism amidst the rococo, and no beat group was more primitive than the Troggs. Their manager Larry Page considered them so lacking in charisma and grace that he renamed the singer and the drummer after the two most stylish people he could think of – Elvis Presley and James Bond. Their debut album was called *From Nowhere – The Troggs* with good reason: not only had this bunch of unknowns sprung into the British and American charts with indecent haste, but they came from the small market town of Andover. Drums went thump. Thump. Thump-thump. The guitar line was three chords, played forever, no solo, no flash, childishly simple, and Reg Presley's voice was as frustrated, rough and unadopted as Lee Brilleaux's ten years later. Here was another example of classlessness – cultural, rather than economic – busting into the mainstream, trashing ordinary cultural categories, boxes and distinctions. Yet even here, in the midst of this pre-school simplicity, is an unexpected ocarina break – did anyone even know what an ocarina was before 1966?

The Troggs should have been a one-shot band, 'Wild Thing' their sole claim to fame. But it turned out Reg Presley was a decent songwriter who could capitalise on their limitations. 'With a Girl Like You' went one better than 'Wild Thing' and reached number one in the UK. Better were a string of suggestive, direct singles that were considerably less tight than Reg's striped pants: 'I Can't Control Myself' (UK no. 2, US no. 43 '66), 'Give It to Me' (UK no. 12 '67), 'Night of the Long Grass' (UK no. 17 '67). By '68 they were finished as a hit act, but their legacy was strange and unique. They became the first poster boys for some of the earliest and best pop writers, inspiring effusive essays from Richard Meltzer and Lester Bangs, and so became the first in a list of alternative heroes that would later include Big Star, the Go-Betweens and Nick Drake. Reg Presley also turned out to be a literal poster boy for Michelle Pfeiffer – his was the only picture she had on her teenage bedroom wall. And in the nineties he suddenly became a millionaire when his 1967 attempt at flower power, 'Love Is All Around', was revived by Wet Wet Wet and spent fifteen weeks at number one in

Britain. Reg, ever the country boy, spent all the proceeds on crop-circle research.

> Most of us have been raised in the tradition of Tin Pan Alley, where the songs . . . were meant to amuse or beguile, but that's all. They were embellishments on life. What these young people seem to say is that their music isn't just decorative, it comes right out of their world.

The Troggs showed there was still room for raw noise in 1966, but the original Merseybeat stars – number-one shoo-ins just three years before – were floundering. The exception was the Hollies. The Mancunians had started with speedy Searchers-like covers of Maurice Williams's 'Stay' and the Coasters' 'Searchin'' in '63, but by the mid-sixties had found they preferred to document the romance of the everyday, whether it was in a school playground ('Carrie Anne'), a strip club ('Stop Stop Stop') or on the morning commute ('Bus Stop'). In '66 they covered Evie Sands's 'I Can't Let Go' – written, like 'Wild Thing', by Chip Taylor – which featured an awesome high harmony from Graham Nash that, for years, I assumed was a top-note trumpet. Nash wrote with Tony Hicks (who had the best haircut of the day, and is maybe British pop's most underrated guitarist) and wood-carved singer Allan Clarke (who always looked ten years older than he was) under the enigmatic group pseudonym L. Ransford. Beyond this the Hollies were a working pop group, pure and simple. They made three great self-penned albums (*For Certain Because* in '66, *Evolution* and *Butterfly* in '67), and had absolutely nothing to say about Vietnam, devolution or Hare Krishna. All, that is, except Nash, who quit in '68, when he decided his lifelong, pint-drinking Manchester mates were too small-time.

> I like the eclecticism of it, its freedom to absorb any and all musical styles and elements, like old blues [he plays 'Hanky Panky'], or a high Bach trumpet ['Penny Lane'], or a harpsichord ['Society's Child'] or even a string quartet ['Eleanor Rigby'] . . . Then I like the international and interracial way it ranges all over the world, borrowing from the ragas of Hindu music ['Love You To'] or borrowing from the sensuality of Arab cafe music ['Paint It Black'].

Outside Britain and America, modern pop also ruled. By 1966 local scenes had developed which mimicked Anglo beat but frequently took on their own unique flavours. Almost anywhere you went, a country had its own Beatles and more often than not, because teenagers were usually running the scene, they were pretty good. Sweden had a ridiculous number of groups for a country of just eight million people and the best – the Mascots and Tages – tended towards Kinks and Zombies melancholy; Holland grew its hair longest, liked its beat rawest, and groups like Q65 (their best song title: 'I Despise You') and the Outsiders – led by the ghostly Wally Tax – had a delicate menace; from Greece came the sweetly sad Bluebirds; Austria had the snotty Slaves, with their ragged single 'Shut Up'.

Some of the best, and most regionally specific, non-Anglo-American pop came from France. It had developed its own complex scene, yé-yé, at the turn of the sixties, which developed from the nation's inordinate love of the twist plus a fondness for girl-group sounds. Cute blondes did best – France Gall, Sylvie Vartan, Gillian Hills – but fiercer females – Cléo, Clothilde, Jacqueline Taïeb – got to cut records too, backed by thudding, fuzzy garage bands; they tended to sell less, but they were terrifically rough compared to their British and American counterparts. France did things its own way, producing pop records that ridiculed pop, most of which were written by the chain-smoking Serge Gainsbourg;* in France, uniquely, it was also perfectly OK for their pop stars to cut right-wing protest singles, like a bunch of juvenile Barry

---

* Gainsbourg has proved a long-term influence, but one who barely registered in Britain or America at the time, despite scoring a UK number one ('Je t'aime . . . moi non plus') in 1969 (it rather appropriately reached number sixty-nine in the States) and writing a Eurovision winner for France Gall in '65. As pop prankster, general cynic, provocateur and talented musician, Gainsbourg has posthumously assumed the mantle worn in the late sixties by Frank Zappa – the difference in the longevity of their influence is mostly down to the fact that Gainsbourg clearly loved pop and Zappa didn't; he was anti-pop. Both toyed with the form, but Gainsbourg was capable of writing truly beautiful songs, ones that reached into the darkness beyond the Top 40, without the need of raspberry-blowing to proclaim their otherness. With over forty years' distance, it's hard to work out what Zappa was trying to achieve.

Sadlers* – among the biggest were Johnny Hallyday's 'Cheveux longs idées courtes' and Jacques Dutronc's 'Restons français soyons gaulois'. Just one of their sixties stars crossed over, selling records in the UK and US. The willowy Françoise Hardy was their biggest (and tallest) export. Though many of her record sales were probably down to the gorgeous Jean-Marie Périer photos that adorned her sleeves,† Hardy was very good – her songs were sad and simple, her voice like the sound of petals falling from a flower. She scored a Top 20 UK hit with 'All over the World', and it became an anthem for British soldiers serving abroad (in peacetime manoeuvres, of course, not Vietnam). Everybody was in love with Françoise. She was the art-school Bardot. Dylan and Jagger serenaded her, but they barely came up to her waist, and she ended up marrying local hero Jacques Dutronc. France in the sixties could afford to be so insular – its pop stars were beautiful, its sound unique.

Still, the world revolved not around Paris, but the 'rain grey town' mentioned in the Byrds' 'Eight Miles High': London. Once the Rolling Stones broke through in '64, R&B groups had taken over the beat scene, initially taking their impetus from the Chicago blues singers Brian Jones loved – Muddy Waters, Elmore James – before moving on to contemporary soul – Motown, Otis Redding, James Brown – by 1965. Unlike their Liverpool antecedents, these groups developed fast out of their primal club sound. It surely helped that almost all of them were from, or near, the capital; their music reflected and absorbed the cultural mood, keeping the momentum going.

Working with Motown's clangorous backbeat and Chicago blues' dentist's-drill guitar lines, London groups picked up an aggressive,

---

* Staff Sergeant Barry Sadler's 'Ballad of the Green Berets', a US number one in 1966 (and weirdly a UK number twenty-four – who the hell bought it?), had a regulation martial beat but a delivery that failed to stir, either towards or against the war it was presumably promoting. Certainly it wasn't actively offensive, unlike Victor Lundberg's 'An Open Letter to My Teenage Son' (US no. 10 '67).
† Another quirk of French pop in the sixties is that there were no singles, only EPs in thick, glossy sleeves. Compared to the blank 'company bags' that housed most British and American singles, they looked extremely desirable – they also explain why many French sixties pop stars were more about a cool image and ravishing looks than callow talent.

angular sound with a penchant for guitar feedback along the way. Fed
on purple hearts and sundry other uppers, with a plethora of clubs to
keep them awake all night, they created a uniquely British noise which
was retrospectively tagged 'freakbeat'. It was pioneered by the Stones'
successors as house band at the Crawdaddy Club, the Yardbirds. Blond,
beaky singer Keith Relf had possibly the worst pitching of his generation, but this didn't matter so much when he had the capital's best
guitarists to distract a listener's attention. Tired of straight blues, the
Yardbirds had roped in tablas and a harpsichord to create the moody
'For Your Love' and scored a number-two hit in '65. Their guitarist Eric
Clapton quit in disgust, but they hired young session man Jimmy Page
in his place and got even better, with a string of dark, loud, dusky Top
3 hits: 'Evil Hearted You', 'Heart Full of Soul', 'Still I'm Sad' and the
apocalyptic, proto-psychedelic 'Shapes of Things' in '66. 'My eyes just
hurt my brain,' sang Keith Relf, over washes of feedback and drones. It
felt like quite a step on from 'Little Red Rooster'. Later the same year
they released 'Happenings Ten Years Time Ago', by which point Jeff
Beck had joined as a second guitarist. It sounded like duelling fighter
planes, a three-minute wig-out, but the Yardbirds' superiority in fire-
power didn't help them, and they never managed another hit, eventually calling it a day when Relf quit in '68. Page carried on with the New
Yardbirds, who had morphed into Led Zeppelin by the end of the year.

Out in Ilford were the Small Faces, smart-dressing, pill-popping
short-arses who cut a series of abrasive soul-influenced 45s, the best
of which was 'All or Nothing', a UK number one in '66. Singer Steve
Marriott was a fidgety ball of energy and, once he discovered halluci-
nogenics and mellowed a little, the Small Faces singlehandedly created
cosmic music hall ('Itchycoo Park', 'Lazy Sunday'). After splitting the
group in '68, Marriott wasted his soulful wail in blues-rockers Humble
Pie in the seventies, while the others hooked up with Rod Stewart,
dropped the prefix and became the Faces.

Over to the west, in Shepherd's Bush, were the Who, who you couldn't
have made up: if the Hollies were the straightest, then the Who were the
wildest. After Pete Townshend heard the blunt brutality of 'You Really
Got Me' in '64, he knew exactly how he wanted his nascent beat group

to sound and wrote 'I Can't Explain' as part tribute, part parody – it reached number eight in '65.

Everything about the Who was skew-whiff: they were comprised of an oikish, fighty singer, an art-student guitarist with a complex about his nose, a jazz bassist and a surf-crazy drummer who thrashed around his kit with no regard whatsoever for dancers' feelings. Their untogetherness is what I like most about them. They were also managed by the odd pairing of Chris Stamp (brother of actor Terence) and Kit Lambert (son of classical composer Constant). Somehow, these two also produced most of the Who's records from their imperial phase:* they ended up drum-heavy, with vocals sometimes disappearing from the mix, John Entwistle's bass used for counter-melody colour, and Townshend's guitar constantly on the edge of feeding back. This was all for the good, and made their instantly recognisable singles leap out of transistor radios. 'I like the blatantness of pop, the speed, the urgency,' Lambert told the *Observer*, by way of explanation. Pete Townshend wrote all of their singles, and his subject matter was unlike anybody else's: seaside simpletons ('Happy Jack'), masturbation ('Pictures of Lily'), divorce ('A Legal Matter'), cross-dressing ('I'm a Boy') and total disrespect for your elders ('My Generation'). For three years they were never out of the UK Top 10, although they could never quite reach number one, falling one place short on two occasions: 'We're always beaten to the top by the dead or the half dead,' said Entwistle in '66. 'Good old Jim Reeves did it on us last time ['I'm a Boy'], and before that ['My Generation'] it was the singing pimple, Ken Dodd.'†

Kit Lambert sowed the seeds of progressive rock when, presumably

---

* Shel Talmy produced their first three – 'I Can't Explain', 'Anyway Anyhow Anywhere', 'My Generation' – and the first album, which included their anthem, 'The Kids Are Alright'. An American based over here, Talmy was also responsible for all of the Kinks' singles up to 1967, as well as Coventry girl group the Orchids' raucous 'Love Hit Me' and Davy Jones and the Lower Third's droning freakbeat 'You've Got a Habit of Leaving'. He decided to save what was left of his hearing by working with Roy Harper (1968's 'Come Out Fighting Genghis Smith') and producing Pentangle's first three albums. Almost everything he touched is worth investigating.
† At the time of writing, Dodd has survived Entwistle by a decade.

inspired by his dad, he suggested to Townshend in '66 that he should try writing a 'rock opera'. 'A Quick One While He's Away' was a ten-minute 'suite' on their second album, but their third album was the keeper: *The Who Sell Out* made real Townshend's claim that they were 'pop art'; there were songs about acne creams and deodorants, and everything was linked by pirate-radio-station jingles. On the cover, Daltrey was pictured in a bath of cold baked beans. It was a busy concept, and could have ended up horribly wacky, a London scenester smug-in, but Townshend had saved some of his prettiest melodies for tracks like 'Our Love Was' and 'Sunrise', and his most explosive guitar effects for 'Armenia City in the Sky'. *The Who Sell Out* was an overwhelming, wraparound experience, the most consistent and thrilling album of the year. Unfortunately, this very '66 record was released at the end of '67. London had moved on: 'People aren't jiving in the listening boxes in record shops any more like we did to a Cliff Richard "newie",' moaned the prematurely aged Townshend.

> Then I like some of the new sounds, purely as sound, that are coming out of pop music – the arresting impact of a consort of amplified guitars ['Good Day Sunshine'] . . . Now that's not just cheery, that's very unortho-dox . . . We never used to find that in pop music – it's new . . . sort of tart, pungent . . . Now the point I want to make is such oddities are not just tricks or show-off devices – in terms of pop music's basic English, so to speak, they are real inventions.

In mid-'66 the now London-based Beatles released a single with McCartney's 'Paperback Writer' on the A-side and Lennon's 'Rain' on the flip. 'Paperback Writer' was a crazed tribute to the Beach Boys, with multi-tracked high harmonies that predicted the disco-era Bee Gees, which would prove impossible to perform live. It was a groundbreaking single, for at this point the studio took over from the stage as the pri-mary way people consumed pop. 'Rain' was possibly the densest Beatles recording. At all times, it sounds disorientating. Ringo's drumming is always slightly behind and off the beat, which he never plays the same way twice. The vocals are drawn out, tired in every possible way, and the way Lennon sings 'sun-*shine*' was the complete blueprint for Oasis. McCartney's bass is so fluid it flows off the turntable; Harrison's guitar circles and swirls like oppressive cloud cover. And, right on the tail, the tape gets flipped and Lennon's vocal comes out backwards. British psychedelia is invented right here.

> What about Gershwin? What about Duke Ellington? 'Sophisticated Lady', with those rich, chromatic parallel seventh chords? Yes, but that's the whole point. This pop generation has rejected that old chromatic sound as too sophisticated, the sound of an older, slicker generation . . . This new music is much more primitive in its harmonic language. It relies more on the simple triads, the basic harmony of folk music.

The girl-group sound, with its storytelling and naive tales of heartbreak, had become America's suburban folk music. It had survived Merseybeat by adapting to the nascent Motown sound (the Chiffons' 'Sweet Talkin' Guy', the Shirelles' 'Last Minute Miracle'), but by 1966 had entered its terminal phase. For once, a dying pop trend reached its apogee just as it turned from ripe to rotten. The Red Bird label – formed by Leiber and Stoller in 1964, and funded by doo-wop lover and Frankie Lymon producer George Goldner – was one of the dozen best the music industry has ever produced.

For such a short-lived label, started at precisely the wrong moment (weeks after 'I Want to Hold Your Hand' was on *The Ed Sullivan Show*), Red Bird was incredibly successful. It scored a US number one with its very first release – the Dixie Cups' stripped back, sweet, but impossible to resist wedding song 'Chapel of Love' – and barely paused for breath: the Jelly Beans' aching 'I Wanna Love Him So Bad' (US no. 10 '64), the Ad Libs' jazzy finger-snapper 'The Boy from New York City' (US no. 8 '65) and Bessie Banks's original, intensely sad version of 'Go Now' (a UK number one for the Moody Blues in January '65). Best of all were records by the Shangri-Las, myrmidons of melodrama, two sets of sisters – the blonde Weiss sisters, the brunette Ganser twins – from Cambria Heights in Queens. It could be because I first heard the song when I was six or seven,* a highly impressionable age, but I've never

---

* A perennial fairground favourite in the UK, it reached number three when it was reissued in 1972, and number seven just four years later.

perceived 'Leader of the Pack' (US no. 1, UK no. 12 '65) as a camp gag.
There are no affectations in Mary Weiss's delivery on this blow-by-blow
account of the grisly death of her boyfriend. Her singing voice, high and
quite piercing, is one of the most emotive on record, while her spoken-
word episodes on 'I Can Never Go Home Anymore' (US no. 6 '66) and
'Past, Present and Future' (US no. 59 '66) are positively haunted; on
the former her mother dies, on the latter ('don't try to touch me') she
suggests something worse. Pete Townshend has cited it as his favourite
pop single of all.

Just as the classic American girl-group sound began to dip, a new breed
of British girl singer had emerged in the mid-sixties: Dusty Springfield,
Sandie Shaw, Cilla Black, Lulu, Marianne Faithfull, Petula Clark, all – in
their varied ways – totems of late-twentieth-century British social history. There had been British female singers before, of course, but it often
seemed like only the fine details separated Alma Cogan (ballgowns) from
Edna Savage (married a wrong 'un), and Marion Ryan (she had twins
– more of them later) from Helen Shapiro (just fourteen, but with a crazily deep voice). These girls had rarely been major stars, and had almost
zero autonomy. By 1966 the way British girl singers were presented had
changed. They all had their own jobs: Cilla Black was the girl next door,
a Scouser with a slightly crooked fringe, flat chest and buck teeth; Dusty
Springfield was sophisticated and heavily bouffant – she'd forged her
own identity by studying the Brill Building catalogue, and she yearned
to record in the States; Petula was continental, a survivor of pre-rock and
child stardom who had an apartment in Paris and could probably show
you a thing or two beyond French kissing; Marianne was demure, well
spoken and sexy, with a quavering folkie voice, definitely out of your
league; Sandie was working-class and achievable – as a fashion role model
for girls and as a potential date for boys; Lulu was a Glaswegian bundle
of fun who could holler like a cross between Brenda Lee and the girl in
the Trio advert. Between them, they had it all sewn up.

The best singer, by a distance, was Dusty Springfield, a vision in
monochrome on *Ready Steady Go!*, eyes sooty with mascara. Originally
she was part of a folk trio called the Springfields; when she heard the
Exciters' girl-group screamer 'Tell Him' (US no. 4 '63) on a trip to New

York, she knew she had to make a break. Within weeks her knicker-bocker glory of a debut 'I Only Want to Be with You' (UK no. 4 '63, US no. 13 '64) was on the radio – and it hasn't been off the radio since. It liberated the Sandies, Lulus and Twinkles by reinventing the American girl-group sound for the girls of Bradford, Bellshill and Bournemouth. 1966 provided both Dusty's biggest hit, 'You Don't Have to Say You Love Me' (UK no. 1, US no. 4), which she had heard while compet-ing in the '65 San Remo song festival, and her best, the philosophical 'Goin' Back' (UK no. 10), written by Goffin and King. The lyric ('I'm returning to a place where I was young enough to know the truth') is perfectly matched by Johnny Franz's arrangement – compressed piano intro, muted woodwinds, a fast burst of brass. The vocal is soft, playful, seductive, an invitation to eternal happiness. It's not outrageous to sug-gest Dusty Springfield is the most emotionally engaging singer Britain has ever produced.

For every Dusty there were a dozen Glo Macaris, Martha Smiths and Cheryl St Clairs, teenagers shunted into Pye studio B for two hours one morning in 1966. A couple of singles usually emerged, a bunch of promises, then came marriage, kids and a chest in the attic with a few photos and some scratched discs with a bright-pink label, curios from a misspent youth that was over before it began. Lorraine Silver from Golders Green was just twelve when she cut the graphic 'Lost Summer Love', a Wigan Casino classic some years later. Dee King* ('It's So Fine') got her break by dint of running Birmingham group the Ivy League's fan club; then there was Maxine Darren from Manchester ('How Can I Hide It from My Heart'); Deano from Cardiff ('Baby Let Me Be Your Baby'); Nita Rossi from Bournemouth ('Untrue Unfaithful'); Jenny Wren from Dudley ('Chasing My Dream All over Town'); Truly Smith from Warrington ('My Smile Is Just a Frown Turned Upside Down'). They all cut one or two heart-rending singles, paeans to pain, gave us the essence of their teenage frustration. Almost without exception, they were washed up at seventeen.

---

* Dee became a successful TV actress in the seventies and eighties after she changed her name to Diane Keen.

The London hinterlands were particularly flush with pale-lipped singers. Essex alone gave us Hornchurch's Tammy St John, Purfleet's Pamela Blue, Southend's Antoinette and Dagenham's Sandie Shaw. Sandie rose above the also-rans after her manager, Eve Taylor, found 'Always Something There to Remind Me' on a song-shopping trip to the States. The Lou Johnson original, all side-street stoicism, collar turned up against the rain, had been pure New York, but with the Breakaways' chattering backing vocals, Kardomah cafe strings and Sandie's aching performance, the song's location became Streatham, Bolton, Walsall; this was the story of any girl in any town, any suburb, choking back tears at the bus stop outside the Mecca ballroom. Sandie and songwriter Chris Andrews then came up with one of the strongest runs of British singles ever: 'Girl Don't Come', 'I'll Stop at Nothing', 'Long Live Love', 'Message Understood', 'How Can You Tell', 'Tomorrow', 'Nothing Comes Easy', 'Run', 'Think Sometimes about Me', all UK Top 50 hits from '64 to '66. They were as close as pop got to British New Wave cinema: there was Sandie being chatted up by fast worker Albert Finney at the bar; there she was again, bespectacled this time, eating oranges on a park bench with Tom Courtenay. And she was the carefree beatnik who wanted to take her prevaricating boyfriend on the milk train down to London in *Billy Liar*, the girl who was pregnant at seventeen in *A Kind of Loving*, the girl who somehow made it onto TV in *Smashing Time*. She was all of them at the same time. Sandie Shaw conveyed the small dramas and private disappointments of girls outside Swinging London looking in.

'She's not really pretty in the accepted sense of the word,' said a columnist in *Fabulous* in 1965, 'but she's really got something. I think she's a knockout person.' Sandie did it for all the girls left stood up in the rain, for all the girls on Pye who never had a hit, the Lorraine Silvers and Tammy St Johns, the ones who evoked the rainy-street pathos of the rest of England in 1966. By the end of the decade she'd married a fashion designer, and even had her own range of shoes. All of this became possible with London as the pole star of pop culture.

Another Pye girl, Anita Harris, sang an obscure Burt Bacharach song called 'London Life' in '66: 'In this cold umbrella weather, boys and girls keep warm together . . . this London life is the life for me.' Not everyone was buying into this self-celebratory scene. At the end of the year, the Kinks released 'Dead End Street' (UK no. 5, US no. 73): 'We both want to work so hard, we can't get a chance.'* Within a year the pound would be devalued and the British economy in freefall. On the flip side of 'Dead End Street' was 'Big Black Smoke': if the A-side was about the indigenous working classes, the flip detailed, with the relish of Hogarth, a naive arriviste's descent into the gutter – 'Every penny she had was spent on purple hearts and cigarettes.' As it climaxes in a head-spinning drunken swirl, Dave Davies plays the grotesque town crier, screaming '*Oh yea!*' until the sorry girl puts her hands over her ears, closes her eyes and blocks out London.

Ray Davies was a sly writer, with an eye for small details. The Kinks could have followed a similar path to the Who if they'd wanted – they'd created the freakbeat template after all. But in late '65 Davies wrote four songs for a semi-acoustic EP called *Kwyet Kinks* and one of them, 'A Well Respected Man', was a slice of lower-middle-class observation straight out of Orwell's *Keep the Aspidistra Flying*. When it became a US Top 20 hit in early '66, Davies felt emboldened. His incisive satire made him the Wyndham Lewis of his day. In 1965 he had suffered a nervous break-down; during his recuperation he listened to Frank Sinatra, while taking note of the spiralling fame and prestige of his contemporaries (the Kinks, it should be noted, did extraordinarily badly from industry dealings in spite of their success). The first song he wrote on the other side of his breakdown was 'Sunny Afternoon' (UK no. 1, US no. 14 '66), which blended the blear of Sinatra's bar ballads with the Lovin' Spoonful's dap-pled drowsiness (their first '66 hit, 'Daydream', must have had a heavy radio presence) and a lyric about the poor-little-rich-boy Establishment. Was it about old money or new? Who was guilty of 'drunkenness and cruelty'? It could have been about an heir to a coal-mining fortune or a newly rich bass guitarist. The Kinks knew that swinging London

---

* Other non-swinging-sixties London songs include Donovan's 'Young Girl Blues', Lorraine Silver's 'Happy Faces' and – atmospherically if not directly lyri-cally – Jackie Trent's 'Where Are You Now'.

– especially in its *Sgt Pepper* fashions – was about imperial decline, an end, not a beginning. Look out, they said, here come the seventies.*

There are astonishing key changes, even tempo changes, astonishing cadences, unequal phrase lengths, the works.

'Dead End Street' ushered in a brief period of English social realism with a cartoonish bent: there was Cat Stevens's 'Matthew and Son' (UK no. 2 February '67), the Beatles' 'Penny Lane' (no. 2 March '67), Pink Floyd's 'Arnold Layne' (no. 20 April '67), the Who's 'Pictures of Lily' (no. 4 May '67) and the first David Bowie LP, which was peppered with gravediggers, adult babies and girls with a military fetish. All of them were a twisted response to an image of Britain emulsified in Roger Miller's 'England Swings' (US no. 2, UK no. 13 '66); these songs evoked a weird, repressed island where men in raincoats lurked in the bushes. Duncan Browne's 'On the Bombsite' was a gorgeous baroque single on Immediate that didn't chart, but was a tidy reminder that, yes, there were still bomb sites in London twenty years after the war. Britain was no longer a world power. Old military outfits were on sale in junk shops, picked up by the new anti-war generation. The fictitious England that existed in American imaginations – somewhere between *Oliver!* and *Uncle Fred in the Springtime* – was vividly and hilariously portrayed in Herman's Hermits' movie *Mrs Brown You've Got a Lovely Daughter*: starring Peter Noone as a Dickensian urchin with only a greyhound for company, it mangled the English language ('you saucy knave!') to its own ends. *Mrs Brown* was released in 1968, more than a year after the ground had shifted in the US: England had swung its last swing. Now California called the tune.

---

* When the seventies arrived, Ray Davies ceased cloaking his satire. Starting with an album called *Lola versus Powerman and the Moneygoround*, his decline was horribly swift and though there was the odd glimpse of his once pin-sharp writing skills ('Moments' in '71, 'Father Christmas' in '77, 'Better Days' in '81), the Kinks' dense concept albums became incredibly hard work to listen to. At the same time, curiously, they became a major stadium act in America.

ENDLESS SUMMER: THE BEACH BOYS

The Beach Boys had been the biggest noise of 1966. At the year's end, with the *NME* readers' poll rating them best group, ahead of the Beatles, they were putting the finishing touches to their *Smile* album. Its centre-piece would be 'Surf's Up', the song premiered in Leonard Bernstein's *Inside Pop*. With 'Good Vibrations' they had put themselves on another plane to anyone else: 'At present our influences are of a religious nature,' said Carl Wilson, and nobody questioned him. 'Not any specific religion but an idea based upon that of Universal Consciousness. The concept of spreading goodwill, good thoughts and happiness is nothing new, but it is our hope. The ideas are there in "God Only Knows", "Good Vibrations", "Heroes and Villains" and it is why the new LP is called *Smile*.' The February issue of *Rave* revealed: 'The Beach Boys hope to return to Britain in May, and we can be certain of one thing when they do – they'll bring all that's futuristic in pop music '67.' No one doubted this for a second.

The world waited for *Smile*. And waited. In the spring of '67 Capitol issued the two-year-old album track 'Then I Kissed Her' as a UK single, and it reached number four. Beyond that, nothing. The Beach Boys were due to headline the Monterey festival in California in June. It would be the non-pop world's first real glimpse of the flower generation. If 1966 had been about the common cause, with everyone rallying behind Brian's 'Good Vibrations' while hoping to emulate it for the good of all mankind, Monterey unintentionally built a wall that would take years to dismantle. Jimi Hendrix, Janis Joplin, the Who and Otis Redding would all take a major career step at Monterey. All could be regarded as 'heavy'. The Beach Boys were 'soft'.* When the line-up was announced, Brian Wilson – with a bunker mentality and the weight of the expectant, impatient pop world on his mind – panicked. A few weeks earlier the Beatles had released *Sgt Pepper's Lonely Hearts Club Band* to the widest acclaim of any modern pop album before or since – 'a milestone in pop music', *Record Mirror* had called it. Almost immediately, *Smile* was abandoned and the group pulled out of Monterey; the critical plaudits went instead to the Jimi Hendrix Experience, making their US debut. 'You will never hear surf music again,' drawled Hendrix. He wasn't kidding. By the end of '67 the Beach Boys were history. They had sold a million copies of every American album they released from 1962 to 1966; 1968's *Friends* could only shift twenty-three thousand copies.

* * *

Brian Wilson was pop's own Charlie Brown. He had been a sensitive boy, attuned to pre-rock harmonists the Four Freshmen on his radio, and clouted by his father Murray for the slightest misdemeanour. He grew up with younger brothers Dennis and baby Carl in Hawthorne, California, a nondescript adjunct to Los Angeles. Along with cousin

---

* As was the soulful Laura Nyro, who appeared clad in a black cape and, with her female backing singers, recalled a modern Chiffons. She got one of the worst receptions at Monterey. Legend has it she was booed, but footage released in the last ten years shows nothing worse than a tepid response, which was still enough to have the singer visibly welling up.

Mike Love, they sang harmonies around the kitchen table.

Beyond the Four Freshmen, their primary influences were Chuck Berry and the beach: Dennis loved to surf, Brian loved to watch the girls. Augmented by schoolfriend David Marks, the Wilson clan broke through with Brian's very first composition, 'Surfin'', a US number-seventy-five hit in March 1962.

Surf music, fast instrumentals with juddering post-Duane Eddy guitar simulating the feel of shooting the curl or catching a wave, had first broken cover with Dick Dale's 'Let's Go Trippin'', a US Hot Hundred hit in 1961, and it was an entirely localised sound, the California equivalent of Scottish bagpipe music. What bagpipe music didn't have, though, was the promise of sand and warmth and bikinis, a teenage Utopia, and so by 1962 surf music had infiltrated the Midwest and east coast. In 1963 it went global as the Surfaris' 'Wipe Out' and the Chantays' 'Pipeline' – gibberish jargon to the non-surfer – were Top 20 hits in Britain. The Beach Boys took this sonic thunder and added the Four Freshmen-styled harmonies they had sung since childhood. It should've sounded a bit daft, a one-off novelty at best, but instead this combination came over as the promise of a never-ending summer. Their subject matter was limited to youth, sun, girls, cars and surfing. Singles like 'California Girls' and 'Surfin' USA' are still brought out every April at the first hint of spring sunshine. They are still exactly what you need to hear to know that winter is over.

The Beach Boys' second single, 'Surfin' Safari', went Top 20; their third, 'Surfin' USA', reached number three. Surfing wasn't a local craze any more, and Brian Wilson – the group's chief songwriter – was turning out three albums a year of the stuff. The supply of hits – 'Surfer Girl', 'I Get Around', 'Fun, Fun, Fun' – seemed inexhaustible; he even gifted pals Jan and Dean a US number one with 'Surf City' (his dad *really* tore into him for that show of disloyalty). Brian was a one-man group and a super-producer all in one. In almost all his best songs – 'In My Room', 'The Lonely Sea', 'The Girls on the Beach', 'The Warmth of the Sun' – the music's sunny demeanour was tempered with an ache. Best of the lot was 1964's 'All Summer Long', both joyous and sad, a requiem for teenage kicks and Hondas in the heat. Amidst this thick cocktail of confused emotions, Brian Wilson's main memory of the summer is captured in the opening, *Animal House*-like couplet: 'Sitting in my car outside your house, remember when you spilt Coke all over your blouse?'

Brian Wilson's friend and drug buddy Loren Schwartz later recalled there was 'not an ounce of guile or malice in him'. His music was both immature and universal. He was an adult child, a genuine naif, breaking off from songwriting to watch episodes of *Flipper*, the dolphin whose young sidekick Sandy would invariably learn a life lesson which made Brian cry. On the Beach Boys' 1965 album *Today!* was a stumbling but beautiful song called 'In the Back of My Mind' that revealed Wilson was 'so happy at times that I break out in tears'. His emotions, whatever really was in the back of his mind, seemed to come out without any filter for what was deemed cool, or appropriate, or even musically acceptable, which is what made the Beach Boys' music the most emotionally satisfying in the whole modern pop canon.

The same album's 'She Knows Me Too Well' opened with 'Sometimes I have a weird way of showing my love', a line that wouldn't shock in the catalogues of Nick Cave or the Jesus and Mary Chain, but was pretty unsettling in the hands of the car-crazy Californians. Brian was aiming for Johnny Mercer but coming up proto-indie. Maybe with this in mind he turned to an untried lyricist called Tony Asher for help on the 1966 album *Pet Sounds*. Again, Wilson seemed unaware of any concept of roots credibility; Asher described himself as 'a nothing who had never done shit'* save write jingles for Mattel toys and Gallo wine.

Pet Sounds, released in May '66, was a song cycle, a love affair that began with 'Wouldn't It Be Nice' ('We could be married, and then we'd be happy') and ended with the gentle apocalypse of 'Caroline, No' ('Where is the girl I used to know?'). Nik Cohn described it as an album of 'sad songs about happiness', which is only partly true. Astonishing productions like 'Don't Talk (Put Your Head on My Shoulder)' are more complicated than that. The bassline is a beating heart, the ride cymbal is

---

* Asher wrote lyrics for Roger Nichols and the Small Circle of Friends in 1967, a west-coast soft-harmony act whose sole album is, in many ways, a twenty-something sequel to *Pet Sounds*. He was then badly hurt in a car crash which ended his brief music career.

a ticking clock; beyond that there is very little. 'Listen, listen, listen . . .' sings Brian, and then the strings dip down, like the singer's heart dropping into his stomach. He knows that this is it, these are the last hours they will spend together. He wants the moment to last forever, and it isn't a happy moment.

In 1964, while on tour, he had written a letter to his young bride Marilyn, ending it 'yours 'til God wants us to part'. With Tony Asher's help, the sentiment was built up into 'God Only Knows'. It's impossible to exaggerate how beautiful this song is. Everywhere, it takes risks. The opening line is 'I may not always love you', but the sentiment is that real love is all-consuming, it's frightening. The moral of the story is that love is about total surrender and without it there is no reason to live. Towards the end of the album is an extraordinary insight into Brian Wilson's darker thoughts, 'I Just Wasn't Made for These Times', on which his insecurities and shortcomings are carefully transcribed by Tony Asher and backed by an almost atonal harpsichord, plucked bass and theremin. Though he was the leader of the biggest pop group in America, though he was married to a thoughtful and loving woman, though he was only twenty-three, there was something incredibly old and incredibly melancholy within Brian Wilson. 'Sometimes I feel very sad,' the song goes, and no amount of convoluted Bob Dylan or Joni Mitchell wordplay is as effective or affecting.

The first cracks had appeared in 1964, when he found himself crying on a plane, unable to fly. He was replaced on tour by Glen Campbell* and, given time to mature in the studio, came up with *The Beach Boys Today* in 1965 and *Pet Sounds* in '66. When every insider from brother Dennis to Leonard Bernstein claimed the follow-up, *Smile*, was going to be five times better, expectations went through the roof. Dylan was a lone wolf with no dependants. There were four Beatles, so their load could be borne more easily. Also, strangely, no one made cosmic claims about what masterpiece they might be concocting in the aftermath

* As a thank you, Brian wrote and produced the single 'Guess I'm Dumb' for Campbell, which, recorded immediately before *Pet Sounds*, is a match for pretty much any track on that album.

of the wildly celebrated *Sgt Pepper* (which, seeing as these recordings included 'I Am the Walrus' and George Harrison's visceral noise collages 'It's All Too Much' and 'Only a Northern Song', is rather surprising). Brian Wilson was on his own, with some members of his own group deeply suspicious about his new music. Mike Love had warned him, 'Don't fuck with the formula,' when he first heard the backing tracks for *Pet Sounds*, and even forced one of the song titles to be changed from the hep 'Hang On to Your Ego' to the simpler 'I Know There's an Answer'. Brian himself would have been happy to turn back the clock, goof around in a little Honda and sing Four Freshmen songs for fun. He didn't mind being called a genius, but the family and record-company pressure, combined with his fondness for LSD, eventually tipped him over the edge.

In the UK, *Pet Sounds* had been greeted with unbridled awe, and reached number two in the album chart, only kept off the top spot by the *Sound of Music* soundtrack. Paul McCartney heard it, claimed it to be the greatest record ever made, and in a moment everybody wanted to know where Brian Wilson was heading next. Six months later, with the teen-age symphony 'Good Vibrations' number one worldwide, they got some idea – somewhere very different but at least as revolutionary as *Pet Sounds*.

During that summer Wilson had met a young session musician around Hollywood with the exotic name of Van Dyke Parks. 'I met Van Dyke at my friend Terry Melcher's house. I talked to him for a couple of hours and I said you have a good way with words. You seem to be very poetic, do you think you could write some lyrics? And he said sure, I probably could, so he came over to my house a couple of weeks later and we wrote "Heroes and Villains", "Surf's Up", "Wind Chimes" . . . it came together very quick, we wrote very fast.' At this point the new album, all written in the fragmented style of 'Good Vibrations', was to be called *Dumb Angel*, 'but Van Dyke said we need something more jovial and he thought of *Smile*. So I agreed. I said *great title*, let's go with it!'

The key word on *Smile* was humour – Wilson felt that the moment someone laughed they lost self-control, and that moment was a spiritual experience. He and Parks wrote their songs in a sandpit built in Brian's living room. At the same time, *Smile* would be an American travelogue, from Plymouth Rock to Diamond Head, in time as well as distance. Its ambition had no precedent; no idea seemed too oblique.

During the recording, Wilson decided that everybody involved had to be healthy. One night he dumped all of his living-room furniture and replaced it with blue tumbling mats, and out of this came the song 'I'm in Great Shape'. He wanted to create the feeling of 'being healthy in the morning, paradise in the morning in Hawaii'. So he opened a health-food shop called The Radiant Radish. He had to be talked out of opening a twenty-four-hour table-tennis shop soon after.

If opening shops as part of the creative process seemed wild, it was nothing alongside a piece of music called 'Mrs O'Leary's Cow'. Part of a suite called 'The Elements', representing fire, it was a terrifying atonal cacophony which abruptly ended the good vibrations and pushed Brian into a well of paranoia: he was convinced the music was responsible for a string of fires across Los Angeles. When his fellow band members returned from a fabulously successful tour of Europe to hear what their leader had been up to, they were horrified by the concrete abrasiveness of 'Mrs O'Leary's Cow'. Brian's confidence evaporated, Van Dyke Parks split the scene in the face of band hostility towards his evocative lyrics, and *Smile* was dumped. There's no doubt that, had *Smile* been released in late '66, it would have taken pop down a completely untrodden track. But in June '67 Brian Wilson pulled the group from their Monterey performance. He then left both *Smile* and the Beach Boys behind and, like Gerald at the end of *Women in Love*, walked off into the snow.

* * *

Post-Monterey, the Beach Boys flushed the bad karma of *Smile* out of their system with the emasculated *Smiley Smile*, the same songs that had been abandoned after a year's work, only this time recorded over ten days with a bag of weed and a portable tape recorder. Barely three months later came *Wild Honey*, an about-turn into DIY blue-eyed soul which confused the hell out of a pop public wondering how to come down from their summer '67 high.

In the early seventies, isolated from his band and beset with mental and pharmaceutical problems, the touchstone album for American pop's erstwhile golden boy was Randy Newman's *Sail Away*, and in particular the title song. Newman was painting a picture of America as broad and fanciful as the golden, perfect California dream outlined by Brian Wilson ten years earlier, but in the Watergate era.

By this point, Brian was living in his bedroom, overweight, lank-haired, creatively stymied by bandmates and inner demons. Though he was ill, he was still expected to earn a living for the Beach Boys. It was hard to run away as they were essentially his family. They waited for him to snap out of his deepening depression throughout the late sixties and seventies. Only music could end Brian's crisis, though, and he knew that if he carried on listening to *Sail Away* he could draw on it. The song was about how a free spirit can be tricked and trapped by economic greed: 'We will cross the mighty ocean . . . it's great to be an American.'

In 1971 Brian Wilson wrote a song called "Til I Die' for the *Surf's Up* album: 'I'm a leaf on a windy day, pretty soon I'll be blown away. How long will the wind blow? Until I die.' But he didn't die; he went into deep freeze, and only re-emerged at the turn of the twenty-first century. By this time Dennis and Carl were dead, and Mike Love – for his part in the collapse of the Beach Boys – was possibly the most reviled person in all of pop. Things were different. Away from the old, poisonous environment, surrounded by well-wishers, and with the help of a bunch of fans who were also a tidy power-pop band called the Wondermints, he was finally convinced to revisit *Smile* and play it live.

Crawdaddy's Paul Williams encapsulated the feel of the Beach Boys' music in three words: warmness, serenity, friendship. For this reason, there is more love directed at Brian Wilson than anyone else in this book. One of the most poignant moments of the 2004 *Smile* shows at the Royal Festival Hall wasn't musical at all. As Brian left the stage to a standing ovation his shirt caught on something; he tried to walk off, his feet kept moving, but he was held back. Everyone wanted to run on stage and help him, wanted to help Brian Wilson. After what seemed an age he noticed what was wrong, but not before he had appeared, in front of two thousand people, as a lost little boy, Charlie Brown aged sixty-five, bumbling and bemused.

THE GOLDEN ROAD: SAN FRANCISCO AND PSYCHEDELIA

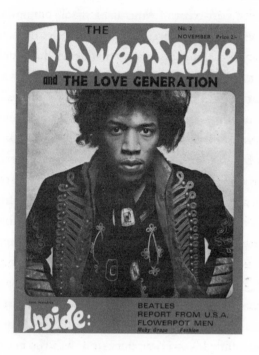

The sixties were like science fiction.
Paul Kantner

The Beatles first took acid when John, George and their girlfriends had
their drinks spiked by their dentist, one John Riley, at a dinner party
in 1965. The four of them left the party unaware of what they'd taken,
and entirely ignorant of what LSD could do. They got into George's
Mini, he drove into the West End, and they all went to the Ad Lib, a
club with fur-lined walls which was on the top floor of a building on
Leicester Place – on the way up they all thought the lift was on fire, and
ran in screaming. After a few rum and Cokes, George somehow drove
them back to his home in Weybridge: 'We were going about ten miles

an hour,' John Lennon told *Rolling Stone* in 1970, 'but it seemed like a thousand and Patti was saying, "Let's jump out and play football."' Back at George's place, John was convinced the house was a submarine and that he was driving it: 'God, it was just terrifying, but it was fantastic.' The Beatles were among the very few people in Britain to have taken LSD, but on the west coast of America, a whole community was going through a similar lysergic experience.

Psychedelia was where modern pop first decided it could look beyond the dancefloor. It was all about inner space, although it was grounded in one specific city – San Francisco. And, like that city's best beat writers,* it leaned towards the rediscovery of a sense of wonder, it set out in search of a new sensory excitement. It was a leap into the unknown.

In many ways the San Francisco scene resembled the Liverpool beat boom of four years earlier. Both cities looked west, out to sea, separate from the rest of the country; both were known to be left-leaning and politically active; and both had a large dollop of civic pride which rubbed off on the young, who were happy to follow and support their local acts. Where Liverpool had cellars, San Francisco had ballrooms – the Avalon, the Carousel, the Longshoremen's Hall. Why San Francisco? It was a big city but small enough to sustain a scene – not manic like New York, not spread out like Los Angeles. One major difference from the Mersey boom, though, was that the Frisco bands were frequently not natives: Janis Joplin had arrived from Texas, Steve Miller from Canada. San Francisco was a post-war beacon. Drawn to the city as Dada's creators had been drawn to Zurich, incomers saw the city as neutral ground where you could walk the streets and not get your head kicked in for having hair that grazed your collar. The beat scene, which was centred around Lawrence Ferlinghetti's City Lights bookstore and publishing imprint, drew in small-town outcasts, intellectuals and would-be intellectuals, and they soon built a small hipster community in the low-rent Haight-Ashbury district.

In the rambling Victorian houses, bands lived together (just like the

---

* Specifically there was Richard Brautigan, the writer and poet who ended up recording a spoken-word album for the Beatles' Apple label.

Beatles did in *Help!*) and could play for kicks, practise, experiment, with no real plans to go out and work as jobbing musicians as the Searchers or the Hollies did. There was an acceptance of bohemian values, a more relaxed playfulness than pop had seen before: Moby Grape were even named after a punchline – what's big and purple and lives in the ocean? Unsurprisingly, the music was initially a little ramshackle. With most bands drawing on blues, folk, country and jazz, the result was not unlike an improv extension of folk rock – if there was a Top 20 forerunner to the SF sound it was the east coast's Lovin' Spoonful. The Beau Brummels, early US adopters of Beatle haircuts, had been the first Bay Area group to score nationally with 'Laugh Laugh' (US no. 15) and 'Just a Little' (US no. 8) – both melancholy, fogged Merseybeat – in '65; more typical were the Warlocks, who started out similarly Beatle-bound but, on stage, stretched their songs out over six, seven, eight minutes. In 1966 they changed their name to the Grateful Dead.

It wasn't any predilection for jazz or even the sea air that fuelled this localised creativity. Above all else, the San Francisco scene was about acid. Another oddball drawn to the Bay Area was a Russian-speaking, bee-keeping former ballet student from Kentucky called Owsley Stanley. Enrolling at Berkeley in 1963, he discovered LSD for himself, learnt how to make it, then began cooking it up and handing it out to friends and the favoured; all people had to do was stick out their hand and maintain eye contact, and he'd keep pouring them acid that was very strong and very pure.

The San Francisco bands* weren't even aiming to make records, let alone hits. This musical freedom was new and, with acid leading the musicians on, it had no boundaries. A go-for-broke philosophy developed; the laces of conventional chord changes and song structures were loosened and came undone. It's hard to know whether the Jefferson Airplane's 'White Rabbit' (US no. 8 '67) is one long verse, one long chorus or – climbing ever higher, increasing in intensity from its ominous

* They were now called 'bands' rather than 'groups', a subtle change of terminology that suggested outlaw status, a bunch of people with a single vision who relied on nobody else.

fidgety intro to its climactic cry of 'feed your head' – just riffing on
Ravel's 'Boléro'. Whichever, it doesn't sound much like 'She Loves You'.

The Jefferson Airplane, led by ex-model Grace Slick and the gentle guitarist Marty Balin, were the first band to make a noise nationally. They had their own bumper stickers made that read 'The Jefferson
Airplane Loves You'. After becoming a local cause célèbre with much
support from the *San Francisco Chronicle* (where the Airplane's manager Bill Thompson just happened to work) they headlined the Human
Be-In at the Polo Grounds, Golden Gate Park, in January '67, where
speakers included Jerry Rubin, Allen Ginsberg, Lawrence Ferlinghetti
and Timothy Leary. Participants were urged to bring flowers, beads,
costumes, feathers, bells, cymbals, flags and food to share. The Jefferson
Airplane entertained, while the A&R men from LA and NYC looked
on. By this point people had messianic expectations for LSD. They
didn't want to talk about what a hellhole of homeless, drug-addled teens
Haight-Ashbury was rapidly becoming, they wanted to talk about their
hopes. They wanted to talk about how there would be universal love in
the near future, and how we'd all go back to farming. Cattle, they said,
would be grazing in Times Square in the year 2000.

Canadian Steve Miller had a clearer head. He noted that the city's
flower-power scene was largely a social trip; the Airplane weren't playing
that much music and spent as much time handing out flowers as they
did rehearsing. If these lightweights can get a deal, figured Miller, so can
I. Capitol signed the hastily assembled Steve Miller Band for $50,000.

The most enduring psychedelia has a tightness, even if it remains
structurally weird. Donovan's 'Sunshine Superman' (US no. 1, UK no.
2 '66) still sounds gently, warmly lysergic; late-in-the-day cash-in 'Green
Tambourine' by the Lemon Pipers (US no. 1, UK no. 8 '68) has enough
vim (and sitar, and wild percussion) to keep it on the radio in the twenty-
first century. This is not true of the vast majority of San Francisco-scene
recordings. Much San Francisco psychedelia failed to communicate the
highs it was meant to soundtrack. It could sound self-indulgent, strung-
out, little more than a twenty-minute variation on a Bo Diddley line. Yet
the SF bubble was secure in the knowledge of its own superiority – the
drugs also enabled musicians to say, 'We know something you don't.'

As it turned out, the best psychedelic group on the west coast were down the road, in a city that hip San Franciscans regarded as the capital of everything manufactured – Los Angeles. They were called Love, and they had two leaders: a mixed-race hardnut R&B guitarist called Arthur Lee and a blond boy-toy with an unfashionable love of Broadway and flamenco called Bryan MacLean. They began as a fierce six-piece garage band who dropped acid and lived together in a house called the Castle, previously the home of Bela Lugosi.

Their name was ironic. Lee was rumoured to have killed a roadie, and two other members – Ken Forssi and Johnny Echols – paid for their drug habits by robbing donut stands. Recording their first album in January '66, engineer Bruce Botnick remembers that Lee was 'so high all the time that he wasn't high. He had achieved what they call clear light.' Yet once they'd cemented their place as the toughest, punk-est folk-rockers in LA with the insanely intense hit '7 and 7 Is' (US no. 33 '66), their music transformed into a unique, incredibly delicate form of psychedelia. For their second album, *Da Capo* in early '67, they were reinforced with a flautist called Tjay Cantrelli, and their drummer Alban 'Snoopy' Pfisterer switched to harpsichord. Arthur Lee, possibly as a non-generic side effect of taking hallucinogenic drugs, stopped roaring like an ursine Jagger and instead modelled his vocals on crooner Johnny Mathis. Essentially they sounded like off-kilter easy listening, a Herb Alpert, Tijuana Latin sound with flecks of feedback and lyrics like 'Oh the snot has caked against my pants.' Love's song titles were a way into their elliptical, gently apocalyptic netherworld: 'Alone Again Or', 'Orange Skies', 'Stephanie Knows Who', 'Andmoreagain'. When Lee and MacLean combined with arranger David Angel on *Forever Changes* at the end of 1967, they created something no one in San Francisco had managed – a melodic, concise, hypnotic album.

Though acid may seem revelatory for the first two or three trips, it starts to become a hall of mirrors thereafter. Love's *Forever Changes* has an inexact beauty: someone randomly shouts 'Face!' in one song; the needle jumps deliberately, repeatedly, on the fade of 'The Good Humor Man He Sees Everything Like This'; the guitar wig-out of 'A House Is Not a Motel' ends in mid-air; 'Andmoreagain' climbs to a lyric of 'And you don't know how much I love you', and its sudden conventionality is shocking, genuinely moving. *Forever Changes* is exquisitely arranged, but everything is slightly out of place. When the Manson gang wanted to unsettle Beach Boy Dennis Wilson, they broke into his house, moved three or four things around in the living room, then left. *Forever Changes* is similarly intimidating. It is certainly mind-altering. On the back of the album cover the band stand around, laughing at an off-camera gag, looking like they could be posing for a men's clothing catalogue. Arthur Lee, though, is looking straight at the camera, holding two parts of a broken vase. What's wrong with this picture?

Love's masterpiece peaked at 152 on the *Billboard* album chart.* 'We all thought we were on a rocket ship that was going to continue to go straight up,' said Bryan MacLean. 'I thought this was always going to be my life.' The band disintegrated in 1968; Lee's subsequent career was rarely more than disappointing, while MacLean never made another record.

Psychedelia, meanwhile, was absorbed and processed, with ruminants like the Doors chewing it over and spitting it out in a radio-friendly format. Psychedelic bands were singing about a world that the majority of listeners had never experienced – tuning in without either turning on or dropping out. In London, the 14 Hour Technicolor Dream festival at Alexandra Palace was peopled not only by flower children and a hungry media, but by confused mods who had turned up to see what the fuss was all about.† Those who didn't buy into it went home, dug out their Tamla 45s, began to scour junk shops and market stalls for more mid-sixties thrills, and helped to lay the roots of the northern-soul scene.

In the States, mysticism was used as a cloak. The Doors dropped a few quotes from Lorca and teen-rebel fodder into their interviews: 'The

---

* Britain loved *Forever Changes* – considering the group never played outside California, let alone touring in Europe, its number-twenty-four chart placing in early '68 is miraculous.
† Naysayers may well have been impressed by the Flies, a tough-sounding act who bridged the gap between tight, soul-flecked beat and trippy Anglo pop. Playfully cynical about the whole event, they chucked flour rather than flowers at the audience, which guaranteed they were never invited to another festival.

most loving parents and relatives commit murder with smiles on their faces,' said singer Jim Morrison. 'They force us to destroy the person we really are.' Morrison dared you to point and laugh at such pronouncements, and wrote the primary rule for all of pop's future satyrs and self-taught poets, from Lou Reed to Patti Smith to Nick Cave: stare down your detractors, and don't blink.

On stage Morrison was saturnine and wore tight leather pants. Cold and aloof, he would pout and sneer at the audience; he never smiled. The Doors, said Australian writer Lilian Roxon, had 'poetry, violence, mystery, suspense and terror'. That they moved swiftly from the underground to pop crossover was a major shock to their loyal LA fans, many of whom rapidly disowned them, but it was no surprise to anyone else because – amid the oedipal tracts and suggestions of the satanic – they wrote some prime whistleable pop. Two of their best singles – 'Light My Fire' (US no. 1 '67) and 'Touch Me' (US no. 3 '69) – came from guitarist Robby Krieger, and were covered to great effect by José Feliciano and French yé-yé girl Katty Line respectively. It wouldn't have happened to the Grateful Dead. On top of this, Morrison could roar or whisper, his voice was deep, chocolate brown, he was a new kind of crooner. 'Riders on the Storm' (US no. 14, UK no. 22 '71) could have been Mel Tormé singing a Frankie Laine cowboy song if it wasn't for the rain-sodden backing track, the neon blur of electric piano and lines like 'There's a killer on the road, his brain is squirming like a toad.' Some felt betrayed by rock's first poet – even their producer Paul Rothchild quit midway through sessions for the final album, *LA Woman*, allegedly calling it 'cocktail music'. But what had people expected of the Doors? That their unsmiling demeanour and loud, organ-heavy rock could bring deliverance, that it was 'real' unlike the studio-bound Lemon Pipers? There's no such thing as a discourse that delivers only truth. So 'Riders on the Storm' sounded like Frankie Laine – so what? No one was betrayed.

Anyway, the Doors never cracked jokes, became the first major rock act with a logo, usually included an epic closing track on each of their albums ('The End', 'When the Music's Over', 'The Soft Parade'), and were hugely successful. In these respects, they created a new American rock template. In their wake came San Diego's Iron Butterfly, whose portentous album *In-a-Gadda-Da-Vida* sold twenty-five million copies solely on the strength of its seventeen-minute-long title track. Yet, in the heavy stakes, both the Doors and the 'Fly were trumped by a Long Island act called Vanilla Fudge, whose shtick was to re-cut hit records – the Supremes' 'You Keep Me Hangin' On' (US no. 6, UK no. 17), Cher's 'Bang Bang', the Beatles' 'Ticket to Ride' – at half speed, adding wounded-lion vocals and overloaded church organ to increase the angst. They also recorded a soulfully strained 1967 Coke jingle – an unorthodox way to stick it to the Man. Quite possibly they were the most hilarious group of all time. Their second album, *The Beat Goes On*, attempted to condense the entire history of music, from Mozart to Elvis via Stephen Foster, inside half an hour. You had to admire their ambition, but such a grave undertaking needed gentle hands to guide it, maybe a George Martin at the helm; the Fudge had George 'Shadow' Morton, the man who had discovered the Shangri-Las and written 'Leader of the Pack'. Morton was a great producer, but subtlety really wasn't his strong point. Tracks on *The Beat Goes On* were interspersed with quotes from Winston Churchill and Franklin D. Roosevelt – an early example of sampling – as well as the four members of Vanilla Fudge. Kids were wide open to this stuff; those who had taken acid had their critical faculties impeded, while non-trippers believed their turned-on friends. Vanilla Fudge's weight and density found plenty of takers and created stoner rock, loud music to pass out to; they are godfathers to Black Sabbath and, in turn, Monster Magnet and Soundgarden.

Acid was not freely available in Britain in 1966. There was no Owsley in Bradford or Bracknell. Instead, the influence of psychedelia was largely third-hand, via the in-the-know (essentially the Beatles) or the drug-inspired music that made it onto the pirate stations ('Good Vibrations', the Association's 'Along Comes Mary'). An emergent, homegrown strain of psychedelia came from Cambridge. The Pink Floyd were well-spoken, decidedly middle-class boys who played at devastatingly loud volumes, with oil-lamp projections adding another dimension to the off-kilter sound. 'We're a very young group, not in age, but in experience,' they would coyly say. 'We can't go on doing clubs and ballrooms. We want a brand-new environment, and we've hit on the idea of using a big top. We'll have a huge screen 120 feet wide and forty feet high and project films and slides.' Singer Syd Barrett had a mop of curls and an intense look of obtuse ambition. Bassist Roger Waters claimed coolly that they weren't interested in chart positions, but Barrett wrote songs like 'Arnold Layne' (UK no. 20 '67) and 'See Emily Play' (UK no. 6 '67) to augment their freeform cacophony, and they were gently weird but incredibly catchy. Syd Barrett wanted to be a pop star. But in 1967 he ingested vast amounts of acid, which derailed his plans after just three singles and one magical album. *The Piper at the Gates of Dawn* defined a thoroughly English take on psychedelia, a mix of dark, driving floor-fillers ('Lucifer Sam'), space rituals ('Astronomy Domine') and twisted nursery rhymes ('The Gnome', 'Bike', 'The Scarecrow') with Lewis Carroll lyrics that suggested spiked cups of Earl Grey. When Barrett stood on stage, unable to sing a note, his bandmates took him to see R. D. Laing and were told there was nothing he could do to help. Barrett had given himself permanent brain damage. Having to cut loose from their stricken songwriter in mid-'68, the remaining band members decided to try and scratch out a living, playing their mumbled, unmelodic jams on the student circuit. As it turned out, this would be their salvation.

The influence of Floyd and *Sgt Pepper* was all over the British pop of late '67 and '68: the woody sadness of the Mellotron – first heard on 'Strawberry Fields Forever' – was the defining sound of the year, along with lyrics about wishing wells, steam trains and honey for tea. Birmingham band Traffic had emerged in the spring of '67 with 'Paper Sun' (UK no. 5), a tough mod sound with a sitar hook, but 'Hole in My Shoe' (UK no. 2) was the full *Alice in Wonderland*, English psychedelic flowering: 'I walked through the sky where an elephant's eye was looking at me from a bubblegum tree.' There was a Mellotron, a spoken interlude about a giant albatross narrated by a small child, and a strange, wellington-boots-through-mud rhythm track. It was tremendously over the top. Keith West's 'Excerpt from *A Teenage Opera*' roped in a whole kiddie chorus, as well as balalaikas and cornets, for an absorbing

Toytown Spector sound which reached number two in the autumn – producer Mark Wirtz hinted that the 'opera' was complete but it soon became clear he'd been caught out by the excerpt's success. Still, if you're looking for a British equivalent to *Smile*, the fragments that remain of the *Teenage Opera* make it a good call.

Beyond this handful of hits were 45s by short-lived groups like Ice ('Anniversary of Love', 'Ice Man'), the Virgin Sleep ('Secret') and the Fairytale (who created a creaking-floorboard sense of unease on 'Guess I Was Dreaming') – all of them had probably been playing Motown covers in '66, or had been Swinging Blue Jeans soundalikes in '64. The main difference between them and their US counterparts was that they were only given deals of one or two singles, and so condensed all their ideas inside three minutes; American bands had a forty-minute album to play with, stretching their initial ideas to breaking point almost as soon as they opened their mouths. While Tintern Abbey's 'Vacuum Cleaner' or the Factory's droning 'Path through the Forest' pick you up, disorient you gloriously for three minutes, then drop you back in your armchair before the kettle's even boiled, the careers of American bands like Autosalvage, Clear Light and Mad River were stillborn; their albums remain largely unloved, with blues jams and freaky guitar work-outs extended to fill the empty inches on the vinyl. While this format created the possibilities of psychedelia, from which an elemental, pan-global music could be created, any band that had just one good idea was always going to sound stronger on a seven-inch single than on an album. Among those who ultimately benefited from a frugal record company were the Beautiful Daze ('City Jungle'), the Calico Wall ('Flight Reaction') and the Caretakers of Deception ('Cuttin' Grass'), who were all offered just a solitary single on which to promote their singular psychedelic vision.

British psych records were generally more red-blooded. This was down to superior studios, a love of angles and musical briskness among musicians, and the 45 factor. And yet the American acts were almost always more out on a limb, with a more radical musical and linguistic vocabulary. Put simply, they sounded more like a revolution than Pink Floyd, or anything Britain – with a child's kaleidoscope pressed tightly to its eye – had to offer. If a group could blend the two distinct styles, chances were the alchemy would provide a psychotropic journey without equal – and so it proved.

The golden ticket arrived in the hand of Animals' bassist Chas Chandler when Keith Richards's girlfriend Linda Keith told him about a wild but shy guitarist she'd seen at Cafe Wha? in Greenwich Village. Chandler was about to quit his disintegrating group and looking to manage someone: Jimi Hendrix – with the name and the face of a ready-made star – suited him just fine. He brought his charge back to London and harnessed him to bassist Noel Redding and drummer Mitch Mitchell. If the Jefferson Airplane wanted to explore your mind, the Jimi Hendrix Experience sounded like they wanted to tear through it on a silver rocket. Chandler was smart enough to know that his feral boy – who had already been sacked from a few tight, touring R&B groups for being too musically wayward and unreliable – would have the most impact if he was contained by three-minute singles and by his two bandmates, similarly untamed but instilled with a zipped-up British aggression. His plan worked: almost incredibly, they gelled like no trio before or since.

In no time the Jimi Hendrix Experience scored four UK Top 20 hits – 'Hey Joe', 'Purple Haze', 'The Wind Cries Mary', 'Burning of the Midnight Lamp' – that made everything else in 1967 sound as lightweight as balsa wood. The music poured out of Hendrix's fingers, he made it look so effortless. He also happened to be an A-grade showman; he claimed to be from Mars, dressed outrageously, was both boyishly cute and sexual as hell, and he had a laugh in his voice as infectious as Alma Cogan's. Jimi Hendrix, the original dandy highwayman. 'Rock is so much fun,' he said. 'That's what it's all about – filling up the chest cavities and empty kneecaps and elbows.' He filled them up with guitar music that recalled the noise of roaring lions, Spitfire dogfights and racing-green Ferraris tearing around Brands Hatch.

Yet without Chas Chandler maybe none of this would have happened. Hendrix needed to be kept on a tight leash, without which his psychedelic pyrotechnics – which he happily alloyed to anything from *Sgt Pepper*'s title track to the Troggs' 'Wild Thing' to the *Coronation Street* theme* – might have been dripped randomly, wastefully, over aimless jams. The inevitable split happened in '68 after three Experience albums and one more single, a roof-lifting take on Bob Dylan's 'All along the Watchtower' (UK no. 5, US no. 20 '68), which soundtracked the paranoia and viciousness on the streets that year as well as anything.

Hendrix, though, was utterly outside of and totally uninterested in the disciplines and mechanics of hit singles. 'I don't want to be a clown any more. I don't want to be a "rock & roll star",' he told *Rolling Stone*'s Sheila Weller in late '69 as he ate a Theragran and drank a shot of tequila in milk for breakfast. By then he was free of Chandler and Redding, keeping Mitchell on as a part-timer, indulging his tastes for the avant, and mixing with jazzers and black militants who he worried didn't take him seriously. The ensuing *Band of Gypsies* album was flabby. Adrift without the Experience, he died in 1970.

If much of the San Francisco scene's music is forgotten, its myth was hugely influential, redirecting pop's geographical focus from Britain to the American west coast for a whole decade. Concretely, it gave us the rock concert. Until the late sixties, package tours ruled in the UK, and sock hops in the US: you got to see a lot of star names perform a few songs through a sound system more suited to announcing train delays than psychedelic rock. In San Francisco in 1966 they became 'concerts', announced by posters with vivid colours, swirling fonts and wild imagery; bands had their own sound systems built to accommodate the volume of the new music. One promoter, Bill Graham, bought up all the ballrooms, including the Carousel, which had been owned by members of the Grateful Dead and Jefferson Airplane. The early boho fantasy of right-on, acid-inspired socialism buckled and the era began of the rock concert as money-spinner rather than mere promotional tool for recorded matter.

San Francisco was also the birthplace of FM rock radio, playing album-based music for the first time – even the pirate-radio stations in

---

* Hendrix morphed the *Coronation Street* theme, a melancholy piece of trad jazz which he heard soon after arriving in Britain, on the Experience's debut album, *Are You Experienced*: it's the unlikely root for the liquid jazz-rock of 'Third Stone from the Sun'.

Britain would leaven their more outré 45s with Tom Jones to keep the mums on board. In the States, the fact that few FM radio receivers were owned by the general public left a void for the counterculture to fill with music that was largely ignored by mainstream AM radio. First out of the blocks was Berkeley's KPFA, which had broadcast Allen Ginsberg's 'Howl' in its entirety in 1956; by '67 it was playing the Grateful Dead's side-long 'Dark Star'.

Meanwhile, out in the San Francisco suburbs, sci-fi fan and rock 'n' roll enthusiast Greg Shaw was producing a mimeographed sheet called *Mojo Navigator* (or, to give it its full title, *Mojo-Navigator Rock and Roll News*) full of ravings about the music he loved. Until now, reviews of modern pop had rarely been more analytical than 'solid beaty number', tucked away as a snippet of news between tour dates and adverts. *Mojo Navigator* was full of valuable secret info, and the expanding psych scene gave Shaw more meat to sink his teeth into. There were few completists, scholars and connoisseurs around in 1966. Records were simply forgotten as soon as they dropped off the chart. Greg Shaw was the first person to connect an amorphous gaggle of pop fanatics and give them a black-and-white photostat they could look to for inspiration and succour. Soon it was followed by Paul Williams's *Crawdaddy*, Jann Wenner's *Rolling Stone* and, in March '69, by *Creem*; high-quality, modern pop journalism was no longer the preserve of *Esquire* or the *Sunday Times*.

And there was more. The looseness of San Francisco's collar allowed the idea of an all-girl band, playing their own instruments, to become part of the scene without being patronised. While others did exist (the British-based Goldie and the Gingerbreads, ragged sister act the Shaggs from Fremont, New Hampshire, and Michigan's Pleasure Seekers – featuring a young Suzi Quatro – who played at army camps for returning Vietnam vets), the Ace of Cups were possibly the first not to be seen as eye candy or novelties.* They were more like a counterculture Shangri-Las: 'Glue' was an anti-capitalist screed – 'Hello, ladies, are you feeling

---

* Jimi Hendrix told *Melody Maker* in December '67 about 'this girl group, Ace of Cups, who write their own songs and the lead guitarist is hell, really great'. It's too bad they never made any records at the time – their demos were finally released in 2003.

unloved, unwanted and miserable? If you had our product, everyone would love you!' backed by yells of 'It's bad for you, but buy it.'*

And more, again – San Francisco also provided the first group looking for direct inspiration from pop's immediate past. The Flamin' Groovies had no time for mind expansion but were intent on keeping the no-nonsense recent past – whether it was Lovin' Spoonful jug-band music or Merseybeat stomps – alive in '67. Their long career was patchy but they scored at least one genuine tears-on-the-Mecca-dancefloor master-piece, 'Shake Some Action', in 1976.

Then there was Country Joe and the Fish, whose mix of cool jazz, folk and heavy politics made them possibly the ultimate SF band. It seemed as if they came and went in the Summer of Love, with a memo-rable Monterey set and scrapbook album (*Electric Music for the Mind and Body*), but they had been in there right at the beginning. The Fish's major contribution was their DIY approach, self-produced records and tapes that they had stuffed into manila envelopes back in 1965, as if their music was mail art. As the '67 sun faded, the reality of big business left them drained. 'We were like this little dreamland,' sighed Country Joe McDonald. 'It was a rare moment for those of us who made music, being in this really happy environment full of really intelligent people.'

Beyond this, there was simply a lot more water to swim in. It felt like San Francisco had given modern pop a sixth and a seventh sense, some-thing that even the hep parents who dug Elvis and the Beatles couldn't really get their heads around.

* San Francisco's socialist dream was largely wishful thinking, even in its Haight heyday. At the Monterey festival, Big Brother and the Holding Company decided not to allow D. A. Pennebaker's film crew to film and record them without pay-ing them, and ordered the crew to turn their cameras off. They played two more songs – including 'Ball and Chain' – the following night purely for the cameras. The counterculture born in San Francisco, the international utopian move-ment, was genuinely popular with the masses – popular enough to be co-opted by Coca-Cola as early as 1971. The New Seekers' 'I'd Like to Teach the World to Sing' was written for the Coke ad by Roger Cook and Roger Greenaway, and wistfully predicted a future of 'apple trees and honey bees and snow-white turtle doves'. This was how the regular world saw hippies; this was pop's final distilla-tion of Kerouac, Kesey, Leary and Love. It was a UK number one.

POP GETS SOPHISTICATED: SOFT ROCK

Picture yourself in a boat on a river. Close your eyes; what do you hear? There's the mesmeric sound of a distant harpsichord. Slowly, it is joined by a string quartet, a Spanish guitar, some echoed exotic percussion. And then, like celestial birdsong, four-part harmonies. The sound is light but yearning, delicate but hugely evocative: it could be winter outside but in your ears it's June.

Pet Sounds and *Sgt Pepper* were greeted as landmark records on release, not just as albums that were more a suite than a collection of songs, but in their instrumentation and musical complexity. They didn't rock in the way that Little Richard, the Swinging Blue Jeans or the Kingsmen rocked. They included found sounds and time changes and songs that lasted more than five minutes without degenerating into blues jams. You might well hear fuzz guitar in the mix but you were just as likely to hear piccolos and bass harmonicas and marimbas.

'Pop Trend: Sophisticated, Serious' ran a *Billboard* headline in September '67. The term 'progressive rock' had yet to be coined, but there were clear signs of progress on 'sophisticated, serious' records like the Young Rascals' 'Groovin'' (US no. 1, UK no. 8 '67) and the Association's 'Never My Love' (US no. 2 '67). Soft rock evolved from a variety of sources, notably surf (the Beach Boys) and folk (the Mamas and Papas), but it also provided an opening for a bunch of mavericks who may have adored the Beatles but were never going to stand behind Marshall stacks and bellow. These writers had a strong sense of the Great American Songbook and, quite often, sharp humour: Randy Newman, Curt Boettcher, Van Dyke Parks. A harmony outfit called Harpers Bizarre mixed Simon and Garfunkel covers ('Feelin' Groovy') with Cole Porter ('Anything Goes') and appeared on their album covers behind the wheel of a Ferrari or clasping a glass of brandy by candlelight. 'I write with a flourish of Hassidic melodies,' said the Association's Terry Kirkman. 'I'm moved by Stravinsky and Copland. I think in those terms when I produce and arrange.'

From Greenwich Village, the Mamas and Papas were torchbearers for soft rock. They surfaced with 'California Dreaming' in early '66 (US no. 4, UK no. 23), a single that summed up a feeling: it was reaching forward for something, someone, somewhere over the rainbow; the sound was pure sunshine but there was more than a hint of sadness in it.* Visually they were cartoonish, with plus-size Mama Cass Elliot and impossibly pretty Mama Michelle Phillips hogging the camera; sad-eyed Denny Doherty and John Phillips, who looked like a mean cowboy and

---

* The Mamas and Papas' sound was hugely influential, with acts like the 5th Dimension (who added a touch more soul), Millennium (a touch more rock) and Free Design (a touch more jazz) working around their template. The upbeat feel of these groups has earned them the retrospective label 'sunshine pop', though, given the deep darkness in John Phillips's life story, it doesn't seem entirely appropriate.

was married to Michelle, were the Papas. They harmonised like a dream, they were 'now people', and quickly scored two more transatlantic hits with 'Monday Monday' (US no. 1, UK no. 3) and 'I Saw Her Again' (US no. 5, UK no. 11), loaded with *ba-ba-ba*s, celestes, cellos and a perceptible warmth.

Off stage, John Phillips was also responsible for putting the Monterey festival together in '67, and wrote a heat-hazed anthem-cum-advert for it called 'San Francisco (Be Sure to Wear Some Flowers in Your Hair)', which became a UK number one for his old New York folk buddy Scott McKenzie. For eighteen months the Mamas and Papas were golden. One night, though, Michelle and Denny slept together, John found out, and that was pretty much the end of the group. Their demise came swiftly after Monterey, which, though Phillips could hardly have known it would happen, was the first time the public audience sensed a divide between pop and rock, between soft and hard. Monterey cut modern pop in half, and both halves would eventually be diminished by being unable to interact with the other – this would cause an impasse that pervaded the early seventies. So John Phillips sowed the seeds for the Mamas and Papas' downfall as surely as Michelle and Denny's tumble. Still, in just over two years they had managed to record four albums and – with their cover of the Five Royales' 'Dedicated to the One I Love' (US no. 2, UK no. 2 '67) – created the sexiest lullaby you ever heard.

If you wanted to pick one person who summed up the new school of soft rock, there was Harry Nilsson – scholarly, engaging, super-melodic, as fond of Broadway and booze as he was of the Beach Boys and the Beatles, and smart without being a show-off. The singer with the looks of a Swedish businessman had been quietly writing ('Cuddly Toy' for the Monkees, 'Paradise' for the Shangri-Las) and occasionally recording for nearly a decade when he burst onto the scene at an Apple press conference in 1968. When asked who their favourite American artist was, the Beatles replied in unison, 'Nilsson!' And their favourite American group? '*Nilsson!*'

It turned out that their press officer, Derek Taylor, had given them each a copy of an album he'd picked up in the States, Nilsson's debut, *Pandemonium Shadow Show*; it was a mix of vaudeville, classy orchestrated pop, cockeyed humour and the odd Beatles cover, delivered with Harry's sweet three-octave treatment. The Beatles were enamoured. The press were caught on the hop and hurriedly tried to get some info on this mysterious figure – to their horror they discovered Nilsson had never even played live. He told callers, 'My amateur status is still intact, thank you.'

The following Monday morning, Nilsson received a phone call at seven o'clock: 'Is that Harry? This is John.' 'John who?' 'John Lennon.' 'Huh?' 'Your record is fucking fantastic, man. I just wanted to say you're great.' The next Monday at seven, Paul McCartney also phoned to rave about the album. Nilsson later recalled, 'I got up early the following Monday and waited for Ringo to call. He didn't.'

Beatle patronage built an instant profile for Nilsson. In '72 he peaked commercially with the Grammy-nominated *Nilsson Schmilsson* album, and invented the power ballad by covering Badfinger's 'Without You' (US and UK no. 1) in an opulent Italianate style, with a delicate piano-led verse and an earthquake of a chorus, testing his high notes and showing off his range. Fame and fortune battered him, though, alcohol wrecking his health and his angelic voice, which was little more than a croak by the late seventies. Soft-rockers were no less vulnerable than hard-rockers.

A little further out were the Neon Philharmonic. In the seventies Paul Weller would contrarily tell fans to vote Tory, and Eric Clapton intrigued us with his views on immigration, but in the late sixties it was safe to assume most politically involved musicians were left-leaning – pop was anti-war and the draft threatened its audience, let alone its musicians.* From their two bizarre albums, it would be hard to gauge where the Neon Philharmonic stood. They were the brainchild of Tupper Saussy, a jazz pianist who had studied with Oscar Peterson in the early sixties, made money from ad jingles and had a pet monkey called Thelonious Monk. In 1968, fascinated by the new orchestral direction

---

* The Beatles' 'Taxman' was an exception – anti-state individualism wasn't branded 'libertarian' as readily in the late sixties, as it suffused the counterculture. Retrospectively, George Harrison's song sounds like an anthem for future tax exiles like Rod Stewart and the Rolling Stones.

pop was taking, he hooked up with singer Don Gant and the Nashville Symphony Orchestra to create the Neon Philharmonic. Straight away they had a Top 20 hit with 'Morning Girl'; spooky titles like 'Are You Old Enough to Remember Dresden' and 'A National Anthem for Rent to Emerging Nations' didn't stop three Grammy nominations.*

There was no 'Without You' up Saussy's sleeve, however. By the early seventies he was back working on jingles for Purity Dairy and writing kids' books. He also wrote *The Miracle on Main Street*, a book that claimed income tax was unconstitutional; after refusing to pay it, he was sentenced in 1985 to a year in prison. Then he vanished. Saussy was on the run for ten years. By now a hero to the libertarian right, he would leave cryptic messages on the internet from his Washington State hideout. Occasionally, disguised in a wig, he played the piano in a Seattle shopping mall. Finally captured in 1997, Saussy served fourteen months – just enough time to finish his next book, *Rulers of Evil: Useful Knowledge about Governing Bodies*. 'I was gifted with the abilities to do what three persons do,' he claimed.

If you wanted to find the source of soft rock's love of recherché arrangements and improbable instrumentation, you only had to peek into one of the Brill Building cubicles. Burt Bacharach and Hal David were the Powell and Pressburger of pop, causing a quiet revolution that would only be fully appreciated after their heyday. Bacharach had been writing out of the Brill Building since the late fifties, when he had two consecutive UK number ones with Perry Como's 'Magic Moments' and Michael Holliday's 'The Story of My Life'. Both featured cute, whistled hooks and were cosy as a Swiss wood cabin at Christmas, but neither gave any real suggestion of what was to come. Bacharach slowly began to add askew flute trills, trumpet stabs and bass-note pushes; the sound became more New York but decidedly upmarket at the same time – he was especially fond of the baion beat pioneered by Leiber and Stoller. Inside the Brill, with 'a closed window, no view, no air, and Hal smoking

---

* Saussy and Gant also wrote and produced Roy Orbison's 1969 state-of-the-nation single 'Southbound Jericho Parkway'. Seven minutes long, with no recognisable verse or chorus, it traces the family fallout from a businessman father's suicide. No sunshine at all, this was a very dark record.

all over the place', Bacharach wrote and arranged the mordantly sensual 'Baby It's You', a US Top 10 hit for the Shirelles in 1961. Other heart-breakers from this period that didn't chart included Adam Wade's 'Rain from the Skies', Chuck Jackson's 'I Wake Up Crying' and Dee Clark's 'You're Telling Our Secrets', the sounds of strong men in purgatory, wronged, battered by tympani and teased by pizzicato.

When Bacharach and David began working with backing singer Dionne Warwick in 1962, she kept bugging them to write her a solo single. After the third or fourth broken Bacharach promise, she snapped, 'Don't make me over!' and they had the title of her first hit. Warwick was an improbable-looking woman with a jutting jaw, Martian hair and wide, oval eyes that conveyed no emotion whatsoever. In this, she was the perfect foil for Bacharach's ever more oddly constructed songs, with their staccato trills and cool, clipped, offbeat rhythms. 'One-level records always made me a little bit uncomfortable after a while,' said Bacharach. 'They stayed at one intensity. It kind of beats you up, you know? It's like a smile. If you have a great smile, you use it quick, not all the time.'

Dionne Warwick realised she didn't have to stay intense and shout all the time to make an impact. 'Walk On By' (UK no. 8, US no. 6 '64) had chords that dived and plucked and ate away at you, but it never got over-excited – which was quite impressive for a song whose dialogue ran 'Each time I see you I break down and cry.' It was exquisite, modern and mini-mal, like a piece of white plastic furniture. Bacharach-produced Dionne Warwick albums were an essential component of any sixties apartment.

As Bacharach's awkward, orchestrated influence percolated under the more acclaimed Beatles/Stones noise, a bunch of pop pin-ups took their cue and became similarly more intriguing and more baroque. The son of fifties singer Marion Ryan, Barry Ryan emerged with twin brother Paul in '66, and as a duo they cut a bunch of unremarkable minor UK hits; things got interesting in '68, when Paul decided to concen-trate on the writing and Barry on the singing. Clearly, Barry Ryan was a meat-eater. He arrived like a Brontëan hero on horseback, whip in hand, with the heavily orchestrated five-minute potboiler 'Eloise' (UK no. 2) in late '68. Everything he sang was an imminent apocalypse, and when he reached a chorus the veins stuck out on his neck like knotted rope. His songs were post-Bacharach and 'Hey Jude' sophistico-pop with enigmatic titles like 'Magical Spiel', 'The Hunt' ('Go! Tally ho!') and 'Kitsch' ('It's a beautiful word, it's a beautiful lullaby'). Working on his stall in Kensington Market, it's a safe bet Freddie Bulsara was paying close attention. In a row, they sounded ludicrous but, taken one at a time, Barry Ryan 45s were like a bareback gallop through a forest. Their grandiloquence soon wore down listeners, which was a great shame, and he'd switched to bubblegum like 'Can't Let You Go' by '72. They still love him in Germany.

Scott Walker's combination of florid woe and arthouse angst was more piquant still. In 1965 John Maus and Scott Engel were playing the Hollywood club scene when their friend, Standells drummer Gary Leeds, had the idea for them to try and crack Britain: he'd recently played there with P. J. Proby and knew how, as if they were latter-day GIs, British girls freaked out at the sight of boys with a Californian sun tan. The unrelated trio became the Walker Brothers and Walkermania ensued, incredible adulation over a twelve-month period from late '65 that saw them cut melodramatic smashes like 'Make It Easy on Yourself' (no. 1 September '65), 'My Ship Is Coming In' (no. 3 January '66)* and 'The Sun Ain't Gonna Shine Anymore' (no. 1 March '66), heavily influenced by Spector's Righteous Brothers productions but somehow more heartfelt, certainly more European. The Walker Brothers had arrived as equals (John Walker had taken lead vocal on the first UK 45, 'Pretty Girls Everywhere') in 1965, but split just two years later with Scott the undoubted star and John feeling sidelined and unloved.

Continental tendencies were writ large on Scott Walker's five startling solo albums between 1967 and 1970; intense Jacques Brel interpretations (emotionally bettered by no one) sat alongside towering, Mahlerdaubed self-written songs like 'Big Louise' and 'Boy Child'. Here was a willingness to get lost. Walker abandoned himself in hymnal, orchestral

---

* The heavily compressed piano intro on 'My Ship Is Coming In' seems to start mid-phrase and bears no relation to the rest of the song; in this way it suggests the lyric is wishful thinking, desperation even, as Scott tries to convince his girl that she'll soon be able to 'throw away that shabby dress'.

pop – hit records wouldn't reach such levels of red-eyed religiosity again until Orchestral Manoeuvres in the Dark's *Architecture and Morality* in 1981. Given his own TV show, Scott Walker sat on a stool and looked deeply hurt, modern pop's most existential star. His voice was a Bournville baritone and his lyrics were beautiful and opaque ('Night starts to empty, that's when her song begins'), but also urban, surreal and everyday ('Screaming kids on my knee, and the telly swallowing me'). Somehow, Scott Walker managed all this while playing the industry game; though he quoted Camus in his sleevenotes, he also got Jonathan King to write them. This way, rather astonishingly, he managed to score a UK number-one album in 1968 with *Scott 2.**

For a short while he was the biggest pop star in Britain. At one point he escaped to a monastery, but was evicted by the monks when teen scream-ers tried to break in. Cancelled gigs and heavy drinking began to take their toll. Washed up commercially and artistically by 1975, the Walker Brothers resorted to re-forming. They decided to get a flat together at the Stamford Bridge end of the King's Road. It only had two bedrooms. Scott wanted the small, dark, back bedroom at the top of the stairs; John had the master bedroom; Gary built a tent in the living room. With their brittle yet strong affection for each other and wildly differing personali-ties, they couldn't have been more like real brothers if they tried.

In 1967, as well as being adored by teenagers, *Sgt Pepper* was feted by the *Sunday Times* and Scott Walker was the housewives' choice. There was room for soft-rock innovators who could bridge the generation gap, unite the teenagers and the older sceptics Leonard Bernstein had helped to win around. A handsome twenty-one-year-old Oklahoma boy called

---

* Unlike Barry Ryan, Scott Walker's mystique and reputation have grown expo-nentially since the seventies, built initially on the dark majesty (and long unavail-ability) of his first five solo albums but helped by a move away from pop into adventurous, if ugly, avant-garde records. His tracks on the Walker Brothers' 1978 album *Nite Flights* heavily influenced Bowie's *Lodger* the following year. It has been a fascinating route for a singer first brought into public view on the *Eddie Fisher Show*, though albums like *Tilt* and *The Drift* are weighed down by violent, misanthropic lyrics. Loneliness is the cloak he chooses to wear, but it would be good to hear him, maybe just once more, let the seriousness slip and adapt his avant tendencies to a three-minute single.

Jimmy Webb rose to the challenge. He had started out at eighteen, writing for Motown – 'it was like shining shoes', he told the *NME* in 1969. One song he wrote was called 'By the Time I Get to Phoenix', and it was clearly a cut above album filler, but Motown didn't have a clue what to do with it. What did it represent? Freedom, loss, the whole of America condensed in those quirky names – Phoenix, Albuquerque and Oklahoma – as the protagonist ends up hundreds of miles from his girlfriend's sour tears. It was romantic, it had no real chorus, and the geography in the narrative was a little out, but it felt like ten years of someone's adult life inside 150 seconds. It sounded like a whole movie. It was an incredible achievement for a teenager.

Johnny Rivers cut the song in '66 and was so enamoured of Webb's work that he bought out his contract with Motown and set him to work with pop-soul harmony group the 5th Dimension. His hunch paid off, and the first Webb-penned 5th Dimension hit was 'Up, Up and Away' (US no. 7 '67), the *Charlie Bubbles* of pop songs, with a hot-air balloon as the ultimate escape route. It entered the US chart just as Glen Campbell's version of 'By the Time I Get to Phoenix' gained traction; when Frank Sinatra called the latter 'the greatest torch song ever written', Jimmy Webb was suddenly hailed as the biggest thing since Lennon and McCartney.

Things peaked very quickly for Webb. He cut an album called *The Magic Garden* with the 5th Dimension that was a proper song cycle, an event, orchestrated and complex; it seemed Webb had absorbed the American songbook – from Stephen Foster to Burt Bacharach – without being remotely derivative. *The Magic Garden* was nothing, though, compared to a song he wrote while ensconced in actor Richard Harris's beach house for a month. 'MacArthur Park' was, in 1968, the longest single that had ever reached the American or British Top 10 (it peaked at two and four, respectively). It was an elaborate mansion of a song, with doors opening onto a new room full of unexpected treasures every thirty seconds or so. And, being a Jimmy Webb song, it was deathlessly romantic: 'I recall the yellow cotton dress foaming like a wave on the ground around your knee, birds like tender babies in your hand, and the old men playing checkers by the tree.'

Sung by Harris in an oak-aged warble, it came out in May 1968, just
as the battle lines were drawn in Paris, in Mexico, in pop. Instead of
being acclaimed for his daring, Webb was pilloried, particularly for the
line 'Someone left the cake out in the rain'. What did it mean? asked
the hippies, as if they had suddenly morphed into their grandparents.*
Webb had more up his sleeve. Glen Campbell's 'Wichita Lineman',
'Galveston' and 'Where's the Playground Susie' all trumped 'MacArthur
Park' for emotional punch in 1969, and in the same year there was an
astonishing divorce album called *The Yard Went On Forever*, sung again
by Richard Harris. But Webb had his pride. He took the post-Monterey
route, ditched the orchestration, sang his own songs in his cracked,
slightly unpleasant voice, fell in line, and eventually became accepted
as a serious rock artist.

1968's predominant trend was to get hairier, heavier, more long-
winded. A lot of writers felt disenfranchised. They had only just got to
grips with the über-English trappings of homegrown psychedelia, especially its mournful evocations of Victoriana, its village-green gentility,
and its church bells softly chiming: like the Left Banke and the Zombies
they wanted to get softer rather than harder, and were not about to fly
their freak flag. The majority of English baroque records were made
between 1968 and 1973 – while Lennon and McCartney got more raucous and rootsy, and Led Zep ruled the student unions, the harpsichord
trickle-down took its time to reach the provinces.

The quintessential English baroque group was Honeybus. Though
they only had one hit – 'I Can't Let Maggie Go', a UK number eight in
'68 – its melancholy air ('she flies like a bird in the sky') hung in the seventies ether when, for years, it accompanied a woman in a hot-air balloon advertising Nimble, a processed bread for slimming. They hailed
from industrial East London, an area full of bone-crushing factories
and animal-fat recyclers but not renowned for pop groups, especially
ones of such a gentle disposition. 'We all liked Mozart and all that,' said

---

* It was pretty obviously a metaphor for a broken relationship, with no one to
blame. There were far stranger lines in 'MacArthur Park' – 'Pressed in love's hot
fevered iron like a stripy pair of pants' – but the cake took the biscuit, and rock-
ists have used it as an example of pop's meaninglessness ever since.

guitarist Colin Hare, who had actually been born in baroque-friendly Bath. Their singer and songwriter Pete Dello 'convinced us to use woodwinds and strings but we didn't need much persuading. It didn't bother us that nobody else seemed to be doing it because we wanted to do our own thing. We weren't easy to pigeonhole.' Any chance of lasting commercial success seemed to have ended when Dello left while 'I Can't Let Maggie Go' was still on the chart – he abhorred the idea of touring. Though their momentum was lost, Hare and bassist Ray Cane carried on as if nothing had changed and turned out to be pretty good songwriters themselves; they got as far as completing one great album, *Story* in 1970, a full two years after their sole hit, before folding.

From moment to moment, what it is that constitutes pop shifts and changes; it's always contradictory. Soft was always likely to be squished by hard, though, and by 1970 a Honeybus album sounded twee and ancient. In 1968 Lennon had started to refer to McCartney's more whimsical moments as 'granny music'; George Harrison went even further and drafted Cream's Eric Clapton in to give the Beatles added rock bathos on *The White Album*. Seriousness – an element of pop which had periodically surfaced, on Del Shannon's 'Runaway', say, or the Shangri-Las' 'Past, Present and Future' – was now seen to trump everything else. 'They offer THEMSELVES', ran the *Record Mirror* review of *The White Album*, 'without much show-biz artifice.'

The Association had no time for 'Yer Blues'. 'Today we're exposed and cross-indexed tastewise,' said their leader Terry Kirkman in '68. 'There's a general potpourri of music. But I think an awful lot of white musicians ought to finally admit to themselves that they aren't black.' A seven-piece west-coast group, they were initially produced by Curt Boettcher, a kind of junior Brian Wilson who was behind a string of pop-dreamscape albums (most notably the Millennium's 'Begin'), but the Association's 'Along Comes Mary' was his and their starting point, a US number eight in 1966. It's hard to know why they have fallen off the critical map so completely – 'Cherish' and 'Windy' were both US number ones, while 'Never My Love' is apparently one of the ten most played pop songs on American radio, ever. It could just be because they wore suits and their name was so blank. Kirkman was clearly frustrated by the fact they

weren't taken more seriously: 'Lots of times you really want to break the
amplifier. You want to make it so loud you can't stand it.'

Pet Sounds and *Sgt Pepper* and 'MacArthur Park' should have been
instruction manuals for the early seventies, but largely the lessons were
junked. Why was this? It had started to become unfashionable not to
write and perform every aspect of your music in the mid-sixties; by the
divisive year of 1968 it was seen as a sure sign of insincerity if you didn't
pull all the levers yourself. Also, orchestration was associated with the
older generation, the Mantovani lovers: parents, teachers, bosses.

Still, soft rock didn't die completely when the calendar reached
January 1st 1970 but, with less and less interaction with the hard-rock,
album-orientated world, it significantly lost its cutting edge and was
abandoned by the next generation of McCartneys, Boettchers and Brian
Wilsons, who instead turned to singer-songwriter stylings. With a gen-
eration's finest minds otherwise occupied, soft rock ceased to provoke
and so ceased to progress. Detractors may have laughed at 'MacArthur
Park', but it was unavoidable. The next wave of soft-rockers were more
easily ignored. Take Bread. They were based around songwriter David
Gates, who had penned some exceptional girl-group 45s (Maureen
Evans's 'Never Let Him Go', the Girlfriends' 'Jimmy Boy', Connie
Stevens's 'Lost in Wonderland'), as well as 'Saturday's Child' for the
Monkees. They had an FM-friendly air to their melodic pop and racked
up a long list of hits, starting with 'Make It with You' (US no. 1, UK no.
5) in 1970. They were nobody's favourite group, though – too square,
somehow a little unsatisfying, a little too nerdish – but Gates had faith,
knew his best songs ('Guitar Man', 'If', 'Everything I Own') came in
shades of blue with unexpectedly morose twists,* and he wasn't ashamed

---

* 'Guitar Man' (US no. 11, UK no. 16 '72) is an unlikely counterpoint to Bowie's
'Starman' – it could be the song playing on the radio immediately before Ziggy
beams down with his 'hazy cosmic jive'. You assume it's about an unreachable
rock star until it reaches its climax, where you realise his star is waning, his audience disappearing. 'If' (US no. 4 '71, and a UK number one for Telly Savalas in
'75) was even starker, a tale of creepily devoted love which becomes darker with
each verse: 'If the world should stop revolving, spinning slowly round to die,
I'd spend the end with you.' Savalas's version positively relishes this notion – no
wonder he made such a good Bond villain.

of his classical nerdiness: 'I'd say Bread are unique – people doing things that come totally naturally to them musically. As a kid I took in everything – Beethoven, Ravel, the lot, and I guess all that knowledge has to come out in some form every now and again.' *The Best of Bread* went five times platinum in 1973, and David Gates didn't really care if he sounded like the uncoolest kid at school.

Like Bacharach and David, Neil Diamond had emerged from the Brill Building, first charting with Jay and the Americans' ray of Latin sunlight 'Sunday and Me' (US no. 19 '65), then writing a couple of major Monkees hits ('I'm a Believer', 'A Little Bit Me, a Little Bit You'), while simultaneously recording his own Latin-flavoured discotheque pop ('Cherry Cherry', US no. 6 '66). Before any of his contemporaries, he began to write introspective New York songs: 'Brooklyn Roads' led him to the west coast, where he scored a brace of all-time karaoke classics ('Sweet Caroline', 'Cracklin' Rosie') before 'I Am I Said' (US no. 1, UK no. 4 '71) solidified his unique singer-songwriter/Vegas stylings: ever the New Yorker, Diamond described it as 'autobiographical and psychoanalytic. There are two stories to the song really. Firstly, it's a search for roots, and secondly it's a cry for acceptance, and that's what it's all about.' You can see how he struck a nerve in the me decade.

Diamond was a rare Brill Building survivor, though. With a musical based on the Frank Capra film *Lost Horizon*, even Bacharach and David lost their commercial grasp in the seventies. The soundtrack, sung by a cast including Peter Finch, Liv Ullmann and Charles Boyer, was roundly destroyed by the press. *Newsweek* called it 'excruciating', and soon Bacharach and David were suing each other over a royalty issue.

The strongest soft survivor of the Monterey split was the A&M label. Herb Alpert had started it in the early sixties with arranger Jerry Moss, and they struck gold in 1962 with Alpert's 'The Lonely Bull' (US no. 6), a daft cod-Mexican instrumental. Implausibly, Alpert and his Tijuana Brass became one of the biggest album acts of the sixties. The records were crisply produced, the girls on the covers looked fine – notably on *Whipped Cream and Other Delights*, which was a very sweet temptation and sold over six million copies.

A&M formed a link back to pre-rock, to Les Baxter and the trave-logues of Jo Stafford and Mantovani, via percussive Latin exotica. Once the Tijuana Brass broke, A&M signed the Baja Marimba Band, the weightless Hispanic harmonies of the Sandpipers, and Sérgio Mendes and Brasil '66, whose chic, lush bossa-nova versions of Bacharach's 'The Look of Love' (US no. 4 '68) and the Beatles' 'Fool on the Hill' (US no. 6 '68) seemed to absorb the diffuse LA light, their sound always slightly vague and unsettling. But the act that took A&M into the seventies and kept the soft flag flying were a sibling act from Downey, California, called the Carpenters. Karen sang and played the drums, Richard grinned behind a keyboard. They looked like the history of apple pie, but there was a hint of sulkiness in Richard's demeanour that suggested some-thing wasn't quite right. Besides, given the right material, Karen had one of the warmest, saddest voices pop had ever produced – and the right material came from Paul Williams ('Rainy Days and Mondays', 'We've Only Just Begun', 'I Won't Last a Day without You'), Bacharach ('Close to You', US no. 1, UK no. 6 '70) and Leon Russell, whose 'Superstar' (US no. 2, UK no. 18 '71) was a wrist-slashing groupie song that made the fine line between fan and pop singer feel like a chasm. It turned out that Karen wasn't happy at all as a pop singer, psychologically tortured, forced to admit her solo disco album wasn't even worthy of release, and in the end she starved herself to death. Is that sadder than a heroin OD? I think it probably is.

CRYING IN THE STREETS: DEEP SOUL

In the late sixties white teens wanted to be taken seriously as grown-ups, and so fashioned a new music that showed they now had concerns that were a little more weighty than the ones in 'Summertime Blues'. But what also shaped politics and pop in the sixties was that black *adults* were demanding to be respected as grown-ups – to be allowed to vote, to gather in desegregated spaces with everyone else. What was simultaneously so powerful and so strange was that modern pop was often a weapon for both white kids and black adults. If it was unselfconscious fun for a Troggs fan, it was something sharply different for a James Brown fan. 'I'm a man,' sang Muddy Waters – but when the Yardbirds covered it (US no. 17 '65), or when the young David Bowie named his group the Mannish Boys after a Waters song, it had a very different political freighting.

When modern pop exploded in 1966 and '67, launching a thousand possibilities for future musics, Southern soul music began to turn inward. Motown would tip its hat to psychedelia with the Supremes' darkly chaste 'Reflections' (US no. 2, UK no. 5 '67), replete with cosmic sound effects, but in the South Sam Cooke's swan song 'A Change Is Gonna Come' had become a blueprint for a more sensitised sound. This was tagged 'deep soul' and it was an end in itself, where there was nothing else but to simplify, distil, intensify. The more intense it was, the better.

The rise of soul had been inextricably linked with civil-rights marches and Black Power, which led to an increase in black pride across America as the sixties progressed. There was no longer a need to hide behind veiled lyrics (the Impressions' 'It's All Right') or to use graphics on record sleeves rather than black faces (the Marvelettes' 'Please Mr Postman', Barbara Lewis's 'Hello Stranger'). 'A Change Is Gonna Come' had been a US Top 20 hit in 1964, posthumously; it had a lyric of great sadness but also one of potential salvation. Sam Cooke had written a song about the black experience for black people; it was genre-defining, not only for its lyric and intense delivery but also for its post-doo wop 6/8 time signature and churchly atmosphere, both of which would be major ingredients of deep soul.

Ben E. King asked the question 'What Is Soul' in 1967. It's a tough one.* A gut reaction might involve terms like 'honest', 'authentic', 'natural'; these are problematic words in pop because there's as much emotional truth in the Monkees' 'I'm a Believer' – written by Neil Diamond, performed by session musicians on an hourly rate – as there is in Irma Thomas's 'Wish Someone Would Care'.† Each song can say just as

* Ben E. King certainly doesn't give us much of an answer – after a few lines about it being 'deep within us, it doesn't show', we soon realise the song is a chat-up line rather than an explanation: 'Hold me tight, so tight I can't breathe, can't you feel it girl? This is soul!' Atlantic Records issued an answer to King's question with a compilation called *This Is Soul* in 1968 that included Aretha Franklin's 'I Never Loved a Man', Carla Thomas's 'B-A-B-Y' and Otis Redding's 'Fa Fa Fa Fa Fa (Sad Song)'.
† Irma Thomas's shocking, starkly intimate 'Wish Someone Would Care' had been a US number-twenty hit in 1963. It started with a long wordless wail before Irma composed herself to tell us how she was 'sitting at home alone, thinking about my past', leaving little doubt that she was singing from personal

much about your life. Maybe the answer to King's question lies in the sense of being privy to something secret – listening to a vocal performance so intense that you feel that you're sharing someone's private pain and anguish.

The man who coined the term 'deep soul' was a British collector called Dave Godin, a shy man who nonetheless left a large impression on pop. He had gone to Dartford Grammar School, where he'd encouraged a young Mick Jagger to listen to R&B. He then set up the Tamla Motown Appreciation Society in 1964, became the label's British consultant later that year and described the second-hand 45s he sold to soul fans from Lancashire with a taste for driving beats and basslines as 'northern soul' – that stuck, too. He was gentle and private, and found he got the most pleasure from music when it was slow and fervent: 'Deep soul often seems to me to be one of life's true blessings, a tonic for the heart, so powerful and honest that it can redeem and rescue.' For Godin, a classic deep-soul performance consisted of little more than vocal, bass pulse, clipped guitar and rich organ chords. Unlike other strands of soul, energy was funnelled away from the dancefloor and into the performance, which was always central. Take Reuben Bell's 'It's Not That Easy' – the backing is uncluttered, almost perfunctory, allowing Bell's anguish to strike as close to your heart as possible.

If the genre had a figurehead, it was Otis Redding, who had blossomed into the Stax label's premier star. He was stocky, rather stiff on stage and not obviously handsome, but there was an ache to his voice that sounded like Little Richard in utmost remorse. His torment was reflected in his song titles: 'Pain in My Heart', 'Mr Pitiful', 'I've Been Loving You Too Long', 'Chained and Bound', 'Try a Little

---

experience. A film isn't necessarily more enjoyable if it's based on a true story. Likewise, a song isn't necessarily any better or any more heartfelt, or convincing, because it was written by the singer. You may fancy the power of 'Wish Someone Would Care' is enhanced by the knowledge that Irma Thomas had three children and was twice divorced before she turned twenty, yet on the follow-up, 'Anyone Who Knows What Love Is (Will Understand)', the performance is tender, even more heartbreaking. It was written by Randy Newman, a Jewish songwriter from a middle-class LA background whose family spent their summers holidaying in Thomas's home town of New Orleans.

Tenderness'. Even his uptempo efforts were full of biblical woes. He was an unexpected guest at the Monterey Festival in the summer of 1967 and immediately became a major star. His 'got-ta! got-ta!' gospel-fired catchphrase didn't impress white critics: Redding 'worked hard', said Dave Marsh. He 'strained in achievement, no ribbon for that'. Marsh accepted Redding had cut a pair of fine live albums, but sniffed that both were 'in front of white audiences, of course'. Redding's reputation never quite recovered from these attacks of inverse racism: all he had done was to play a pop festival where the white kids loved him, and then he was killed when his plane crashed into Lake Monona in Madison, Wisconsin, on December 10th 1967. Pity poor Otis, unable to defend himself.* The gloomy seascape 'Dock of the Bay' (US no. 1, UK no. 3 '68) was a huge posthumous hit. Possibly his finest single was a ballad called 'I've Got Dreams to Remember'. It's underplayed, all sad aban-don. Redding was only twenty-six when he cut it but he sounds like an old, old man, alone on Christmas Eve, nothing left but photographs and memories.

Deep soul rarely had any major impact on the chart, but the excep-tions were striking – Percy Sledge's 'When a Man Loves a Woman' (US no. 1, UK no. 4 '66) – happened to be your actual genre arche-type: church organ, wailing vocal, minimal brass like a knife through the air. Star quality and artistic value aren't synonymous, but modern pop being popular entertainment it helps if they go hand in hand, and

---

* There's a lot of snobbery in pop. Soul snobbery is a particularly strong strain, and Otis Redding's is not an isolated case. Take Diana Ross, always seen as the most Broadway-conscious of Motown's singers. In 1971 she cut a single called 'I'm Still Waiting'. Ross sings it in an airy, sweet voice; she seems to be telling the audience about her one true love, and that 'love has never shown its face' since the day he left her. Yet this isn't the message that comes across from her performance at all. Instead, we get the feeling Ross has walled herself in; her detached voice – especially on a chillingly blank spoken part – implies that her childhood sweetheart is nothing but a handy excuse, someone to blame for a life of lonely disappointment. Quite possibly the man is a complete fiction. Neither Flo Ballard nor Mary Wilson, her fellow Supremes, could have made the cold, still heart of 'I'm Still Waiting', with its jumble of self-denial and self-loathing ('I'm just a fool'), work as well as Diana. It's moving and unsettling; it's a faultless performance.

the gap-toothed Percy Sledge (has any US number-one hit-maker had a less likely name?) was no Hollywood pin-up. He scored a monster hit because 'When a Man Loves a Woman' was an intense, arresting 45, something that had an extra urgency – even though it shared the airwaves with 'Wild Thing', 'Paint It Black', 'Paperback Writer' – that forced you to stop and pay attention. The budget for the single was so small that a woefully out-of-tune trumpet couldn't even be re-recorded.

This was music from the outside – created by, but then opting out of, the modern pop story. We'll be encountering more genres that feed into and out of pop as the story continues, but deep soul was the first departure, and its presence was a quiet constant from '66 onwards, as long as you knew where to look. Etta James recorded 'I'd Rather Go Blind' in 1967 as the B-side of her US Top 20 hit 'Tell Mama'; it was picked up by British blues-rock band Chicken Shack and became a spotlight song for their cool-voiced singer Christine Perfect. Deep soul was also the music that David Bowie's character in 'Young Americans' was trying to conjure up when he sang, 'Ain't there one damn song that can make me break down and cry?' It floated in and out of other pop forms, blending with country on Dorothy Moore's extraordinarily moving, subtly devastating 'Misty Blue', a UK number six in 1976 which has some of the best phrasing of any pop single: 'Listen to me, sweet baby,' she implores, and you're caught up in her story, you can't do anything else. Deep soul also grazed rocksteady on Ken Boothe's fire-breathing 'The One I Love' in '67, and even touched the cabaret soul of Tom Jones on his 1967 cover of Lonnie Donegan's 'I'll Never Fall in Love Again' (UK no. 2 '67, US no. 6 '68).

There are only the odd, creased monochrome shots of deep-soul singers like Doris Allen, Barbara West or Danny White; they seem as distant and dusty as the early blues singers, and it's terribly easy to romanticise them. So unknown are the personalities involved that the first biography of the genre's one star name, Otis Redding, appeared as recently as 2001. Maybe this is why deep soul rarely troubled the charts, but it provided a fistful of 45s which are the first you should reach for to solve arguments with classical or jazz buffs about the emotional heft of pop music. Here's a cut-out-and-keep list of songs to listen to on your own, curtains drawn, on a winter night; confront your worst fears, use these songs as therapy: George Perkins's 'Cryin' in the Streets', Timmy Willis's 'Easy as Saying 1-2-3', Doris Allen's 'A Shell of a Woman', Billy Joe Young's 'I Had My Heart Set on You', Betty Greene's 'He's Down on Me', Nelson Sanders's 'Tired of Being Your Fool', James Carr's 'The Dark End of the Street', O. V. Wright's 'That's How Strong My Love Is'. Hear Betty Harris's 'What Did I Do Wrong' or Irma Thomas's 'Wish Someone Would Care' and you can understand why people like Dave Godin devoted their lives to it.

I CAN'T SING, I AIN'T PRETTY AND MY LEGS ARE THIN: HARD ROCK

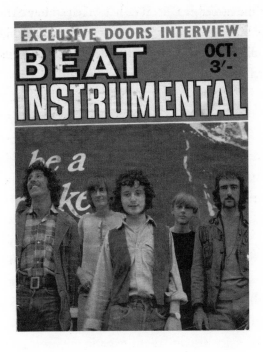

It's intriguing to wonder where pop might have gone if the Beatles hadn't done an about-turn on the brilliant colours and dayglo, utopian dreams of 1967, if they had followed Jimmy Webb's path rather than Eric Clapton's. John Lennon's send-up of the emerging British blues-rock sound on *The White Album*, 'Yer Blues', indicates they weren't entirely at ease with it, and the album was a big messy mix of different stances, stabs and attempts at ways out of modern pop's sudden impasse. Still, 'Yer Blues' also showed that they didn't need a weatherman to know that the wind was blowing away from Strawberry Fields, heading somewhere murkier and darker. Down to the Dartford delta. In 1968 the Rolling Stones, finally, became the more significant musical force.

The turning points had less to do with the Beatles and the Stones than with external factors. In November '67 the pirate stations which had fed British pop culture since 1964, playing 45s in daylight hours while the BBC broadcast specially recorded light music, were closed down by the government. Radio Caroline, Radio London and a dozen other stations which had been legally broadcasting from international waters, a few miles off the British coast, were put out of business by the Marine Broadcasting Offences Act and replaced by a single station, the state-owned BBC Radio 1. Straight away, even though it took most of the popular pirate DJs with it, this was regarded as the sound of the Man, a line in the sand between them and us. Ergo, the pop played on Radio 1 became unsound to support, which was tough on classy acts like the Bee Gees, the Hollies, Dave Dee, Dozy, Beaky, Mick and Tich, the Love Affair and Manfred Mann. These were safety-first acts as far as Radio 1 was concerned. The Who, on the other hand, had released their magnum opus, *The Who Sell Out*, at the end of '67; unsurprisingly, Radio 1 had hardly been keen on playing a record that glorified the departing pirate stations, and they also ignored Pete Townshend's next effort, a quite beautiful song about greyhound racing called 'Dogs' which stalled at number twenty-five in spring '68, ending a three-year run of Top 10 hits. Licking their wounds, the Who disappeared for a whole year, returning with the game-changing *Tommy*.

For pop radio in Britain, then, experimentation was out. Instead, there were now middle-aged DJs like Pete Murray – who had been on Radio Luxembourg when the very first hit parade was published in 1952 – and former singer Jimmy Young, with his squeaky jingle, 'What's the recipe today, Jim?' No competition, no threat, no danger. Just apple crumble for all.

Within a few months of Radio 1's launch came the Paris uprising, the anti-Vietnam demo outside the American embassy in Grosvenor Square that spilled over into violence, the Black Power salutes in Mexico. The inarticulate rage of the '68 generation fizzed around the figure of Mick Jagger. There he was, in Grosvenor Square; that was him, singing 'Street Fighting Man' (which the Stones were prevented from releasing as a single in the UK by their nervous record company, Decca), showing which side he was on. Still, these were mere glimpses. Anyone who fought through the loud but woolly vocal on 'Street Fighting Man' – a production technique which made the song seem even fiercer, and was later copped by Slade for most of their hits – would hear an ambivalent star rather than a catalyst for revolution. The Stones were content for everyone else to get involved, to get their heads cracked by batons and boots, but they would remain apart, totems for the cause, posters on the student-union wall. Modern pop may have seemed thoroughly politicised at the end of the sixties, but it was a confused jumble of ideologies.*

These events widened the division between pop and rock. (A truce has only occasionally been called since, but it's no coincidence that when there has been one – 1978, 1981, 1989 – it has tended to benefit everyone, and modern pop has jumped forward instead of circling, turning to its past or turning on itself.) In 1968 the interdisciplinary hopes of Leonard Bernstein looked to be dashed. The UK album-chart-toppers of 1968 showed a generational battle line (Val Doonican, Andy Williams and Tom Jones up against the Beatles, Simon and Garfunkel and Otis Redding) which only became more extreme in '69 (Ray Conniff, the Seekers and the late Jim Reeves on one side, with Cream, Jethro Tull and the Moody Blues on the other). By cutting out both softness and orchestration – which gave it access to different kinds of emotional presence – hard rock began to gel around belligerent self-pity and bullying cliché. Running away from the conflicts and complexity of modern pop as a whole, the result was that rock entered an anxious cycle of increasing loudness and heaviness.

The most obvious musical influence on the switch from orchestrated fantasies to heavier roots music was Bob Dylan's *John Wesley Harding*. Dylan had been away from the public eye for almost two years when it appeared at the beginning of '68. The Beach Boys had been the first major act to throw the dreamscape gears into reverse with their home-recorded, minimal soul album *Wild Honey* in November '67, but

---

* By 1971 John Lennon was funding ultra-leftist organisations and dressing in military fatigues. Mick Jagger was a tax exile, wining and dining the Nicaraguan model Bianca Pérez-Mora Macias. Both were still seen as figureheads to the underground, whose blind faith in rock stars was boundless.

Dylan's return, no matter how low-key, was so hugely anticipated that it could hardly fail to be an influence. With its acoustic guitars and light skittery drums, rural myths and sepia country feel, *John Wesley Harding* instigated a return to the source: folk, country, blues and jazz. It seemed necessarily adult in a world where only the naive seemed optimistic, with its veiled Vietnam references ('I Pity the Poor Immigrant') and enigmatic prophecies of imminent doom ('All along the Watchtower', 'The Wicked Messenger'). *John Wesley Harding* also rejected the urban. Carnaby Street and 1967 Utopia would soon be satirised in a few bitter British movies – *The Untouchables, Joanna, The Guru* – which only foresaw self-destruction.

A conservative, self-preservative, back-to-basics stance also suited the Rolling Stones' situation, post-Redlands bust. The Stones finally emerged from the Beatles' shadow – where they had dwelt as late as Christmas '67 with the post-*Sgt Pepper* prettiness of 'She's a Rainbow' – by reacquainting themselves with the blues that had brought them together in the first place. This time around, they lost the ethnographic librarian stance of 'Little Red Rooster' and Brian Jones's buttoned-up purism. Jones was still in the band but, by 1968, could barely function due to his cognac swigging and chain-smoking of joints – Jagger described his eyes as looking like they'd gone over a lemon squeezer. Aside from the yowling sitar on 'Street Fighting Man', Jones's input was entirely absent from their 1968 recordings.

Emboldened by having pushed the Establishment to the very brink in the court room, Keith Richards now seized the reins. Catching fire with twin dark party hits 'Jumpin' Jack Flash' (US no. 3, UK no. 1 summer '68) and 'Street Fighting Man', the Stones cut the bluesy *Beggars Banquet* (1968) and *Let It Bleed* (1969), which included a cover of Robert Johnson's 'Love in Vain'. Tellingly, it sounded like the Rolling Stones rather than a Delta homage, taking the eeriness of Johnson's song and imbuing it with '69 nihilism. The louche 'Honky Tonk Women' (US and UK no. 1 summer '69) featured a proto-hip-hop beat* and

---

* Proto-hip hop, but it's impossible to sample unless you want to spend hours screwing about to make Charlie Watts's drums 'n' cowbell hit the beat. Another

found them back on familiar territory, in the arms of a bevy of women. But it was a *Let It Bleed* album track, 'Gimme Shelter', that confirmed their transformation from Dartford upstarts gatecrashing parties in Chelsea to blackhearted soothsayers. They'd seen the inside of a cell, after all.

This new/old direction can also be put down to manager Andrew Oldham's departure. They were a blues-rock band before he stumbled across them and they reverted to type when he left. Spearheaded by the Stones and Eric Clapton, a British blues boom emerged in '68 as the flip side to '67's flower power. In '64 the Yardbirds had been the Rolling Stones' only real rivals on the R&B scene, largely due to Clapton, their thin-lipped, close-cropped kid guitarist who had a permanent look of suspicion in his eyes. He was also the most technically proficient blues player Britain had yet produced.

Clapton had quit the Yardbirds before the purple Indian baroque of 1965's 'For Your Love' was even in the shops, dismayed by what he perceived to be a sell-out. He then joined John Mayall's hardline, Chicago-styled Bluesbreakers. Mayall was to British blues what Ken Colyer had been to British trad jazz. His band was a photocopying exercise, with Clapton given free rein to let loose on the Freddie King lines he'd learnt down pat. To give Clapton credit, he soon tired of this, and probably regretted leaving the Yardbirds in a strop, because when two jazzers called Jack Bruce and Ginger Baker came knocking in 1966, he left Mayall to join them in a blues-jazz improv trio called Cream. Their main problem was their total confidence in their greatness – the clue was in the name. Bruce had a theatrical voice which, on heavyweight numbers like 'Sunshine of Your Love' (US no. 6 '68), was rubbery and slightly reminiscent of David Whitfield. What Cream had in abundance was volume; by 1967 they were hugely popular, and a flock of imitators – notably the super-heavy American trio Blue Cheer, whose cover of Eddie Cochran's 'Summertime Blues' was Vanilla Fudged to the

---

record it kept at number two which pointed to future rhythms (though it was yet another with a dark and deathly aura) was Robin Gibb's 'Saved by the Bell', the first hit record to use a drum machine.

power of ten – forsook the subtleties of the blues entirely for Cream's powerplay.

One 1969 single, in a year of albums, bridged the gap between the soft-rock adventurers and the blues-rock recidivists. Thunderclap Newman were barely a band at all; they had been put together by the Who's Pete Townshend to get the songs of his drummer pal Speedy Keen* on record. Their first single was called 'Something in the Air' (UK no. 1, US no. 25 '69), and it was a beautiful, fatalistic, post-Grosvenor Square call to arms: 'We've got to get together sooner or later.' Keen's voice was high, straining to be heard over the pub-piano playing of bearded GPO engineer Andy Newman and some heroic French horns. 'Hand out the arms and ammo,' implored Keen in his decidedly non-violent voice, 'we're gonna blast our way through here' – just two years on, the flowery passivity of Scott McKenzie's 'San Francisco' was a wilted memory. Off the chart and out in the margins was another astonishing 45 by British four-piece Fresh Air called 'Running Wild'. Buoyed by valley-bottom handclaps and a razor-sharp, dissonant guitar hook, it doesn't deviate from 1969's anti-urban drift, but has a proto-punk snottiness that much of the year sorely missed: 'Young fools from greener places, flocking to rush in, light up the old man's face with hate behind the grin. He thinks he'll win, but we're running wild, running wild . . .' After three minutes of libertine biker roar, it dissolves into wild, wordless bellows and fierce distortion that anticipates Hüsker Dü and My Bloody Valentine's vacuum-cleaner psychedelics in the eighties. You can dance to it, too. Both 'Running Wild' and 'Something in the Air' possibly stood out because they refused to be defeated. Neither equated heaviness with significance. After all, it's always easier to be bleak than optimistic. These bands were trying harder.

The biggest new British name of '68, Fleetwood Mac, were altogether more limited than Cream – which was a blessing. Drummer Mick Fleetwood and bassist John McVie laid down a steady but basic beat and could have sounded like it was Ealing '63 all over again, dated

---

* Keen had written 'Armenia City in the Sky', the mindblowing opening track on *The Who Sell Out*.

and slightly silly, if it wasn't for their sad-eyed guitarist and singer, Peter Green, who turned out to be one of the very best. For a start, he was no purist and Fleetwood Mac soon progressed from being the best pub band in the country to Britain's foremost progressive-blues act. Green did not cleave to classic blues forms or chord progressions. 'Black Magic Woman' (UK no. 37 '68) was spiced and smoky enough to be covered almost immediately by Santana in the States; a cover of Little Willie John's 'Need Your Love So Bad' (UK no. 31 '68) was elevated by a Siamese-cat string section; 'Albatross' was as much influenced by Hank Marvin as it was by Muddy Waters, and was a UK number one in January '69; and 'Man of the World' (UK no. 2 May '69) was a crushingly gorgeous ballad that showed a rather fragile pop star, neither mannered nor self-pitying, but one we should probably keep an eye on. What's more, B-sides like 'Someone's Gonna Get Their Head Kicked In Tonight' showed they had a sense of humour, and were more likely to be on the terraces at 3 p.m. on a Saturday than quoting Ginsberg to first-year students in a smoky bedsit.

In the States, a bunch of Bay Area bayou-obsessed guys in plaid were 1968's biggest new act, concocting a Southern fried boogie sound that – in less talented hands – would become a hard-rock staple in the seventies. Creedence Clearwater Revival, though, were thrilling, and had a rabid work ethic. Led by the moptopped John Fogerty, they released an unfeasible number of albums – six between '68 and '70 – and scored a run of tight, loud, instant-classic hit singles, something almost no one else managed in those years: 'Proud Mary', 'Bad Moon Rising', 'Green River', 'Who'll Stop the Rain', 'Up around the Bend', 'Have You Ever Seen the Rain', 'Long as I Can See the Light', all Top 5 American hits.* Fogerty's voice channelled Little Richard (check that 'yeeeeah!' on the end of gospel rocker 'Long as I Can See the Light'), and solos were Nashville-tight. Improv, if that's what you fancied, was reserved for album workouts like 'Keep On Chooglin'' and a cover of 'I Heard It through the Grapevine'.

---

* Creedence never had a US number one, with no fewer than five of their singles stopping at number two, though 'Bad Moon Rising' spent three weeks at number one in Britain.

As America's hottest act of 1969, they headlined the year's biggest festival, Woodstock; unfortunately for Creedence, this meant having to follow the jam-crazed Grateful Dead and they ended up playing at three in the morning, by which time most of the crowd was asleep. They worked far too hard – one of their albums was called *Cosmo's Factory* to reflect their incessant schedule – and they acrimoniously fell apart at their peak in 1971; brothers John and Tom Fogerty never spoke again.

'I can't help it 'bout the shape I'm in,' sang Peter Green on 1969's 'Oh Well' (UK no. 2). 'I can't sing, I ain't pretty and my legs are thin.' If much of the new blues rock/hard rock was ugly, this was because music that spoke to its audience in painful and ugly times necessarily reflected and exhibited ugliness and pain. One facet of this was to look as unpretty and unpop as possible. Mac looked entirely attainable to girls, no question. A lot of the new bands in town had formulaically unattractive names, including Hard Meat, Toe Fat, Creepy John Thomas and Fresh Maggots. The sweaty likes of Joe Cocker and Jethro Tull's Ian Anderson looked like men you'd see on a park bench, the kind your mother would lead you away from at speed.

Pop mags didn't know where to turn.* No wonder people put leather-lipped Mick Jagger on a higher pedestal than ever. The Stones, riding a wave, now broke the traditional bond between performers and audience, the one that fed both parties' needs and wants; they turned the pop concert into a battlefield. The aloofness of their early days had hardened by 1969 into something more directly sexual but also more vicious – the incendiary 'Sympathy for the Devil' and 'Gimme Shelter' seemed torn from the Aleister Crowley book of demonic Albion. Playing with fire, the band's strange new game seemed to permeate the atmosphere

---

* For a brief period girls' magazines like *Jackie*, and even music mags – notably *Fabulous* – largely abandoned pop, focusing instead on actors like Robert Redford, Pete Duel and Jack Wilde. The Monkees, as late as 1970, were still valid pin-up material in spite of their ever slipping chart positions as there were so few newcomers to replace them. The glossy pop monthly *Rave* folded in 1970; the following year, the weekly inkie *Sounds* was set up as a 'left-wing *Melody Maker*' by former *MM* writers Jack Hutton and Peter Wilkinson. The trend was for things that looked like the news, like something significant, not for pin-ups and hot gossip.

post-Grosvenor Square and My Lai: it seems queer that Charles Manson's murderous set discovered hidden messages in Beatles songs as unambiguous as 'Piggies' when the Stones had released 'Sympathy for the Devil' in the same month.

All around, the mood grew black in '69: 'The way things are going they're going to crucify me,' sang John Lennon on one of the Beatles' chirpier cuts that year; Creedence delivered the ominous 'Bad Moon Rising', an old-world warning, just as Neil Armstrong took a giant leap for mankind; Jethro Tull sang, 'Nights of winter turn me cold, fears of dying, getting old,' on their melancholic number-one album, *Stand Up*, spokesmen for the state of pop in 1969. Playing a private party at a castle in rural Germany, Peter Green caved in to bad acid and mental demons, an event borne out in the ultra-heavy, cackling terror of 1970 single 'The Green Manalishi (with the Two Prong Crown)': it would be Fleetwood Mac's last hit for years, as Green left, retired from music to grow his fingernails, and wandered the streets of Richmond, Surrey, unshaven, unwashed and unrecognised for years. The rest of Mac, in need of solace, initially switched to playing sweet Buddy Holly covers – and things infinitely more gentle than 'Oh Well' or 'The Green Manalishi' – on *Kiln House* (1970). Drafting in American guitarist Bob Welch they made a fresh start with the prophetically titled album *Future Games* in 1971 – their time would come again.

It felt like a conflict with no rules and no aims had been gradually stoked by the Stones, and the grisly, public denouement at Altamont speedway stadium was a logical conclusion. Looking desperately around for some positive news, half a million people attended the 1969 Woodstock festival. Musically, it was nothing compared to Monterey, but optimists saw it as the turning of a page rather than a full stop on the hippie era. The highlight was John Sebastian's acoustic set, gently reviving the Lovin' Spoonful's seemingly lost-forever goodtime sound. People were already nostalgic for the sixties, and they hadn't yet ended.

Woodstock was mimsy. Altamont was hell. It was where the Stones' vision of America, gin-soaked ballroom queens from Memphis and the like, met with harsh reality. Brian Jones's body had finally given in that summer, and the Stones had played a free tribute show in Hyde Park.

They had hired local Hell's Angels as security. These heavy-looking hair-
ies had 'Hell's Angels' written on their leathers, in case you couldn't tell
who they were meant to be – they were pure panto compared to the
American variety, who were mostly Korea and Vietnam war veterans,
yet the Stones went ahead and booked the Angels to man the crowds at
their last American gig of the year, at Altamont, on December 6th 1969.
The Frisco and Oakland chapters would flank their Satanic Majesties
on stage.

I love the notion of myth in pop, and I'm guessing Jagger and
Richards do too. But this was the cruellest way to dispel the myth of
California, heartland of surf music and endless summers. Altamont
was the climax to something John Phillips had unleashed at Monterey
– the manufactured Utopia of classlessness. 'The Rolling Stones are
still a little bit in 1965,' reckoned David Crosby; 'to them an Angel is
something between Peter Fonda and Dennis Hopper.' In reality, they
were combat-hardened killers. First, the Angels knocked the Jefferson
Airplane's Marty Balin unconscious *while his band were on stage*. After
dark, as the Stones played 'Midnight Rambler', their security guards
killed a black kid in the crowd called Meredith Hunter. Altamont, a
valley in the desert full of dead cars, was where the sixties pop dream
ended. It was a self-made trap. It was stupid and awful and captured in
Gimme Shelter by the Maysles brothers, who less than six years earlier
had filmed the Beatles' first trip to the States. A witness to the horror,
Chris Hillman of the Byrds and the Flying Burrito Brothers, described
Altamont as 'the worst scenario you could imagine. I thought that day
was the end of the 1960s – it had come from the wonderful innocence
of the Beatles and Gerry and the Pacemakers to this.'

The Rolling Stones kept their heads down, re-emerging in 1971 with
'Brown Sugar' (UK no. 2, US no. 1), another party anthem, and the
saucily named *Sticky Fingers* album. They now had a corporate logo,
designed by Andy Warhol. Heavy vibes were banished. Nearly four decades later they are still a party band, have barely changed, give or take
the odd foray into disco. It's only rock 'n' roll. You wonder if Altamont
still preys on their minds, if they remember their naivety, their belief in
their own power crumbling so horribly, so finally in front of them, with

Jagger's words sounding useless, feeble, trembling over the PA: 'Brothers and sisters, why are we fighting?'

For modern pop, Altamont was a decisive break – the end of innocence. There was a darker side, we knew it to be true. One group picked up on this and, rather than look as ugly as possible to show their commitment to the devil's music, they decided to cloak their lyrics with Hobbitry, their artwork with pagan symbols, and dress up like sex gods. Girls didn't fancy Ian Anderson or Peter Green much, but they sure as hell fancied Robert Plant and Jimmy Page. Led Zeppelin also happened to play harder and heavier than any other band in 1969, with a pummelling, punishing drummer in John Bonham. Genuinely, they were scary. With bombast, Celtic mythology and blouses undone to the waist, Led Zep cleaned up while the Stones were still white-faced with post-traumatic stress. It was no coincidence that in 1965 Page had replaced fun-hating Eric Clapton in the Yardbirds, where he honed his electric dreams via their string of white-hot hit singles. And it was also no accident that, in Peter Grant, Led Zeppelin had the most clued-up, unyielding manager in pop since Andrew Oldham. Everything about them – their aura, their instrumentation, their artwork, their manager – was the heaviest. 'I must admit I haven't listened to it straight yet,' said *Rolling Stone*'s John Mendelsohn, reviewing *Led Zeppelin II* – 'I don't think a group this heavy is best enjoyed that way.'

BUBBLEGUM IS THE NAKED TRUTH:
THE MONKEES

The twin promise and tragedy of the sixties was the emergence of a modern pop field in which *anything* was possible. Some time in 1967, its radical unity had broken down, and the extremes had begun to harden in opposed camps – the idea of progress began to define itself against the idea of mere manufactured pop.

The Monkees are one of pop's greatest conundrums. They are seen as the first boy band, but they could (after a fashion, and to varying degrees) all play instruments and write songs. They were the Pre-Fab Four, a deliberate copy of an existing group, but that was only in their scripts. They became a cog in a multinational machine, broke free to create hits entirely on their terms, but were eventually brought down by the hipsters they so wanted to be seen on a par with. They were blamed for ruining pop's innocence, yet their best songs are its quintessence.

Ultimately, they affirmed the Brill Building – and, tangentially, Motown – as the secret motor of the best sixties pop, and also showed Monterey to be the decade's great fulcrum of failure – dethroning the Mamas and Papas (despite their role in setting it up), destabilising Brian Wilson, and putting in their place all kinds of self-satisfied, under-achieving acts.

Let's start with some statistics. Between the end of 1966 and the spring of 1968 the Monkees were the biggest pop group in America, if not the world. Their albums spent thirty-seven weeks at number one in the US, and they scored both 1967's biggest-selling US single ('I'm a Believer') and its third biggest ('Daydream Believer'). *More of the Monkees* is still one of the twenty best selling albums in America. Outside of the States, things barely let up. In Britain, 'I'm a Believer' was number one for seven weeks in early '67; in Japan, they outsold every non-Japanese act in the sixties, then pretty much repeated the feat when they had a revival there in the seventies. Although they only made records for three years – cramming in nine albums, plus dozens of unreleased tracks – they had a huge pop presence until the mid-eighties, and that was all because they had their own TV show.

Already I'm tripping myself up. The Monkees didn't *have* their own TV show, *The Monkees* was the TV show. They were four actors, and they were playing a band who aspired to be the Beatles. Micky Dolenz had been a child star – as Corky he was the main attraction of US TV show *Circus Boy*. By September of 1965 he was struggling to find work as a young adult when he answered an ad in the *Hollywood Reporter* from Raybert Productions. 'MADNESS!! AUDITIONS Folk & Roll Musicians-Singers for acting roles in new tv series,' it read. 'Running parts for 4 insane boys, age 17–21.' When he got there, Dolenz was faced by a desk lined with Coke bottles; behind them, almost totally obscured, sat TV producers Bob Rafelson and Bert Schneider. Dolenz looked at the producers, raised an eyebrow, then carefully, slowly, moved one of the bottles along the table. 'Checkmate,' he said, and got the job.

The 'four insane boys' hand-picked by Rafelson and Schneider – Micky Dolenz, Davy Jones, Michael Nesmith and Peter Tork – were chosen because the series was 'about the guys we were looking for. They didn't have to play the roles – they had to be themselves.' For the young actors, this blurred fiction and reality dangerously: imagine if the characters in *Star Trek* were named William Shatner, Leonard Nimoy and DeForest Kelley – how would this have affected the actors psychologically? As far as the public and most critics were concerned, the group wasn't a TV construct, the group was as real (and as instantly famous) as the Beatles.

When Rafelson and Schneider successfully pitched their show to Screen Gems in 1966, they hadn't thought too hard about the music for *The Monkees*. The storyline would usually involve Peter acting the dummy, Davy falling in love with a teenage cutie, Micky doing a James Cagney impression and Mike being the mature voice of reason. At some point there would be a couple of songs. It was colourful, it was done at breakneck speed and – thanks to Rafelson and Schneider's subversive side – it had a dollop of Dada and it was very funny. The new Marx Brothers, said John Lennon.

The music, including the self-descriptive theme ('We're the young generation, and we've got something to say'), was initially written by jobbing writers Tommy Boyce and Bobby Hart, but soon Brill Building overlord Don Kirshner was brought in, and he smelt big money in the project. The star names of the early sixties – Goffin and King, Mann and Weil, Carole Bayer, David Gates, Russ Titelman – got their first phone calls in months. 'We'll outsell the Beatles,' said Kirshner, and everybody coughed and looked the other way. Session musicians were brought in – the cream of the crop: James Burton and Glen Campbell on guitar, Al Casey on bass, Larry Knechtel on piano, Hal Blaine on drums. It was the whole Spector 'wrecking crew', the 'Da Doo Ron Ron' '63 team brought back together. *Newsweek* called them 'direct videological descendants of the Beatles', even though, from the session musicians' perspective, it must have seemed like the Beatles had never happened. All the boys had to do was add vocals – Kirshner took care of the rest.

Boyce and Hart's plaintive folk jangler 'Last Train to Clarksville' was released as a single just before the series aired. By the time the eighth episode was broadcast, it had replaced ? and the Mysterians' '96 Tears' as the number-one single in America.

The Monkees' timing was perfect. They arrived just as it became clear that the Beatles were no longer cute moptops; in 1966 they had become 'bigger than Jesus' and sprouted facial hair.* The Monkees plugged a gap, fulfilling a need the pop public had for a sweet-faced smiling beat group. As such, with *Revolver* released just prior to the Monkees' break-through, most '66 scenesters thought they were nothing but a put-on, a drag, phoney. The Beatles were kings of the art world; the Monkees were four Johnny Restivos. As a genuine pop phenomenon, the Monkees were put under incredible scrutiny. 'I can only speak for myself,' Davy told the *NME* in January '67. 'I am an actor and I have never pretended to be anything else . . . No one is trying to fool anyone! People have tried to put us down by saying we copy the Beatles. So, alright, maybe *The Monkees* is a half-hour *Hard Day's Night*. But we read that the Who are working on a TV series. Now who's copying who?'†

By February 1967 the Monkees were getting twelve million viewers on US TV, and were simultaneously number one in the British and American album and singles charts. No one had done this before. They had sold six million albums and five million singles in four months. Don Kirshner's prediction had come true in double-quick time.

And at this point something quite unexpected happened.

---

* Facial hair was no laughing matter. When the Monkees' *Headquarters* album appeared in 1967, it featured a picture of the band sporting three weeks' growth. Colgems hurriedly withdrew the album and replaced the photo, lest it scare pre-pubescent fans.
† This was true – Brian Epstein's Subafilms was in discussions with the Who about a Monkees-style series, according to the January 28th 1967 edition of the *NME*. It never got off the ground. Nor did pencilled-in copies starring Haircut 100 or Supergrass. Time and cost aside, any other TV series starring a group would end up being compared to *The Monkees*, and would almost certainly pale. When it did eventually happen – with S Club 7 in Britain in the late nineties – the results were so anodyne and forgettable that most people listening to their singles were unaware there even was a TV show.

The *Saturday Evening Post* wanted to run an exposé on how the Monkees were manufactured, fake, duping the kids, and to their surprise Michael Nesmith was broadly in agreement: 'The music happened in spite of the Monkees. It was what Kirshner wanted to do . . . Tell the world we don't record our own music, but that's us they see on television. The show is really a part of us. They're not seeing something invalid.'

A few weeks later, Micky Dolenz was interviewed by a relative heavyweight, Cliff Michelmore, on the BBC's *24 Hours* show. 'Does it worry you that you are, in effect, a manufactured pop star?' asked Michelmore. 'No, not a bit,' said Micky. 'Because we weren't. I was discovered going to school, LA Trade Tech. Mike was discovered in the Troubadour singing to fifteen people every night. Peter was discovered in Greenwich Village singing to two people every night. And Davy was trying to get a job singing to anybody in LA. No, we're not a manufactured group. Where do you draw the line?'

Unsurprisingly, this all went down like a lead balloon with Don Kirshner. In January 1967 he had heard rumblings of discontent in the group and had flown west – something he only did under extreme duress – with a quarter-million-dollar cheque for each Monkee. That'll placate the ingrates, he thought. Instead, they were belligerent, insisting on recording their own songs and playing on their own records. Kirshner's lawyer drily reminded them that they were all committed to contract, to which Nesmith put his fist through a partition wall and said, in his best Clint Eastwood voice, 'That could've been your face.'

Kirshner relented, a little, and Nesmith hired Chip Douglas, fresh from arranging the Turtles' 'Happy Together', to produce a session on which the Monkees would finally get to play. Chip would become their musical director. Don Kirshner, though, had no intention of releasing these sessions. Why should he listen to these failed musicians and child actors? Hadn't everything he had planned for them been a number-one hit? Sod them, he thought, and sneaked out the next single in Canada hoping no one would notice: 'A Little Bit Me, a Little Bit You', backed with 'She Hangs Out', featured just loyal Davy and a bunch of session musicians. It was a bad miscalculation. When Screen Gems discovered what he had done, they decided the four actors were of greater worth to them than Kirshner and he was duly sacked.

Davy, Peter, Micky and Mike were now no longer four kids playing a part; just three months after the first episode of *The Monkees* aired, they were a fully functioning pop group. Micky quickly learnt to play the drums – 'It's not exactly brain surgery,' he reasoned – and in spring '67 they shut themselves away in RCA Studios on Sunset Boulevard for three weeks to record their third album. The results should have been a disaster, DIY at best; instead, they produced *Headquarters*, quite the most morning-fresh album of the era, with tinges of country and folk rock and a tangible sense of gleeful freedom. Dolenz's 'Randy Scouse Git',* renamed 'Alternate Title' to become a number-two UK hit in the summer of '67, was a wigged-out vaudevillian précis of their time in England, where Dolenz had just met his future wife; 'You Just May Be the One', 'Sunny Girlfriend' and 'You Told Me', Nesmith originals, are distilled California sunshine with hints of Texas that effectively pre-date the biggest-selling American records of the seventies; Tork's 'For Pete's Sake' was a love-generation song strong enough to become the end titles music for their second season. The greatest compliment you can pay *Headquarters* is that almost nobody would have guessed the circumstances in which it was made without being told. It's a miracle of a record.

Their fourth album in just over a year, *Pisces, Aquarius, Capricorn & Jones Ltd*, saw the four bringing in outside musicians and, briefly, considering doing a whole album of Harry Nilsson songs – he was the only contemporary songwriter the thrown-together-fast friends could agree on. It produced another massive single, Goffin and King's paean to suburbia 'Pleasant Valley Sunday' (US no. 3, UK no. 11), with its sly opening line, 'The local rock group down the street is trying hard to learn their songs'. But by the start of '68 the show was losing viewers and it was cancelled, with the last episode going out in the States in March (directed by Micky and called 'The Frodis Caper', the last three

---

* The title was a reference to British comedy series *Till Death Us Do Part*. Dolenz had caught it while he was over and been amused and confused when Warren Mitchell referred to his TV son-in-law Tony Booth as a 'randy Scouse git'. The subject of Mitchell's ire grew up to be Tony Blair's real-life father-in-law.

minutes of it were taken up by Tim Buckley's debut performance of his magical 'Song to the Siren'). By this point, the Monkees' feature film *Head* (originally titled *Untitled*) was well into production.

Head was a suicide note. Rafelson and Schneider wanted to kill their creation in a cinematic car crash. The TV commercial for the movie featured a close-up shot of an unsmiling, balding, sleazy and anonymous man – after thirty seconds he smiled, and the word 'HEAD' appeared on screen. It was a parody of Andy Warhol's 1963 film *Blow Job*, which most Monkees fans, it was safe to say, hadn't seen. The film itself opened with Micky Dolenz committing suicide, jumping from a suspension bridge before being bathed in psychedelic solarisation and carried away by mermaids. This scene was played out to the tune of Goffin and King's elegiac 'Porpoise Song', a heavy, baroque creation orchestrated by Spector sidekick Jack Nitzsche which was a final, fond farewell to not just the Monkees but the sixties.

Did anyone care? Of course not. Rafelson and Schneider acted as if the whole movie was sarcastic (it wasn't), the fans didn't want to see their heroes die, literally, amid shots of Viet Cong assassinations and exploding Coke machines, and the Monterey scenesters weren't about to suddenly tune in. A cover of the Byrds' 'Wasn't Born to Follow' was recorded for the soundtrack; Rafelson and Schneider saved it instead for their next movie, *Easy Rider*, which they didn't have to pretend was all a bit of a put-on. Bob Rafelson's official line after *Head* premiered was: 'I grooved on those four in very special ways while at the same time thinking they had absolutely no talent.'

The Monkees had no map, no rules – they had to forge their own path. They had shown with *Headquarters* that they understood pop better than Screen Gems. But by the end of 1968 this was not enough. When the first *Monkees* show had aired in September '66, there had been no separation between the 'pop' audience and the 'rock' audience; by the time *Head* premiered in November '68, they were two different worlds. The Monkees were seen as lowest-common-denominator moneymakers, harbingers of bubblegum.

The Monkees' immediate influence was felt in a bunch of songs written by a fabulously cynical New York pair called Jerry Kasenetz and Jeff

Katz.* They teamed up with Neil Bogart, late of Cameo Parkway, who had started a new label called Buddah and created a run of super-commercial hits in 1968 and '69, most of which used the Monkees' 'Stepping Stone' as a musical base, then added lyrics that would easily reverberate around the playground: 'Yummy Yummy Yummy', 'Simon Says', '123 Red Light', 'Gimme Gimme Good Lovin".† This was a return to pre-psych basics – garage-band simplicity, riffs and hooks, and in Britain the Equals ('Baby Come Back') and Tommy James and the Shondells ('Mony Mony', surprisingly their only UK Top 30 hit) both benefited from this with 1968 number ones. Kasenetz–Katz's Super K productions were intentionally basic; their lyrics messed with food and love – hence, it was tagged bubblegum – but it took an old hand to make the ultimate hit in this short-lived shock-tactic genre. As the Brill Building cubicles emptied and Ellie Greenwich licked her wounds in her New York apartment, ex-husband Jeff Barry packed his cowboy hat and headed for California. Old Golden Ears Don Kirshner welcomed him back into the fold, and together they concocted a song, which it was only too easy to imagine Davy Jones singing, called 'Sugar, Sugar'. It was given to the Archies, a cartoon group that couldn't answer back or punch holes in walls.

'Sugar, Sugar' is one of pop's most beautifully constructed singles. It's sweet, of course, and takes a while to stretch beyond the rather obvious sugar, honey and candy-girl references, but when it does it catches fire

---

* Their Super K production outfit scored their first hit with the Music Explosion's 'Little Bit of Soul' (US no. 4 '67): *Billboard* reported that for Eric Burdon and the Animals' album *Winds of Change*, 'producer Tom Wilson spent long hours in April through July in three different cities around the world to come up with the finished product. *Little Bit of Soul* by the Music Explosion [was recorded] in about an hour.' Kasenetz and Katz's last hurrah was a spiky attempt at Led Zep bubblegum, Ram Jam's 'Black Betty' (UK no. 7 '77).
† Though it's presumed Kasenetz and Katz put together most of their bands, the Ohio Express ('Yummy Yummy Yummy', 'Chewy Chewy') were very real, a garage band who seemed quite happy to munch on the nasal, repetitive fare Buddah fed them. At the far end of the Super K empire, future 10cc star Graham Gouldman had a short stay writing for Kasenetz and Katz. His only success was 'Susan's Tuba' ('ooby dooby dooba, Susan's got a tuba') for Freddie and the Dreamers, a sizeable European hit, though none of the group appears on it, not even Freddie – Gouldman sang lead.

and it then becomes clear that the song is all a prelude to sex: 'I'm gonna make your life so sweet,' coos Betty Archie, so deeply and huskily it's barely audible, then the line is repeated by excitable Veronica Archie in a precocious squeak, before singer Ron Dante, lead Archie, brings it all back home with real, human desire ('Aaaaaaaah, *SUGAR!*'); the record fades just as it introduces a final hook to snare you, with joyous *ba-ba-ba*s straight out of the Mamas and Papas' locker. It's so good you want to hear it all over again the moment it finishes. It's the kind of single the auto-repeat function on a Dansette was made for.

Christmas 1969 saw teenagers getting their own stereo hi-fi record players, built for long-playing albums; their Dansettes were discarded, handed down to their younger brothers and sisters. In Britain, eight weeks of 'Sugar, Sugar' at no. 1 was followed by six weeks of Rolf Harris's 'Two Little Boys'* as 1969 bled into 1970; the severance between album-based rock and 45-led pop was complete, and the Monkees were held responsible for the inanity at the heart of our singles chart.†

Even now, though 'I'm a Believer' is regarded as a classic, and Dolenz's vocal one of the best blue-eyed soul performances ever, they are tarred as the first boy band, precursors of the Bay City Rollers, New Kids on the Block, Westlife.‡ If only other boy bands were as good, or at least as self-aware. After *Head*, the Monkees hobbled on, shedding members (Tork in '68, Nesmith in '69) until 1970, by which time the shows were already being rerun, keeping them in the minds of pre-teens for more than a decade to come. Their later albums were patchy, a little sad. But

---

* Though it was a regular on the BBC's *Junior Choice*, 'Two Little Boys' was a World War One song about the death of a childhood friend in battle. John Lennon sent a telegram to Rolf Harris congratulating him on having a Christmas number one with an anti-war song in the year of My Lai. Harris later said, 'Lennon got it,' but the point seemed lost on everyone else.

† One of Jonathan King's better musical gags was to try and bridge this real or imagined divide by recording a heavy-rock version of 'Sugar, Sugar' under the name Sakkarin – it was convincing and danceable enough to reach number twelve in 1971.

‡ Hugely successful Irish balladeers the Bachelors – with eighteen UK Top 40 hits in the sixties – were the true forefathers of Westlife, and their catalogue is just as devoid of interest.

against the odds Davy Jones came up with his best-ever effort for their 1969 album *Instant Replay*: the autobiographical 'You and I' has a lyric and a production made all the richer and more bittersweet by the guitar-playing of Neil Young, a pop star whose stature would only grow with the passing years: 'In a year, or maybe two, we'll be gone and someone new will take our place. There'll be another song, another voice, another pretty face.'

PART THREE

top 50

Week ending January 3rd, 1970

1	(1)	TWO LITTLE BOYS Rolf Harris
2	(2)	RUBY Kenny Rogers and First Edition
3	(3)	SUGAR SUGAR Archies
4	(6)	SUSPICIOUS MINDS Elvis Presley
5	(5)	MELTING POT Blue Mink
6	(4)	YESTER-ME Stevie Wonder
7	(7)	ALL I HAVE TO DO IS DREAM Bobbie Gentry/Glen Campbell
8	(8)	WINTER WORLD OF LOVE Engelbert Humperdinck
9	(10)	TRACY Cufflinks
10	(12)	WITHOUT LOVE Tom Jones
11	(13)	ONION SONG Marvin Gaye/Terrell
12	(16)	GOOD OLD ROCK AND ROLL Dave Clark Five
13	(14)	LEAVING Roger Whittaker
14	(9)	CALL ME NUMBER ONE Tremeloes
15	(15)	LOVE IS ALL Malcolm Roberts
16	(11)	THE LIQUADATOR Harry J. All Stars
17	(22)	BUT YOU LOVE ME DADDY Jim Reeves
18	(19)	LONELINESS Des O'Connor
19	(21)	GREEN RIVER Creedence Clearwater Revival
20	(24)	NOBODY'S CHILD Karen Young
21	(18)	SOMETHING/COME TOGETHER Beatles
22	(20)	WITH THE EYES OF A CHILD Cliff Richard
23	(27)	SWEET DREAM Jethro Tull
24	(17)	WONDERFUL WORLD, BEAUTIFUL PEOPLE Jimmy Cliff
25	(28)	LOVE'S BEEN GOOD TO ME Frank Sinatra
26	(23)	HIGHWAY SONG Nancy Sinatra
27	(30)	SOMEDAY Diana Ross and Supremes.
28	(22)	RETURN OF DJANGO Upsetters
29	(37)	IF I THOUGH YOU'D CHANGE YOUR MIND Cilla Black
30	(40)	REFLECTIONS OF MY LIFE Marmalade
31	(25)	OH WELL Fleetwood Mac
32	—	SHE SOLD ME MAGIC/Lou Christie (Buddah 201 065)
33	(33)	BILJO Clodagh Rodgers
34	(31)	I'M GONNA MAKE YOU MINE Lou Christie
35	(38)	SEVENTH SON Georgie Fame
36	(41)	BOY NAMED SUE Johnny Cash
37	—	HITCHING A RIDE/Vanity Fare (Page One POF 158)
38	(39)	GIN GAN GOOLIE Scaffold
39	—	GOOD MORNING STARSHINE/Oliver (CBS 4435)
40	(32)	I'LL NEVER FALL IN LOVE AGAIN Bobbie Gentry
41	—	RUB A DUB DUB/Equals (President PT 275)
42	(49)	MY WAY Frank Sinatra
43	—	HOLY CITY/Moira Anderson (Decca F 12989)
44	(35)	HE AIN'T HEAVY Hollies
45	(50)	HERE COMES THE STAR Herman's Hermits
46	(42)	PROUD MARY Checkmates
47	(34)	COMING HOME Delaney and Bonnie
48	(43)	ROBIN'S RETURN Neville Dickie
49	(46)	JE T'AIME Jane Birkin
50	(36)	WHAT DOES IT TAKE Jnr Walker, All Stars

Published by Cardfont Publishers Ltd., 7 Carnaby Street, W.1.
Distributed by Surridge Dawson Ltd., New Kent Road, S.E.1.
Printed by Pendragon Press Ltd., Old Tram Road, Pontllanfraith,
and C. J. Mason & Sons Ltd., Bristol BS13 7TP.

1970: EVERYTHING'S GONE GREY

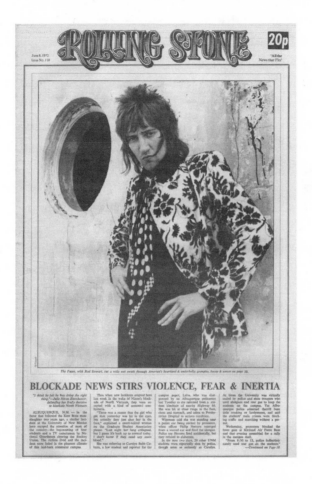

I still get the same old yearning tearing my heart inside out
And now there can't be any doubt
I'm still not over you.
    Pickettywitch, 'That Same Old Feeling'

There's a school of thought that sees a modern pop revolution occurring every ten years: rock 'n' roll taking over in '57, psychedelia in '67, punk in '77, house in '87. The flip side to that is the ten-year lull. 1960 had seen the brave new beat at bay, rock 'n' roll on its knees. Ten years on, things were worse still. By 1970 pop had become a country of melancholic introspection, underachievement and lost idealism.

Pop was in denial that the sixties were over. The Beatles' split, made official by Paul McCartney on April 10th 1970, caused widespread mourning; without the group who had focused pop for seven years internationally, it now suffered a total loss of direction. In need of spiritual renewal, record buyers initially turned to the quasi-hymnal: there was 'Let It Be', the Beatles' swansong, and Simon and Garfunkel's 'Bridge over Troubled Water', then came the musicals *Godspell* and *Jesus Christ Superstar*. Norman Greenbaum's Christian bubblegum rocker 'Spirit in the Sky' was a transatlantic number one. Church aside, the only other places to look were over your shoulder or down at your feet. For those inclined to the latter there was heads-down, no-frills hard rock, which had begun as an extension of the blues revival but was taken in heavier directions by Led Zeppelin, Birmingham's Black Sabbath, teenagers Free, and Deep Purple, a group put together by the Searchers' Chris Curtis before he was kicked out by the other members for his unreliability.* Student unions in Britain saw cross-legged audiences listening to heavy bands in tight tie-dyed shirts with names like Jody Grind, Levee Camp Moan and Titus Groan.† Where to go next? The old dependables didn't have the answer. Think of any of the major names of 1968 – Lennon, McCartney, Byrds, Airplane, Stones, Who, Kinks – and consider the quality drop in their output between then and 1971, when Don McLean wrote 'American Pie', his broadside about the end of a

---

* Picking up Curtis from his flat, the other members of Roundabout – as the first line-up of Deep Purple was known – were surprised to find he'd covered everything in tin foil to confuse anyone who might be spying on him. He was living in complete darkness: the windows were blacked out, and every time he turned the lights on the foil-covered bulb blew up.
† A rocksploitation film from 1970 called *Permissive* shows the true horror awaiting students who were just too young to have made it to college in the sixties. Everyone and everything looks greasy. Titus Groan and Comus play to kids who look as if they're playing a predetermined role, just as surely as their bowler-hatted father and pinafored mother.

golden era. As for the new names, much of their music sounded bored and boring: Pink Floyd scored a UK number-one album with *Atom Heart Mother*, which Roger Waters quickly condemned as 'horrible'; Neil Young's 'Out on the Weekend' ('think I'll pack it in and buy a pick-up') suggested modern pop was flatlining.

One thing the old and new guard were in agreement on was that whatever came next would be album-shaped. Pop had never been an album format until the late sixties. The album may have pre-dated the 45 by a year but it had been the stage for Frank Sinatra's song cycles, for *A Kind of Blue*, for Glenn Gould or the *Sound of Music* soundtrack. Mostly, modern pop albums of the fifties and early sixties were overloaded with filler – usually rush-recorded covers of contemporary hits – and only sold to the wealthy or obsessive fan. *The Freewheelin' Bob Dylan*, *Rubber Soul*, then *Pet Sounds* and, most significantly, *Sgt Pepper's Lonely Hearts Club Band* were the milestones that led to albums becoming a format of choice. This had coincided with psychedelia's stretching out; by 1969 a group like Led Zeppelin could become stars without even releasing singles.* 1969 was the first year when albums in Britain outsold singles, which, very quickly, became derided by rock fans and rock musicians as purely commercial ventures, an industrial by-product. Standing at a bus stop with *Atom Heart Mother* (cow in field, no text at all) under your arm looked considerably cooler than clutching a 45 on the Parlophone label (how very mid-sixties). Singles were now for parents and kids.

By 1970 the UK singles chart had become a house full of yellowing newspapers. Motown reissues were constantly in the Top 20, as soul fans who had been raised on uptempo floor-fillers rejected the new, darker sounds of urban America; the Miracles' 'Tears of a Clown', a track from their 1967 *Make It Happen* album, went all the way to number one. Records seemed to hang around the Top 20 for months, and there were lengthy stays at the top for Mungo Jerry's 'In the Summertime', Freda

---

* The profit margins on albums were considerably greater. Led Zeppelin's manager Peter Grant figured that if you wanted 'Whole Lotta Love' badly enough, you'd fork out £1.99 for *Led Zeppelin II*. There was little more to Led Zep's album-only aesthetic than that.

Payne's 'Band of Gold' (both six weeks) and the reborn Elvis Presley's ballad 'The Wonder of You' (seven weeks), a 1959 hit for Ray Peterson and Ronnie Hilton. Mungo Jerry were the breakthrough act of 1970, an attempt to breathe new life into the goodtime jug-band sound of the Lovin' Spoonful, refracted through the post-flower-power free-love vibe: 'If her daddy's rich take her out for a meal,' they advised. 'If her daddy's poor just do what you feel.' Singer Ray Dorset had an afro, manly side-burns, a vicious gap-toothed smile, shoulders like girders and a voice that could switch from elfin warble to gargling bare-knuckle boxer. They had no drums, sounded like a one-man band with a pub piano on the side, and pressed their singles as value-for-money, ten-minute-plus EPs – great for your pocket, less so for your hi-fi. 'In the Summertime' was followed to the top by 'Baby Jump', maybe the grubbiest number one ever. Manic Jerry Lee Lewis-style piano tried to push along a song that sounded like a JCB stuck in a claypit, as Dorset leered, 'She wears those see-through dresses, she likes to wear her stockings black, and if I see her tonight you can bet your life I'll attack.' This was more the work of a potential stalker than a pin-up. So grey and sludgy, such an uncomfortable listen.

It was downtime for pop. A new wave of British songwriting teams who had emerged on Denmark Street in '67 and '68 seized their chance and, in the absence of new heroes, they hogged the remainder of the Top 20, bringing rare glimpses of daylight: Cook/Greenaway, Hammond/Hazlewood, Carter/Stephens, Fletcher/Flett, Macaulay/McLeod. The Brit Building. These cats certainly knew their way around a studio: super-sessioneers and fine harmonists, they spurned jams and classical-inspired suites for fluid, upfront basslines, clean *Seaside Special* brass – more mussel shells than Muscle Shoals – florid strings and tight melodies. This was Britain's version of bubblegum; while the Kasenetz/Katz team had always seemed cynical and intentionally short-term (and was largely extinct by 1971), the UK output seemed much more crafted, bright and uplifting, the sound of sunset yellow. Edison Lighthouse's 'Love Grows (Where My Rosemary Goes)' was the year's first UK number one and it was a soufflé of a single, one sustained hook (a pretty great one), and it owed nothing to the album chart's prevailing hard-rock sound whatsoever. The singer was a session man called Tony Burrows who was so anonymous that he also sang a run of hits for White Plains ('My Baby Loves Lovin'', 'I've Got You on My Mind', 'When You Are a King'), the Brotherhood of Man ('United We Stand'), Butterscotch ('Don't You Know') and Pipkins ('Gimme Dat Ding') without record buyers being any the wiser. The only singles he couldn't buy a hit with were under his own name.* Burrows was so ubiquitous in 1970 that he appeared three times on the same *Top of the Pops*.

Brit Building music was optimistic, innocent, functional. These records may have been as glamour-free as Pink Floyd, but it's hard to think how a single like White Plains' 'When You Are a King' (UK no. 13 '71) could be improved, wheezing along on barrel-organ minor chords before exploding like a mass of butterflies emerging from a cornfield.

If there was a problem with this school of writers it was that they seemed solely in the business of writing hits, amassing cash and investing in golfwear. None of them were, as Leonard Bernstein had described 1966 pop, 'grasping at the unattainable'. This is where a team like Murray/Callander (Vanity Fare's 'Hitchin' a Ride', Tony Christie's 'Las Vegas', Paper Lace's 'Billy Don't Be a Hero') differed from Mann/Weil, who had been striving to make a political statement that would sell (the Crystals' 'Uptown', the Animals' 'We've Got to Get Out of This Place'), or Leiber/Stoller's promotion of R&B, or Goffin/King's public dissection of their relationship. The days when musical ambition was married to the three-minute single were over; with no need to overstretch themselves, the self-contained Brit hit machine purred along while pop's progressive tendency were split over where to go next.

One single bridged the gap between the two factions. Matthews' Southern Comfort were led by ex-Fairport Convention singer Ian

---

* Of Burrows's many solo singles 'Melanie Makes Me Smile' and 'Every Little Move She Makes' are at least the equal of his hits and highly recommended. In the wake of his 1970 chart domination, Burrows reckons he was 'banned from BBC Radio for two years. That was the period when I had the solo records, and I really and truly couldn't get played. We had no commercial radio in those days, just the BBC.'

Matthews, and their sole hit, 'Woodstock' (UK no. 1 October '70), had been written by Joni Mitchell immediately after the festival. The arrangement's musty, pastoral mood suggested Woodstock in Oxfordshire as much as upstate New York; Mitchell's lyric was quite specifically about something lost, the slight desperation of the chorus – 'We've got to get ourselves back to the garden' – hinting that it'll never happen. Of course, it might also come across that way because Joni wrote it having been unable to get to the Woodstock festival because of the traffic, but from this distance it does sound remarkably like an elegy.

The growing split between singles and albums is revealed by taking a look at the British number ones of 1970. Aside from the generation-spanning 'Bridge over Troubled Water' and sore thumb 'Voodoo Chile' (issued as a 'tribute' within days of Hendrix's death) in the singles list, and the various compilations on the album side, the split is complete and the modern pop consensus dead:

SINGLES

Edison Lighthouse	'Love Grows (Where My Rosemary Goes)'
Lee Marvin	'Wand'rin' Star'
Simon and Garfunkel	'Bridge over Troubled Water'
Dana	'All Kinds of Everything'
Norman Greenbaum	'Spirit in the Sky'
England World Cup Squad	'Back Home'
Christie	'Yellow River'
Mungo Jerry	'In the Summertime'
Elvis Presley	'The Wonder of You'
Smokey Robinson and the Miracles	'The Tears of a Clown'
Freda Payne	'Band of Gold'
Matthews' Southern Comfort	'Woodstock'
Jimi Hendrix Experience	'Voodoo Chile'
Dave Edmunds	'I Hear You Knocking'

ALBUMS

| Led Zeppelin | *Led Zeppelin II* |

Various	*Motown Chartbusters Volume 3*
Simon and Garfunkel	*Bridge over Troubled Water*
Beatles	*Let It Be*
Bob Dylan	*Self Portrait*
Moody Blues	*A Question of Balance*
Creedence Clearwater Revival	*Cosmo's Factory*
Rolling Stones	*Get Yer Ya-Ya's Out*
Black Sabbath	*Paranoid*
Pink Floyd	*Atom Heart Mother*
Various	*Motown Chartbusters Volume 4*
Led Zeppelin	*Led Zeppelin III*
Bob Dylan	*New Morning*
Andy Williams	*Andy Williams' Greatest Hits*

Listening to albums also meant you didn't have to get out of your chair every three minutes. They suited the heads, sweating in their digs to heavyweight stoner material from Pink Floyd and Black Sabbath, as well as the bucolic world of the early seventies' failed revolutionaries. The singer-songwriter tones of Cat Stevens, Melanie and Gordon Lightfoot provided homespun philosophies; Carole King – transposed from the Brill Building to the west coast – was now an earth mother. They provided balm for the walking wounded, the sixties fighters burned by the events in Chicago and Hornsey in '68 and the return of Republican and Conservative governments in 1969/70 who were unwilling to take the fight forward with the Weathermen or the Angry Brigade. *New Morning*, Carole King's *Tapestry*, and *Bridge over Troubled Water* all pointed to resolution. Dissenting voices were welcome but thin on the ground. The brittle, nihilistic debut album by Loudon Wainwright III was one: monochrome and proto-punk on the cover, he tried to stir to things up – 'Earth is a mystery mother,' he sniggered, 'but then again so is Mom.'

Records were made all the worse by new twenty-four-track studio technology that had yet to be mastered by most producers used to smaller mixing desks; vocals and individual instruments would be recorded on separate tracks, leaving them sounding flatter, lifeless, caked in festival mud. Trying to revive the spirit of Woodstock, as if it had been a new dawn rather than a sunset, festivals sprouted in unlikely spots like Maidstone aerodrome and Bickershaw, a pit village near Wigan. The first free festival, soon to become a seventies staple, was at Shepton Mallet, where the Pink Fairies and Hawkwind – long-haired groovers relentlessly in search of inner space – played on a flat-bed truck adjacent to the Bath Blues Festival, where Led Zeppelin were headlining and commanding a fee of £20,000. In America, the Powder Ridge Rock Festival was scheduled to be held over the first weekend in August at a ski resort in Connecticut. It was cancelled, but a crowd of thirty thousand arrived anyway. A volunteer doctor on the site declared a 'drug crisis. Woodstock was a pale pot scene. This is a heavy hallucinogens scene.' The water butts were spiked with any drugs people felt free enough to share. The Black Panthers gave a speech as a thunderstorm brewed and there were bad trips all round.

Flash was out. So similar-looking were the cheesecloth- and denim-wearing singer-songwriters* that it only took a twist, a strip of tartan, a flat cap or a pair of oversize glasses and you stood out like a vicar in a tutu. Gilbert O'Sullivan dressed like an Irish schoolboy from the thirties, which – along with sentimental hits like 'Claire', dedicated to a six-year-old – distracted from a rather black worldview made commercial by a fine sense of semi-detached suburban detail. 'Alone Again (Naturally)' was his biggest hit, a rare American number one about suicide; 'Nothing Rhymed' (UK no. 8), his first hit in 1970, threw in references to Bonaparte Shandy, apple pies and starving Africans; 'We Will' (UK no. 16 '71), with its nods to football, church, Uncle Frank and Auntie May, even suggested he could be pop's Alan Bennett.

The main problem was his voice, which was reminiscent of Paul McCartney with a heavy cold. Gilbert also turned out to be a rather bitter man, as well as an arch-sentimentalist. When the public shunned

---

* This generic look, with no distinguishing visual marks, is the easiest explanation as to why so many artists revered forty years later – Judee Sill, Nick Drake, Vashti Bunyan, Linda Perhacs – slipped through the net at the time.

him in the mid-seventies after one too many jaunty romps, one too many dad jokes, he blamed his management and disappeared in a sulk. The pleasures of 'We Will' would be historically outweighed by songs like 'Ooh Wakka Doo Wakka Day' (UK no. 8 '72) that just weren't built to last. The title of one compilation – *The Berry Vest of Gilbert O'Sullivan* – gets to the heart of the problem.

Elton John had been around for a while, playing piano for such unpromising-sounding acts as Bluesology and the Bread and Beer Band. To supplement his low income he was also a session pianist (that's him on the Hollies' 'He Ain't Heavy, He's My Brother') and anonymously sang covers of current hits for budget supermarket compilations (his recording of Bob and Marcia's 'Young, Gifted and Black' was quite something). By 1970 he had a solo deal with the tiny DJM label, and nobody expected much to happen except his best mate and lyricist, Bernie Taupin. Just a year earlier, they'd tried to write an entry for the Eurovision Song Contest called 'Can't Go On Living without You'. Sung by Lulu as one of six entries on national TV, it came sixth. Elton's diary entry for April 22nd 1969 read: 'Got home tonight to find that Auntie Win and Mum had bought me a car – Hillman Husky Estate – superb!!'

Short, short-sighted, far from hirsute, the reinvention of Watford FC season-ticket-holder Reg Dwight was a thing to behold. First, he decided that, rather than compete with the likes of sweet baby James Taylor in the pin-up stakes, he'd come over so outrageously that you'd forget all about his thinning hair and his indoor complexion: he started sporting a Julius Caesar crop, huge sunglasses, yellow and green velveteen trousers, a white ruffled Liberace shirt, a blue serge waistcoat, white patent leather boots and, to top it off, an enormous Donald Duck badge on his lapel. Then he wrote a very 1970-sounding mope called 'Your Song', which made the Top 10 in America before repeating the feat in Britain a few months later. On tour stateside, Quincy Jones shook his hand. Suddenly, little Reg was a star.

The rapidity of Elton John's breakthrough was largely down to his crazed stage antics. He'd jump on his grand piano, mashing it with his feet, reviving the spirit of Jerry Lee Lewis. 'Jagger and Lennon', he said, 'show you that living an ordinary life is only boring. I love Jagger. Being outrageous on stage is part of it for me, I have to, because ordinarily I'm such a quiet person.' Yet his music – gospel-inspired and largely ballad-led – reflected the bedroom-bound Reg who would occasionally leave the house to potter around Watford in his Hillman Husky.

'My roots are listening to records. All the time. I live, eat, sleep, breathe music. Neil Young, the Band, the Springfield, the Dead, the Airplane. I feel more American than British. Really.' He wasn't kidding. Those were no Hertfordshire vowels on 'Your Song': 'I hope you don't mind' became 'I hawp yi dawn maand'. He should care if I mock. Elton turned out some beautiful, post-Spectorian things on his seventies hot streak – 'Goodbye Yellow Brick Road' (US no. 2, UK no. 6 '73), 'Someone Saved My Life Tonight' (US no. 4, UK no. 22 '75) – and he made so much money he could afford to splash it on Watford FC, helping to lift them from the fourth division to European contention. No matter how Hollywood he got his friends still called him Reg, even after fifty-six American Top 40 hits.

Another veteran of the sixties British R&B circuit was Rod Stewart. He liked football, too, and could have turned professional, but instead he found himself a band that needed a helping hand. After losing Steve Marriott in 1969, the Small Faces had become the Faces, and Rod – late of the Hoochie Coochie Men, Steampacket, Shotgun Express and the Jeff Beck Group – was another lad about town, the Sam Cooke of Highgate who sang with a rasp that was urgent enough for the heads and the soul boys but could also bring the birds down from the trees, and frequently did.

Rod had made all the classic Anglo pop moves – bought Little Richard records, joined a skiffle group and auditioned for Joe Meek – before he became an active supporter of CND, joining the Aldermaston Marches from 1961 to '63, entertaining the protestors with early Dylan songs and getting himself arrested at sit-ins for his trouble. His main motivation wasn't to see the red flag flying over Downing Street, though, but to meet and bed girls. One day in 1963, after Rod and his mates accidentally set fire to a squat in Hampstead, his mum threw his much-prized but rarely washed rollneck and jeans on the fire, and Rod split the beatnik scene to become a mod. When his career finally picked up momentum in 1969, he divided his time between solo and Faces albums and turned out to be a natural storyteller. He had an ear for the sound palette of blues, soul and folk, and could work them into something that sounded working-class, English, shrouded in a muted brown North London mist. 'Maggie May', a US and UK number-one single in '71, didn't even have a chorus, just a yarn that kept you hooked for four full minutes before its mandolin coda. He'd invented his own myth before the single hit the run-out groove, the bruised lover who can seduce an older woman but, heck, if she packs him in there's always the pool hall and the lads. A year later he reprised the affair on 'You Wear It Well' (UK no. 1, US no. 13 '72), on which he gently ribbed his ex while still eating his heart out, trying to get back with her: 'You wear it well, a little old-fashioned . . . but that's all right.'

This appealed to boys and girls, men and women, and Rod Stewart became a superstar. By 1975 he had also become a tax exile, moving to LA, cutting the blustery, antiseptic single 'Sailing' (UK no. 1, US no. 58 '75), and causing outrage among his fans. 'Rarely has a singer had as full and unique a talent as Rod Stewart,' wrote Greil Marcus, 'rarely has anyone betrayed his talent so completely.' The other viewpoint was that rarely does a working-class kid from the Archway Road get to move to California, dine on champagne and be fed grapes by blonde nubiles. He may have betrayed his talent, but he wasn't betraying his roots – if his strike rate slowed, it was no great shock. Besides, his demise was in no way instantaneous. As late as 1981 he could still sit you down, spin a yarn and keep you fascinated. Set to a quickfire electro backing, 'Young Turks' (UK no. 11, US no. 5 '81) – about two eloping New Jersey kids – was an anthem for the Pepsi generation: 'Don't let them put you down, don't let them push you 'round, don't let them ever change your point of view,' winked Uncle Rod. I won't spoil his curious cautionary-cum-celebratory punchline.

Rod and Elton, Zeppelin and Purple, they all pointed to a future, to something specifically seventies, but it was all in shades of grey compared to the myriad colours of the late sixties. The elephant in the room was the Beatles, now in four pieces. Initially it was the unlikely lads who looked as if they might have come out of the break-up best: Ringo released the stellar 'It Don't Come Easy' 45 (UK and US no. 4 '71) and at a stroke trounced all his Beatles novelty efforts, while George sounded like a free man with nothing but open spaces on his mind on the vast but vastly successful *All Things Must Pass* triple album and its lead single 'My Sweet Lord', an international number one. It wouldn't last. By the time of *Living in the Material World*, his second album a full three years later, it was already clear that he'd been stockpiling songs for *All Things Must Pass*, while offloading tosh like 'Savoy Truffle' onto the later Beatles albums.

John Lennon initially released the bleak *Plastic Ono Band* album as therapy, which was hard work, quite un-Beatles and very 1970, though much of it sounded whiney and little more than self-pitying when stacked alongside the raincloud of breakdown albums scattered through the seventies.* 'I don't believe in Beatles,' he sang, to slam that door shut. Things improved with his mood on two scorching singles – 'Instant Karma' (UK no. 5, US no. 3 '70) and 'Power to the People' (UK no. 7, US no. 11 '71) – and the almost homely *Imagine* album in '71. Beyond that, jewels like 'Mind Games' and 'Number Nine Dream' were rare, scattered over the rest of the decade. *Double Fantasy*, his last album issued shortly before his death in 1980, was a thin stew of icky philosophies mushed in a blender until they resemble puréed carrot and peas. His taste for Maoism had been displaced by rich-man domesticity, and his efforts on *Double Fantasy* were shown up by the contributions of his wife Yoko Ono, whose scratchily erotic 'Kiss Kiss Kiss' sounded very New York 1980. Lennon's 'Beautiful Boy' sounded like he wished it could be 1970 again (here's another unwritten rule of modern pop – never write songs about your kids).

People who had pinned their hopes on Paul lighting the way in the darkness of the new decade got to hear him sing 'I want a home, I want a sheep, I want to get me a good night's sleep' on good days and snidey songs about his ex-bandmates ('Three Legs', 'Too Many People') on bad. Having paved the way for the seventies with *Abbey Road*'s

---

* Nick Drake's *Pink Moon*, Big Star's *Sister Lovers*, Marvin Gaye's *Here, My Dear*, Gerry Goffin's (unlistenable but heartbreaking) *It Ain't Exactly Entertainment*.

studio-stretching collage in '69, he generally retreated into campfire cosiness; *Ram* was *Abbey Road*'s spiritual successor, arguably his best album of the seventies, and he never lost his deceptively easy melodic gift.* But sonic innovation and tub-thumping were behind him. Who could blame him? He must have been knackered. All four, in every way, were ex-Beatles. The early seventies was a post-Beatles world.

* As soon as the seventies ended, and punk had meant no one would ever again look to him for innovation, he produced the electro-minimalism of *McCartney II* in 1980, mixing avant instrumentals ('Front Parlour') with trademark winsomeness ('Waterfalls') to great effect, especially when it was stacked up against Lennon's 1980 retro wimp rock on *Double Fantasy*. The first decade of the twenty-first century likewise saw him write more emotionally open songs than he ever had before ('Memory Almost Full') and mixing art and commerce on the Fireman projects. When he's gone, Paul McCartney will be everyone's favourite Beatle.

AN ENGLISH PASTORAL:
BRITISH FOLK ROCK

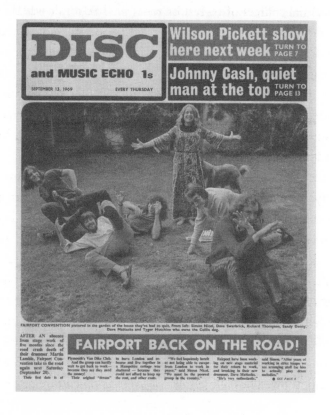

When I write songs I often picture myself standing on a beach, or standing on a rock, or a promenade or something. I just put myself there sometimes and without even realising it I find myself describing what I'm looking at and often it's the sea. I keep promising myself I'll put myself somewhere else when I'm writing songs but I really can't think of anywhere that's nicer than that.

Sandy Denny, *Sounds*, 1973

Modern pop may have been well defined – well established in the market, certainly – in the early seventies, with its hard-rock albums and soft-bubblegum singles, but in its divided state, post-Beatles, it was deeply wanting. Throughout the first half of the decade there was a furthering of this split, and a withdrawal – especially in America – from any potential sources of revival or renewal. The result was that music on the outside of the mainstream started to become more important – sounds from beyond the Anglo-American ambit, from various points in the past (the twenties, the fifties, the seventeenth century), from the suburbs rather than the city centre, from Jamaica, from truculent electric noise, from ultra-black funk. As deep soul had done, different musical strains started to pass close to planet pop without landing, causing a fuss without ever seizing control.

British folk rock was an early indicator of things to come. It was music made in a bubble, a space free of commercial and even chronological constraints; much of the British folk scene was making music that possibly nobody wanted in the belief that, some day, someone would. It was a pocket of idealism that – when it worked its way through – emerged in a striking and unexpected way. By the turn of the seventies folk seemed to be everywhere in Britain, informing children's TV (*The Changes, Children of the Stones, The Owl Service*) and cinema (*Witchfinder General, The Wicker Man*). The cover of *Led Zeppelin IV,** a painting of an old farmer on the wall of a derelict house in an urban wasteland, showed how close folk was to the pop-culture pulse.

---

* Led Zeppelin's isolated Welsh home, Bron-yr-Aur, was only ten miles from where acid-folk group Trees rehearsed and the same distance from Cader Idris, in the same Snowdonian territory as Alan Garner's novel *The Owl Service*. This had been turned into a disturbing children's television series in 1969, with Gillian Hills – an Anglo-French yé-yé singer who had made an exquisite, breathy folk-pop 45 called 'Look at Them' in 1965 – as the flame-haired reincarnation of Blodeuwedd, a mythical woman made from flowers. Mixing the occult, the class system and adolescent sexuality, it found a counterpart in the Christian-baiting, anti-Establishment horror film *The Wicker Man* three years later. Both couched eroticism and nature worship in eerie, ivy-hung acoustic folk, the music of the ages made new. It declared victory for the pagans. No wonder it kept its head down – the *Wicker Man* soundtrack wouldn't get an official release until the nineties.

British folk rock was a side effect of the post-psychedelic search for roots and escape from pop's perceived plasticity, quite different from the American twelve-string and protest-based variant of 1965. Partly it reflected the move from urban to rural. Swinging London was over, the scene had become stale, it made sense to decamp to a cottage where, chances were, you wouldn't get busted. It had filtered through from a Soho club movement, the stars of which coalesced in a supergroup, Pentangle, in 1968. In their wake came a bunch of contemplative outsiders, without the flash or confidence to have made it in pre-hippie pop, who were brought out of themselves by the musical and social freedoms of the late sixties; shy kids who could barely make eye contact when they went to buy a paper suddenly found themselves with an album deal just because they owned an acoustic guitar.

In some respects the folk-rock movement was barely pop at all, but at the turn of the seventies it had real commercial clout: if the Band could move out to Woodstock to reconnect with America's past, then idylls in Dorset, Hampshire or the Scottish borders could be just as inspiring to London-based acts on a post-flower-power comedown – we had the hedgerows, we had the Tudor houses, we had the crofts, we had the country pubs. We weren't short of history and inspiration. By the early seventies British TV soundtracks were often folk-based, Fairport Convention were high in the album chart and Polydor had launched a subsidiary called Folk Mill. This was different from 1968's rock retrenchment – it was an attempt to forge a way forward through musical archaeology and Apollonian productions.

The roots of British folk rock had been another offshoot of the beatnik trad-jazz boom – while some had followed Chris Barber's blues train, others connected with the acoustic guitar. The post-war, left-leaning folk clubs, led by the dry, dogmatic figure of Ewan MacColl, had produced two firestarters in Anne Briggs and Shirley Collins,* the English wife of American song collector Alan Lomax; their a cappella visions were taken a step forward in the early sixties on collaborations

---

* Shirley Collins's voice is so close to the soil of Albion that a German admirer once complimented her by telling her she sounded 'like a potato'.

with Bert Jansch and Davy Graham, guitarists who saw no boundaries between folk, blues and jazz.

Davy Graham was something new under the sun. Born in Hinckley, Leicestershire, to a Guyanese mother and Scottish father, he was a heroin addict with restless feet who had travelled to Africa and India in the late fifties, returning with a new way of tuning his guitar – DADGAD – and a tricksy melody he had written called 'Anji'. Released on an EP in 1962 by the folk label Topic, 'Anji' soon became the standard by which all guitar players were judged. With Shirley Collins, Graham cut an album called *Folk Roots New Routes* in 1964, which was the first time anyone had taken traditional English songs like 'Reynardine' and given them a guitar backing.* Folk, jazz and blues merged; Miles Davis, modal music and North African scales all fed into *Folk Roots New Routes*. Art-school kids turned off by the growing commercialisation of the blues by the Rolling Stones and their ilk were understandably hooked.

By 1964 the Soho scene – featuring John Renbourn, Roy Harper, Martin Carthy and US émigrés Paul Simon and Jackson C. Frank† – was strong enough for a string of clubs to play host to the new folk movement; upstairs rooms at the Prince of Wales Feathers on Warren Street and the King and Queen on Foley Street were colonised, and the Les Cousins club on Greek Street became the folk equivalent of the Cavern. The best of these acts appeared on the Transatlantic label – the producer, Bill Leader, recorded many of them in his Camden Town flat on a Revox tape recorder, using blankets and egg boxes for soundproofing.

---

* Traditional British folk singers never had a guitar, electric or acoustic – the trad form was a cappella. So the sixties folk-club fear of 'going electric' never made sense. Instead, the hardliners should have been against the guitar altogether.

† Frank was in a school fire as a kid, in which most of his classmates died. When he turned sixteen, he collected a load of compensation money and came over to London. He stayed on an even keel for long enough to make the best record of the Soho folk era, his self-titled album on Columbia, which included his own theme tune, 'Blues Run the Game'. The tragic nature of his life and wasted talent is about as extreme as it gets: Frank had long been homeless, broke and blind in one eye – shot randomly by a stranger for fun – by the time he died. The only other recordings he made (in the early seventies) were released posthumously, and included the busted but beautiful 'Marnie'.

John Renbourn remembered a session for the touchstone *Bert and John* album with Leader 'setting up the tape machine in the sink and having us play in the broom cupboard'. It was small-time, but it was intense.

King of this world was Bert Jansch, a Glaswegian with a look of total concentration beneath a black curly mop. He rarely spoke, a man of mystery – the fact was he had very little to say. He loved a pint and he loved his guitar, and women adored him (he loved this as well). His best-known song was 'Needle of Death', written for Davy Graham; it was cold, unromantic and hypnotic. It was on Jansch's self-titled first album, which featured a stark black-and-white photo of the tousled Bert on the cover. Even the pirate stations wouldn't touch it – its legend spread purely by word of mouth.

By 1966 the brightness had been turned up in London. Al Stewart wrote a song called 'Swiss Cottage Manoeuvres', Jansch and Renbourn cut 'Soho', Roy Harper wrote 'Freak Suite' about the scene's focal point, Greek Street. A wide-eyed boy from St Albans called Donovan wrote 'Sunny Goodge Street', 'Hampstead Incident' and 'Sunny South Kensington', three of the greatest odes to sixties London. His tuning was learnt from Jansch, but his voice and his curly locks brought to mind Chatterton or Byron; Donovan's was a refined bohemia that took folk out of Soho clubs and all the way to number one in the US in '66 with 'Sunshine Superman'. Some of the Soho crowd thought him a copyist and a fake Bob Dylan;* when he was made to look foolish by Dylan, like a fourth-rate imitator, in D. A. Pennebaker's documentary *Don't Look Back*, it became apparent that – in spite of what Donovan may have thought – the two had little in common. One was a hummingbird, one was a hornet.

Initially, he had been under the wing of a North London manager/ producer called Peter Eden, who sensed Donovan could be Britain's first

---

* A tipsy Jansch claimed in 1970 that Donovan's management would call on him and buy tunes to give to their charge. This seems extremely unlikely – Donovan had an easy way with a melody, while Jansch's talent was all in his guitar-playing. His only obvious attempt at writing a hit was 'Woe Is Love My Dear', a 1967 orchestrated single that was too subtle to work on the radio and on which he sounded too constrained.

folk superstar; Eden secured him a run of appearances on *Ready Steady Go!* which got him two fast hits with 'Catch the Wind' and 'Colours' (both UK no. 4 '65). Contract disputes then stalled Donovan's career, so he swanned off to the States in late '65 and came across San Francisco's fledgling psychedelic scene. Heading home with a stash of new songs and lysergic inspirations, he went to work with hit-machine producer Mickie Most* and was rarely off the charts for the next four years. Though his base was still folk, which could be quite straight-ahead and Soho-style on album tracks like 'Young Girl Blues' or 'Sand and Foam', Donovan's A-sides ranged from the 'blow your little mind' psych 'Sunshine Superman' (US no. 1, UK no. 2 '66) to the dope-addled New Orleans jelly roll of 'Mellow Yellow' (US no. 2, UK no. 8 '67) and the childlike, bassoon-led 'Jennifer Juniper' (UK no. 5 '68). Best of all was the very strange 'Hurdy Gurdy Man' (UK no. 4 '68), a piece of hard-edged, eerie psychedelia, with Donovan's voice sounding like it had been recorded under water, as if he was Ophelia's kindred spirit.

He was a very gentle man. In 1967 he told the *NME*'s Keith Altham, 'All the really beautiful things happen so slowly that we hardly ever see them – the clouds, the tides, birds, the wind rising. All things are fascinating and inspiring if you only give yourself the time to watch. It's at those times I get my inspiration.' He wasn't scared to write albums for children – not one, but two.† In a way he epitomised the late sixties as concisely as Eddie Cochran had the late fifties and, when the calendar

---

* Most's success was phenomenal – he'd already scored number ones, almost back to back, with Herman's Hermits and the Animals in '64, and would go on to boss the glam scene with his RAK label. I'd grant him more space if I could only find some common thread. Where's the link between Eric Burdon's wailing 'House of the Rising Sun', the pitter-patter beat of 'I'm into Something Good', Donovan's stoned, nearly legal 'Mellow Yellow' and Mud's 'Tiger Feet'? Search me. Most seemed to know exactly what the public wanted, no more, no less. In this respect, he probably had a better ear for a hit than anyone else in this book.

† 1967's *For Little Ones* (released in the UK as part of the double set *A Gift from a Flower to a Garden*, along with *Wear Your Love Like Heaven*) and 1970's *HMS Donovan* both have moments colourful and haunting enough to give a child with a vivid imagination some wild dreams. The cover of *HMS Donovan*, with sailor-suited Don looking as if his face is melting, surrounded by jabberwocks and all manner of weirdness, is more nightmarish.

turned to January 1st 1970, his career died like a butterfly in winter.

Donovan was the key link between the Soho cellars and the folk-rock boom. He led the way to a pharmaceutically informed music that was open to Albion's mythic past, a mixture of the bubbling Soho folk scene and psychedelic rock. He had an arranger called John Cameron, who augmented his songs with excellent jazz musicians – notably Jamaica-born flautist Harold McNair, the secret star of the *Mellow Yellow* album. He was as comfortable toying with jazz ('The Observation') as he was with Arabic and Indian styles ('River Song'), and all of this was rooted in solid rock session work: 'Hurdy Gurdy Man' featured soon-to-be Led Zep members Jimmy Page and John Paul Jones, with ex-Tornados drummer Clem Cattini at his busiest; 'Barabajagal' (UK no. 12 '69) was turned into a flaming floor-filler thanks to the backing of the Jeff Beck Group. And yet Donovan was allied so closely to flower power his career couldn't survive the transition into the new world of folk rock he had pioneered.

Other Soho folk survivors ganged together and, with some fanfare in the press, created the scene's first star attraction. Bert Jansch and John Renbourn – after Jansch's failed attempt at a pop crossover in '67 with the *Nicola* album – met up with clear-voiced singer Jacqui McShee, a bear of a bassist called Danny Thompson and nimble jazz drummer Terry Cox. Calling themselves Pentangle – the name had spooky connotations, definitely not flowery – they were as unreadable as a stone circle. 'There's one thing we never talk about – music,' said Jansch in 1970. 'We never talk music to each other. You understand? It's like, we talk about what we're going to do next. Where we're going, what bars we're going to visit, whether we can have a game of golf at all, or who won the football . . . never music.' The exceptionally pretty 'Light Flight' was used as the theme to TV series *Take Three Girls*, and their career had lift-off; it was a perfect musical evocation of escape from the city, buying the ticket, boarding a train at Marylebone and – into the wordless dream of its middle eight – drifting far away. With their perceived heads-down heaviness, Pentangle walked streets where softie pop star Donovan was forbidden. They may have been cold as ice but, on *Basket of Light* or *Solomon's Seal*, they had the keys to a secret garden.

Up in Muswell Hill, meanwhile, were a group of middle-class kids

who rehearsed above a dentist's surgery in a house on Fortis Green called
Fairport. They called themselves Fairport Convention, which tripped
off the tongue as smoothly as Jefferson Airplane, and they turned out
to be far more approachable and less intimidating than Pentangle. The
rich, lightly psychedelic mix of their first album in '68 featured Joni
Mitchell covers, Byrds-like harmony and a lovely singer called Judy
Dyble. They may have been US-fixated, but already you could sense
oak and brocade in Fairport's music. In fact, they sounded exactly like
the Arts and Crafts house in which they played.

In what was to be the first of many line-up changes, Dyble left in
1968; manager Joe Boyd then introduced the group to Wimbledon-
born folk singer Sandy Denny, whose voice was so astonishingly pure
and strong that she had no equal, and Fairport had no choice but to
invite her into their home.* Denny was a tomboy with waves of red
hair; she sounded warm, comforting, ancient and modern, and suited
the group's temperament perfectly. As their new singer she quickly
bossed the group towards an English sound – 'Nottamun Town' was the
first traditional folk song they recorded, on a BBC session in June '68.

By their third album, which had the oblique but quite perfect title
Unhalfbricking, Fairport Convention had one foot in Home Counties
suburbia, the other in seventeenth-century Suffolk. Richard Thompson's
west-coast guitar lines flowed around Sandy Denny's liquid, centuries-
old voice, and everything clicked. By the spring of '69 Fairport were
on *Top of the Pops* (with a perverse French-language cover of Dylan's 'If
You Gotta Go, Go Now') and looked set for stardom. Then one night,
returning to London from a gig, their van came off the M1: drummer
Martin Lamble and Richard Thompson's girlfriend Jeannie Franklin
were killed. According to the *NME*'s Chris Welch, clubs around the
country played their prophetic 'Meet on the Ledge' in tribute.

Once he got out of hospital, bassist Ashley Hutchings, who had
escaped the crash with a broken nose and cheekbone, went to as many

---

* Judy Dyble resurfaced as half of Trader Horne, with former Them guitarist
Jackie McAuley. Their one album, the very delicate *Morning Way*, works like a
fairy tale. It's good medicine if you like your folk rock from the winsome end of
the spectrum.

folk festivals as he could, talking late into the night with traditional and revival musicians, obsessing over the English Folk and Dance Society's archive at Cecil Sharp House in Camden Town. It may have been therapy, but it resulted in their best-selling album, *Liege and Lief*, which was almost entirely made up of traditional folk songs. Coming out just five months after the crash, it was impressive, slightly academic, and inevitably lacked the clear-eyed sense of fun of their earlier albums. *Rolling Stone* called it 'a nice album to accompany sitting by the fireplace or staring vacantly at a candle flame'. Narrowing their vision, they had created a folk-rock template (Trees, Steeleye Span and the Woods Band couldn't have existed without it), but destroyed themselves in the process. Thompson ('Meet on the Ledge') and Denny ('Who Knows Where the Time Goes', 'Autopsy') had already proved they were very talented songwriters. Unsurprisingly, they both quit soon after *Liege and Lief*. Fairport would carry on selling records and playing to folk lovers for decades to come, but their muse was gone.

Peeking out of glades, glebes and garden sheds were gentler souls and wild eccentrics: Heron, Trader Horne, Nick Drake and Vashti Bunyan* created music that seemed to use birdsong and fresh air as instruments – Vashti once admitted apologising to a piece of broccoli after she'd picked it. There were other folk discontents who tended towards the apocalyptic. Michael Chapman, Bill Fay and Roy Harper were visionary descendants of social outcasts like Augustus John and Peter Warlock, genuine mavericks who probably didn't subscribe to Donovan's petal-strewn image of the world.

An also-ran of the Soho scene, Roy Harper was an unlikely sonic voyager. He'd been in the RAF, in prison and in Lancaster Moor Mental Institution before he headed to London with his guitar. 'If you're a wild

---

* Nick Drake and Vashti Bunyan were among the lucky few to benefit from the verdant melancholy of Robert Kirby's arrangements. They reflected and amplified the profound loneliness in Drake's music, brought a skip to Bunyan's 'Just Another Diamond Day'; he also arranged John Cale's 'I Keep a Close Watch' and Keith Christmas's 'Forest and the Shore', two songs whose majesty is akin to standing on the top of the Long Mynd.

animal,' he told *Rolling Stone*, 'there's only one thing you want to do. That's escape.' He became the life and soul of the party, the ultimate giggling stoner, sharing Pink Floyd's manager, Peter Jenner, and guesting on their *Wish You Were Here* album. Led Zeppelin were similarly enamoured of his untamed spirit, paying tribute with 'Hats Off to (Roy) Harper' on their third album. Harper himself never seemed to keep his pants on for long enough to make a great album until 1971's *Stormcock*, which was made up of four lengthy songs, accompanied by David Bedford's luxuriant strings and Harper's whirlpool of echoes and delays. It was breathtaking.

A year later, Harper was doing a screen test to play a fictional pop star. He was up against stiff competition, from Ray Davies and Marc Bolan, but director John Mackenzie picked him to play Mike Preston in his 1972 big-screen debut, *Made*.* How Mackenzie must have wished he had plumped for the Bopping Elf or the saturnine Davies – Harper was such a handful that at one point he stuck a magnet inside the tape box containing potential spin-off hit 'Valerie's Song', erasing half the track. Asked to re-record it, he sang 'Shitty city, shitty city' over the blank parts. Radio 1 received the single with raised eyebrows. The single, and the movie, undeservedly sank in a sea of indifference. Roy Harper returned to the margins.

Outselling Fairport, Pentangle and everyone else in British folk rock were Lindisfarne. 'Lady Eleanor' was the most successful UK folk-rock single of all, reaching number three in 1972. It floated on finger bells, a warm organ swell and a picked mandolin, with its tales of the dead dancing in soft meadows softened by a more radio-friendly chorus than 'Valerie's Song' or 'Needle of Death': 'It's all right, Lady Eleanor, it's all right.' Lindisfarne's music wasn't a product of chewing on blades of grass in the shade of an old oak tree, however. Their mythical visions were fed on stout, and their album *Fog on the Tyne* went all the way to number

---

* Mackenzie was a BBC *Play for Today* veteran who went on to make *The Long Good Friday*, and his cinema debut is bleak beyond belief. Carol White plays Valerie, a downtrodden single mum who meets hippie Mike – all flaxen hair and cheeky grin – on Brighton beach as he is being interviewed. When Preston, having rubbed noses with her, turns Valerie's plight into a hit record, everything goes dark.

one in 1972. The title track, though not a hit, became their best-known
song and replaced images of the siren Lady Eleanor with 'sickly sausage
rolls'. Relentless touring built their audience. 'We'll never work as hard
as this again,' said guitarist Si Cowe in 1973, 'it's killing the magic. And
it's not doing us much good either.' He lifted up his jumper to show a
Melody Maker journalist his shingles: 'It's a nervous complaint. We've all
had something.'

A scene based around myth, ancient history and nature's magic wasn't
built to last. Some of the records made under the folk-rock banner –
Oberon's 'Nottamun Town', Stone Angel's 'The Bells of Dunwich', the
Water into Wine Band's 'Harvest Time' – were recorded in makeshift
studios and pressed in tiny amounts; they were as localised and obscure
as a deep-soul 45 from Shreveport or a rockabilly single from Wink,
Texas. Decades on, they sound as lost and adrift from the modern world
as Cecil Sharp's field recordings of the twenties: campfire get-togethers
on Box Hill, saved for the ages, packaged on coarsely pressed vinyl.

Fairport Convention's ever-changing line-ups and the steady drop in
the quality of their albums matched the decline of folk rock in the mid-
seventies; musical stasis, an increasing bearded geniality – sausage rolls
washed down with warm ale* – and lack of serious intent ran it into the
ground. There were two number-one albums in 1976 by folk singers –
Max Boyce and former Transatlantic act Billy Connolly – both of whom
had switched to comedy to become more commercially successful. The
previous year, Mike Harding had charted with the horrible 'Rochdale
Cowboy' (UK no. 22), and Steeleye Span had a Christmas novelty hit
(UK no. 5) with the pub singalong 'All around My Hat'. The secret,
cobwebbed path trod by Sandy Denny, Vashti Bunyan and Roy Harper
was lost in a haze of beery burps. Blame the fog on the Tyne. Steeleye
Span's 1976 Mike Batt-produced album was the final straw: possibly a
well-intentioned but misguided attempt at futuristic folk, it dabbled in

---

* Folk became associated with CAMRA – the Campaign for Real Ale – in the
mid-seventies. It was driven into a craft-brew corner by the end of the decade,
and only resuscitated in the great 'world music' niche-market move of the late
eighties. Pubs may have helped to destroy folk rock, but they would feature positively in another strand of British pop later in the mid-seventies.

reggae and boogie, attempting to give folk a contemporary, space-age twist – they called it *Rocket Cottage*. What the hell were they thinking?

Punk – a music from which magick and myth were banished – was as much a bullet in the post for folk rock as it would be for the more easily savaged progressive rock. Its last hurrah, and a strange mixture of truth and legend, lay in a poignant story resulting from the 1978 National Theatre production of Flora Thompson's *Lark Rise to Candleford*. The live soundtrack was provided by husband and wife Ashley Hutchings and Shirley Collins. During the rehearsals, Hutchings began a relationship with one of the younger cast members and, like a character from a centuries-old ballad, Shirley Collins had to carry on singing each night while watching her marriage disintegrate in front of her. She was, literally, struck dumb: Alan Lomax's sidekick, and Davy Graham's co-conspirator, never sang on stage again nor made another record. Shirley Collins became her own part of mythic folklore.

FREDDIE'S DEAD: ELECTRIFIED SOUL

At a 1966 press conference, Bob Dylan had told the world he thought Smokey Robinson was 'America's greatest living poet'. Presumably Smokey was quite tickled, rather proud, but his response was not reported. While America had *Hit Parader* and *Tiger Beat* and the UK had *Rave*, *Fabulous* and various inkies, they were produced for an almost entirely white market, and interviewed almost exclusively white singers. No one expected soul singers to come up with much in interviews beyond 'We love your beautiful country' and, truthfully, the Motown machine had done little to dispel this preconception. Sly Stone changed all that.

Sly and the Family Stone were the most goodtime group since the Lovin' Spoonful. Their spirit was irresistible. The Spoonful had been white New Yorkers in a different age. Sly and the Family Stone were the first pop group in which black and white, male and female came together, and they emerged in 1967 as race riots raged in Detroit leaving forty-three dead. Within a year they had changed soul music entirely. How? It's all there in their first hit, 'Dance to the Music' (US no. 8, UK no. 7 '68): thumping fuzz bass, doo-wop harmonies, propellant drums,* topped off with a Minnie the Minx yell of 'All the squares, go home!'; inside three minutes, every singer and every instrument get their moment in the spotlight. It had the feel of a Sunday-school riot, the same giddy spontaneity as 'Be-Bop-a-Lula', with its random, exultant shouts. Motown was made to look lumbering, embarrassing by comparison, and its reined-in performers appeared like marionettes alongside the sheer joyous freedom of the Family Stone. While Motown acts played the Copa, covered Rodgers and Hart and wore processed hair for Berry Gordy's perception of black/white crossover appeal, the Family Stone effortlessly exuded Oneness. They were Everyday People, and their music was all about celebration.

Sly Stone must have wondered why no one had come up with the recipe before. He took the live excitement of the Stax soul revue, grafted on James Brown's functional, rhythm-as-a-pure-state funk, and mixed in the heightened airs of psychedelia (the Family were from San Francisco, after all). But it's not just that no one else had thought of it; no one else could have made it quite as tight and loose and blessed and blithe-spirited. Visually, he could have pushed sexy Rose and tomboy-cute Cynthia to the fore – as Ray Charles had done with his Raelettes – but Sly wanted a family, equals on every level.

Sly Stone, brother Freddie, sister Rose, teenage Italian American drummer Greg Errico, slap-pop bass pioneer Larry Graham, Motown-loving saxophonist Jerry Martini and a Californian forest fire of a trumpet player called Cynthia Robinson went from mere stars to superstars at Woodstock in '69, the year they had back-to-back US number ones ('Everyday People', 'Everybody Is a Star'). Sly didn't want to do lounge, like the Temptations, or stick to the Apollo, like James Brown – he wanted to do concerts. He also dressed the Family Stone in polka dots, stack heels, space-suit silver and eye-popping fluorescents, so it looked as if the next decade had already arrived. In the meantime, he was making a name for himself as the new Stagger Lee – a wrong 'un. During

---

* 'Dance to the Music' could be the most sampled Top 10 hit in pop, either used as a bed for other loops or brazenly, as on Primal Scream's 'Rocks' (UK no. 7 '94); the beat is deathless.

an engagement at a Vegas stripclub called the Pussycat a' Go Go, Sly took up with the white girlfriend of the club owner, incurring a barrage of racist threats. He told this story from the stage that night and got a standing ovation, followed by a police-escorted route out of town.

When Sly Stone changed the rules, Motown didn't slouch. By the end of '68 the Supremes had hit back with 'Love Child', Diana Ross singing like a girl from the Brewster Projects for the first time since 'Where Did Our Love Go': 'Started my life in an old, cold, rundown tenement slum. My father left, he never even married Mom.' It was their first American number one in over a year.

Still, sonically 'Love Child' was classic Motown. Standing in the shadows was Norman Whitfield, who saw an opportunity to rewrite the Motown template when Holland/Dozier/Holland quit the label over a financial row in '68.* Whitfield was a former pool-hall punk from Harlem who had first got work in the quality-control department at Motown before succeeding Smokey Robinson as the Temptations' producer in 1966. He loved to play in the studio: Sly Stone's breakthrough loosened him up, as did the departure of the Temptations' nominal lead singer David Ruffin in 1968 – later that year Whitfield used each Temp in turn on the spooky, oddly structured 'Cloud Nine' (US no. 3, UK no. 15). It borrowed the Family Stone's 'Higher!' lines but subsumed their defiance, yearning and pride into a smackhead's private realm; if it didn't make the trip sound all that appealing, it certainly didn't admonish. Soon there were wah-wah pedals, pools of echo, funky basslines and social commentary all over the vocal group's records – 'Psychedelic Shack' (US no. 7, UK no. 33 '70), 'Ball of Confusion' (US no. 3, UK no. 7 '70), 'Papa Was a Rolling Stone' (US no. 1, UK no. 14 '72) – and they effectively became the Norman Whitfield Chorale. Eddie Kendricks soon left to regain his identity in 1973, and the group swiftly lost momentum.†

---

* Berry Gordy's power is revealed by the fact that HDH couldn't write under their real names, unveiling their own Invictus and Hot Wax labels while hiding behind the Dunbar/Wayne pseudonym. Their talents could stand the subterfuge and they updated the HDH sound for Freda Payne ('Band of Gold'), Chairmen of the Board ('Give Me Just a Little More Time') and the Honey Cone ('Want Ads').
† Whitfield's social commentary took the Temptations so far away from their

Whitfield's single best record, though, was recorded with the sensitive Marvin Gaye. He'd cut it back in '67, but Gladys Knight's version of 'I Heard It through the Grapevine' (US no. 2), recorded at the same time and full of piss and vinegar, had been released in its place. Marvin Gaye's deeply paranoid, much slower take had to wait until late '68, and became the darkest Christmas number-one hit in US pop history. A stray snare set the scene, like the gunshot intro to 'Like a Rolling Stone', only this time, quite differently, it was followed by near silence; we were in the domain of a lost and troubled singer rather than one who could see through walls and bring down governments. Next came a muted electric piano that sounded like it was being played in a haunted house, the soft tribal thud of a bass drum suggesting smoke signals and bad omens, Jack Ashford's rattlesnake tambourine and, finally, Marvin Gaye, his anguish unbottled in the most intense confessional: 'Oooohh, I bet you wonder how I knew, about your plans to make me blue.' For the conspiracy theorist there are clues everywhere. 'I Heard It through the Grapevine' was Sly-derived, but while the Family Stone's 'Stand!' was scaling the mountain ('Stand! You've been sitting much too long, there's a permanent crease in your right and wrong'), this stared into the abyss.

With Sly Stone, a black political consciousness had entered American pop. Just as protest in white rock was on the wane, Sly encouraged fellow soul musicians to pick up the slack. Marvin Gaye had felt he was on a short leash from the get-go, and his Motown labelmate Little Stevie Wonder, the boy genius who'd had a US number-one single back in '63 with 'Fingertips', was now coming of age. Taking Sly's lead and having Norman Whitfield's stormcloud soul as back-up, Gaye and Wonder challenged Berry Gordy's authority and asked for more autonomy. They wanted to make albums, personal statements, no more pat dance routines. Wonder began with 'Where I'm Coming From' and 'Music of My Mind' (both 1971), writing, producing and playing virtually every instrument: here was jazz, funk, Latin and soul, lusty and liberated.

---

familiar habitat they had to plead with him for a love song, and got it with 'Just My Imagination' – another US number one in February 1971.

Always the optimist, he was also a spiritual crutch and – most gently – advised against drugs ('Too High') and dreaming about the other man's grass ('Living for the City'). By the time of *Talking Book* in '72 and *Innervisions* in '73 he was in a perfect world, entirely of his own making, and this endeared him to a white audience who saw him as a genius, separate from other black artists. There were reasons why he stood out. His blindness had kept him away from the rest of the Motown family, his voice had no gospel or group-vocal grounding, and so he pitched it against other instruments, which he was usually playing. He loved to work in the studio, twiddling knobs on new gear rather than bonding with other black musicians. He was a master of sound textures (no one had thought of using a clavichord as a rhythmic instrument before 'Superstition' in '72), and in this seemed closer to white progressive acts, while also being more prodigiously talented. Even forays into MOR ('Isn't She Lovely') couldn't hurt his reputation.

As a spiritual leader, though, even Wonder didn't come close to the Francis of Assisi-like spirit of Curtis Mayfield. Having gently paved the way with the Impressions in the sixties, he went solo in 1970 and proceeded to block out the sun with tales of urban squalor. Don't worry, he smiled, 'if there's a hell below we're all gonna go'. So Curtis wasn't as white-media-friendly as Stevie, and didn't write anything Bruce Forsyth was likely to cover. Sometimes he was all positivity ('Move On Up'), or at least optimistic ('We Got to Have Peace'), but mostly his beautiful, cracked, feline voice was now used as a counterpoint to vicious stories: 'Right On for the Darkness', 'Short Eyes', 'Hard Times'. By the time *There's No Place Like America Today* was released in '75, he had largely abandoned melody for message.

With the release of *There's a Riot Goin' On*, the Family Stone's dense, rambling and rewarding 1971 LP, black politics bled directly into American pop; it debuted at number one on the US album chart and sold half a million copies inside a month. It was in bars, cars, and on the radio in the kitchen. 'Runnin' Away' ('to get away') and another US number one, 'Family Affair' ('you're all broke down'), were a long way from the spirit of Woodstock. Two years on, 'Everybody Is a Star' had been inverted – *There's a Riot Goin' On* belonged to everybody as surely as 'Stand!' did, but this time nobody was a star. Like the records being made by the solo Beatles, *There's a Riot Goin' On* was the diary of a man raking over his personal troubles, with fans pounding at the door, in an attempt to find and define himself. For connoisseurs of breakdown albums, it was one of the very best, and it made a full-length album from the blueprint of Norman Whitfield's Temptations singles.

This was conscious soul, and its best practitioner was Marvin Gaye. Like Creedence Clearwater Revival, he seemed wise in an age of hotheads by seeing both sides of an argument, not screeching 'Fuck the pigs' or settling for black jive speak. 'I can remember as a child I always kept myself to myself and I always dug nature,' he told *Disc* in 1971. 'I used to fool around with worms, beetles and birds and I used to admire them, while the other kids were playing sports. It was like some strange force made me more aware of nature. Those kids playing sports were also showing love – love for sport. And if we could integrate all types of love into one sphere we'd have it made.'

His voice was calm, his appearance saintly: 'I spent three years writing, producing and reflecting. Reflecting upon life and upon America especially – because that's where I live – its injustices, its evils and its goods. I think if I had to choose another profession I'd like to be a judge.'

On the cover of 1971's *What's Going On* he wore a black coat, collar turned up against the rain, brow lightly furrowed. Marvin Gaye wanted to alert the world to 'fish full of mercury', and how we had to Save the Children. He had spent two years mourning the death of his singing partner Tammi Terrell from a brain haemorrhage in 1969 and had been a lost soul. 'I did this record not only to help humanity but to help me as well, and I think it has. It's given me a certain amount of peace.'

What's Going On was electrified and politicised, a gentler, more hopeful suite of songs than *There's a Riot Goin' On* whose three attendant singles ('What's Going On', 'Inner City Blues', 'Mercy Mercy Me') all reached the US Top 10. Curtis Mayfield's score for blaxploitation movie *Superfly*, a number-one album in '72, spawned the bleak US number-four single 'Freddie's Dead', about a coke dealer going for one last job, while Stevie Wonder's 'Superstition' was a black cloud over the dancefloor, and another US number one in '72. In the fifties the Weavers had been blackballed for their political views; in the eighties anarcho-collective punk group Crass would be conveniently airbrushed from the chart while selling hundreds of thousands of records.* Yet in the seventies articulate black musicians, established stars, were scoring number-one hits with state-of-the-nation addresses while Nixon was sweating in the White House. I imagine the CIA had a few bulky dossiers on the subject.

The productions on these records were expansive, symphonies were created from ghetto life, and hope sprang from this new public platform for black politics. Bill Withers, in his butterscotch-coloured sweater, was a more intimate alternative, even if his message was essentially the same on 'Harlem', 'Use Me' (US no. 3 '72) and 'Lean on Me' (US no. 1, UK no. 18 '72).† His voice was warm and homely, and he looked as if he'd be more at home in a garden shed than on stage. Using similarly stripped-back production, Timmy Thomas's 'Why Can't We Live Together' (US no. 3 '72, UK no. 12 '73) was hard to miss; it cut through the airwaves with an ear-piercing one-note organ motif and just a beat-box for company – no guitar, no bass, 'no more wars, no more wars, just a little peace in this world'.

There was no message to Funkadelic beyond 'Free Your Mind . . . And Your Ass Will Follow', and neither group name nor song title needed much dissection. Post-Family Stone, they dressed like Marvel-comic characters in the Age of Aquarius and made long, loud progressive and polyrhythmic jams that owed as much to Jimi Hendrix as they did to James Brown. Underpinning the extravagance and silliness was the airtight rhythm section of Billy 'Bass' Nelson and drummer Tiki Fulwood. They had originally formed as a nameless backing group

---

* Crass's singles were excluded from the chart on the grounds that they were too cheap and therefore contravened BPI rules. Meanwhile, sanctioned major labels sold 'double singles' by the likes of Nick Heyward, the Farmer's Boys and the Teardrop Explodes for the price of a regular 45.
† 'Lean on Me' was a soulful caress – 'Call on your brother if you need a hand' – that would later be quoted in Dexys Midnight Runners' more agitated but equally moving 'Plan B' in 1981.

in the mid-sixties for George Clinton's barber-shop harmony act the Parliaments; it was hard to imagine their Perry Como-like roots when you saw Clinton arrive on stage in an inflatable silver car, or heard the 1969 space-age, Temptations-influenced wig-out 'I Bet You'. 'We were down in Tunbridge Wells,' Clinton told *Blues & Soul*, 'and just walking down the streets people were stopping and staring. They were even coming out of shop doorways to take a look.' The wonder is these acid-munching weird-beards got a gig in Tunbridge Wells in the first place. 'We psych ourselves in the dressing-room before we go on,' explained Clinton. 'We do that by singing bull of any kind, or it could be a riff or a harmony we concentrate on. Sometimes we really work ourselves up so much there's a danger of hurting ourselves.'

Hard and spacious, the early Parliament/Funkadelic combine – or P-Funk – came closest to a hit with a single from their 1970 album, *Osmium*. 'The Silent Boatman' had been written by County Durham-born Invictus Records stablemate Ruth Copeland, who they backed on tour in 1971.* It's a terrible shame she got written out of their story, as Copeland could switch from weeping folk song to full-on Southern-soul lung power, and cut two astonishing albums – *Self Portrait* and *I Am What I Am* – with P-Funk backing her. Without Copeland, or someone else with similar pop smarts to ground their eccentricities, they turned into George Clinton's ever-expanding circus, absorbing and acquiring members of other groups, like the JBs' Bootsy Collins and the Detroit Spinners' Philippe Wynne; on records like 1973's *Cosmic Slop* they were still a highly sample-delic outfit, a mine of loops and lifts for future generations, but were aimless, eventually grooving themselves into a dead end.

1972 may have felt like a dawn for black consciousness but this is pop, not politics, and electrified soul's peak was brief. Five-minute epics like the Temptations' 'Papa Was a Rolling Stone' were soon abandoned, stretched out instead into albums. Isaac Hayes's prescient *Hot Buttered*

---

* She dated their guitarist Eddie Hazel, so maybe they split up and she was excommunicated from Clinton's family. History doesn't record, and Copeland has since become one of pop's most elusive figures.

Soul had set the template for this style back in 1969 (just four tracks, two of which passed the ten-minute mark), and record companies sniffed album-shaped profits from the new sound. Following *What's Going On* and *Superfly* came dense epics like the Temptations' *Masterpiece* and the O'Jays' *Ship Ahoy*, not bad records at all but adding little to the palette.*

Soul rapidly became as splintered as white rock. By 1973 Gaye had gone back to bed ('Let's Get It On'), and Wonder gave the first indication that he could write the easiest of easy listening ('You Are the Sunshine of My Life'). Both were US number ones, so neither the public nor the record companies seemed to mind, but Black Power seemed to be off the airwaves as quickly as it had arrived. A less militant singer would eventually break down the racial barriers of seventies pop; in 1973 he was already a star. In the unlikely world of teenybop pop was the political phenomenon that Sly Stone and black America had been hoping for – a black Elvis, an artist with the possibilities of turning racism completely on its head. But his astonishing story will come, in a few chapters' time.

Meanwhile, the man who set Gaye, Wonder and Mayfield free, helped them burrow underground to bring conscious soul overground, went off the radar completely. The endless recording sessions for *There's a Riot Goin' On* burned him out, and drugs did the rest. 1973's *Fresh* was stale; 1974's *Small Talk* aptly named. After a twenty-year hiatus Sly Stone finally appeared on stage again in Perugia, Italy, of all places. Now sixty-four, but looking much older, he was wearing a neck brace beneath

---

* The exception that proves the rule is the Isley Brothers. Veterans who had recorded the original versions of 'Shout' in '59 (covered by Lulu in '64) and 'Twist and Shout' in '62 (covered by the Beatles a year later), they had a stint at Motown (unsuccessfully at home, but producing two UK Top 5 hits in 'This Old Heart of Mine' and 'Behind a Painted Smile') before venturing into funkier territory with 'It's Your Thing' (US no. 2 '69). Always a little late to the party but hugely talented, they drafted in little brother Ernie on guitar in 1973 and sailed off in a psychedelicised direction with 'That Lady' and an extraordinary cover of Seals and Crofts' 'Summer Breeze'; the atmosphere on their '73 album *3 + 3* was not unlike Jimi Hendrix guesting on *What's Going On*. They scored a UK number-ten hit with the eco anthem 'Harvest for the World' as late as 1976, by which time their peers had all moved into disco or been reduced to playing oldies on the chitlin circuit.

a high-collared top. It was nothing to do with his excessive lifestyle – he'd taken a fall from the Beverly Hills clifftop where he lived. He was bruised, beaten, broke, but you could still make out he was the carefree catalyst of '68. 'I had a plate of food in my hand,' he smiled, 'and when I landed I still had a plate of food in my hand. That's the God-lovin' truth. I did not drop a bean.'

STATE OF INDEPENDENCE: JAMAICA

The search for new sounds was within and without pop. Folk rock had been hidden in the gorse on an English heath, but there was another whole world out there, beyond Britain and America, for modern pop to explore. People were yearning for something new, something entirely unfamiliar to revive and renew the spark. Mods at clubs like the Flamingo on Wardour Street had been in on a secret as far back as 1963, when they danced to an exotic, imported music they called 'blue beat'. At the time it seemed like little more than flavouring, like Latin booga-loo, the Cuban-based sound which gave Ray Barretto a one-off hit with 'El Watusi' (US no. 17 '63); Jamaican blue beat's moment seemed to come and go with Millie's 'My Boy Lollipop' (UK and US no. 2 '64). Both were an inkling of modern pop's globalism to come, but Jamaica would make its chart presence felt much more heavily than Cuban or African sounds.

By 1969 the skinhead movement – working-class youth, some of whom were ex-mods, all of whom were violently opposed to rock's dancefloor unfriendliness – had clutched Jamaican music to their bosom. Blue beat (known in Jamaica as ska), rocksteady and reggae – these local micro-genres were a parallel world of pop, born in a tiny British colony. In the early seventies the skinheads helped to place this music in the UK charts. With a foot in the door, it quickly worked its way into the UK/US modern pop narrative.

The island of Jamaica is 145 miles long and fifty miles wide. Its population is roughly the size of Glasgow's. Safe to say, it punches above its weight as a major pop player. Outside of Detroit, it has produced more floor-friendly music than anywhere in the world; for rhythmic invention, there is no Anglo-American parallel.

In spite of its remoteness, street glamour and exoticism, Jamaican pop has been largely boiled down to one term ('reggae') with one figurehead (Bob Marley). This is like reducing the history of British pop to blues rock, with Rod Stewart as the all-conquering, ale-drinking, feather-cut hero of the story. In reality, Jamaica's pop path weaves around and away from the British and American models, quite distinct, but just as intricate. And confusing. Its first incursions into the British charts in 1967, for instance, included singles like the Skatalites' 'Guns of Navarone' (no. 36) that were already several years old. Its most influential export – dub reggae – accounts for just one UK Top 10 hit, Rupie Edwards's 'Ire Feelings' (no. 8 '74). And the man most associated with Jamaican music, Bob Marley, spent his golden years away from the street music of his homeland, honing a mainstream sound that would appeal to rock fans in Britain and America rather than Jamaicans.

Prior to the early sixties Jamaica's influence on pop was almost non-existent. The main sound of fifties Jamaica was mento, a close relative of Trinidad's more widely exported calypso. But jump-blues and rock 'n' roll records – especially those produced in New Orleans – began to make their way south, wriggling around Cuba, landing in the port of Kingston by the turn of the sixties. This coincided with the urbanisation of the island, with thousands leaving rural areas for the capital. The island's class divide meant that live bands were beyond the reach of most of the population, so, at the weekend, Kingstonians organised dances in the open spaces called 'lawns' all over the city; sound systems – essentially mobile discos – replaced live music. The better the bass, and the more distinctive the sound, the more popular the sound system became.* Rivalries built up – the most popular were Duke Reid's Trojan and Clement 'Coxsone' Dodd's Downbeat. With radios scarce, this was how most Jamaicans heard the new American sounds of the fifties.

As American pop moved on from rock 'n' roll and R&B into the Brill Building sound at the turn of the sixties, there was a demand for new R&B material which, if America couldn't provide it, Jamaica would. Prince Buster, Coxsone Dodd, Duke Reid and Chris Blackwell – whose family had run the Crosse & Blackwell tinned-food empire† – started producing 45s for the local marketplace, and Blackwell scored the first local hit with Laurel Aitken's New Orleans soundalike 'Boogie in My Bones'.

It was Coxsone Dodd, though, who inadvertently started a revolution. In 1959 he called a meeting with guitarist/arranger Ernest Ranglin and bassist Cluett Johnson in the backroom of the Dodd family liquor store and explained how he wanted a more distinctively Jamaican feel to his next recordings. So, using a mento-style guitar chop to emphasise the off beat, the trio recorded 'Easy Snappin"‡ and instantly created a

---

* Sound-system hits – and inspirations for ska – include the walking bass and easy dancefloor action of Nina Simone's 'My Baby Just Cares for Me' (producer Coxsone Dodd was particularly fond of jazz) and Fats Domino's 'Be My Guest'. The more popular R&B records in Jamaica hinted at ska before it happened. Rosco Gordon from Memphis had patented a style he called 'back to front boogie' by emphasising the second and fourth beats of the bar: his 'T Model Boogie' was a ska blueprint, while 'Just a Little Bit' was a Merseybeat favourite when it was covered by the Undertakers. Obscure threads like this between the States, Jamaica and Britain are such a joy to discover.
† Chris Blackwell's wealth came from his mother's side of the family – she was a sugar-cane heiress, and the inspiration for Pussy Galore in the James Bond movie *Goldfinger*.
‡ It was Ranglin's record, but he didn't want his name anywhere near it: 'It was ghetto music and in Jamaica they put that music down. I also had to be playing

local variation on R&B, the brass-heavy, onomatopoeically named ska.

Dodd and Duke Reid had enough cash to make trips to America and pick up new tunes to cover, but their rivals had to get itinerant work as sugar-cane cutters to get a US visa. Cecil Bustamente Campbell, under the adopted name of Prince Buster, couldn't even make it as a cane cutter – the dock authorities said his hands were too soft – and so he determined to create his own Jamaican sound. He recorded a song called 'Oh Carolina' in 1959 with Rastafarian teenagers the Folkes Brothers which owed nothing to American pop. The boys sang in Jamaican accents; this was rebel music. It was 'Heartbreak Hotel' to the 'Rock around the Clock' of 'Easy Snappin''. When you consider Ernest Ranglin didn't even want his name on a record because the new rhythm was so strongly connected with the underclass, Buster's sociopolitical move was incredibly bold; he called himself the Voice of the People, and nobody argued.

Ska exploded in 1962, the year Jamaica became fully independent from Britain, when its goodtime feel was perfect for the atmosphere of positivity on the island. Anything uniquely Jamaican was embraced. Derrick Morgan's 'Forward March' and the Skatalites' 'Freedom Sound' soundtracked the dawning of a new era; Jamaican expats in London played the new sounds at house parties in Notting Hill Gate, and white mods picked up on this underground excitement. In 1962 three labels were launched to release Jamaican music in Britain: Blue Beat, a purely ska label and home to Prince Buster and Laurel Aitken; Island, baked-bean magnate Chris Blackwell's creation; and R&B, based in a shop on Stamford Hill.* Prince Buster toured the college circuit. Eventually, in

---

at the society functions and the hotel dances and there they would be looking down at me. Maybe I wouldn't get enough work. You had to walk the line.' 'Easy Snappin'' came out credited to pianist Theophilus Beckford.

* R&B didn't stand for rhythm and blues, but was the initials of Rita and Benny King, a Jewish couple who opened their shop in 1959. A few years later they started releasing Jamaican singles on their own labels – first the parent label, R&B, and then subsidiaries King, Ska Beat, Giant, Hillcrest, Caltone, Jolly and Port-O-Jam. While Benny looked after the shop, beehived Rita travelled to Jamaica to buy the tapes and meet the acts. The couple's roster would go on to include Laurel Aitken, Delroy Wilson, Derrick Morgan, Dandy Livingstone, Ken Boothe, the Wailers, the Maytals and the Skatalites. The shop was almost unique

1964 Blackwell-produced Millie Small hit with 'My Boy Lollipop'.

According to Derrick Morgan, 'You might sell five thousand records in Jamaica, but you'd sell a lot more over there.' Britain became a shop window for Jamaican rhythms, even if it lagged behind. By 1967, when Prince Buster ('Al Capone', no. 18) and Desmond Dekker ('007', no. 14) scored Top 20 hits in Britain, Jamaican pop had changed, become more mid-paced and supple, pushed brass to the back and syncopated its basslines. The result was rocksteady. It was silk smooth, its lyrics and diction crystal clear and, unlike ska, it was largely about wooing, cooing, and broken hearts. It was all about seduction. A generation of crooners (Ken Boothe, Derrick Harriott, Keith and Tex) and harmony groups (the Heptones, the Techniques, the Paragons) appeared. Coxsone Dodd's Studio One label had the Heptones, whose 'Equal Rights' was playfully political ('Every man has an equal right to live and be free . . . take a tip from me, don't hang him from a tree'), but Duke Reid's Treasure Isle label became the Motown of rocksteady, with a constant supply of hits from Alton Ellis (the genre-defining 'Rock Steady' and 'Girl I've Got a Date'), Dobby Dobson ('Loving Pauper') and the Techniques ('I'm in the Mood for Love', 'You Don't Care'). Though rocksteady's instrumentation was much closer to Anglo-American pop – guitar, bass, drums, three-part harmony – than ska had been, oddly it took even longer to filter through, eventually becoming the basis of the late-seventies British variant known as lovers' rock (the finest example being Janet Kay's 1979 number-two hit 'Silly Games') and the source of Blondie's 'The Tide Is High' (a US and UK number one in 1980 originally recorded by the Paragons).

The kind of American soul sound that the rocksteady acts had been influenced by came from New York and Chicago, and was typified by Johnny Nash's lush, smoothly emotive 1965 single 'Let's Move and Groove Together'. Nash stands as a key neglected figure in terms of popularising Jamaican music – for a start, his cover of 'Stir It Up' (UK no. 13 '72) introduced the music of Bob Marley to the UK charts two

---

in stocking so much Jamaican music, and became something of a social club and community hub. It eventually closed in 1984 when Rita and Benny retired.

years ahead of Eric Clapton's cover of 'I Shot the Sheriff'. He had first travelled to Jamaica in early 1968, and was introduced to the local scene by a group called the Wailers. Immediately impressed, Nash planned to break rocksteady in the States. He cut the gorgeous 'Hold Me Tight' (US and UK no. 5 '68) and signed the three Wailers members – Bob Marley, Bunny Wailer and Peter Tosh – to a publishing and recording contract with his JAD label. In 1972, while promoting his hit 'I Can See Clearly Now' (UK and US no. 5) in Britain, he brought the Wailers over as a backing group. They hooked up with Chris Blackwell, signed to Island, and recorded the *Catch a Fire* album; when Marley – at this point without dreadlocks – delivered the tapes to Island in the winter of '72, Blackwell sensed that, with a concerted push, the Jamaican sound could break into the rock mainstream. Keyboard player Rabbit Bundrick (late of blues-rockers Free) and guitarist Wayne Perkins (who would go on to play with the Rolling Stones and Eric Clapton) were drafted in to make *Catch a Fire* less overtly Jamaican, still rootsy but with a smoother European veneer. Tosh and Bunny Wailer were excised, and the songs were made less bright and perky, rhythmically squarer, so as to be closer to Anglo-American rock sounds. The dreadlocks appeared, the ganja was smoked, and a global audience of serious-minded rock fans was won over by this carefully marketed music. The intricacies of Jamaican music, for an easy sales patter, would remain hidden behind a dope and rasta mask. Here, Blackwell told the rock world, is your Jamaican Hendrix.

Marley's subsequent elevation to godhead (and he is the most famous Jamaican of all time – nobody on the island would deny him that) isn't that perplexing in one sense – he wrote simple, anthemic, mellow brotherhood songs like 'One Love' ('let's get together and feel all right'). But it is quite amusing. People had been yearning for something other, for something they perceived to be real or authentic since Monterey drew a line between supposed serious and non-serious pop. What they got, and what they happily accepted, was Bob Marley, who was as niche-marketed and musically simplified as the Bay City Rollers.

Besides, it wasn't as if Britain and America couldn't handle unvarnished Jamaican pop. Desmond Dekker's 'Israelites' had been a UK number one in 1969 – the sheer oddness and exoticism of it struck the British public forcefully, and its lyrical incomprehensibility was a part of its attraction. It was followed into the UK Top 10 by Dekker's similarly alien 'It Mek' (no. 9 '69), the Upsetters' pure groove 'Return of Django' (no. 5 '69) and a stream of sweeter 45s: Jimmy Cliff's 'Wonderful World, Beautiful People' (no. 6 '69), Bob and Marcia's 'Young, Gifted and Black' (no. 5 '70) and Dekker's second-biggest hit, 'You Can Get It If You Really Want' (no. 2 '70). These last three were overdubbed with strings in the UK by Johnny Arthey, who had written the theme to kids' TV series *The Double Deckers*. Arthey's reggae handiwork was dubbed 'the Willesden Sound', a sound which purists and critics perceived to be watering down Jamaican roots music for white European tastes. More likely is that Arthey was mimicking the sweet sound that African American Johnny Nash had introduced with 'Hold Me Tight' in '68, at that point the only Jamaica-produced record to have made the UK Top 10. Nash, then, was indirectly responsible for the most lauded and the most reviled reggae in the UK, neither of which had much to do with what was happening in Jamaica.

Ah yes, reggae. I've deliberately avoided the term until now as it wasn't coined until 1968, and certainly wasn't a catch-all term for Jamaican music.* Coxsone Dodd, once again, can stake a claim to its creation. He imported an echo unit from Britain and used it on Larry Marshall's otherwise unremarkable 'Nanny Goat'. The familiar 'chang' of the off-beat guitar now sounded more like 'chang-ah', or 'skanga', or 'reggae' if you wanted to verbalise it. Hammond organ was introduced, the beat sped up, and a jerky dance called the reggae took over in '68. The percolating organ of Harry J's 'The Liquidator' (UK no. 10 '69) marked it out as something different from rocksteady, but the real difference between reggae and its Jamaican pop forerunners was the freedom to improvise. The music suddenly had more space.

Osbourne 'King Tubby' Ruddock would take the nascent reggae sound in a quite unexpected direction. Like Joe Meek before him and

* The reggae era lasted from 1969 until 1983, when dancehall became the dominant rhythm.

Juan Atkins later, Tubby was an indoors type who loved to tinker with anything electrical. He cut discs at Treasure Isle, as well as having a popular sound system. One day in 1969, having been given access to Treasure Isle's master tapes, he cheekily ran off some acetates – or dub-plates – with virtually all the vocals removed. Later that week, singer Dennis Alcapone went to see Tubby's sound system, with star turn Ewart 'U Roy' Beckford: 'Tubby did it quietly. Him and U Roy start the dance off as normal, and after a while he play "You Don't Care" by the Techniques, then he switch it to the dub version and, after a couple of lines, all the crowd could hear was pure rhythm. Then U Roy come in toasting, and they went nuts.' The best sound systems had always given their crowd something extra, something they couldn't hear anywhere else, but U Roy's patter and Tubby's tape manipulation opened up new vistas – right here, for starters, is the beginning of hip hop – and they were justifiably proud when the first 45 they released, 'Wake the Town', was a massive Jamaican hit: 'Wake the town and tell the people about this musical disc coming your way!'

Tubby's genius was to grasp reggae's new freedom and give it an entirely new dimension, music for the mind as well as the feet. He trans-formed drums into a melodic instrument. San Francisco psychedelia had tunnelled itself down into something thin and silvery; Tubby's dub was a dark space you could climb inside.

His main rival in dub was Lee 'Scratch' Perry, a skinny four-foot-eleven character with a penchant for 'I'm mad, me' self-promotion who played Salvador Dalí to Tubby's André Breton. Armed with only a four-track ¼-inch TEAC reel-to-reel, a Mutron phaser and a Roland Space Echo, Perry piled on sound effects like crying babies and thunderclaps; on the Upsetters' 'Black Ipa' he twists and tweezers the horns until they sound like both a children's toy and something entirely alien. He also had pop smarts and scored UK hits with the Upsetters' 'Return of Django' and Susan Cadogan's 'Hurt So Good' (no. 4 '75). Perry was also smart enough to know that if he created a myth of madness – claiming that he drank bottles of tape-head cleaning fluid for fun – then people would remember his name. It worked. But Perry didn't invent dub, he just knew how to play the media.

Neither Tubby nor Perry had anything like the impact of Bob Marley, though, because Marley fitted a preconception about Jamaican culture that suited a white audience. This misunderstanding, or patronising view of Jamaican pop, was summed up on the Clash's best record, '(White Man) In Hammersmith Palais' (UK no. 32 '78): in it, Joe Strummer goes to see a show by Ken Boothe expecting intense roots reggae, but instead feels alone and confused at a cabaret show which everyone else is lapping up. It is a moment of self-awareness and embarrassment unparalleled in pop. This gulf between white expectations of black culture and what the black audience wanted was bridged by Bob Marley.

Without Marley as a figurehead, though, it's hard to imagine hard-edged records like Althea and Donna's 'Uptown Top Ranking' (UK no. 1 '78) becoming hits. As time progressed, his benign smoky presence on the walls of student dorms softened Europe and America for reggae to affect and gently transform modern pop. Fifteen years later, in 1993, there would be two dozen Jamaican-made singles in the charts, the biggest of all being Shaggy's 'Oh Carolina' (no. 1). This, the first of four number ones for Shaggy, was an irresistible, chug-a-bug update of the Prince Buster-produced Folkes Brothers single that had soundtracked Jamaican independence back in 1962. Jamaican pop didn't need Chris Blackwell-style manipulation or Johnny Arthey's sweeteners any longer.

IT CAME FROM THE SUBURBS:
MARC BOLAN AND DAVID BOWIE

At the Flamingo on Wardour Street in 1962, American servicemen mixed with young Jamaicans from Notting Hill and younger mods from London's outer ring, all outsiders, finding common ground in the fresh blue beat of Derrick and Patsy's keening 'Housewife's Choice', the popping Hammond-organ jazz of James Booker's 'Gonzo' and the live stylings of a former Larry Parnes protégé called Georgie Fame. Two kids hopped up on pills and cappuccinos from the New Piccadilly cafe represented their district: Mark Feld came from the Jewish neighbourhood of Stamford Hill, wore his curly hair greased down into an immaculate side parting and had recently featured, aged thirteen, as one of London's most stylish self-inventions in the gentlemen's magazine *Town*; this gave him bragging rights over David Jones, a Beckenham kid who wore his hair in a pompadour, had different coloured eyes and played saxophone (unsuccessfully). They stood in the shadows, in opposite corners of the club, trying not to chew on their cheeks too much, trying not to be intimidated by their rivals. Feld and Jones looked smart, but no smarter than the mods of Finsbury Park, Chiswick, Plaistow or White City. Impatiently, they drank their Coke.

Once in a while a bit-part player comes along and changes the course of pop. Someone still largely unknown to the pop public, like Chelita Secunda. One day in early 1971 Chelita, the wife of Marc Bolan's manager Tony Secunda, decided that Marc – formerly Mark, formerly Feld – was very pretty and was wasting his looks in nettle-dyed vests and flared jeans. They went into town and hit her favourite boutiques, picking up feather boas, Zandra Rhodes tops and beautifully embroidered jackets that hung exquisitely on his tiny frame. And when they came home with their booty, she threw glitter on his cheeks. Chelita transposed her look to Bolan, and glam took off from there.

What pop needed in 1970, more than anything, was a new consensus act to give it direction, effectively a new Beatles; in 1970 it still seemed possible that a new Beatles would eventually appear – it was just that nobody knew where they were hiding. So when, backstage at *Top of the Pops*, Chelita Secunda dabbed her magic dots of glitter under Marc Bolan's eyes, people were happy to believe the answer was Stamford Hill. Just over a year later Marc Bolan and T. Rex were the subject of the first high-street cinema pop movie since the Beatles' heyday. That *Born to Boogie* was directed by Ringo Starr* just seemed to confirm the passing of the torch.

As Bolan cruised through '72 with a brace of number-one ('Telegram Sam', 'Metal Guru') and number-two singles ('Solid Gold Easy Action', 'Children of the Revolution'), an old sparring partner was coming up on

---

* Ringo also released a single called 'Back Off Boogaloo', a blatant T. Rex tribute, and scored his biggest-ever UK hit – number two in 1972.

the rails with an album called *Ziggy Stardust and the Spiders from Mars*.

Marc Bolan and David Bowie both grew up in suburban London; both had brushes with UK rock 'n' roll (Bowie as sax player in the Joe Meek-recorded Konrads, Bolan serving soft drinks at the 2i's when he was ten); both had been mods, then hippies; both were on the make, eager to please, peacocks, poseurs, part-time models. And both had released a string of flop records in the sixties that meant they were familiar to every A&R man in the land but to pretty much no one else. In both cases this toughened them, prepared them to play the game in the seventies; had either of them broken through any earlier they might have fizzled out quickly. Bowie's early songs smelt of woodsmoke over the suburban fence, of railway stations, platforms and waiting rooms – the golden road to London Town. He sketched the suburban-mod theme better than any of his contemporaries on a trio of 1966 singles: 'Can't Help Thinking about Me', the sarcastic 'I Dig Everything' and the funereal 'The London Boys', with its references to pill-popping, queasiness and losing face.*

As Bolan vacillated between garage blues ('The Third Degree') and folk mysticism ('The Wizard'), Bowie got a deal in 1967 with Decca's new progressive offshoot Deram and cut his first album. He'd moved to the Smoke and outgrown mod. It came across as a mixture of music-hall grotesque and Geoffrey Fletcher's pencil sketches of underclass London. 'I was the world's worst mimic,' he smiled later, in his 1973 pomp. 'I mean, I was Anthony Newley for a year. He stopped his world and got off, which is terrible, because he was once one of the most talented men that England ever produced . . . there's a lot of *Monty Python* in there – left-handed screws and right-handed screws.' The Newley-indebted Deram album remains a curio, the least intense work in his entire catalogue. Soon after it was released – and bombed – he was setting up the Beckenham Arts Club (little more than a pub backroom with a couple of speakers and a knackered sofa, but already he had the vocabulary to draw people in) and studying mime.

* Bolan also recorded a single called 'London Boys' in 1976 which was an up-tempo stomper, but looked back to the mod era with similar unease: 'Changing life's patterns to get to the top. And when you get up there, you don't know if you're there or what.'

The magnetism of Bowie and Bolan meant that they could both afford to stumble and fall several times, knowing that, eventually, each would pick up devotees. Bolan found his feet, and his warbling voice, on the 1966 single 'Hippy Gumbo'. Whether he had become a star or not, this would still stand out as one of the weirdest singles of the decade. Bolan stirs the cauldron of almost atonal strings, chanting, 'Hippy gumbo he's no good, chop him up for firewood'. Parents led their children away from this tiny, twinkle-eyed figure, the Pied Piper of Hackney. Others were quite taken with his new direction. He was briefly talked into becoming a member of Leatherhead troublemakers John's Children, cutting one classic 45 in 'Desdemona' ('Lift up your skirt and fly') in 1967 before heading further into the woods, acoustic guitar in hand. His new band – a duo with the studiously stoned bongo player Steve Peregrin Took – was called Tyrannosaurus Rex, and they quickly became darlings of Britain's hippie underground, heirs to Tolkien with their spooked poetry and intense bongo-smackery. In small doses – 'Debora',* 'The Seal of Seasons', 'Child Star' – they were thrilling, and quite unique. Bolan finally tired of the limited scope of a duo after four albums, introducing electricity and shortening the band's name on 1970's *T. Rex* album. Peregrin Took was ousted in favour of Mickey Finn, purely on the grounds that he was prettier.

Bowie snapped out of his arts-lab reverie in time to soundtrack the 1969 moon landing with the song that, even now, is his signature tune – 'Space Oddity'. It was a one-off – the album of the same name was loaded with feathery things like 'Letter to Hermione' – but gave us the ingredients that made Bowie the perfect face for the seventies: as Major Tom the spaceman, adrift and confused, semi-fictional, schizophrenic. Swathed in Mellotron by producer Gus Dudgeon, with butterfly-wing delicate drumming from ex-Tornado Clem Cattini, it was a masterpiece and felt like a bigger hit than the UK number five it became in the summer of '69.

Bolan and Bowie were now names, almost, and finally collaborated

---

* 'Oh Debora, you look like a zebra' puts 'I don't want clever conversation . . . I love you just the way you are' in the shade as a backhanded compliment.

under the aegis of producer Tony Visconti on a 1970 follow-up to 'Space Oddity', 'The Prettiest Star'. It was poignant and oddly backwards-looking; Bowie may have been singing it to the rising star on guitar, who was about to eclipse him entirely, rather than to his new girlfriend Angie. It was also melodically confused – gorgeous, but never a hit. Weeks later Bolan, now on a rock 'n' roll primitivist trip, cut 'Ride a White Swan', with a lyric about wearing a tall hat like a druid in the old days alloyed to a three-note Chuck Berry riff. Over and done inside two minutes, it was simplicity itself and genuinely exciting, and it was number two in the 1970 Christmas chart. All over Britain, people were getting their first colour television sets. A snooker programme called *Pot Black* became hugely popular, simply because people wanted to see the brightly coloured balls – if someone appeared on, say, *Top of the Pops* in a colourful costume, then they might really cause a commotion. Enter Chelita Secunda.

'I've suddenly tuned into that mental channel which makes a record a hit and I feel at present as though I could go on writing number ones for ever . . . the secret ingredient is "energy",' Bolan told *Record Mirror* as 'Hot Love' hit number one in spring '71. 'Let's face it, the majority of pop hits that make it are a permutation on the twelve bar blues and I've found one that works.' In the future he saw himself as 'a science fiction writer who sings' – you get the feeling Bowie was taking notes. On the way up Bolan had been an empathetic character because, even as an underachiever, he was rich in ideas, smart and full of desire. He was Jewish working class from the East End, but far from playing up to this he entreated his fans to 'keep a little Marc in their heart' with the effete light tenor of a RADA trainee.

The strange magic of T. Rex's 1971 album *Electric Warrior* is partly to do with its reliance on acoustic guitars and restraint. It is also among the most sexually charged albums ever released in Britain: *Electric Warrior* audibly pants, yet also leans on cellos and the eerie banshee backing vocals of ex-Turtles Flo and Eddie for its power; it is dark, tangled up, a sensualised version of the pixie poesy of Tyrannosaurus Rex, only now 'she was born to be my unicorn' has become 'you've got the teeth of a hydra upon you, you're dirty-sweet and you're my girl'. It's quite a feminine, witchy sensibility, closer to Kate Bush and Stevie Nicks in its allure than the Doors or Scott Walker. His songs played with your sense of perspective. At their best they had a curiously disorienting quality. 'Cosmic Dancer' could be a fey boast – 'I danced myself right out the womb, is it strange to dance so soon?' – yet given its time-shifting lyric ('I danced myself into the tomb'), and wrapped up in a haunted string section, it seemed to be as much about loss, absence and regret.

By the start of 1972 Bolan was Britain's biggest pop star, the Slider himself. He had his own new record label (T. Rex Wax Co., which went through EMI), his third number-one UK single with 'Telegram Sam', and 'Get It On' (retitled 'Bang a Gong' so as not to alienate prudish radio stations) was nudging the American Top 10. On the face of it, he should have taken America by storm: he wrote melodic but riff-born rock songs that could charm bikers and birds. The *Born to Boogie* movie captured the reasons why he didn't click. He looks sweet enough but miscalculates his young audience by attempting Hendrix guitar wiggery – born to boogie he may have been, but he couldn't touch the spaced-out avant-rock style of Hendrix, and ended up looking rather brattish; just as he was seemingly set as a superstar, he allowed his ego to get the better of him and let the mask slip. Worse was to follow. He had been a vegan for years but fame brought with it new desires for cocaine and champagne – Bolan ballooned.* By the time 1973's *Tanx* came out he looked more Elvis than elfin. His long-term girlfriend June left him and pulled a Samson move by ruining his beautiful locks, giving him an old-lady perm just before she walked out. Bolan never had another Top 10 hit.

Bowie appeared far less likely to break America. The Anglophile crowd on the west coast adored him, but he seemed way too fragile and art-school for mainstream success. In 1970 he had paid a visit to Andy Warhol's Factory to meet his heroes. Hearing there was a rising English rock star at the door, the artist let him enter. In lieu of a mundane hello, Bowie began to mime. Warhol was nonplussed, turned to his assistant and asked, 'Should we laugh?'

---

* Bolan was unlucky it affected him this way; cocaine made Bowie stick-thin.

Like Bolan, Bowie wanted to work on your eyes as well as your ears. As T. Rex broke through in '71 he released his fourth album, *Hunky Dory*, which paid blatant tribute to Dylan and Warhol while leaving room for his best, most individual songs ('Changes', 'Life on Mars', 'Kooks') since 'Space Oddity'. 'The Bewlay Brothers' was terrifying, Major Tom lost in orbit, lost in his thoughts, degenerating into lunacy on its closing vari-speed wail, 'I'm starving for me gravy!' It also contained a line which became Bowie's manifesto: 'He's chameleon, comedian, Corinthian and caricature.' For the sleeve artwork he had taken pictures of Marlene Dietrich to the photo session, though the results were more Bloomsbury than Hollywood. No matter, he'd get there soon enough.

Watching from the wings, Bowie listened and learnt. As he had done with Major Tom in 1969, he decided to build his music around an image rather than just a specific sound and a carrier bag full of influ-ences. He created an alter ego – the sci-fi rocker Ziggy Stardust – which enabled him to become a star before he had more than a handful of fans. His second masterstroke, one-upping Bolan's glitter, was to drop the bomb on the implications of male make-up: I'm bisexual, he told the press, and caused instant pandemonium. *The Rise and Fall of Ziggy Stardust and the Spiders from Mars* (1972) was at once more alien and more inclusive – 'Oh no love, you're not alone' – than T. Rex's contem-poraneous *The Slider*. As '73 got into its stride, Bowie's star ascended – 'Jean Genie', 'Drive-in Saturday', 'Sorrow' and the reactivated *Hunky Dory* track 'Life on Mars' all went Top 3. So did Bolan's singles, but crucially none of them made number one as they had done with such ease in '71 and '72.

Bolan was so sweet to his fans – with the Christmas flexidisc messages ('Have a good Christmas, a real good Christmas, and . . . don't cry!') and extra bonus B-sides (including songs as cosmic as 'Jitterbug Love', which he surely regretted not saving for an A-side) – that he could only slip from his high '72 perch. Bowie was wily, and killed the Ziggy Stardust character on stage in '73, leaving the crowd wanting more. 'Give me your hand!' he wailed to his fans at the climax of 'Rock 'n' Roll Suicide', and they felt his love, his outsider empathy. But this was his theatre training, the Anthony Newley of 'What Kind of Fool Am I' reborn for the glam age. Bowie wasn't fake, but he'd never give himself to the public, or prostrate himself to be stroked like Bolan. He'd been in the theatre too long to make a mistake like that. When the *NME* asked if the Ziggy Stardust saga could be made into a film, he said, 'I would not want to shatter anybody's private movie.'

Emasculated by his ex, rejected by the press, Bolan trumpeted a new idea – the 'intergalactic soul' of '(Whatever Happened to the) Teenage Dream' in 1974. It was complex, featured the gospel back-ups of Pat Hall and Gloria Jones, and impressed with its Dylanesque lyrical weave. But – like its creator – 'Teenage Dream' was not as light on its feet as it should have been. When Bowie trumped his concept with the 'plastic soul' of 'Young Americans' and 'Fame' (US no. 1 '75) a year later, he sounded understandably bitter: 'I really dig David Bowie. I like his songs and we have a good head thing . . . but we don't make love. To make love wouldn't be repulsive to me, it would just be a bit of a bore.'

What pop really needed in the seventies turned out to be someone to reflect a fractured world, one where chaos was just a kiss away – not a consensus band. Not a new Beatles. Bowie understood this and Bolan didn't. Bowie was all about confusion, angles, ch-ch-ch-changes. By 1977 Bolan was embracing the punks, who, in turn, loved him back. He toured with the Damned and got his own TV show, *Marc*, on which he introduced schoolkids to the Jam and Generation X. On the last episode in the series he introduced a special guest, David Bowie, who sang his new single, 'Heroes'. They attempted a new song together – 'Standing Next to You' – which lasted a few bars before Bolan, heady with his new role of Punk Godfather and giddy from the cold drinks in the green room, stumbled off the stage. The moment died in a few splutters and giggles.

Neither his current single – 'Celebrate Summer' – nor Bowie's 'Heroes' made the Top 20, though one of them sounded like the future and the other sounded like 1972. While Bolan was theoretically on the way back, the physically wasted Bowie spent 1977 simply trying to stay alive. After three years on a diet of milk and cocaine, he looked like a silent-movie ghost. He had moved to Berlin, the city that reflected the rifts, the barriers and the disillusion of the seventies better than any other, and saved his life. *Low*, released in the spring, was his masterpiece, and possibly the blankest, loneliest record in all of pop. 'Sound and Vision' gave him a UK Top 3 hit and it sounded like little that had gone before: it didn't swing but it rocked (in the cradle sense), like a machine-operated hammock. Only some fiercely bashed dustbin drums, miked up to sound simultaneously very loud and very small, could disturb a supine Bowie, who waited a good minute, humming and sighing to himself, before summoning up the strength to sing. Somehow, in spite of its morphine-pumped nihilism, it was a pretty single. The follow-up single, 'Be My Wife', wasn't and went nowhere: 'Please be mine, share my life, stay with me, be my wife.' It is needlingly needy.

When punk rock came to town, and Bolan played up his part in its lineage, RCA came up with a perfect marketing slogan: 'There's old wave, there's new wave, and there's David Bowie.' He didn't need to shout about it. With the Berlin trilogy – *Low, Heroes, Lodger** – Bowie laid the groundwork for the sound of the eighties.

A few weeks after they had briefly kissed and made up for the cameras, Bolan was killed as his car took a bend too fast in Barnes, south-west London. That elfin face was destined never to turn thirty. Bolan remains forever the 20th Century Boy, remembered for his corkscrew hair and kissable lips. Which is maybe for the best, because the long-running battle between the North London mod and the South London mod was already over.

---

* *Lodger* wasn't recorded in Berlin, but the three albums were of a piece, and 1979's *Lodger* is dreadfully underrated. By the time of 1980's *Scary Monsters* Bowie had survived punk to become a hero to the New Romantics, New Poppers and electropop pioneers (notably Gary Numan); 'Ashes to Ashes' gave him his first number-one hit (excluding the reissue of 'Space Oddity' in '75).

DELUXE AND DELIGHTFUL: GLAM

It's 1974. The scene is a transport cafe on the A5 just outside Towcester, Northants. Lorry drivers in donkey jackets sit by steamed-up windows, drinking dirt-brown tea from smoked-glass cups as wonderful Radio 1 plays the intro to Mud's latest single, 'The Cat Crept In'. It's just a tinny Alba radio, but as the song begins, as if by magic, a pop group appears. It's Mud. They jump on the tables, cavorting, sticking out their tongues, hamming it up in full panto-glam regalia. There's singer Les Gray, his back hunched from hod carrying, his Elvis shades getting a little greasy in the grey-green atmosphere, and his lecherous, bum-pinching smile familiar to the whole caff; Dave Mount, the double-drumming drummer who made 'Tiger Feet' 1974's best-selling single, twirls his sticks and batters a kettle as his eyebrows threaten to fly off his head; Rob Davis on guitar, with a perm straight out of *Crossroads* and Gypsy Rose Lee's earrings, wears powder-blue, faux-satin bell bottoms that flirt dangerously with plates of black pudding and fried eggs; and there's Ray Stiles, the bassist, smiling like a Cheshire cat in his blue crêpe brothel creepers. His band are number two in the chart after a decade of slogging around pubs in Carshalton. Hell, they'd barely made it out of

Surrey before Mickie Most signed them to his RAK label a year before, got Nicky Chinn and Mike Chapman to start writing their A-sides, and their run of hits began with 'Crazy', 'Hypnosis' and 'Dynamite'.

Outside, the rain beats down. In London's Square Mile, in Welsh pit villages and in the mill towns of Lancashire, the three-day week is screwing with the economy. In America, the Symbionese Liberation Army has kidnapped heiress Patty Hearst and the president has been impeached. In a cafe just outside Towcester, everyone's having such a raw time that Rob Davis doesn't even care when he stands on a squeezy bottle of brown sauce and it squirts right up his trouser leg. The scene is not very glamorous, but it's very glam.

David Bowie lived in a spaceship, primed and ready to whisk you off to some blank alien planet where everyone was bisexual and lived on soma ('Don't laugh babe, it'll be alright'). Mud were quite at home in a greasy spoon, with a copy of the *Racing Post*, winking at the waitress. Both were glam, even though few realised it at the time.

The hippie counterculture was politically committed to the present tense and largely mistrusted theatrics. Take the first issue of British underground music monthly *Let It Rock* in October '72, which devoted its cover story ('The Great Pretender?') to an annihilation of Bowie – 'Bowie on stage looks *fantastic* – no more, no less' – while elsewhere it took three critics to pick over John and Yoko's right-on but almost unlistenable *Some Time in New York City* (conclusion: 'There's something important here'). Glam – garish, ultra-commercial and colourful as a Dulux paint chart – was its worst nightmare. And while Bowie and Bolan were media-savvy enough to keep most of the counterculture music press on side, the glam acts who followed in their wake were all about jumping on tables, wearing the spangliest outfits and treating the *Top of the Pops* studio like a home from home. Whether miming their hits astride a motorbike, or descending to the stage on a crescent moon, or throwing custard pies at each other, the likes of Mud, Wizzard, Suzi Quatro, Gary Glitter, Slade and Sweet picked up on certain lines of Bowie and Bolan's glam manifesto – the Bo Diddley riffs, the glittering artifice, the outrageous make-up, the tremendous sense of fun – and rewrote them with an abundance of exclamation marks.

Top of the Pops was reborn in the early seventies. Though it had been running since 1964, it was always seen as a bit of a drag, not as exciting as ITV's *Ready Steady Go!* or as cool as an art/pop show like *Late Night Line-Up*. Now it was inadvertently on one side of the fence, with the BBC's own *Old Grey Whistle Test* – on the arts-led second channel, BBC2, to indicate something alternative and heavyweight – on the other side, the rock side. *Top of the Pops* and glam went hand in hand. *The Old Grey Whistle Test*'s Whispering Bob Harris declared Roxy Music, the first big glam act to emerge after Bolan and Bowie, too 'computerised'. You could see what he meant. Glam reduced pop to shorthand. It used trigger terms like 'teenage' ('Teenage Dream', 'Teenage Rampage', 'Teenage Lament '74') and 'rock 'n' roll' ('Rock 'n' Roll Winter', 'The Golden Age of Rock 'n' Roll' and – best of all – 'I Didn't Know I Loved You 'Til I Saw You Rock 'n' Roll') just like pop had done in the late fifties. In fact, glam was just like rock 'n' roll.

Unlike Beatlemania, T. Rextasy did not lead to a bunch of Bolan clones. Possibly no one felt they were pretty enough to compete. Neither were there many acts doing a Bowie,* though his chameleon changes were mimicked on a more prosaic level by Chicory Tip, who went from denim rockers to full Martian costume overnight, and Mud's Les Gray, who felt quite at home slipping into a suburban Elvis impression midsong. There was no blueprint for glam. If anyone had to define glam in 1972, they would have described a new pop sound with a retro-futurist feel – a collage of rock 'n' roll drive, electronics and space-age lyrics which occasionally mentioned jukeboxes and Chuck Berry. In a nutshell, they were describing Roxy Music.

Bowie had pushed the door ajar, and Roxy Music took full advantage. They were very much British art-school, but unlike the R&B acts

---

* New Zealand provided Bowie-alike Alastair Riddell's band Space Waltz, briefly a sensation with their NZ-only number one 'Out on the Street'; Britain only had Casino (one blinding single called 'Crazy'), Roderick Falconer (two albums of brave new world paranoia) and Steve Harley's Cockney Rebel, who dumped the glam shtick early on. Their single 'Sebastian' – a flop in Britain but number one in the Netherlands – was a preposterous, cake-out-in-the-rain moment. I still can't work out if it's actually good.

of the sixties or the progressive smart alecks, they majored in British Pop. While the Who had bluffed their 'pop art' sound with reference to obscure auto-destructive artist Gustav Metzger, Richard Hamilton and Joe Tilson taught Roxy Music – literally. And while they had an egghead on keyboards called Brian Eno, with a bank of synths straight out of Cape Canaveral, he was counterbalanced by louche front man Bryan Ferry. Old-time glamour was his angle, and Roxy Music – their name redolent of crimson Hollywood, suburban Vitralite and neon – was his band. Ferry wore tuxes, sometimes sequinned, and screwed his eyes right up tight when he sang, as if he was going to hiss very loudly. As the song progressed he'd perspire gently, and his brilliantined hair would fall over his forehead. He looked just like a coke fiend from an F. Scott Fitzgerald novella, which was entirely the idea.

Eno's full name was Brian Peter George St John le Baptiste de la Salle Eno* and, silver threads aside, his face betrayed a refined, arch and rather haughty man. While an art-school student he had pinned up a handwritten note outside the staff room: 'Brian Eno will be conducting tutorials in his office today. Any staff member needing advice or guidance please feel free to come and see me.' Eno, with a head full of ambient whirs and clicks, quit Roxy in '73 as it became clear that Ferry was running the show. And Roxy just got better: their first two albums revealed a little too much of their art training, and Eno's departure led to a finer, more unified sound. On 'All I Want Is You' (UK no. 12 '74) the saxophone and guitar wheel-spins sounded like a souped-up Ford Capri, while 'A Song for Europe' basked in its continental drift, the finale of *Death in Venice* as imagined by Warhol and Spector.

Roxy Music were glamorous, in a slightly tortured way, and they plastered gorgeous models in unlikely poses – sweaty and wasted – on their album covers to ram home the point. Mud, on the other hand, were merely glam. How they got to be tagged glam in the first place was largely down to the hit-writing machine of Nicky Chinn and Mike Chapman. Simply, they saw the adulation, the magazine covers, the

---

* This, it should be noted, is a name he gave himself, not the one he was given at birth. His dad worked for the Post Office.

cold hard cash that T. Rex generated in '71 and '72 and they wanted in. Up to this point, Chinnichap had worked on a Brit Building formula. Sweet were their most successful act with their Latin-soused bubblegum hits 'Funny Funny', 'Poppa Joe' and 'Co Co' (UK no. 2 '71); beginning with 'Little Willy', they threw in recycled twelve-bar blues riffs, turned up their amps ever louder, and for the next three years produced the most taut, diamond-hard run of singles by any seventies band.

Sweet's first single had come out in '68. By '72, when glam was reaching its full potential, they were a fearsomely tight live act. After the nudge and wink of 'Little Willy' and 'Wig Wam Bam' ('Wham bam bam, gonna get you in my tent'), both of which reached number four in 1972, they moved in for the kill with 'Block Buster' in January '73. Klaxons announced an important record; Chinn and Chapman had decided to fuse Sweet's bubblegum to T. Rex's glam muscle and Bowie's theatre. It was camp as Christmas but, manipulated by backroom boys with an eye on the big prize, it was absolutely magical. Frenzied gibberish, the best since Little Richard. Buster was someone who had to be blocked, but the lyric didn't suggest why, it just implied some kind of apocalypse: 'you better watch out if you've got long black hair'.

Who the hell was Buster? Just the first in a line of preposterous glam characters. T. Rex (again) had got the ball rolling with Telegram Sam in '72, who was soon joined by Mud's Dynamite ('Nobody knew her name but she turned up just the same/ There was a knock on the door, a thump on the floor and the party turned insane') and Kenny's Fancy Pants ('She's a rocker, she's a shocker . . . when she hears a beat she goes wild'). Following 'Block Buster', Sweet got two more cute little demons from Chinn and Chapman: the man at the back who said 'Everyone attack and it turned into a Ballroom Blitz', and the terrifying but irresistible sounding 'Hell Raiser': 'Mama you don't understand, every time I touch her hand it's like I'm burning in the fires of hell!' Wrong crushes, one and all. In Britain they were big; in Germany, Sweet were the biggest pop noise ever. They only began to stumble when they wrote their own songs and decided to be a second-rate Led Zep instead of a first-rate Sweet.

The British Top 20 was entirely won over by glam's frantic noise, to an extent not seen since Merseybeat. As the British music press tied themselves in knots over the moral issues raised by glam, or glitter rock, or 'fag rock' (thanks, *Beat Instrumental*), it dictated both the singles chart and, effectively, pop culture as lapels grew wider, cars looked flasher and Britain let its hair down and finally forgot the war. In the States, with the exception of Anglophile shock-tactic rocker Alice Cooper, glam meant less than zero.* The 1973 number ones show two countries who – soul aside – were as far apart as they'd ever be in the modern pop era.

UK

Sweet	'Block Buster'
Slade	'Cum On Feel the Noize'
Donny Osmond	'The Twelfth of Never'
Gilbert O'Sullivan	'Get Down'
Dawn	'Tie a Yellow Ribbon Round the Ole Oak Tree'
Wizzard	'See My Baby Jive'
Suzi Quatro	'Can the Can'
10cc	'Rubber Bullets'
Slade	'Skweeze Me, Pleeze Me'
Peters and Lee	'Welcome Home'
Gary Glitter	'I'm the Leader of the Gang (I Am)'
Donny Osmond	'Young Love'
Wizzard	'Angel Fingers'
The Simon Park Orchestra	'Eye Level'
David Cassidy	'Daydreamer'/'The Puppy Song'
Gary Glitter	'I Love You Love Me Love'
Slade	'Merry Xmas Everybody'

* America also had the ill-fated Jobriath, whose music sounded more like Elton John's campest moments, and the New York Dolls, who looked like *Exile on Main Street*-era Stones and played a rough, sloppy glam variant that intrigued London clothes-shop operator Malcolm McLaren enough for him to become their manager. The raggedness of single 'Jet Boy' excited a few, but their records sold poorly and they had dissolved into drug chaos by the time glam started to fade. Their one antagonistic *Old Grey Whistle Test* performance lingered in the memory, though, and despite the paucity of their catalogue they became a touch-stone for British punk.

USA

Billy Paul	'Me and Mrs Jones'
Carly Simon	'You're So Vain'
Stevie Wonder	'Superstition'
Elton John	'Crocodile Rock'
Roberta Flack	'Killing Me Softly with His Song'
The O'Jays	'Love Train'
Vicki Lawrence	'The Night the Lights Went Out in Georgia'
Dawn	'Tie a Yellow Ribbon Round the Ole Oak Tree'
Stevie Wonder	'You Are the Sunshine of My Life'
The Edgar Winter Group	'Frankenstein'
Paul McCartney and Wings	'My Love'
George Harrison	'Give Me Love (Give Me Peace on Earth)'
Billy Preston	'Will It Go Round in Circles'
Jim Croce	'Bad, Bad Leroy Brown'
Maureen McGovern	'The Morning After'
Diana Ross	'Touch Me in the Morning'
Stories	'Brother Louie'
Marvin Gaye	'Let's Get It On'
Helen Reddy	'Delta Dawn'
Grand Funk Railroad	'We're an American Band'
Cher	'Half-Breed'
The Rolling Stones	'Angie'
Gladys Knight and the Pips	'Midnight Train to Georgia'
Eddie Kendricks	'Keep On Truckin''
Ringo Starr	'Photograph'
The Carpenters	'Top of the World'
Charlie Rich	'The Most Beautiful Girl'
Jim Croce	'Time in a Bottle'

Glam schlam. There's a lot of fine songs in that list but, essentially, the States were still pretending the Beatles hadn't split – Lennon was the only ex-Fab not to score a US number one.

T. Rex had created a future, Bowie had painted it self-destructive ('We've got five years'), and into their invention poured Detroit rocker Suzi Quatro – a girl in no make-up and Elvis '68 leathers, the perfect mirror image to all the fey boys – and Roy Wood, formerly of the Move, given a fresh paint job as the leader of Wizzard. Beyond the Top 40 were wannabes and cash-in merchants, loaded with novelty and comic-character names, and all as disposable as gum: Spiv, Hector, Jook, Chunky, Crunch, Smiffy, Screemer, Zipper and Zappo. The sound most readily mimicked by these acts was Sweet's, which also – for reasons that didn't extend beyond outright snobbery – was the least applauded by the critics. 'Block Buster' (comic-book fun) had kept Bowie's 'Jean Genie' (pop with pretensions) at number two – the songs shared the exact same Muddy Waters riff, but Bowie's was deemed more acceptable by the *NME* and *Sounds*, presumably because he had written his own lyrics.

The Bowie/Roxy glam axis – short on custard pies, high on Genet references – fitted the seventies rock critic's post-*Sgt Pepper* world more comfortably than Sweet and Mud, whose *It's Better than Working* album title didn't suggest much familiarity with Lorca. Nobody came in for a tougher time than a portly blue-eyed soul singer known as Paul Raven until glam's sequinned glove beckoned. Born Paul Gadd, he was, like Bolan and Bowie, another sixties refugee, though his first single had appeared as far back as 1960. Teaming up with producer Mike Leander, Gadd produced the bone-crunching 'Rock 'n' Roll Parts 1 & 2' (UK no. 2, US no. 7 '72), all caveman grunts, guitars like hornets and drums treated with echoes that Joe Meek might literally have killed for. Thinking of a suitable name for this studio project, Gadd and Leander discarded Horace Hydrogen and Terry Tinsel before settling on Gary Glitter. What seemed a one-off eulogy to primal noise and dancehall action (you weren't meant to dance to James Taylor or Genesis) became one of pop's unlikeliest pin-ups. Even the neanderthal backing group, the Glitter Band, had hits of their own ('Angel Face', UK no. 4 '74; 'Goodbye My Love', UK no. 2 '75) and – with *Rock 'n' Roll Dudes* – turned out one of the half dozen best albums of the genre.

The oikish end of glam was taken to an extreme by a band who were

Sweet's only rivals in the post-T. Rex world – Slade. A Wolverhampton group guided by Jimi Hendrix's former manager Chas Chandler, they were unlikely superstars but, as Bolan's star faded in '73, they became the most beloved group in the country. Dickensian singer Noddy Holder had a voice like John Lennon screaming down the chimney of the *QE2*; rosy-cheeked bassist Jim Lea looked as if he lived with his mum and bred homing pigeons; Dave Hill on guitar had the most rabbity face in the world; while drummer Don Powell chewed gum and stared into space – even after he'd been in a horrific car crash and lost most of his memory, he looked exactly the same. With no hint or possibility of pin-up potential, they saw the Titus Groans and the Amazing Blondels, the prog noodlers, the folk archaeologists and the questing space rockers and thought, sod this, let's get pissed and have a really, really good time.

Chas Chandler's Slade productions were simultaneously airtight, fierce and murky – they contain an insane amount of energy. And they revitalised the UK singles chart. No one had gone straight in at number one since the Beatles with 'Get Back' in 1969, but Slade managed it three times – 'Cum On Feel the Noize', 'Skweeze Me, Pleeze Me', 'Merry Xmas Everybody' – in 1973. Very much in the premier league, they made a miserabilist movie about the industry called *Flame* in '74, cut their most varied album (*Old New Borrowed and Blue*), then tried to turn America on to their beer 'n' cigs power pop. But like T. Rex, they didn't click. By the time they got home, the scene was greyer, their profile had wizened, and they called their 1976 album *Whatever Happened to Slade?* It seemed that nobody knew.

Since then there have been many pratfalls, regrettable stabs at metal ('Lock Up Your Daughters'), stadium ballads ('My Oh My'), would-be football anthems ('Give Us a Goal') and even Celtic rock ('Run Runaway') to counter the odd stellar moment ('Radio Wall of Sound'). But 'Merry Xmas Everybody' has kept Slade on the radio, at least once a year, and reminded everyone how much dunderheaded, giddy fun they had been in the first place. If you took a survey tomorrow, Slade could well be the best-loved band in English pop history.

Only two groups could rival Slade in nailing the Blitz spirit that pervaded Britain's seventies slough. A notable fan of Mott the Hoople in their early days was a London-based student by the name of Benazir Bhutto. Another was David Bowie. They were from the hinterland between Wolverhampton and the Welsh border, and were a pleasant enough band without suggesting they'd ever catch fire. Three albums in, they called it a day in 1972. Enter Bowie. He pleaded with them not to split. Singer Ian Hunter – a Dylan freak and ale drinker from way back – laughed, 'Give us a hit and we'll think about it, Dave.' So Bowie gave them 'All the Young Dudes' (UK no. 3 '72). It was the equivalent of Brian Wilson giving Jan and Dean 'Surf City' (US no. 1 '63), handing over the secret manifesto of the movement. Hunter screamed out lines like 'I don't need TV when I've got T. Rex' with such openness, his voice crackling with mirth, knowing this song would make their career: 'I've wanted to do this for years and years,' he cackled over the fade and, true to their word, Mott stuck together and got ten times better.

They self-mythologised to a ridiculous degree. Giving themselves nicknames like rock 'n' roll action heroes – Overend Watts,* Ariel Bender – they aimed for the sky and hit the pub ceiling. Their albums tended towards drunken introspection, yet they understood and celebrated pop's magic on 45s, getting it across merrily as tears of joy watered down their pints and filled their ashtrays on 'All the Way from Memphis' (UK no. 10 '73), 'Roll Away the Stone' (UK no. 8 '73), 'The Golden Age of Rock 'n' Roll' (UK no. 16 '74). Every one was a pocket pop-history chapter. And just when it was about to get boring, just as glam had run its course, they split in 1975.

Like rock 'n' roll, and rave to come, glam's lack of a manifesto allowed all kinds of oddballs a stab at glory. Not glam at all but somehow the epitome of where British pop was at in 1972, this seems a good place to bring in Stavely Makepeace. Led by ex-navy man Nigel Fletcher and pianist Rob Woodward, they recorded in Woodward's front room in Coventry allegedly under the influence of Gene Vincent and Elvis: their two dozen singles sound precious little like either of them, or anyone

---

* His mates knew him as Pete Watts, but his full name was Peter Overend Watts. So it wasn't exactly a nickname – it just sounded like one.

else for that matter. What they did sound like was Dada, and they took their clumsy noise all the way to number one.

Their 1969 debut – '(I Wanna Love You Like a) Mad Dog' – sounded like a one-man oompah band, phased to simulate a psychedelic experience, peddling the kind of nudge-wink sexual filth Marie Lloyd had once been up in court for. Three years later they penned a woozy pub instrumental called 'Mouldy Old Dough'. It wasn't up to Stavely Makepeace's 'serious' attempts on the chart, like 'Mad Dog' or 'Tarzan Harvey', they reckoned, so they released it under the pseudonym Lieutenant Pigeon, and gave themselves a parallel career. Woodward's mum Edna was drafted in as a second pianist, and when it made number one in 1972 she became the oldest person to appear on *Top of the Pops*. If it weren't for the Makepeace/Pigeon delineation, nobody other than Woodward and Fletcher could tell which of their records were meant to be novelties. Lieutenant Pigeon cut three albums in short order – *Mouldy Old Music*, *Pigeon Pie*, *Pigeon Party* – while 'Mouldy Old Dough' topped the charts from Belgium to Australia, taking the sound of a country in severe depression around the world. Miners' strikes? Rampant inflation? Crack open a Party Seven. Grin and bear it. 'Mouldy Old Dough' is the brownest record ever made.

As glam counted for so little in the States, brothers Ron and Russell Mael decided to move to the UK and test their helium rock 'n' roll on a British audience. Sparks made no sense whatsoever: Ron had a Hitler moustache and scared children; Russell had a curly mop and piercing eyes; their breakthrough hit, 'This Town Ain't Big Enough for Both of Us' (UK no. 2 '74) sounded like Sweet playing a Chinese folk melody and featured glam's loudest, most exciting instrumental break (gunfire, Russell's screams, dive-bombing power chords). The Maels picked a crack British backing group who they inexplicably sacked after one fine album, *Kimono My House*. They would survive into the twenty-first century and – after experiments with swing-band revivals, Giorgio Moroder and ambient minimalism – remained just as impenetrable.

It's one of the more obscure puzzles of pop as to why so many stars of glam (and metal) came from the Midlands. I still can't work it out. Birmingham's Roy Wood wasn't first out of the blocks, not even third or fourth, but in his own way he was as significant to glam's long-term influence as Bolan or Bowie. They introduced otherness via androgyny and sexual confusion; Roy Wood – musically and physically – showed how you could change who you were entirely. Bowie invented characters, but you had a handle on who David Bowie was behind the mask. Who on earth was Roy Wood?

Unlike his glam contemporaries, Roy Wood had been a star in the sixties. The Move were a distillation of Birmingham beat groups under the aegis of manager Tony Secunda, and Wood was their chief songwriter. They began as a Who knockoff (debut 45, 'Night of Fear', a UK number two at the end of '66; 'I Can Hear the Grass Grow', UK number five in '67), with power-pop riffs and gigs that ended in fireworks, but within a year they had gone hippy-dippy with 'Flowers in the Rain', another number two, and then started '68 with a switch into Duane Eddy basslines and Buddy Holly melodies on 'Fire Brigade', a number three. This was largely seen as bandwagon-jumping at the time – they also went 'heavy' with the dreadful 'Brontosaurus' in 1970 – but Roy Wood was not one to sit still. By 1972 he was not only in the Move but had formed the pseudo-classical Electric Light Orchestra with Jeff Lynne and started the glam-leaning Wizzard. He also found time to release his first solo album. This wasn't the CV of a dilettante – Roy Wood loved pop. He was a super-fan. He wanted to be all of pop, all at the same time.

His best 'solo' single was 'Forever' (UK no. 8 '73), on which he sounds like the 1968 Beach Boys on the first verse, then 1959 Neil Sedaka on the second. You have to concentrate to see the join. In Wizzard, Wood buried himself under garish make-up and frightful hair. Their hits sounded awesome and opulent, heavy on the Spector percussion, all bells and whistles. They also had some beautiful lyrics, delving into pop's past, asking the serious questions: 'Will Dion still be so important to you on your wedding day?' The very best was 'Angel Fingers', a number one in 1973, which combined pre-rock innocence with back-seat fumbling. It also included possibly my favourite line ever: 'If I could get a job with that cool rockin' band, you'd notice me with that red guitar in my hand.' There it is. The entire pop myth in one couplet.

'I always feel that you should keep singles as commercial as possible so that people can walk down the road and whistle a song,' he said in 1973. 'But on albums I think you can afford to show people what you can do.' If glam was about snubbing rock's post-Monterey seriousness, then Roy Wood was the shapeshifting king. Was he the Wizzard, or a rock 'n' roll revivalist? Which was his real voice?

It's easy to see why he wasn't taken to heart by *The Old Grey Whistle Test* or the *NME* ('Shut up Roy, that's not rock 'n' roll!'), but it was also pretty obvious that neither Robert Plant nor Mick Jagger sang in their real voice. The best glam caused an uncomfortable itch in the increasingly cosy and fast-hardening music industry* by flying in the face of rock orthodoxy, whether it was Mud invading a transport cafe or thirty-something Gary Glitter, bouffant and pop-eyed, bulging out of his sequinned suit.

And it all evaporated very quickly. Nothing usurped glam, people just woke up one day in early 1975 and realised it was over. So Sweet went heavier, Mud turned to disco, Gary Glitter became a pantomime villain. Marc Bolan, its creator, was still cherubic but chubby, a spurned cupid, doomed to endlessly revisit the sound of '72. It's too bad that, as its originator, he alone missed the point – glam wasn't considered, or classy, or built to last. The trip from 'Ride a White Swan' to Sweet's false new dawn 'Fox on the Run' (UK no. 2 '75) took five years, as Bowie had predicted. Glam was constantly aware of its own mortality, and that is what made it so enjoyable.

---

* It was notable how many of glam's big names were on smaller labels – Bell, RAK and Polydor in particular. The *grande dame* EMI signed T. Rex (from the independent Fly label in '71, when they were already the biggest pop group in Britain) and album-based, serio-glam acts Cockney Rebel and Queen; CBS had Mott the Hoople. At the same time as glam was breaking, a new label called K-Tel was licensing hit singles on the cheap from EMI and CBS to create *20 Dynamic Hits*, which became the biggest-selling British album of 1972. It seemed like the majors were embarrassed by chart pop.

THE SOUND OF PHILADELPHIA: SOFT SOUL

With pre-rock harmony and doo wop as its precursors, disco and house as its offspring, Philadelphia soul is the fulcrum of modern pop.

Philadelphia soft soul and Glitter Band glam shared a loved of spangly suits, but while the genres and the primary audiences (glam was for white kids, soft soul was for black adults) were musically poles apart, there was another connection between the two – a professional showbiz overlap. Both genres rewarded hard-working acts who had struggled in the sixties but finally made it in the seventies.

The one time I went to Philadelphia was in search of a record shop that I'd heard about with aisle upon aisle of 45s, catalogued and ripe for the picking – it was a collector's paradise. We drove out from New York with the O'Jays' 'Back Stabbers' and Blue Magic's 'Sideshow' on the stereo and eventually we found the shop. But the owner was a jerk, he wouldn't let us browse, and it turned out to be a wasted journey (one great discovery: 'Tell Him' by the Drew-Vels). More shocking than the cantankerous record-store owner was the state of the city: Philadelphia – home to the

Delfonics, Harold Melvin and the Blue Notes, the birthplace of luxuriant, soft soul – was a mess. There was street upon street of semi-derelict
clapboard houses, their occupants sat bored stiff on the porch, and the
neighbourhoods got incrementally poorer until we found the holy grail
record shop – which was itself protected by metal doors and Fort Knox-
like security grilles. The music and the environment just didn't tally.

It wasn't until I was back in New York that I worked it out. The
Sound of Philadelphia is all about aspiration. James Brown had spoken to working-class black America in the sixties, but not everyone in
that constituency wanted to hear songs about black power or the ghetto
any more than white working-class Britain wanted every Kinks song
to sound like 'Dead End Street'. Philadelphia, more than any other
American city, liked a lot of spangle in its suits, a lot of sugar in its tea,
and the acme of this came with what producer Thom Bell called the
'beat concerto' sound.

This brand of soul's constituent parts wasn't unique to Philadelphia.
Leiber and Stoller had created the strings- and baion-beat-based 'There
Goes My Baby' for the Drifters in 1958; this had been expanded on in
a more ornate style by Italian American Teddy Randazzo in the mid-
sixties (notably with Little Anthony and the Imperials' 'Goin' out of My
Head' – US no. 6 '64 – and the Royalettes' 'It's Gonna Take a Miracle')
and then by Charles Stepney, more darkly, more intriguingly, at the end
of the decade with the Dells and the Rotary Connection at Chess.*

* Randazzo and Stepney are both unique voices in pop who really deserve more
than a footnote: the former was a New Yorker who took Bacharach's baton and
ran with it. Restrained emotion through clipped verses and florid choruses was
his speciality – his Italian roots were clearly audible. Randazzo's biggest UK hit
was Cupid's Inspiration's 'Yesterday Has Gone', a number four in 1968. Charles
Stepney was the vibes player in a jazz trio when he met the Dells, who convinced
him to do orchestration on their next single, 'O-O, I Love You' (US no. 61 '67);
they soon scored a brace of Stepney-produced hits ('Stay in My Corner', 'Oh
What a Night'), the only Top 10 hits of their six-decade career. His jazz background then helped to make the production on four-octave Minnie Riperton's
1969 album *Come to My Garden* one of the most sensuous and exotic this side of
Laura Nyro. Stepney was in discussions with Michael Jackson and had just finished work on Deniece Williams's *This Is Niecy* when he died of a heart attack in
1976 – Williams's 'Free' gave him a posthumous UK number one in 1977.

Yet, unlike other cities, Philadelphia never regarded this sound as a passing trend. The city absorbed the atmosphere of these records, and thrived on the warm hues that vocal harmony and orchestration brought to soul; it was hooked on melancholy, but was no less heartfelt than its electrified cousin.

Soft soul's opulence and depth stood out in the early seventies. This was an era of twenty-four-track, heavily carpeted studios, when every instrument was recorded separately and deliberately cut flat, waiting for the producer to work his magic. The sound that sprang from Philadelphia was sonically much closer to studios like Gold Star in LA, where Phil Spector, Jack Nitzsche and Brian Wilson had created their finest work; the secret was to record large numbers of musicians playing together. The Philly producers liked orchestration, but they liked it with an R&B feel. They wanted a groove just as much as James Brown did. Listen to the Delfonics' 'Ready or Not (Here I Come)' or the Stylistics' 'You Are Everything' – these songs occupy the space in which they were recorded. Played alongside Neil Young's *After the Gold Rush*, or even *There's a Riot Goin' On*, they sounded impossibly lush and heartbreakingly pure, richer than anything that had gone before.

You would never have thought this likely in 1959, when Philadelphia made its first impression on modern pop with Dick Clark's *American Bandstand*, the nation's top TV show. A local independent label called Cameo Parkway took advantage of the TV studio on their doorstep; while they connived to force Bobby Rydell onto the world, Cameo also discovered Chubby Checker, and he started a whole new wave of post-rock 'n' roll pop with 'The Twist', a US number one in 1960. The dance tore off like a bushfire in pop's most parched year, and Chubby became a short-term superstar, the King of the Twist.

Chubby and Cameo Parkway had followed one of pop's golden rules – make it as simple as possible. Jiving was hard work but the twist was a piece of cake, and you didn't even need a partner – you could do it all by yourself. All you had to do was follow Chub's simple instructions: pretend to dry your back with a towel while stamping out a cigarette with both feet. By the end of 1962 everyone around the world from Petula Clark ('Ya Ya Twist', UK no. 14) to Frank Sinatra ('Everybody's

Twistin", UK no. 22) to the Isley Brothers ('Twist and Shout', US no. 17) was reading from Chubby Checker's instruction manual.

New dance crazes spread across the country from Philadelphia on a weekly basis (froog, frug, snake, monkey, jerk, lurch). Cameo Parkway, meanwhile, was building a whole empire from the trend. Chubby himself scored with less viable dance moves on 'Pony Time' (US no. 1 61) and 'The Fly' (US no. 7 '61), before 'Let's Twist Again' (US no. 8 '61, UK no. 2 '62) made the beat go international. Cameo Parkway's other acts were fed variants that were derivative but catchy, and milked that cow as fast as they could: Dee Dee Sharp ('Mashed Potato Time'), the Orlons ('The Wah-Watusi') and the Dovells ('Bristol Stomp') all reached number two with their debut hits. As Motown would a little later, Cameo Parkway had found a hit formula and dominated the American chart. Unlike Motown, the brains behind Cameo Parkway – in 1962 America's most successful pop label – were Bernie Lowe, who had played piano on Paul Whiteman's *TV Teen Club* in the forties, and Kal Mann; their industry breakthroughs had been writing 'Toyland' for Nat King Cole and 'Teddy Bear' for Elvis Presley. While Berry Gordy had his weekly panel meetings to decide which singles would be received, Cameo Parkway's Bernie Lowe played acetates to his teenage daughter Lynne. Hats off to Lynne Lowe, then, for her impressive strike rate from 1961 to 1963 – seventeen Top 10 hits, including three number ones.

When the British Invasion hit in '64, Cameo Parkway, stranded in mashed-potato land, began to back-pedal frantically, signing random British acts (including the Kinks, but only for their first two singles) and dipping into the emergent soul scene. In mid-sixties Philadelphia there were local, non-Cameo hits bubbling through, like Barbara Mason's 'Yes I'm Ready' (US no. 5 '65) and Brenda and the Tabulations' 'Dry Your Eyes' (US no. 20 '67). They had a distinct feel: orchestrated, almost hymnal in their hushed intensity, and clearly connected to the doo-wop and girl-group sounds that most of the US was now shunning in favour of Anglo beat and folk. Cameo Parkway already had the acts (Checker, Sharp, the Orlons), and soon the backroom at Cameo included a trio of boys who had a better long-term grasp on what the kids wanted than Kal Mann, Bernie Lowe or even Lynne Lowe.

While they didn't land any major hits, writer/producers Kenny Gamble and Leon Huff, and arranger Thom Bell – all former members of a Cameo Parkway house band called the Romeos – used their time at the label as an apprenticeship for building the definitive Philadelphia sound. Bell, twenty-three when he arrived at Cameo, was middle-class ('We didn't eat steak all the time, but we didn't eat beans all the time either') and something of a prodigy – he could play drums, piano and the flugelhorn by the time he was eight. The new Philly sound he concocted with Gamble and Huff included French horns, harps and tympani, and it worked best when there was an expressive falsetto (Eddie Holman's 'This Can't Be True') or a female voice of poise and piercing power (Dee Dee Sharp's 'I Really Love You') to carry the emotion. If the label had been smart they'd have got the trio's names in blood – but the label wasn't smart.

When Cameo Parkway went bust in 1968, engineer Joe Tarsia bought one of their old studios and changed its name to Sigma Sound. Gamble and Huff – who had both been supplementing their pay from Cameo Parkway by working at the local hospital – moved right in, striking gold fast with the Intruders' novelty soul 'Cowboys to Girls' (US no. 6 '68) and reviving former Impression Jerry Butler's career with 'Only the Strong Survive' (US no. 4 '68); as Curtis Mayfield went further into black politics, mounting the barricades with 'Choice of Colors' and 'We're a Winner' in '69, his former teammate Butler was rebranded with homely wisdom and silky strings. Philadelphia DJ George Woods knew Butler had a penchant for ice sculpting and dubbed him the Ice Man. The moniker suited his sonorous, adult voice just as surely as earlier, eye-of-the-storm hits like 'Make It Easy on Yourself' (US no. 20 '62) and 'Need to Belong' (US no. 31 '63).

Thom Bell went further with the Delfonics' 'La La Means I Love You', a US number four in '68 that opened with the softest tympani, seemingly struck with marshmallow beaters, and the sound of weeping bouzoukis; his Delfonics productions took the sweet soul of Barbara Mason into an ethereal new world – a combination of the childlike ('la la la la la', 'ready or not, here I come'), the celestial and the sensual. If Brian Wilson was set to abandon his sonic adventures with the stripped-back *Wild Honey* and *Friends*, Bell was happy to pick up the magic wand and apply it to street-corner vocal groups. The 'Eleanor Rigby'-like jagged intro of 'Ready or Not' (US no. 35 '69), the slow-motion waterfall of 'Didn't I (Blow Your Mind)' (US no. 10 '70) and the lush, extraordinary adaptation of Barry Mann's 'When You Get Right Down to It' were all breathtaking, gauzy like a David Hamilton photo, florid as Bell's classical training would allow. *Blues & Soul* magazine dubbed the Delfonics 'America's No. 1 sophisticated soul group', but once they parted ways with Bell in '72 the hits seized up. Direct beneficiaries were the Stylistics, another Philly act for Bell to toy with whose singer, Russell Thompkins Jr, had an extraordinary falsetto and a look of genuine surprise whenever he hit the high notes.

As Roy Wood's productions and Chinn and Chapman's vignettes understood and revived the spirit of true, daffy rock 'n' roll, Thom Bell's work could be considered mature doo wop. It was opulent, yes, but it was never showy. He was thoughtful, followed no rules, loved Burt Bacharach and Shep and the Limelites equally. Working in the seventies with Dionne Warwick, he told *Blues & Soul* that he 'had this constant feeling that there was a connection between her and a cat. Just take a look at her: she has a feline grace, she's slinky. Even her facial features – those eyes, the cheekbones. So for about three weeks, I studied all the books I could find on cats and their behaviour and saw how it related to Dionne.'

Kenny Gamble was always the businessman of the ex-Cameo Parkway three. He also married Cameo's prize catch, the fierce-eyed Dee Dee Sharp. He set up his own label, Gamble Records, and scored a few hits with the Intruders, though the label's best 45 – the Baby Dolls' shy, keening 'Please Don't Rush Me' – was a flop; they had no staff and hits slipped through their fingers. Working for Atlantic they cut a whole album with Dusty Springfield, a sweet, crisp collection called *From Dusty with Love*, from which 'Brand New Me' was a Top 30 hit in the US in '69, and gave Archie Bell and the Drells irresistible dancefloor fillers with 'Here I Go Again' and '(There's Gonna Be) A Showdown', the former fired by a sitar-guitar that would soon become a Philly staple. Gamble started another label, Neptune, this time with major distribution through Chess, but again it died. He began to get frustrated, and set his mind to finding a way out. 'We'd been really brought down by the Neptune situation,' Gamble told *Blues & Soul* in '73. 'But when we recovered we thought "hell man, they're the ones who've blown it, not us." We *know* the music's good, we *know* it's what people want. So we began talks with another company, a big corporation, who had the resources to get the sound we'd nurtured and nursed and developed to the mass public.'

Soul, as a black art form, had held onto its independence, without labels being co-opted by the corporations, for a long time, much longer than rock 'n' roll had managed. But, just as mom-and-pop shops were closing in black districts of Philadelphia and all over America, so the independent labels started to disappear, and fast, in the early seventies. Chess was swallowed up in 1969 by GRT, passed on to All Platinum in 1975, MCA in the eighties, and is now part of the omnipotent Universal; Stax, over a barrel thanks to an obscure clause in their contract with distributors Atlantic, failed in 1975, despite having number-one hits with the Staple Singers' 'I'll Take You There' and Isaac Hayes's 'Shaft' just a couple of years earlier. Kenny Gamble's deal with Columbia, a label with a tiny proportion of black pop artists in 1970 (the most prominent were Sly and the Family Stone and Santana, the biggest seller was Johnny Mathis), was prophetic. The freshly minted label was called Philadelphia International Records; the time for humility was over – this really was the sound of their city. Over the next three years PIR became the best-selling soul label in the world. 'We have tried to follow the Motown pattern of establishing a home away from home for writers,' explained Gamble. 'We have fifteen writers' rooms. We have guys who, like I did, come in here after school and write for two or three hours a day. We write, produce, and above all we teach.'

Who were the label's superstars? The O'Jays struck gold first with the astonishing 'Back Stabbers' (US no. 3, UK no. 14 '72). It had the sleek guitar, the congas, the strings that had already become Philly ingredients, but it added the urban paranoia of Marvin Gaye's 'Inner City Blues', black mistrust of black and the agony of love previously dealt with by the Four Tops' 'Bernadette'. On top of all this, it had an outrageous piano intro, part Brazilian, part Rachmaninov, which stopped

you in your tracks before the brass burst in – 'Ba! Ba! Ba! Ba-ba . . .
BAAH!' – like James Bond. Then things calmed down, just a little. It
was majestic.

Gamble and Huff's answer to the Supremes was the Three Degrees,
who'd had a small hit called 'Gee Baby (I'm Sorry)' in the girl-group era
(US no. 80 '65), released a few crackers in between (1968's excellent
'Collage' is one of the few singles you can file under girl-group psych)
but were strictly C-list when they signed to PIR. Singer Sheila Ferguson
was ninety per cent hair and lipgloss, the other ten per cent being her
eyes, and she used her assets with slo-mo Marilyn Monroe moves. Her
voice, likewise, was all seduction, coming over softly like Diana Ross
on 'Take Good Care of Yourself' (UK no. 9 '74) one minute, then belt-
ing out the chorus of epic heartbreaker 'If and When' the next, as the
other two Degrees billed and cooed around her. One of the great long-
distance smoochers, 'When Will I See You Again' (UK no. 1, US no.
2 '74) was their biggest hit, but 'Year of Decision' (UK no. 13 '74)
was their best: 'Yes, this is the year to open up your eyes,' they sang as
Watergate unfolded and America prepared to bail out of Vietnam. It
had the Impressions' sense of friendly persuasion – you didn't have to
actually name Richard Nixon in the lyric to make your political point.

Billy Paul, already on the edge of forty when he signed to PIR, burst
into town selling medicine for the afflicted, with his wide-brimmed hat
and an endless grin. He took Paul McCartney's 'Let 'Em In' and Elton
John's 'Your Song' and turned them into a kind of festival gospel, ridiculously upbeat, joyous to an irritating degree. His biggest hit, 'Me and
Mrs Jones' (US no. 1, UK no. 12 '73), was like a Del Shannon single in
reverse – Billy was happy to be on the run, 'holding hands, making all
kinds of plans while the jukebox plays our favourite song'. Such was his
bonhomie that he made cheating sound not only acceptable but a whole
heap of sunny fun.

Rather more racked were Harold Melvin and the Blue Notes, who
had recorded one of the great singles on the cusp of doo wop and soul,
'Get Out (and Let Me Cry)' in 1964. 'Club work was how we ate,'
said Melvin; hits didn't bother them. So when Gamble and Huff first
approached them to record for PIR, they were unfazed: 'Working with

Kenny and Leon would mean a month with no pay.' But PIR was on a roll, and gave them 'If You Don't Know Me by Now' (US no. 3 '72, UK no. 9 '73), a tense, 6/8 ballad of devastating doubt and suspicion that burst into life from the very first second; there is no intro. Lead singer Teddy Pendergrass also had the saddest scream since Levi Stubbs, and the Blue Notes were later given Gamble and Huff's sexiest songs ('Satisfaction Guaranteed', 'The Love I Lost') as a reward for finally acquiescing.

Girl trio First Choice ('Smarty Pants', 'Armed and Extremely Dangerous') and the Intruders ('Win, Place or Show') got the daft songs with playground-friendly lyrics, snatches of horse-racing commentary or TV detective themes, anticipating hip-hop corn like Doug E. Fresh's 'The Show'. They were daft, but all of them were Top 50 UK and US hits.

Was it all down to Gamble, Huff and Bell? Couldn't just anyone have used the same studios and session musicians and come up with the same magical formula? No. Producer Peter DeAngelis took Eddie Holman's skyscraping falsetto into Sigma Sound and cut a revival of Ruby and the Romantics' 'Hey There Lonely Boy'; with a gender change and all the Philly details – even the French horn – present and correct it made number two in the US in early 1970, and number four in Philly-hungry Britain four years later. It was beautiful. But DeAngelis had recorded it as an afterthought, as a Holman album track, and when he tried to follow his fluke hit he couldn't, crushing Holman's power with a hundred-weight of strings, burying him under easy-listening gloop. Holman, who had created the very first Philly sound 45, 'This Can't Be True', with Gamble, Huff and Bell in 1966, deserved better.*

Could anyone outside Philadelphia create anything as luscious? They certainly gave it a go. By 1973 the smooth, aspirational sound had taken over other cities. Eugene Record took the Philly sound to the Midwest and made the Chi-Lites an even smoother proposition: the sentimental

---

* Holman's other great recording under DeAngelis's instruction was 'I Surrender', a 1969 throwaway B-side built on brass stabs, sparse rhythm guitar, minor chords and an imploring, acquiescent vocal: 'Here is my heart darling, take it . . . I surrender my love to you.'

but two-million-selling 'Have You Seen Her' (US and UK no. 3 '72) had an epic monologue intro that was closer to Rod McKuen than Isaac Hayes, while 'Oh Girl' (US no. 1) added Southern harmonica and a Nashville piano sound to the stew. No one-trick balladeers, the Chi-Lites cut the swampy, mellow electro-soul 'Stoned out of My Mind' (US no. 30 '73), the calypso-flecked 'Too Good to Be Forgotten' (UK no. 10 '74), cutesy school-love ballad 'Homely Girl' (UK no. 5, US no. 54 '74) and a truly odd disco-dub song with blasts of twenties jazz brass called 'You Don't Have to Go' (UK no. 3 '76), and – like the Turtles in the sixties – became one of the most versatile pop groups, soul or otherwise, of the seventies.

West-coast operator Barry White did even better. First off, he took three girls, named them Love Unlimited, and came up with 'Walking in the Rain with the One I Love' (US and UK no. 14 '72), an almost narcotic love song with a four-note keyboard hook straight out of an Italian giallo, topped with meteorological sound effects and a husky spoken intro – it was a masterpiece.* White himself was not an obvious pop star but, emboldened by his production success, he cut a single of his own. Critics were suspicious of this jewellery-laden ex-con. They accused him of plagiarising Isaac Hayes's million-selling *Hot Buttered Soul*, which was hardly a crime (it was more mystifying that no one else had done it); he made the Hayes sound simpler, to the point, more pop. And then the critics said his subsonic, unmusical voice was comical, a gift for impressionists, and this time, maybe, they weren't wrong. And also they said that his girth, his powder-blue suit, his perma-sweat, his pompadour were laughable. So what? He didn't look or sound like any-one (OK, he sounded a *bit* like Isaac Hayes) and this is why he reached number three in the States, straight away, with 'I'm Gonna Love You

---

* Nat King Cole's 1960 'two act' album *Wild Is Love* had been a part-spoken, part-sung forerunner but, most likely, White used the sole album by a sweet-voiced Philly girl group called the Fuzz as a blueprint. They had cut one major hit, 'I Love You for All Seasons', in 1970 and their sole album was made up of upbeat love ballads, occasionally bordering on danceable ('I'm So Glad'), and linked by spoken-word soliloquies to the Boy – it was as if the Chiffons had grown up and developed an appetite for Valium (this is meant to sound like a good thing).

Just a Little More Baby'. Also, it was the most blatant record about sex to date – with White muttering and groaning right in your ear, and the backing dark, slow, almost scary until its sweet string-led outro – that had been made to date in the US. No one said that about Hayes's *Hot Buttered Soul*. Barry White was set up, and he scored a long list of hits with long, long titles – 'You're the First, the Last, My Everything' being the biggest, a transatlantic 1974 number one. He was also responsible for an instrumental US number one as the Love Unlimited Orchestra with 'Love's Theme' in '74, one of the earliest disco hits, and you fell for its April uplift even when you knew it was nothing but soft-porn Mantovani. 'The real superstars are the people who buy the records,' Barry White would say, sweating charm as he bought another Cadillac.

By 1976 soul was mutating into disco, and Philly's ingredients were in the hands of less talented chefs. Philadelphia International was disco's bedrock, the musicians creating the rhythmic template with Harold Melvin's 'The Love I Lost' (US no. 7 '73), and the epitome of the genre's high camp with 'TSOP (The Sound of Philadelphia)', *another* PIR number one in the spring of '74, this time for their MFSB session men,* with a little help from the trilling Three Degrees. With its history and its mastery of the raw materials the label should have bossed disco, but instead it was all but dead by the time the *Saturday Night Fever* soundtrack was breaking sales records in '78.

What went wrong? Kenny Gamble simply got greedy. Like Berry Gordy before him, he wouldn't share the spoils, and the musicians all left; his plan to create another Motown in record time had come back to haunt him. The Three Degrees left Gamble, rubbing his nose in it by recording the *3D* and *New Dimensions* albums† with the new disco king, Giorgio Moroder, in 1979. One of the last great Gamble and

---

* MFSB stood for Mother Father Sister Brother – or Mother-Fucking Sons of Bitches, depending on who you believe.

† These albums did nothing in the States but they gave the girls a whole new run of hits in Britain with 'Giving Up Giving In' (no. 12 '78), 'A Woman in Love' (no. 3 '79), 'The Runner' (no. 10 '79) and 'My Simple Heart' (no. 9 '79). The latter's playful Bacharach/Philly-isms clearly showed the respect Moroder had for Gamble, Huff and Bell.

Huff records, ironically, was the Jacksons' 'Show You the Way to Go' in '77, their first UK number one after leaving Motown. Michael Jackson watched the producers 'like a sponge with eyes', knowing that there was no one better at their craft – mastering a rich, inclusive studio sound. Two years later he concocted *Off the Wall*, at that time the biggest-selling album ever by a black artist, and one that was unintentionally coached by Philadelphia's masters.

PROGRESSIVE ROCK (AND
SIMPLER PLEASURES)

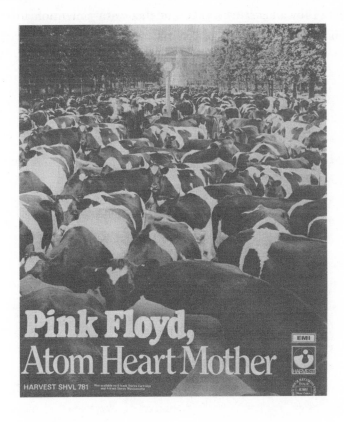

The music is immediate yet technical. It threatens to throttle
the ears and mind with its complexity of styles and expressions.
Advertisement for Gentle Giant's *Free Hand*, *Melody Maker*,
1975

Creating intelligent pop music is not an inherently noble endeavour,
though it may have seemed so in the early seventies. Norman Whitfield
concocted ever more elaborate Temptations singles, and electric soul
warriors like the Isley Brothers and sophisticates like Gamble and Huff

playfully reinvented soul in a post-Beatles era. For rock, a vastly more dispersed field than soul in the early seventies, the challenge to progress its sonic invention was grave.

The Beatles had been the role models for an ever-changing, forward-looking pop. It was a given, from the perspective of the music press, that pop would not only consistently come up with new sounds but new, more *adventurous* sounds. Commercialism and bubblegum were seen as regressive, and new British music mags – *Sounds, Let It Rock* – were set up purely for the rock fan. Within the major labels there was also an element of sniffiness: with the sounds of 'Sugar, Sugar' ringing in their ears, and flush with the profits of ever-increasing album sales, they set up various labels for the burgeoning British underground: Polydor begat Vertigo, Pye created Dawn, RCA glowed Neon.* The buzzword was 'progressive'.

Conceptually, the most influential album in the wake of *Sgt Pepper* had been the Who's 1969 album *Tommy*. With encouragement from manager Kit Lambert, Pete Townshend had been banging on about creating a rock opera since their second album, *A Quick One*, in '66. In keeping with previous Who albums, *Tommy* featured some crackling electric power pop ('Pinball Wizard', 'I'm Free'), and a few comedy moments for Moony and Entwistle to let fly ('Tommy's Holiday Camp', 'Fiddle About'), but it was stretched to double-album length in order to accommodate the album's overriding concept (deaf, dumb and blind kid finds deliverance in amusement arcades). As a pop record *Tommy* is patchy; as an opera it is badly executed on every level of pacing, plot and characterisation. But it wasn't received this way in a world hungry to move forward.

Eighteen months before *Tommy* was released, Birmingham R&B group the Moody Blues had been asked by their label, Deram, to record an album with the London Festival Orchestra in order to showcase the company's latest studio equipment. The group's brief moment in the sun had come with a cover of Bessie Banks's 'Go Now', a UK number

* The majors weren't necessarily favouring art over commerce – the profit margins on albums were much greater on albums than singles.

one back in early '65, but they had barely sold a record since, and had lost their main singer and songwriter Denny Laine, who went solo in early '67. To Deram, the 1967 Moody Blues must have seemed desperate, a group on their last legs who would have done anything – including a stereo test record, effectively an album-length advert – to keep their contract. Hats off to the Moodies, then. They took full advantage of the opportunity to create their own *Sgt Pepper*: *Days of Future Passed* was loaded with Mellotrons, snatches of poetry and minor-key whimsy, wrapped up neatly as a suite to give it added gravitas. At times it was overly precious but it was cleverly sequenced (from 'The Day Begins' to 'Nights in White Satin'), songs overlapped, and it was clearly meant to be listened to in a single sitting. 'Nights in White Satin' also provided their first hit single in years (UK no. 18, US no. 6), a quill-penned ballad that sat midway between eerie, breast-beating sincerity and Barbara Cartland.

Tommy and *Days of Future Passed* were rock's first concept albums. A few years after the American experience, British groups started to focus exclusively on album-length pieces, as opposed to three-minute songs, using the Moody Blues' sunny template and the Who's angularity rather than Vanilla Fudge's leaden, blues-based sound. Essentially an extension of British psychedelia, progressive rock was deeply rooted in Albion. Groups used instrumentation, phrasing and rhythms – as well as song topics – that they had learnt playing folk, jazz and blues; inevitably, many of the musicians had been trained in classical music. It lacked the lyrical earnestness of the singer-songwriters, and had more in common with Monty Python than James Taylor, but there was a seriousness of intent. Much maligned since, it could be very beautiful.* On the other hand, musical chops were essential, which resulted in some of pop's most tedious, self-indulgent music, and this has led to the entire genre being sharply unfashionable ever since its mid-seventies decline.

In 1971 Jon Anderson of Yes summed up the ambition, frustration and limitations of the progressives: 'I think there is this feeling within

---

* Exhibit A: Van Der Graaf Generator's 'Refugees', which epitomises a golden, early-seventies utopian sensibility: 'West is Mike and Susie'.

Yes that we'd really like to stand for something very positive in music. I mean, we're in an odd position at the moment – I look at the Beach Boys and think of the incredibly important things they did to music, and we want to do those same things and yet often we feel we'll never be able to break through and stand for something in that way.' The key problem with assessing the legacy of the progressive bands is trying to work out whether they actually were of greater significance than acts – say White Plains, or Tony Orlando and Dawn – knocking out three-minute singles, whether their pretensions were matched by their achievements, whether they embodied anything beyond what they were.

Jon Anderson may have been an unlikely front man, tiny, with a slightly alien face and a shrill high voice midway between that of a Canterbury chorister and a children's TV presenter, but he was a romantic,* and he wanted to write romantic songs about Albion. 'I don't know why the only acceptable songs about England have only been folk songs. I wrote a song about Accrington, which is near where I come from, and everyone cracked up about it. Somehow it's all right and very romantic to write a song called "Cincinnati" – that sounds cool – but not a song about Bolton.'

Genesis, with their portentous one-word name, were the prog archetype, and 'Musical Box' (from *Nursery Cryme*, 1971) – a Victorian murder and rape fantasy – was the genre benchmark. On stage, singer Peter Gabriel would change costumes and voices mid-song, throwing in the odd mime or monologue for good measure. Genesis defined 'rock opera' and it's not hard to see why some pop fans, impressed by scope and scale, would have considered their albums a cut above the latest Slade three-minute transistor-radio anthem. Opera is the sum of all the performing arts mulched to become a whole greater than its parts; on *Selling England by the Pound* it might have seemed they were channelling Noël Coward, Edward Elgar, Tubby Hayes and *Sgt Pepper*, as if they were genuinely progressing pop, leading it out of Tin Pan Alley with a theatrical smile, creating some new, higher art form.

* 'She brings the sunshine to a rainy afternoon, she puts the sweetness in and stirs it with a spoon', the opening couplet of 1969's 'Sweetness', is a peach.

Alternatively, it could be said that Genesis were a decent pop group with neat chord changes who mistook archness for intelligence; with its rather patronising references ('Easy now, sit you down, chewing through your Wimpy dreams' – can you picture Peter Gabriel in a Wimpy bar?) *Selling England by the Pound* is very sixth-form. Their magnum opus, the twenty-three-minute 'Supper's Ready' from *Foxtrot*, has deserts of desiccated organ and drum twiddles, leading nowhere but the run-out groove. When they were concise – the soft, warm whisky-mac halluci-nations of 'Carpet Crawlers' from *The Lamb Lies Down on Broadway* (1974), or the rag-week cuckooness of 'I Know What I Like' (a rare single, and number-twenty-one hit, also in '74) – they were English as tuppence and all you'd want them to be. Unfortunately their philosophy of constant progression, ever heavier and more theatrical sounds, and the demands of their fans led to longer and longer suites, more opaque sci-fi lyrics, more luminous flower costumes. Almost inevitably, Peter Gabriel quit in 1975. If Peter Sellers couldn't pull off the multiple roles he had in *Lolita* and *Dr Strangelove*, what chance Gabriel with his ever more complex rock operas?*

In the States, Genesis were less than a sensation. Beer cans were thrown. According to *Melody Maker*, they were heckled with shouts of 'Boogie!' Mike Oldfield avoided this problem by never taking the stage. He recorded the almost entirely instrumental *Tubular Bells* on a bor-rowed ¼-inch Bang & Olufsen reel-to-reel tape recorder. A collection of pretty melodies strung together as a suite, it was a number-one album in 1974, selling close to three million copies. Parts of it were used in a milk advert on TV; parts of it were used for 'interpretive dance' classes in British schools; parts of it were used on the soundtrack of *The Exorcist*. It may have featured 'The Sailor's Hornpipe' and Oldfield's neander-thal grunts,† but there was an overriding melancholy, and Oldfield's

---

* They didn't doubt their own abilities. Sat in the studio listening to a playback of Gabriel's first solo album, King Crimson's Robert Fripp, after a suitably rever-ential silence, muttered, 'A cosmic concurrence.' Producer Bob Ezrin turned to them both and burst out laughing.

† *Tubular Bells* was the breakthrough album for Richard Branson's Virgin label. Unsure about a totally instrumental record, Branson asked Oldfield if he

folk roots (he had been in an acoustic act called the Sallyangie in the late sixties) meant he never lost sight of the album's melodic thread. On the minus side, according to a review in *Let It Rock*, it had 'no sex, no violence, no ecstasy; nothing uncontrolled, nothing uncontrollable'. *Tubular Bells* was high-class library music – it could mean whatever you wanted it to mean. The sequel, the less melodic, more elongated *Hergest Ridge*, was another number one, but still Oldfield hid himself away; by the time he appeared on the cover of *Ommadawn* (1976) he looked a lot like Jesus.

Oldfield was chronically shy. *Melody Maker*'s Karl Dallas interviewed him, sprawled on a bed, apparently quite relaxed, in 1974. At the end of what Dallas felt had been a pretty amicable chat, Oldfield whispered, 'I feel as if I've been raped.' To overcome his problem, he did a course in exegesis in 1978, cut his hair off and transformed himself into a confident rock superstar. He'd taught himself to fly. He'd bought himself a Lear jet. He met Dallas again and told him, 'I'm fed up being a romantic . . . I was determined to have a very bad time in order to work out a few things. I have now completed that process, and have chosen to have a good time.' The result was Europop hits like 'Guilty' and 'Moonlight Shadow' (UK no. 4 '83) – the new Oldfield sound was so different, friendly and bubbly, you half expected him to change his name to Micky Oldfield. Good for him. But most of his fans preferred the bearded, romantic, bad-time Mike.

The only prog act to outsell Mike Oldfield was Pink Floyd. The rump of the post-Syd Barrett group had seen out the sixties with a low-key film soundtrack – for Barbet Schroeder's *More* – that in part was the golden vision of Albion that Jon Anderson was striving for. 'Green Is the Colour', 'Cirrus Minor' and 'Cymbaline' used organ, acoustic guitar, flute and birdsong to paint watercolours of summer afternoons by the River Cam in the shade of a weeping willow. They had evicted their acid-fried singer in 1968, after his mental collapse, and replaced him with a somewhat calmer Cambridge boy called Dave Gilmour, who was

---

could sing on just one track – the petulant Oldfield's answer was the 'caveman' section.

just back from a spot of male modelling in France. Gilmour was also an old friend of Barrett's, which made the regrouping guilt-edged and uncomfortable, but Floyd soldiered on and Barrett moved back in with his mum.* Everyone felt embarrassed. Things were so bad, they almost talked to each other about it.

Initially the new-look Floyd aped the departed singer's style, to no small psych-bubblegum effect, on a couple of singles called 'It Would Be So Nice' and 'Point Me at the Sky' (both worth seeking out, though they are written out of official Floyd history), but neither reached the Top 50. Rudderless, personality-free, it was hard to see what else they could do or where else they could go.

Visually, Pink Floyd had always gone for anonymity. They had never spoken on stage, played extended instrumental passages (not jazz, no real solos – they were the first to admit they didn't have the ability), and drenched both themselves and their audience in a lightshow which rendered them largely invisible. Barrett had been their Tigger, bouncy and cute, as well as their songwriter, their singer and their pin-up potential. Without him they became entirely faceless. Without him there really should have been no Pink Floyd. So they decided to make this total anonymity their calling card. American arthouse act the Residents would make great play of their mystery line-up in the seventies, masquerading as giant eyeballs and developing a cult audience; Pink Floyd's Nick Mason could have walked naked around Woolworths in 1973, as one of the biggest-selling pop stars in the world, and only been screamed at by traumatised shoppers.

The first sign that things might somehow work out was when Pink Floyd were asked to improvise live, in the BBC studio, as Neil Armstrong and Apollo 11 were launched from Cape Kennedy in 1969.

* Pop's ultimate lost boy, Syd Barrett kept it together long enough to make two albums of what would now be called outsider art. While living at his mum's house in Cambridge, growing fatter and balder, he became the founding father of indie dropout culture. Both *The Madcap Laughs* (1969) and *Barrett* (1970) are engaging but unsettling listens. Syd Barrett's lack of classic song structure and incapability to extend the sound experiments of *The Piper at the Gates of Dawn* makes them a simpler (ergo, easier to mimic) but far less exciting inspirational flavour.

The horse-faced Roger Waters had now assumed control. He was a far less frivolous, hedonistic soul than Barrett, and the future of the group was signposted by an arresting line on *More*'s 'Cymbaline': 'apprehension creeping like a tube train up your spine'. Musically, they became more of an obvious extension of pastoral English psychedelia than most of their contemporaries. 1971's *Meddle* opens with the minor-key atmospherics and ground-shifting dubbiness of 'One of These Days', followed by the brushed-organdie pastoral 'Pillow of Clouds': 'Sleepy time in my life with my love by my side.' Other times, they echoed the booster rockets of Apollo 11 – 'Careful with That Axe, Eugene' was a long day's flight into deep space; there was no aim, there was no captain of the ship.

In fact, very little went on, and that was almost the point – this was a group who were perpetually adrift, diffused and sad. They were permanently in Syd Barrett's shadow, and grew more racked with guilt over their lost friend with each incrementally bigger-selling album they released. Gradually, Roger Waters's vision became more focused. The higher their record sales climbed, the greater Floyd's fame, the more he felt a social and political responsibility. Waters spoke with a clear, deliberate voice about the things that inspired him, chiefly his father's death in World War Two ('a wrenching waste') and childhood friend Barrett's decline. No group wore the deep-blue cloak of rock's new gravitas more heavily than Pink Floyd.

Their British post-Barrett renaissance had begun with the 1970 number-one album *Atom Heart Mother*, which added a beered-up brass band and posh girls' choir to their saucerful of secrets; 1971's *Meddle* contained the twenty-plus-minute 'Echoes', a prog-rock high-water mark; American FM stations picked up on another of their soundtracks, for 1972's *Obscured by Clouds*. When their eighth album, *Dark Side of the Moon*, was released in '73, wrapped in a jet-black sleeve, it was Waters's all-time statement and made everything thus far feel like an apprenticeship. The demos were recorded in his garden shed in Islington, but the finished album was a stereo surround-sound spectacular, a treat for your hi-fi, with effects flying from left to right, deeper and beyond. To the accompaniment of cash registers, plane crashes, banshee backing vocals and ticking clocks, it was also hard work, largely tuneless, with misery and paranoia to spare. There were no flutes. *Dark Side of the Moon* reflected the downer vision of large parts of British and American youth in the years of Chrysler crisis and Grunwick grind – 'You're older, shorter of breath, and one day closer to death.' It sold forty-five million copies; *Sgt Pepper*, the Beatles' eighth album and similarly cup-overflowing creative peak, sold a mere thirty-two million.

When they finally laid Syd Barrett's memory to rest with the karmic 'Shine On You Crazy Diamond' in 1975, they lost their *raison d'être* for good. More rock theatre, ever greater, emptier extravaganzas, replaced their self-flagellating desire to drift, and the only way they could agree to go forward was by hiding behind pyrotechnics and flying pigs. It seemed that they hated being themselves.

As Fairport Convention's ale-sodden decline mirrored that of folk rock, so Pink Floyd's mid-seventies – plateauing and then turning towards self-parody – traced prog's failure.* Its flame would be kept alight by a teenage Pink Floyd fan, nurtured by Dave Gilmour since she was fourteen, who signed to EMI while they were counting their profits on *Wish You Were Here* but didn't release her first record until 1978. Everything about Kate Bush was English, autumnal and sensual, from her lyrics ('Driving back in her car, watching the wipers washing the leaves away') to the definitive photo of her head, shoulders and auburn curls entwined in ivy. She swooped and wheeled like a White Lady of legend, a ghost from a Kentish folk tale paying a visitation to the 1970s. Her best work combined the theatre of Genesis ('Wow'), the folk melodies of *Tubular Bells* ('The Man with the Child in His Eyes'), Jon Anderson's search for 'meaning' ('Running up That Hill'), Floyd's anti-war leanings ('Army Dreamers', 'Breathing'), even King Crimson's ultra-tricksy rhythms ('Sat in Your Lap'). All of these titles were Top 20 singles – her songs never outstayed their welcome.

Concision aside, where Bush's work differed from pretty much all

---

* See also Yes's *Tales from Topographic Oceans*, Gentle Giant's *Interview*, a 1976 concept album about the futility of being in a rock band, and Emerson, Lake and Palmer's fitfully funny trashing of Mussorgsky's *Pictures at an Exhibition*.

progressive rock is that so much of it was about sex. What her break-through single 'Wuthering Heights' (UK no. 1 '78) gave to rock's pro-gressive quarter was a woman's perspective and sensuality in what was a very male, insular music; this, combined with her litheness, sense of adventure, mystique and melodic gift, meant Kate Bush alone was equipped to ride out the new-wave storm.

There was almost nothing on the first three Kate Bush albums that couldn't have passed for a 1973 recording, and yet she bloomed in the post-punk era as the progressive giants split (Moody Blues, Jethro Tull) or jumped ship – Genesis into pop funk, Yes into electro pop. 'The essence of sensuality and child-like wonder or screeching wood nymph?' asked the *NME*; the answer – which explained her influence on female pop and her elevation to the top of Sunday-supplement English Eccentric lists – was 'Both'.

While mid-seventies America was content to keep Jethro Tull, the Moody Blues and Emerson, Lake and Palmer on a permanent coast-to-coast tour, it strangely never developed its own strain of progres-sive rock. Overt cleverness was channelled in a slightly different way by Todd Rundgren. Ridiculously talented, he was like a one-man Yes and, similarly, wanted to take the music of the sixties groups he loved – chiefly the Beatles and the Who – and stretch it out as far as he could. At first his solo albums were indebted to Laura Nyro's white-soul piano balladry; with the 1972 double *Something/Anything?* he perfected his blue-eyed soul shtick ('Sweeter Memories' and 'Hello It's Me', which was a US number five) but also had a go at super-compressed power pop ('Couldn't I Just Tell You'), neo-Merseybeat ('I Saw the Light', a UK turntable hit that somehow only got to number thirty-six), Motown/bubblegum mash-ups ('Wolfman Jack') and tasteless odes to groupies ('You Left Me Sore'). Its schoolboy grubbiness was easily overlooked, though, and when Rundgren discovered LSD relatively late in life, the result was 1973's *A Wizard, a True Star*. No pussyfooting, he now took on all his musical loves (bits of Gershwin, Weimar cabaret *and* a fight between electronic dogs) and made a red-blooded synth stew. The first side crammed in a dozen tracks, squeezed and pulsing with gonzoid energy – it messed with your head, it felt like there was an electrical storm outside your window. There was even room for hankie-wringing soul covers on Side 2 (the Impressions' 'I'm So Proud', the Delfonics' 'La La Means I Love You', the Miracles' 'Ooo Baby Baby'), a necessary breather which reflected the Philly sounds on the chart.

'There's a reason I'm so erect!' he squealed. The effervescent noise of *A Wizard, a True Star* predicted Prince in its playful R&B fizz, and a swathe of twenty-first-century electropop acts from the Avalanches to Hot Chip, but when it came out Todd Rundgren was on his own. 'Todd does shine,' said the sleevenote. 'Go ahead and try to ignore him again . . .' Like Bowie and Roxy in Britain, these were Technicolor sounds in an overcast age, and in 1973 Rundgren seemed geared for stateside superstardom. To promote 'Hello It's Me', his first Top 5 US hit, he went on the soul show *Midnight Special*, introduced by the Four Tops, in sequin-strewn, green peacock plumage; the glitter above his eyes looked like shiny reptilian scales and his shoulders sprouted feathery wings. He looked like a cross between Ming the Merciless and a glam gecko. O'Jays fans were not won over. There was a reason why glam rock remained a UK-only flavour in 1973, and Rundgren's outfit would have been too hot even for Mud's Rob Davis. In the space of five minutes, he went from potential saviour of all our tomorrows to that most demeaning of tags, the quirky cult hero.

Steely Dan were musicians more consummate and well schooled than the self-taught progressives in Britain. Their music came from a culture where high-end jazz had been common on radio and TV, one from which you could actually graduate as a musician in jazz (at Boston's Berklee School of Music, which had been established in 1954). They were craftsmen, smart to the point of glib, and heartless in their jazz name-drops ('Rikki Don't Lose That Number' was based on a Horace Silver riff). An augmented duo of ex-session men Donald Fagen and Walter Becker, they ticked so many cred boxes it's no surprise journalists loved them. Steely Dan had an intellectual layer that never really existed in the UK, highly professional but also knowledgeable, witty and subversive. They were part of a wisecracking, nonconformist New York tradition that dated back to Leiber and Stoller (who, by the seventies, were writing off-kilter show tunes like 'Is That All There Is'), and would inform the air of CBGB in '76 and Brooklyn in the 2000s: 'I learned music theory and harmony at music college,' said Donald Fagen, 'even though I ended up with a degree in literature. When we met, we both realised we listened to late-night jazz shows and be-bop music. I hated rock and roll.'

Steely Dan's records were immaculately presented, heavy on the electric piano, not a hair out of place. It takes some major dude attitude to have a song on your debut album that opens with 'Thelonius my old friend, step on in and let me shake your hand', but they didn't flinch. The question has to be why they didn't just play the jazz they loved, and the answer – visible at the early, shaky shows – was that they weren't good enough. So, throwing in a bit of pop to lighten the load, they were probably as surprised as anyone when it worked so well: they had hits in America ('Do It Again', US no. 6 '72, 'Reeling in the Years', no. 11 '73, 'Rikki Don't Lose That Number', no. 4 '74, 'Peg', no. 11 '77) because they telegraphed to a demographic just as clearly as Grand Funk Railroad did with their fundamentalist blue-collar rocker 'We're an American Band' (a Todd Rundgren-produced number one in '73). What's more, unlike the more po-faced British progressives, they clearly had a sense of humour. 'People who take their clothes off [at concerts] are into rhythm,' Fagen told *Melody Maker* in 1973. 'We're into that.' Despite being intentionally unlovable, people really love them. I've tried hard. I think, as with ninety per cent of jazz, I might like them a lot more one day.

They weren't widely copied, but Manchester's 10cc were as close as Britain got to its own Steely Dan. And 10cc had more hits – including three number ones – because they were more human, more fallible, and leaned towards the multi-part song structures and odd chord changes of '66 Beach Boys rather than Horace Silver. 'It's hard to define what 10cc is,' drummer Kevin Godley told the *NME* in 1973. 'It's our particular form of humour and I think it's a reaction against the introverted "corridors-of-my-mind" stuff we've been getting in the last two or three years . . . it's not just straightforward silliness or parody.' They had been around the block: Eric Stewart (in the Mindbenders), Graham Gouldman, Kevin Godley and Lol Creme (in the Mockingbirds) were veterans of the Manchester sixties scene,* while Gouldman had also done a stint as a session man for Kasenetz-Katz. In 1970 they built their own Strawberry Studios in Stockport, where they latched onto any passing trade, be it Neil Sedaka, Leslie Crowther or Manchester City FC. Once in a while they released singles under pseudonyms for fun: Doctor Father gave us the atmospheric, lost-in-Borneo yarn 'Umbopo'; 'Naughty Nola', an instrumental that sounded like electrified milk bottles, was by Lol; and as Grumble they reheated 'Da Doo Ron Ron' to no great acclaim. In 1972, as 10cc,† they cut a doo-wop spoof called 'Donna' (UK no. 2 '72), both tribute and novelty – it was smarty-pants stuff ('Oh Donna, you make me break up, you make me break down Donna'), not a loving homage in the style of Wizzard, but simple and ultra-catchy.

Analysing the success of 'Donna', Eric Stewart furrowed his brow and declared, 'We've decided that everything we've done so far has worked on its own terms, but we're still only working within the limits that have been set up during the last ten years of rock and roll, from the Beatles to 10cc today. And it's time to transcend all that, if we can.' They could. Freestyling in their own studio, they peaked with 'I'm Not in Love', a UK number one in 1975, where all their cleverness was corralled into a lagoon of vocal harmonies and a sad puddle of a lyric: 'I keep your picture up on the wall – it hides a nasty stain.' It worked like a faulty mixer tap, alternating warmth and chilliness in its repressed yearning and subsequent bitterness. Though 10cc may have learnt their moves from Steely Dan, 'I'm Not in Love' was ever so English.

By the mid-seventies it must have seemed to fans of Gene Vincent, or the Supremes, or Desmond Dekker, as if rock had been purloined and turned abstract by greatcoated students. Since the Teddy Boys adopted rock 'n' roll, British pop's progress had depended on its position as the

---

* Graham Gouldman had written some of the era's most melancholy, storytelling 45s: 'Look through Any Window' and 'Bus Stop' for the Hollies; Herman's Hermits' 'No Milk Today' and 'East West'; 'Heart Full of Soul', 'For Your Love' and 'Evil Hearted You' for the Yardbirds. All sounded influenced by his Jewish upbringing in Salford, and all were huge hits.
† Jonathan King – who had signed them to his UK label – had a dream in which an act called 10cc were the biggest band in the world. It sounded better than Grumble, anyway.

core of male teen culture. But outside the cloisters occupied by Genesis, Yes and Gentle Giant was a teen subculture – the bovver boys – who rejected this tradition, feeling *Tubular Bells* said nothing to them about their lives. They didn't feel remotely inspired to form a band. Eventually, this led to the dead zone of 1975 and '76, a period when no vital new sound came along to replace glam and prog at the end of their cycles. It may have felt like the British pop era – essentially the Beatles era – was winding up.* It was time to look abroad for new thrills.

West Germany had no musical heritage, at least none that it was comfortable with so close to the war. As the sound of schlager – oom-pah, bierkeller pop – dominated the German chart, musicians decided to create a brand-new sound by using the newest musical instruments they could find. If prog was maximalist on pretty much every level, bands like Neu!, Cluster and Can were its opposite, with a stripped-down aesthetic based on modern synthesizers (the first stop for anyone trying to create something entirely new in the seventies) and repetition, which built energy as a tension-containing machine from the endless chunk-a-chick-a of modern industry. Compared to Pink Floyd's pyrotechnics, it was very off-the-cuff. Spontaneity was key. One morning, soon after singer Malcolm Mooney had left the band, Can members Holger Czukay and Jaki Liebezeit were enjoying a coffee at a pavement cafe in Munich. They heard a commotion and looked up to see a wild-looking Japanese man singing on the street corner; his name was Damo Suzuki. They asked him to join Can immediately. Suzuki made his debut that night. No prog qualifications required.

---

* One possible way forward was to make modern music that was 'Beatlesque', an adjective that would become common in the ensuing decades. British prog-poppers Supertramp ('Dreamer', 'Give a Little Bit', 'Breakfast in America') were clearly in thrall to Paul McCartney's songs for *Magical Mystery Tour*, specifically 'Your Mother Should Know' and 'Fool on the Hill', while Cleveland band the Raspberries impressively merged the Who's pyrotechnics with 'Twist and Shout'-era Beatles to score US Top 20 hits with 'Go All the Way' and 'I Wanna Be with You'. Most successful were the Electric Light Orchestra, or ELO – the group Roy Wood had formed, then quit, in 1972. Under Jeff Lynne's leadership they made a career largely out of condensing and regurgitating *Abbey Road* on singles like 'Mr Blue Sky', 'Wild West Hero' and 'The Diary of Horace Wimp'.

Can were canned as 'Krautrock' by the British press, regarded as an interesting sideline but something of a novelty – so far beyond traditional rock boundaries, referencing Stockhausen and John Cage, that they simply didn't fit any pop criteria. Smart, brave, funny, relentless, it really was a new kind of music. That was an achievement in itself. The influence of Can and Neu! in particular would slowly, slowly permeate Anglo-American pop, not taking a real hold for the best part of two decades. In 1975 a lank-haired kid in Manchester called Mark Smith had already decided this was the sound for him: 'Repetition in our music and we're never gonna lose it' would become the Fall's one-line, Kraut-born manifesto.

YOUNG LOVE: WEENYBOPPERS
AND BOY BANDS

THE OFFICIAL

PARTRIDGE FAMILY FAN CLUB

58 Parker Street, London WC2B 5QB, Fan Club Secretary, Susie Miller

*Above: There are times when even David likes to climb onto a desk
and just talk about things*

Once Marc Bolan had unleashed the erotic, once he'd told twelve-year-old girls that he wanted to be a jeepster for their love, emotional anarchy was sure to follow. It was partially contained by a new breed of pop star, one aimed largely – if not solely – at pubescent girls.

Teen screams had followed Frank Sinatra and Dickie Valentine, been amplified by the Beatles, then the Monkees, and somehow quietened by the dawn of the seventies. But the sixties' social revolution affected everyone, whatever age, and the next time a teenybop act was put together it was set to be considerably more charged and specifically targeted than planting a woolly hat on Michael Nesmith's head.

The Jackson 5, a family band of good-looking boys led by eleven-year-old Michael and managed by father Joe, cut effervescent playground soul crafted by the Motown machine, and had four US number ones ('I Want You Back', 'ABC', 'The Love You Save', 'I'll Be There') in 1970. They opened the door for an even poppier, even younger family band, MGM's Osmonds, to become the biggest pop act in the UK, where the Jackson 5 had a few Top 10 hits but never a number one – it almost certainly helped their cause that the Osmonds were white. The Jackson 5 and the Osmonds were both real bands who played real instruments, but in both instances the focus was on the youngest, cutest member. Pubescent girls didn't care about chops, didn't care that 'Puppy Love', 'The Twelfth of Never' and 'Young Love' (all UK number ones) were uncool oldies, didn't even care that the young Donny Osmond's triple-tracked unbroken voice had no great emotional heft. Boys cared a lot, but that was irrelevant.

Clearly this was a very different pop game from what had gone before, one which possibly *did* have a magic formula for success. For managers and record labels this was a difficult learning curve – getting inside the minds of pre-teen girls – and it took decades for them to work it out: when they did, in the boy-band era of the late nineties, it become the most dominant style in pop and has shown no sign of letting up. The seventies, though, was an era of freakish experimentation. Most of the teenybop artists of the seventies weren't old enough to buy a pint; some were too young to write their own songs, too young even to get on a bus without their mum. Elvis, Billy Fury, the Beatles and T. Rex had been pin-ups who were moulded – by management, by record companies – but not contrived; the Monkees had been put together, and were wildly success-ful, but then revolted and got even better. Boys in their early to mid-teens didn't have the wherewithal to say 'No sir, I will not,' and, in the wake of the Osmonds' success, record companies signed up battalions of them.

Most of them made quite awful records, but David Cassidy was not one of them. A little older and wiser than Donny Osmond, Cassidy was blessed with a girlish mane, thick mink eyelashes and golden Cali skin. He was also a smooth article – five minutes with him and a girl had a past. At first he was an actor and landed a role in an apple-pie sitcom called *The Partridge Family*, about a travelling family band. But he just happened to have a honey-dripping voice. Whenever he opened his mouth, birds suddenly appeared. He was the most swooned-over pop star, by his co-stars, by his tour manager, by boys and girls from six to sixty. Walking on the Paramount lot one day he was spotted by two of the *Brady Bunch* actresses. They fell to their knees and screamed.

The first *Partridge Family* spin-off single, in 1971, was a rickety circus tune with a neat minor-to-major twist called 'I Think I Love You', and it went straight to number one in America. Very quickly, David Cassidy was all over teen magazine *Tiger Beat* – they hadn't had anyone quite so desirable since the Monkees.* And in the tradition of the Monkees, Cassidy didn't want to play ball. He was obliged by his TV contract to make records for Bell, never getting an advance from the label, not even for his solo recordings. When *Rolling Stone* approached him for an interview in 1972, he saw it as his chance to bare all – quite literally. Annie Leibovitz shot him naked, from the waist up, with just a hint of pubic hair. Even now it would be a sensation, truly subversive, an über-pop figure on the cover of the number-one underground paper. 'There are people who carry around that issue of *Rolling Stone* and think it's the coolest thing that's ever been done,' Cassidy said. But parents didn't think so. Crucially, nor did his ten-year-old fans, who loved cuddly, misty-eyed David, not post-coital David with all that body hair. He had violated the trust of young America. Bob Hope pulled out of a planned Cassidy TV special. His profile plummeted, and he never scored another Top 20 American hit.

Luckily, he had only just broken in Britain, where girls were less likely to baulk at his naked torso, and so Cassidy became the all-time pin-up all over again. Teenyboppers in Britain, like British pop fans in general, were altogether more dedicated and obsessive. In short order, he had a number-two hit in '72 with soft-rocker 'Could It Be Forever', followed by number ones with 'How Can I Be Sure' and 'Daydreamer'. His

---

* It's notable that pop was not the only source of pin-ups between 1969 and 1971: Paul Newman, *Alias Smith and Jones* star Pete Duel, even *Please Sir* actor John Alderton were flirted with by *Rave* and *Fabulous*, as chart sensations Jethro Tull and White Plains were never going to be the stuff of teenage fantasies.

wispiest, breathiest hit was called 'I Am a Clown'. Poor, sweet, forlorn, sexy David – marshmallows could've bruised this sound.

Musically it hasn't always scaled the heights of Cassidy's powder-puff tower, but one of the best things going for the teenybopper boom was its iconoclasm. This wasn't part of the *NME*'s plan for rock in the seventies – it wasn't meant to be like this. It had been hijacked. And whenever this happens, whenever the gatekeepers try to keep newcomers from getting into the party, pop is the eventual winner.

In 1974 Charles Shaar Murray reviewed an Osmonds show for the *NME*. He was sniffy about everything from the ticket price to the band's musicianship – 'the best instrumentalist is Merrill, who's about up to the standard of an average Marquee support band guitarist'. Refusenik Murray was just like Irving Berlin – that is, the Irving Berlin who tried to ban Elvis's version of 'White Christmas' for being musically unsound. Teenybop pop found the rock press on enemy territory. They didn't get it, and teenybop pop certainly didn't need them – it was all over kids' magazines like *Look In* and *Jackie*, where readers and punters were the same people.

Stared out by hundreds of under-sixteen girls and suspicious ushers at the Rainbow, Murray reported how the audience was 'weeping and wailing with a terrifying intensity . . .' It was a female reaction to pop that he couldn't understand, and would prefer to silence with muso grumblings. The Osmonds as an entity (their solo records were usually covers of fifties ballads, often pre-rock, universally unimaginative) cut some of the hardest-ever teenybop 45s: 'Down by the Lazy River' (US no. 4), a version of Joe South's 'Yo-Yo' (US no. 3), 'Goin' Home' (UK no. 4) and, best of all, the eco-warrior wig-out 'Crazy Horses' (UK no. 2, US no. 14). They took the Jackson 5 sound, sped it up, threw in some pedal-heavy guitars and growled as fiercely as their sexless Mormon upbringing would allow.

David Cassidy and Donny Osmond both later made the classic move into grown-up pop, even scoring a couple of major hits (respectively, 'The Last Kiss', UK no. 6 '85; 'Soldier of Love', US no. 2, UK no. 29 '88). Groundbreakers for a new style, a new era, they survived and still play to an ever-ageing crowd. Lower down the food chain were manager/producers keen to discover the next Donny or David before he had any musical savvy or ambitions of any kind. EMI A&R man Colin Burn searched high and low for a British Donny, and ended up signing his son, Darren.* Larry Page, who had managed the Kinks and discovered the Troggs, gave us the simian James Boys from Upminster, who looked like a pre-teen Supergrass and sang straight, unquestioning nursery pop like 'Roly Poly', 'Shoog Shoog' and 'Lo-Lo-Lollipop'. Even fat, freckled Jimmy Osmond, who made number one in the UK with the unctuous 'Long-haired Lover from Liverpool' in late '72, might have drawn the line. Asked by the BBC what reasons young girls might have for screaming at boys whose balls had yet to drop, the older James boy smartly replied, 'Dunno – ask 'em.' Jonathan King presented the far more appealing Ricky (son of Marty) Wilde, who cut some hyper, kid glam ('I Wanna Go to a Disco', 'Teen Wave') and later wrote a run of stunning bubble-punk hits for his sister Kim; another King protégé, Simon Turner, also outgrew his master and ended up recording soundtracks for Derek Jarman and David Lynch.

When it became clear that no one was about to step into Donny Osmond's baby shoes, the poster-boy age went up a few years. David Essex was the total package. He was a natural charmer, playing up his Canning Town background something chronic on 'Hold Me Close' (UK no. 1 '75) and its follow-up, 'If I Could' – 'Oh we could have a lark, picnicking in the park' – as if he was Burlington Bertie from Bow reborn in a white polyester suit. He also made some very good records. A stage-school boy, Essex had cut his debut as far back as 1965 but, unlike Bolan and Bowie, his profile was non-existent† until his manager

---

* He was the star of a BBC *Man Alive* programme called *Twinkle Twinkle Little Star* which showed just how out of his depth the precocious, middle-class ten-year-old was when confronted with real-life ten-year-old girls. Given Cook and Greenaway's decidedly adult 'Something's Gotten Hold of My Heart' to launch his career, poor Darren was doomed, back at school, a failed pop star at twelve. Eventually he cut one great glam 45 called 'Summertime Time', but by then his five minutes were already up.

† A bunch of singles for Fontana, Pye and Decca lack the intrigue of Bolan and Bowie's pre-fame catalogue. 'Thigh High' from 1966, a music-hall ode to kinky boots, takes the cake.

landed him a part in *That'll Be the Day*, a porridge-grey evocation of fifties rock 'n' roll Britain. Essex played Jim MacLaine, a teenager with a great deadpan delivery and a raging libido. Over the end credits ran an original song called 'Rock On'.

'Rock On' was all about what wasn't there. The rubbery bassline was an echo of something played in 1956, caught like a sound corked in a bottle and released as a gas twenty years later. The whole song was akin to a spectre in a photograph, with its cat-ghost strings and Essex's half-asleep vocal summoning a lost era with random signifiers – 'Hey, shout, summertime blues'. There were more questions than answers – 'Where do we go from here? Which is the way that's clear?' – and 'Rock On', caked in echo and confusion, effectively, quietly, was the sound of Britain in 1973.

So was he an avant? Not quite. Essex's producer was Jeff Wayne, and the two had been working on ad jingles for products like Us deodorant and Pledge furniture polish for a few years – the latter (as 'Bring in the Sun') even made it onto his first album. Besides, he was ever so pretty and became teen-scream material just as the *NME* ran their first serious feature on him; the rock media dropped him like a hot potato, equating him with Donny Osmond just weeks after they had called him 'the English Dr John'.*

It didn't matter to the *NME* that sequels like the Dixieland glam of 'Lamplight' (UK no. 7 '73) and stuttering heartbeat of 'Stardust' (UK no. 5 '74) were almost the equal of 'Rock On', Essex was suddenly a girls' singer. He had the wisdom to turn this into subject matter: 'Gonna Make You a Star', his first number one in '74, was a pithy put-down ('Well, they say he's into his music, but I don't believe it. He just doesn't seem to understand the rock media') and became a youth-club classic in the process.

David Essex posters started to get taken off bedroom walls almost as soon as he released *Out on the Street* in '76, a concept album that was to the alleys of Stepney what Bowie's *Diamond Dogs* was to the ballrooms of Mars. The lead single, 'City Lights', was a seven-minute, string-driven

* As a fifties New Orleans rocker, Mac Rebennack had written Jerry Byrne's electrifying 'Lights Out'; by the late sixties he was Dr John, 'the night tripper', who played spooky swamp blues and whose stage show involved Mardi Gras costumes and voodoo ceremonies.

piece of dark disco, as quietly apocalyptic as a mugging. Radio hated it, and it settled at number twenty-four and died, effectively killed by its own ambition. Girls felt betrayed by his new direction, his apparent desire for serious acclaim – didn't David respect their adoration? Didn't he understand that their love could always be withdrawn, that it was transferable? The next time anyone noticed David Essex he was playing Che Guevara in *Evita*, older, bearded, not being screamed at. Eventually, almost inevitably, he landed a part in *EastEnders*. And once in a while he still made great records that sounded like nothing else on earth – the Weimar electro pop 'Me and My Girl (Night Clubbing)' from '82 – but mostly he played up to the mums, made enough money to buy a house in New England and a flat in London. He was happy with that and nobody got hurt.

It wasn't Essex, or Cassidy, or even the Osmonds who were to be the blueprint for future pin-up boy bands. Zero creative control, nothing to rock the boat, something for girls from eight to eighty (ignoring the ones between sixteen and sixty) – it was the Bay City Rollers, deflowerers of Scotland, and they would have no cosy Osmond/Cassidy afterlife. Their hits began in 1974 as fifties-fitted glam-lite ('Remember', 'Shang-a-Lang', 'Summerlove Sensation', 'All of Me Loves All of You' – all Top 10), with lyrics that looked to an idealised past. The Rollers had hits written by Bill Martin and Phil Coulter, veterans of Eurovision (who had written 'Puppet on a String' and Cliff Richard's 'Congratulations'); they had their own TV show, *Shang-a-Lang*, complete with passionate audience; and they had a recognisable and easily mimicked image – the Osmonds had teeth, the Rollers had tartan.

This effective combination worked wonders for them. None of the Rollers was especially talented,* or even especially pretty, and it seemed to sum up the paucity of pop in 1975 that they merited such hard love and worship for eighteen months. Catching a bus as an eleven-year-old boy in 1975 was to run the gauntlet, there being a strong chance of every young female on board loudly singing 'Bay City Rollers we love

---

* Debut album *Rollin'*, a number one that pre-dated their brace of number-one singles, included some self-penned songs. One of them, 'Just a Little Love', is sweet, shambolic and fragile, an unlikely precursor to the Glasgow indie sound of the eighties.

you', tartan scarves in the air, their newly discovered sexual energy being publicly released en masse.

They scored 1975's biggest-selling British single, a cover of the Four Seasons' 'Bye Bye Baby', which stayed at number one for six weeks. It was followed by 'Give a Little Love', another number one and a landmark in its own sappy way – with its too-easy chord changes and Mattel-pop trundle from verse to chorus, this was the prototype boy-band ballad.* Presumably it was aimed at expanding the Rollers' audience to an older demographic – you can almost hear the lighters being waved in the air.

But the cracks started to show very quickly. According to their manager, Tam Paton, the Rollers kept their peachy complexions by drinking pints and pints of milk. Paton was old-school – like Maurice Levy, like Bill Sykes. In a Channel 4 documentary twenty years later, Rollers singer Les McKeown was brought face to face with Paton: exasperated by Paton's flaky excuses about the Rollers' lost millions, McKeown resorts to asking, 'Where's my fucking money? I want my fucking money.' Paton lived in luxury from the Rollers' first flush of fame until his death in 2009. McKeown remembers Rollermania – never sleeping, not having Christmas off, the band being given speed to keep them going. Paton also forced his charges to go through the humiliation of guesting regularly on a US kids show called *The Krofft Superstar Hour*.†

* The move from teenybop to grown-up pop would be eliminated by Boyzone and Westlife, who scored twenty UK number ones between them by recording ballads that appealed simultaneously to soft-hearted pubescent girls, their mums and their grandparents (who were old enough to remember the Bachelors' Irish ballad hits of the sixties). Westlife – Shane Filan, Mark Feehily, Kian Egan, Nicky Byrne and Brian McFadden – had their milksop style perfected on their debut single, 'Swear It Again', in 1999. Feehily explained the Westlife rules to the *Guardian*: 'A piano intro, Shane starts the song, the drum beat kicks in for the second verse. I sing the second verse and maybe the middle eight, then there's a key change, a gospel choir and some ad-libs, the end.' They upset the art/commerce equilibrium. One day I may get round to trying to appreciate their craft, but not just yet.
† Oddly, the Rollers only had hits in the States with their tougher 45s: 'Rock 'n' Roll Love Letter', 'Money Honey' and – pick of the bunch – the foot-stompin' 'Saturday Night', which made number one but flopped completely in Britain. Its chanted chorus became the base material for the Ramones' 'Blitzkrieg Bop' and, thus, their entire career.

Their co-star was a green-faced woman called Witchiepoo. They looked like they were about to cry in every scene. Far worse, McKeown ran over and killed a near neighbour, seventy-six-year-old Euphemia Clunie. And the band played on.

What pervades the Rollers' records, and what a nostalgic air freshener fails to cover the smell of, is the cynicism. After a bracing start with their early 45s ('Shang-a-Lang' still has a Womble-esque idiot joy), the records are rarely more than tepid, and no one – least of all the group – sounds as if they enjoyed making them. The hack work of 'Give a Little Love', the sleazy Paton back story, the drugs, the death, the inevitable fallout and lifelong bitterness – was any of it worth it?*

By contrast, boy bands of the eighties and beyond – and there was a mighty long gap between the Rollers and the next major teenybop bands, New Edition in the States and Bros in the UK – seemed to enjoy what they were doing. New Kids on the Block looked like B-boy wannabes, and their lame but child-friendly beats matched their aspirations. Beyond them, Boyzone and Westlife quietly went about their business with professionalism and an air of confidence, certain that their music had a stamp of quality. In this way, they were entirely pre-rock, more in tune with David Whitfield than David Essex.

But what Bolan had made explicit, and what Cassidy was lambasted for, would be built upon in the nineties by Take That. At first they seemed like just another manager's plaything, Muscle Marys with cute faces who took an eternity to score their first hit. This, it turned out, was in their favour – by the time 'A Million Love Songs' reached number seven in '92 they had assumed their roles: there was singer/writer Gary Barlow, the rather clumsy, pudgily earnest front man; Mark Owen was the girlishly pretty one; Howard was hirsute; Jason was chiselled; and

* McKeown was talked into putting the death of Euphemia Clunie out of his mind, both for his sake and for the sake of the band. 'They didn't see it from a helpful, human way,' he told the *Guardian* in 2005. 'It wasn't like, "We're going to get through this together", it was more like, "We need you on stage tomorrow, you wee cunt, so you better stop fucking crying."' In 1982 Paton was convicted of gross indecency with two teenage boys and served a three-year sentence. In 2007 he was accused, but cleared, of raping Rollers guitarist Pat McGlynn in a hotel room in 1977.

Robbie was the class clown. While they still played hard to the gay audience (packing the 'Pray' video with homoerotic imagery, calling up gay icon Lulu for a guest spot on 'Relight My Fire' – both UK number ones in '93), they had something for everyone. Take That weren't for children – these were real men and, once they ditched the overtly queer videos, they became beloved entertainers. After a ten-year hiatus they came back in 2006, by which time Barlow's songwriting had matured and his puppy fat had gone. Off the bat they released three singles ('Patience', 'Shine', 'Greatest Day') which all reached number one; all had an easy charm and milkman-ready melodies, and all trounced the hits they had scored in the nineties. They became the first – and, to date, only – teenybop act to mature, to naturally grow older with their fans, expanding their appeal and becoming the everymen of pop in the process; twenty years on from their first hit, the statesmen-like Take That could still pack out arenas.*

The Bay City Rollers, meanwhile, have skidded through alcoholism, prison sentences, court cases. You rarely hear their music, even on oldies stations. Their significance was more about female bonding than it was their music, and in this respect they maybe had as much of an influence on girl groups as Frankie Lymon had twenty years earlier – I'd lay money on Bananarama being fans for a start. Progenitors of riot grrrl? That's probably stretching it. But if you found yourself in the terrible state the former Rollers ended up in, then you'd be clutching at straws for your place in pop history too.

---

* Cliff Richard is the only comparable pop figure. He grew older with his audience and expanded it likewise when he hit his eighteenth or so year in the business with 'Devil Woman' (UK no. 8, US no. 6 '76) and later the new pop canary 'We Don't Talk Any More' (UK no. 1, US no. 7 '79). From the nineties onwards, though, his appeal narrowed more and more until it was largely limited to women around his own age. His legacy – saturnine pin-up in the fifties, clean-living movie star in the sixties, bouffant balladeer in the seventies and reborn MOR synth-popper in the eighties – became more tarnished with each passing year until he was pop's favourite punchline, its softest target; claiming he was 'the most radical rock 'n' roll singer Britain has ever seen' due to his clean-living lifestyle didn't help. Take That's revival has been based on humility – it'll be interesting to see what the public's perception of them is in another ten years.

SEE THAT GIRL: ABBA

The office is just what you'd expect of a Swedish record company whose main attraction is Abba. It's all bright, clean, stripped pine efficiency. The only thing in the entire room that doesn't fit with the squeaky clean image is a big, almost life size painting. It's of a schoolgirl in a gymslip, crisp white blouse unbuttoned, and one breast is exposed. Her discreet and presumably masturbating hand has slipped under her skirt. The style is ultra realism. It's the only sign of decadence in the whole Abba operation.

Mick Farren, *NME*, 1976

Abba: The Movie opened in 1977. My whole family went to see it on a Saturday afternoon. Unlike T. Rex, or Gary Glitter, or anyone who had starred in their own movie since the Beatles tore the heart out of the Brill Building world with *A Hard Day's Night*, this was a pop film about a group with universal appeal. Still, it was hard to pinpoint exactly why Abba had got *so* big – if 'Money, Money, Money' hadn't stalled at number three, *Abba: The Movie* would have been released on the back of six straight number ones. It came, it went. I'd forgotten everything in it apart from the songs and Agnetha's metallic blonde hair and blue satin pants by the following day. It was boring.

Compared to Elvisitis, Beatlemania or even T. Rextasy, Abba's planet-conquering success was a conundrum. What did we have? A striking but sulky blonde, a slightly saucier brunette who most of the time looked like she'd just baked a cake, and two men – definitely not boys – who were stereotypical seventies uncles. To a hard-nosed journalist who couldn't give two hoots about their music, there was one outstanding feature: they were Swedish. Let me paint a picture.

Modern pop was an Anglo-American affair until the late seventies. Britain had more in common with the States – through proximity and, especially, language – than the rest of Europe. Britain absorbed and mirrored the American sound, spitting out the bits it didn't get or didn't like, and this was how American pop was filtered and passed on to mainland Europe. Paul Revere and the Raiders couldn't buy a hit in Britain? Then there was no hope for them anywhere else on this side of the Atlantic. European countries added their own spin to this by adding ingredients – melody, harmony and rhythms – from their own folk and music-hall traditions. Sometimes this worked well, as in France, where yé-yé became a style all of its own, and in Italy, where writers like Gino Paoli and producers like Ennio Morricone concocted a rococo, cinematic ballad style. It also created a hellish kitsch, devoid of all black American influence, known as schlager, a polka-based music which was pop's dominant European style in the sixties and seventies.*

---

* The reggae boom in Britain at the end of the sixties meant this influence slowly trickled down to mainland Europe. Boney M were the result: 'Rivers of Babylon'

All of this was a mystery to most locally holidaying Britons until the Eurovision Song Contest suddenly became a significant annual event, like the FA Cup Final. As was true in international football for many years, Britain had stood by and watched every other country compete with each other, sure in the knowledge that British pop was inherently superior. For years, Europe had its own culture of song festivals which were alien to Britain. Songs from, say, the San Remo festival were identifiably Italian – that was where Dusty Springfield first heard 'Io che non vivo', her only UK number one when it was retitled 'You Don't Have to Say You Love Me'. Britain was content to throw these festivals bones like Kenneth McKellar's Caruso-in-a-kilt 'A Man without Love', our 1966 Eurovision entry. The following year, the BBC decided to up their efforts, screening all potential British Eurovision entries on the prime-time *Rolf Harris Show*, with the hip and continental* Sandie Shaw singing each one. When Bill Martin and Phil Coulter's 'Puppet on a String', mulching every cliché of European pop, won the contest at a canter, it set a template: dumber than dumb nursery lyrics, and a backing that sounded as if it was played on a euphonium and a xylophone. Presto. The fabled Eurovision sound. It was all our fault.†

By the time Abba entered the contest with 'Waterloo' in 1974, Eurovision had become horribly predictable. Britain's recent entries had seen the sultry Clodagh Rodgers sully herself with 'Jack in the Box' and Olivia Newton-John – on the verge of becoming a major country-pop

---

certainly had as much oompah as it had skank. This odd variant on the British and American black experience was finally killed off by the international success of hip hop.

* Sandie was easily the most successful British sixties girl on the continent, recording in French, Spanish, Italian, German and Portuguese. Some of her very best songs – 'Com'e bella la sera' (Italy), 'Toy' (Portugal) – were only released in those territories.

† 1965's winner had been 'Poupée de cire, poupée de son', a galloping Franco-Spectorian yé-yé number sung by France Gall and written by Serge Gainsbourg. The patronising pan-Euro parping of 'Puppet on a String' both created and confirmed Britain's xenophobic ideas about European pop music. And let's not forget it was chosen as our entry by the British public, ahead of four classy songs: 'Tell the Boys', 'Had a Dream Last Night', 'Ask Any Woman' and the heart-stopping 'Cry Myself to Sleep'.

star in the US – singing the none-stompier 'Long Live Love', seemingly
backed by the elephant orchestra from *Dumbo*. Abba comprised two
songwriters of some years – Björn Ulvaeus and Benny Andersson – and
their attractive girlfriends. They had the easy appeal and tightness of a
family act. And they ignored the Eurovision norm by whacking together
something that started like 'Da Doo Ron Ron', then quickly worked
itself up into a brassy glam-popper with the odd Rachmaninov flourish
from Benny on the piano. Roy Wood must have rubbed his beard and
nodded appreciatively. It was as obvious a winner as 'Puppet on a String'
had been in '67, and it rewrote the rules for future Eurovision entries.

So Abba's influence made the Eurovision Song Contest a lot more
palatable for the next few years. That would not be enough to cement
their place in the pantheon, not even for an avid telly watcher like me.
Britain was ready to discount them as another Eurovision flash in the
pan like Vicky Leandros ('Come What May', no. 2 '72) or Anne Marie
David ('Wonderful Dream', no. 13 '73); it didn't take to follow-ups
'I Do I Do I Do I Do I Do', or 'So Long', or 'Ring Ring'. The reaction in Britain and America – using one of only two Swedish cultural
totems they could think of (the other was to compare them to Ingmar
Bergman, and that wouldn't work, not just yet) – was to summon up
porn references: 'Belly to belly, butt to butt, Sweden sends us rock and
roll smut' ran a headline in *Phonograph*. As for the teen mags, Abba were
far too old. Bearded Benny and gnomic Björn couldn't even have been
the fantasy subject matter of their own 'When I Kissed the Teacher'.

But then 'SOS' turned up on the airwaves. It was certainly European,
it lilted and swayed on a soft Mediterranean breeze, its descending
piano intro recalled Georges Delerue's Truffaut soundtracks. And it was
a second hit, a number six in the UK and – more impressively – a
number fifteen in the States. Shaking off their lowly Eurovision tag,
they presented an eponymous album, a clean start, that no one could
ignore: *Creem* said, '"SOS" is surrounded on this LP by so many good
tunes that the mind boggles.' The *NME*'s Mick Farren reckoned 'their
closest antecedents are the early days of Motown, or maybe Philles. It's
the structure that produces the music that I'm talking about – and also
the fact that a frightening amount of work goes into each one of their

records.' From their log cabin in the Stockholm archipelago, Ulvaeus and Andersson now spent six years writing a collection of songs which were the best planned, best edited, most hook-filled, polished, economically tight hits of their era – maybe of any era.

A year after 'SOS', they made a record that placed them amongst the greats. 'Dancing Queen', from its split-second cascading intro in, never wastes a second. Counter-melodies were Abba's best friends, and this fitted one into every conceivable nook and cranny – a string line here, a glissando there. 'Dancing Queen' also had a precipitous drop, in the style of T. Rex's greatest singles, from major to minor almost as soon as the vocal comes in, leaving just enough time for the vital 'oooooh' to glide into your ear just before it pulls your heart down to your stomach with 'you can dance, you can jive . . .' It's a rare and magical achievement.

Abba were magpies, always seemingly one step behind pop fashion but not slow enough to spoil the flow. They embraced disco in '79 with 'Voulez-Vous' a year after *Saturday Night Fever* was the genre's commercial peak, and mimicked California's hazy sloth with 'Name of the Game' in '77, just as punk rendered it passé. Even the nu-Spector sound of breakthrough hit 'Waterloo' had been perfected a year earlier by Wizzard. Yet their mastery of the studio (nothing has ever sounded more well drilled and glossed than an Abba production) and Stockholm's distance from the heat and the action of Anglo-American pop ensured a subtly unique and removed sound; imitators from the Netherlands (Luv) and Britain (Brotherhood of Man, the Dooleys), aping the high, tight sound of the Agnetha/Frida vocals, sounded shrill and weedy without the production meat and might of Ulvaeus/Andersson.

Their influences were hard to divine, and the men gave little away in interviews, but Agnetha and Frida's harmonies were a mix of plangent Swedish folk and the high nasal cries of the Hollies, who had been bigger in Sweden than anywhere else. No one musician stands out on any of their hits because they don't sound like anyone played an instrument on them; they all sound like a music box carved from ice. The most unusual ingredient in Abba's strange magic was the coming together of the two couples, who then both split once the group had become the most successful singles act in the world. Much has been made of the internal ruptures and jealousies that informed Fleetwood Mac's *Rumours* but, hell, this was nothing but a night on the couch compared to the full-on nervous breakdown of Abba's post-split ballads.

'The Winner Takes It All' (UK no. 1, US no. 8 '80) is an adult pop song. No room for doubt, this was the story of someone put through the mill, pop's equivalent of *Scenes from a Marriage*, with its grisly, unresolved feelings of love, memories, jealousy and confusion. 'I don't want to talk', it starts, as anyone going through a divorce invariably does before opening up with indecent candour. Its most naked moment is sung with an awful mix of hope and bitterness, just as the music dips to near silence, allowing its desperation to sound as raw as possible: 'But tell me, does she kiss like I used to kiss you?' It's the sound of the Shangri-Las grown up, two kids upstairs asleep, a bottle of red wine open on the kitchen table. Sung by Agnetha, alone at the microphone, to her ex-husband in the control booth, 'The Winner Takes It All' was pure musical theatre, but frightening because it was clearly real – anyone listening knew they were intruding on the private grief of an ex-couple – and it outsold all of their singles from the previous two years.

It was their late masterpiece. With their relationships asunder, the group struggled on for a couple of years, ending with an album (*The Visitors*) and ultra-realist single ('The Day Before You Came') that piled dread and foreboding into their sound.* They released a compilation optimistically called *The First Ten Years*, then put their career in the deep freeze.

And when Abba went to sleep, a swathe of pop went to sleep. A sound and image that was toothpaste-clean with a gentle suggestion of filth died with them. It happened very fast. Abba's final year saw several remarkable records that were clearly based on the Ulvaeus/Andersson model – Tight Fit's 'Fantasy Island' (UK no. 5), Bardo's tricksy UK Eurovision entry 'One Step Further' (UK no. 2), Bucks Fizz's 'My Camera Never Lies' (UK no. 1) – but these were also born of new pop,

---

* 'The Day Before You Came' is like *CSI*. Who is the stranger who appears the next day? The man of her dreams? Her murderer? It sounds a lot like death. I'm prepared to ignore the fact that Abba released one more single ('Under Attack') before they disappeared, because this is the career-closer to beat them all.

the bright new sound of '82, with a knowing wink that Abba simply didn't possess. Abba were classicists, right down the line. They didn't belong any more and bowed out at the perfect time.

So what had made Abba so big? Nobody has ever worked harder, that's all. Yes, they were talented, but Björn and Benny have confessed that they wrote twelve songs a year, sweated over them and released them all; there are no hidden, rash attempts at post-punk or reggae lurking in Abba's vaults. It was all they did. There were no outside productions, and God knows they didn't spend too long thinking of what to wear in photo shoots. The end result was a catalogue that seemed oddly out of its time – of any time – because it was, and remains, timeless. Hard, honest toil. It's not romantic but, like police work, it's where ninety-nine per cent of the results come from.

BEYOND THE BLUE HORIZON:
COUNTRY AND WESTERN

EAGLES: Tequila Sunrise (Asylum AYM 520).
From their "Desperado" concept album comes the
Eagles' latest laid-back gem, an oh-so-languid lazy
lilter which features sleepy singing, gentle guitar,
slithering steel, "Tumbling Tumbleweeds"
touches, and a trace of influence from their
feathered friends, the Byrds . . . . aaahhh-uurrr-
umm, I think I'll just lay me down and rest awhile,
so sleepy, mmmmm, mmmm MMMUSIC PICK.

We stand today on the edge of a New Frontier – the frontier of the 1960s, the frontier of unknown opportunities and
perils . . . Beyond that frontier are uncharted areas of science
and space, unsolved problems of peace and war, unconquered
problems of ignorance and prejudice, unanswered questions of
poverty and surplus.
      John F. Kennedy, 1960

Of all the musical genres in this book, country and western is the only
one that pre-dates and survives the modern pop age. From the fifties
through the eighties and nineties, it developed on a parallel track, the
two musics bumping together frequently, feeding into and from each
other, like wary neighbours. I decided to bring it in at this point of
the story as, commercially, it peaked in Britain in the mid-seventies
when Glen Campbell, Slim Whitman and the late Jim Reeves topped

the album charts; Tammy Wynette's 'Stand by Your Man', the ultimate lost housewife anthem, became a number-one single;* and country rock – a post-Monterey, roots reaction to bubblegum – became a radio staple, with the Eagles especially dominant. I did think about leaving it out completely, but this proved to be impossible because, when you get right down to it, country music is the underfelt of modern pop.

Almost every genre in this story so far has withered in its effectiveness after a while, been absorbed or usurped, or at least stopped adding significant new ideas to the mix; the chart lifespan of any new genre is usually five years from start to finish but can be as short as two years (Merseybeat), twelve months (skiffle) or even less (acid house). There can be no such assumptions about country; divided against itself, it has endless internal arguments about what it is exactly. Come what may, even now, it remains the lingua franca of white American pop, the imagined language of the ordinary man or woman. Many of its key songs are about survival, and this probably isn't a coincidence.†

Country's appeal beyond the Southern states of America is provided by an incredibly attractive shared canvas of memory. It reminds people of home – but since many of the people drawn to it have never lived in or even seen Abilene, or Death Valley, or El Paso, this is a very curious fact. One possible explanation is its longevity. It's always been around, in some form: from silent Western movies that go back as far as 1901, to games of cowboys and Indians with Gene Autry as the soundtrack, to Glen Campbell's panoramic stories of Wichita, Galveston and Phoenix. This is a large part of its appeal, a compelling combination of affection for childhood pleasure with grown-up domestic-scale tragedy and difficulty. Not bohemian tragedy, as sung about by Carole King or Elton John, but unpaid bills, broken marriages, alcoholism. Country dealt

---

* Tammy Wynette's 'D.I.V.O.R.C.E.' also reached the Top 20 in '75, and was followed by Billy Connolly's comedy cover, which provided yet another number one.
† There's a large contingent who believe bluegrass is the one true country music. Bluegrass is a high-chord, fast-picked banjo style devised by Bill Monroe from Kentucky – 'the blue grass state' – in the late thirties. 'It's pure, it's clean,' Monroe declared in 1976. 'There's no sex in it.'

with these issues with controlled emotion, and this appealed to sensibilities far away from Texas – the British stiff upper lip, the Swedish culture of *lagom*, the Ghanaian appreciation of cool and reserve, they would always make room for the stoicism of a singer like Jim Reeves over the ballyhoo of Gene Vincent.

If we can cast our minds back to the start of this tale, we might remember that modern pop had arrived at, and out of, a mid-fifties generational clash within country, when its youthful wing had embraced elements of forties black pop and melded them with the music they knew best. Contrary to orthodox rock thinking, country music had never been merely foolish, sexless and sentimental, and it thrived, in spite of the rock 'n' roll rebellion, because it was there to deal with complicated adult responses. Unlike most modern pop of the late fifties and early sixties it wasn't, necessarily, built for teenagers. If you look at Western movies from the early years of modern pop, they were dealing with similar complexities – *High Noon, The Searchers, Shane* – and were some of the genre's high points. Country music, like Westerns,* is a part of the age-old American dream – an impossible dream – a mix of absolute individualist autonomy ('home on the range') and civic peace ('Abilene, Abilene, prettiest town I've ever seen, women there don't treat you mean'). While kids like Johnny Cash, Johnny Burnette and Elvis Presley set up their own youth-led new town, with souped-up Chevys, coffee bars and soda joints lining the streets, there was still the old West territory down the road, ruled by the sheriff of Nashville, a place where a more conservative form of country continued to rule, quietly.

When rockabilly swallowed up a generation and led them away from the Grand Ole Opry, the conservative heart of Nashville and country music, older practitioners stepped back, thought hard and long about what to do next, and came up with a new pop strand of their own. One

---

* Singing cowboys make up the 'western' part of the country-and-western equation, not movies – both cowboy ballads and hillbilly country would be played on the same radio stations in the thirties and forties, leading to their musical merger. The term was officially recognised by *Billboard* in 1949, when the country-and-western (C&W) chart replaced the hillbilly chart.

where you could hear all the words. Sensible music for maturer, wiser heads.

Countrypolitan, born just as Kennedy made his frontier speech in 1960, was the beginning of what became known as the Nashville sound, a breakthrough, a smooth version of country with international adult-orientated appeal which still thrives today. It meant the end of the road for a decades-old template: cowboys were out, strings, twilit piano and butter-soft drums were in. Jimmie Rodgers's nasal singing, yodelling and fiddles were unwelcome here, and a hint of pedal steel and the patented slip-note piano of Floyd Cramer would now be quite enough distinctive flavouring. There was a crack team of Nashville session musicians on hand to provide the backing. The producers of this music were slick and businesslike, the ad men of country music, quite convincing and quite cold. *Record Mirror* met the first names of Nashville when they visited London in 1962: 'Chet Atkins, we noted, was the tall handsome one in the blue suit. Floyd Cramer, the tall handsome one in the grey suit.'

Chet Atkins was a guitar picker and producer who had been discovered by one Steve Sholes, the man who had taken Elvis Presley from the local Sun Records to the global RCA Victor label in 1956. It was a measure of Chet's standing – and of country's commercial reach – that Sholes rated him a more important discovery than Elvis. In 1962 Atkins produced more than half of RCA's hits, in all genres. His production style smoothed out all of country's creases and was widely copied. If a performer was good enough, this production created a warm sitting room of sound, a suitable venue for someone like the post-army Elvis, who, when he wasn't in Hollywood, was in Nashville creating hits with Atkins like 'She's Not You' (US no. 5, UK no. 1 '62). In the same league as Elvis was Patsy Cline. A tough cookie, she referred to herself as 'the Cline' and everyone else as 'hoss' – except for Elvis, who she called 'the big hoss'. When Nashville's WSN asked where she got her distinctive style from, she told them, 'Oh, I just sing like I hurt inside.' In short order, she had US Top 20 hits in 1961 and '62 with 'Crazy', 'I Fall to Pieces' and 'She's Got You'. The Nashville sound has its detractors, but its hushed minimal backing was all Cline needed as she lived the lyric, cracking up, disintegrating in front of us. Friends said that she would cry at the end of recording sessions. Soon after cutting 'Sweet Dreams' in 1963, a plane carrying her crashed into a forest in Camden, Tennessee, and she was killed.

If Patsy Cline was a singer you pictured at home, thumbing through a photograph album, hands shaking as she turned the pages, then Brenda Lee was the woman alone at the bar, glued to a glass of whisky, too far gone for any man to dare chat her up. Cline and Lee shared another countrypolitan producer, Owen Bradley, who clearly liked his girls to sound racked. Brenda Lee was just four foot nine, and broke through with 'Sweet Nothin's' (UK and US no. 4 '60) when she was just fifteen; unlike Cline, she had previously fooled around with rockabilly ('Rock the Bop', 'Dynamite', 'Let's Jump the Broomstick'), which suited her Wanda Jackson-like gravel tone and earned her the name Little Miss Dynamite. She scored her biggest hits with distraught ballads like 'I'm Sorry' and 'I Want to Be Wanted' (both US no. 1) but was pop-savvy enough to mix up her output with Brill Building songs ('Dum Dum', US no. 3 '61; 'Speak to Me Pretty', UK no. 3 '62; 'Here Comes That Feeling', UK no. 5 '63), Italian balladry ('All Alone Am I', UK no. 7 '63) and even tough post-Merseybeat ('Is It True', US and UK no. 17 '64) and Motown ('Time and Time Again').* Yet, in spite of her varied singles discography, she was Nashville to the core. 'I do not like recording in any studio but the ones I use in Nashville,' she told the *NME* in 1963, 'because the surroundings and the people are familiar. I use studio musicians including Floyd Cramer and we all know our limits and capabilities. I think it's only fair to everybody, including myself, to stick to the usual routine.'

While Patsy Cline and Brenda Lee had urgent voices, nonchalance

---

* A little later, the young Dolly Parton experimented with the girl-group sound in 1965 and '66 for two strong singles, the Shangri-Las-influenced 'Don't Drop Out' and anguished soul thumper 'Busy Signal'. The country/pop/soul interactions of the mid-sixties also created two of the very best northern-soul singles, Barbara Mills's 'Queen of Fools' and Bobbie Smith's 'Walk On into My Heart'. Alabaman Sandy Posey sang back-ups on Percy Sledge's 'When a Man Loves a Woman' before scoring three US Top 20 hits of her own, the best of which – 'I Take It Back' – had a Patsy Cline weepie chorus allied to a sassy spoken-word verse straight out of the Ellie Greenwich songbook.

was seen as a major virtue in countrypolitan. This explains the incredible success of Jim Reeves, who spent 322 weeks on the UK singles chart in the sixties, with twenty-six Top 50 hits. The most popular BBC radio show of the era was *Family Favourites*, which involved letters between soldiers abroad and their loved ones back home, and was broadcast just as the nation was sitting down to its Sunday roast. Reeves was a regular, with at least one song a week. His music was comfort food, his voice had a pre-rock, lullaby quality that made him the first international country star; he was Gentleman Jim, always the stoic, never known to raise a voice in anger.

In many Westerns, the sheriff – lovable Jimmy Stewart, upstanding Gary Cooper – is racked with thoughts of bitterness, revenge and anger, but this always plays under the surface. Outwardly, all that is visible is noble restraint. On Jim Reeves's first major hit, 'He'll Have to Go' (US no. 2, UK no. 12 '60), he phones his wife from a bar – presumably he's tipsy, and he knows she's at home with another man. They may even be in bed together. This was a pretty radical lyric for a year which also gave us 'My Boomerang Won't Come Back' and 'Tie Me Kangaroo Down, Sport'. But throughout the song Reeves never once sounds pissed off or particularly cut up; he just calmly tells his wife to end the affair, and his sangfroid is the song's strength. On other songs, however, his calm control means something else entirely: 'Welcome to My World' (UK no. 6 '63) has an especially florid Nashville production and sounds, at first listen, like the warmest of invitations. The problem is that Reeves has built the world entirely for one person, and it's not himself. He sits there waiting in this dreamscape, placid, blank, with that gentlemanly half-smile on his face. Dig deeper into Reeves's catalogue and it becomes disturbing on a Patrick Bateman level.

Jim Reeves's death in 1964, again in a plane crash, sealed his fame; his waxy face would never grow old. Posthumously his music continued to accompany Sunday lunches through the sixties and seventies, and 'Distant Drums' even gave him a UK number one in 1966. It turned out that he wasn't quite the gentleman the photos suggested, given to bouts of petulance, complaining about the condition of the pianos on a 1963 UK tour, sleeping around. 'I don't like to see women messing

around with Jim,' his wife told singer Ginny Wright, 'and I don't want
to know anything about it.' Reeves was cited in a paternity suit, and
it was then revealed he was incapable of having children. In the most
child-focused, baby-boom era, this must have affected his personality
and possibly accounts for that voice – so warm and huggy, like a big sad
teddy bear, entirely devoid of sexuality.

* * *

The US is highly unusual in not having a city from which the nation's
pride flows. Instead, it has several big cities, and all tend to be held in
varying degrees of disregard – it has no London, Paris, Rome, Athens, no
core metropolis in which the nation's sense of self is invested. The heart
of America, instead, is in the mythic West, beyond the frontier, over the
horizon. Yet it is when country cheekily tries on the city's clothes that it
reaches out to modern pop and causes tremors that affect both musics:
western swing in the forties, rockabilly in the fifties, country rock in the
sixties and seventies.

In the city you have to know how to speak and look, how to fit
in, how to subtly change your behaviour from one neighbourhood to
another – it is not a matter of choice but a need. Country musicians
who moved to California to find work in the sixties knew this to be
true, and their new perspective informed a generation who wanted
their country with a little more zip, a little less factory air than Chet
Atkins's white-walled studio allowed. Countrypolitan hadn't been
to everyone's tastes. It hadn't been what the Lovin' Spoonful's John
Sebastian had in mind when he wrote about the 'Nashville Cats' (US
no. 8 '66) who 'play clean as country water'. 1966 was the year in which
Southern musicians, reared on both country and rock 'n' roll, started to
reclaim it from Atkins and Owen Bradley and their slick orchestrated
arrangements. The Monkees' Michael Nesmith ('Papa Gene's Blues',
'Don't Wait for Me'), the Byrds' Gene Clark and Chris Hillman ('Time
Between', 'The Girl with No Name') and Buffalo Springfield's Stephen
Stills all wrote identifiably country songs as album tracks. 1966 was
also the year Lee Hazlewood became a recognised name in pop and

country circles – with an international number-one hit, he was hard to avoid.

Born in Mannford, Oklahoma, Lee Hazlewood was the son of an oil man who had spent his childhood flitting across the South, and in the late fifties produced Duane Eddy's run of bowel-shaking guitar instrumentals. His voice was like a whisky-soused Johnny Cash, and he cut his own sardonic *Trouble Is a Lonesome Town* in '63, a concept album about the residents of a fictional Southern outpost called Trouble – Jim Reeves was probably not a near neighbour. Hazlewood's break came when he gave a song to Frank Sinatra's hitless daughter Nancy in '66 and told her to 'sing it like a fourteen-year-old who goes with truckers'.

'These Boots Are Made for Walking' combined camp, humour and sass, Carnaby Street's kinky boots with a plain-speaking country undertow. From that tomcat descending bassline in, it was irresistible. Nancy and Lee then embarked on a series of psychedelic cowboy duets ('Summer Wine', 'Some Velvet Morning', 'Sand'), none of which matched the commercial clout of 'Boots' (six weeks at number one in the UK in '66), but all of them had a dark knowingness, playing up the duo's image of hard-living cowboy and leather-booted siren. Where 'Boots' had been Adam West's *Batman* meets *The Mod Squad*, Bobbie Gentry's 'Ode to Billie Joe' (US no. 1, UK no. 13 '67) was somewhere between *The Waltons* and *Deliverance*. It was ridiculously cinematic, every line loaded with swampy Southern references: 'black-eyed peas', 'Choctaw Ridge', 'they bought a store in Tupelo', 'another sleepy, dusky Delta day'. Both records were almost cartoonish and both were recorded in Los Angeles; Gentry, like Hazlewood, was a true Southerner with her own highly individual take on the country myth. 'Ode to Billie Joe' could only have been written by someone who had crossed over the Tallahatchie Bridge and could see a tough country life for what it really was – the older generation in Gentry's songs sound bitter, callous, cold. Billie Joe's dead? Well, he 'never had a lick of sense – pass the biscuits, please'. It was number one in the States for a month in the autumn of '67, a down-home downer after the Summer of Love. In person, Gentry was even sassier than Nancy Sinatra, with a jet-black bouffant and a honeyed croak of a voice. And, like Hazlewood, she didn't stick around, marrying a multimillionaire and retiring in the early seventies. It's too bad that her six-album career was so short.

Glen Campbell was another displaced Southerner working in California when he cut Jimmy Webb's 'By the Time I Get to Phoenix' in 1967. He must have felt as uncomfortable as Jon Voight in *Midnight Cowboy*, and all his best songs were thumbnail sketches of the South. Among the best were 'Gentle on My Mind', with Glen as a drifter, serenading from a distance the one girl who never tried to tie him down; 'Galveston' (US no. 4, UK no. 13 '69), which could have been set in either the civil war or the Vietnam war ('I can see her standing by the water . . . looking out to sea . . . is she waiting there for me?'); and 'Wichita Lineman' (US no. 3 '68, UK no. 8 '69), the everyday tale of a man fixing phone lines which nevertheless features the most beautiful line in the whole pop canon, one that makes me stop whatever I'm doing every single time I hear it – 'I need you more than want you, and I want you for all time.'

Hazlewood, Gentry and Campbell were all Southerners trying to make a living outside of Nashville's straitjacket. Internal flights became more affordable in the mid-sixties, and the modern world created a new wave of less localised country writers. Glen Campbell worked with John Hartford (who wrote 'Gentle on My Mind') and Chris Gantry ('Dreams of the Everyday Housewife'); Elvis worked with Jerry Reed ('Guitar Man') and Mickey Newbury ('An American Trilogy'); Tom T. Hall wrote Jeannie C. Riley's conservative-bashing 'Harper Valley PTA' (US no. 1, UK no. 12 '68), while Joe South came up with the philosophical 'Walk a Mile in My Shoes' and 'Games People Play' (employing a very un-Nashville sitar), as well as Lynn Anderson's strangely chilly 'Rose Garden' (US no. 1, UK no. 3). They dominated the late sixties, but another crop of transplanted Southerners were set to conquer the seventies.

Central to country and western is the myth of the frontier, the point at which settled domestic life and chaotic, perilous adventure meet. The actual, official frontier was closed in 1894: there was no more land left to move into, or to steal. In 1960 Kennedy had made his speech, which relocated the central mythical site of the frontier somewhere in the liberal political imagination. No one exemplified this brave new internal adventure more than the Band.

The stream of country influence on post-Beatles pop became a flood after Bob Dylan's touring band, then known as the Hawks, spent 1967 in Woodstock. Staying in a huge, pink-washed house for $125 a month, they improvised a home-recording studio in the basement and shut themselves away from Monterey, psychedelia and flower power. Dylan, who lived only a few miles away, would call round most evenings, and they would run through a bunch of songs that ranged from ancient folk numbers to things they wrote on the spot (the results would be boot-legged as *Great White Wonder*, and later became known as *The Basement Tapes*). They began to grow moustaches and beards and wear tall hats. Their neighbours called them the Band, and it stuck. They looked old and wise beyond their years.

Four fifths of the group were Canadian, but they were at pains to point out their backwater woodedness: Arkansas-raised drummer Levon Helm was the only Southerner; bassist Rick Danko, the son of a wood-cutter, claimed to have grown up without electricity but with a wind-up Victrola, and 'always wanted to go to Nashville to be a cowboy singer. From the time I was five, I'd listened to the Grand Ole Opry, the blues and country stations.' Guitarist Robbie Robertson 'used to listen to country music a lot' and wrote songs that crossed Brer Rabbit with Grimm's fairy tales.*

The Band's yarn-spinning felt natural and cosy in 1968 alongside the brash bubblegum of the Ohio Express's 'Yummy Yummy Yummy'. 1968 was also the year in which Martin Luther King and Robert Kennedy were assassinated; these Canadian kids dressed up in bootlace ties and hobnail boots, with promo pics shot in sepia tones, may have

---

* *Rolling Stone* summed up the impact of their first album, *Music from Big Pink*, with a remarkably prescient review in 1968: 'The Band dips into the well of tra-dition and comes up with bucketsful of clear, cool, country soul that wash the ears with a sound never heard before. *Music from Big Pink* is the kind of album that will have to open its own door to a new category, and through that door it may very well be accompanied by all the reasons for the burgeoning rush toward country pop, by the exodus from the cities and the search for a calmer ethic . . . by the thirst for simple touchstones and the natural law of trees.'

been less connected to their lyrics than the Monkees were to 'Pleasant Valley Sunday', but – to a world cowering in fear of 1968's urban revolution and decay – the Band's prairie tales seemed as reassuring as Slim Whitman's 'Rose Marie' had been in the post-war, pre-rock era, and a genuine alternative. That they were blessed by Bob Dylan didn't hurt them either, and they were canny enough to include his – as yet unheard – 'I Shall Be Released' on their 1968 debut, *Music from Big Pink*.

Their song titles – 'Whispering Pines', 'Up on Cripple Creek', 'Acadian Driftwood' – blended the old pioneer stories with Kennedy's new frontier spirit, and sated what *Rolling Stone* called a 'hunger for earth-grown wisdom'; they opened a door. *Creem* was less kind about the new wave of country-rock frontiersmen, calling them 'city boys who've suddenly taken to wearing spurs and howling at the moon', but the Band's influence was instantaneous. The most prominent country-ward moves came from Bob Dylan, who brought out the liberal left's favourite country star, Johnny Cash, to sing on his 1969 album *Nashville Skyline*, and Crosby, Stills and Nash, whose debut album added smooth harmonies to the Band's driftwood potage. Beyond this, the Rolling Stones cut 'Honky Tonk Women' in '69 and then, if its inspiration wasn't already clear, they recast it as 'Country Honk' on *Let It Bleed*; the Bee Gees wrote the cowboy lament 'Don't Forget to Remember' in '69 and 'How Can You Mend a Broken Heart', a country-soul US number one in 1971; the Byrds – who had dropped country-flavoured songs onto most of their previous albums – abandoned their cosmic progression entirely in favour of country on 1968's *Sweetheart of the Rodeo*; another forebear, Michael Nesmith, quit the Monkees and formed all-out country-rockers the First National Band in 1970; in the same year, Elton John sang about those good old 'Country Comforts', which was soon covered by Rod Stewart. When the Beatles split, a lonely Ringo Starr made an entire country album called *Beaucoups of Blues*.

At the heart of the seventies hippie Utopia was the original American dream: the idealised land of the settler, the gold-rush world of the old West. The Band sang about 'The Night They Drove Old Dixie Down'; Bob Dylan sang about 'Country Pie' and yearned for a home on the range. In the UK, the poverty and a real sense of loss (through loss of jobs and large-scale redevelopment of cities) in the seventies meant there was as ready a market as there was in the States for music to nurse people through the bad times. The idyll that Dylan, the Band and their alternative-lifestyle cohorts were in search of was really not that far from the desires in mainstream country – 'What I've got in mind', sang permed Nashville singer Billie Jo Spears, 'is a small cafe, out of the way.' She shared space in the UK singles chart of 1976 with Dolly Parton, Don Williams, the Eagles and another transplanted Canadian, J. J. Barrie; K-Tel issued *20 Town & Country Greats*; EMI put out the TV-advertised *Country Life* compilation. By this time, the misty-eyed American mindset of country and western had become an international dreamscape.

The Eagles were the group who joined up the remaining dots between country, western and the new frontier. Don Henley had come to Los Angeles from Texas, where he had been the token hippie in an otherwise straight town, and joined a band named Shiloh. Glen Frey was a soul fan from Detroit who had followed a girl to California and stayed. They were spotted at LA nightspot the Troubadour by ex-Stone Poney Linda Ronstadt,* who plucked them both for her backing band. In 1970 they decided to go it alone as the Eagles, with a little writing help from other Troubadour regulars J. D. Souther and Jackson Browne. Following in Crosby, Stills and Nash's slipstream, they played with sensitivity but weren't averse to aggressive, clean-cut rocking. Their timing was perfect.

On 'Take It Easy' (US no. 12 '72), 'Witchy Woman' (US no. 9 '72) and 'Peaceful Easy Feeling' (US no. 22 '72), steel guitars and banjos were swaddled in denim, and the result was just as smooth as countrypolitan. The lyrics – 'I like the way your sparkling earrings lay against your skin so brown, and I wanna sleep with you in the desert tonight' – were simple, noble cowboy fare, much like a more forward Jim Reeves. They were low-profile, they wore blue jeans and sneakers and had a platonic, California-tanned, sun-loving image. *Rolling Stone* reckoned they were 'full of desert loneliness'.

* The Stone Poneys' 'Different Drum', a Michael Nesmith song with flashes of baroque in its strings and harpsichord arrangement, was a US Top 20 hit in 1967. It was unquestionably country-flavoured, Ronstadt's voice having a similar emotional catch to Patsy Cline's.

It's worth recalling the good press the Eagles received at the time, because it has been largely airbrushed from history. '*Desperado* is an American version of *The Rise and Fall of Ziggy Stardust*,' said Barbara Charrone in *Sounds*. 'Like Bowie's portrait of life as a rock star, *Desperado* draws a perfect analogy with the lawless gunman and the renegade rocker.' *Melody Maker*'s Chris Charlesworth claimed 'there are few bands who can match them in the vocal harmony department and fewer still who can capture the ambience of California so well . . . I'm hard pressed to name any other band that can boast a drummer with the vocal talents of Henley. Only the Beach Boys can really match them for the number and variety of voices available.'

The Eagles became the biggest-selling country act of the seventies, which – internationally – was the biggest decade for country music. Somewhere in between the Eagles and the blonde-beehived Tammy Wynette fell Olivia Newton-John ('Have You Never Been Mellow'), Linda Ronstadt ('You're No Good'), Don Williams ('I Recall a Gypsy Woman') and John Denver, who had four US number ones – 'Annie's Song', 'Sunshine on My Shoulders', 'Thank God I'm a Country Boy', 'I'm Sorry' – all of which also topped the country chart. Denver wore denim, like the Eagles, but had a blond mop and granny glasses, and looked for all the world like the kid most likely to be bullied at school. Former Sun Records veteran Charlie Rich, who had the bearing of an American eagle and an intimidating mane of grey hair, didn't see the Colorado kid as part of the family. At the Country Music Association's awards in 1975, Rich was meant to open an envelope and announce that Denver was CMA Entertainer of the Year; instead, he set fire to the envelope.

On the Eagles' 1975 fifty-nine-city tour, some eight hundred and fifty thousand people paid $5 million to see them. Their *Greatest Hits* album has since sold forty-two million worldwide; in the US its twenty-nine million sales make it the neck-and-neck all-time number one alongside Michael Jackson's *Thriller*. The Eagles' phenomenal success is down to their city slickery as much as their country stylings: as well as wearing cowboy boots and having super-smooth harmonies, they had a logo like a hard-rock band. They could slip into pretty much any category

American pop fans wanted. This slipperiness is part of what has kept country as America's best-selling musical genre.*

Country has changed in the last forty years from being an essentially local network of male musicians into a full-blown industry, still largely independent of modern pop moves; quite possibly this is what Chet Atkins always envisaged. In the twenty-first century it continues to absorb stars from other genres which have ceased to be part of mainstream chart pop – Jon Bon Jovi and Lionel Richie would both feature on the *Billboard* country chart in 2012. While their recent albums still wouldn't be coded 'country' to British ears, they fit the soft, rock-ballad genre which is now a major part of the Nashville sound.†

Country remains as riven as it was in the fifties: these days alt country, like bluegrass, sells itself as the 'real thing', only to a different audience. A fan of the former wrote on a message board that 'mainstream country is for people who don't like country music, they just like singing about how country they are. Alt country is for people who love country music, and when they sing they don't have tell you how country they are.' In 1973 the Eagles had worn spurred boots and posed as cowboys on the back cover of *Desperado*; in 2009 the smug Easton Corbin scored a huge hit with 'I'm a Little More Country than That'. Songs about small-town life remain as popular in the States as ever, even though most of the population live in cities. The opposing wings, the bickering keepers of the flame, are as starstruck as each other – on every level, country music remains a mass American fantasy.

---

* Hip hop overtook it in the nineties, but country re-established its lead in the 2000s.
† This isn't a totally new phenomenon: a bunch of first-generation rock 'n' rollers wound up being country artists (Jerry Lee Lewis, Wanda Jackson, Carl Perkins, Johnny Cash); and a pile of folk-rockers became mainstream country (a late vindication for the Byrds' significance in forging country rock was that Chris Hillman's Desert Rose Band became one of the best selling country acts of the eighties). Country seems to be pretty good at sucking up influences from outside itself and selling them back.

BEFORE AND AFTER THE GOLD RUSH:
LAUREL CANYON

At the end of 1968 Penny Valentine, one of the best pop journalists in Britain, spent an afternoon in a Bayswater flat with three singers: David Crosby (ex-Byrds), Stephen Stills (ex-Buffalo Springfield) and Graham Nash (ex-Hollies). She reckoned they were 'not making pretentious music, they are not trying to shatter our minds, but to clear them'. She heard no blues, no heaviness, just a few songs that 'lie somewhere in the

Simon & Garfunkel/Buffalo Springfield category, and yet are really a whole new personal, gentle, persuasive power'. Valentine was only with them for three hours but 'came away from that flat more excited and elated than by anything I've heard, seen or talked about in the music scene since I first saw the Beatles'.

David Crosby had proved to be the bridge between the Los Angeles and San Francisco scenes at Monterey; when he got on stage at the festival to sing with Buffalo Springfield he also effectively evicted himself from the Byrds. The Springfield's Stephen Stills was closest to Crosby, and had a few of the group's best songs on his CV, including the scene-encompassing 'For What It's Worth' (US no. 7 '67). They would harmonise at parties thrown by Mama Cass Elliot and the Monkees' Peter Tork, both considerably wealthier than Crosby or Stills. Nash, meanwhile, had led the jobbing Hollies from Merseybeat ('Stay'), through folk rock ('Look through Any Window') to psychedelic pop ('On a Carousel'), all of which they excelled at, with a five-year unbroken string of UK Top 20 singles to prove it. Then Nash presented the group with hippie anthem 'Marrakesh Express', at which point the other Hollies – with conventional cigs in their coat pockets – got cold feet. Graham Nash decided to leave his band, his wife and his kids in Manchester and start a new life in a new city. He left it all behind for Crosby, Stills and Nash and for California, specifically for a sparsely populated valley in greater Los Angeles called Laurel Canyon.

Imagine an evening in New York: the shadows are long and the light is soft, but its edges are clean and strong. In Los Angeles the light glows differently, more brightly, and the edges blur. When America's pop HQ shifted from New York to LA at the turn of the seventies, the whole process of making pop music shifted with it. New York is over-caffeinated. People shout. Things get done. LA has a mantra of *mañana*. In 1969 it was the perfect home for sleepy troubadours with time on their hands and money in the bank; Crosby, Stills and Nash and LA were a perfect fit.

This may sound mean, but it's the truth. Besides, their 1969 debut was proof – it sounded exactly like a set of sunrises. Crosby's 'Guinnevere' was especially lovely, with dark thrummed chords on meshed guitars; its unsettling passing notes underscored something that sounded exactly as a song by a former Byrd should have sounded in 1969* after living through folk rock, Monterey, bad acid, lost women and dwindling fame. It was different, mellow and smudgy. The world hadn't changed for the better after all; outside things weren't all all right, they really weren't. This was balm for the Vietnam protest veterans. 'Seagulls circle endlessly, I sing in silent harmony.'

As Penny Valentine noted, something had to give. Bands were either getting heavier and hairier or heading to the supper clubs,† neither of which signalled anything forward-thinking or particularly thrilling. CSN felt both familiar and different. Here were three songwriters with track records, all capable of cutting their own solo material, who also happened to harmonise like the first rays of dawn. *Crosby, Stills & Nash*, their eponymous debut, was released in May '69 and went four times platinum as it slow-burned through the seventies.

The singer-songwriter quickly became the most successful economic model in the history of entertainment. They wrote, sang, frequently performed alone, and sold albums rather than singles. Unsurprisingly, record labels saw dollar signs and put out albums by any Californian longhair with a battered Martin acoustic. Most didn't make it, but many of the real delights were to be found among the also-rans. Karen Beth sang as if she had hearing problems, with a slightly choked, weirdly affecting voice that gave her debut album a lost-in-the-woods quality; for some reason she called it *The Joys of Life*. Linda Perhacs was discovered by her Kapp Records A&R man while he was having root-canal surgery and his dentist happened to mention that his lithe assistant had written a few songs; her sole album, *Parallelograms*, outspooked even

---

* After driving en masse to Crosby's house in late '67 to tell him he was out of the band, the Byrds cut one more great album – the segued, soft and dreamlike psych *Notorious Byrd Brothers*, maybe their best record – before getting side-tracked by country rock. By 1969 they featured no original members bar Roger McGuinn and were once again reliant on Bob Dylan ('Ballad of Easy Rider') for their A-sides.

† This would be the fate of the pre-psychedelic beat groups. Places like Batley Variety Club, in a small Yorkshire town, became a home from home for the likes of the Searchers and the Hollies, and would provide them with a regular income until retirement age.

Karen Beth with its dead space, occasional clashing chords and Perhacs's fragile, clear-mountain vocals. Bob Brown made a piece of leaf-green folk/jazz and called it 'The Wall I Built Myself'; Marc Jonson's *Years* crammed every lover-spurning, toe-stubbing incident of his twenty-two summers into thirty-five minutes of primal-scream therapy with added strings and harpsichord; Kathy McCord used jazz legends like Hubert Laws on her one album of lullabies and the odd fuzz-guitar wig-out; Nancy Priddy was very pretty, had a voice to match, was the subject of Stephen Stills's 'Pretty Girl Why', and created a downer folk/off-Broadway amalgam called 'You've Come This Way Before' shortly after giving birth to her daughter, actress Christina Applegate. None of these records sold enough to break even, and lay forgotten in bargain bins until pop historians rehabilitated them in the nineties under the banner of 'acid folk'.

Why didn't they sell? Because these records embarrassed the paying customers with too many personal failures, rambunctious emotions, lost moments and memories that were far too vivid. The traumas of the rich and famous are so much more interesting than our own, or Karen Beth's for that matter. Carole King, on the other hand, had famously split from her Brill Building co-writer and husband Gerry Goffin; she had written beautiful songs that had soundtracked teenage lives and by 1971 she had come out of her destructive relationship with Goffin as a wealthy Laurel Canyon celebrity with a sack full of introspective lyrics and her melodic instinct intact: her *Tapestry* album was the hit of the year, the single 'It's Too Late' also a number one in the States. We wanted to share her pain. Maybe we could learn from it.

Handsome and skinny but similarly bruised, James Taylor was next in line for a million-selling Laurel Canyon album on the strength of his being King's sometime beau. His hit 'Fire and Rain' (US no. 5 '70) was a still, small story of a friend's death and pretty much set the tone for the singer-songwriter confessional. The cover of Carole King's *Tapestry*, meanwhile – long unkempt locks, cheesecloth shirt, soft furnishings, softer cat – epitomised both the cosiness and the domesticity of the singer-songwriters. It was a twenty-something equivalent of the womblike hush that had engulfed rock 'n' roll in 1959, with Taylor and King as the new Fleetwoods. There was no danger, just comfort, and people needed that after a decade of war, assassinations and inner-city turmoil, just as they had needed the balm of Perry Como and Doris Day in the early fifties. There was more sexual openness in Laurel Canyon pop than there was in *Calamity Jane*, but not necessarily more sex, or indeed insight. The singer-songwriter message was 'Everybody hurts'.

Two former members of Buffalo Springfield gave us the best and worst examples of the genre. Neil Young, peeking out from beneath his curtain hair like a cross between a startled deer and an eagle-eyed Action Man, had a definitive line in self-pity, exaggerated fivefold by his high, wobbly Canadian voice: 'I went down to the radio interview, found myself alone at the microphone.' Poor lamb. But the whine, the easy shifts from barstool rockers like 'Cinnamon Girl' to French horn-haunted oddities like 'After the Gold Rush' to gibberish that sounded weighty ('Don't let it get you down, it's only castles burning') showed a singular strength. And when his 1972 *Harvest* album sold like umbrellas in April, Young celebrated by recording a live album of previously unheard, uniformly cloud-grey material called *Time Fades Away*. 'I'd rather head for the ditch than the middle of the road,' he said. The result of *Time Fades Away* and its darker-yet sequels *Tonight's the Night* (about a personal apocalypse) and *On the Beach* (ditto, on a national level) was that, having lost ninety per cent of his fans overnight, he built another audience who twigged that he was America's Roy Harper, a contrary sod who would later side with Ronald Reagan on Farm Aid and would rarely be less than interesting. If I had to pick two highlights from his career, they would be 'Like a Hurricane', a torched rewrite of Del Shannon's 'Runaway' which features the simplest, fiercest guitar solos of the decade, cleanly volcanic, and 1974's 'Albuquerque', a story of escaping the city in a jalopy, with no particular place to go: 'I'll stop when I can, find some fried eggs and country ham.' Like the Band's historical fictions, it anticipated an alt-country movement which was decades away.

Stephen Stills made for a less convincing victim. CSN had become instant superstars in 1969 when their debut album was released. By the

time of their 1970 follow-up *Déjà Vu*, they were kings of the hippies,*
but Stills was already struggling with fame. On '4 + 20' he described it
as 'a different kind of poverty' from that of his father, but one that was
enough to leave him 'just wishing that my life would simply cease'. Stills
sings the song very well, with the voice of a weary pioneer, picking out
new territory in a post-rock-group world. Even so, he was a twenty-
four-year-old millionaire with cars, girls and an endless supply of booze
– and fried eggs and country ham – at his disposal. You can understand
why the phrase 'Never trust a hippie' was coined.

David Crosby ended up, uniquely among these mumbling troubadours, as a spokesman. And he was maddening. Jackson Browne recalled
how 'he had this legendary VW bus with a Porsche engine in it, and that
summed him up – a hippie with power!' Crosby loved the grand statement, no matter how idiotic – 'the era of the guitar virtuoso is over,' he
told *Rolling Stone* in February 1969, a few months before Neil Young's
solo-heavy *Everybody Knows This Is Nowhere* became one of the year's
most influential albums.

Outside of the Hotel California, Vietnam rolled on, the Weather
Underground wrecked corporate headquarters and the Symbionese
Liberation Army fought the American 'fascist insect' that somehow mirrored the 'many-coloured beast' of Stephen Stills's '4 + 20'. Some people were still angry, anyway. You can hear a hint of '68 ire in Jonathan
Edwards's 'Sunshine', a US number four in '72 which emerged as the
last vestige of hippie resistance to Uncle Sam: 'He can't even run his
own life, I'll be damned if he'll run mine.' And there was still Loudon
Wainwright III, though he had quickly become bogged down in novelty
protest; his sole hit single, 'Dead Skunk' (US no. 16 '73), stank out his
back catalogue for years.

Inside the nourishing hive of Laurel Canyon, Joni Mitchell was queen
bee. A muse to both Crosby and Nash, Mitchell was the prototype for
pretty much every female singer-songwriter; she was a cut above the

---

* The original fifties definition of the word 'hippie' was someone who wants to be
hipper than everyone else in the room. It's unsurprising, then, that CSN fell out and
tore each other apart so quickly. Adding Neil Young to the line-up in 1970 hardly
helped. Among these elemental hippies, Nash turned out to be the lukewarm water.

winsome likes of Melanie and, boy, did she know it. She was nobody's fool
and proclaimed as much quite loudly. You are not hiding your light under
a bushel if you appear on an album cover dressed as Vincent Van Gogh.
Mitchell had surfaced in 1967, moving to Los Angeles from Toronto, and
written 'Both Sides Now' (covered by Judy Collins), 'Chelsea Morning'
and 'I Don't Know Where I Stand' (both covered on Fairport Convention's
first album). The girl was talented. The real problem for her was that
other people always made her songs sound more lovable. She had a habit
of cramming more words in than were actually necessary, and delivering
them in a flustered schoolma'am voice that killed their radio friendliness –
quite likely this was intentional. They ended up sounding rather like this:

> The last time I saw Richard
> Was Detroit in '68, and he told me
> Allromanticsmeetthesamefatesomedaycynicalanddrunkandboring-
>   someoneinsomedarkcafe . . .

It thought it was a little cleverer than it was, and sabotaged a lot of her
charms. On songs like 'Carey' she would cast nets and pull in lives lived
to capacity, in Paris, New York or Venice Beach; her lyrics exuded intelligence ('You don't like strong women 'cos they're hip to your tricks')
and her music was so richly detailed and immaculately laid out that
it had no immediacy whatsoever. Once in a while she would use her
wordplay to puncture the immaculate arrangements, write something
catchy – like 'Big Yellow Taxi' (UK no. 11, US no. 67 '70) – and deliver
it as if it were a fart gag. Her best record was *The Hissing of Summer
Lawns*, which is also maybe the most self-descriptive album title in all
pop, apart from *Trogglodynamite* by the Troggs.

Carole King's crossover notwithstanding, entry into the hallowed
inner sanctum of Laurel Canyon was not automatic for the singer-
songwriters of an earlier era. Though Joni Mitchell accepted Jimmy
Webb, the author of 'Up, Up and Away', singing on his *Letters* and
Land's End albums, others were snootier. 'I wasn't welcomed with open
arms everywhere I went,' Webb said. 'I came into a Joni session one night
and Eric Andersen was lying under the piano having had a bit too much
to drink. He raised up on one elbow and said, "Oh, it's Mr Balloons."

I mean, you had to prove that you were a dyed-in-the-wool left-winger and that you had been to the barricades, whereas I'd achieved fame with very outspoken middle-of-the-roaders like Glen Campbell, who had John Wayne on his television show. I came into this world of exquisite artists having to explain that I used drugs and was really very hip.'

Other oldies tried their hand at moving with the softer times: Ellie Greenwich's 'Let It Be Written, Let It Be Sung' was tasteful, dull, and a depressing failure for the queen of Brooklyn songwriters. 'People wanted conversational,' said Jimmy Webb. 'People like Joni were fishing beneath the thermal clime.'

Time moved slowly in this sub-thermal environment. As glam came and went in Britain, CSN became CSNY and expanded the singer-songwriter sound back into conventional band form. The diffuse LA edges blurred soft rock and singer-songwriter. One new band had the gall to call themselves America. They ripped off the CSN sound wholesale and were hated by the press but, as they were still teenagers, their wide-eyed innocence on songs like 'Ventura Highway' (US no. 9 '72) and 'Tin Man' (US no. 4 '74) was rather more endearing than the twenty-something navel-gazing of their elders. Besides, they had a great back story, being rich kids who had met at school in England, initially managed by mod DJ legend Jeff Dexter and later produced by George Martin. 'Horse with No Name' (US no. 1, UK no. 3 '72) was an ecology song that was quite the most dreamlike single of the year, clip-clopping past burnt-out cars across the endless plain of the future. Crosby, Stills and Nash would have thrown in a reference to Nixon, or Stephen Stills's milk bill, but America kept everything clean and sunny and effortless and, for this most pop of reasons, they had racked up six US Top 10 hits by 1975.

CSN's immediate legacy was that everyone mimicked their name. You had Cashman, Pistilli and West; Cotton, Lloyd and Christian; Loggins and Messina; in Britain the Shadows morphed into Marvin, Welch and Farrar.* You half expected Peter, Paul and Mary to grow their hair and re-form as Yarrow, Stookey and Travers. The slightly blunter

---

* MWF's two albums contain some gorgeous Anglo–west coast harmonic pop; imagine CSN but with an extra ex-Hollie.

Seals and Crofts wrote the era's finest, most sun-kissed CSN-alike. 'I come home from a hard day's work and you're waiting there, not a care in the world': 'Summer Breeze' remains the ultimate commuter dream. Seals and Crofts were Texans and, like America, their lighter touch came from being able to ape the Laurel Canyon sound without being close to the inner sanctum.

As the decade progressed, modern pop began to putrefy, partly because the Laurel Canyon singer-songwriters got richer and, consequently, lazier; LA provided them with a plateau of self-celebratory success. As it had been before rock 'n' roll, pop music was just *there*, like buildings, or roads, or other things of permanence you take for granted. Even in these bland times some things jumped out of the kitchen and tasted less like vanilla blancmange: Seals and Crofts came up with another beauty in the mantra-like, blue-eyed soul hit 'Get Closer' (again, it's a whole summer inside three minutes thirty); Cliff Richard used pop's new smoothness to relaunch himself with his best-ever hit, 'Miss You Nights' (as singer-songwriter confessional lyrics go, 'children saw me crying' is among the rawest); while Fleetwood Mac reinvented themselves with the addition of a young Californian couple.

Their story is maybe the most extraordinary and unlikely in all pop. From a position of being the biggest group in Britain in 1969, a series of catastrophes had befallen them. After Peter Green had lost his fragile grasp of the rope he quit the group, soon after the terrifying 'Green Manalishi' went Top 10. Next, the cherubic Jeremy Spencer went out to buy a paper while they were on tour in the States in February 1971; en route, he was hijacked by a cult called the Children of God and left the Mac on the spot. There was a year-long gap between 'The Green Manalishi' and 'Dragonfly', the forgotten jewel in their catalogue, a 1971 single with a heartbreaking guitar line and warm pillow of percussion, the sound of the saddest Sunday. It was the work of Danny Kirwan, who by now was their main guitarist, but he liked to drink, so much so that one night he smashed his Les Paul to bits, refused point blank to go on stage and got the boot. In stepped Bob Weston, who quietly began having an affair with Mick Fleetwood's wife; his position soon became untenable.

By now it was truly a miracle the group still existed. The original rhythm section of bassist John McVie and drummer Mick Fleetwood remained a constant, bolstered by ex-Chicken Shack singer Christine McVie (née Perfect) in 1970 and a year later by American singer/guitarist Bob Welch, who, after a few albums of diminishing commercial returns, convinced the group to relocate to California in 1974. When Welch quit (for once, not in a haze of sexual or opiated confusion), the rump Mac came across a curly-topped, wild-eyed, saturnine character called Lindsey Buckingham, who had made one album with his high-school sweetheart, Stevie Nicks.* Somehow, Buckingham's guitar-playing – never showy, melodic, abrasive but melancholy – felt like a continuation of all the Macs that had gone before; in spite of Nicks's full Hollywood persona, they still frequently sounded like a walk beside a sea shore on a windy day, collar pulled up against the spray. 1977 album *Rumours* was all about love affairs, seen from different angles (the two couples in the group were both separating as they wrote and recorded it – they couldn't resist making life difficult for themselves). Like *Pet Sounds*, it was perfectly cohesive, with various shades of optimism (Christine's 'Don't Stop' and 'You Make Loving Fun') set tight against the weary (Stevie's 'Dreams'), the anxious (Lindsey's 'Second Hand News') and the desolate ('Gold Dust Woman' – Stevie again). The production, given their lush harmonies, is remarkably spare – the intro and guitar break on 'Dreams' (US no. 1 '77) are as stark as the production on 1968's 'Albatross'; Lindsey Buckingham, like Peter Green before him, knew how to wring maximum emotion from a few notes.

The Buckingham/Nicks era of Fleetwood Mac proved to be a starting point for a new soft rock. It was smooth, and ticked as precisely

* Stevie Nicks's witchy personality was a construct that looked both back to glam and forward to new pop. She never wasted a word in her lyrics, was always ready to emphasise her lace-veil spookiness with ever-present scarves and Tarot cards, and it gave Mac a new dimension which nevertheless fitted the windswept, sea-salty atmosphere of previous incarnations; maybe Peter Green had foreseen the group's future with 'Black Magic Woman' in 1968. Away from the group Nicks could lay this on too heavily ('Leather and Lace', a duet with Don Henley, US no. 6 '81), but with Buckingham lurking over her shoulder she could still evoke frosted window panes and doomed Brontëan love – see 'When I See You Again' from 1987's *Tango in the Night*.

as an atomic clock. This west-coast sound may have lacked the *ba-ba-bas* of its sixties forebear, and the American economy wasn't yet out of the woods, but people no longer needed anything quite as intimate and overly sharing as James Taylor.* And it soundtracked America – there was no escaping the forty-million-selling *Rumours*; you couldn't listen to the radio for thirty minutes without hearing something from it. Apocalypse had been postponed. Whatever might be happening in Britain, also at a financial breaking point, it wouldn't affect the States just yet.

The Eagles' 'Hotel California' (US no. 1, UK no. 7 '77) was meant to be a damning description of the self-regarding, suffocating freedom of Laurel Canyon life, one that Crosby, Stills and Nash had unintentionally nailed with a cute, troubling couplet on their first album in 1969: 'You are living a reality I left years ago, it quite nearly killed me.' Pop is escapism, but transfer this ethos into an entire community and it quickly stagnates. The post-Woodstock cosiness that created *Tapestry* became incrementally more crafted, more precise, more balanced, and the music got duller and duller. Sat on a yacht on the cover of their 1977 album *CSN*, the incredibly wealthy Crosby, Stills and Nash looked just like the enemy of 1967, just like the Man.

The LA sky in 1976 was flawless, as if a nip-and-tuck surgeon had removed the creases. LA was the industry. And CSN now looked and smelt like the industry rather than the underground. The Laurel Canyon scene was rank, sloppy and happy to peddle such weak fare as James Taylor's gutted version of the old Marvin Gaye hit 'How Sweet It Is' (US no. 4 '77). Desiccated, devoid of joy, it was time for pop to go back home to New York.

---

* Retrospectively, this sound has been termed 'yacht rock'. This is partly because it suited the lifestyle of someone wealthy enough to enjoy smooth music while out for a sail; partly because sailing was a popular leisure activity among the wealthier California musicians; and partly because of a spoof TV series called *Yacht Rock* from 2005 which fictionalised the lives of late-seventies soft-rockers. Its anthem is the gorgeous 'Sailing' by Christopher Cross, an entirely aquatic single from 1980, just like a flotation tank (and a lot cheaper).

1975: STORM WARNING

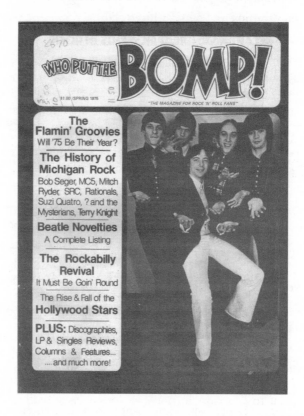

There's gonna be a rock star backlash . . . We're moving into a grit cycle, a revulsion against excess.
Rock Follies, ITV 1976

The best-selling singles in Britain, 1975:

1 Bay City Rollers, 'Bye Bye Baby'
2 Rod Stewart, 'Sailing'
3 The Stylistics, 'Can't Give You Anything (But My Love)'
4 Windsor Davies and Don Estelle, 'Whispering Grass'

5 Tammy Wynette, 'Stand by Your Man'
6 Bay City Rollers, 'Give a Little Love'
7 David Essex, 'Hold Me Close'
8 Art Garfunkel, 'I Only Have Eyes for You'
9 Roger Whittaker, 'The Last Farewell'
10 10cc, 'I'm Not in Love'

Beneath the pavement, the beach; beyond the city, the jetty. 1975 was a year of tame pop – the tamest ever – and myriad novelties. Glam dissolved fast as Slade tried to crack America and the Sweet began to write their own songs away from Chinn and Chapman's keen guidance. Chinnichap's big new stars were Smokie ('If You Think You Know How to Love Me', UK no. 3), who came from Bradford but sounded like an Eagles covers band playing on a sightseeing boat; they went on to have ten more sleepy Top 20 hits. Rod Stewart became a tax exile, scoring a number-one album (*Atlantic Crossing*) and single ('Sailing') that acted as a glossy goodbye to impoverished Britain. Everything sounded clean and empty. 1975 was typified by David Essex's 'Hold Me Close', a dry, small sound, like music hall in a doll's house. Cute, harmless, but impossible to dance to. The best-selling record of the year, a genuine phenomenon, was a re-recording of a Four Seasons flop from ten years earlier. Think what the Walker Brothers had done with Frankie Valli's 'The Sun Ain't Gonna Shine Any More', then play it next to Rollermania's defining 45. From '66 peak to '75 trough, pop had lost its way badly. Looking at Britain's ten biggest-selling singles, Tammy Wynette's reactionary rally-ing cry was a six-year-old recording; only the Stylistics could get you on your feet, and the year's best major hit, 'I'm Not in Love', was sensuous as hell but narcotically numbed.

America had it even worse. At number one were the Doobie Brothers' 'Black Water' (a Creedence-type tribute to the South, only sapped of all energy); John Denver's 'Thank God I'm a Country Boy' ('Got me a fid-dle, eggs on the griddle' – this was America sticking its fingers in its ears and closing its eyes, on the verge of surrender in Saigon, imagining itself inside a Foghorn Leghorn cartoon); Linda Ronstadt's 'You're No Good' (a retread of Betty Everett's and the Swinging Blue Jeans' smoking 1964 single, overcooked and turned to slurry). In any other year, these records would have struggled to make the Top 20 – none of them registered at all in the UK Top 50.

What had happened? Well, for starters, the industry should never have moved to California. The laissez-faire environment sent it to sleep; by 1975 rock was neutralised, and pop – whether bubblegum, glam, soft or teenybop – gave you little more to chew on. Linda Ronstadt's gutless covers (she also cut the Everlys' 'When Will I Be Loved', Chuck Berry's 'Back in the USA' and Martha and the Vandellas' 'Heatwave') typified the lack of spirit. At least the UK had gone through glam and prog. America, from its new salad-crunching power base in Los Angeles, had spent all of the early seventies creating what became known as 'classic rock'.*

Classic rock was more of a business model than a genre. The establishment of a canon (by industry and by critics) led to fifties and sixties recordings being repackaged with tags like 'Rock Roots', as if the Small Faces had been nothing more than baby steps for Humble Pie, and the Yardbirds a nursery for Led Zeppelin. By 1975 the huge sales of Humble Pie and Led Zeppelin led the industry to this conclusion (which proved to be lazy, and bad guesswork). There were refuseniks who, very soon, would seem like seers.

Radio also played its part in the emergence of classic rock. The turn-of-the-decade switch to stereo FM in the States – without the static of mono AM – had led to a new kind of radio programming, one which was still recognisably pop but wore a lightly furrowed brow – the music had to have its roots, however vague, in hippie. So the Moody Blues were in, but the Osmonds certainly weren't. Classic rock was music that appealed to advertisers, drivers and young parents. It was written up in *Rolling Stone*, which managed to be both countercultural and crushingly

---

* The term 'classic rock' was not bandied about at the time; it was a given that this was simply 'real music'. It wasn't until 1983 that KRBE in Houston was set up to play nothing but album tracks from the late sixties to the early seventies. Classic rock in late-seventies Britain only meant a series of huge-selling albums by the London Symphony Orchestra. Their track listings – 'Whole Lotta Love', 'Bohemian Rhapsody', 'Nights in White Satin' – neatly reflected the still nebulous American definition.

conservative. It was also unforgiving, very male and very straight. Even now, magazines like *Mojo* and radio stations like Planet Rock will adhere to the mid-seventies classic-rock rules; they will deify Led Zeppelin's hard-rock thunder but think Sweet are a bit silly.* Decades later, this really shouldn't matter. But it does – classic rock's influence is deep, its hold is vice-like and, without a viable alternative to challenge it in the early seventies, its rules had been set in stone by 1975. For once, the American singles chart was not the place to find pop's unlikely heroes. There was no Dion or Monkees or Creedence around to make school days go faster. There *was* disco, but we'll deal with that later.

In the old American music centres, things decayed; the future was not so much cancelled as postponed while people struggled to cope with the present. Motown left Detroit as its population plummeted and its once grand city centre became a rusting hulk. Down in Memphis, Elvis stayed home, recording ever mushier ballads at Graceland, and barely saw the streets of his home town, where Stax Records, through heinous mishandling, went bust in 1975. New York City, meanwhile, had gone bankrupt and – with central government refusing to help – had been officially left to rot. Deep in the ruins things were stirring; out of desperation, or as a reaction to the sap that surrounded them, a few citizens of these great cities decided they wanted to hear something that sounded like whatever the opposite of the Eagles was. In Memphis, former singer with blue-eyed soul act the Box Tops ('The Letter', US no. 1, UK no. 4 '67) Alex Chilton helped his band Big Star to invent the power-pop genre, using sharp Who edges and bright Beatles harmonies on 1974's *Radio City*. Their sensibility, said Bud Scoppa in his *Phonograph* review, was 'a tangle of hip affectations, mid-sixties mannerisms, teenage sagaciousness, jaded cynicism, and yearning romanticism'. Writers loved it, but Big Star were signed to Stax, which was already on the rocks, and *Radio City* sold a ridiculously small number of copies. By 1975 Chilton was taking Big Star into a smack- and depression-led

---

* I can't hear much difference in the sound of the groups, aside from industry in-tray shuffling. One of them was marketed as an albums band and one as a singles group. One for teenagers, one for kids. It seems astonishing now how easily people were taken in by the packaging, without trusting their own ears.

place on 'Holocaust', 'Nighttime' and 'Kanga Roo', love songs that were cut with feedback and deliberately amateurish musicianship. Chilton was trying to create music that sounded like the exact moment before he expired. Rejected by every label in 1975, then bootlegged and known by only a small clique of believers, the album was eventually released as *Big Star Third/Sister Lovers* in 1978.

In terms of decline, the Detroit area had a head start on Memphis and New York. It had been in a state of upheaval since riots in 1967 – almost two hundred thousand whites left the city in the next two years, and economic desolation happened concurrently. The musical reaction came from the MC5 and the Stooges; both used dirty guitar sounds and ground out repetitive riffs like engines with faulty exhausts – you could choke on this sound, and it was way too greasy for radio. It was enough of a jolt to earn the MC5 a *Rolling Stone* cover in 1969, before their first album was even released. 'Kick Out the Jams', one of pop's great titles, proved to be a noise in search of a tune. People wanted them to be great, but they spluttered and died. The Stooges were much better. They were led by the ferrety Iggy Pop, who was a circus freak of the old school. He spent much of his time on stage topless, contorting his body, flexing his muscles. Their titles alone – 'Dirt', 'I Wanna Be Your Dog', 'No Fun' – suggested the Stooges were the group least likely to kiss corporate ass. Elektra A&R man Danny Fields saw them at the University of Michigan student union in September '68 and thought they were the sound he'd been waiting to hear all his life. Repetition, repetition, repetition: they were as automated and relentless as the Motown machine in its prime. Play 'Going to a Go-Go' after 'Loose' and you'll see what I mean; both are one-chord wonders.

The Stooges sought power and release through sheer noise and endless, precision-made groove. This is what made the first two Stooges albums so refreshing and influential, first to David Bowie ('Rebel Rebel' is, essentially, a Stooges knock-off), then in punk (the Sex Pistols covered 'No Fun'), and then to dozens of acolytes in the eighties. The very same qualities meant they were rejected out of hand in 1969.

The first album's stand-out track was 'I Wanna Be Your Dog', written over breakfast by guitarist Ron Asheton after Danny Fields told them they needed at least one actual tune. Elektra got John Cale in to produce it, he added an insistent one-note piano line and tambourine to give it zip, and they had the hardest, angriest record of 1969. 'So messed up' served as an opening line and a career manifesto. You imagined the Stooges were constantly grinding their teeth as they played. Their second album, 1970's *Fun House*, had no tunes whatsoever, nothing but a groove, nothing but raw power; their third album, *Raw Power*, on the other hand, was all hooks and hits, but it came out in 1973. They had taken years off in between, been usurped by another Detroit act called Alice Cooper, become smackheads, become completely messed up. 'I'm the world's forgotten boy,' shouted Iggy, now aged twenty-six. They split again.

Reviewing *Raw Power* for *Let It Rock*, Simon Frith thought it was the best album of '73 (along with *Tubular Bells*) but concluded that Iggy Pop sounded 'a little silly, and a little sad. However much Iggy may prance, he doesn't really know what to do about America and he doesn't really like to think about it.' Iggy toyed with pop for decades after the Stooges split, living large on their legend, but he always seemed a bit panto without his band. He became Bowie's drugs buddy, shouted at journalists who offered him coffee (he was clean of *all* drugs, he insisted), fornicated with a giant teddy bear on children's TV and generally acted like a wally. Just when you were set to dismiss him, just when you thought that his doing a car-insurance advert was the final straw, he'd turn on the charm again, remind you of the basic, thrusting glory of 'Search and Destroy', and all was forgiven. In 2007 the Stooges got back together for a third and final time, recording an album called *The Weirdness*. 'After forty years of making fucking records,' Iggy wept to the press, 'I really cared on this one.' Enough already.

New York was where the biggest and best nihilists were. Like the Stooges, the Velvet Underground were similarly intrigued by pure noise and didn't feel much kinship with the Great American Songbook. They were formed by two mean-faced contrarians. Charismatic Welshman John Cale, who could have been the new Richard Burton in a parallel world, went to New York to do a postgrad course in modern composition on a Leonard Bernstein scholarship. Entirely uninterested in pop, he had joined La Monte Young's Theatre of Eternal Music. Among other new methods of creating music, Cale and the Theatre once sustained a single note for days; another time they screamed at a plant until it died. Lou Reed had fought his way out of a troubled Jewish upbringing that included ECT with a radio show called *Excursions on a Wobbly Rail.* He also played guitar and got himself a publishing deal in 1964 with budget label Pickwick, on which he released an unhinged dance-craze single under the fake band name of the Primitives. 'The Ostrich' didn't catch on like 'The Twist', but it did well enough to earn Reed an appearance on TV; Cale was invited to back him in the fictitious Primitives. Reed revealed to Cale that 'The Ostrich' had been written by tuning all six guitar strings to one note. The Welshman was impressed, and soon the Velvet Underground were recording avant-pop like 'Heroin' ('it's my life, it's my wife' – they made it sound great) and 'I Heard Her Call My Name'. There is a point on the latter, immediately after Reed sings 'and then my mind split open', where you can actually hear a tear in the space–time continuum. This was 1967, but it was also 1977. And 1987. Reed and Cale had somehow created a noise so brand new that it tore a hole in pop's natural state of progression, so sharp and freakish and heart-piercing that it makes me burst out laughing every time I hear it. It sounded like the future, and nobody (bar the young David Bowie, at home in Beckenham) was listening. 'I Heard Her Call My Name' was violently and gleefully against what the west coast of 1967 – that is, the whole pop world in 1967 – stood for. No peace, no easy options. And yet it was a song of unrequited love with sweet, ghostly harmonies backing Reed as he sings, deluding himself, 'I know she *cares* about me, I heard her call my name.' This was pop, but not as anyone – Warhol and Bowie aside – would have recognised it in the year Procol Harum's 'A Whiter Shade of Pale' and the Beatles' 'All You Need Is Love' were all over the radio.*

* Václav Havel's battered copy of the Velvet Underground's second album, *White Light/White Heat,* did the rounds in communist Prague in the early seventies, inspiring local art-rockers the Plastic People of the Universe; it could be claimed that the Soviet bloc was ultimately broken up by the power of the guitar solo on 'I Heard Her Call My Name'.

In 1975, with the Velvet Underground long dissolved, Reed made an album called *Metal Machine Music*. It was four sides of feedback, that was it. That was all. In 1975 it was succinct. It was an end – the 'ultimate conclusion of heavy metal', according to Reed's notes. Most importantly (because you'd never want to actually *listen* to it, trust me), *Metal Machine Music* was a statement. Lester Bangs, writing in *Creem*, was the only journalist to understand this at the time. 'Any idiot with the equipment could have made this album, including me, you or Lou. That's one of the main reasons I like it so much.' He also called Reed 'an emblem of absolute negativism'.

A magazine called *Punk* was launched in 1975. The first issue included a large piece on *Metal Machine Music*. It existed to celebrate a new scene being played out in clubs like CBGB, Zeppz and Max's Kansas City, by bands like the Ramones, Blondie, the Marbles and the Patti Smith Group. Unquestionably, they were the children of the Velvet Underground, and Lou Reed – surely with no small sense of pride – was usually in the crowd. Intriguingly, none of these bands sounded anything like each other. The Marbles, now all but forgotten, were Beatles nuts playing power pop, while the Ramones aimed to condense Beach Boys, Phil Spector and Shangri-Las hits into recidivist ninety-second bursts with antagonistic titles like 'Now I Wanna Sniff Some Glue'. On paper they may have seemed as backward-glancing as the Marbles. They had the ferocity of the early Kinks, the pace of the early Who, named themselves after the young McCartney's stage name – Paul Ramon – and played as fast and loud as possible, no gaps between the songs. Leather jackets, T-shirts and jeans; they felt like the entire history of music (blues and folk aside) pummelled, broken down into pieces and recast in bubblegum. It didn't feel like it was looking backwards at all; it felt more like an art project on how to distil modern pop's essence.

The Ramones' debut album in early '76 was incredibly primitive, the most unprofessional-sounding major-label record the seventies had seen. It had no solos; it was a simple, straight line of energy, and it became the single biggest influence on UK punk – a teenager in Deptford called Mark Perry was so moved by its excitement he started the *Sniffin' Glue* fanzine.

In short order the Ramones made three rama-lama albums (*Ramones*, *Leave Home*, *Rocket to Russia*), and scored a few minor UK Top 40 hits ('Sheena Is a Punk Rocker', 'Swallow My Pride', 'Don't Come Close') which the radio wouldn't touch; in the States 'Rockaway Beach' (no. 66 '78) was their only sniff of a hit. In interviews ('What does brevity mean?') they came across as sweet and extraordinarily naive: 'We're playing pure rock 'n' roll with no blues or folk or any of that stuff in it,' explained Johnny Ramone. But then drummer Tommy Ramone left in '79 and it turned out that it had been high concept after all, with Tommy as the secret mastermind: 'My function with the Ramones was as a producer and an organiser,' he told Timothy White in 1978. 'There was never anything like the Ramones before. We used block chording as a melodic device, and the harmonies resulting from the distortion of the amplifiers created countermelodies. The hypnotic effect of strict repetition, driving the music like a sonic machine . . . it's very sensual. It was a new way of looking at music.' After Tommy left, the Ramones' sonic machine continued on cabaret autopilot for twenty years until Joey, Johnny and Dee Dee had all died.

Then there was Talking Heads, whose odd vibe resulted from a bunch of male musicians all trying to impress bassist Tina Weymouth with their chops. Television attempted to reinvent guitar solos with zero flash, and Patti Smith was a hippie poet who ended up in the CBGB gang by dint of having a song called 'Piss Factory'. Which leaves Blondie, who were Brill Building pop reinvented for a John Waters movie, catfights in velvet. Aside from the Ramones, Blondie were the most photogenic and the most vital of the new New Yorkers. Television had the technical ability, Talking Heads had the brains, but Blondie had the lot. Patti Smith used to stand at the front of their CBGB shows just to stare out singer Debbie Harry – I imagine she might have been jealous.

The past was being raked over, reanimated. A New Yorker of a previous generation, Phil Spector, had sat out most of the seventies, feeling – justifiably – that he'd done his work and he'd done it well. In 1975 he began to reissue his early-sixties productions, most of which had been out of print for the best part of a decade. In a masterstroke of self-publicity which doubled as disaffection with FM radio and the predictability of classic rock, he started to wear a button badge that picked up on a different strand of '75 conservatism: it read 'Back to Mono'. Backing him up was an underground network of pop fanzines which, while hoping and trusting that something fresh and energising would soon emerge, were in thrall to the sixties. Greg Shaw's *Who Put the Bomp*, his successor to *Mojo Navigator*, led the way. Britain had *Dark Star*, led by Steve Burgess, a cheerleader for Big Star and former Byrd Gene Clark.

In the north of England, a mutation of late mod lived on. There was a BBC radio programme in 1975 called *Northern Soul: Fact or Fiction?* This fierce local scene was all about secrecy, cover-ups, and the folk heroes weren't the singers but the DJs. Its centres were unlikely venues in unfashionable provincial towns – Wigan Casino, Blackpool Mecca, the Torch in Stoke. Aside from the Mecca, which spun contemporary but obscure records like Voices of East Harlem's 'Cashing In', it was all about sixties soul, slight variations on the classic Motown sound. Occasionally, a record would become big enough to warrant a reissue and then chart – Tami Lynn's 'I'm Gonna Run Away from You' (UK no. 4 '71) was originally released on Atlantic in '66, while Frankie Valli and the Four Seasons' 'The Night' (UK no. 6 '75) had been a flop during their brief stay with Motown in 1972. Northern soul was all about obscurity, one-upmanship, the subtle, the impenetrable. You could see this as outsider art, or purism, or as unbearably precious. In New York Lenny Kaye, guitarist in the Patti Smith Group, put together a double album of garage-rock 45s called *Nuggets* which made forgotten 45s like the Remains' 'Don't Look Back' available to a new generation, and ignited a new interest in garage punk.

What *Nuggets* and northern soul signified was that there was an almost bottomless well of great sixties records – way too many for even the best ten per cent to have all been hits – and that what had occurred on the fringes just a few years earlier was more worthwhile than pretty much anything happening in the Top 10 in 1975. Just a year earlier the Stylistics had cut the heart-stoppingly lovely 'You Make Me Feel Brand New' (US no. 2, UK no. 2 '74) with the cool, classical help of producer Thom Bell. But, after splitting with him in late '74, they had taken soul into grim new territory with 'Sing Baby Sing' (UK no. 3 '75), a hideous song of forced jollity with a soft Eurovision under-belly. Possibly sensing endgames, James Brown had recently decided it was time to stake out his place in pop's lineage and had taken to calling himself the Godfather of Soul. It was a fair shout. He had been there back in 1956 with the Little Richard-inspired R&B ballad 'Please Please Please'; again with his barked dancefloor orders on 'Night Train' (US no. 35 '62); he had sung high and sweet on the soul ballad 'Prisoner of Love' (US no. 18 '63); and he had slowly moved into ever harder, crisper polyrhythmic singles, his vocals operating on a purely percussive level, culminating in 'Give It Up or Turnit a Loose' (US no. 15 '69). By 1975, though, he was increasingly sidelined, first by silky soul (he wrote 'Get Up Offa That Thing' as a dig at Barry White), and then by disco, while self-destructive comments (he publicly sup-ported Nixon in '72 and lost a swathe of his audience) and tax debts burdened him further. For the first time in a decade, he failed to score a number one on the R&B chart. He turned to ballads (the exqui-site 'People Wake Up and Live', the slightly unsettling 'Kiss in 77'), but his career seemed to be in decline. Kids in parts of bankrupt New York City, however, deified him. Fans of Philadelphia and aspirational disco associated Brown's music with bad times, with poverty, a lack of civil rights, with the ghetto; the soundtrack in the South Bronx in '75 wasn't 'Sing Baby Sing' but the harsher, tricksier 'Give It Up or Turnit a Loose', 'Funky Drummer' and Brown's early-seventies productions for Lyn Collins ('Think') and Bobby Byrd ('I Know You Got Soul'). These weren't especially old records – just three, four, five years – but they had been discarded and reclaimed just as surely as the obscurities on *Nuggets* or the manic Detroit soul being played at Wigan. James Brown's ghetto deification would have long-term repercussions.

The drug of the day in Laurel Canyon in 1975 was coke, enough to take your septum out. Its high price reflected its users' wealth. At Wigan, and in other northern-soul strongholds, the drug was speed; on Canvey Island it was beer. Cheap and, in moderation, cheerful. The earliest backlash against staid Laurel Canyon rock in Britain came from the London hinterland – Essex, the most ridiculed county in England, the Anglo equivalent of Staten Island. It made perfect sense that Dr Feelgood were keen to convey their Canvey, Essex, locale on their debut album, *Down by the Jetty* (a clever title which also evoked Baltimore docks and Louisiana swamps), and to wrap the record inside a monochrome jacket with a clean, simple typeface in the era of bubble writing.* On the sleeve they wore Southend suits and ties, and grimaced in the face of a North Sea gale; musically, they revisited the London R&B scene of the mid-sixties, energetic and boozy, with no songs lasting over three minutes. Growing up in a town full of modified shacks, out in the Thames delta, it was easy for Dr Feelgood to fantasise about the States and, in turn, write their own Canvey Island blues songs – jagged 45s like 'She Does It Right', 'Roxette' and 'Back in the Night' were enough to fuel the pub-rock scene twenty-odd miles up the Thames.†

Singer Lee Brilleaux looked a good deal older than his twenty-five years; he was the original Essex spiv, in a gravy-stained white suit, and had the kind of voice you might hear if Ford Cortinas could sing. His foil was guitarist Wilko Johnson, who – bug-eyed, mouth agape – looked like an oversize, menacing Muppet as he darted back and forth across the stage. Wilko also played brutal guitar lines with great precision, as economical as Steve Cropper – his sharpness on songs like 'She Does It Right' would be echoed in the post-punk rhythmic riffs of XTC and Gang of Four a few years later.

---

* The monochrome simplicity of both picture and layout of the Patti Smith Group's *Horses* bore a startling similarity to Dr Feelgood's *Down by the Jetty*, an album Blondie drummer Clem Burke had picked up on a trip to England and was loudly touting to his scenester mates. Already, in a very small way, there was a kinship felt between the London and New York undergrounds.
† As a reaction to the stadiums the likes of the Who and the Rolling Stones were now playing, a bunch of pubs – the Nashville Rooms in Hammersmith, the Hope and Anchor in Islington – started to put on regular nights. The music was initially undemanding country rock – American band Eggs Over Easy started the trend with a residency at the Tally Ho in Kentish Town in 1971, where they were soon followed by Nick Lowe's Brinsley Schwarz and the slightly more aggressive Ducks Deluxe – but Dr Feelgood upped the ante, playing faster and harder, and were soon followed by Southend's Eddie and the Hot Rods, who cracked the Top 10 in '77 with the perfect pub/punk/power-pop amalgam 'Do Anything You Wanna Do'. The pub-rock scene created a ready-made gig circuit for punk.

Against the grain, with Led Zeppelin's *The Song Remains the Same*
and Rod Stewart's *A Night on the Town* just behind them, Dr Feelgood's
third album, *Stupidity*, was a UK number one in '76. It looked like
their future was secured. Then, just before an electrifying performance
of 'Lights Out' on *Top of the Pops* in May '77, Wilko quit. Lee Brilleaux's
growl and *Sweeney*-like charisma alone weren't enough to keep up the
momentum and their star dimmed. Yet their brief burst of success in
'75 and '76 suggested people really, really wanted something a little
more energetic than Pink Floyd's *Wish You Were Here*, something more
immediate, a little more violent.

Dr Feelgood's commercial success was an exception: most random
bursts of disaffected 1975 noise disappeared into cardboard boxes –
discarded by critics, underpromoted by the industry – and were only
unearthed two or three decades later by modern pop archaeologists.
A few of these isolated attempts to break free, to extemporate mid-
seventies angst, are astonishing. Spunky Spider had maybe the ugliest name ever; their bawled tale of sexual failure, 1973's 'You Won't
Come', features a gargled Lee Brilleaux-like vocal over a wall of fuzz
guitar, pierced by dive-bombing electronic shards. No one has any idea
who Spunky Spider were or what they were hoping to achieve. Almost
as unlikely is 'Do the Clapham', a piece of '75 thug rock played by the
fictitious Kipper in the soft-porn comedy *Confessions of a Pop Performer*.
Meanwhile, Cleveland, Ohio, gave us 'Agitated' by the Electric Eels
('I'm so agitated, I'm so agitated, I'm so agitated that I'm so agitated'). In
Brisbane, the frigid, isolated capital of Queensland, Australia, a bunch
of stout lads called the Saints had heard quite enough stodgy rock – 'As
long as you had a satin jump-suit and a copy of [Free's] *Fire and Water*,'
said singer Chris Bailey, 'you could probably make it on some level or
other.' They set about recording a primal, two-minute 45 called '(I'm)
Stranded' which arrived by ship months later in a very different Britain,
one crying out for such acts of open rebellion. Across the world, pop
lovers were agitated. Monthly magazine columns, compilation albums
and button badges were a start, but the fun had only just begun.

PART FOUR

TOP 50 SINGLES

◇ = FORECAST
● = MILLION (PLATINUM)
○ = ½ MILLION (GOLD)
○ = ¼ MILLION (SILVER)
● = SALES INCREASE OVER LAST WEEK
£ = MUSIC WEEK, MARCH 18, 1978

DISTRIBUTORS CODE
A – Pye, C – CBS, W – WEA, E – EMI, F – Phonodisc, H – H.R. Taylor, L – Lugtons, R – RCA, S – Selecta, X – Clyde Factors, Z – Enterprise, CR – Creole, G – Spartan, P – Pinnacle, V – Virgin, M – Mosaic (Scotland)

This Week	Last Week	Wks. on Chart	TITLE	ARTIST	LABEL & NO.	PUBLISHER	PRODUCER
£● 1	1	6	WUTHERING HEIGHTS Kate Bush		EMI 2719	EMI/Kate Bush	Andrew Powell
£ 2	2	7	TAKE A CHANCE ON ME Abba		Epic EPC 5950	Bocu	B. Andersson/B. Ulvaeus
○ 3	5	5	DENIS Blondie		Chrysalis CHS 2204	EMI	Richard Gottehrer
○ 4	3	8	COME BACK MY LOVE Darts		Magnet MAG 110	Carlin	T. Boyce/R. Hartley
○ 5	4	10	WISHING ON A STAR Rose Royce		Warner Brothers K 17060	Warner Brothers	Norman Whitfield
£ 6	8	6	BAKER STREET Gerry Rafferty		United Artists UP 36346	Island/Belfern	H. Murphy/G. Rafferty
7	7	5	I CAN'T STAND THE RAIN Eruption		Atlantic/Hansa K 11068	Burlington Music	Frank Farian
○ 8	6	7	STAYIN' ALIVE Bee Gees		RSO 2090 267	RSO/Chappell	Bee Gees/Richardson/Galuten
○ 9	9	8	MR. BLUE SKY Electric Light Orchestra		Jet UP 36342	United Artists/Jet	Jeff Lynne
◇10	18	4	MATCHSTALK MEN & MATCHSTALK CATS & DOGS Brian & Michael		Pye 7N 46035	Gt. Northern Songs/EMI	Kevin Parrott
11	12	4	IS THIS LOVE Bob Marley & The Wailers		Island WIP 8420	Rondor	Bob Marley & The Wailers
£12	14	7	EMOTIONS Samantha Sang		Private Stock PVT 126	RSO/Chappell	B. Gibb/Richardson/Galuten
£13	21	3	ALLY'S TARTAN ARMY Andy Cameron		Klub 03	Copyright Control	Pete Shipton
£14	15	6	FANTASY Earth Wind & Fire		CBS 6056	Chappell	Maurice White
○15	10	7	JUST ONE MORE NIGHT Yellow Dog		Virgin VS 196	Lazy Lizard/Heath Levy	Kenny Young
£16	22	4	LILAC WINE Elkie Brooks		A&M AMS 7333	Chappells	Mike Batt
17	11	5	FREE EP		Island IEP 5	Blue Mountain Music	Free
◇18	13	10	FIGARO Brotherhood of Man		Pye 7N 46037	Tony Hiller/ATV Music	Tony Hiller
19	28	4	RUMOUR HAS IT Donna Summer		Casablanca CAN 122	Heath Levy	G. Moroder/P. Bellotte
£20	27	3	EVERY 1'S A WINNER Hot Chocolate		RAK 270	Chocolate/RAK	Mickie Most
◇21	33	2	I LOVE THE SOUND OF BREAKING GLASS Nick Lowe		Radar ADA 1	Rock Music	Nick Lowe
£22	25	6	JUST THE WAY YOU ARE Billy Joel		CBS 5872	Joelsongs	Phil Ramone
○23	16	4	LOVE IS LIKE OXYGEN Sweet		Polydor POSP 1	Sweet/Carlin	Sweet
£24	26	5	GLAD TO BE GAY Tom Robinson Band		EMI 2749	Konkwest/EMI	Chris Thomas
○25	17	10	IF I HAD WORDS Scott Fitzgerald/Yvonne Keeley		Pepper UP 36333	B.U. Music/RAK	Jonathan Hodge
◇26	35	3	WALK IN LOVE Manhattan Transfer		Atlantic K 11075	Rondor	Tim Hauser
27	19	7	5 MINUTES Stranglers		United Artists UP 36350	April/Albion	Martin Rushent
◇28	36	7	WORDS Rita Coolidge		A&M AMS 7330	Abigail	David Anderle
£29	31	3	WHENEVER YOU WANT MY LOVE Real Thing		Pye 7N 46045	Screen Gems/EMI	Ken Gold
◇30	42	2	FOLLOW YOU FOLLOW ME Genesis		Charisma CB 309	Gelring/Hit & Run	D. Hentschel/Genesis
£31	50	2	CHELSEA Elvis Costello and Attraction		Radar ADA 3	Plangent Vision	Nick Lowe
○32	20	4	HOT LEGS/I WAS ONLY JOKING Rod Stewart		Riva 10	Riva	Tom Dowd
33	32	4	BABY COME BACK Player		RSO 2090 264	ATV Music	D. Lambert/B. Potter
◇34	41	3	WHAT'S YOUR NAME WHAT'S YOUR NUMBER Andrea True Connection		Buddah BDS 467	DJM	Michael Sager
£35	38	2	NEWS OF THE WORLD Jam		Polydor 2058 995	And Son	Vic Smith/Chris Perry
36	24	3	WE'VE GOT THE WHOLE WORLD Nottingham Forest/Paper Lace		WB X 17110	Barry Mason/Marksman	J. Fiddy
£37	39	3	SOMETIMES WHEN WE TOUCH Dan Hill		20th Century BTC 2355	ATV	M. McCauley/F. Mullin
38	37	3	CLASH CITY ROCKERS Clash		CBS 5834	Nineden/Riva	Micky Foote
39	23	4	DRUMMER MAN Tonight		TDS 1	G.O.A.L.	Andy Arthurs
40	34	4	SPREAD YOUR WINGS Queen		EMI 2757	EMI/Queen	Queen
◇41	43	2	I'LL GO WHERE YOUR MUSIC TAKES ME Tina Charles		CBS 6062	Chappells	Biddu
42	NEW ENTRY		IF YOU CAN'T GIVE ME LOVE Suzi Quatro		RAK 271	Chinnichap/RAK	Chinn/Chapman
43	NEW ENTRY		THE GHOST OF LOVE Tavares		Capitol CL 15960	ATV	Freddie Perren
£44	46	5	IF IT DON'T FIT DON'T FORCE IT Keelee Paterson		International INT 544	Sutran/Miller	Larry Farrow
◇45	48	2	SINGIN' IN THE RAIN Sheila B. Devotion		EMI 2761	Big Three/Big Three	
46	46	2	RHIANNON Fleetwood Mac		Reprise K 14430	Intersong	Fleetwood Mac/K. Olsen
47	44	2	TOO HOT TO TROT/ZOOM Commodores		Motown 12 TMG/TMG 1096	Jobete/UK	J. Carmichael/Commodores
£48	47	2	STAY WITH ME BABY David Essex		CBS 6063	Tro-Essex	Bert De-Coteaux
49	NEW ENTRY		AUTOMATIC LOVE Vibrators		Epic EPC 6137	April/Momentbest	Viv Maile
£50	49	2	READY STEADY GO Generation X		Chrysalis CHS 2207	Copyright Control	Martin Rushent

Top 50 compiled for Music Week and BBC based upon 250 from a panel of 375 conventional record outlets by the British Market Research Bureau Ltd.

COURAGE, AUDACITY AND REVOLT: THE SEX PISTOLS

There was a time when John Lydon was a Pink Floyd fan. Living in a council flat in Finsbury Park, he listened to Pink Floyd, to Can, to Jamaican dub and to Van Der Graaf Generator. Outside his window, London was wasting away. The post-war shine of socialism, the optimism evinced by the Shadows' 'Wonderful Land' just over a decade before, was tarnished and muddy. Public housing was mean and colourless. Buildings were filthy, bins overflowed, everything smelt, everything was dirty. No one seemed to care enough to do anything about it. Hanging on in quiet desperation – it was the English way.

Pink Floyd certainly didn't appear to care, or intend to do anything about it. They seemed content to point out, from a distance, that people frittered their lives away, owing their souls to the company store. Moneyed and pretentious was how Lydon started to read their stance; Floyd had a cocksure, self-satisfied aura of greatness – it suddenly struck him that they thought they were so great, in fact, there was no room for anybody else. One day, he cut off his Gilmour-length locks, got a marker pen and wrote 'I hate' across the top of his Pink Floyd T-shirt.

The Sex Pistols were, initially, a figment of Malcom McLaren's imagination. One of the most divisive figures in this saga, McLaren had been at Croydon Art College in 1968 and organised a sit-in; he was the perfect suburban situationist. He believed in Guy Debord's maxim, 'In the future, art will be the overturning of situations or it will be nothing.' The situation McLaren wanted to overturn, he soon realised, was how pop was being created and consumed. Kicked out of college, by 1971 he was running a clothes shop called Let It Rock (nothing to do with the magazine), and selling vintage fifties gear. Larry Parnes was in the mix with Guy Debord in shaping McLaren's stance. He didn't want to be Billy Fury – he knew he was too pasty, curly and puffy-cheeked – but he could be an impresario.

Let It Rock became Too Fast to Live Too Young to Die, and then, when McLaren tired of the oikish Ted clientele, it became Sex. With Vivienne Westwood, he stocked ever more outrageous clothing under the Seditionaries label – one shirt featured the hood worn by the Cambridge Rapist, then terrifying the city, and beneath it the legend 'Brian Epstein found dead August 27th 1967 after taking part in sado-masochistic practices . . . S & M made him feel at home'. McLaren was in awe of his forefathers, but at the same time had a Freudian desire to destroy them.

By the mid-seventies modern pop had become part of Debord's Society of the Spectacle, uninvolving, uninspiring, just there, on supermarket shelves offering you the lame beats of the Bay City Rollers, the numbing muzak of Mike Oldfield's *Ommadawn*, the whinnying of wealthy west-coast hippies. McLaren knew that no one really wanted this, that he couldn't be the only one who'd had enough, who wanted to kick over the statues. What he needed was a group to mould, and he thought he'd found them in the New York Dolls on a trip to the States. Closer to home, though, was a bully beef of a lad called Steve Jones who frequented the Sex store – he had a band playing covers of Small Faces and Who songs with amateurish gusto. McLaren thought they could take on the Bay City Rollers if only they could find a front man. John Lydon, in his customised 'I hate Pink Floyd' T-shirt, walked in one day and got the job by leaning on the shop jukebox and miming to Alice Cooper's 'Eighteen'. He was rechristened Johnny Rotten.

Punk brought the issue of class back into pop. What the Beatles had started, the Sex Pistols carried on. Johnny Rotten said, 'I regard myself as working-class, but I know damn well working class doesn't regard me that way,' and later, 'Why are the working class so angry, lazy and scared of education? Why are they so scared of learning and stepping outside their clearly defined class barriers?'

Johnny Rotten, like no one since Elvis, affected the cultural temperature. 'I had no ambitions. I knew I was just sick of a lot of things and had no way of expressing it.' The Sex Pistols' music and nihilist stance expressed revulsion at a passive country on its knees, with *Love Thy Neighbour* and *Mind Your Language* passing for entertainment on TV, with BBC Radio 1 avoiding anything that could be construed as underground (including ninety-five per cent of reggae); they sounded as sore and angry as an unlanced boil. 'I was frightened going near a microphone,' said Rotten, 'I was shocked the way it sounded, what I sounded like.' Not as shocked and frightened as everyone else would be.

Rotten called things as he saw them, which could have been embarrassing – he could have sounded like a finger-wagging student or a terrace yob or a junior Enoch Powell, but he was clever. Bored and clever. And he dealt with the press by ignoring them as much as he could, calling them 'spiteful and childish and stupid'.

There was plenty to rail against in the Britain of 1976, and the irritation popped up in the strangest places. A children's comic called *Action*

– featuring killer shark Hookjaw and post-apocalypse teen-gang story
'Kids Rule OK' – caused outrage and was pulled a year later. Before
Action, the number-one boys' comic in Britain was *Warlord*, which
still had World War Two as its key source. *Action*, with its heavy anti-
authoritarian tone and extreme violence, was launched in February
'76 and was the perfect ten-year-old schoolkid's primer for the musical
upheaval ahead.

The upheaval was crystallised by an appearance on Thames Television's
Today programme, an undemanding early-evening show with a Moog
version of the Association's 'Windy' as its theme and an avuncular presenter called Bill Grundy. The Sex Pistols only appeared because Queen
dropped out at the last minute and EMI's promotions man Eric Hall,
not wanting to miss a promotional TV slot, put another group on the
show. Grundy appeared to be drunk. He goaded the band into swearing. He chatted up their mate Siouxsie Sioux. 'You dirty fucker!' said
an unimpressed Steve Jones. 'What a fucking rotter!' *Action* comic was
stronger stuff, but this incident was enough to cement the legend. 'THE
FILTH AND THE FURY', ran the *Daily Mirror* front page the following day. EMI, panicking, withdrew the Pistols' first single, 'Anarchy
in the UK', which was at a lowly number thirty-eight. McLaren was
beside himself with joy. Here was the situationist event he had craved,
turning the mushiest teatime TV show into an antagonistic event which
so enraged one viewer he put his foot through the TV screen. And it only
happened because Freddie Mercury and Brian May were out Christmas
shopping.

'Anarchy in the UK' had some of the best lyrics in pop – almost
every line's a soundbite ('Your future dream is a shopping scheme' being
maybe the most insightful). But, musically, it was almost nothing like a
blueprint for punk; behind Lydon's ear-piercing, Establishment-baiting
voice, it was slow, it had a conventional guitar break, it was hard to pogo
to. 'God Save the Queen', eventually released in June '77, was faster,
harder, more direct, all about the power chords. And by the time it was
released, it had an expectant public – 'God Save the Queen' entered the
charts at number eleven, climbed to number two, then fell back the following week. It was an abrupt and unexpected drop. Rod Stewart's 'The

First Cut Is the Deepest' stayed at the top for a fourth straight week. *Top of the Pops* refused to mention the title of the song at number two.

Conspiracy theorists have cried foul ever since. Did 'God Save the Queen' sell enough copies to get to number one?* Malcolm McLaren always claimed as much. He was wise enough to know pop needs its martyrs: if the Establishment (the market-research company BMRB, the BBC, the government even) had fiddled the Top 10, then so much the better – it kept the group and its fans as outsiders. 'God Save the Queen' became a cause célèbre.

McLaren, who understood where Little Tich and Max Bygraves fitted into British social history as well as he understood Larry Parnes and Gene Vincent, happily played up the group's theatrical side. Rotten came across on stage like a mix of Albert Steptoe and Richard III, noble but very pissed off. Off camera, McLaren's dealings with the music industry were just as short and sharp; they had been signed to three different record labels – EMI, A&M and Virgin – by the time of their second single (all much to Rotten's amusement, which gave him the inspiration for 'EMI' on *Never Mind the Bollocks, Here's the Sex Pistols*, a UK number-one album in November '77). This was played up by McLaren as a money-making master plan after the fact, but 'Anarchy in the UK' and 'God Save the Queen' had more in common with Serge Gainsbourg's porn-pop hit 'Je t'aime . . . moi non plus';† they were simply too hot to handle.

The mainstream press were unimpressed by the group's collage

---

* It suits the Sex Pistols myth to say 'God Save the Queen' was stopped from getting to number one by the authorities. Beyond the fact it was number one in the *NME* chart, and that an unverified source told Virgin label boss Richard Branson it was outselling Rod Stewart's 'The First Cut Is the Deepest' (the eventual number one) by two to one, there is no evidence for this. And yet it reached number two on a chart that only registered sales in a certain number of shops. As well as the BBC and IBA, the single was banned by W. H. Smith, Boots and Woolworths, three major chain stores which chart compilers BMRB would have relied upon. That 'God Save the Queen' even reached number two is a miracle.
† Released on Fontana in 1969, 'Je t'aime . . .' had reached as high as number two in the UK chart before the label, Philips, got cold feet and withdrew it. Independent label Major Minor stepped in at once and took the single over the finishing line to number one.

artwork or capitalist-baiting lyrics. They saw the dyed hair, the safety pins, the torn shirts, and thought the Sex Pistols were only about destruction: 'Get pissed! Destroy!' Their beer-glass-chucking mate John Ritchie was exactly that, a caricature. He was shy around girls and loved his mum, but as alter ego Sid Vicious he was little more than a nihilistic thug with a leather jacket and a pretty face, punk's poster boy and a dumb prick. Sid joined on bass (he couldn't play, but that wasn't really the point) when Glen Matlock was sacked in spring '77, and things rapidly disintegrated. At a gig in Dallas, Sid was headbutted but carried on playing, blood pouring down his face like a badge of honour. 'Look at that,' sighed Rotten, 'a living circus.'

The pivotal moment for the Sex Pistols' – and punk rock's – musical momentum came with the arrival in London of American band the Heartbreakers. They were fronted by Johnny Thunders, formerly of the New York Dolls. They brought heroin into a very innocent drug scene (speed and beer) and changed it overnight. Subway Sect sang, 'We oppose all rock 'n' roll'; the Heartbreakers – with first single 'Born to Lose' coupled with 'Chinese Rocks' – clearly *were* rock 'n' roll. As if it was still World War Two, they appeared glamorous to the blushing British punk groups purely because they were American; they flashed their smack like so many silk stockings, took over the London scene and dragged it down with them. The Heartbreakers were ugly ghosts of one of McLaren's earlier social experiments, and re-emerged to haunt him. Rotten had invited Sid Vicious in, but it was McLaren who encouraged him to become a circus freak, and bequeathed him the consequences.

Rotten pulled the rug from under McLaren by leaving the Sex Pistols at the end of their '78 US tour. All of pop waited on his next move, as it had done with the post-army Elvis and the post-crash Dylan. Listen to Johnny. Johnny Rotten will know what to do.

At home he had a huge reggae collection. In the summer of '77 he had appeared on Capital Radio with Tommy Vance (this in itself seemed miraculous – most people assumed he'd trash a studio like a Tasmanian devil as soon as he walked in). 'Just play the records,' he told Vance, 'they'll speak for themselves. That's my idea of fun.' He played music by Lou Reed and Nico but, ever the contrarian, said he didn't like the

Velvet Underground. He played Can and he played Augustus Pablo. He loved reggae, and said he loved the look of pre-release reggae sevens, the idea that you could buy records with little or no clue as to what was on them. That was another kind of anarchy.

Anyone listening to the show may not have been too surprised by his post-Sex Pistols move. McLaren claimed ownership of the name 'Johnny Rotten' so he reverted to his real name, John Lydon. With bassist Jah Wobble and guitarist Keith Levene he formed Public Image Ltd, and they released 'Public Image' as their first single; Levene's waves of disorienting, spin-cycle guitar were underpinned by a two-note dub bassline burrowing up from under your feet and between your legs. The drumming was relentless, machine-like, no cymbals, no improv. Above all this was Lydon's tale of crisp revenge, sweet and merciless. He felt as chewed up and spat out, as abused by his manager as Les McKeown. McLaren could rewrite the Sex Pistols' history as much as he liked, but Public Image was all Lydon's – the beginning, middle and end* of the story would all be written by him.

A number-nine hit in October '78, 'Public Image' sounded like the future – it took a decade for anyone (My Bloody Valentine, Ride) to make guitars sound as intangibly and emotionally unsettling, and for dub (Primal Scream, Underworld) to be absorbed into guitar music as successfully. All that, and it's a beautiful manifesto: 'I'm not the same as when I began. I will not be treated as property.'

Some days I think 'Public Image' is the most powerful record ever made.

The Sex Pistols wanted to destroy rock, something Lydon made a decent fist of with Public Image Ltd. The Clash, the Pistols' only real rivals, wanted to save it. 'It ain't punk, it ain't new wave,' said guitarist Mick Jones, 'all the terms stink. Just call it rock 'n' roll.' As pretenders to the Sex Pistols' throne, the Clash were presumably pleased as punch with the new back-to-basics direction the Heartbreakers had introduced. Jon Savage wrote about a gig in Harlesden in March '77: 'All I

---

* No end in sight as yet. Lydon reconstitutes the PiL line-up every so often and still plays a powerful, lengthy set. There's no doubting his work ethic.

can think of, when the Clash come on, is that they jettisoned their great Pollock look for a more militaristic uniform of zippers and epaulettes. It makes them look like rock stars.'

Their singer, Joe Strummer, joined the Clash after quitting pub-rockers the 101ers, and prior to that was involved in the Maida Vale/Notting Hill hippie squat scene. The rest of the band were West and South London working class, and milked this heritage with photo shoots under the Westway – the last gang in town, speakers of the truth. Strummer claimed to carry a knife at all times, and felt a confused kinship with Notting Hill's black community which he channelled in their first single, 'White Riot' (no. 38 '77). It was written out of envy for the black anti-police riots in the late seventies. The Clash were ready to pick up sticks.

Behind all this bad-boy behaviour was manager Bernie Rhodes, and he was probably the most interesting thing about the Clash. He also managed Subway Sect, from Mortlake, the oddest of all first-generation punk groups. They wore V-neck jumpers and guitars were held high like Gerry and the Pacemakers, while the lyrics suggested Rimbaud and contained no 'yeah', no 'baby', no Americanisms at all. 'We dye all our clothes grey, in a big bath,' said singer Vic Godard. Even Rhodes, sadly, couldn't steer them into the charts.

Saying that you liked the Sex Pistols or the Clash was as loaded a statement as whether you preferred the Beatles to the Stones: working-class versus middle class, art school versus Establishment, *Top of the Pops* versus *The Old Grey Whistle Test*, rock versus pop. But which was which? Johnny Rotten wrote 'I hate' on his Pink Floyd T-shirt with his own felt-tip pen; Joe Strummer wore jackets with slogans – 'sten guns in Knightsbridge', 'hate and war' – thought up by Bernie Rhodes and spray-painted by Sebastian Conran.*

The Sex Pistols could be viewed as a calculated project, structured round a theory largely favoured by student radicals, but the effect they had on modern pop and society beyond was entirely real. Yet the Clash

---

* Definitions of the punk aesthetic are numerous, but my favourite is George Berger's in *The Story of Crass*: 'If you want to deface a Pink Floyd t-shirt with "I hate . . ." you have to own one in the first place.'

were considered more politically based and socially dangerous in the US than the Pistols, who were largely seen as a contrary boy band spoiling for a punch-up. The manufactured nature of the Clash's image shouldn't bother me – I think the Monkees are one of pop's greatest achievements – but hearing the Clash's 'I'm So Bored with the USA' at a distance, it's hard not to roll your eyes. Often, they were plain silly: 'We ain't never gonna get commercial respectability,' they told the *NME*, proudly. The difference between the Sex Pistols and the Clash is that Strummer would have got defensive, maybe even flashed his blade, if you pointed out the incongruity of the Conran connection; Rotten wore Vivienne Westwood gear, or even full Ted regalia, and didn't give a toss what you thought. The Clash set out parameters, which is one reason it took them ages to find a drummer ('They gotta believe in what's happening,' Jones explained to the *NME*. 'They gotta tell the truth'), and then squirmed like politicians when they were caught busting their own manifesto.

They ended up recording a double album (*London Calling*), a triple album (*Sandinista*), and then a brace of classic-rock, American radio staples in 'Rock the Casbah' and 'Should I Stay or Should I Go'; they became part of the rock canon. The Sex Pistols' tiny recorded legacy has been selected, dissected, inspected and rejected so much since the mid-seventies that it seems almost impossible to work out what they were all about. Ask forty punk-rockers how they define punk and you'll get forty different answers, and they'll all be right. The Sex Pistols, though, really did stand for something. Here's what it was.

On what turned out to be their final British tour, in December 1977, there were just four shows, with four more cancelled due to illness or political pressure. The last one was at Ivanhoe's in Huddersfield. Before the evening show, the Pistols played a matinee for five hundred kids under fourteen. Their parents were striking firemen who, already in the middle of a recession, could expect a Dickensian Christmas.

The Sex Pistols turned the club into a grotto, filling the place with sweets and copies of their LP, *Never Mind the Bollocks, Here's the Sex Pistols* – kids of ten were running about in 'Never Mind the Bollocks' T-shirts. There were tables of fruit – pomegranates and oranges; there was a talent competition, which was won by a girl reading a Pam Ayres poem. The children were handed skateboards, the single most desirable 1977 Christmas present. Craig Mallinson was a teenager, the son of a striking fireman, and he told the BBC, 'They came on and sang "Holidays in the Sun". Sid Vicious spat on the kids and Johnny had to tell him that we weren't proper fans – we were just little kids! Johnny Rotten just loved it. He seemed really happy. He put his head in the cake at the end. He licked his fingers, passed it around, and then put his head in and got it all in his hair.'

Footage of the Huddersfield gig will make you laugh out loud. It may not have been on the scale of Live Aid, but its ethics were unquestionable, and it has had a positive, lasting impact on the community: Huddersfield Town football fans still sing 'I wanna be HTFC' to the tune of 'Anarchy in the UK'. On a wall of the building where Ivanhoe's used to be, graffiti reads, 'Anarchy in the KU'. Never mind the spelling – people in Huddersfield remember Christmas Day 1977. As a showing of solidarity, a small act of charity, outsiders playing for outsiders, and the very real power of pop, the thought of it can just about break my heart.

CRANKED UP REALLY HIGH: PUNK ROCK

The 600-strong line, which last Monday straggled across two blocks outside London's 100 Club in Oxford Street, waiting for the Punk Rock Festival to start, was indisputable evidence that a new decade in rock is about to begin. Two 18-year-olds from Salisbury were at the front of the queue. 'I've been waiting for something to identify with,' says Gareth, hopping up and down. 'There's been nothing for years. I just want to be involved.'

Caroline Coon, *Melody Maker*, October 1976

Before 'God Save the Queen', pop was recreational, occasionally a calling; afterwards, it was a religion. I was in Notting Hill's Record and

Tape Exchange one day in 1978 and there were two punk girls at the counter, one flustered and giggling. 'God, it's so embarrassing,' she said as she flogged her copy of Eddie and the Hot Rods' *Life on the Line*. And this is Eddie and the Hot Rods we're talking about, not Yes or Donny Osmond. Barbers were full of longhairs getting five, six, seven years' growth cut back to nothing. By 1980 no man in Britain had long hair, not even Roy Harper.* And, like a new religion, pop after punk had no singular vision; it split into more factions than ever before. Punks versus Teds, punks versus skins; there were street punks with their orthodox icons like the safety pin and the sacred leather jacket, and anarcho punks, vegan, almost Lutheran, closer to the hippies than they cared to admit.

Pop had been a dirty word since the late sixties and was still a dirty word in '77 – it would remain one for a few years hence. No one in a punk group was flying the flag for Abba, David Soul or Smokie. Although these were the names that dominated the UK chart in 1977, they just weren't as despised as Pink Floyd, Rod Stewart or (most of all) the Stones. Punk rock† was there to overthrow classic rock, the development of a stratospheric scene of global celebrity which had arrived at the end of the sixties, post-Monterey, and grown throughout the seventies – the ex-Beatles were in this zone, joined by other Britons like Rod Stewart and Elton John as well as the upper echelons of the Laurel Canyon crowd. It was a bit like a retirement home, a bit like the Hotel California the Eagles sang about, and its lack of creative impulse was maddening.

Exactly how punk rock could end classic rock's dominance wasn't clear. Punk was as much about what wasn't there as what was. Stewart Home described it as 'a receding object; as one approaches, it disappears'. It was stripped of most Americanisms; it was also stripped of pretty much all black influence. Prog and metal may have been the result of a blues/rock fusion, a coming together of the international underclass, but punk rock disowned it all – it was wrapped up in what the new generation saw as

---

* The Human League's Phil Oakey had long hair in 1980, but only on one side of his head.
† 'Punk rock' was the terminology used in 1977, and this is more than just a technicality: 'punk' was what it became during the anti-rockist early eighties.

rock's collective failure. Instead, it found its own underclass and kindred musical spirit in Jamaica and in West London's immigrant population.

The Clash were largely to blame for punk's Maoist 'year zero' take on pop history. A few older acts – the Velvet Underground, Stooges, Flamin' Groovies – were permissible, but even a sonic reducer like Neil Young was locked out of the love-in, presumably on the grounds of his long hair. Soon, even the pub-rock R&B acts who paved the way for punk, like Eddie and the Hot Rods, were expelled from the party – they wore flares. 'Like trousers, like brain,' said Strummer. This was pop's own Cultural Revolution – the present was all that mattered. 'No Elvis, Beatles or Rolling Stones in 1977,' sang Strummer. By 1978 there were no Sex Pistols either, which left the Clash as the punk movement's unelected figureheads.*

Clearly the Clash loved the USA, and loved rock 'n' roll. Strummer's insistence on purity of line was naively genuine, as was the openness of his politics and his sympathy with underdogs – the body-popping kids of the Bronx, the Sandinistas in Nicaragua, the kids who bought independent singles in the Rough Trade shop. But eventually their contradictions grew more tiresome, and when Strummer decided to get back to basics one more time, kicking over the statues with a green mohican and an album called *Cut the Crap* in 1985, everyone winced.

The Damned were much more fun than the Clash: Dave Vanian dressed like a vampire, Captain Sensible was permanently pissed and wore granny specs, while Rat Scabies was the loon drummer to beat them all. They were great, and they didn't take themselves remotely

---

* This may be a good time to mention that the word 'punk' is slang that refers to weak or poor kids acting tough. The term 'punk rock' initially related to 1960s garage punk, was referenced by Nick Tosches and Dave Marsh (in 1971, when writing about ? and the Mysterians in *Creem*), and was also in usage in Britain (it has an entry in Dave Laing and Phil Hardy's 1975 *Encyclopedia of Rock*) before it was reappropriated in 1976. The phrase possibly hung in the air because the Sex Pistols and Eddie and the Hot Rods were playing 1960s garage-punk covers in their live sets: the Monkees' 'Stepping Stone', Dave Berry's 'Don't Gimme No Lip Child', ? and the Mysterians' '96 Tears'. Besides, '76/77 British punk had more in common with the Trashmen's crude, intense, hyped-up 1963 hit 'Surfin' Bird' (US no. 4, also reissued in the UK in '76 on a K-Tel album called *Goofy Greats*) than it did with Television, Talking Heads or early Blondie.

seriously. The problem with this was that, despite releasing a run of super-fast, super-excitable 45s ('New Rose', 'Neat Neat Neat', 'Stretcher Case Baby', 'Problem Child', 'Don't Cry Wolf'), nobody else took them seriously either; none of their singles charted, and they split in '77 before re-forming in '79 to finally chart with 'Love Song' (UK no. 20) and the Farfisa-led bubblegum of 'Smash It Up' (UK no. 35). The Damned were also one of the few groups who dared to reference the past – they tried to get Syd Barrett to produce their second album, *Music for Pleasure*, but had to settle for another Floyd member, Nick Mason.

British punk's most significant legacy is DIY. The best thing to come from the year-zero mentality, DIY seized the means of production, initially with the xeroxed *Sniffin' Glue*, Mark Perry's fanzine that bypassed the music press to deliver the news from punk's London frontline.* Buzzcocks' *Spiral Scratch* EP, recorded with producer Martin Hannett for the borrowed sum of £500 and released on their own New Hormones label in January '77, was the green light – for the first time in British pop, you could ignore the major labels and not worry about losing the roof over your head if the record didn't sell.

When Chuck Jones was once asked who he made cartoons for, adults or children, he said, 'We made them for ourselves.' Desperate Bicycles' 'Smokescreen', released in the spring of '77, was a record entirely about itself ('It was easy, it was cheap, go and do it!'). The group admitted they were formed 'specifically for the purpose of recording and releasing a single on our own label'. Their second single, 'The Medium Was Tedium', railed against the industry ('Just another commercial venture!') with as much righteous anger and humour as 'Anarchy in the UK', only this time the drums were made of cardboard, and Steve Jones's guitar had been replaced with Nicky Stephens's Winfield organ: the sleeve boasted that the complete cost of recording and pressing a few hundred copies

---

* It should be remembered that, before punk, any alternative to chart pop was a secret, something that was given, at best, a small weekly slot on BBC2's *Old Grey Whistle Test* and coverage in the *NME*, *Sounds* and the monthlies *Zig Zag* and *Let It Rock*. But rarely in TV adverts, and barely on the radio. Punk wanted pop to be everywhere, for everyone. In time this happened – though whether you really want to hear the Damned as you shop in Sainsbury's or Marvin Gaye's 'Sexual Healing' as you wait in the family-planning clinic is a moot point.

of 'Smokescreen' was £153. 'If you can understand, go and join a band.' The floodgates opened.*

DIY related to punk in the way skiffle had to rock 'n' roll. Strange, redundant keyboards were a common feature, as punk had laid waste to anything outside the guitar/bass/drums set-up and this old gear was going cheap (Martin O'Cuthbert's *Vocal Vigilante* EP lists a Dubreq Stylophone and a Crumar Performer as his instruments, both highly desirable now but obsolete technology in the post-punk heat of February '78). The look was monochrome, handmade, an A4 photocopied sleeve wrapped around a hand-stamped seven-inch single.

Like the folk-rock scene of a few years before, DIY was fiercely localised, largely because the music industry and London were so closely tied. One of the genre's most directly emotional singles was by Hornsey at War. Then there was the Good Missionaries' 'Deranged in Hastings', and 'Wickford's So Boring' by Grinder. These were truly private projects. No one expected their records to reach beyond their home town's boundaries, so contact addresses rarely appeared on the sleeves. It was far more common to find a list of pressing plants, printers and costs worked out to the penny – the Desperate Bicycles' £153 was the real benchmark of DIY. Competition over who could function on the smallest budget was intense.

If the DIY side of punk had a centre, it was the Rough Trade shop at 202 Kensington Park Road, which opened in '76. Some of the new independent labels, like Small Wonder (in London), Factory (Manchester) and Fast Product (Edinburgh), had collectivist ideals and a profit-sharing relationship with their acts. An infrastructure was built of independent labels and independent distribution. The *NME* and *Sounds* soon had weekly columns on cassette albums. This was about as far removed from corporate rock as you could ever get. To quote Hornsey at War, 'They won't play this on the radio because it poses a threat.' Far closer to the Situationist International – hand-printed, self-promoted – than

---

* John Hammond claimed that Bob Dylan's first album cost $402 to record, his point being that great music doesn't need excessive time and money. Likewise, the raw-throated, thrilling vocal performance John Lennon turns in on 'Twist and Shout' only came about because the Beatles had to record all fourteen songs for their debut album in a day – 'Twist and Shout' just happened to be the last one.

the Clash and their deal with CBS, DIY was the last hurrah of the Angry Brigade, and good hippie aesthetics.

Even the DIY aspect of punk can cause an argument in an empty room. It had been there at the start of punk, with its fanzines (*Sniffin' Glue* first appeared in the summer of '76, swiftly followed by *Ripped & Torn*, Jon Savage's *London's Outrage* and Jonh Ingham's *London's Burning*) and record labels (the London-based Stiff and Chiswick led the way, New Hormones and Fuck Off followed). But the release of the Clash's 'Complete Control', a tirade against CBS on a CBS single, though seen as a victory, only showed how hard it was to overthrow the major labels. DIY can be viewed as either a situationist solution – overturning rival orders – or a retreat, a concession of defeat, which would lead directly to the indie ghetto.

It began to wind down when the leading bands either got writer's block (like Lincolnshire's Instant Automatons) or became musically proficient (Scritti Politti). Between '81 and '83 there was a growing focus on dance rhythms, a move away from outsider attitude and tactics, and the music began to close in on the mainstream. Bristol's Pop Group provide a case study as they splintered in 1980, producing a batch of new groups, all heavily rhythmic – the Mafia, Maximum Joy, Pigbag and Rip Rig and Panic, whose singer, Neneh Cherry, completed the process by becoming a star at the end of the decade: how to get from the Rough Trade shop to Buffalo Stance in three easy stages.

The way punk was perceived in people's houses, on the radio and on television, was quite different from how it was seen in the Rough Trade shop. Jon Savage has argued that punk was primarily about sexuality and gender, but the misogynistic Stranglers were in the charts, and on *Top of the Pops*, on a regular basis. This is how 1977 looked to Joe Public:

Dec. '76	The Sex Pistols, 'Anarchy in the UK', no. 38
Apr. '77	The Clash, 'White Riot', no. 38
Apr. '77	Television, 'Marquee Moon', no. 30
May '77	The Ramones, 'Sheena Is a Punk Rocker', no. 22
May '77	The Stranglers, 'Peaches'/'Go Buddy Go', no. 8
June '77	The Sex Pistols, 'God Save the Queen', no. 2

June '77	The Jam, 'In the City', no. 40
July '77	Jonathan Richman and the Modern Lovers, 'Roadrunner', no. 11
July '77	The Sex Pistols, 'Pretty Vacant', no. 6
July '77	The Jam, 'All around the World', no. 20
July '77	The Saints, 'This Perfect Day', no. 34
July '77	Television, 'Prove It', no. 25
July '77	The Stranglers, 'Something Better Change', no. 9
Aug. '77	The Ramones, 'Swallow My Pride', no. 36
Aug. '77	Eddie and the Hot Rods, 'Do Anything You Wanna Do', no. 9
Aug. '77	The Adverts, 'Gary Gilmore's Eyes', no. 18
Sept. '77	The Boomtown Rats, 'Looking after Number One', no. 11
Sept. '77	Generation X, 'Your Generation', no. 36
Oct. '77	The Stranglers, 'No More Heroes', no. 8
Oct. '77	The Clash, 'Complete Control', no. 28
Oct. '77	The Sex Pistols, 'Holidays in the Sun', no. 8
Oct. '77	The Tom Robinson Band, '2468 Motorway', no. 5
Nov. '77	Elvis Costello and the Attractions, 'Watching the Detectives', no. 15
Nov. '77	The Jam, 'Modern World', no. 36
Nov. '77	Jonathan Richman and the Modern Lovers, 'Egyptian Reggae', no. 5
Nov. '77	The Tubes, 'White Punks on Dope', no. 28
Nov. '77	The Boomtown Rats, 'Mary of the Fourth Form', no. 15
Dec. '77	The Banned, 'Little Girl', no. 36

This list includes any Top 40 hit that could loosely be described as punk or new wave: the Tubes were pranksters whose song title alone was enough to incur a Radio 1 ban, and the Tom Robinson Band's trucker boogie was somehow enough to convince *NME* writers Julie Burchill and Tony Parsons (in their book *The Boy Looked at Johnny*) that he was the future of punk, however wrong-headed that may now seem. Those quirks aside, it's interesting to see just how open-minded first-generation punks were. No safety-pin and mohair clichés, and only the Boomtown Rats and the Banned (with a reedy cover of the Syndicate of Sound's garage hit) seem like chancers. Of the American acts, it's heartening to see the uncommercial Television as the most popular prior to Blondie's arrival with 'Denis' (UK no. 2 '78) the following spring, and odd that the Ramones couldn't crack the Top 20. The belated success of the Modern Lovers, led by Velvet Underground groupie Jonathan Richman, influenced the nascent Postcard acts and the UK jangle pop that emerged in the early eighties; they had one more hit with the hopelessly romantic, very gentle 'Morning of Our Lives' (no. 29, Jan '78), and even managed a *Top of the Pops* appearance later in '78 singing the virtually a cappella 'New England' live in the studio.

Considering 1977 is punk's year zero, this doesn't seem a long list, and absentees (the Damned's non-appearance, even though they had been first out of the blocks with 'New Rose' in November '76) are immediately apparent. The chart positions aren't mindblowing, either, but consider two things: almost none of these records received any airplay beyond John Peel's late-night Radio 1 show; and sheer weight of numbers (thirteen Top 40 entries over the school summer holidays) made punk a needling but unavoidable presence.

Now let's take a look at the records that hit the Top 40 in the three months leading up to Public Image's post-punk green button:

Aug. '78	The Stranglers, 'Walk On By', no. 21	
Aug. '78	Jilted John, 'Jilted John', no. 4	
Aug. '78	Plastic Bertrand,* 'Sha La La La Lee', no. 39	

* Belgium's Plastic Bertrand was the unlikely cover star of the first issue of *Smash Hits* in September 1978, while Sham 69 provided its first centre-spread poster. A spiritual successor to *Fabulous*, it was the idea of Nick Logan, who had been editor of the *NME* and would go on to launch *The Face* in 1980. The instant success of *Smash Hits* indicated how much pop had revived since punk – just as the Beatles had launched and helped to sell magazines in the mid-sixties, so Blondie, then Gary Numan, and then the stars of new pop would make *Smash Hits* an irreverent, essential alternative to the weekly papers. In the eighties it spawned

Aug. '78	The Rezillos, 'Top of the Pops', no. 17
Aug. '78	The Jam, 'David Watts', no. 25
Sept. '78	Blondie, 'Picture This', no. 14
Sept. '78	Siouxsie and the Banshees, 'Hong Kong Garden', no. 7
Sept. '78	Buzzcocks, 'Ever Fallen in Love', no. 12
Oct. '78	The Boomtown Rats, 'Rat Trap', no. 1
Oct. '78	Sham 69, 'Hurry Up Harry', no. 10
Oct. '78	Public Image Ltd, 'Public Image', no. 9

Aside from a late-flowering classic punk 45 (Siouxsie and the Banshees – the last of the first wave to put a record out), these can be divided up into power pop (Blondie, Buzzcocks), cover versions of sixties hits (the Jam, Plastic Bertrand, the Stranglers), and novelty records (Jilted John, the Rezillos, Sham 69). Daytime Radio 1 was still happier playing singles from the *Grease* soundtrack, which dominated the summer charts with sixteen weeks at number one broken only by a five-week spell for the Commodores' grandparent-friendly ballad 'Three Times a Lady'. 'Rat Trap' ended this run, effectively becoming the first 'new wave' number one, though this multi-part, saxophone-led Springsteen knock-off suggested Bob Geldof's group had been using punk as a foot in the door, waiting for the moment when – after four Top 20 hits – they could unleash what they really wanted to do. Given things had come to this pretty pass, Public Image Ltd were a necessary new start – punk had done its job, now the fun could really begin. As John Lydon sang on 'The Flowers of Romance', 'I'll take the furniture, start all over again.'

Did punk wipe out all of pop's prehistory? Clearly not. Was that what everybody wanted? Probably not. Danny Baker was co-editor of *Sniffin' Glue*. Did he get his hair cut off for the cause? Did he hell. The girls thought his thick dark curls were reminiscent of David Essex and he wasn't going to mess about with his pulling power just because he quite liked Subway Sect – pop was still about teenage boys trying to get into teenage girls' knickers, even after punk.

---

imitators including *Number One*, *Big!* and the BBC-sponsored *Top of the Pops* magazine.

As with most popular uprisings, punk didn't conquer – it had been an impossibly wide coalition that began to crumble as soon as the media built punks up to be Britain's folk devils. The disparate elements behind its ascent had only ever agreed on the fact they were against the status quo. The Sex Pistols and the Clash were diametrically opposed. Public Image Ltd suggested one way out of this impasse. Buzzcocks and New Hormones provided another, the dawn of a new sensibility, with their graphic designers Linder and Malcolm Garrett as precursors to post-punk's visual sensibility. For those who wanted to eliminate rock from the equation completely, Jonathan Richman and the Modern Lovers' gentility provided a third way, which would evolve in the eighties and beyond.

Disco had a far broader base of support than punk, and its chart positions were vastly more impressive, yet it was the latter which shaped British culture (music, TV, comedy, art, personal politics) for decades to come. Punk rock, the Sex Pistols and the DIY boom gave a free pass to kids to start making music again, and the opportunity for female musicians and writers (Caroline Coon, Julie Burchill, Jane Suck) to work towards equal status. Beyond this, punk's intertwining with reggae and dub had consequences which reverberate through to the end of this story and beyond. Disco's influence remained firmly on the dancefloor.

PLEASANTLY ANTAGONISTIC: NEW WAVE

Some people didn't use the term 'punk', or even 'punk rock'. Some people got it confused with the kind of music that the *Daily Mail* referred to as 'punky', and called the whole thing 'new wave'. It had originally been coined by French cinema-savvy Malcolm McLaren as a term for the new British music before Caroline Coon cemented the phrase 'punk'. It was then used in *Sniffin' Glue*'s October '76 issue as an expression to encompass the whole scene – not just the music, but the clubs and the clothes. Phonogram Records then released a compilation called *New Wave* in 1977 that included proto-punk American acts like the Dead Boys, Ramones, Talking Heads and girl group the Runaways, and the name stuck as a modern pop-genre term.

In America, 'new wave' isn't seen as a half-cocked term at all, but instead as a catch-all for British music in the immediate post-punk era, usually with an electronic element to it. Minor acts from the early eighties like the Thompson Twins would later be hailed as 'new wave' by house and techno pioneers. Some of the more stereotypically new-wave acts who had one foot planted firmly in pre-punk soil, like the Fixx and Wang Chung, unsurprisingly did much better in the US than they did at home.

In Britain, though, 'new wave' was a term used by A&R men and softer DJs and journalists; they referred to *all* punk rock as new wave, as well as the loosely related music which wore similar clothes. This lumping together of a bunch of different musical strands certainly made things simpler for the likes of Radio 1's old guard and, commercially, it made sense for the acts: you had actual punk rock (the Sex Pistols); you had new music that would have happened anyway, that was perhaps reluctantly dragged through the new-wave door (Television); there was not-quite-new music that would have happened anyway and opportunistically pushed its way through the new-wave door (Boomtown Rats); then there was not-quite-new stuff that would have happened anyway, but recognised that punk had opened a door for it (Elvis Costello); and, a little later, you had genuinely new stuff with an electronic pulse (Buggles, New Musik).

In 1977 new wave meant overgrown kids raking it in by impersonating nasty little kids. Step forward the Stranglers, formerly known as the Guildford Stranglers, who amassed a tidy run of twenty hit singles between 1977's outrages and 1983's return of the old order, including six top tenners. Formed in '75, they gigged constantly and had a sizeable following for their Monday-night residency at the key pub-rock venue the Nashville by the summer of 1976. One night the Sex Pistols supported them and, without needing to update their brutish image, the Stranglers fell naturally into punk's slipstream. They were nasty bastards. 'Five Minutes', a no. 11 hit from '78, had some of the ugliest lyrics – 'they killed his cat and they raped his wife, and in their eyes there was screaming hate' – ever heard on Radio 1.

Who 'they' were wasn't exactly clear. The Stranglers certainly didn't seem to share the leftist leanings of most first-generation punks. Their first hit, 'Grip', had included a line about doing a two-way stretch and, looking at them, you'd guess there might have been an element of projection in 'Five Minutes'. They looked like they'd do *Top of the Pops*, jump into their Cortina, pull stockings over their heads and hold up a chippie on the way back to Surrey. A gang, but not the way the Clash were a gang: there was no romance with the Stranglers. It seemed likely they had no friends, none at all. On top of this they seemed *really* old – singer Hugh Cornwell had been the bass player in a sixties Highgate band called Emil and the Detectives, alongside Fairport Convention's Richard Thompson, playing Bo Diddley and Howlin' Wolf covers;* drummer Jet Black was a year older than the Shadows' Jet Harris, a guitar hero when most '77 punks were still being bottle-fed. Only French bassist Jean-Jacques Burnel looked under thirty, and his rumbling, aquatic basslines – like a pub-brewed Duane Eddy – were what gave their beefy songs a unique flavour, topped off by human walrus Dave Greenfield's organ sprigs. Their thuggishness was compelling, their singles like a set of dirty postcards, and a 1978 take on 'Walk On By' was one of the half-dozen most effective Bacharach covers. They even mellowed in time, showing their advanced age with the '67-sounding pop-psych lullabies 'Golden Brown' and 'Strange Little Girl', both Top 10 hits in '82. Quite possibly they had been listening to Pink Floyd and Donovan while they were in Wormwood Scrubs.

The Stranglers' ultraviolence was not something you would associate with other new-wave acts. Most, like the Boomtown Rats, looked rather like Showaddywaddy on their way to a swingers party. People who were generally scared of punk rock saw new wave as a way of depoliticising the new music: referring to Talking Heads as new wave meant colour-coding them, a little more beige than the Sex Pistols, a little less blood-red than the Damned. New-wave music was largely adrift from punk's moral bearings. But by the time its practitioners ended up on *Top of the Pops*, alongside David Essex or Donna Summer, they looked rather similar and adhered to a style thought of as 'punk' (wild eyes and skinny ties) by most viewers. It joined some but not all of punk's dots in a slightly cock-eyed manner (see the Regents' '7 Teen', or the Leyton Buzzards' 'Saturday Nite beneath the Plastic Palm Trees', or Tonight's 'Drummer Man'), and this meant that new wave provided a few real gems, quite by accident, as well as a whole lot of piffle.

* Emil and the Detectives also covered the Everly Brothers' 'Man with Money', a tough number that would have suited the Stranglers to a tee.

For a genre that was basically punk boiled down, its threatening elements removed, new wave somehow had its own musical logic and boundaries. The vocals tended to be performed in a self-conscious, permanently surprised manner, an exaggerated hangover from glam, with Sparks' 'This Town Ain't Big Enough for Both of Us' as the unspoken blueprint; choruses ended with hysterical question marks, while, on a record such as Lene Lovich's 'Lucky Number' (UK no. 3 '79), you got the impression the singer was continuously jumping on and off a chair to avoid a mouse. In the background, punk's power chords were often augmented by cod-reggae rhythms – a third-generation photocopy of the real thing via the Clash – and a Blondie/Costello toyshop organ. The look was like the undead (bulging eyes, mouth agape, with furrowed brows indicating at least two decades among the living) in tight-fitting suit jackets, leather ties and spray-on Lee Coopers. New-wavers often had careers that lasted into the eighties, while punk-rockers were frequently burnt out by the turn of the new decade, or had moved on to something entirely new like Buddhism (Poly Styrene) or working for the Royal Mail (Vic Godard). Punk had structural hatred, revolution in its heart; new wave had its magpie eyes on the big cash prize.

The new-wave band who had the genre's spirit, sound and comical contradictions in a bottle were the Boomtown Rats, who had a spirited punky hit in '77 with 'Looking after Number One'* (UK no. 11) before settling into their groove. Singer Bob Geldof felt outré enough to get away with ripping up a picture of John Travolta and Olivia Newton-John on *Top of the Pops* when 'Rat Trap' deposed 'Summer Nights' as the UK's number one in November '78. Their next single was also a number one, and bigger yet; an important record, even. 'I Don't Like Mondays' blended Elton John balladry with righteous ire about a playground shooting in San Diego. It was as morally vague as the Stranglers' 'Five Minutes', but Geldof was an angry man. Things going wrong made him blunt and vengeful. The parlous state of the world meant his

---

* The lyrics ('I'm alright Jack!') were proto-Thatcherite, and one particular line ('Don't give me charity') would have sounded self-contradictory coming from Geldof a few years later.

focus soon drifted away from the Rats. They remain one of the few acts, huge in their day, who are now resolutely unlovable. They were ersatz in the clumsiest way – why listen to 'Rat Trap' when you've got 'Born to Run'? How did they fool us all?

It was easier to see how the Police got away with it, scoring four UK number-one singles between 1979 and '83 – three moody blond dudes, not that ugly, and a pared-back sound that was instantly recognisable. Singer Sting had a high, mewling voice that, appropriately, sounded a little like the whine of a police siren. They hit their stride on fourth single 'Message in a Bottle', economical and irresistible, enthusiastic whoops not out of place, and it was a UK number one in the summer of '79. But the feeling that something wasn't quite right crept in early. Sting's faux-Jamaican accent was always problematic, and he did himself no favours in a 1979 *Smash Hits* interview. Did the Police have a master plan? Yes, said Sting. 'We'll try and beat the Beatles. I'm interested in appealing to a great mass of people without going for the lowest common denominator, which is dead easy – you become Gary Glitter.'

The dumb lyric to 'Walking on the Moon', their second number one in '79, was compensated for by impressively spacey dub holes in the production. By the following summer the Police were big enough to go straight in at number one with 'Don't Stand So Close to Me'. The lyric this time wasn't lazy but tortured: former teacher Sting drew on his experience, relating the story of an illicit classroom affair, and shoe-horning in a reference to Nabokov to show us how well read he was. Sting seemed to wind his bandmates up as much as his detractors.* In 1983 he had a dream in which he looked outside his bedroom window to see three blue turtles, stranded on their backs, gasping for air. He interpreted this as the death of the Police, quit the group and called his first solo album *The Dream of the Blue Turtles*. This wasn't meant to be funny.

Most often, new-wave acts simply took advantage of the new rock

* Initially the Police was drummer Stewart Copeland's band. Sting took over songwriting duties once Andy Summers replaced Henry Padovani as guitarist. Resentment simmered quite openly, and Copeland once got through a whole tour by shouting a monosyllabic cuss word at Sting every time he hit the snare.

rules and adapted their existing style to suit. Skeletal guitarist Ric Ocasek and bassist Benjamin Orr had been in a Crosby, Stills and Nash-like folk-rock group called Milkwood in '72 but, under the name Cap'n Swing, had progressed to Velvet Underground covers by '77. They then worked hard on their image, emphasising Ocasek's gaunt, almost alien presence, and hid him behind huge mirror shades to make him look like a human fly; dressing in red and black they relaunched themselves, with new-wave economy, as the Cars. Their love of pop lore and Anglophilia was borne out on their first album, which was recorded in London with sly references to new kids in town, dancing under stormy skies and 'suede blue eyes'. Described in MTV's *Who's Who in Rock Video* as 'cool, mysterious and slightly vulnerable', they peppered their power pop with slick harmonies, rockabilly riffs and melodic synth lines, and on 'My Best Friend's Girl' (UK no. 3, US no. 35 '78) and 'Just What I Needed' (UK no. 17, US no. 27 '79) they managed to both predict eighties American AOR and echo *American Graffiti*'s processed rock 'n' roll history – call me a lowbrow, but I reckon some of their teen beat lyrics ('I don't mind you coming here and wasting all my time, 'cos when you're standing oh so near I kinda lose my mind') were worthy of Buddy Holly.

A slew of balding and/or bespectacled singer-songwriters appeared from the suburbs to take out their physical shortcomings on the public. Graham Parker also wore shades at all times but peddled soul-based pub rock ('Hey Lord Don't Ask Me Questions', UK no. 32 '78) that was agitated but had no lasting effect. Elvis Costello wore a surgically enhanced arched eyebrow and wrote pun-packed songs while singing as if he was standing in a fridge; 'The only two things that matter to me,' he said, 'the only motivation points for writing these songs, are revenge and guilt.' With his mad-owl stare and over-tight suits, Costello symbolised the difference between punk rock and new wave. His songs were strong, he evoked sickly London on its knees, he gave love a bad name, and if punk hadn't happened he'd have maybe been Kilburn's own Bruce Springsteen. But the Sex Pistols opened the door and so the likes of Costello were blown in and snapped up and packaged as easily processed punk-lite. 'He's a very young, unassuming, talented person,'

said Costello's American A&R director, Gregg Geller. 'We certainly succeeded in creating a kind of mystique about him. He can be kind of
pleasantly antagonistic.'

Like a caricature of a caricature, there was Joe Jackson, who changed
genre with each album and confused absolutely everyone. Initially he
barked like a pissed-up accountant, all thick-necked and red in the face,
and scored bitter-love hits with 'Is She Really Going Out with Him' (UK
no. 13 '79) and 'It's Different for Girls' (UK no. 5 '80). But off stage he
was smart and unassuming. In '82 he released the *Night and Day* album,
which included New York City's unofficial, neon-pretty early-eighties
anthem 'Stepping Out', a Top 10 hit in Britain and America. *Night and
Day* blended lounge jazz with lyrics about cancer and break-ups, and
it was good enough to make his strange journey – from cod reggae to
jumpin' jive to Big Apple anthems – worthwhile, if not comprehensible.
He reckoned that American radio stations loved him because 'people
were looking for an alternative to the established American rock star
groups which wasn't disco. Something new which wasn't punk. They
picked up on Costello, the Police, and me. I think a lot of these people
want to appear hip and play something new and English.' While his
favourite band were Public Image Ltd, *Night and Day* sounded like a
superior Billy Joel – this may not have been Jackson's intention.

The *NME* reckoned that XTC and Squeeze were heirs to the Kinks
and Small Faces, a new, classically English pop. The former started out
as the most bug-eyed, itchy new wave imaginable ('This Is Pop', 'Life
Begins at the Hop') before switching to a bucolic sixties sound, marred
by Andy Partridge's mannered vocals, which somehow suggested he
hated his audience. Squeeze were harder to work out – they hit big in '79
with kitchen-sink playlets 'Cool for Cats' and 'Up the Junction' (both
UK no. 2), made the exemplary Kentish concept album *Argybargy* in
1980 ('My mother didn't like her, she never peeled the spuds'), dabbled
with Camden Town country and western ('Labelled with Love', UK
no. 4 '81), then got progressively more serious, added pun upon pun
to every song and, quite self-consciously, grew up in public. Keyboard
player Jools Holland eventually became the official face of grown-up
music in Britain on his BBC series, *Later . . . with Jools Holland*.

But if new wave was generally Pepsi to punk's Coca-Cola, with Britain's half-arsed rebels soon to be sweetly absorbed into the John Hughes era, a few unlikely acts emerged who acted as a bridge between punk and the eighties' new pop to come. The more genuinely strange included synthesizers, which, for a start, meant they weren't just former country-rockers with a squirty flower in their lapel. New Musik were a bunch of borderline geriatrics led by Tony Mansfield, who looked like a field vole in a check suit. They had a clear love of both the Beatles – unmentionable as an influence in 1979 – and electronics. Similar were the Buggles, the new wave's Peter and Gordon, who had a UK no. 1 with the prescient 'Video Killed the Radio Star' in 1979. Both groups were all clean-cut, straight lines, and as zippy as Tupperware. They had melodies you could slice cheese with, and a retro-futurist melancholy: the Buggles sang of B-movie memories ('Elstree') and 'Living in the Plastic Age' ('I wish my skin could stand the pace!'), while New Musik served up Brill Building pop with a dollop of cold war angst on 'This World of Water' and 'Living by Numbers' (UK no. 13 '80) – 'they don't want your name, just your number.'

The Buggles saw themselves as well beyond punk's scruffiness, 'a total rejection of all those poor recordings,' singer Trevor Horn told *Smash Hits*, 'the banal songs, "Babylon's burning yeah yeah yeah" and that type of thing. That's why we took a different line and almost went the opposite way to most new-wave bands. We felt that it was about time somebody started making good, well-produced pop records again.' In this, they predicted new pop, the most exciting sound of the early eighties, and just when it looked like they had found a new way forward, going back to early-seventies Brit Building pop and covering it in dayglo dots, the Buggles went and screwed with the whole linear progression of the thing by joining Yes in 1980.

I've been hard on new wave, but it did give some stranded singers of a former age the chance to reinvent themselves without dyeing their hair green. Robert Palmer was a debonair singer from Batley, Yorkshire, who, prior to 1980, was mainly known for making records that had naked girls and high-life photos on the cover. They sold relatively poorly. The synth boom and the new minimalism saw him step back and record the bleak and repetitive electro ballad 'Johnny and Mary' (UK no. 44 '80) about a couple's bleak and repetitive life; it was moving and catchy. Then he asked Gary Numan to guest on his *Clues* album, which was bolder than Pete Townshend or Ray Davies or Mick Jagger ever got. Best of all, he cut a single called 'Some Guys Have All the Luck' (UK no. 16 '82), whose chorus was pure drivetime but whose verse was made up of nothing but hiccups, growls and unhinged squeaks. Like new wave as a body of work, it wasn't about to shape the future of pop or rock or disco. Yet it was fast fun and, dear lord, it made for a hilariously diverting three minutes on *Top of the Pops*.

In the end, new wave was the sound of the old order trying to come to terms with punk. And often succeeding, commercially at least. Post-punk and new pop took the signals and flares, the politics and inspiration of punk, made music that throbbed and oscillated, that wept rain rhythms, that conquered the charts with string sections and references to sex and death, while nodding to Smokey Robinson and Jacques Derrida. Over the next four or five years, this would result in some of the bravest, most truly inspiring pop music ever made; elemental stuff that took punk from a fourteenth-floor council flat and spirited it to previously unimagined musical realms. New wave, on the other hand, took punk no further than a shopping centre in Harlow.

SUPERNATURE: DISCO

In 1968 Andrea True arrived in New York as a wide-eyed innocent with the age-old American dream of becoming an actress. She'd been a boarder at St Cecilia Academy, an all-girl Catholic school in country-music capital Nashville. She was clean and pure as she packed her case and headed for Broadway. Clean, pure Andrea True. Any ideas where this story is going?

After a while she got herself a bit part in *The Way We Were*, but that wasn't going to pay two years' rent. For a leggy blonde, though, roles in *Illusions of a Lady* and *Deep Throat 2* certainly were. True started to divide her time between porn and directing low-budget commercials.

At no point did she think about singing until, while filming in Jamaica in 1975, she found herself stranded during the country's political crisis: no one was allowed to leave the island with any money. Not wanting to lose her hard-earned cash, True asked a friend called Gregg Diamond to fly in and produce a track for her, which she would finance with her $400 acting fee; maybe she could use the track in her next movie. Diamond was no big shot, but he was capable. A journeyman drummer, his career highlights included sessions with Joey Dee and the Starliters and James Brown. But by '75 he'd decided to give production a try. The sum of all he had come up with when True called was one basic backing track, with himself on piano and brother Godfrey on drums. He arrived in Jamaica, and True breathily cooed some hastily written lyrics over his demo: 'How do you like your love? How do you like it? More, more, more . . .' As luck would have it, also staying in Diamond's hotel was the calypso star Mighty Sparrow, whose horn section added some suitably loose parps, and that just about used up True's fee. They flew home, Diamond's lawyer arranged a deal with Buddah Records in New York, and DJ Tom Moulton mixed the track at Philadelphia's Sigma Sound studio. 'More, More, More' – with possibly the only transcendental cowbell break in pop history – ended up as a hypnotic, saucy floor-filler across Europe. It went Top 5 in Britain and America in the spring of 1976. Andrea True, by now in her mid-thirties (or 'twenty-six with a bullet', as she told the press), never had another major hit and returned to the world of porn in 1980.

There are two ways of approaching disco. One is that it was all about surface, for good or bad. To the mid-seventies music press and many soul fans it was rootless, as visceral as cornflakes, an end to the struggle, a precipitous drop into vapidity. Porn actresses could have huge disco hits recorded on a whim. Donna Summer, one of the very few stars to emerge from the genre's amorphous anonymity, described her performance on her first hit, 'Love to Love You Baby', as 'Marilyn Monroe singing, not me. I'm an actress.' Disco picked up on Bowie's cold distance from the art of pop, kept the artifice, removed his furrowed brow and stuck a smiley face on his Kentish forehead; it was all about pleasure, the end rather than the means. It was often gay, European, machine-made,

female-led (Cerrone's 'Supernature', Voyage's 'From East to West').
Disco couldn't have been further away from serious, male-dominated,
dues-paying classic rock (Lynyrd Skynyrd's 'Sweet Home Alabama',
Bruce Springsteen's 'Thunder Road') if it had taken a three-year course
in contrariness.

Another view. Disco boomed when the Vietnam war entered its terminal phase. When the last American boarded a helicopter out of Saigon
in April 1975, Elton John topped the American chart with his paean to
the home of disco, 'Philadelphia Freedom'; the record it replaced was
Labelle's 'Lady Marmalade', a song about sexual abandon sung by a
sixties girl group – Patti Labelle and the Bluebelles – reborn in feathers
and garish space bikinis. The message was that the war was over and the
freaks had won. From this vantage point, disco is as political as punk.
More than John and Yoko, Bob Dylan or Phil Ochs, Elton, Labelle,
Donna Summer and Chic knew how to celebrate the end of the Far
East conflict that had cleaved American society in two. Democracy had
won; outsiders could at last emerge from the underground. America
now began a long cocktail party that lasted until the end of the seventies, and disco was its soundtrack.

While disco eventually fell harder and faster than any other major pop
trend, it permanently altered the way pop was processed; for the first
time the pulse of pop became the most important factor in a hit record,
and that hasn't gone away. You can go back to the amplified snare that
opens 'Rock around the Clock'. You can go back to Bo Diddley, who
rode his patented chunka-chunk maracas and locomotive rhythm for a
lifetime without usually bothering with a topline melody. Most significantly, you can go back to James Brown, whose style was to take a song
and strip it of its fineries, pare it back until it was just a husk, nothing
but shouts and rhythmic stabs. 'Papa's Got a Brand New Bag' (US no. 8
July '65) had dispensed with verse and chorus structure and cut through
the air like a knife; it could have been two, three, thirty minutes long –
the endless beat, wound up tight and impossible to resist, was all that
mattered. But disco brought the pulse into the pop mainstream, and it
took over completely. Disco was populist, it knew no shame.

So the beat was fundamental to disco, but there was more to it.

Its roots were, once again, in New York. And we can thank the city's homophobic laws and a chicken plucker from Philadelphia for its creation. Men were forbidden from dancing together in New York until the 1960s; at clubs on Fire Island flashlights were shone at dancers to make sure they weren't doing anything as subversive as even holding hands. Chubby Checker's 1960 US number one 'The Twist' had been the very first record to encourage dancing solo, and so became a sensation at New York gay club the Peppermint Lounge. Soon the club's house band, Joey Dee and the Starliters, wrote their own anthem, 'The Peppermint Twist', which was another number one in January '62. The Lounge now became the hottest club in town, attracting – much like Studio 54 nearly two decades later – the A-list likes of Jackie Kennedy, Audrey Hepburn, Truman Capote, Marilyn Monroe, Judy Garland, Noël Coward, Frank Sinatra, Norman Mailer and Greta Garbo, and all of them were in thrall to Chubby Checker's choreography. Discotheques began to spring up around the world.

Kenny Gamble and Leon Huff had cut the first true disco record – Harold Melvin and the Blue Notes' 'The Love I Lost' – at Philadelphia International in 1973, but their heartbeat, the MFSB orchestra, left for New York after a financial dispute. Reborn as the Salsoul Orchestra they cut definitive disco, string-heavy instrumentals with the occasional female vocal and the ever-present hissing hi-hat of drummer Earl Young which were universally based on Gamble and Huff's blueprint. When they weren't with Bob Blank at his perfectly named Blank Tape studio in New York, the musicians recorded at Philadelphia's Sigma Sound studios; it was almost impossible to tell an MFSB production from a Salsoul one. PIR had been usurped by the older, wiser industry town further up the eastern seaboard.

The Philadelphia musicians' lack of loyalty to their home town shouldn't surprise us. Disco was essentially rootless; it was the beginning of pop's internationalisation, something that would grow exponentially with the house revolution. Take one of disco's greatest practitioners, Giorgio Moroder. He came from Val Gardena in the Dolomites, a culturally mixed area of Italy that has as much of a taste for Wiener schnitzel as pasta and meatballs. Donna Summer was a Bostonian, part of the

cast of *Godspell* performing in Munich when she met Moroder. He had
a notion of updating Serge Gainsbourg's softcore hit 'Je t'aime . . .' and
cut 'Love to Love You Baby', a panting, orgasmic three-minute single.
The spirit of 1975 was for longer records, something pioneered by DJ
Tom Moulton, who used spliced reel-to-reel tapes to give his favourite
dance records – South Shore Commission's 'We're on the Right Track',
Patti Jo's 'Make Me Believe in You' – more space to breathe. When the
head of Casablanca Records, Neil Bogart,* heard 'Love to Love You
Baby', he asked Moroder to make it longer – fourteen minutes longer.
'He liked the song so much', said Moroder, 'he wanted to have a long
version of it. The official story is that he was playing it at a party and
people wanted to hear it over and over. I think he was doing something
. . . other than dancing.'† With Summer simulating two dozen orgasms
over Moroder's ebbing, flowing, super-clean extended electro backing,
the frankly pornographic 'Love to Love You Baby' hit number two in
the US as *Linda Lovelace for President* was playing in the country's main-
street cinemas.

An eighteen-minute song was never going to become a radio-airplay
hit – disco was the first genre that created hit records through club spins.
Disco's first UK number one, in 1974, was George McCrae's 'Rock Your
Baby', a Miami production from the same stable as KC and the Sunshine
Band's ecstatic hit with a telltale title, 'Queen of Clubs' (UK no. 7 '74);
neither received Radio 1 support until they were already in the Top 10.
Bobby 'DJ' Guttadaro of New York club Le Jardin was largely responsible for Disco Tex and the Sex-o-Lettes' 'Get Dancin'' (US no. 10, UK
no. 8) and the Love Unlimited Orchestra's 'Love's Theme' (US no. 1,
UK no. 10) becoming hits in 1974 – and he received gold discs from the
record companies to acknowledge the fact.

---

* Bogart had also been head of Cameo Parkway when it went down in 1967, four
years after Chubby Checker's last Top 20 hit.
† Orgasmic girl vocals became common currency after the success of 'Love to
Love You Baby'. Two of the best came from Salsoul and Prelude producer Patrick
Adams: Musique's 'In the Bush' (UK no. 16 '78) was as rapid-fire and single-
entendre as Donna McGhee's 'Do as I Do' was silky and seductive, based on the
groove of the Rolling Stones' 'Miss You' (US no. 1, UK no. 3 '78).

The same companies were slower to pick up on Tom Moulton's reel-to-reel innovations. 'Love to Love You Baby' was a hit in its three-minute form – you had to buy Donna Summer's album to get the full session. In 1974 Moulton was selling tapes of seamless hour-long mixes of soul and early disco for $50 a go; crafted with vari-speed record decks and careful tape splicing, these were fraught constructions and Moulton's first attempt took him eighty hours to get right. The first label to cotton on to his underground success was Scepter, home in the sixties to the Shirelles and Chuck Jackson. They let Moulton loose on Don Downing's 'Dream World' and BT Express's 'Do It 'Til You're Satisfied', which he stripped back and rebuilt starting with the drum track and bassline, creating space, drop-downs, euphoric peaks – the alchemy of dance music. As if inventing the remix wasn't enough, the wizard Moulton then discovered the new physical format for his concoctions. In early '75 he mastered his mix of Al Downing's 'I'll Be Holding On'. The studio had run out of seven-inch acetates, though, so Moulton made do with one of the twelve-inch ones that until now had been exclusively used for albums. The dynamics, bass and clarity of the mix were light years ahead of the groove-crammed seven-inch singles – soon, Moulton cut all of his mixes on twelve-inch, and the industry followed suit.

Moulton, like most disco pioneers, is hardly a household name. Nor is Bob Casey, a soundman at Infinity (a former envelope factory at 653 Broadway) who solved the problem of records jumping when the dancefloor heaved. Inspired by the suspension on his 1947 Packard, he suspended the turntables with elastic bands, something which became the norm until laptops and iPods signalled the vinyl endgame for DJs.

Donna Summer, though, did become a star. The Goddess of Love, no less, was her soubriquet. 'Love to Love You Baby' had been a symptom of the need for longer records in discotheques and bedrooms. If Summer and Moroder had never made another record, their hit would still be wheeled out as often as 'More, More, More', accompanying footage of Britain's pre-punk decadence: mirror balls, polyester, men in macs, wife-swapping, a squeaky-bum soundtrack for a country still struggling with its sexual identity. But then came 'I Feel Love', which was something else entirely, the sound of now and tomorrow, *still* tomorrow; it was highly mechanised and deeply sensual, with the most unlikely chord changes, and minimal lyrics to rival the Ronettes' 'Be My Baby' – 'Ooooh, you and me, you and me, you and me . . . ooooh, I feel love, I feel love, I feeeeel love.' Here was the future, and it seems to me that we still haven't caught up with 'I Feel Love', still don't fully understand it.* It cemented Donna Summer's status; by the end of the eighties she had scored fourteen US Top 10 hits, and four number ones, including a Dionysian remake of Jimmy Webb's 'MacArthur Park'.

Summer aside, the genre's only real star act was Chic. And try naming their singers. Chic were effectively Bernard Edwards and Nile Rodgers, smart arses with the chops and slyness of Steely Dan but with an understanding that the simplest way to get a message across on the dancefloor is to title your songs 'Dance, Dance, Dance', 'Good Times' and 'Everybody Dance' (rather than 'Bodhisattva', 'Haitian Divorce' or 'Bad Sneakers'). They were originally called Allah and the Knife Wielding Punks, which gives you some idea of their politics, but changed to Chic because it had four letters, like Roxy, who they adored, and Kiss, who were maybe America's hottest rock act in 1977 (and who Bernard also dug, rather unchicly).

Chic were all for celebration, but their evocations of American escape fantasy stood closer to the edge than most. Check out these lines: 'Stepping to our favourite tune, the good times always end too soon' ('Everybody Dance'); 'On your ladder I'll be a peg' ('I Want Your Love'); and, most terminally, 'At last I am free, I can hardly see in front of me' ('At Last I Am Free'). 'Good times – our new state of mind.' What was this, a psychology test? Well, yes. Disco could be so much frothy foot fodder, even its staunchest admirers would agree, but Chic were not going to be part of the pattern on the wallpaper.

Underpinning their pre-millennial tension were backing tracks of supernatural grace. So confident were Edwards and Rodgers of their

---

* This makes 'I Feel Love' one of a very select group of pop records – maybe a group entirely made up of 'I Feel Love' and 'Good Vibrations'.

guitar/bass/production skills that they took up an offer to produce a washed-up French yé-yé singer called Sheila, third-division even at her peak, who had most recently been terrifying the dancefloors of Europe with a disco-fied 'Singin' in the Rain' (UK no. 11 '78). The result was 'Spacer' (no. 18 '79), a silvery miracle, a zooming aerodynamic flight path of a record with one of pop's most flirtatious intros. Sheila? Yes, *that* Sheila. Good God. These boys were trouble.

Chic hit big in 1978, the same year that *Saturday Night Fever* glued – for one time only – celluloid and vinyl together in one trans-arts, mega-bucks package. With 'Do Ya Think I'm Sexy' (UK and US no. 1 '78) and 'Miss You' (UK no. 3, US no. 1 '78), Rod Stewart and the Rolling Stones joined in by 'going disco'. This was quite a media event, as if they had suddenly started singing in German. Unlike Stewart or Jagger, though, Chic's run of Top 10 hits still didn't guarantee Edwards and Rodgers could get into Studio 54; humiliated by the club's exclusive-cum-fascistic door policy on New Year's Eve, they went home and wrote a song with a chorus that ran 'Aaaaaahhh . . . *FUCK OFF!*' Amending the lyrics slightly to 'Freak out!', 'Le Freak' became their only US number one. Chic peaked in '79. So did disco. 'Le Freak' became the biggest-selling single in Atlantic Records' history, hitting the top of the Hot Hundred in early December '78 and hanging in there over the Christmas period and into mid-January. It marked an astonishing eight-month period in which every American number one was a straight disco record, with the exception of last-dance smoochers by Peaches and Herb and the Bee Gees. In June Anita Ward's 'Ring My Bell' deposed the Bee Gees' 'Love You Inside Out'. It was an infuriating record, Ward's heliumated, come-hither squeaks buoyed by a relentless syndrum, on the beat, *every* beat. So thin and spindly it was almost a novelty record, this was disco in its decadent phase.

'Ring My Bell' was followed at the top by Donna Summer's 'Bad Girls' (her second of three US number ones that year), then Chic's 'Good Times'. In many ways 'Good Times' rang the bell on Anita Ward and disco lite, warning that nothing lasts forever: 'A rumour has it that it's getting late. Time marches on, just can't wait.' It would gently usher in a new era when it was sampled at the end of the year on the Sugarhill

Gang's hip-hop breakthrough 'Rapper's Delight'. A year later it provided the pizza base for Grandmaster Flash's 'Adventures on the Wheels of Steel', and Edwards and Rodgers's rhythmic wellspring had smoothly, elegantly invented the future.

Yet by the time 'Rapper's Delight' was in the UK Top 3 at Christmas, 'disco' had become a term of abuse. Since 1978 the back pages of American classic-rock haven *Rolling Stone* had featured ads for T-shirts that bore legends such as 'Death to disco' and 'Shoot the Bee Gees'; one shock jock, WLUP in Chicago's Steve Dahl, had even run into a teenage disco and physically broken a copy of Van McCoy's 'The Hustle' on the night that McCoy died of a heart attack.* This liberal-faggot music was fine for New York's Sodom on the Hudson, but in the rust belt they wanted their rock back.

While 'Ring My Bell' was number one, Dahl got a call from the Chicago White Sox baseball team. They were having a rotten season and, on July 12th, they were planning a 'Disco Demolition Derby' to spice up the game against the Detroit Tigers. The game was a sell-out, with fifty thousand inside Comiskey Park and fifteen thousand locked out with disco records to destroy. 'Disco sucks,' they chanted. 'Disco SUCKS!' At half-time, Dahl – in full army fatigues – blew up a box containing ten thousand disco records, and the place went ballistic. The pitcher's mound was destroyed. There were bonfires everywhere,

---

* There is an ignoble American tradition – lost, thankfully, to history in the digital age – of breaking records that don't conform. In January 1958, at KWK in St Louis, station manager Robert Convey purged the station of 'undesirable music' with a Record Breaking Week; all rock 'n' roll records received a 'farewell spin' and were then ceremonially smashed on air. This made a satisfying noise with 78 shellac, but when John Lennon dared to suggest the Beatles were regarded by most kids as more significant than the church in 1966, the accompanying moral panic was satisfied with bonfires. The interview was five months old when it was picked up by Birmingham, Alabama, DJs Tommy Charles and Doug Layton of WAQY. They initiated a ban-the-Beatles campaign when Lennon refused to back down and simply clarified the quote – 'I said we meant more to kids than Jesus did, or religion. I wasn't knocking it, or putting it down. I was just saying it as a fact.' Starke in Florida had the distinction of becoming the first place in the US to actually burn Beatles records; 'They've got to buy them before they can burn them,' sniggered George Harrison.

urinating in the outfield and oral sex on the home plate. The White Sox forfeited the game. Simultaneously, the Knack's bubblegum riff-rocker 'My Sharona' broke disco's eight-month run of number ones and, with a sense of finality, ended up as America's best-selling single of 1979.

Maybe Sheila B. Devotion's 'Singin' in the Rain' did suck. And abominations like Disney's *Mickey Mouse Disco* album (featuring 'Macho Duck', in which Donald joins the Village People) made Frank Sinatra's 'Everybody's Twistin'' sound like 'The Lark Ascending'. But disco didn't go away because its roots were too deep, it had already changed pop fundamentally. The genre's main acts – the Bee Gees, Donna Summer, Chic – suffered major sales dips, but only the term 'disco' died; the venues now became 'clubs'.

At 84 King Street, west SoHo, in the echo-riddled spaces of a concrete parking garage, DJ Larry Levan was taking the sound back underground, away from the Studio 54 elite and part-timers. Once again, it was home for an extended family of outsiders, it was intimate, and soon became a religion. The Paradise Garage kept the flame burning, becoming the touchstone club for future generations. Levan's innovative set lists – Taana Gardner's 'Heartbeat', the Nick Straker Band's 'A Little Bit of Jazz', Change's richly atmospheric 'Searching', things he had made himself, things made exclusively for him – set the benchmark higher, higher.

A generation of British kids, weaned on disco, were also just setting out in defiance of Chicago's disco inferno. Londoners Hi Tension had released a brace of Top 20 hits in 1978 ('Hi Tension', 'British Hustle') which laid the groundwork for the specific UK sound of Britfunk – a singer with no vibrato, a popping funk bassist, the occasional vocoder, and a keyboardist who kept sneaking in Herbie Hancock jazz moves. Freeez explored both Stevie Wonder and the blank spaces of Factory's post-punk on 'Southern Freeez' (UK no. 9 '81); better still were Linx, who showed a clear understanding of Michael Jackson, Latin percussion and *Grange Hill* lore on 'Intuition' (UK no. 7 '81) and 'So This Is Romance' (UK no. 15 '81).

In the South Bronx they were playing a new game with new toys; on the Lower East Side the art-school crowd were fiddling with hi-hats and disco's unexplored spaces; in London, teenage Bowie fans were using disco as a template for something else again. And in the rockist rust belt – Chicago, where the funeral pyre had been built, and beneath the twinkling hubcaps of Detroit – the mirror ball slowly turned 360 degrees; the next revolution was already under way.

ISLANDS IN THE STREAM: THE BEE GEES

Billboard US number ones, 1978:

The Bee Gees	'How Deep Is Your Love'
Player	'Baby Come Back'
The Bee Gees	'Stayin' Alive'
Andy Gibb	'(Love Is) Thicker than Water'
The Bee Gees	'Night Fever'
Yvonne Elliman	'If I Can't Have You'
Wings	'With a Little Luck'
Johnny Mathis and Deniece Williams	'Too Much Too Little Too Late'

John Travolta and Olivia Newton-John	'You're the One that I Want'
Andy Gibb	'Shadow Dancing'
The Rolling Stones	'Miss You'
The Commodores	'Three Times a Lady'
Frankie Valli	'Grease'
A Taste of Honey	'Boogie Oogie Oogie'
Exile	'Kiss You All Over'
Nick Gilder	'Hot Child in the City'
Anne Murray	'You Needed Me'
Donna Summer	'MacArthur Park'
Neil Diamond and Barbra Streisand	'You Don't Bring Me Flowers'
Chic	'Le Freak'
The Bee Gees	'Too Much Heaven'

The elephant in the discotheque is the Bee Gees.

Their dominance of the charts in the disco era was above and beyond Chic, Giorgio Moroder, even Donna Summer. Their soundtrack to *Saturday Night Fever* sold thirty million copies. They were responsible for writing and producing eight of 1978's American number ones, something only Lennon and McCartney in 1963/64 could rival – and John and Paul hadn't been the producers, only the writers. Even given the task of writing a song called 'Grease' ('Grease is the word, it's got groove, it's got a meaning,' they claimed, hoping no one would ask, 'Come again?') they came up with a classic. At one point in March they were behind five singles in the American Top 10. Not including these number ones, their 1978 hits also include Samantha Sang's 'Emotion' (US no. 3, UK no. 11) and Tavares's 'More than a Woman' (UK no. 7), both radio staples to this day. In 1978 they accounted for two per cent of the entire record industry's profits. The Bee Gees were a cultural phenomenon.

Three siblings from an isolated, slightly sinister island off the coast of north-west England, already in their late twenties by the time the *Fever* struck – how the hell did they manage this? Pin-ups in the late sixties, makers of the occasional keening ballad hit in the early seventies, the Bee Gees had no real contact with the zeitgeist until, inexplicably, they had hits like 'Nights on Broadway', 'Stayin' Alive', 'Night Fever', and the zeitgeist suddenly seemed to emanate from them. This happened because they were blending white soul, R&B and dance music in a way that suited pretty much every club, every radio station, every American citizen in 1978. They melded black and white influences into a more satisfying whole than anyone since Elvis. Simply, they were defining pop culture in 1978.

Like Abba, there is a well of melancholic emotion, even paranoia, in the Bee Gees' music. Take 'How Deep Is Your Love' (US no. 1, UK no. 3 '77), with its warm bath of Fender Rhodes keyboards and echoed harmonies that camouflage the cries of the lyric: 'We're living in a world of fools, breaking us down, when they all should let us be . . . How deep is your love? I really need to know.' Or 'Words' (UK no. 8 '68), with its romantic but strangely seclusionist 'This world has lost its glory. Let's start a brand-new story now, my love.' Or 'Night Fever', their transatlantic '78 number one, with its super-mellow groove and air-pumped strings masking the high anxiety of Barry Gibb's vocal; the second verse is indecipherable, nothing but a piercing wail with the odd phrase – 'I can't *hide*!' – peeking through the cracks. It is an extraordinary record.

Total pop domination can have fierce consequences. Elvis had been packed off to the army; the Beatles had received Ku Klux Klan death threats – the Bee Gees received the mother of all backlashes, taking the full brunt of the anti-disco movement. Radio stations announced 'Bee Gee-free weekends'; a comedy record called 'Meaningless Songs in Very High Voices' by the HeeBeeGeeBees became a UK radio hit. Their 1979 album *Spirits Having Flown* had sold sixteen million copies and spawned three US number-one singles ('Too Much Heaven', 'Tragedy', 'Love You Inside Out'); the singles from 1981's *Living Eyes* – 'He's a Liar' and the title track – reached thirty and forty-five on the US chart respectively, and didn't chart in Britain at all. Almost overnight, nobody played Bee Gees records on the radio, and pretty much nobody bought them. The biggest group in the world at the end of 1978 went into enforced retirement three years later. Could they rise again? Of course they could.

In the beginning, there was big brother Barry and twins Robin and Maurice Gibb. They were born on the Isle of Man but moved to Manchester as children. And they were trouble, especially Robin, who loved setting fire to pretty much anything. He progressed quickly from bedclothes to advertising hoardings. One day a member of the Manchester constabulary came knocking and suggested to their parents that it was time to think about emigrating. Manchester's problem became Australia's, but the Gibbs started to channel their pyro activities into vocal harmonies – with no New York subway stations available, they practised their art in public conveniences: 'We always looked for the best toilets in town,' said Maurice.

Encouraged by their band-leader father, the brothers became a child act at working-men's clubs, doing comedy routines and singing between races at the local speedway track. These were hard crowds to please. Bill Gates, a local DJ, began to promote them and they took their name from his and Barry Gibb's initials – the Bee Gees. By 1960 they were on TV, singing 'My Old Man's a Dustman'. Their mum made their stage clothes. None of this exactly screamed international success.

It's easy to forget that the Bee Gees were child performers and that they grew up in such an odd, isolated way. Foraging, they found things they liked on the radio and absorbed them – the Everly Brothers, the Goons, Lonnie Donegan. Old Super 8 footage shows them goofing around, but you never see any other kids playing with them, just the three brothers. They only started playing in front of teenagers (who, sales figures suggest, were largely unimpressed) when they became teenagers themselves. This airtight upbringing informed their insularity, their prickly, defensive behaviour, and many of their deeply strange early recordings: songs like 'Holiday' (US no. 11 '67) and 'I Started a Joke' (US no. 6 '68) suggest they were beamed down from another planet, aliens who had been given tiny scraps of information about what pop music was all about and were bravely trying to piece it together. By the time they left Australia, heading for the docks of Southampton in January 1967 to try and make a name for themselves back in Britain, they had released eleven singles, and none of them had meant very much at all. One of them, the admittedly excellent 'Wine and Women', had made it as far as number nineteen in Australia, but only after the group gave $200 to their school friends to buy copies. That was it. They sent tapes of their latest songs to Brian Epstein. For a failed fraternal comedy act, you had to admire their nerve.

Then something odd happened. Midway through their three-week voyage they heard that their eleventh single, 'Spicks and Specks', had gone to number one in New Zealand. And when they docked, they discovered that Brian Epstein's sidekick Robert Stigwood was very interested in their tape. The raffish Stigwood booked them into a basement rehearsal room and asked them to write a hit. This sudden run of good luck seemed to desert them when there was a power cut. Finding themselves with no electricity, stuck in darkness at the bottom of a lift shaft, they came up with 'New York Mining Disaster 1941'.

'Robin's voice . . . still makes me go cold when I listen to him,' his mother once said, presumably meaning it as a compliment. There is something shivery as well as alien about the early Bee Gees records. As a child in the early seventies I had cassettes of the Beach Boys' *Greatest Hits* and the sixties-era *Best of Bee Gees*. The similarity in the bands' names led me to twin them, but musically and visually they were complete opposites. The Beach Boys, pictured smiling on a high-contrast bright white cover, sounded like essence of summer; the Bee Gees, murkily shot on an old boat, no smiles, all shades of brown, were entirely autumnal. And what did their name mean, I wondered? It sounded like 'Beach Boys' but drained of its meaning, mumbled, opaque – it suited the heaviness and obscurity of the music, rich in ninths and fully orchestrated, with hints of Celtic melancholy. So young, so sad.

In 1967 the Bee Gees were teenagers, literally straight off the boat, and Stigwood opened up the world to them. 'The most significant new musical talent of 1967', he called them. He threw down the challenge, and they thrived under pressure. 'New York Mining Disaster 1941' gave them a US and UK Top 20 hit straight off. Clearly they were storytellers, and their third single, 'Massachusetts', about a weekend hippie trying to hitch a ride to San Francisco but ending up homesick and

stranded, was number one in Britain and all over Europe by the end of
'67. Quickly they were compared to the Beatles, but their love of soul,
and Bill Shepherd's heavy-drape arrangements, gave them a distinctive
and intense mournfulness. Stigwood asked them to write a song for Otis
Redding – he had no intention of passing it on to Otis but wanted to see
what they were capable of. The result was 'To Love Somebody', only a
number-seventeen hit in the US and a number forty-one in Britain, but
a hardy blue-eyed soul perennial. There was an emotional depth to their
songs that gave them a rare advantage over the Beatles. George Martin
had also produced the Action, a Kentish Town group who had worked
up anglicised, uptight versions of things like the Marvelettes' 'I'll Keep
Holding On' and Bob and Earl's 'Harlem Shuffle'; the Bee Gees, in
their own way, set themselves somewhere between the Beatles and the
Action. Nobody else was staking out this territory. By late '68 they had
released three albums, scored a second UK number one ('I've Gotta
Get a Message to You', about a prisoner on death row, apparently written with Percy Sledge in mind) and a swathe of continental European
number ones: 'World', 'Words', 'I Started a Joke' ('which started the
whole world crying'). Eighteen months after docking in Southampton
they were white pop's greatest hope.

Still, they were brothers, and cooped up together they started to
fight. Barry loved pot, Robin loved pills, Maurice was always out
boozing with Oliver Reed, Alan Bates and Ringo Starr (who could
blame him? Just months earlier he'd been a fifteen-year-old Beatles
fan-club member). This chemical imbalance led them to split after
1969's *Odessa*, a wildly ambitious double album housed in a red velvet sleeve. Robin, unmoored, more or less unhinged,* quit the group
and cut a solo single called 'Saved by the Bell' (UK no. 2 '69). Over

---

* In late '68 Robin was involved in the Hither Green train disaster in South
London, in which forty-nine people died. After their carriage turned upside
down and they were thrown clear, Robin and his fiancée had to pull less lucky
survivors and bodies from the wreckage. A few months later they were married.
On their honeymoon they were trapped in their lodge by an avalanche for several
days, not knowing if anyone knew where they were. 'The pathos has been there
ever since,' said Barry years later.

a primitive drum machine he'd found in Soho, his ethereal vibrato sang a sad-spaniel song that made 'New York Mining Disaster 1941' sound like 'Surfin' USA'. In short order, he cut two albums of similarly vast, equally downbeat material (*Robin's Reign* and the still unreleased *Sing Slowly Sisters*). Singing with closed eyes, a cupped hand over his ear, he may have seemed a delicate flower on stage but he didn't lack ambition. He had 'completed a book called *On the Other Hand* which is to be published soon', the *NME* reported. '"I'm a great admirer of Dickens."' In the few weeks between leaving the Bee Gees and hitting the chart with 'Saved by the Bell' he wrote more than a hundred songs. 'I'm also doing the musical score for a film called *Henry the Eighth*,' he told *Fabulous*, 'and I'm making my own film called *Family Tree*. It involves a man, John Family, whose grandfather is caught trying to blow up Trafalgar Square with a homemade bomb wrapped in underwear.' In July '69 the *NME* announced that Robin was 'fronting a 97-piece orchestra and a 60-piece choir in a recording of his latest composition "To Heaven and Back", which was inspired by the Apollo 11 moonshot. It is an entirely instrumental piece, with the choir being used for "astral effects".'* Robin Gibb was still only nineteen years old.

With his solo career, Robin had tried to leave home but found he couldn't; the filial pull was too strong. When the Bee Gees first appeared in '67, the depth of their songs cut through on the radio like a beacon through fog. By 1970, though, they were the fog, lost in overambitious, undercooked records (Maurice and Barry both cut mopey, unreleased solo albums). Right at the end of the year, they got back together. Initially the reunion worked beyond anything they could have hoped for – the first two songs they came up with were 'Lonely Days' and 'How Can You Mend a Broken Heart', autobiographical, self-healing songs which reached number three and number one respectively in America. Their success led the Gibbs to abandon their sky-reaching orchestrated pop, and they settled for an easy country-ballad sound which threw up

* None of these projects materialised, and it would be logical to think that Robin was trying to get good press with a few outlandish claims. Except 'To Heaven and Back' finally surfaced on bootlegs in the late nineties and was just as out there and vast as you might expect.

the occasional gem ('Run to Me', UK no. 9 '72) but had entirely run itself into the ground by 1974. In a valley, they went back to soul, were paired with producer Arif Mardin and came up with an exquisite album called *Mr Natural*, whose title track and lead single, 'Charade',* were the best things they'd cut in years. They sounded contemporary again. For the follow-up, 1975's *Main Course*, Mardin took them to Criteria studios in Miami. Barry picked up the rhythm of the car wheels as they crossed a rickety bridge to the studio; transcribed, the rhythm became 'Jive Talking', their first US number one in four years. Most significantly, Barry ad-libbed a falsetto while recording 'Nights on Broadway'. Mardin's ears pricked up – 'Can you scream in tune?' he asked.

And with that question, Arif Mardin launched their second coming.

Five years of thrillingly urgent falsetto disco later, having crested the wave and crashed to the shore, they were unsaleable. With no one buying records bearing the name 'Bee Gees', they decided to work undercover, cutting records with Jimmy Ruffin ('Hold On to My Love', UK no. 7 '80), Barbra Streisand ('Woman in Love', UK no. 1 '80), Dionne Warwick ('Heartbreaker', UK no. 2 '82), Kenny Rogers and Dolly Parton ('Islands in the Stream', US no. 1 '83), Diana Ross ('Chain Reaction', UK no. 1 '86). It was a pretty successful subterfuge.

Their fall had partly been their fault – by the time of *Spirits Having Flown*, their look (chest hair, teeth, medallions, teeth, horrid logo, more teeth) was preposterous and widely lampooned, and on 'Tragedy' (a transatlantic no. 1 in '79) there was none of 'Night Fever''s subtlety or the emotional glide of 1975 single 'Fanny (Be Tender with My Love)'; instead the Euro-bombast of acts like Boney M was sneaking in. Still, Trevor Horn – soon to have his first number one with 'Video Killed the Radio Star' – was probably taking notes. On the single's flip side was something else entirely. 'Until' is almost too heartbreaking to listen to; the antithesis of the A-side, it curls upwards over Manhattan in a balloon built solely out of Aero-bubble keyboards and Barry's orphaned vocal, gently drifting over the skyline and out of sight. It marked a farewell to their golden era.

---

* If 'Charade' was a city, I'd move there tomorrow.

By 1987 the dust had settled and the Bee Gees felt confident enough to make another record under their own name: 'You Win Again' – which sounded like a Christmas carol created in a shipbuilding yard – was another UK number one. With this third breakthrough, the Bee Gees staked their claim as the most consistently successful and gently shapeshifting group of the modern pop era. When the most easy-going brother, Maurice, died in 2003, the group effectively ended. Through the nineties they had still scored the odd UK Top 10 hit ('Secret Love', 'For Whom the Bell Tolls', 'Alone'), and their final, aptly titled, peek-over-the-shoulder single 'This Is Where I Came In' reached the Top 20 in 2001. That's thirty-four years of hits. No wonder they felt underappreciated.

Through it all, they were never fashionable. They made some diabolical mistakes, so bad that you'd think it was some kind of cosmic joke. Take 'Fanny (Be Tender with My Love)' – no one else could have come up with such an ugly title (why not 'Annie', for God's sake?) for such a beautiful song. Then there were the celluloid disasters. *Saturday Night Fever*, which grossed $350 million, was followed by a musical adaptation of *Sgt Pepper's Lonely Hearts Club Band*, a move so illogical (the Gibbs were famous for writing their own songs, and the Beatles were not exactly fashionable in post-punk '79) it may have all been a dream – as with Barry and Maurice's awful 1969 TV movie *Cucumber Castle*, *Sgt Pepper* is buried so deep that even YouTube can't find it. And here's another Gibb peculiarity: they defined disco, yet released no twelve-inch singles until, paradoxically, their ill-advised rocker 'He's a Liar' in '81.

None of this makes any sense until you remember their upbringing: cocooned, with extreme arrested development, they had no instincts for cool pop moves. With ill grace, they'd always point the finger when things went wrong, always be the first to build themselves up (on 1973's *Life in a Tin Can* – 'the best thing we've ever done, we think, and everyone who's heard it agrees'. No, it was entirely unmemorable), or chide a fellow act in decline (Maurice on John and Yoko: 'They say "power to the people" but charge enormous prices for seats at their concerts'). Blaming anyone but themselves. Blaming it all on the nights on

Broadway. They would walk out of interviews on a regular basis and, until the end, found it hard to understand their place in history after the almighty eighties backlash. So they were childish and childlike. Forgive them. They wrote a dozen of the finest songs of the twentieth century. The Bee Gees were children of the world.

ROUTINE IS THE ENEMY
OF MUSIC: POST-PUNK

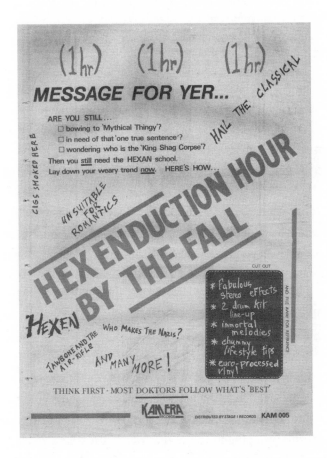

The truth of it is, I didn't know how much I loathed rock and roll, how much I deeply resented it – that was part of the motivation behind PiL – that deep resentment, and a longing for new forms.

Keith Levene, Public Image Ltd

I hate rock and roll like I hated school. I hate it because, like school, it parades before you the capitulation of the individual

under the pressures of convention and the outside world.
People get broken, friends get straight, they stop rebelling and
gradually start edging closer to normalcy. Rock stars and their
audiences blindly perpetuate and correspond to each other.
Rock becomes a habit. People collect rock like they collect
stamps or old clothes. They can't break off the habit and face
that frightening foe called change.
  Dave McCullough, *Sounds*, 1979

Punk had put music back on the streets but with no road map. People
knew what they loved, what they hated, and why they felt passionate.
Post-punk was a free-for-all, love in a void. If punk was the sound of
kids from council estates, post-punk was the sound of post-war architecture itself. It was abstract, sometimes confused, frequently surprising.

From 1964 up to 1977 Britain had fashioned modern pop as the
multinational lingua franca. The Beatles, David Bowie and Elton John
travelled the world as a sound recognised and agreed on as something
we all shared. With post-punk, the UK unilaterally revolted against the
lingua franca, and the vanguard of British music vanished from the
international pop landscape: Siouxsie Sioux was not Sandie Shaw; PiL's
'Death Disco' would not be heard on cruise ships. There was a huge cost
to be paid for the embrace of a consciously anti-communicative avant-
garde line as the way forward, however strikingly fruitful it was locally.
Which it was – the agenda was terrifying, but more than worthwhile.

'You've got to keep learning and keep discovering and keep going forward all the time,' said Bruce Smith of the Pop Group. The shift towards
non-rock forms, bringing in values that were antipathetic to classic rock,
would utterly transform modern pop. It eschewed the relentless speed
of the remaining straight-ahead punk groups, with their power chords
played so fast that the poor little drummer boy struggled to keep up, and
decided it was much more rewarding to dance in inner space.

Post-punk groups also didn't tend to look like any groups that had
gone before. They didn't pose in a traditional way; in photos they had
more in common with the surrealists, existentialists or Dadaists than
someone who had just signed to Chrysalis and was about to play the

Keele University freshers' ball – it's no coincidence that many of these groups were only seen in monochrome. All of this gave them a sense of danger, romance, of unknowable things. When you finally heard them, chances were you'd be disappointed. They might sound a bit like PiL (Section 25), or even a bit like Chris Rea (the Psychedelic Furs), but once in a while someone like Joy Division came along and then it would be unlike anything you'd heard before and your faith was restored.

Post-punk was a secret garden, and John Peel's Radio 1 show – post-punk's main platform, outside of the music press – seemed to provide new paths, new life forms within it on a weekly basis. Radio 1's daytime DJs were Noel Edmonds, Tony Blackburn, Paul Burnett, Kid Jensen and Dave Lee Travis, none of whom gave much indication of their personal taste, and seemed as happy to play Boney M as Buzzcocks. Peel was clearly a pop obsessive. His show was on late every night, between ten and twelve, after programmes as random as the military-brass show *Listen to the Band* or live commentary on an FA Cup fourth-round replay. Like *Top of the Pops*, the Peel show informed school conversations – most importantly, it included sessions specially recorded for the show. These could be by acts without a record deal, ones you'd read about in the *NME* but – if you were too young, or too far from the action – had never heard before. With things moving fast and in so many directions, the Peel sessions were a way of making sense of the new scene. They would be recorded onto cassettes and swapped at school, at gigs, a secret underworld, an alternative pop universe, beyond the reach of the music industry.

Liverpudlian Peel was the fly in the ointment at the BBC. He had his first DJing experience in sixties California, where anybody with an English accent was automatically fast-tracked to the top. Returning to Britain, he presented *The Perfumed Garden* on Radio London. When Radio 1 was launched in September '67, he took over *Top Gear* from Brian Matthew and it became a hippie haven, wall-to-wall Tyrannosaurus Rex. The late-night slot was his – out of harm's way, as the BBC saw it, where he could (and did) play *Tubular Bells* from beginning to end if he so desired.

The Peel show became a totem for the punk generation as soon as he played the Ramones' 'Judy Is a Punk' in May '76; in October he aired a session by the Vibrators, and then one by the Damned, before either group had a record out (nor had any other British punk act). Peel's show was the only place on Radio 1 where you could hear 'Anarchy in the UK'. Astonishingly, the BBC rewarded him with a nightly hour-long extension to the programme. After the watershed, under the covers, a balding man fast approaching forty became a teenage hero.

His favourite group, and the one who would record more Peel sessions than anyone else, was the Fall. Their truculent leader Mark E. Smith combined a love of M. R. James's ghost stories, Wyndham Lewis's Vorticist manifesto and an anti-fashion stance – flares, tank tops, cheap beer and fags. Smith was witty, bloody-minded, and had little time for any music beyond Can, Lou Reed and sixties garage punk. His contemporaries got a kicking on songs like 'Slags, Slates, Etc.' ('The Beat, Wah! Heat . . . male slags'), and audiences weren't treated any better; on 1980's live *Totale's Turns* album, he asks someone, 'Are you doing what you did two years ago? *Yeah?* Well, don't make a career out of it!' Though band members were sacked or quit, and the line-up changed constantly, the Fall were the definition of independent music.

Factory Records' Tony Wilson described their sound as 'urban folk', though Ewan MacColl would never have approved; it was the sound of trashed cotton mills, speed abuse and plastic bags caught on the branches of stunted trees on Burnley estates. It could also be very funny, which set it apart from much post-punk. Their *Grotesque* album painted a picture of England in 1980, a land of container drivers, cash and carry and the liberal classes who 'talk about Chile while driving through Haslingden' with its 'sixty-hour weeks and stone toilet back gardens'. It included a political murder mystery, 'New Face in Hell', with fine kazoo work. Smith mulled over what was wrong with this country on 'English Scheme'. His conclusion: 'Peter Cook's jokes, bad dope, army careers, fancy groups . . . if we were smart we would emigrate.' They went on to record more than thirty albums and, smart as Smith was, he stayed in Manchester.

John Peel played cuts from a bunch of new DIY compilations with names like *East of Croydon*, *Norwich: A Fine City* and *Avon Calling*. Regionalism was one of punk's victories – while it had been a given in

American soul and sixties garage punk, pop in Britain had always been London-centric. But by 1979 Liverpool, Manchester and Glasgow all had quite distinct sounds.

The Pop Group were from Bristol, and they were the embodiment of post-punk. Many assumed their name was ironic – instead it was a challenge thrown down to every other pop group. They first surfaced on a summer '78 Peel session. Their politics were anarcho-syndicalist, they claimed to owe nothing to the past, they binged on dub reggae, free jazz and itchy funk. Most impressively, they figured out their sound from scratch – none of the group could play a thing when they formed in May '77. Bristol was out on a limb, which gave the Pop Group the same invigorating isolation that the Saints had had in Brisbane. 'They have no contemporaries,' said the 1978 *NME Book of Modern Music*,* 'and carry few, if any, comparisons, forcing audiences to respond on imme-diate instincts. It's a very open music and an unexpected, inexplicable pleasure.' The Pop Group were on the cover of the *NME* in September '78, before they had a record out.

In 1979 they released their first single – produced by Dennis Bovell, who was best known for his work with Jamaican poet Linton Kwesi Johnson – and it was called 'She Is Beyond Good and Evil'. It fea-tured free-jazz blowing, deep dub holes and guitars that scratched out a partially sketched Memphis rhythm. Above this Mark Stewart's echo-drenched vocal proclaimed: 'I'd exchange my soul for her, there's no antidote for her . . . western values mean nothing to her.' The single's absolute weirdness was liberating; as promised, this was a new form of pop. They played shows for Amnesty International, Rock Against Racism, a fundraiser for Cambodia, and, in the process, the Pop Group quickly locked themselves into a formula that soon became more depressing than liberating. A year later came an album entitled *For How Much Longer Do We Tolerate Mass Murder*. Now the lyrics were crystal clear, the dub was gone, and everything sounded as skeletal as trees after

---

* This appeared in weekly instalments, shortly after the softback *NME Encyclopedia of Rock* was published, reinforcing the wall between punk and all that had gone before.

a forest fire: 'All that we ask for is our very own garden of Eden. All that
we get is a garden of interballistic missiles.'

All of their early promise dissolved on first listen, their flow had
stiffened and calcified – compared to the Fall's 'New Face in Hell' it
was embarrassingly dogmatic and predictable. On their 1979 album
Y, they had refused the comforts of form itself: on the second, they
sheepishly accepted that the one form they wanted to nurture was the
political earnestness of the radical student newspaper. Just the act of
releasing records had made them part of the system, which led to deep
self-criticism and, inevitably, their demise. Absolute refusal ended in
absolute silence. They were a magnificent, preposterous failure.

Joy Division's post-punk was less a total repudiation of rock than
a rewriting of it. They were modern pop viewed through night-vision
goggles – grainy and murky. Like the Pop Group, the *NME* put the
barely born Joy Division on their front cover in summer '79. It was an
atmospheric Kevin Cummins shot, and the group had their backs to the
camera. Joy Division were signed to Factory, a Manchester label started
by local TV presenter Tony Wilson. With Bauhaus-inspired sleeve
designer Peter Saville and pharmacist-by-day producer Martin Hannett,
Factory had an integrated and entirely distinctive look, feel and sound.

Joy Division's *Unknown Pleasures* had been released in the late summer
of 1979. Like the early Pop Group, its sound revelled in space – in this
instance the underpasses, the empty streets of post-industrial Victorian
Manchester. It had haste. Producer Martin Hannett was not averse to
stripping the songs back, adding reverb that made everything sound like
it was recorded in a deserted cotton mill, and sneaking in sound effects.
It also had guitar parts that were simple but – with Hannett's fondness
for effects and chemically induced trickery – had hints of a dark psychedelia. This was brought out further on their 'Transmission' single at
the end of the year. In no time Joy Division were the most influential
sound in town.

They weren't without contemporaries: Public Image and Siouxsie
and the Banshees were likewise twisting guitar and bass sounds, working in dark and difficult territory. And there were nods to the forbidden pre-punk era: the spectre of Spector can be heard in the chorus of

'Atmosphere' ('Be My Baby') and in the guitar line on the tail of 'Love Will Tear Us Apart' ('Then He Kissed Me'), while 'Novelty' pinned Cream's 'Badge' to its raincoat. Joy Division's melodies tended to be carried by bearded bassist Peter Hook, who played his lines an octave higher than usual; their sound was echoing, abandoned, the buzz of a streetlight and the low purr of the city always in the background.

Singer Ian Curtis based his phrasing on Jim Morrison, and moved easily from a whisper to a scream.* On stage he was taut, with an electric wiriness. He would look to the skies in agitation, deliver the chorus of 'She's Lost Control', then break into a windmill dance, sweat on his brow, grey eyes glazed. If it caught you at the wrong moment – say, if you were a Buzzcocks fan watching Joy Division as a support act, and you were impatient to hear 'Orgasm Addict' – this was pretty comical. But as their songwriting improved, and took you deeper into the woods, Curtis as compelling front man and Joy Division as masters of a new sound became undeniable. They joined an elite list of acts that were so plainly superior to everything around them that it became too obvious to call them your favourite group: the Beatles, Led Zeppelin, the Sex Pistols, Joy Division.

Joy Division were not relatable to most teenagers; they were about exceptionalism and self-isolation. Was this how anyone else felt? Did they engage with teenage ennui like Nirvana or Morrissey, or high drama like Goffin and King? No. 'She's Lost Control', 'Decades', 'The Only Mistake', these songs were a private apocalypse, closer to the unknowable despair of Roy Orbison.

'Transmission', almost as soon as it came out, started to appear in pop stars' all-time top-ten lists; Wah! Heat's Pete Wylie said in *Smash Hits* that they would listen to it backstage to get themselves going before they played. 'Love Will Tear Us Apart', released in July 1980, went beyond number one in the independent chart and reached number thirteen on

---

* In 1979 and 1980 issues of the *NME*, the Doors are mentioned frequently, treated with exactly the same weight (an influence, untouchable canon) as the Velvet Underground. Their critical fall from grace coincided with Oliver Stone's 1991 biopic, which (unintentionally) painted Morrison as a drunken ass with a Native American monkey on his shoulder.

the *actual* chart; their second album, *Closer*, entered the album chart at number six. *Unknown Pleasures* had been monochrome, restless, investigating new spaces. By contrast, *Closer* was as black and dense as oil. The four songs on Side 2 were funereal, climaxing in the stately, icy 'Decades': 'Here are the young men,' groaned Curtis, 'a weight on their shoulders.' Factory owner Tony Wilson saw Joy Division as a group that would earn gold discs, grow in wealth and importance, play Wembley and Madison Square Garden. But this would never happen; Ian Curtis had hanged himself a few weeks before 'Love Will Tear Us Apart' was released.

This branch of post-punk, described by Jon Savage as English Gothic, was a landscape of steely rain, bare wintry trees and dirty snow, like a Lowry without people. Under Joy Division's dark wing were a nest of groups playing in the shadows, and most of them came from the industrial north: Comsat Angels (Sheffield), A Certain Ratio (Manchester), Sisters of Mercy (Leeds) and Liverpool's Echo and the Bunnymen. The latter were blessed with a fierce drummer, Pete de Freitas, and a guitarist, Will Sergeant, who wasn't afraid to play Hank Marvin-like single-note guitar solos, minimal and lightly psychedelic. Then they saw *Apocalypse Now* and never recovered; their pretty, tousle-haired singer Ian McCulloch now believed himself to be next in line to Brando and Jim Morrison. This new psychedelia and intense self-belief led to one of 1981's best albums, *Heaven Up Here*, which hummed ominously throughout, like a distant overhead helicopter.

U2 were dubbed a 'flashy Irish showband' by the *NME* but, like the Bunnymen, had a guitarist called the Edge who could play his guitar just like ringing a bell, harmonics a speciality. Their first album, *Boy*, came out in October 1980 and could be summed up by one of its song titles, 'Shadows and Tall Trees'. Martin Hannett produced their third single, '11 O'Clock Tick Tock' (released in the same month as 'Love Will Tear Us Apart'), added an eerie children's choir to the Edge's fire, and the results suggested they really might be Joy Division's sonic successors. The Cure, having released the Palitoy power pop 'Boys Don't Cry'*

---

* This isn't meant as an easy insult. 'Boys Don't Cry' is a terrific song, and should have been a hit in 1979, but the guitar and drums – hear that cymbal

as recently as June '79, were never the same after *Closer* came out: their 1981 album *Faith* may as well have been called *Even Closer*. The Cure took Joy Division's angst and channelled it in a more teenage, sulky way. Singles like 'Charlotte Sometimes' and 'The Hanging Garden' packed in an album's worth of melancholy and flanged guitars inside three minutes, but it was all somehow powdery and a little slight. The Cure were more about stubbing your toe than taking your life.*

By using the examples of Joy Division, Echo and the Bunnymen or Liverpool's brass-driven, psychotropic voyagers the Teardrop Explodes, and adding the textured guitar work pioneered by Public Image's Keith Levene and Magazine/the Banshees' John McGeoch, here were ways for modern pop to go forward, ways that avoided the rock clichés that made *Sounds'* Dave McCullough feel sick, and ways which wouldn't tie themselves in philosophical knots as the Pop Group had done. With a few subtle adaptations, though – after a few sweaty, large-scale gigs, after the word 'baby' began to sneak back onto the lyric sheet – these sounds could be all too easily tweaked to re-emerge as pre-punk rock, as if nothing had changed.

* * *

I hope it never gets that big again. I hope nobody gets so big that they have to play to two hundred thousand people in a field. What happens if you're the two hundred thousandth person? What can you possibly hope to see?

Jake Burns, Stiff Little Fingers

Tony Wilson had imagined Joy Division playing stadiums. By 1983 Echo and the Bunnymen were playing at the Royal Albert Hall; by

---

go *tish!* – sound like they were bought at Hamley's.

* Robert Smith's miserabilism, it turned out, was a much more sensible way through teenage angst than Ian Curtis's. Curtis wore his inexperience like an angry badge of bold courage and radical difference, but Smith survived into his less self-absorbed twenties, when he recorded much lighter, more radical and, arguably, much better singles like 'The Caterpillar' (UK no. 14 '84) and 'Close to Me' (UK no. 24 '85).

the end of the decade the Cure were playing the MTV awards at the Universal Amphitheatre in Los Angeles. But it was U2 who grew into the world-swallowing pop group Wilson had wanted his charges to become. By 1988, when they released *Rattle & Hum*, they were the biggest-selling act in the world. They had become a complete inversion of everything post-punk had appeared to stand for: backward-looking, triumphalist, built for arenas. Bono had climbed up the stage curtain when they played the Moonlight in West Hampstead in 1980; now he stood on top of a towering speaker stack, messianic, wagging his finger, promising a cure-all for the cold war and the common cold. *Rattle & Hum* managed the unlikely and awful feat of patronising the future. 'Music's become too scientific,' said the Edge in 1988, 'it's lost that spunk and energy that it had in the fifties and sixties. And that quality, that missing quality is something we were trying to get back into our own music. What I like about "Desire" [the first single from *Rattle & Hum*] is that if there's ever been a cool number one to have in the UK, that's it.'

U2 rejected post-punk's own rejection of pop as lingua franca, its hunkering down in regional particularity, and its raised finger to populist communication. While they were aware of how exciting this all was, U2 were also aware of how much it was throwing away; 'Desire' was a recycled Bo Diddley riff which turned 180 degrees on post-punk's anti-rockist beliefs. Their all-things-to-all-people generality made them an international success story but, from 1983's *War* onwards, it became increasingly hard to tell what U2 stood for, or what their purpose was – their vastness and their complete avoidance of detail made them hard to read, let alone love. One day someone will explain to Bono that pop is always more expressive when it is trying to mend a broken heart than when it's trying to save the world.

Unlike U2, Joy Division were an important group to like, and have stayed that way ever since. Very few groups since have tried to sound like them,* but they were the most significant influence of their genera-

---

* For a while, every other act on Factory – Section 25, Crispy Ambulance, A Certain Ratio, Tunnel Vision, the Names – sounded quite a lot like Joy Division, but then most were also produced by Martin Hannett. The unwanted legacy of

tion. They made you want to form a group, or write something, but not necessarily something that read or sounded like Joy Division. In this, they were the most abstract influence of an abstract pop era.

Post-punk was pop without boundaries, without signposts of any sort, and not everyone was brave enough to see it through to the next stage. How do you 'sing' when all conventions of music are meant to have been smashed? Ian Curtis, Ian McCulloch, Mark Stewart, Mark E. Smith, Robert Smith and Bono all ended up with highly distinctive voices, but were any of these voices the solution? In the end, post-punk groups found themselves facing exactly the same difficulties their predecessors had come up against – in time, almost all were defeated by the problems of scale: what do you do when your records go from single to album, your career goes from six months to six years, your fanbase from the local pub to the local arena?

You couldn't blame the Edge for panicking and reverting to rockist moves, and U2 became huge in America while the Pop Group remained of minor cult interest. Yet the less cowardly moved on, in unexplored and often unexpected directions, some looking to the past and some looking to America. They found a way of harnessing the abstract energy and scoring Top 10 hits without needing a guest appearance from B. B. King.*

---

their English Gothic was its stubby cousin, goth. Though blaming Joy Division for the rise of goth is as cruel as blaming Jimi Hendrix for heavy metal.

* The beneficiaries of their efforts wouldn't surface for many years. Post-punk was picked up by the young groups at the turn of the century – the scratchy Pop Group end of the spectrum – and this in turn led to a re-evaluation and reissues for the Glasgow school (Orange Juice, Josef K, Fire Engines), New York's no wave (Liquid Liquid, ESG) and the Ze roster, while Leeds's political funk-scratchers Gang of Four re-formed to play far bigger shows than they ever had first time round. Even now, it is the single biggest influence on new young guitar bands, though it is now devoid of political chemistry. Post-punk needed years to bed in, to be appreciated, to inspire. And, for this to happen, it needed to be heard outside of the intense pop politics of the late seventies – between 1978 and 1981, there was simply too much going on. The latter-day groups may record for independent labels for reasons of peer cool rather than as an attempt to up-end the music industry but, if nothing else, they have elevated and validated the efforts of their forebears.

BACK TO THE FUTURE:
TWO TONE AND MOD

Everyone's praising us and saying, 'Great album, but can they follow it?' – so I do tend to get paranoid about it. I think the best thing for us is to go back to doing something really simple, even more simplistic than we've done in the past, towards the old R&B roots of the stuff we was doing.

Paul Weller, *Melody Maker*, 1979

Not everybody wanted to hit fast forward and shape the twenty-first century twenty years early. Post-punk's open door simultaneously attempted to shut out rock while allowing in the past, which had been forbidden ground since the Clash had declared year zero.

There were two main beneficiaries of this schism. First, the Jam, who had always looked to the sharpness of sixties mod imagery as much as they had to punk's two-minute buzz, something that had separated them from the year-zero ideologues, damaged their punk credentials and initially worked against them. They hailed from Woking, Surrey, the site of Britain's first mosque and the town where the Martians landed in H. G. Wells's *The War of the Worlds*. But there was little that was futuristic about the Jam. Rat-thin Paul Weller was the introverted leader of the first punk-generation group to appear on *Top of the Pops*,* a writer of lyrics like 'staring at a grey sky, try to paint it blue, teenage blue'. He was pop-savvy, and his group were heavily Who-influenced. Their following grew exponentially with the release of the 1978 album *All Mod Cons*; its artwork was a scrapbook of nostalgic sixties imagery. The era it evoked had only existed fifteen years earlier, but it felt like several generations. Reissues were randomly released in the late seventies, and they were largely greatest-hits packages – you couldn't walk into a shop and buy the Who's first album, nor any of the Kinks' sixties albums. Weller had a key and he was scattering clues to a lost world. In 1978 the Jam performed the Kinks' 'David Watts' on *Top of the Pops* and suddenly their fans were buying Lambrettas, turning up at their shows decked out in voluminous green parkas; Weller had singlehandedly created a mod revival.

This isn't quite as cosmically odd as it may sound. It's often overlooked that a large part of punk's aesthetic had been its razor-edged look, and this was largely borrowed from the mods of the sixties. The early punk sound, likewise, had the tightness and brevity of the Who, Kinks and Small Faces – the Sex Pistols had even covered the Who's 'Substitute'. Punk, it should also be remembered, was over very quickly. And punks were proud that it was over, proud that they had moved on before it was killed by stereotypes and part-timers. Sixties mod had

---

* They were introduced by DJ Kid Jensen, who paid due respect by mentioning 'new wave'.

been much the same. Also, not all punks were ready to embrace the headspace of *Metal Box* or *Unknown Pleasures* – some still wanted verse/chorus structures and danceability in their pop, and this is where the mod revival found its support. Mod was one of punk's constituent parts, sonically the main ingredient, so while it appeared backward-looking it was an easy and in some ways logical next step, and it blew up in 1978.

So were these new mods checking out the latest French films, scouring the jazz-import section of Dobell's or picking up on new American short-story writers? No. Unlike their forefathers, the mod revival was about the audience as stars. They marched through towns singing 'We are the mods'; they wore parkas as uniforms, and saw the early-sixties seaside battles with rockers as the high point of original mod. Few, if any, mod revivalists were autodidactic or style leaders. Paul Weller, looking out on a sea of green when the Jam played in 1979, was quite uneasy with this.

Many of the new mods were younger brothers of punks who just wanted a riot of their own – punch-ups with Teds in Clacton, that sort of thing. Possibly the second-best mod-revival group were the Purple Hearts ('Millions Like Us', no. 57 '79), and, while they could write existential lyrics like 'My life's a jigsaw, what am I here for?' they also pulled down their trousers and farted when they were interviewed on TV. No backstage discussions of Joseph Losey, Tommy Nutter or John Coltrane for these boys.

The other main beneficiary of the post-punk peek over the shoulder was 2 Tone, a Coventry label set up by mad-eyed, gap-toothed Jerry Dammers. His own group, the Specials, were a mixed-race act whose timing couldn't have been better. As the mod revival blossomed, it created a parallel skinhead revival – again a short-haired, short-lived working-class cult from the sixties that had fed directly into punk's edge and energy. Specials singer Terry Hall had seven-stone-weakling vocals which sounded neatly blank alongside Dammers's finger-wagging lyrics and the sped-up ska backing – this was more of a Punky Reggae Party than anything Bob Marley or the Clash had envisaged. Their first single, 'Gangsters', reached number six in August '79;

by February 1980 their live version of 'Too Much Too Young' was number one.*

The *NME* called the Specials' debut album 'a speed and beer-crazed ska loon, all coitus interruptus jerks, raucous party soundtracks sugar-coating moralistic homilies about sexual and other social mores. The adolescent intensity comes across as patronising.' Lyrically they wanted to have their cake and eat it, humiliating young pregnant girls on 'Too Much Too Young' ('try wearing a cap!') while recreating the horror of a rape scene (narrated by Rhoda Dakar) on 'The Boiler' – the first Top 40 hit that really dared you to listen to the end. The Specials' worldview was bleak. But these were tough times.

Quarantined from second-wave mod and ska, but another mode of anti-intellectual class and style, were the various strands of continuity punk. Those slightly too young for the first wave of punk, whose older brothers might have seen the Clash in '77, carried on as if nothing was changing. Some grew their mohicans taller, dyed them dayglo colours and became internationally known for their appearances on London postcards; the most dayglo and pointy-headed were the Exploited, a Scottish group who made it onto *Top of the Pops* and into the Top 40 with the breakneck-speed 'Dead Cities' in 1981. They called their album *Punk's Not Dead* (here's another rule of pop – if someone claims something is 'not dead', it definitely is. Likewise, if somebody claims a scene *is* dead, it definitely isn't).

Others cut their hair as short as possible. Taking the violent, oik-ish aspects of punk and deleting everything else were groups christened 'street punk' by *Sounds'* Garry Bushell but more usually called 'Oi!' Like mod, Oi! was about audience as mass. Oi! groups were stuck in a '77 timewarp and had a blunt thuggishness. Many were from London's East End and all of them were working-class and white. The Cockney Rejects, wearing West Ham shirts on stage, had a Top 40 hit with the club's anthem, 'I'm Forever Blowing Bubbles', in the spring of 1980.

---

* At a little under two minutes, 'Too Much Too Young' was also the shortest number one since the sixties, the Beatles' 'From Me to You' being the last sub-two-minute single to top the chart, in 1963.

Mawkish East End sentimentality and boot-boy punk with a dash of music hall – quite a combination. It would have been more diverting if nothing else was going on, but in 1980 there were more than enough groups pushing forward, exploring and creating new worlds to keep Oi! in the shadows.

While the Cockney Rejects were just happy to defend West Ham from all comers, and certainly weren't racist, others sailed too close to the wind for comfort. Slap-happy National Front skinheads began to flood Sham 69 gigs, eventually causing the group to discontinue; when the same thing happened at a Specials show, Terry Hall took to the stage on his own and sang 'Doesn't Make It Alright' until the beer bottles and racist chants subsided.

Just behind the Specials were a raft of other ska acts who also scored instant chart success in late '79. From Birmingham, and also on 2 Tone, the Beat anticipated the Afro-influenced pop of Paul Simon's *Graceland*, and their songs ('Mirror in the Bathroom', 'Hands Off She's Mine', 'Too Nice to Talk to') were interchangeable goodtime stuff. UB40, again from Birmingham, specialised in super-bleak lyrics ('Food for Thought', 'The Earth Dies Screaming', 'One in Ten', a cover of Randy Newman's 'I Think It's Going to Rain Today') over needle-eye thin, minor-key reggae, usually complemented by an electric harpsichord. Their rainy confusion and sense of resignation summed up 1980 as well as any-thing in pop – it was a rare year when the national mood could send a reissued 'Theme from *M.A.S.H.* (Suicide Is Painless)' to number one midsummer. Like most of their contemporaries, UB40 were stumbling by 1983, but were then unexpectedly offered a velvet bag of gold coins marked 'Red Red Wine'. The Neil Diamond song – which had been a reggae hit for Tony Tribe (UK no. 46 '69) – was from an album called *Labour of Love*, versions of songs the group had grown up with, and it was easily their best seller, diverting their career into a form of post-punk cabaret. Fourteen Top 10 hits, including four number ones, followed,*

---

* One of the number ones was with Chrissie Hynde ('I Got You Babe'), another with Pato Banton ('Baby Come Back'). As more time passes, it becomes harder to recall that for a while UB40 were subversive – hell, they had a Top 10 hit called 'The Earth Dies Screaming'!

and all bar two were cover versions. They were so lazy it sounded as if they had all been recorded on a keyboard with a special UB40 preset; by the time of 'Can't Help Falling in Love' (no. 1 '93), Ali Campbell sang as if he couldn't even be bothered to pronounce consonants.

Bad Manners were true fairground fare; listening to them was like being on a waltzer when you've had three pints and desperately need to find a toilet. Singer Buster Bloodvessel came across like a cross between *Ghostbusters*' Mr Stay Puft and Archie Rice, John Osborne's music-hall monster in *The Entertainer*. They gave the world 'Lip Up Fatty' (no. 15 '80) and a two-speed ska ballad in 'Special Brew' (no. 3 '80), and ended up with more hits than any ska group bar Madness. A joke, but a slightly frightening joke.

Madness themselves were a well of nostalgic optimism. Even their debut on 2 Tone, 'The Prince' (no. 16 '79), was a tribute to Prince Buster. It commenced a run of twenty straight Top 20 hits, and the Nutty Boys brought such un-nutty subject matter as schooldays, mixed marriages and homelessness onto *Top of the Pops*, assisted by videos that echoed *Help!*-era Beatles. They were the new Coasters: 'Night Boat to Cairo' was 'Little Egypt', 'My Girl' was 'Poison Ivy', and 'Baggy Trousers' channelled 'Charlie Brown''s playground twist. The clunky productions of Clive Langer and Alan Winstanley made some of them unwieldy, but on 'Our House' (no. 5 '82) and 'The Sun and the Rain' (no. 5 '83) song-writer Mike Barson wrote himself into the Great English Songbook. When they broke up in 1986, the *NME*'s Mark Sinker wrote that 'they were a group who made growing up and the getting of wisdom as public, palpable – and silently painful – as could ever have been imag-ined . . . from pre-adolescent kids-gang japes, to post-political weary adulthood, seven earning lads changed to seven earning dads.' Their Englishness and openness was what finally did for them; as the eighties wholegrain-soul era of Paul Young and Wet Wet Wet was ushered in, Madness sounded like they were stranded on a bomb site, and too cute for the CD age. They belonged on seven-inch singles.

Madness's longevity was the exception – mod and ska were born to be short-lived crazes, as they had been first time around. What seems odd from this distance is how revered these revivalists have become, as much if not more so than their sixties predecessors. Ska became a massive pop force some two decades later in the US, with Gwen Stefani and No Doubt reaping the commercial benefit. Paul Weller, meanwhile, became the UK music media's most respected spokesman of the early eighties. The Jam created an astonishing sequence of jagged pop singles, from 'Strange Town' in early '79 to 'Beat Surrender' three years later. Ever the contrarian, Weller called his first bona fide classic single 'Going Underground' – which is exactly where they weren't going; in March 1980 it became the first single in seven years to go straight in at number one.

In a rare combination of heavy commercial success and the highest peer respectability, the Jam were a band apart. Weller set up his own label (Respond, which signed Dolly Mixture, the best girl group of the era) and publishing house, Riot Stories. He never lost sight of how he had seen pop as a kid – back then he had taken the train from Woking to London just to walk around, capturing the sounds of the city streets on a cassette recorder. With the Jam, he capped ticket prices and always made sure their shows finished early enough for fans to catch public transport home. Musically, they forged forward with acoustics and atmospherics, pulling away from their mod roots and, like Madness, growing ever more English without losing their ire. On the Tamla-tracing 'A Town Called Malice', their third number one in '82, Weller sang affectingly of a past and present England disappearing before his eyes: 'Rows and rows of disused milk floats dying in the dairy yard. A hundred lonely housewives clutch empty milk bottles to their hearts, hanging out their old love letters on the line to dry.'

Of their less well remembered hits, 'Funeral Pyre' (no. 4 '81) was remarkable, a relentless, drum-drubbing, chorus-free 45 that sonically matched the fear, mistrust and hatred stalking pre-Falklands Britain: 'As I was standing by the edge I could see the faces of those who led, pissing themselves laughing.' The more successful the Jam got, the more political Weller became. In conversation he was always defensive, coming across as almost wilfully dim, scared to pronounce French words properly in case he looked like a sell-out. But, on record, he kept on burning: 1980's *Sound Affects* album was their most varied, acerbic and melodically strong. It included the heart-tugging 'Monday'. Seemingly recorded by producer Vic Smith on a deserted Surrey heath, 'Monday' is at once a yearning, everyday classroom/office crush ('Oh baby I'm dreaming of Monday, oh baby, when I see you again'), while also reflecting Weller's shy, retiring, raging persona: 'When I start to think that I'm something special, they tell me that I'm not. And they're right . . . I will never be embarrassed about love again.'

Sticking to his script, to keep things extremely sweet, Weller split the biggest group in the country at the height of their powers, just after his best blue-eyed soul effort 'The Bitterest Pill' reached number two in summer '82. 'Beat Surrender', the farewell single, was the Jam's third to go straight in at number one, a feat which had only been achieved by one act in British pop before. 'I'd hate us to end up old and embarrassing like so many other groups do,' said Weller, telling the press before he'd informed his bandmates. 'I want us to finish with dignity. What we have built up has meant something. For me it stands for honesty, passion, energy and youth. I want it to stay that way and maybe exist as a guideline for new groups coming up to improve and expand upon.'

He quit at just the right time. Weller's career has been up and down since, mixing the sublime and the gorblimey, but he's rarely been dull, and he would be the last person to relive his glory days by re-forming the Jam. Having turned fifty, his 2010 album *Wake Up the Nation* was his most adventurous since *Sound Affects*.

The Jam's contemporaries came to stickier ends. Jerry Dammers faced a mass mutiny from the Specials when Terry Hall, Neville Staple and Lynval Golding left to form Fun Boy Three. They scored a string of oddly muddy brass-honk hits before splitting spectacularly in 1984 on Channel 4 TV show *The Tube*; while playing the Doors' 'The End' absolutely straight, they set fire to an American flag. At the end of the song, Terry Hall leaned in to the microphone and asked: 'Does anybody get the joke?'

Terry Hall, Paul Weller and Jerry Dammers, none of them was a run-of-the-mill pop star. Yet as eccentrics and wilful personalities they paled alongside Kevin Rowland. Dexys Midnight Runners emerged at the end of 1979, also from the Midlands, also with a leaning towards the soulful sixties (Stax rather than ska), but they turned down an opportunity to sign to 2 Tone, going with ex-Clash/Subway Sect manager Bernie Rhodes instead. 'We liked the fact that everybody hated him,' said Rowland. 'If somebody is hated by a lot of people then there must be a lot of good in them.'

Kevin Rowland, over six foot, an Irish-bred bruiser, was wont to come up with such contrary statements. Dexys were built on controversy. Their first album, *Searching for the Young Soul Rebels*, began with the sound of a radio dial scanning the airwaves, settling briefly on the Specials' 'Rat Race', the Sex Pistols' 'Holidays in the Sun' and Deep Purple's 'Smoke on the Water' before Rowland roared to his eight-man team, 'For *God's sake*! Burn it down.' Very quickly, they reached the top – number one in the spring of 1980 with second single 'Geno' – and very quickly it fell apart; 'There, There, My Dear' reached a more than respectable number seven, but 'Keep It Part Two (Inferiority Part One)' was too intense, an uneasy listen. It failed to chart at all that autumn and the entire group, bar Big Jim Paterson, left Rowland to form two other brass-led combos called the Bureau and Blue Ox Babes. 'I just had something to say,' says Rowland. 'I was disappointed with success – we were still cramped in a minibus on hot summer days. I did not think in any way that "Keep It" was difficult. It was truthful, one hundred per cent truthful. "Geno" had been a number one – so I thought if you like that amount of emotion, try *this* amount of emotion.'

Rowland licked his wounds, dropped the donkey-jacket look for that of a prize boxer, and released his best record yet in 'Plan B': 'Bill Withers was good for me, pretend I'm Bill and lean on me.' Strong, romantic, who could resist? Almost everyone, as it turned out. 'Plan B' stalled just inside the Top 75, but by the summer of '82 Dexys were back at number one with 'Come On Eileen', repeating the feat in the States, where the Jam and the Specials had barely sold a record. It's the all-time wedding song, ironic when you consider how dirty and personal the lyric is: 'These people round here wear beaten-down eyes, sunk in smoke-dried faces. But not us, no, not us. We are far too young and clever.'

The parent album *Too-Rye-Ay* was a best-seller, reaching number two and staying on the UK chart for just under a year. They had survived and prospered. The follow-up album, *Don't Stand Me Down*, was an astonishingly personal and beautiful record. The problem was it came out three years after 'Come On Eileen': 'I remember coming out of the studio thinking "That's the best I can do".'

Don't Stand Me Down emerged in a far less open era than *Too-Rye-Ay*. New wild-hearted outsiders like the Smiths and the Jesus and Mary Chain were entirely ignored by Radio 1. When Rowland appeared on TV interviewed by Muriel Gray, she was obsessed by the fact he was wearing a Brooks Brothers suit. Meanwhile, radio could afford to turn a blind eye – there was no single.

'It was a stupid mistake,' Rowland sighed. 'I wanted "This Is What She's Like" to be the single, a ten-minute single. The manager said, "Good idea, or . . . no single at all?" It was a chance to be like the groups of the early seventies, like Led Zeppelin. I thought that would be great, but I wasn't sure. There was a new guy at Mercury and he was like, "*What?*" That was it. I said, we're *definitely* not releasing one. Mercury went with *Don't Stand Me Down* for about a fortnight. Then they moved on to something else.'

The album tanked, only to be reassessed in a kinder climate as a lost classic. 1985, after all, was no time for mavericks. The Specials' *In the Studio* did similarly badly, and even Paul Weller's Style Council weren't guaranteed a Top 10 position for just any old single. But, before those hard-getting-harder times, there would be more than a few diverting pleasures and a whole slew of new heroes.

A SHARK IN JET'S CLOTHING:
AMERICA AFTER PUNK

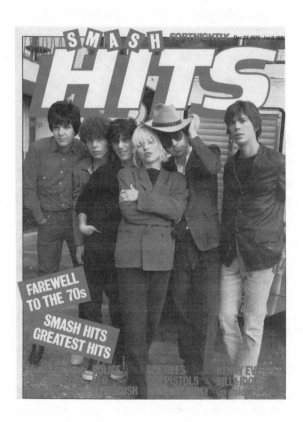

Darby Crash had one of the sweetest punk names ever, and his story distils the difference between British and American punk. Crash sang with the Germs, an LA punk band who made a fierce noise but were fatally indebted to UK punk's worst clichés. Nazi jewellery? Check. Smack habit? Check. Sid Vicious, the twit, was James Dean for these kids. When the Germs broke up in 1980, Crash and Pat Smear formed the Darby Crash Band – a tired, dreary, pre-punk appendage of a name. Sensing that even his footnote in the punk annals was slipping away, Crash injected a huge amount of heroin into his veins and pinned a note to his bedroom wall that read, 'Here Lies Darby Crash'. You'd have called him a professional fuck-up, only his timing was horrible. Crash killed himself on December 7th 1980. The next day John Lennon, the long-haired sell-out, the dinosaur, the commie-turned-capitalist apologist, and pop king of the pre-punk world, was shot dead; any column inches a small-time suicide may have received were lost.

Darby Crash's life and death were as much a pop artifice as the career of Bucks Fizz, or New Kids on the Block, or Milli Vanilli.* American punk initially treated the new music as an excuse for all manner of spoilt-brat behaviour – upset your parents, do the V-sign at teacher, draw a swastika on your cheek. The herky-jerky wackiness of new wave also blended into the US punk aesthetic: the B-52's pioneered the cute girl/annoying boy vocal style (later perfected by the Sugarcubes) which, with their atomic-age bouffants, only distracted from some rich Brill Building-spun songcraft ('Give Me Back My Man', 'Roam', 'Song for a Future Generation'); from Akron, Ohio, Devo wore flowerpots on their heads and made Talking Heads seem naturalistic; the Dickies played old TV themes very, very fast. Check the crowd in the video for Blondie's 'Dreaming' for its high poseur factor and play it alongside the Sex Pistols' Huddersfield footage. Spot the difference. Punk in the US copped the anti-Establishment attitude of Britain while missing its situationist liberation. In June '77, with 'God Save the Queen' still in the chart, Mark Perry's Alternative TV were already renewing, switching from first-generation punk's two-chord howl: 'If my band don't relate to punks I'm sorry, I apologise, but I'm never going to change. I'm into Zappa and Can and jazz.'

Punk affected America very differently from the way it affected Britain. Again, the size of the country meant there was no obvious hub, and there was no Sex Pistols equivalent. It was niche and didn't threaten the charts, let alone the government. Things moved at a snail's pace.

---

* In 1990 Milli Vanilli's producer Frank Farian told reporters that front men Rob Pilatus and Fab Morvan didn't sing on the records. The media attention meant Milli Vanilli's Grammy was withdrawn, their career was over, and the shamed Pilatus turned to crime and drugs. He died of a suspected overdose in a hotel room on the eve of a comeback tour in 1998.

America took the speed, the shouting, the DIY aesthetic of UK punk, and burrowed deep, pared it back until, years and years later, it came up with something uniquely American called hardcore, by which time most British observers had long since turned away.

Post-punk New York was all-embracing, and altogether different from the rest of America. It also had a head start; it was as if post-punk happened there *before* punk – prior to the Sex Pistols swearing at Bill Grundy, Blondie, Patti Smith and Talking Heads had created sounds that would inform the music of the late seventies and early eighties. Blondie's 'Heart of Glass' – a number-one single – was the beacon pointing to a way forward from two-chord Ramones punk. On the west coast, and in the Midwest, disco may have sucked, but not in NYC. Instead, as it faltered in the 1979 mainstream, disco was absorbed into a more intriguing dance-driven, post-punk noise. Beyond Blondie it may have had little Top 40 sway, but it was a crucial step forward. New York label Ze released a compilation called *Mutant Disco*, which was a succinct description of New York's vision for pop life after punk. With Reagan in control in America and Thatcher in Britain, it felt like any minority needed all the help it could get to survive the new decade.

ESG – or Emerald, Sapphire and Gold – never cut a 'Heart of Glass'-size hit but were the quintessence of New York in 1980. From the South Bronx, they were four sisters called Scroggins, of Afro-American/Cherokee/Irish descent. ESG covered all racial and sonic bases with a tight, super-minimal, super-rhythmic pop (two-note basslines, one-note guitar solos, cowbells all over the shop); they supported the Clash, played the last night at the Paradise Garage and were produced by a visiting Martin Hannett. 'You're No Good' applied Hannett's space shuttle-cum-grain silo deep, deep sound to a haunted rewrite of the Supremes' 'Where Did Our Love Go'. It was quite astonishing, an *NME* Single of the Week. But the Scroggins girls were too sweet, and loved their mom too much, to move out of the Bronx – 'All we want to do if we make a lot of money is buy her a house. That's all. And some furniture to put in it.' They continued to play live, their B-side 'Moody' became a second national anthem in New York clubs, and they got sampled to death, but

ESG would stay a New York secret for another decade and a half.*

Ze Records was a more self-conscious link between CBGB and Studio 54, and fancied itself as channelling Andy Warhol's Factory to boot. Its offices were above Carnegie Hall. If Joe DiMaggio had been the doorman and Woody Allen their analyst it couldn't have been more New York. Ze's founder was the heir to the Mothercare fortune, a Jewish Iraqi called Michael Zilkha, who was beetle-browed and wore a moneyed smile. He'd been to Westminster School and then Oxford, where he switched from economics to French because he wanted to read Balzac in its original form. Zilkha put his entire inheritance into Ze and trusted his instincts. 'The only stipulation I make is that the rhythm should go boom-chuck and there should be black vocalists on the record,' he said, and everything about Ze bore his stamp. It was witty without being smart-arsed, colourful without being lurid. Avant electro mambo. And eventually, after three years of consistent flops,† Ze got big with Kid Creole and the Coconuts' *Tropical Gangsters*.

'I don't give a damn about having the hippest record label in the world,' declared Zilkha, 'I'd much rather have the hits.' August 'Kid Creole' Darnell wore zoot suits, his backing singers wore bunches of fruit, and *Tropical Gangsters* couldn't have been timed better for a new-pop UK audience.‡ 'Stool Pigeon' sounded like a herd of elephants (one ridden by Carmen Miranda) storming down Broadway; 'Annie, I'm Not Your Daddy' was like 'Billie Jean' retold by Lenny Bruce ('See, if I was in your blood then you wouldn't be so ugly'); 'I'm a Wonderful Thing'

---

* Among the acts who have sampled ESG's tiny catalogue are Public Enemy, Ice-T, Marley Marl, LL Cool J, Ice Cube, Miles Davis, Tricky, DJ Shadow, the Beastie Boys, Q-Tip, TLC, the Wu-Tang Clan, Ja Rule, Notorious BIG and Tupac Shakur.

† These include Cristina's beautifully bleak festive single 'Things Fall Apart', which failed to chart in spite of heavy play on late-night Radio 1. At least it now receives annual spins at the most fun Christmas parties. Gorgeous and dry-humoured, with a poker-faced delivery, Cristina deserved to become famous. Husband Zilkha was possibly less than keen for this happen, and was happy for her to remain a cult singer.

‡ The group were formed from the remnants of Dr Buzzard's Original Savannah Band, who had peddled a similar blend of zoot-suit swing and high-life disco for some years – check the sublime and self-descriptive 'Sunshower'.

had Darnell as superlover, clawing and slapping his way through his little red book. All three were UK Top 10 hits in '82, though they meant
zip in America. Darnell was sweetly relaxed. 'People in America would
say, "What did you do to get that sort of coverage?" I just said, "I put
out some crazy music and it found a following."' No fool, he moved to
England in the mid-eighties and has stayed here ever since.

With hindsight, you can draw a line from seventies classic rock,
through the more knowing college rock of the eighties and on to grunge.
You can also draw one that goes from disco through electro and on to
house and techno. Parallel lines. The only point at which they cross is in
post-punk, and Blondie were the apogee of this cross-pollination.

From the misty, water-coloured memories of people old enough to
remember, you could get the impression that every edition of *Top of
the Pops* from 1978 was chock full of wonderful post-punk weirdness
and guns-a-blazing disco delights. The reality, at least in February '78,
was ELO's Beatle pastiche 'Mr Blue Sky', the Brotherhood of Man's
own-brand Abba, and a bunch of pub-rockers called Yellow Dog singing down a telephone in a faux-Jamaican accent. Glamour was virtually
non-existent. Then Blondie appeared and it was immediately clear what
pop had been missing.

Blondie looked like a gang, self-contained and self-assured. Most
importantly, the gang was led by a girl, an exotic blonde. There were
tough-girl precursors: the Shangri-Las, who had been mismanaged so
badly they lost the right to use their own name; the Runaways, pup-
peteered by svengali Kim Fowley; and Suzi Quatro, who had the leather
and the look, but it always seemed like the band were her minders.
Debbie Harry, it was quite apparent, was the leader of this gang. The
song Blondie played on *Top of the Pops* in February '78 was a piece of late
doo-wop fluff called 'Denis', originally a US Top 10 hit for Randy and
the Rainbows fourteen years earlier. They made it hard and shiny, and
it went to number two in Britain. They reappeared on our screens a few
weeks later with '(I'm Always Touched by Your) Presence, Dear', a love
song to a kid with ESP, and upped the exotic stakes. A few months later
they released an LP called *Parallel Lines* and Debbie Harry became the
biggest pop star in the world. It had been that quick and easy.

Harry had been born some thirty years earlier and was adopted, never knowing her real parents but always believing her mother was Marilyn Monroe. Prior to Blondie, she'd already gone through several lifetimes of experiences: a high-school cheerleader, she moved to downtown New York after leaving school and waited in cafes, then became a Playboy Bunny, made an LP with a group called the Wind in the Willows (imagine a hippie Mamas and Papas), got into heroin, got into yoga, and by 1972 was teaching exercises in a health spa.

She heard about a girl group called Pure Garbage and became obsessed with the idea of them before she'd heard a note of their music; when they broke up, Debbie formed a new group, the Stilettos, with two ex-members. As a waitress at Max's Kansas City she'd hung around with Warhol superstars – now Debbie was partying with the New York Dolls and very much becoming a face on the New York underground scene. The Stilettos were True Confessions trash, tough-girl pop in the Shangri-Las tradition. By the time Chris Stein saw them at the Hobury Tavern in 1974, where the stage was a pool table with its legs sawn off, Debbie was already writing quality songs like 'In the Flesh'.

Stein, a twenty-one-year-old guitarist who'd been in groups since the mid-sixties, hit it off with Harry well enough to join the Stilettos. Now things began to move. Stein and Harry split the group, put an ad in the *Village Voice* that read 'Freaky energy rock drummer wanted' and got Clem Burke, an Anglophile and Rodney Bewes lookalike with a Keith Moon fixation. He had freak energy to spare. They wanted a pianist but ended up with Jimmy Destri and his Farfisa organ, which, it turned out, became entirely essential to the Blondie sound. Gary Valentine became the bassist because he'd written a couple of great songs (one of which was 'Presence, Dear'), and that was reason enough.

'It's not cheap retrospection. We're just living the dreams we had,' said Destri in '76. Blondie hooked up with producer Richard Gottehrer, who had already been behind some of pop's most enduring songs – the McCoys' 'Hang On Sloopy', the Angels' 'My Boyfriend's Back' – and soon he was guiding Debbie's gang through an LP of locker-room put-downs ('Rip Her to Shreds'), 'Be My Baby' drum rolls ('X Offender') and pinched news headlines ('Youth Nabbed as Sniper'). Teen dreams: brazen, stylish, humorous and sexy. Lester Bangs described Blondie as 'unself-conscious fun . . . what rock 'n' roll has always stood for'. In *ZigZag*, Kris Needs said they were 'all the great American pop styles rolled into one, but fuelled with the energy of the super soaraway seventies'.

When they had first arrived in Britain in 1977, Blondie were supporting press darlings Television. It was a marriage of convenience. Journalists frothed at the mouth for Television's intellectualism and Tom Verlaine's new guitar moves, but Blondie – insisting they were merely a pop group – were sidelined. In the *NME*, Tony Parsons was a dissenting voice when he said 'seeing Blondie was like hanging around an amusement arcade while Television made you feel like you were sitting in church'. Always a group to namecheck the 1910 Fruitgum Company ahead of Ray Charles, Blondie loved to throw curve balls, and peppered their pudding with a healthy Warhol-babies cynicism.

Blondie's cute masterstroke on *Parallel Lines* was to use producer Mike Chapman, until that point best known in Britain for writing glam classics like 'Block Buster', 'Can the Can' and 'Tiger Feet', and the marriage of band and producer was one of pop's finest. 'I Know But I Don't Know' was as arch as they ever got, 'Sunday Girl' as classical and 'Heart of Glass' as zeitgeist. In a move of definitive postmodernism, the group named the latter (which had been kicking around since 1975 as 'Disco Song') after a Werner Herzog film none of them had seen. It blended their NYC punk stance with sleek sequenced disco at a time when the two forms were still seen to be diametrically opposed; they had the confidence to toy and taunt with a mirrorball in the video, Destri checking his hair in its reflection. 'Heart of Glass' became their first UK number one. While their next LP, *Eat to the Beat*, released in '79, was in many ways a paler retread of *Parallel Lines*, it did include their most beautiful song, 'Union City Blue'. Chapman's production was impossibly loud and the song was epically evocative ('Skylines, passion, union city blue'), a movie of the mind, part noir and part rooftop party. The unusually structured 'Atomic' was another number-one single: it had no verse. Entirely made up of bridge and chorus – tension and release, tension and release – it was almost pornographic, the Chris and Debbie show.

By 1980 Blondie were international pop stars and could do pretty much anything that took their fancy, making film cameos (*Roadie*, *Union City* and *American Gigolo*), working with Giorgio Moroder ('Call Me', their biggest US hit and only transatlantic number one) and covering old rocksteady tunes (the Paragons' 'The Tide Is High', their fifth and final UK number one). Their wildest diversion was 'Rapture', which moved from a distinctly cinematic first half into a rap that sounded like a Sugarhill Gang remake of 'Monster Mash'. It worked, but the accompanying LP *Autoamerican* was a cultural grab bag that lacked focus and featured a surfeit of saxophones – always a telltale sign. Blondie's decline was swift. *The Hunter*, from 1982, was dire beyond belief, a collection of novelty songs the B-52's would have thought twice about. It sold nothing and Blondie, soon after, were no more.

While they are a constant play on oldies radio and at wedding receptions, Blondie's place in the rock-history books has never been that secure. There are a number of reasons: the hits have been repackaged and even remixed (on the embarrassing *Once More into the Bleach*) so often that it isn't until you hear such obscure but stellar LP tracks as *Eat to the Beat*'s 'Shayla' that you realise how special the records still sound. Secondly, Debbie Harry's solo career was so incomprehensible – working with minor leaguers like the J. Geils Band and the Thompson Twins, and nobody interesting since Chic in 1982 – that it has watered down the relevance of Blondie, especially when record companies continually suggest that Debbie Harry *was* Blondie.

But largely, you suspect, it's down to the fact that some rock writers still can't accept that a cracking blonde was capable of writing some of the best pop songs of the era; they await a *Mojo* retrospective.* The same chroniclers have no such problem lauding the likes of Janis Joplin or Patti Smith, which suggests that if Debbie Harry had looked like a crow then Blondie would be accepted as the finest group of their generation, shapeshifting, forward-looking and endlessly melodic – 'shake and finger pop', as *Smash Hits* dubbed them.

---

* They were inducted into the Rock 'n' Roll Hall of Fame in 2006, but that was still four years after their peers Tom Petty and the Heartbreakers, Talking Heads and the Ramones.

Debbie Harry's grin may have won over men and women alike but it's her music, her sassiness and her obvious strength that made her a lasting influence. Madonna, Courtney Love and the Spice Girls drew deep from Blondie's well. Classic art-school dropouts, they were true pop fans who became true pop stars without sacrificing their true pop ideals. It was quite a feat.

Blondie and Ze provided a rare commercial harbour between the chaos of punk and disco's aftermath and the nascent electro and freestyle sounds of 1983/84. Elsewhere, in parts of the country where disco would remain a cuss word until the twenty-first century, UK punk's trad guitar/ bass/drums set-up was used to find a more conventional path forward.

* * *

Early California punk wasn't just anti-longhair and anti-Eagles – the scene's first single was the Weirdos' nihilistic 'Destroy All Music'. Based around Hollywood's Masque club, other groups soon rose up – the Dils, X, and Darby Crash's Germs, who included a doll-faced drummer called Dottie Danger. All of them played fast, energetic, British-inspired punk and read the imported *NME*. Some of the records weren't bad at all, a garnish to London's '77 red meat, but when John Lydon had said 'I want more bands like us,' this probably wasn't what he had in mind. By 1981, when the Dead Kennedys breached the UK Top 40 with 'Too Drunk to Fuck', Joy Division had been and gone, and New Order were progressing from post-punk to shimmering proto-house. Two-chord punk with go-faster stripes seemed as relevant to pop's present as trad jazz.

Still, some American punk groups kept the faith, reducing their straitjacketed Pistols sound to something that became more muscular, faster still, and this was labelled 'hardcore'. After a while, these groups realised they had to build a new value system in place of the one they'd just trashed: hardcore wasn't anti everything, it was pro plenty. Darby Crash had been a punk caricature. Washington DC's Black Flag and Minor Threat were far more interesting, an inversion of macho rock etiquette; they had a credo of self-will, discipline and clean living, and the musical accompaniment was intense and very loud.

'It's so funny reading interviews with English punk bands,' Black Flag's Henry Rollins told the *NME* in 1982, 'because they're literally disgusted with American bands. They don't dress right, they don't sing about anarchy, nuclear war, or the dole. Or they're rich white kids, their hair is long, and they're wearing sneakers instead of combat boots.' Hardcore gigs had no fancy lights, no theatrics, just musicians hunched over their instruments and keen focus. No one spoke, smoked, drank or interacted. Coming from Washington DC's 'straight edge' scene (no drugs or alcohol), Rollins was an ex-Häagen-Dazs manager and compulsive skateboarder when he met Black Flag in New York. 'I hope what I'm giving is not a macho thing, like David Lee Roth, like "come and get it girls" . . . What I'm trying to get across to people, a girl could do the same thing. It's just a physical and emotional release of energy – it's an intensity. I put myself on the line.' This obsession with self-analysis and primal-scream pop therapy found fewer supporters in the UK. 'I don't understand why American music has to be so military and aggressive,' said Brett Anderson a few years later. 'Look at Henry Rollins; he's like a sergeant major or something.'

Hardcore was no fun at all. But in the super-commercialised early eighties it was easy to see why a section of pop fans looked to the rubicund, unsmiling figure of Black Flag's Rollins, and to Big Black's pale-faced leader Steve Albini. Here are the roots of emo – or emotional hardcore as it was originally known – which would become a chart-topping phenomenon in Britain and America by the early twenty-first century. Unlike Oi! and sundry post-punk British dead ends, hardcore had a manifesto, and if its followers turned twenty and still didn't know what to do with their lives, at least they didn't blindly follow the Sid Vicious school of nihilism.

The Feelies owed nothing to straight edge, or Black Sabbath, or New York mutant disco. Post-punk children of quite another stripe, they did up the top buttons on their polo shirts and couldn't have sounded less intense and emotionally hardcore if they were paid a million dollars. They were from Frank Sinatra's home town of Hoboken, New Jersey, and in 1978 the *Village Voice* hailed them as 'The Best Underground Band in New York'. All this promise and after one album, 1980's *Crazy*

Rhythms, they split – but not before they had left a strong impression on a freshly formed Athens, Georgia, group called REM. Like Subway Sect in Britain, the Feelies understood the more oblique possibilities of punk. Their songs were quite beautifully vague and uncommitted: 'Get a message out to Mary Ann, everything is alright. Get a message out to Mom and Dad, everything is alright.' They had harmonies, layered guitars played with utmost simplicity, sometimes wavering like static on an untuned radio, and underneath were unchanging, trance-inducing drum patterns – essentially they came across like the Monkees playing Television's 'Marquee Moon'.

Meanwhile, the Germs' former drummer Dottie Danger – under her real name of Belinda Carlisle – had formed a new group in LA called the Go-Go's. They started out as rama-lama punk, before signing – like the Feelies – to Stiff Records in Britain, where they spent six months on tour with Madness, picking up on the melodic Jam/Madness/Dexys strain of UK post-punk. Returning home, their first album, 1980's *Beauty and the Beat*, included the waterfall-fresh singles 'Our Lips Are Sealed' (US no. 20 '81) and 'We Got the Beat' (US no. 2 '81). It became the first US number-one album to be written and performed by an all-female band. A year later they were dressed as surfing cheerleaders on the cover of *Vacation*. Here was another way beyond post-punk's impasse. Ze, Blondie, the Feelies, the Go-Go's – they all showed that ugliness really wasn't necessary.

THIS IS TOMORROW: KRAFTWERK
AND ELECTROPOP

Our reality is an electronic reality.
Chris Petit, *Radio On*, 1979

Since the beginning of modern pop, New York and London had taken it
in turns to set the agenda. In the seventies California had tried to forci-
bly suck all the creativity out of both, as well as from renegade outposts
like Detroit and New Orleans, and shift the balance of power onto the
west coast. Pockets of resistance had remained. Liverpool. Stockholm.
Düsseldorf.

There was an unlikely romance to Düsseldorf in the 1970s. Its football team, with the almost Romany name Fortuna Düsseldorf, laid claim to the little obvious glamour the city offered. But in its sleek, blank, slightly detached post-war West German way, this city – the most typical in a forbidding, divided country caught up in the midst of a terrorist campaign – held a compelling attraction. Its very blankness, an empty canvas, inspired a type of music no one in New York or London or California had come close to realising. Düsseldorf was the home of Kraftwerk.

The first electronic hit in the UK had been Frank Chacksfield's 'Little Red Monkey' (no. 12 '53), which featured the clavioline of Jack Jordan in place of Chacksfield's usual lush string sound. High-pitched, whining and eerie, more like a giant pissed-off wasp than a red monkey, it must have cut through the airwaves in 1953 like a ray gun through a pea-souper. Quickly forgotten, 'Little Red Monkey' lacked the stickability of Britain's single most important piece of electronic music, the theme tune for the children's TV series *Doctor Who*. Ron Grainer's melody was recorded by an anonymous collection of musicians and technicians in a BBC Maida Vale studio known as the Radiophonic Workshop.* Beamed out with suitably cosmic visuals to a pre-teen audience from 1963 onwards, it's safe to say this thirty-second burst of electronica was the basis for a revolution that started at the turn of the eighties.

There would be other fleeting diversions into electronic music during the sixties – Max Crook's musitron on Del Shannon's 'Runaway' and the clavioline on the Tornados' 'Telstar' came before it, Moog squiggles by Micky Dolenz on a couple of '67 Monkees tunes, and the Beatles' squelchy noises on *Abbey Road* came soon afterwards – but the *Doctor Who* theme remains arguably the most influential electronic record ever made.

In these early electronic experiments you could detect the sound of progress and optimism. Electronic pop could have been the sound of the

---

* They remained anonymous by BBC diktat. This could have been a socialist show of solidarity, but was more likely imposed to stop independent minds getting ideas above their station. The mental challenges of running their own electronic playground while knowing they had to remain in complete obscurity were enough to drive two of its brightest minds – Delia Derbyshire and John Baker – to drink and an early grave.

space age, if only someone had tried to streamline it by taking out the rock affectations and leaving a pure electronic heartbeat. In 1972 one group scalped the guitars, torched the drumkit and left the Moog to ride alone, not just placing it centre stage but making it the heart of their sound, the reason for their existence. The name of the group? Chicory Tip.

OK, so 'Son of My Father' (UK no. 1 '72) lacked gravitas. It was still the first international hit written and produced by Giorgio Moroder. I was seven years old in 1972 and its newness sounded strange and important. Chicory Tip didn't write their own songs, looked slightly embarrassed to be electro-bubblegum pioneers, were deemed a novelty act and only managed a couple more Moog-powered Top 20 hits. Kraftwerk, on the other hand, were the biggest rupture in pop since 1955. In 1975 'Autobahn' delicately made everything else look try-hard or plain dull.

How did Kraftwerk differ from the synth pioneers before them? There were no furrowed brows, as you had with Silver Apples' repetitive oscillations or Tangerine Dream's sleepy soundscapes; no attempt to mimic existing instrumentation like Walter Carlos and his million-selling *Switched On Bach*; no squelchy camp like Hot Butter (whose instrumental 'Popcorn' was a US number one in '72) or Chicory Tip. Kraftwerk made synthesizers sound effortless, and – crucially – they made them seem part of our world. Their power was the reversal of expectation; they humanised synthesizers through their intensity of melody and tone. 'We are not into morality, but realism. We're not trying to create some kind of safe, "Baby I love you" kind of atmosphere, but to put some realism into it,' Ralf Hütter told *Interview* magazine in 1977. They were romantic realists, though, and described 'Autobahn' as the sound of cars singing. Kraftwerk sparkled where forebears frowned. Unlike Walter Carlos, they didn't pretend that synthesizers would replace entire orchestras or could be programmed to write future symphonies. They already sounded utopian. The perfection of the future was already here with 'Autobahn', a UK number-eleven hit in 1975, pop's most fallow year. The effect of 'Autobahn' on David Bowie was enormous; his influence on the electric eighties was, in turn, exponential.

Kraftwerk were metric where progressive rock had been indecipherably imperial – pounds, shillings and pence, farthings, guineas, emersons, lakes and palmers. English in the most clotted way. 'They sound so detached,' reckoned a bemused *NME* in '76, 'the kind of guys who could blow up the planet just to hear the noise it made.'* Their image was robotic, which helped to confirm their detractors' worst fears about cold, mechanical, efficient German electronic music, yet 1977 album *Trans-Europe Express* was an excursion across a trashed, transforming continent that conveyed hope, sympathy and unity just thirty years after the war. The music and the artwork were geometrical – machine music, machine art, from the pulse waves of their (UK only) debut album sleeve to the constructivist red/black/white of 1978's *The Man-Machine*.

Wasn't a constructivist sleeve rather the opposite of futuristic? Yes, because in spite of their clear, far-sighted construction, Kraftwerk's songs were frequently looking back to Germany's past, Europe's past. On the insert for 1975's *Radioactivity* they dressed not at all like robots, but like members of a thirties swing band in front of a pointedly vintage but super-modern microphone. Kraftwerk were political, thoughtful, at a time when most British and American music, disco aside, was decidedly inward-looking. Few groups have set themselves so far apart from pop and yet done so much for it. And they drove on, barely releasing anything new but sounding like the sound of *now*, right through the eighties and into the techno explosion.

'Autobahn' was Kraftwerk's only UK Top 40 hit in the seventies. 'Are "Friends" Electric' by Tubeway Army spent a month at number one in the spring of 1979.

Tubeway Army were fronted and created by a shy boy with bad skin and a receding hairline called Gary Webb. Heavily leaning on David Bowie's impassive turn as Mr Newton in *The Man Who Fell to Earth*,

---

* More suspicious yet was Britain's Musicians' Union. By 1976 it had put an end to miming on *Top of the Pops* as it claimed it put real, dues-paying players out of business. An MU representative, who bands nicknamed Dr Death, insisted that every *TOTP* guest re-recorded their single or played it live on the show with session players – the results were risible and viewing figures slid. But even more than miming, the MU hated synthesizers. Synthesizers broke the laws of labour: all you had to do was wave a hand, press a button, and out came a sparkling fresh fountain of sound. The machine did all the work for you. In the mid-seventies many saw synthesizers as decadent.

Webb became Gary Numan, filling in his pockmarks with chalk-white powder and dyeing his thinning hair jet black. Tubeway Army had already recorded a middling new-wave album in 1978 when, while working one day in the studio, Numan found a Korg synthesizer. He pressed a key; the volume and frequency made the whole room shake. Numan decided to utilise this new machinery at once.

A short sleevenote on the Japanese release of 'Cars', the first single under Numan's own name, poetically explained his future-shock appeal: 'he is a man who escaped from a black hole, now heading for an endless journey'. Jon Savage saw him in a lineage that stretched beyond Kraftwerk, beyond Bowie, back to 'the ice cream fiction' of the Tornados' 'Telstar'. 'Numan's success', he wrote in *Melody Maker* just after 'Cars' gave him a second number one, 'has shown that, in pop, plagiarism doesn't matter: what does is being on the ball.' On stage Numan created theatre, robots around him, dressed in alien uniform, and he acted out freeze-frame pop-star poses. You could call it proto-voguing; you could also, quite easily, imagine him pulling the same poses in front of his bedroom mirror. He was a very suburban extraterrestrial.

In spite of the dystopian settings in his songs, Gary Numan turned out not to be cold at all. He was childlike, happy to explain his odd private world to *Smash Hits*: 'On stage, the robots are pyramid-shaped . . . you say "robot" and people think of something that does this [gesticulates mechanically] and clanks about, and really that's the most unpractical shape you can think of because it's so unstable. It keeps falling over all the time.'

Without a frame of reference for an electronic-music poster boy, the press found him easy to kick, constantly comparing him unfavourably to Bowie. The *NME* called him 'the slug who sold the world'. Bowie himself was deeply suspicious, and had Numan thrown out of a TV studio when he tried to sneak in and watch his hero rehearsing. Antipathy among rock fans was just as extreme: 'I mean, I went to New Zealand once, got off the plane and the first thing I saw, written on the side of a building, was "Numan, Fuck Off". I thought, twelve thousand miles for this!' Yet he bossed the UK charts in 1979, scoring two number-one singles, two number-one albums, and at one point placing three albums in the

Top 20. The reflective *Telekon*, with its synths given atmospheric support by piano and viola, became one of the least commercial UK number-one albums ever in 1980; after this Numan briefly retired, became better known for crashing planes and voting Tory than for his music, and subsided into cult status before a considerable reappraisal in the nineties. 'I think,' he said modestly, 'possibly to a lot of people, I'm a symbol of something new.' In Detroit and the Bronx he really was. As for his strangely personalised sci-fi world, take a look at some of his song titles – 'Me! I Disconnect from You', 'My Dying Machine', 'I Dream of Wires'. They predict the twenty-first-century condition uncomfortably well.

Düsseldorf fitted Kraftwerk like a glove. Conversely, no group in history has been as stigmatised by their home town as Depeche Mode. From Basildon, Essex, their first few singles in 1981 – 'Dreaming of Me', 'New Life' (UK no. 11), 'Just Can't Get Enough' (UK no. 8) – positioned them as a pre-school Kraftwerk. They looked incredibly young, and their music sounded like the 1960s artists' sketches of Basildon New Town come to life – the mums with their bright new pushchairs on gum-free pavements, the clean modernist lines of brand-new hospitals and unthumbed libraries. Their spotlessly clean but historically vacant home town led the British music press to regard them as a novelty; they wouldn't take them seriously for years. Kraftwerk would have wept tears, real tears, to have come from a town so antiseptic. Besides, there has to be true, deep melancholy in a brave new world built, as if over a graveyard, on the shanty plotland settlements of Essex.

Vince Clarke, with hair like a downy duckling, wrote pretty much everything on their debut album *Speak & Spell*, including the gurgling baby synth hook on 'Just Can't Get Enough', but within a year he left, first forming Yazoo, then, in 1985, Erasure, who came across like secondary-school Pet Shop Boys underlings and racked up seventeen Top 10 hits. As close to instant disposable pop as anyone has ever got, it was possible to acquire a bunch of Erasure singles without ever being close to any of them; they were entirely confectionery.

The rump of Depeche Mode, left stranded on an Essex plateau by their sole songwriter, decided to carry on. Dave Gahan's voice grew deeper and more disturbing; curly-topped Martin Gore's wardrobe switched from frilled white smocks to fetish wear. It soon became apparent that they weren't a confection at all, unless you consider leather thongs, smack, religious intolerance and sadistic synth crunch suitable for children. Outside the UK, where no one knew or cared about Basildon and thought it was probably a becastled fiefdom run by Count Dave Gahan, they became one of the half-dozen biggest groups in the world, certainly the biggest synth act; they walked a line between heavy electronica and a strain of goth metal which had yet to be invented.

Having influenced a generation of UK chart pop – Bowie, Numan, Depeche Mode, the Human League, Orchestral Manoeuvres in the Dark – Kraftwerk got their due, or benediction, when 'The Model' became a surprise UK number one early in 1982. It was a melancholy examination of the emotional disconnect of modern communication – it's not until the last verse that you realise the singer is telling us about someone he's never even met.

Rather ironically, by the time 'The Model' reached number one the sound of Düsseldorf was beginning to curl a little round the edges, and after the 'Tour de France' single a year later Kraftwerk were clearly playing catch-up with their own progeny. But 1982 was also the year when their influence made itself most keenly felt, with the arrival of Afrika Bambaataa's 'Planet Rock', Arthur Baker's electro-dub production on Rockers Revenge's 'Walking on Sunshine', and the paradigm shift of electro. 'Planet Rock' in particular took *Trans-Europe Express*'s foundation stone and turned it into a whole plug-in city. As 'The Model' hit number one, the Human League's 1978 single 'Being Boiled', a strange and disturbing noise inhabiting its own half life,* belatedly reached the UK Top 10, eventually peaking at number six; just above it at number four was OMD's 'Maid of Orleans', with an atonal thirty-second intro that was pure Radiophonic experimentation. The electronic revolution had been postponed for long enough.

---

* It's unlikely that any other Top 10 hit in the UK or US opens with the final words – Gary Gilmore's 'OK, ready, let's do it' – of a man about to be killed in the electric chair.

ADVENTURES ON THE WHEELS
OF STEEL: EARLY RAP

If black musicians are getting their inspiration from Kraftwerk,
that shows how low things have sunk.
    DJ Chris Hill, *NME*, Christmas 1983

Tom Silverman was a doo-wop fan, a disco nut, and a record collector
from way back. He used to get his vinyl fix at a shop called Downstairs
Records on 42nd Street. Without blinking, he'd pass the triple-X peep
shows, the card sharps scamming tourists, the pimps passing out flyers
and the junkies inside dumpsters. The shop was a small box-like space:

the counter was to the left, and on a wall to the right you could leave messages and calling cards. It had an intense atmosphere – they never let you listen to anything. One day in 1981 Silverman was surprised to find a new room at Downstairs. The size of a cupboard, it was called the B-boy Room. Records on the wall at ten dollars a pop included the Eagles' 'The Long Run', the Incredible Bongo Band's 'Apache' and a jazz album by Bob James. The kids in the room, all black, all very young, were not only buying these bargain-bin regulars at inflated prices, they were buying *two* copies of each. Silverman was intrigued. He asked one of the kids where the hell they'd heard such an exotic blend of sounds. 'Oh, there's this guy in the Bronx called Bambaataa.'

Sometimes, looking back on pop, you come across stories which seem chronologically distant but turn out to be concurrent. Star session musicians Charlie McCoy and Kenny Buttrey worked on Bob Dylan's *Blonde on Blonde* in 1966; their next job, the very next week, was playing on the soundtrack to Elvis Presley's *Harum Scarum*, an Arabic adventure story that included songs like 'Go East, Young Man' and 'Shake That Tambourine'. McCoy and Buttrey must have felt as if they had jumped back two decades. Yet there is no greater disconnect in the story of modern pop than that between late-seventies pop – Smokie, the Boomtown Rats, *Grease* – and the birth of hip hop. Its evolution, over several years, occurred in solitude in one of pop's twin capitals.

Hip hop was bricolage. It was about making music from found sounds, new pop from old, with nothing but a stack of vinyl, two turntables and a microphone. The DJ, for the first time, wasn't just the trendsetter but the creator of the music. Scratching – dragging the needle back and forth in time to the beat, the invention of New York DJ Grand Wizard Theodore – took tiny splinters of sound from records, melodic or just rhythmic; it was a primitive precursor to sampling. You didn't need a guitar. You didn't even need the three chords Mark Perry gave you on the cover of *Sniffin' Glue*.

Club- and turntable-based, hip hop was a relative of disco, and grew up in tandem, yet it remained entirely underground, unknown outside a few square miles of New York, and only broke cover when disco was brought to its knees by the Knack and irate baseball fans. Unlike disco it wasn't sexy, certainly not romantic, and definitely not sexually ambiguous. Disco had revelled in anonymity – the dancers were the stars; hip hop reintroduced the cult of personality associated with early-seventies rock. Grandmaster Flash even DJ'd with his feet like a Technics Hendrix. And it was more self-referential than any modern pop since first-wave rock 'n' roll.

Hip hop can trace its history back to one man. Clive Campbell was a Jamaican who moved to the Bronx as a kid in the late sixties and missed the sound systems and yard parties, so he decided to throw them in his new neighbourhood. He first caused a sensation at his sister's birthday party at a hall in the Bronx in 1973 by using two turntables to mix records together over a sound system that may have been standard in Kingston but made people's bowels quake in the Bronx. Pretty soon, he discovered that kids danced especially fiercely, with moves based on contemporary kung fu movies and James Brown's athleticism, to short bursts of certain records, the parts that were entirely rhythmic. So he got two copies of these records, placed one on each deck and could then extend these breaks indefinitely. It was pretty primitive – Campbell dropped the needle onto the record without attempting to mix them à la Tom Moulton – but he soon became the only fun in town. The dancers tagged themselves 'break boys', or b-boys; Campbell became DJ Kool Herc, and over old James Brown 45s and his signature tune, the Incredible Bongo Band's cover of the Shadows' 'Apache', Herc started delivering spoken raps inspired by the Jamaican toasters he knew from his home town.

One of his greatest admirers was an ex-Black Spades gang member called Afrika Bambaataa. At the turn of the seventies the South Bronx – cut off from even the rest of the borough by the construction of the Cross Bronx Expressway in the sixties – had become a no-go area, run by rival gangs who based their image on Hell's Angels, the dirtier looking the better. There was no more street-corner doo wop in the Bronx of 1970. Bambaataa had watched the film *Zulu* when he was a kid, and was deeply impressed. Instead of seeing Michael Caine as the hero, he sided with the Africans fighting for their freedom against the British colonialists. He saw his destiny at a Kool Herc party. Pretty soon he became

a rival DJ, discovering his own breaks in the strangest places – Grand
Funk Railroad, the Monkees, Bob James – and he interspersed them
with Malcolm X speeches and his own philosophy, eclipsing his mentor.
In 1975 he organised a landmark 'free jam' to break up the Bronx turf
wars – 'Leave your colours at home!' This was the beginning of his own
Zulu Nation, and the motto was 'Peace, love, unity, and having fun'.
It worked. In no time he had an expanding gang of MCs, DJs, graffiti
writers, b-boys, b-girls, all decked out in natty satin, bright colours, an
alternative for the Bronx youth to the Mad Max decimation of the gangs.

Herc was the godfather, and Bambaataa provided the social glue.
The third crucial name in early hip hop is Joseph Saddler, a proper little scientist who grew up in a house full of girls in Fort Apache, west
of Bambaataa's manor. Instead of being involved in the pitched battles
outside his window, Saddler used to sneak around the rubble, raiding
abandoned cars for radios, apartments for hairdryers – anything that
plugged into the wall, anything he could try and fix with a screwdriver
and a soldering iron. His dad had a huge record collection, which little
Joseph was allowed to look at but never, ever touch. Forbidden fruit.
He became obsessed with vinyl, stayed in his room for months mastering the art of DJing, building his kit, using breaks and other super-
short snatches of songs, actively manipulating the records he spun to
create something brand-new. And when he had a seamless set, he played
out for the first time, expecting instant worship. So sure of his greatness was Joseph that he christened himself Grandmaster Flash. But no
one danced, no one cheered; he got nothing but blank stares. He went
home and cried for a week. Like Joe Meek's 'I Hear a New World' and
Tom Moulton's Fire Island mix before, nobody had known what to
make of it. When he spun again, it was with help from local rapper
Robert 'Cowboy' Wiggins; soon the Glover brothers – Melle Mel and
Kidd Creole (not the Ze Records singer) – were on board, and within
weeks the freshly named Furious Five accompanied Flash at every party
he played, to wild acclaim. Later, *Life* magazine would call him 'the
Toscanini of the turntables'.

In 1977 hip hop was still an incredibly localised scene, barely even breaking into Brooklyn and Queens, let alone Manhattan. Herc, Bambaataa

and Flash largely had the Bronx sewn up until a city-wide power cut that summer; there was widespread looting, and DJ supply stores were among the most heavily ransacked. Within weeks there were enough new DJs in the Bronx to make the scene actively competitive – who could throw the best party? Who could get the most people to throw their hands in the air and wave them like they just don't care? Using electricity tapped from street lamps, the DJ battles echoed the sixties 'battle of the bands' contests that had sprung up across the States in the wake of the Beatles and the astonishing boom in sales of electric guitars. It was a young and totally unauthorised scene. The DJ battles were in parks; there were no police, no adults. It was super-competitive.

The question is, how did these raw, vital dance dens stay off pop's radar for so many years? For one thing, no outsiders ventured into the Bronx in the mid-seventies; it was in such a state of burnt-out desolation that it was used as a 1945 Berlin movie set. Secondly, there were no records. As far as hip hop's instigators were concerned they were playing other people's records, for several hours, and freestyling over the top of them. How do you turn that into your own piece of vinyl? Enter Sylvia Robinson. A pop Zelig, she had first scored a hit as half of Mickey and Sylvia on the cowbell-led 'Love Is Strange' (US no. 11 '57), one of rock 'n' roll's out-and-out sexiest records. She resurfaced in '69 as the creative force behind a bunch of New Jersey-based soul labels (All Platinum, Stang, Turbo and Vibration), co-writing and producing the Moments' million-seller 'Love on a Two-Way Street' in 1970 (US no. 3). By 1973 she was purring her way through 'Pillow Talk' like a proto-disco Eartha Kitt, and scoring a soft-soul hit in Britain (no. 12) and America (no. 3). A few lean years left her on the verge of bankruptcy in 1979, but she gave it one last shot and started the Sugarhill label.

That summer, Robinson was at a party in Harlem, heard some guest rappers with a DJ and knew it was a sound she could sell. The very next week she got session bassist Chip Shearin into the Sugarhill studio and asked him to play the bassline from Chic's 'Good Times' for fifteen minutes straight, with no mistakes. By the end Shearin was sweating bullets. Sylvia told him it would all make sense in the end: 'I've got these kids who are going to talk real fast over it; that's the best way I can describe it.' The Bronx rappers she approached showed no interest, but her son had been chatting to someone who worked in a pizza takeaway and claimed to be a rapper. This is how Wonder Mike ended up as the first rapper ever to commit his verse to vinyl, sounding like a slightly apologetic children's TV presenter as he explained what the hell this new-fangled thing called 'rap' was all about.

Robinson had found two other rappers to make up an amateur trio, unimaginatively tagged the Sugarhill Gang, whose brags made them seem like rather underachieving looters: 'I got a colour TV so I can see the Nicks play basketball!' Still, 'Rapper's Delight' was irresistible, all fifteen minutes of it, and within days of release it had become the best-selling record in New York. In a few weeks it was in the US Top 40, was number three in Britain by Christmas and reached number one in Canada in February 1980.

Sylvia Robinson and the Sugarhill Gang were the Bill Haley and the Comets of hip hop. Almost accidentally, they started a pop revolution. Meanwhile, back in the Bronx, the originators of the sound were outraged, but instead of bitching they got themselves signed up to Sugarhill and made records of their own. Using the house band, most of their singles sounded like KC and the Sunshine Band on the comeback trail. It took Grandmaster Flash to take it up a level with his 'Adventures on the Wheels of Steel'.* If rapping vocals were new to most ears in 1980, this melange of disco (once more Chic's 'Good Times' was the spine), sci-fi ('the official adventures of Flash . . .'), soft rock (a spoken section, sounding a lot like actor Robert Vaughn, taken from the Hellers' 1968 album *Singers . . . Talkers . . . Players . . . Swingers . . . and Doers*), Queen ('Another One Bites the Dust') and Blondie (the Flash-referencing 'Rapture') was a whole new world. No choruses, no

---

* Nobody in Britain had heard of Flash when Debbie Harry name-checked him on 'Rapture' (US no. 1, UK no. 5) at the tail end of 1981. The *NME*'s rave review of 'Wheels of Steel' appeared a whole month after 'Rapture' was a hit – Harry's rap may have lacked for content ('eating cars, eating bars', yadda yadda) after its initial nod to the scene's leading lights but, still, this was an outrageously brave and very cool move. Meanwhile, in Chelsea, her erstwhile rival Patti Smith just carried on quoting Rimbaud's greatest hits, taking no chances on looking uncool.

singing, nothing 'new' at all in fact. Even now, Flash's textures, dextrous scratching and ebb and flow sound thrilling. So daring, so confident, so much fun. In the *NME*, Ian Penman wrote a page-long appreciation of it. The seven-minute, twelve-inch-only single ended with whooping party celebrations, and who could blame Flash? A whole new genre was invented. Those months and years scavenging and soldering paid off in one hit.

Bambaataa, meanwhile, bided his time. 'I don't want to be a star,' he said, 'because stars fall.' So he set himself up to become a legend instead. With rappers the Soulsonic Force – Mr Biggs, Pow Wow, G.L.O.B.E. – he ditched the live Sugarhill sound, and borrowed a synthesizer from keyboard player John Robie and a beatbox from producer Arthur Baker. Inspired by Kraftwerk's *Trans-Europe Express* and the Yellow Magic Orchestra's electro/computer pop, Bambaataa and Baker created 'Planet Rock'. It was eerie and, again, seemed entirely new. On its own it spawned electro, another new modern pop genus. Electro gave American pop a new sense of space, as New York producers mixed dub with Korg and Roland's evolving keyboard and beatbox technology, and created something undeniably futuristic – Bambaataa disciples Planet Patrol and the Jonzun Crew both wore space suits, and it made perfect sense. One of electro's early landmarks was Man Parrish's 'Hip Hop Be Bop (Don't Stop)', a record that featured a colossal bassline, barking dogs and camp, echoing squeals, but no rap at all; somehow it ended up as the record that christened a genre.

Electro bled into soul in the summer of '82. Hip hop aside, b-boys feasted on the pleasures of Evelyn King's 'Love Come Down' (UK no. 7), DJ François Kevorkian's cut-glass production of D Train's 'You're the One for Me' (UK no. 30), and 'Don't Make Me Wait' by the Peech Boys, an outfit assembled by Paradise Garage DJ Larry Levan.

Meanwhile, over in Brooklyn was a record shop, the Music Factory, managed by brothers Dwight and Donnie Calvin. They cut a cover of Eddy Grant's 'Walking on Sunshine' under the name Rockers Revenge. Recorded at Blank studios, like so many Ze hits and almost-hits, it was the Music Factory's number-one best-seller in their own shop. They pressed the records, spun them in the shop and sold them direct to paying customers. Who needed distributors, who needed Tower Records, when you had the hottest record in town?

Like Bambaataa's 'Planet Rock', 'Walking on Sunshine' was produced by Arthur Baker, the man to finally take the sound out of New York and around the world. By the time it reached number four in the UK in the summer of '82 Baker was all over the *NME*, hailed as a new auteur; he was in discussions with Brit funk group Freeez (the resulting single, 'IOU', was a number two the following summer) and the nascent New Order. The South Bronx's isolation, created in the sixties by New York's city planners, rapidly collapsed. Bambaataa organised a European tour with rapper and graffiti artist Rammellzee and Zulu Nation DJ Grand Mixer DST, plus b-boys the Rock Steady Crew and female counterparts the Double Dutch Girls. Hip hop's influence grew apace. With its lean, mechanical sound, its wit and fearless sense of progression, nothing could stop it.

HERE COMES THAT FEELING: NEW POP

We lend enchantment to vulgar material.
  Guillaume Apollinaire

I think it's just taking it back to cabaret – showbiz for showbiz's
sake more than anything.
  Gary Numan

Joy Division seemed like a full stop to post-punk's exhilarating but monochrome and unadorned realism. 'Ian Curtis is dead,' said Orchestral
Manoeuvres in the Dark's Andy McCluskey in 1980, 'and now there's

nothing else to do but dance around his grave.' Curtis's suicide was a
trigger. His death had been a definitive end to an era – things could only
get brighter. It was now or never if the mainstream was to be conquered
by post-punk's philosophies.

The *NME*'s Paul Morley was an architect of new pop. He had championed post-punk, but by the end of 1980, with Joy Division gone,
he wondered out loud where modern pop was heading. Like Andy
McCluskey, he figured the only possible direction was towards 'overground brightness', and in the *NME*'s Christmas 1980 issue he challenged musicians to 'bring life back to the radio, to make the single
count'.* He can't have failed to spot a single called 'Antmusic' by Adam
and the Ants, which had moved up to number seven on the Christmas
chart. Where the Clash had been terrified that *Top of the Pops* would
contaminate them, singer Adam Ant recognised it could amplify his
music and challenge his fans. As Malcolm McLaren had before him,
Adam understood that the formats and possibilities of mainstream
broadcasting, from *Top of the Pops* to *Smash Hits*, were not only available but wide open, and had huge and thrilling expressive potential.
Morley most likely had Adam and the Ants in mind when he declared
that modern pop's new names had 'ambition that is never justified or
considered but that is some grand narcissistic design to grow larger
than life'.

New pop took punk's self-determination and sense of urgency and
married them to values that post-punk had spurned: flash, cash, high
theatre, high chart positions, great image. Like French New Wave cinema, it was born from a love of pop history: for Godard read Horn, for
Antoine Doinel read George O'Dowd. It was the perfect place and the
perfect time – with the public and the charts loosened up and shaken
up, with punk having knocked the industry's confidence, with everyone

---

* Post-punk had split the vinyl market almost down the middle, just as it had
been before punk. While the progressive wing didn't shy away from releasing
singles, they had brought the album back as a desirable format with *Unknown
Pleasures*, *Crocodiles*, *Metal Box*; the Jam, the Specials and the continuity punks
were all singles specialists. As with the progressive/metal split at the turn of the
seventies, this split was largely along class lines.

looking for a way out of 1980's slough of despond* – and a new crop of undesirables were allowed to slip into the charts and onto *Top of the Pops* unmolested. As post-punk had trashed the notion of bands having to move to London to make it, many of the new pop stars came from Sheffield, Leeds, Glasgow. *Smash Hits'* Dave Rimmer said new pop was 'like punk never happened'. But it wasn't really. These new faces were birthed by punk's gleeful independence as much as they were by disco's hedonism and swishy silkiness. New pop sent rock music to the margins. And it had a new language – nobody had used the word 'sericulture' on a Top 10 hit before.

(I roll my eyes at Patti Smith for constantly mentioning Rimbaud, so why do I find it OK for the Human League to use an obscure term for silk manufacture and open a song with the line 'Listen to the voice of Buddha'? Why do I find one good for pop and the other bad? Maybe because Patti Smith was using Rimbaud as a prop, a symbol of rebellion. Quoting Rimbaud meant 'Take me seriously', and it was a trick that worked for her in the long term – she's been a permanent fixture on the arthouse circuit since 1976. The Human League's Phil Oakey turned up to rehearsals with a lyric for 'Being Boiled' that used a word the rest of the group had never heard of. Quite possibly, Oakey didn't know what it meant. But they kept it in, simply because – with no major-label jobsworth to stop them – they could, and because it sounded good.)

New pop was anti-rock, and it was against easy critical respect. Symbols of rebellion (as opposed to actual, living rebellion) were frowned upon. PiL's Keith Levene would have been thrilled that Chuck Berry riffs were entirely absent in new pop – they seemed unnecessary when there was an abundance of exciting eighties soul, dub, lovers' rock, rap and electro to draw on. Lyrically it was OK to sing about sericulture, Jacques Derrida or your favourite shirt. 'Rockism' was a term first coined in an *NME* interview with Wah! Heat's Pete Wylie in 1981: he railed against clichés of production, presentation, sound and stance. New pop

---

* UK number-one albums in 1980 included *McCartney II*, *Peter Gabriel 3*, Gary Numan's *Telekon*, Kate Bush's *Never Forever* and David Bowie's *Scary Monsters*, all of which sound like they are the last stop on the line.

went hand in hand with anti-rockism. It embraced brazen eccentrics like Marc Almond, Julian Cope, Green Gartside and Phil Oakey, but it also found room for the kind of pop acts – the Nolans, Bucks Fizz, Dollar – who had been washed up and binned by punk just a year earlier. There was a new, chart-pop-literate wave of British music writers – Paul Morley and Ian Penman (*NME*), Dave McCullough (*Sounds*), Sunie (*Record Mirror*) and Neil Tennant (*Smash Hits*) – ready to write essays on this new pop Utopia and its endless possibilities.

The man who had fired new pop's starting pistol, Adam Ant, was originally Stuart Goddard. Pale, intense and pretty, he'd lived in a Muswell Hill bedsit. Back then he was in a pub-rock act called Bazooka Joe. They played at Central Saint Martins College of Art and Design on November 6th 1975; the support act, making its debut, was the Sex Pistols. Blown away by the Sex Pistols' brio, Stuart quit Bazooka Joe on the spot, became Adam and started to write songs about fetishism.

Adam and the Ants signed to Decca in 1977, quite possibly because Lulu, the Rolling Stones and Lieutenant Pigeon had all signed to Decca – there was no year zero for Adam. Decca didn't get punk at all (their only other signing was Manchester's thuggish rockers Slaughter and the Dogs) and their first single was the marvellously perverse 'Young Parisians', closer to the Kinks' music-hall leanings than Johnny Rotten's. It was funny and knowing, too: 'Young Parisians are so French – they love Patti Smith.'

Adam was all about strategy. So when 'Young Parisians' flopped and he resorted to releasing his next single, 'Xerox', on the tiny Do It label, he decided to pay Malcolm McLaren £1,000 for some career advice. For his troubles he got very little (a cassette of some Burundian drummers) and lost a lot (his entire band, which McLaren rechristened Bow Wow Wow, with the underage Annabella Lwin as replacement singer).*

That alone would have destroyed anyone with a less than stainless-steel resolve. Adam began to write songs with a sidekick called Marco Pirroni, who looked like the Michelin Man with a gold-blond fringe. He employed two drummers, like the Glitter Band, and they used the

---

* McLaren let two future superstars slip through his fingers – Boy George was also hired and fired as Bow Wow Wow's singer.

one thing McLaren had handed over for his thousand-pound bounty – the Burundi drum sound. 'Sex music for ant people,' he said. 'Ant music for sex people.' Then Adam bought himself a pirate jacket, had an American Indian white stripe painted across his nose and got a deal with CBS. 'Dog Eat Dog', with those punishing drums and guitars like dodgem cars, reached number four in 1980, shortly after his former bandmates' 'C30 C60 C90 Go' limped to number thirty-four. McLaren got the front cover of the *NME* with Bow Wow Wow; Adam and the Ants became the biggest pop sensation since T. Rex.

What made them so exciting is that they were pop about pop. 'None of the ideas are mine,' Adam would say, 'it's just the way Marco and I have moulded them together.' He patented his image with the Merchandising Corporation of America as if he was trying to make himself a one-man Monkees. 'Antmusic' reached the Top 10 in December 1980, in the same week Paul Morley's *NME* clarion call was published, and likewise it was a new pop manifesto: 'Unplug the jukebox and do us all a favour. That music's lost its taste so try another flavour.'

It reached number two. 'Stand and Deliver', which entered the UK chart at number one in April '81 (something that had only happened twice in the previous seven years), was huge, and reinvented Adam as the dandy highwayman: 'I spend my cash on looking flash and grabbing your attention.' No one could deny it. By the summer, with 'Prince Charming' at number one ('Don't you ever stop being dandy'), the Ants were already sounding a little defensive, a little under siege, but no one noticed as they marvelled at the single's Technicolor *Carry On Ken Russell* video, with its voluptuous guest star Diana Dors. Christmas single 'Ant Rap' was a mixture of primitive hip hop, the massed ranks of a thousand Orangemen and a soupçon of harpsichord. Hilarious! In 1981 Adam and the Ants were the teen-scream future dream, part of a rare lineage including the Beatles and T. Rex, and Adam didn't enjoy a second of it. Incrementally his anxiety worked its way into his singles and by the end of '82 they were becoming hard work: one title, 'Desperate but Not Serious', was a little bit of both. His fall was precipitous and by 1985, at Live Aid, Adam was almost a laughing stock. If only he hadn't taken himself and his art so seriously. As it turned out, he had no choice.

An unsettling letter he wrote to *Time Out* in 2002 was the first public suggestion that he had Asperger's syndrome, which retrospectively explained a lot. His records were gleefully giddy, sonically and lyrically on a precipice. Ridicule, he taught us, is nothing to be scared of.

Adam was a lone trailblazer. Just behind him were the regulars at Soho's Blitz club who, for better or worse, ended up tied to each other. If Adam had the look, the glamour and the attitude, then the Blitz kids – suburban scenesters in thrall to Bowie, Roxy and Vivienne Westwood – had the sound of new pop. Often it was electronic, post-Numan, evoking smoky *Third Man*-era Vienna, with fat analogue synth chords to cover the novice bassist or guitarist's deficiencies; the definitive hit in this style was Visage's 'Fade to Grey' (UK no. 8 '81), fronted by Blitz gatekeeper Steve Strange.

To a large extent, new pop was influenced by black American dance music. For years, soul and funk had been largely ignored by white blue-collar America, but they had been crucial to the musical tastes of working-class Britons since Tamla Motown broke in the mid-sixties; clipped funk guitar and popping basslines became the bedrock for even new pop's most orchestrally lavish adventures (ABC's 'Poison Arrow') or cold synth surrenders (Orchestral Manoeuvres in the Dark's 'The New Stone Age'), while northern soul fed Soft Cell's hyped-up beats. New pop also uncovered a yearning for the return of singers, as opposed to post-punk's vocal expressionists (Lydon, Curtis, Rowland); Frank Sinatra was rehabilitated. The Human League's Phil Oakey had been unintentionally responsible for opening this can of worms: Siouxsie Sioux had praised his 'real voice' in 1980, at a time when John Lydon was still the most imitated singer in Britain; he was soon followed by the Associates' Billy Mackenzie ('Party Fears Two', UK no. 8 '82) and Tony Hadley, who led Spandau Ballet to a string of hits with a voice that harked back to the very dawn of modern pop – Al Martino's 'Here in My Heart' played godfather to Spandau's 'To Cut a Long Story Short' (UK no. 5 '81).

From Sheffield, the Human League had originally been cold-wave synth pioneers, with a hatred of guitars, until they split in half in 1981.*

---

* The other half of the group formed Heaven 17 with singer Glenn Gregory and,

Singer Philip Oakey was a deadpan humourist. 'I collect models of Sylvester the cat,' he told *Smash Hits*. 'I have 274 of them.' Left with only 'director of visuals' Adrian Wright from the original League, Oakey chatted up a couple of schoolgirls at a disco, and they joined the group in time for *Dare*, a 1981 album with hooks like steel traps. 'Love Action' (UK no. 3), 'Open Your Heart' (UK no. 6) and 'Don't You Want Me' (UK and US no. 1) were singles so good, so easy and instantly lovable, it almost felt like cheating. Yet they stuttered, only releasing two singles in the next two years ('Mirror Man' and 'Fascination', both UK no. 2), and when they added a guitarist to the line-up in 1984 it was all over.

Haircut 100 were from Kent, wore ski jumpers and belonged to the white-funk axis of new pop. Brass and slap bass were leavened by singer Nick Heyward's kinship with the Monkees: 'Favourite Shirts' (UK no. 4 '81), 'Love Plus One' (UK no. 3 '82) and 'Fantastic Day' (UK no. 9 '82) were rays of breakfast sunshine, and Heyward went on Radio 1's *Roundtable* extolling sixties architecture and telling Kevin Rowland how much 'Plan B' had reminded him of Little Richard. If anyone in new pop still read the *Beano*, it was Nick Heyward. He was doe-eyed and goofy, Beckenham's own Peter Noone, and, in a jealous fit of pique, the rest of the band sacked him in summer 1982. Neither camp kept their boat afloat for long after that.

Orchestral Manoeuvres in the Dark were from the Wirral, which meant they were teased by the Liverpool groups – 'Leo Sayer with synthesizers,' yucked the Teardrop Explodes' Julian Cope. They looked and dressed like accountants, which also got the music press's backs up. And singer Andy McCluskey danced like a wally, like someone's dad impersonating Ian Curtis, which made everyone laugh who wasn't already laughing. Yet they crafted songs like 'Souvenir' (UK no. 3 '81), heartbreaking, romantic electro pop that would have graced the soundtrack to *Un homme et une femme*.* After supporting Gary Numan on tour they scored their first hit with 'Messages' (UK no. 13 '80) and ended the

---

with 'Temptation' (UK no. 2 '82) and albums *Penthouse and Pavement* and *The Luxury Gap*, were almost as commercially successful as the mark-two League.

* The perfect title for 'Souvenir' would have been 'French Film Blurred', but art-school punks Wire had already nabbed it.

year in the Top 10 with 'Enola Gay', a song about bombing Hiroshima that subtly drew attention to the (seemingly constant) early-eighties fear of imminent nuclear destruction. Their subject matter was almost always singular – they wrote songs about a power station ('Stanlow'), an independent nation on a platform in the North Sea ('Sealand'), Joan of Arc ('Joan of Arc' *and* 'Maid of Orleans', both top 5 UK hits) – and they used Korg synthesizers to build chord patterns that were straight out of Vaughan Williams. Their third album was a million-seller, with a sleeve designed by Factory Records' Peter Saville, and a title – *Architecture and Morality* – from a municipal library shelf. As soon as they fell into an old rock cliché, by referring to themselves as an abbreviation of their name – the flat and functional OMD – they got less interesting. By the time they broke America, with the fortuitous placing of the mediocre 'If You Leave' at the climax of John Hughes's *Pretty in Pink* (1985), they were just another eighties synth duo. No more songs about power stations, no distinguishing marks.

In 1981 the least likely Blitz character to have a hit single would have been cloakroom attendant George 'Boy George' O'Dowd. Virgin Records already believed in George, which is just as well because no way did this pouting fellow, with his hands (at least, as Steve Strange suspected) in the pockets of the Blitz clientele, fit anybody's contemporary jelly mould of a pin-up pop star. A year on from 'Fade to Grey', whose success had made him a pusball of envy, George released two singles with his band, Culture Club, which were well received by the press – earning them a *Record Mirror* cover story – but failed to chart. By the time of the third single, 'Do You Really Want to Hurt Me', he'd had a few square meals and got the hang of cosmetics. It reached number one and the all-new cuddly George, a girl/boy conundrum, instantly replaced Adam in the nation's affections. He said he preferred a cup of tea to sex, and with this he even had the nation's grandmothers on his side. Beloved Boy George.

Housed in high-eighties graphics, Culture Club's pop was biodegradable. Lightly soulful ('Time (Clock of the Heart)', UK no. 3, US no. 2 '82) and mallow soft ('Karma Chameleon', UK and US no. 1 '83), it was taken by some as genuinely classic – Dave Rimmer called 1982's *Colour by Numbers* one of the albums of the decade, if not of all time. Loved by the country like a mischievous son, a prodigious daughter, a favourite, soft-haired pet, George had a future wide open as the new Gracie Fields or Cilla Black – and somehow he screwed it up. Disappearing after Culture Club's shamefully weak 1984 album *Waking Up with the House on Fire*, he went into heroin hell before re-emerging with a final UK number one, 1987's weak-kneed cover of Bread's 'Everything I Own'. By the decade's end he wasn't a legend or a national treasure, he was a cult star, DJing in Ibiza and back to cat-scratching gossip. Maybe he was happier that way.

Culture Club's career set a standard of boom and bust which others were depressingly happy to follow. Leeds duo Soft Cell were heavy on red-light, small-hours sleaze, and singer Marc Almond sounded endearingly like Shirley Bassey with a touch of asthma. For a short while they were magnificent: Dave Ball, a keyboard pimp with his pencil moustache and furtive eyes; Almond in leather, looking like a cross between a Jewish mother and a camel. All he needed was a whip to crack – it was perfectly perverted. After scoring five UK Top 5 hits ('Bedsitter' was worthy of Ray Davies, 'Say Hello, Wave Goodbye' of Cole Porter) they committed pop hara-kiri with an unlistenable third album entitled *This Last Night in Sodom*. Almond briefly toyed with a fascinating side project – Marc and the Mambas – which blended heavily rouged Mediterranean originals ('Black Heart') with hushed covers of his teenage heroes (Scott Walker's 'Big Louise', an eggshell-fragile take on Peter Hammill's 'Vision'). Going solo in 1984, he somehow had his pin-sharp sense of kitchen-sink drama pickled by one too many covers. There would be occasional triumphs ('Tears Run Rings', UK no. 26 '88) but too often he would play to the gallery, disco-fied Jacques Brel to order, and rather wasted his talent.

Arguably new pop's greatest triumph was its acceptance and transformation of some strictly old pop acts who wanted in. Kim Wilde had emerged in 1981 with a three-years-too-late budget-Blondie sound she'd bought from a petrol station in Hertfordshire. 'We're the kids in America,' she sang, and it was as catchy as Chinnichap, pastiche bubblepop that time would be very kind to. In 1981, though, it made you screw up your face whenever it came on the radio – 'B-b-but', you wanted to say, 'it's not true. You're clearly from Welwyn Garden City.' No matter. A few months on and Kim's subject matter was the romance of suicide ('View from a Bridge', UK no. 16 '82) and the psychological results of America's 1970s foreign policy ('Cambodia', UK no. 13 '81). The latter, especially, was an astonishing record: morose, phased electronics on the verse with Kim's keening voice implying noir tragedy from the off ('She was an air-force wife, he used to fly weekends, it was the easy life'), blended with a full Cossack lament on the chorus. Her career inexplicably nosedived soon after; she returned in the late eighties with an American number one (a hi-NRG cover of the Supremes' 'You Keep Me Hangin' On' in '87), green fingers and a few classy MOR hits ('You Came', 'Never Trust a Stranger', 'Four Letter Word' – all UK Top 10 in '88) and became Britain's favourite gardener. She smiled a lot more. Everyone was pleased for her. She had always sounded so stressed as a teenage pop star.

More astonishing was the evolution of a bunch of end-of-the-pier acts, real bleached-blonde *Seaside Special* no-hopers. In 1982 Paul Morley claimed that Tight Fit's 'Fantasy Island', a UK number-five hit and a rejected Dutch Eurovision entry, was better than *Led Zeppelin III*. It was an outrageous statement. For Christ's sake, he was saying, let's get away from rock history because 1982 is pretty fucking great. If you were fifteen when you read that, read that the past was less significant than the present, *your* present, it confirmed your place in the world. It both riled the old guard and appealed to young minds. Morley did a good job.

Tight Fit were a trio of models miming to pre-recorded tracks, and 'Fantasy Island' was a glorious one-off with a constantly climbing chorus melody. Bucks Fizz also had Eurovision heritage, but prevailed a while longer. Two boys, two girls, all blond, they won the contest with 'Making Your Mind Up' in '81 and racked up three number ones, including 'My Camera Never Lies', a crazed, jittery mix of new wave and new pop. Possibly the shiniest number one ever, the overlapping vocals, overriding sunniness and (almost over-) abundance of good ideas were reminiscent of 1965 Beach Boys. Ushered in with a near-ambient 'click-click' intro, it jumped to an acoustic-guitar line as hard and glinting as a polished pool ball. 'My Camera Never Lies' was all production over song – buskers wouldn't touch it – but I think that's something to applaud in itself. I mean, how good a song is the Honeycombs' 'Have I the Right' without its floorboard-busting stomps and Joe Meek-gnarled guitar break?

Dollar were very short and very blond, even blonder than Bucks Fizz, and they stole a march by having ex-Buggle Trevor Horn at the controls. David Van Day and Thereza Bazar had managed a brace of hits in '79 ('Shooting Star', 'Who Were You with in the Moonlight') but were flailing in cabaret land when Horn took them on in '81, producing a run of singles that defined new pop's blend of auteurism and greasepaint: 'There was something sweet about them,' said Horn, 'these little people living in this techno-pop world.' 'Mirror Mirror' (UK no. 4 '81) had Van Day and Bazar playing a pair of loved-up budgies; 'Videotheque' (UK no. 17 '82) found them in a cinema, watching themselves as lovers on the screen; and 'Give Me Back My Heart' (UK no. 4 '82) threw the warm vocal breeze of 10cc's 'I'm Not in Love' into the mixture – it sounded like Phil Spector producing the Carpenters' 'Goodbye to Love'. Dollar weren't likely to survive as lovers or pop stars. Their sound was entirely gaseous, and when things toughened up in '83, they left the stage.

Trevor Horn, on the other hand, was so talented he could probably have turned a malfunctioning alarm clock into an international sex symbol. After Dollar he worked with ABC, who seemed built to last, all silk and Sheffield steel. This impression was bolstered by singer Martin Fry, who looked like an emaciated but victorious lion. Their first album, *Lexicon of Love* (1982), was Horn's masterpiece. It was hot, hi-tech soul with knowing references and radio-ready melodies: 'Poison Arrow', 'The Look of Love', 'All of My Heart' – all were UK Top 10 hits in '82. Though he was now using full orchestration, Horn was always big on technology and J. G. Ballard, and *Lexicon of Love* was a romantic but cold soundscape: 'We had this idea that at some future point there'd be a record label that didn't really have any artists – just a computer in the basement and some mad Vincent Price-like figure making the records.'

Yet ABC didn't sustain their momentum. Though Martin Fry told *Smash Hits* he wanted their records to be the sound that future generations would associate with the eighties, their second album – the guitar-heavy *Beauty Stab* – saw them fall fast. The first single from it was the crunching 'That Was Then but This Is Now' (UK no. 18 '83), almost psychedelic in places and heavy on the effects pedals, but it was sunk by a line that rivals Jimmy Webb's 'MacArthur Park' in its notoriety: 'Can't complain, mustn't grumble, help yourself to another piece of apple crumble.' Aztec Camera's Roddy Frame called it the worst lyric he had ever heard. I always assumed that it was meant to be funny – check out the sniggering saxophone that follows it – but that one line was enough to see Fry's dreams of soundtracking the eighties turn to dust.

That honour fell instead to Birmingham's Duran Duran. It's hard to say why this is such a disappointing conclusion. At the start, they were endearingly provincial Blitz kids, and all of them worked at the Rum Runner club, where they eventually became the house band. Their first three singles, released in '81, sourced 'I Feel Love' and Roxy Music for ideas and came up trumps: 'Planet Earth' (UK no. 12) had zip, 'Careless Memories' (UK no. 37) had panache, 'Girls on Film' (UK no. 5) had impact. And flash. They were not ugly, and when the nascent MTV picked them as brand leaders for their 'Second British Invasion' they couldn't fail, eventually scoring fourteen UK Top 10 hits, and eleven in the States.

So why did their music feel so trivial? Possibly because they quickly began to smear the chacka-chacka Moroder rhythm track with pre-punk, hard-rock guitar. Partly because the further they got into their career, the more it sounded like each musician was trying to upstage the rest. Partly because singer Simon Le Bon got progressively more yelpy (it's hard not to wince as he goes for the high notes on 1984's 'Wild Boys'). And partly because – like the hackneyed rockers of old – they indulged themselves in tedious side projects. In this way, they coarsened and inflamed the simplicity of new pop: Arcadia and the Power Station were possibly the two worst groups of the decade. So much huff and puff. You'd hear Arcadia's lead-weighted 'Election Day' (UK no. 7, US no. 6 '85), with its Grace Jones voiceover and authentic old-timey brass, and the clean lines of the Human League's 'Love Action' seemed a long, long time ago.

AMERICAN ROCK (OOH YEAH)

Imagine criss-crossing America in 1981, from Des Moines, Iowa, to Savannah, Georgia, from Pine Springs, New York State, to Tupelo, Mississippi (to see where Elvis was born). You're in a Studebaker, with your wife and kids. Or maybe a convertible coupé with the top down, and at your side is a girl in a denim skirt with long brown legs, a girl who was thumbing a ride and you thought, why not? Either way, the radio's on; it's a local FM station. And either way, the sound of young America on this station is not Blondie, or the B-52's, or Grandmaster Flash and the Furious Five. It is canyon deep, its harmonies are mountain high, it talks of cars and girls with bar chords and Cali-rich piano. It jumps out, it's big and it is super-melodic. It asks, quite directly, 'Do you like, uh, American rock? Well now you're talking!'

People pick a Holiday Inn more for its familiar logo than anything else. For similar reasons, groups like REO Speedwagon, Foreigner and Journey were enormous in early-eighties America. Abroad, they barely registered. This was America (New York aside) looking in on itself, re-establishing its identity in the early Reagan years after being shaken to the core by the successive Kennedy/Johnson/Nixon/Carter eras, years when FM stations had been dominated by British bands, years when disco records could claim the *Billboard* Hot Hundred's top spot for months on end; now it was feasting on a notion of what its rock, American rock, had once been. In fact, it had never been this way, but everyone conspired to convince themselves otherwise.

American rock was the grandchild of an early-fifties state of mind – for Doris Day's 'Black Hills of Dakota' read Bruce Springsteen's 'Darlington County'; for Frankie Laine's 'High Noon', there's the small-town nobility of John Cougar Mellencamp's 'Jack and Diane'. It added a rock beat and a rock style of singing, but the feel and the subject matter were extremely similar. American rock didn't sweat any more than a Marlboro Man sweats. It glistened, and in this respect it's a counterpart to new pop; it was hi-tech and chart-primed. Equally, it was about dressing up, at least metaphorically – Springsteen's factory-floor messiah was as much about role-playing as Adam Ant's dandy highwayman. And as Britain tried to escape rockism, so America tried to escape itself, becoming intensely caught up in imagined notions of freedom and a safe, utopian community, a myth of a myth.

What images does this music conjure up? An auto mechanic in Flint, Michigan, oil on his hands but no real prospects, just happy that the world isn't on fire any more and he won't get drafted ('Your Love' by the Outfield); tan-skinned fourteen-year-olds, sitting on a fire escape after school, and she's crying to their song ('Keep on Loving You' by REO Speedwagon); guys just turning thirty, two kids already, sat in a Chicago bar and reminiscing about their lost youth ('Summer of '69' by Bryan Adams). Every image is gauzy, the film stock suggesting a golden era that is present but somehow already gone. Mostly this music is beautifully, expensively produced, uses all the top session musicians. And occasionally there is a little stab of melancholy, the unlikely tug of a strange emptiness, a slight weirdness, and then you're hooked.

In the early eighties it worked as cruising music. Fifties kids who had just got a licence would have been driving around town on a Friday or Saturday night listening to Alan Freed or Wolfman Jack on the radio.

Instrumentals like the Duals' 'Stick Shift' or Duane Eddy's 'Peter Gunn' did the job back then, guttural rock 'n' roll, mimicking the low rumble of T-birds and pink Cadillacs – or whatever your dad's crappy car was.

A few years later the records on the same radio stations would have been by Grand Funk Railroad or (naturally) America, a spectrum of rock from quite hard to quite soft. More chug than rev. By the early eighties a new car was a standard prize for passing your driving test, and it needed a new teenage soundtrack. So the turn of the eighties marked the return of cruising music and, like the cars, the sounds became more compact and shinier: the steady, solid pace of John Waite's in-the-pocket 'Missing You' (US no. 1, UK no. 9 '84); Rick Springfield's jealous teen trauma 'Jessie's Girl', lyrically an update of Elvis's 'The Girl of My Best Friend' (US no. 1, UK no. 43 '81), and – for that late-night last kiss, leaning against the car – Heart's swollen rhapsody 'These Dreams' (US no. 1 '86, UK no. 8 '88). The band names suggested travel – REO Speedwagon, Boston, Chicago, Foreigner, Journey – and the artwork suggested hotel rooms and space ships, both nothing but a dream to most of the people buying the albums. An American dream.

This brand of American rock had started in 1976 with Boston's 'More than a Feeling' (US no. 5, UK no. 22), a song written for the actress Mariel Hemingway, and you get the idea she'd have been confused but rather flattered by it. There were hints of George Harrison arpeggio on the opening mumbled verse as it faded in, before it exploded with a tightly wound electric snake of a guitar hook, and then hit another level of greatness on a chorus that both echoed 'Louie Louie' and predicted 'Smells Like Teen Spirit'. Pulling away, on the second verse it drifted off into the past, on a Greyhound bus, down a hundred miles of bleak highway, and the world got dimmer and bluer: 'I closed my eyes and she slipped away.' Climaxing with Brad Delp's falsetto scream – which would doom it as a karaoke number – the song ended on an infinite unresolved chorus.

'More than a Feeling' was years ahead of its time,* with a highly buffed

---

* One of the very best garage-punk 45s – part snotty Stones, part psych-out – was the Third Bardo's 'I'm Five Years Ahead of My Time'; it was an exact time

sheen that was all down to the song's writer, Tom Scholz, who played pretty much everything on the record. Every penny he had made from his job working for Polaroid was used to build a recording studio in his basement, and Boston, formed in 1970, took their sweet time to create a unique, aureate sound: guitars harmonised in thirds, Brad Delp's long-held notes, the clean electricity of Scholz's largely home-made effects boxes. The record took Scholz five years to complete, and you can tell. It was trapped between eras. It sounded futuristic, an American rock equivalent to Kraftwerk, even though Scholz cited the Left Banke's 'Walk Away Renee' as its main influence, which, by the time 'More than a Feeling' peaked at number five in the Hot Hundred in 1976, was a spectacularly arcane reference. The story behind 'More than a Feeling', its atmosphere of a lost blue-collar American dream and its high-gloss production laid the blueprint for a new American rock. And, in keeping with the one-shot nature of the genre, nothing else Boston recorded came close.

American rock's exhibit two is REO Speedwagon, who had begun as a covers band in 1967 and chipped away until 1981, when they scored a massive hit album with *Hi Infidelity*; it spent fifteen consecutive weeks at number one in the US, longer than *Purple Rain* or even *Thriller*. The band's history was only interesting for its longevity and gaping lack of thrills: they once approached a singer called Greg X. Volz,* who didn't join them because he had just converted to Christianity; they released a live album titled, with joyless Ronseal efficiency, *You Get What You Play For*; in 1988 their drummer Alan Gratzer retired. Retired! Nobody in rock 'retires'.

REO Speedwagon earned a million-seller through graft and an acknowledgement that they had to gloss up and pop up a little once the seventies became the eighties. They were an archetype who, like Boston, had one stupendous single in them that their whole career hinged on. 'Keep on Loving You' (US no. 1, UK no. 7 '81) was a hard-rock ballad†

---

capsule of 1966. But 'More than a Feeling' is a rare record that can genuinely claim that title as fact.

* Granted, Greg X. Volz's name is quite intriguing. Xavier? Xanthum?

† 'Keep on Loving You' ended up on *Time–Life's Ultimate Rock Ballads*, for which Cronin did the TV commercial.

with power chords held at bay underneath a piano and triangle intro. Singer Kevin Cronin had a featureless, line-drawn face under a mass of permed curls, and he sang through his teeth, which added a weird tension to the song as it built through a sinister, David Lynch-styled verse ('You played dead but you never bled. Instead you lay still in the grass, all coiled up and innocent'). It also suggested maturity, a long-term relationship of unusual depth, and a longevity to match REO's career ('And though I know all about those men, still I don't remember. 'Cos it was us, baby, way before them, and we're still together'). The sustained vibrato of the guitar break starts with a single note held for what seems an impossibly long time, then it dive-bombs in harmony, a sound that punk band Discharge were mastering in Stoke-on-Trent in the exact same month. Its pristine production gave the central theme of 'Keep on Loving You' – 'When I said that I love you, I meant that I love you forever' – a purity that no other REO Speedwagon song could manage. 'Take It on the Run', 'Keep the Fire Burnin'', 'Can't Fight This Feeling' – they also sounded similar, but they all sounded boring.

The sound, the cruise function, was always more important than the song, but when the melodic muse hit these guys – *Abbey Road* fans one and all – it elevated it one notch above. Foreigner's 'Waiting for a Girl Like You' had a synth sensuality both warm and cold, and blended – like Dollar's 'Give Me Back My Heart' – with the ghostly multi-layered harmonies of 'I'm Not in Love'; it chimed with new pop in Britain, and was a UK Top 10 hit as well as a US number two. That the song itself barely existed didn't matter; its twilit icy calm and supplicant eroticism made it one of 1981's definitive singles. Toto's 'Hold the Line' (US no. 5 '78) and Jefferson Starship's 'Jane' (US no. 14 '79) both made it on minor chords, stuttering staccato piano and air-punching. Air Supply* broke the rules by releasing three classic American-rock hits ('Lost in Love', 'All out of Love', 'Even the Nights Are Better'), and their weightless name was apt. John Cougar Mellencamp's 'Jack and Diane' (US no. 1 '82), meanwhile, had short sharp power chords and synth jabs but

---

* Air Supply were actually Australian, though they recorded in the US, which explains their sound and huge US success. They were once described by *Record Mirror*, in a positive light, as 'wimp rock'.

also touched on dreamscape heartland imagery; with lines like 'sucking on a chili dog outside the Tastee Freez', 'Jack and Diane' sounded as roundly and profoundly American to outsiders as *Gidget*, mid-terms and Twizzlers.

'Ooh yeah, life goes on,' sang Mellencamp, 'long after the thrill of living is gone.' It wasn't pretty, but it was almost as evocative of gasoline, torn jeans and the endless road as the opening couplet from a 1980 US number-five hit called 'Hungry Heart': 'Got a wife and kids in Baltimore, Jack. I went out for a ride and I never went back.' Maybe you'll think it's harsh to bunch Bruce Springsteen in with Boston, but the Boss was no stranger to the power of an electronically processed drum kit ('Born in the USA') or a dreamy synth wash ('I'm on Fire'). Besides, if you're talking about creating a cinematic, hyper-real Americana, Springsteen was the king. His songs rolled and kicked and swaggered. They were men's songs and they were rank with small-town heroism. Sometimes they were all beaten up and empty like a rusting pickup – 'The River', 'Downbound Train' – and you fell hard for his loneliness. And sometimes they were selfish – people got abandoned and abused.

Back in 1973 Bruce Springsteen had been all about poetry and, like Loudon Wainwright III a couple of years earlier, he was touted as the new Dylan. It looked like it was going to happen for him as early as 1974, when pop's king magpie David Bowie covered 'It's Hard to Be a Saint in the City'. Critically lauded (*NME*, 1973: 'Was Bob Dylan the previous Bruce Springsteen?') but less than a commercial sensation after two albums, he wrote elliptical songs about the boardwalk life in his native New Jersey: 'with a boulder on my shoulder, feeling kinda older, I tripped the merry-go-round; with this very unpleasing sneezing and wheezing, the calliope crashed to the ground.' Though it got full marks for assonance, 'Blinded by the Light' found Springsteen trying a little too hard.* His lyrics had a weight problem. So for his next trick he returned to his youth, syphoned off the explosive bagpipe intro of Little Eva's 'The Locomotion' (US no. 1 '62), glued it to the sax-party feel

* 'Blinded by the Light' may have sounded stodgy when recorded by Springsteen, but it became a 1976 Top 10 hit in the US and UK when it was pumped full of light disco beats, laser beams and airy harmonies by Manfred Mann's Earth Band.

of Gary U. S. Bonds's 'Quarter to Three' (US no. 1 '61), and wrapped the whole thing up with Spector-like bells and lines like 'the highway's jammed with broken heroes'. It wasn't just small-town New Jersey any more; 'Born to Run' was as big and as busted as America in 1975.

With 'Born to Run' he created something which sounded bigger than anything else around. This is not a surefire way to win credibility but it generally wins fans, and that is the sonic link between Springsteen and the class of '81. 'We were constantly chasing something that was unattainable,' he said. 'We just assumed everything could sound huge.' He wasn't about long hair and satin jackets (he seemed oblivious to style, good or bad) but every time he got introverted his sales dipped. This was a shame because his best moments were frequently his quiet-est. Songs like 'State Trooper' and 'Racing in the Street' were like classic American short stories, while others like 'The River' were more like Joyce Carol Oates's generation-spanning novels: 'Then I got Mary pregnant and man that was all she wrote. And for my nineteenth birthday I got a union card and a wedding coat . . . but I remember us riding in my brother's car, her body tan and wet down at the reservoir.'

Raised on Top 40 radio, Springsteen was as much of a fan-boy rock star as Roy Wood and, in the same way as his unlikely Anglo cousin, he used pop history like a movie set. He'd soaked up 'Like a Rolling Stone' and 'Up on the Roof' both, and understood their power; for him 'pop promised the never-ending now . . . for those three minutes you were lifted up into a higher place of living'. He didn't feel compromised going for either Brill Building urban or heartland rural. He could be the teen rebel ('Your daddy won't let me in') on 'Talk to Me' or the guilty and lust-soaked older lover on 'I'm on Fire'. If you have a certain Americana itch, Bruce Springsteen is the cure. As a result, internationally, he out-sold everyone in this chapter (with one exception).

Springsteen is to American rock as Bowie is to new pop. Nebraska is his Berlin (America is big enough for Nebraska's distance from New Jersey to be more than enough continental divide). As Bowie made a move on commercial salvation with *Let's Dance* in '83, so Springsteen came crash-ing back in '84 with *Born in the USA*. With its army of Fairlights that squished Little Stevie's familiar guitar and Clarence Clemons's rollicking sax breaks, he scored his biggest American hit ever. The bleakness of the album's lyrics (the title track, 'Glory Days', 'Downbound Train') was largely missed in the uncarpeted clatter of the feel-good production. 'I think what's happening now is people want to forget,' he told *Rolling Stone* in 1984. 'There was Vietnam, there was Watergate, there was Iran – we were beaten, we were hustled, and then we were humiliated. And I think people got a need to feel good about the country they live in.' The result was American rock's answer to *Thriller*, the desperate pill sweetened with beyond-friendly synths. *Born in the USA* may well be Springsteen's best collection of songs, but you yearn to hear demos with a lighter touch, without those 'we won the world series' keyboard sounds, without Oliver North on drums. To most patriots the lyric may as well have run, as they did in an Achewood comic strip, 'Born in the USA! I ate a hamburger and said "hooray"!' But the album punched in, did its job, made Americans feel good about themselves, and went fifteen times platinum before it punched out.

Meat Loaf's *Bat out of Hell* sold more, though. Lank-haired greaser Marvin Lee Aday had worked in theatre (*Hair*, *The Rocky Horror Show*), and sung on Ted Nugent's platinum-selling rock blowout *Free-for-All*, before he hooked up with songwriter Jim Steinman when they were touring together on the *National Lampoon Road Show*. On stage, Meat Loaf would encore with 'River Deep – Mountain High', and he sang it like Springsteen meets Mario Lanza, a vast and destructive noise that bulldozed every nuance in its path. It isn't entirely necessary to say much more about Meat Loaf's *Bat out of Hell* other than, released in 1978, it was Springsteen's unwitting progeny and it sold fourteen million copies in the US alone.

Born to Run and *Bat out of Hell* could be seen as the same deal – all revved up with no place to go, small-town teen dreams set to arrangements that rivalled Wagner, let alone Spector. But *Bat out of Hell* was Springsteen's '57 Chevy pimped up and painted luminous pink, *The Phil Spector Story* directed by Richard Curtis. Springsteen's bombast was there because he was angry or excited; it meant he could follow 'The River' with 'Nebraska'. Meat's bombast was inflationary – he was nothing without it. On *Bat out of Hell* the sirens were screaming and the fires were howling. It was passionate, tight, professional, the band worked hard. You got your money's worth. It was also a real-life rocky horror, a musical theme park dreamt up by American rock's own Andrew Lloyd Webber, but that was all irrelevant if you were young, cruising at a steady fifty, a six-pack of Bud on the back seat. All that mattered in the early eighties was that it was American, and it rocked.

JUST A KING IN MIRRORS:
MICHAEL JACKSON

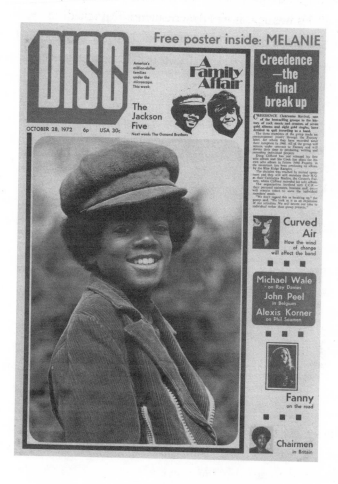

On the same day the Altamont disaster had signalled the death of the sixties, a single entered the American Top 30 that represented rebirth, that pointed to a then unimaginable future for black pop, the triumph of disco, the rise of machine soul, and one of the great Hollywood stories. Its cascading, super-confident piano intro was followed by a choppy, slightly out-of-kilter rhythm section playing as if they *knew* that just round the corner, any second now, a voice was going to come in that you just wouldn't believe. The strings edge up, further up, the drummer nods and we're off: 'Ahhh – haaaaa, ohh woah-a-hoooooo, uh lemme tell you now, ahhh ha . . .'

The miracle of the Jackson 5's 'I Want You Back' (US no. 1 '69, UK no. 2 '70) became more apparent when David Ruffin's version was eventually released, more than thirty years after it was recorded. As the lead singer in the Temptations, Ruffin was Motown's soul man number one, a force of nature, his bad reputation borne out by a ferocious, lived-in voice. You can imagine him hearing the pre-pubescent Michael Jackson's take on 'I Want You Back' – with its strong-man-on-his-knees lyric – and thinking, 'Not bad . . . but I'll show the kid how it's done.' Ruffin strains, sweats, laughs, pleads, 'OHHHHHHH baby give me one more chance!' and it's a tour de force, your feet can't keep still. And yet he doesn't come close to Michael Jackson's joyous, uninhibited take. At the dawn of the seventies here was a boy wonder, a ten-year-old genius throwing down a challenge for the next generation. Here was a star as charismatic and undeniable as Elvis had been.

The Jackson 5 were Berry Gordy's last major success – Motown faltered in the seventies, its sales and creativity outstripped by streetwise funk and sophisticated Philly. But with the Jackson 5, Gordy had his Colonel Parker moment. He spied a new affluent black market, young teenagers, and realised the only idols they had for their bedroom walls were sportsmen. The Jackson 5 became the first black pop idols, and Gordy provided an eager market with posters, fan magazines, T-shirts, lunchboxes, even their own cartoon series. On top of this, within two years of 'I Want You Back' coming out, the Jackson 5 had already sold more singles than any other Motown act.

In the following decades Michael Jackson's career was often painful to watch. He flew higher than anyone, he made terrible mistakes – maybe his biggest pop crime was that he made a lot of uninteresting records. But he was always a star, an inspiration to fans to whom it didn't matter if he was black or white or something else entirely. And in this department he trounced Prince, Madonna, Johnny Rotten, Bowie and everyone else since the Beatles.

If you make a chronological list of all Michael Jackson's singles, 'Billie Jean' sits plum in the middle. Up to this point, in early 1983, he had remained the same Michael Jackson – the symbol of hope and irrepressible energy – that we had first encountered in the week that the Hell's Angels took Meredith Hunter's life in a rundown speedway stadium. 'Billie Jean' was possibly his greatest achievement, too, its panther bassline and sense of impending dread mirrored in a lyric of shame and humiliation at the hands of a fan. Sobbing, and using the tics that would become a cliché long before his death, Jackson was a man on the edge; here was something quite *adult* that we had never heard in his music before, and from this point on nothing would be the same.

From the very start, he had been pawed and possessed. After winning a contest with his brothers at the Harlem Apollo in 1967, aged eight, he was instant hot property. Motown second-stringer Gladys Knight and third-stringer Bobby Taylor pointed Berry Gordy towards the Jackson 5, and he was so impressed that he gift-wrapped them for his girlfriend; their first album was called *Diana Ross Presents the Jackson 5*. Even as a child, the youngest of the five brothers, Michael was thoughtful; in a *Disc & Music Echo* interview in 1972 he revealed that he got an allowance of five dollars a week, and spent most of that on 'art supplies; paint and stuff like that'. Early on, he decided he would be his own boss and make sure no one, not even his demanding parents, could control him. The dancing sensation, the boy who sang the spring-fresh ballad 'Got to Be There' (US no. 4, UK no. 5 '72) with a voice of joyous emotion well beyond his years, was kept for the public eye; he developed a second Michael, furrowed, thicker-skinned and quite private, one that no one could ever reach, deceive or own. Who could blame him?

In the mid-seventies he turned sixteen and his voice broke. The Jacksons recorded an underrated, gently persuasive Gamble and Huff-produced single called 'Show You the Way to Go' (UK no. 1 '77) that lightly stepped forward, with Michael beckoning to you from his shining path to disco redemption. Here was a route out of childhood and into adult life that sounded flower-scented and carefree: put on your bonnet, your cape and your glove, whispered Michael – 'Let me show you, I'll never let you down. Put your hand in mine, we can do it, we can work it out, work it out.' You'd trust him with your life. With the Quincy Jones-produced *Off the Wall* in 1979, his first solo album as an adult, just about to leave his teenage years behind, it really felt like he had the key, he had the secret. 'Don't Stop 'Til You Get Enough' (US no. 1, UK no. 3) is the most dizzying, joyous disco 45 of all, with a vertiginous intro of whirlwind strings and Jackson's whoops. The rest of the record is no slouch either, with his falsetto lead countered by a worn-out Michael in the background, head down, mumbling, beaten by the beat. It's really quite sinister. He sounds as if he could dance until he melted.

With *Off the Wall*, Michael Jackson became a new kind of alpha male, striding out of his school years with the sharpest clothes, the sharpest dance moves in the world, and a voice that could charm the cutest girls. His dates included Brooke Shields and Tatum O'Neal. He gave off an air of super-confidence, like pre-army Elvis. Cooling down after *Off the Wall*'s multi-million sales he cut another album with his brothers (*Triumph*, including 'Walk Right Now' and 'Can You Feel It', both UK Top 10 in '81) and watched on, amused, as a sweet, forgotten Motown ballad from '75, 'One Day in Your Life', went all the way to number one in Britain the same summer. People waited on his next move, certainly, but everything seemed relaxed. He had a nose job. No one minded.

But when *Thriller* finally emerged, almost unheralded, at the tail end of 1982,* it expressed a fear of pretty much everything – bullying ('Beat It'), gold diggers ('Billie Jean'), violence ('Wanna Be Startin' Something'), the supernatural (the title track). Suddenly he was back-pedalling. He isn't smiling on the cover. He looks deep in thought, a little glassy-eyed. Maybe he was having bad dreams, premonitions.

After *Thriller* made him the biggest star in the world, Jackson also became the strangest, the most spaced-out. With plastic surgery (that he denied almost to the end) he started to look less like a human being

---

* This muted reception was due to the choice of first single, a duet with Paul McCartney called 'The Girl Is Mine' which must have seemed a safe bet but was entirely unrepresentative and light years from the chic pleasures of *Off the Wall*. 'Billie Jean' was released as a single the following March, the same month that, dressed in a soon-to-be-ubiquitous black-sequinned jacket, single sequinned glove and black fedora, Jackson performed the moonwalk for the first time on a televised Motown anniversary party. At which point his career went supernova.

than the animatronic lovechild of Ronald McDonald and *An American Werewolf in London*. *Thriller* sold in quantities that are hard to comprehend – you'd expect to see a copy in the corner of any room, in any town, in any country in the world. Somehow he had to follow up the biggest-selling album of all time. Could he ever go back to being the free spirit of 1979's peerless *Off the Wall*? He couldn't, and while his music would become ever more nervous, screwed up tight, his private life began to go in completely the opposite direction.

1987's *Bad* didn't give us any sense of the singer, of why he was bothering. Clearly he didn't *need* to bother at all after *Thriller*'s stratospheric sales. It felt like another push for global domination, this time just for the sake of it. But he was surely reacting to claims that he had turned his back on his roots, working with Paul McCartney, selling out to whitey. Black Muslim leader Louis Farrakhan called him 'cissified'. Jackson worked hard to shake that insult, to reassert his masculinity. He chose to wear a leather jacket; he rarely smiled in photos again.*

His problem was how to become bigger than the biggest; it was a matter of semantics. Paul McCartney attempted to reverse some Lennon/McCartney credits so they read McCartney/Lennon, denying their clean alphabetical consistency; in the mid-eighties Jackson took to calling himself the King of Pop. It didn't seem to matter that the King had been coined some decades before. The King of Pop – that'll do. Astonishingly, the media bought it – to a degree – presumably in hope that their fawning compliance might lead to an interview exclusive. But still this wasn't enough, and a little while later Jackson's people sent out a correction to the media stating that he was now to be referred to as the King of Rock, Pop and Soul, and they sailed hundred-foot-high statues of the deity down the Hudson, the Thames and the Danube to ram the point home. No ordinary pop star, this.

---

* *Bad* was a letdown, but it had a few career highlights. 'The Way You Make Me Feel' was a sweet two-step treat that could've come from a forties musical; 'Smooth Criminal' had a slippery Sir Hiss of a bassline and a catchy, oblique hook – 'Annie, are you OK?' – that rendered it the album's one instant classic. 'Man in the Mirror', which failed to even reach the UK Top 20 as a single, was a piece of vapid self-help that somehow ended up being the song most associated with Michael in the immediate aftermath of his death, recharting at number two.

If *Bad* had been hard to read, 1991's *Dangerous* was full of seriously weird stuff in extremely plain view. On 'Who Is It' (UK no. 10, US no. 14) it became obvious that the megalomaniac hero set in stone and launched down the world's major waterways was not an invention of a CBS marketing man: 'I am the damned, I am the dead, I am the agony inside a dying head.' *Rolling Stone* described *Dangerous* as 'a man, no longer a man-child, confronting his well-publicized demons and achieving transcendence'. It was as if fans and critics alike were unwilling to hear what Jackson was, in his clenched, tortured vocal style, screaming at us.

'Blood on the Dancefloor', released in 1997, was his most remarkable late-period single. Not his best, but a distillation of his style: it was strained, blanched, dehumidified, purified to the point where almost the entire song, as it exists, is a vocal tic. *Dah! Wheeep! Ehh!* There's a story bubbling underneath, one where Billie Jean returns, only this time her name is Susie and she's no longer satisfied with claiming paternity; she wants to kill you. Like late-period Joe Meek, 'Blood on the Dancefloor' sounds like the product of someone on the far edge of sanity. But unlike the Buzz's 'You're Holding Me Down', 'Blood on the Dancefloor' was another UK number-one hit for the King of Rock, Pop and Soul.

It would be his last. There had been allegations before, hush money paid, blind eyes turned, but when another child came forward with lurid tales of 'Jesus juice' at Neverland, it was the tipping point. Statues on the Danube and semantics couldn't save him now, and Michael Jackson spent his final years as a hunted animal, humiliated by an ITV – *ITV!* – reporter, moving to Dubai, a King in exile. Even Elvis never had it this bad, and at least his records kept selling; the last single Michael Jackson released was called 'One More Chance', released in time for Christmas 2003. It entered the chart at five and dropped out of the Top 20 the following week, as if he was an indie band with a hardcore following of a few thousand, as if he was a mere mortal.

Like Elvis he had been caged from an early age, a social scientific experiment – 'How will endless fame and fortune affect the subject?' Like Elvis there was a totality of pop to Michael Jackson – the look, the voice, the dance moves, the complete performance. And like Elvis, he was deemed irrelevant and useless at the time of his death. He wasn't thought to have made a good record in over a decade. Although he was only fifty, no one seemed surprised when his heart gave out.

The day after Michael Jackson died, the front page of *The Times* featured a picture of him before he left the bosom of Motown, before *Thriller*'s fifty zillion sales, before his hair caught fire, before the oxygen tent, the chimpanzee, the sleepovers. Before the rumours that went beyond anything J. M. Barrie ever dreamed up. Remember him this way, the picture said; remember the eleven-year-old genius.

HIGHS IN THE MID-EIGHTIES:
PRINCE AND MADONNA

 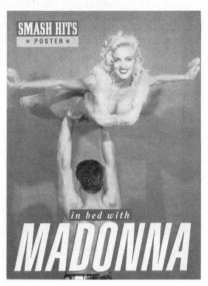

He only knew her for a little while
But he had grown accustomed to her smile.
She had the cutest ass he'd ever seen . . .
　　Prince, 'Girls and Boys', 1986

Q: Why did you decide to go into music?
A: Because music is the main vector of celebrity. When it's a
success, its impact is as strong as a bullet hitting the target.
　　Madonna, *Smash Hits*, April 1987

Twenty-four-hour music television, the brainchild of a TV-spawned
pop star, the Monkees' Michael Nesmith, began broadcasting in August
1981 with the Buggles' 'Video Killed the Radio Star'. MTV was everywhere within eighteen months, marking the beginning of the end of *Top
of the Pops*' reign of unimpeachable power in Britain. If new pop and

post-punk had gleefully and rapidly rewritten rules, taking music forward in a constant revolution of purpose and invention, their aftermath was an era of momentum for its own sake. Things got ever shinier, greed and need replaced innovation: conservatism was a force and a problem both outside and within eighties pop.*

Two new names appeared in this froth of newness. Both stood out from the crowd, both clearly demanded attention, worship, devotion: Prince and Madonna. These were names that couldn't have existed at the dawn of modern pop, names that baited royalty and religion.

Both based their sound on electronically processed dance music, allowing them the opportunity to change style from record to record in a way that seemed innovative, one step ahead of the pack, like Dylan or Bowie before them. Both had egos the size of mansions. Both had a new hunger for success, for money. Both used MTV to become stars, and both used movies (*Desperately Seeking Susan*, *Purple Rain*) to make the jump from stardom to superstardom. Sex! Religion! Gigolo! Whore! Purple! Cone bra! No one could accuse Prince or Madonna of underplaying their hands. And, eventually, both challenged Michael Jackson's place at the very top of the pop empire; by the eighties' end Madonna had (arguably) toppled him in the popularity stakes, and Prince had (certainly) creatively eased past Jackson with the most streamlined, silver-finned R&B of the decade. These were their similarities. In other respects they were quite different.

Prince had first appeared with the itchy falsetto disco of 'I Wanna Be Your Lover' (US no. 11 '79) and was presented – not least by himself – as a teenage prodigy. He grew up in the largely white city of Minneapolis: 'The radio was dead, the discos was dead, the ladies was kind of dead. If I wanted to make some noise, if I wanted to turn anything out, I was gonna have to get something together. Which was

---

* A rare American exception, a new subgenre with genuine weight, was freestyle, a Latin-based electropop sound born in New York and Miami. Although the term wouldn't be coined until a few years later, the definitive freestyle hit was Shannon's 'Let the Music Play', a UK number ten in early 1984. The sound's commercial peak came in 1987, when 'Come Go with Me' by Exposé, 'Show Me' by the Cover Girls and Company B's 'Fascinated' were all major US hits. In spite of a general lack of competition, none meant a thing in Britain.

what we did. We put together a few bands and turned it into Uptown.'

He wanted to be everybody's lover and – unlike most disco acts – was quite at home with lyrics about oral sex, incest and Dorothy Parker. This set him apart. By 1983 he was channelling Sly Stone and the Beach Boys on 'Little Red Corvette' (US no. 6), and a year later *Newsweek* was calling him 'the Prince of Hollywood' as *Purple Rain* – starring Prince as the Kid – grossed $80 million.

Prince was hyperactive, more productive than any major star since the Beatles; some of his most commercial songs – 'Manic Monday', 'Nothing Compares 2 U' – were tossed off as demos for others less prodigiously gifted to take to number one. There was always more in the locker.

Madonna, on the other hand, was the most grasping pop star in history. She was all Blonde Ambition, a triumph of the will. If her roots were always showing (suburban, Italian American, Catholic), it was still almost impossible to feel her soul. Rosaries were for show, crucifixes were worn like candy necklaces; if she ever went to confession it didn't come across in her lyrics. She was a highly sexual, strong woman commodifying her own sexuality. She was a billboard. She was a material girl and proud of it.

And if you listen to *The Immaculate Collection* it succeeds on almost every level. Like Lesley Gore before her – with Quincy Jones, Jack Nitzsche, Thom Bell – Madonna used the best young producers (John 'Jellybean' Benitez, Stephen Bray, William Orbit, Stuart Price) to get to the top and stay at the top. Each step was perfectly conceived, each single a stop on the way to her ultimate destination – iconhood. 'Holiday' and 'Lucky Star', in 1983, were instant club classics, floor-fillers for the masses, with a delicate ache to take 'just one day out of line'; 1984's 'Like a Virgin' and 'Material Girl' (the video for which had her playing Marilyn Monroe for the first time) were pubescent pop, there to antagonise and irritate, and to set up her persona; 'Into the Groove' (her first UK and US number one in '85) was the invitation for everyone to partake, with its cool, crooked finger – 'I'm waiting!' And the world succumbed. A few career-hardening singles later, Madonna could take eighteen months out and return with an event single, 'Like a Prayer', which (because it had to be) was her best yet. At this point, in 1989, she owned pop, and it was hers to lose.

The role-playing had been there from the start. 'There was a real transformation,' said former schoolfriend Kim Drayton. 'In the sophomore year she was a cheerleader with smiles on her face and long hair; very attractive; then by her senior year she had short hair. She was in the thespian society, and she didn't shave her legs any more, you know, like all of us did, and she didn't shave her armpits. Everyone was like, "Oh, what happened to her?"' Dancing became her escape route. The eldest girl in a family of eight children, her mother had died when she was just five. Her dad had been a defence engineer for General Dynamics; he worked long hours, and Madonna didn't get on with her stepmother, who made her help out changing nappies. 'When all my friends were out playing, I felt like I had all these adult responsibilities . . . I saw myself as the quintessential Cinderella,' she said. So she danced in the backyard to Motown 45s with her black schoolfriends, and she went to gay clubs in Detroit where she didn't feel men looked at her like a hard-ass. By the time she arrived in New York and hung out at the Danceteria in 1982, she had the moves if not yet the look or the voice.

Three years on she recorded 'Into the Groove' and, for me, it was her peak. The most sublime example of pop on pop since 'Do You Believe in Magic', it was all about saturating your mind and freeing your body, a three-minute, unrelenting chime of joy: 'Only when I'm dancing can I feel this free'. She came from nothing, a real-life Cinderella, and she made some of the greatest records of the eighties, became a true legend. It's 'Papa Don't Preach' with an exceptionally happy ending.

So why do I struggle to love Madonna? On one level it was her lack of specialness – take away the drive and she's fine, she's good. She's as good as Kim Wilde. Her voice had a squeaky cuteness, a predatory squeaky cuteness that contradicts itself. On another, less personal level, she was a cultural sponge. Once Madonna co-opted a fashion, a look, then it belonged to her. Try imagining anyone who has emerged in her wake pulling off the Monroe look – even someone as big as Christina Aguilera, Kylie Minogue or Lady Gaga: immediately you think, it's a bit Madonna. In this respect, she's been an awful role model for women*

* Like Margaret Thatcher, who, as prime minister, never allowed another woman

and has done a lot of harm without giving much back.

Prince was always more playful, at once generous and controlling, a benevolent dictator – the Tito of pop. He started a label called Paisley Park, writing and producing for the likes of the Time, Sheila E. and Apollonia, the busty co-star of *Purple Rain*; then he spent $10 million building a white modernist Paisley Park studio complex. His jammy fingermarks were all over the label's output, at every level. For the cover photo of the Time's 'Ice Cream Castle' he instructed Paul Peterson to wear an orange suit. He also wanted Mark Cardenas to wear blackface, which was an affectation too far. According to Peterson, 'He said, "If you wear blackface people will notice you." Well, he would have been right there.'

Unlike Madonna, Prince was all contradictions: black funk and white rock, the sound of the future pilfering from the past's cabinet of curiosities, and – like Little Richard before him – unending lust and adherence to the Bible. This was fully realised on 1984's international breakthrough album, the soundtrack to *Purple Rain*. It was put in capsule form on 'Darling Nikki', a violent grind of a track that referenced female masturbation but, if played backwards (Prince had done his Beatles homework), the fade included the spoken lines 'Hello. How are you? I'm fine, because I know the Lord is coming soon.'

It must have caused a few punters who had bought the album for 'Take Me with U' to go bright red. *Purple Rain* was like a condensed CV, each track pointing in a different possible future direction, splendidly and unquestionably announcing the arrival of a legend. The first single taken from it, 'When Doves Cry', was also his first US number one (UK no. 4) and, just for larks, it didn't include a bassline.* 'Take Me with U' was eighties Merseybeat – as if Prince was seeing *Purple Rain* as an update of *A Hard Day's Night* – dressed up with some gorgeous lovelorn strings and a dynamic, slightly disturbing, Brian Wilson-like intro and coda. 'Let's Go Crazy' (another US number one) was synth glam, a vari-speed 'Rock and Roll Part 2' in double time, its lyrics indecipherable

---

MP into the Cabinet, Madonna acted as if she was the only woman allowed in pop.
* 'When Doves Cry' was the first hit single to lack a bassline since Andrew Gold's 'Never Let Her Slip Away' in 1978.

beyond a camp religious intro, panting sounds and a clarion call of 'Let's
go crazy! Let's get nuts!' The title track was a cold, lengthy plod that
resurrected the emotional mudbath of John Lennon's 'Mother' and the
dead-handed thud of the Band; a parody of white rock's self-pity, it may
not be a coincidence that this is the song that brings Prince's character,
the Kid, deliverance in the movie.

Purple Rain spent a dozen weeks at the top of the US album chart.
Prince's place at the table was confirmed when the British press gave him
the kind of nickname which they reserve for only the biggest pop stars,
the ones who can rise no higher: Macca Wacky Thumbsaloft, Dame
David Bowie, Wacko Jacko, Madge and Ponce. You didn't need the
ire of the *Sun* or the *National Enquirer* when *Smash Hits* was there to
remind superstars that no one, but no one, is untouchable.

With the Kid and his busted-up success story, Prince showed a sleight
of hand not seen since David Bowie's Ziggy Stardust. *Purple Rain* was
the pop event of the year, and it was a skin he could easily shed. The
sequel, 1985's *Around the World in a Day*, was built on a bed of the
romantic woozy strings from 'Take Me with U'; from its psychedelically
ornate cover on, it was the Lovin' Spoonful put through a Paisley Park
filter; the title track and 'Raspberry Beret' were sunny-afternoon high
jinks, sweet utopian pop. No wig-outs or workouts, just marshmallows.
It wasn't given a major push, as if Warner Brothers didn't think it could
hold the same crossover appeal as *Purple Rain*. Critically and commercially, in the conservative environment of the mid-eighties, it felt like
Prince was being upbraided for not giving us *Purple Rain 2*, for going
too far. None of the singles from it even reached the Top 20 in Britain.
We should all hang our heads.

Prince shrugged, moved on, and brought two new cohorts to the fore in
1986. 'It is true I record very fast,' he told MTV. 'It goes even quicker now
the girls help me . . . the girls meaning Wendy and Lisa.' Guitarist Wendy
Melvoin could barely contain her pride in *Rolling Stone*: 'I'm sorry, no one
can come close to what the three of us have together when we're playing
in the studio. Nobody!' She was right. By the time of *Parade* in 1986,
and its companion movie *Under the Cherry Moon*, Prince was untouchable. He could indulge his fantasies of upper-class English girls on screen

(Francesca Annis and a young Kristin Scott Thomas were the love interest in *Under the Cherry Moon*) and still come over as impish rather than
creepy. He'd try and be the romantic suitor, try to keep his flies zipped up,
but always had that glint in his eye within a matter of seconds. 'Girls and
Boys' (UK no. 11 '86) was great, but 'Kiss' (US no. 1, UK no. 6 '86) was
greater, a super-parched dancer containing killer eighties map refs: 'you
don't have to watch *Dynasty* to have an attitude'. Within a year Prince
released a double album, *Sign 'O' the Times*,* which contained no filler at
all – he had found Paisley Park hired hands who could keep up with him,
egg him on to greater heights of screwball abandon. 'Starfish and Coffee'?
And a side order of ham. 'Wear something peach or black,' he asked fans
before his 1987 shows. With a new addition, the writhing dancer Cathy
'Cat' Glover, he made the *Sign 'O' the Times* tour the most spectacular of
the eighties, pushing her up against a giant silver heart during 'If I Was
Your Girlfriend' which then tipped up, dumping the two lovebirds backstage. He didn't miss a single beat. And, again, again, he moved on.

Madonna also kept plugging away at a parallel film career, though
she didn't have a predilection for English gents with country houses
to blame for the box-office failure of *Who's That Girl* and *Shanghai
Surprise*.† Given their similar tastes, it's no coincidence that Madonna's
best album, 1989's *Like a Prayer*, bore a heavy Prince footprint. It was
a tightrope-walking blend of the spiritual and carnal; Prince aside, no
one had pulled this stuff off since Elvis. There was even a duet between
the two pretenders to Jacko's throne (the crisp 'Love Song'), which must
have made the King of Pop frown just a little.

Even so, both Prince and Madonna hit a crisis as the eighties turned
into the nineties. Neither had embraced either hip hop's golden age or
the house and techno revolution (which revolved much slower in its

---

* Incredibly, Prince had recorded three 'lost' albums in the short time between
Parade and *Sign 'O' the Times*: *Dream Factory*, *Camille* and *Crystal Ball*.
Unreleased songs like 'In a Large Room with No Light', 'Wonderful Ass' and
the legendary 'Wally' (which no one other than Prince, Wendy and Lisa seems
to have even heard) date from this period – rarity and secrecy are a large part of
Prince's mythology.
† Madonna's nouveau-riche husband Guy Ritchie was still a few years down the line.

homeland).* Both were seen entirely as eighties icons – they didn't have Michael Jackson's prehistory to loosen their ties to that specific decade. Both decided to ratchet up their output.

In Prince's case, this meant reminding everyone of why they loved him in the first place. He remained stubbornly himself, sticking to the landscapes he knew best, sure of his own greatness. First he recorded, then pulled, an album – *The Black Album*. It was bootlegged heavily but was still spoken about more than it was heard. Then he made a third movie, *Graffiti Bridge*, in 1990. It was an almost exact replica of *Purple Rain*, with Prince as the moody singer, sitting on his motorbike, pouting like a lady. All at once, things fell apart. *The Black Album* filtered through and turned out to be quite tedious, all dry-hump funk. *Graffiti Bridge* was a greater error as it was such an overground failure. There were no good songs, Prince looked old, his hair was horrid. Everything about it seemed lazy. For somebody so forward-looking, it was a catastrophic error of judgement.

Madonna, similarly, lost her sense of timing. In the space of what seemed like weeks, she released a career retrospective (*The Immaculate Collection*), a new album (*Erotica*) and a book of photographs called *Sex*. No matter what the new album contained, photos of the world's biggest pop star in the nude were always going to trump it.

You could argue a case for *Sex* being a political move in the culture wars of 1990. The same year saw Robert Mapplethorpe's nudes facing an obscenity trial; was this Madge showing solidarity with the cultural left? It could also be seen as the work of someone who was now being treated as a new strain of feminist by universities, one who was seizing the means of porn production. Or you could argue that she had nowhere else to go – Madonna was as ubiquitous as the Beatles had been; splitting up wasn't an option, but dressing down was.

Looking back, the *Sex* book feels like one of the most radical moves made by anyone in this fifty-year story. But in 1990 it was regarded

---

* The notable exception was Madonna's 'Vogue', a UK number one in 1990, on which she cleverly made the most of her cheerleading background. It's meant to be a rap, but that 'Grace Kelly, Harlow, Jean' sequence is all about her suburban roots, and all the more endearing for it.

generally by those open to it as bad art, as bad porn, and by those against it as a publicity stunt. Either way, releasing the *Erotica* album so soon afterwards was Madge overload and none of the singles from it reached number one. This is a shame, as it was her best album – 'Justify My Love' preceded it and was Madonna at her most sensuous, all spooked Mellotron chords, whispering rather than screaming. The title track was almost as good, a 98 bpm Balearic rhythm topped with a simple but dark three-note piano motif: 'If I take you from behind, push myself into your mind . . .' Well, it worked for me. Other singles from the album ('Rain', 'Deeper and Deeper', 'Bad Girl') were good solid disco pop, based around minor chords, and were notably more mature and less attention-grabbing than anything she'd done before. None of this mattered. She'd got her kit off and that was the entire Madonna story. The album flopped.

How did these icons dig their way out of a hole? Prince got a bigger shovel. He toughened up his sound and added a few more cuss words for 'Sexy MF' (UK no. 4, US no. 66 '92) and 'My Name Is Prince' (UK no. 7, US no. 36 '92), both of which were useful additions to his catalogue, but it still felt like he was playing catch-up. In the eighties his music had been the story; in the nineties his battles with the music industry – writing 'slave' on his cheek, changing his name to The Artist Formerly Known as Prince – became the story, and it was a turn-off. By 1994, when he had a surprise UK number one (his first) with 'The Most Beautiful Girl in the World', he felt like a relic.

Madonna realised that no matter what she did after *Sex*, it would be an anti-climax. Besides, everyone save her hardcore fans had their knives sharpened. So she pretty much disappeared, a queen in exile as grunge and riot grrrl took the heat off her. She started her Maverick record label and signed Alanis Morissette, whose *Jagged Little Pill* album sold thirty-three million copies and moved the discourse of female empowerment on by proxy. By the time she returned with *Bedtime Stories* in '95 she could play godmother to the riot-grrrl scene, and Courtney Love was glad to back her up. With fresh impetus, she cut *Ray of Light* and *Music*, both sonically super-modern; once again she was raising the bar for club-orientated pop. She wore the crown.

SOME KIND OF MONSTER: METAL

In the mid-eighties you couldn't move for shock pop tactics.

The Rolling Stones and the Doors had telegraphed rebellion, but not in the same MTV-friendly way as Madonna. Her outrageous acts – singing about teenage pregnancy, kissing a black man while wearing a crucifix – were calculated to wind up both conservatives ('Of course we're horrified!') and liberals ('Of course we're not shocked!'). Different genres developed their own media-friendly rebels, whether it was indie (the Christian-baiting, riot-inciting Jesus and Mary Chain) or hip hop (the Beastie Boys' casual sexism and penchant for VW pendants). There was no real sense of danger, though, nothing that would see its perpetrators threatened with national service, or prison, or worse.

The climate of predictable outrage was perfect for heavy metal, which had been around for more than a decade but hit a commercial peak in the mid-eighties with Bon Jovi, Aerosmith and, ultimately, Def Leppard's world-swallowing *Hysteria* album. Metal is starter-pack rock. It works as both a gateway to other forms of modern pop, via volume, speed and power, and as a model of pure escapism – the roar of the fairground, the cheap thrills of the slasher movie, sex and horror. Besides, as off-the-peg rebellion, it's a lot more fun than Bob Dylan or Crass. It seems indestructible, and has defied all musical cataclysms. It is also deeply conservative, with its own canon, its own heroes, a true metal code of conduct. Along with country, it's quite likely it will outlast every other genre in this book.

Metal had been born at the start of the seventies, when kids were given two choices over which form of heavy rock they liked. In Britain, this was roughly dependent on the number of O-levels they got. Grammar-school kids tended to go for the clever end, the progressive end, which got progressively cleverer until it imploded in a fog of maths in the mid-seventies. Metal was much simpler. It was formulated, which didn't mean the musicians lacked technical ability (check Deep Purple's 'Fireball' for early, highly dextrous metal) but did mean it was easier to follow. Progressive rock was an exercise in aesthetic subtlety; it was only there for people who were willing to put the time in. There was nothing to get with heavy metal – it was loud, it pissed off parents, and it was largely working-class. Black Sabbath's *Master of Reality* album came with a competition form: 'In 10 words or less, explain why you love Black Sabbath's music.' Metal was not out to test your faculties, it was there to dim them, to blot out all that teenage shit with sheer volume.

The *NME*'s Keith Altham had met Black Sabbath in 1971 and described them as 'four typical Northern lads without pretention or affectation who are busily playing hard, exciting rock and enjoying themselves while others enjoy their music'. Altham was speaking from a London perspective when he described Sabbath as northern. Like Led Zeppelin's Robert Plant and John Bonham, they were from the Birmingham conurbation, and had a similar self-deprecating, down-to-earth camaraderie. The West Midlands was the birthplace of metal.

Black Sabbath had acquired their name when Geezer Butler crashed one night at Ozzy Osbourne's house. Ozzy lent him a Dennis Wheatley horror novel, which included a chapter called 'Black Sabbath'; he left it on the bedside table and fell asleep. In the middle of the night, Geezer was woken by a noise and saw a hooded figure at the end of his bed. He woke up in the morning in a cold sweat, looked at his bedside table and, yes, the book had disappeared; Geezer has told this story a million times and it never seems to have occurred to him that the hunched figure might have been Ozzy in his dressing gown.

Contrasting with beer boy Ozzy and his puff-pastry face was the continental look of guitarist Tommy Iommi. His matador moustache and penchant for wearing black gave him a stately look. He had lost two fingertips while working his last-ever shift in a sheet-metal factory before leaving to become a full-time musician; most impressively, he used hardened leather caps to replace them.

Iommi gave Black Sabbath – and, in turn, all of metal – direction. One night he saw a queue around the block outside a Birmingham cinema for a Hammer horror movie; no one, thought Iommi, is making horror *music*. Let's give the people what they clearly want. Black Sabbath's music was perilously slow, Iommi's power chords were murderous (guitar tuned down to accommodate his broken fingers), and Butler's lyrics evoked evil and suffering without bothering to dig into Led Zeppelin's book of Welsh mythology or clamber up Bob Dylan's watchtower. Outside in the cold distance of 1970, metal's wind began to howl. Sabbath's 'War Pigs' was the original stoner-rock anthem, with a political slant that nobody, save maybe Richard Nixon, could possibly disagree with. It may have rhymed 'masses' with 'masses' in the opening couplet but it had huge appeal to boys left in the cold, by the 1970 chart pop of Pickettywitch and Edison Lighthouse on one hand and by brainiac prog on the other. Sabbath even scored a number-four hit single with the unusually mid-tempo, though still pitch-dark, chug of 'Paranoid'.

Sitting at number two in the same 1970 UK chart was Deep Purple's 'Black Night', its A-grade riff borrowed from the Blues Magoos' moody garage-punk hit '(We Ain't Got) Nothin' Yet' (US no. 5 '66). Purple were a different proposition; they sounded like they were having fun playing together for a start, and they always left room in their songs for a Blackpool Tower organ solo from Jon Lord or an ear-burrowing Ritchie Blackmore guitar break. They took 'horror music' to another level with 'Child in Time' on 1970's *Deep Purple in Rock*, a ten-minute epic about Vietnam with singer Ian Gillan's unnerving, wordless high-pitched wail for a chorus. In Gillan they had the classic metal singer with his precise, clipped pronunciation, and his manly, manly voice: 'There once was a woo-mun, a stra-a-ange kind of woo-mun, the kind that gets written down in hiss-toe-ree.'

While hard rock would maintain its quality and status, heavy metal hit the rocks around 1972; in Britain, glam assimilated its riffs and power, and added light and glitter where there had only been darkness. In the States, Rolling Stones-based boogie acts like Aerosmith and Lynyrd Skynyrd flourished. The former were fronted by Steven Tyler and Joe Perry; their fans were labelled the Blue Army because of their liking for top-to-toe denim. Tyler and Perry were labelled the Toxic Twins because of their obvious desire to be compared to the Glimmer Twins, Mick and Keith, and because of their industrial-scale drug abuse. Perry 'started studying the folklore of opium as a sacrament and really got into it'. *Rocks* in 1976 was their fourth straight platinum album, but during the sessions, in spite of Perry's touching faith in narcotics as a creative source, he could barely play guitar for ten minutes without vomiting and needing a lie down. Tyler had become so paranoid that he recorded the rest of the band's conversations. America's hardest, rock-ingest band promptly fell off the map for the best part of a decade.

'It is now 1976', wrote Lester Bangs in *The Rolling Stone Illustrated History of Rock and Roll*, 'and heavy metal seems already to belong to history.' Holding the hard-rock fort in Britain through the mid-seventies were Status Quo, who wore denim, filled stadiums and had a loyal blue army of their own. They also played heads-down, mindless boogie, relentless and unswerving, but Quo's hard rock had more in common with Neu! or Kraftwerk than it did with the Stones or Aerosmith: 'Paper Plane' (no. 7 '73) and 'Down Down' (no. 1 '75) were their best singles, four minutes of drone and power chords welded to Francis Rossi's nasal Surrey whine. The lyrics were entirely irrelevant, the repetition was everything – the opening seconds of 'Caroline' (no. 5 '73) could almost be Steve Reich.

Queen appeared in an extended gap between Led Zeppelin albums and, like Status Quo, never went away. More flamboyant rock than pure metal, with a penchant for both the Beatles' experimentalism ('Killer Queen', UK no. 2 '74) and melodicism ('You're My Best Friend', UK no. 7 '76), not to mention cold funk (the low-selling *Hot Space* album in '82), they were a singles hit machine that didn't relent until singer Freddie Mercury's death in 1991. Three- or four-part harmonies topped backing tracks that were more studio-sharpened than any catalogue this side of Todd Rundgren, and Mercury was rock's most impressive front man since Robert Plant. Yet somehow they remained hard to pin down – the other three band members always looked bored, and this wasn't a pose, they genuinely looked as if they were clocking in every time they took the stage or appeared on *Top of the Pops*. Unlike Quo or Aerosmith – let alone the Stones or Led Zep – they seemed entirely detached from pop. Beyond their hits, all anyone seemed to know about them was that Mercury had been born Freddie Bulsara, in Zanzibar, and that Brian May had built his own guitar, the Red Special, in a shed with help from his dad. It always seemed a touching detail for a group who otherwise seemed closer to a multinational company than a pop group.

Thin Lizzy, an Irish act with a penchant for phenomenally exciting singles, were easier to warm to. They broke through with a heavy folk hit ('Whisky in the Jar', UK no. 6 '72), but 1973's 'The Rocker' ('I'm a rocker! *I'm a rocker!!* I'm a roller too, baby') became their anthem, amped-up power pop without a wasted second. And in the red-hot summer of '76, as an alternative soundtrack to Demis Roussos's feta cheesecake 'Forever and Ever' (UK no. 1), they gave us 'The Boys Are Back in Town' (UK no. 6). It sounded like the band were riding bareback through the city walls to deliver us cool water and cold beers, to lay waste to Demis and the Rollers and J. J. Barrie, to everything puny on Radio 1.

Neither Thin Lizzy nor Queen turned out to be any kind of signi-
fier, just isolated hard-rock cases. In the late seventies, though, fired
by punk's energy and volume, metal unexpectedly returned. Kids
whose older siblings were into punk but who loved the noise and the
parent-baiting swearing were attracted to metal's survivors (Sabbath),
latecomers (AC/DC), hard-rock weirdos (Motörhead) and, especially,
to a bunch of pub acts who would soon be christened the New Wave
of British Heavy Metal, or NWOBHM: Iron Maiden, Def Leppard,
White Spirit, Diamond Head, Samson, Saxon, Tygers of Pan Tang.
Many were compiled on an album called *Metal for Muthas*, which
reached number twelve in the UK album chart but felt bigger. This
time around, post-punk played the role of progressive rock, the clever
kids' choice, with goth as some kind of mediator. Metal wouldn't fade
away again – this time it would crystallise into distinct scenes. As with
country, all of these factions considered themselves to be keepers of the
flame: my metal is more metal than your metal.

Almost every NWOBHM singer sounded like either Robert Plant
or Ian Gillan; it was as if the Tories had invited impressionist Janet
Brown to a party conference to recite a Margaret Thatcher speech. Yet
another Birmingham band, Judas Priest – who had been hovering in
the background since the mid-seventies – became the most popular of
this crop in America, while East London's rough-edged, faster-paced
Iron Maiden were the biggest in Britain. Their debut 'Running Free'
(UK no. 34 '80) burned faster and fiercer than any other NWOBHM
record; eventually, Iron Maiden would score the UK's sole raw-metal
number one, 'Bring Your Daughter to the Slaughter', in 1991.

Any UK Top 20 from 1980 or '81 would likely feature at least one metal
hit; a good percentage came from Deep Purple splinter groups: Rainbow
('All Night Long', 'Since You've Been Gone', 'Can't Happen Here');
Whitesnake ('Fool for Your Loving', 'Don't Break My Heart Again'); and
Gillan ('New Orleans', 'Mutually Assured Destruction', 'Trouble'). There
was no longer any room for Thin Lizzy's mid-seventies subtleties.* The

---

* Thin Lizzy felt they had to bend to metal's new rules to survive and released
some of their worst singles, including 'Killer on the Loose', which was released as

look, for fans and bands alike, was now unwavering – off-blond curls, denim, leather, gothic script. Though there was a glamour attached to metal's front men, which made it more exotic than other contemporaneous teenage noise, metal was still about wearing a uniform – like mod and Oi! – with the audience as part of the performance. And when the fans turned sixteen, they moved on.

America was slower to develop its own metal bands, but by the early eighties, as Britain embraced NWOBHM, US metal began to manifest itself as a glam variant: Alice Cooper, Sweet and the New York Dolls were touchstones for Twisted Sister, Poison and Mötley Crüe. UK glam had barely registered stateside in the early seventies, as it ate up the British charts. Some American metal acts like Great White (Ian Hunter's 'Once Bitten Twice Shy') and Quiet Riot (Slade's 'Mama Weer All Crazee Now' *and* 'Cum On Feel the Noize') raided the British glam hits of a decade earlier, scoring US Top 10 hits and, in Quiet Riot's case, almost five million album sales. The Americanised Ozzy Osbourne – fresh out of Sabbath, and now biting the heads off bats on stage – became a role model with his new, softer band, Blizzard of Ozz. Make-up was worn, and Ozzy came across as a demonic counterpoint to Adam Ant. 'Crazy Train' and 'Mr Crowley' gave Blizzard of Ozz American hits in 1980; with guitarist Randy Rhoads's choppy melodic riffs and Ozzy's voice double-tracked and harmonised over synths, Blizzard of Ozz were closer to Foreigner's adult-orientated rock than Black Sabbath's murk. Metal's sales figures went higher and higher.

One reason for metal's accelerating popularity in the eighties was MTV. Like Duran Duran's yachts-and-models lifestyle, the excess of metal bands' live shows translated beautifully to the florid new medium. Generally, the more excessive the act, the better they sold. 'Don't forget,' said Bon Jovi's A&R man Jerry Jaffe, 'most of this genre of music . . . is the lowest common denominator entertainment. It's bread and circuses

---

the Yorkshire Ripper terrorised women in the north of England. A happier result was that Slade's career was revived after they played the Reading Rock Festival in 1980, opening their set with 'Merry Xmas Everybody'. 'We'll Bring the House Down' (no. 10 '81) and 'Lock Up Your Daughters' bore a strong NWOBHM stamp.

for the common people. Record companies are trying to make money. In the same way that *Porky's* made money, a record company can make money on Mötley Crüe.'

Secondly, the late-eighties metal generation was explicitly about sex and horror-movie props – denim was abandoned as bands appeared in high heels, fishnets, heavy make-up and long back-combed hair. This was cross-gender rebellion that picked up more female fans than metal had ever had in the seventies. It didn't hurt that Skid Row's Sebastian Bach, Guns n' Roses' Axl Rose and Jon Bon Jovi were very pretty. There was also a glossiness to eighties metal that simply hadn't existed before. British band Def Leppard created their 1987 album *Hysteria*, a transatlantic number one, as a state-of-the-art recording that would make as much sense to someone in Tunisia as it would in Idaho or Shrewsbury. Metal's rootlessness, like disco's, appealed to the misunderstood outsider. With singles like 'Animal' (UK no. 6, US no. 19 '87) and 'Pour Some Sugar on Me' (UK no. 18, US no. 2 '87) – using new pop synths and Mutt Lange's mainstream eighties production – Def Leppard showed how many of these outsiders there were in the world: *Hysteria* sold twenty million copies.

Though it could now be heard on TV soundtracks and ad jingles, metal once again took up the rebellious middle ground it had staked out in 1970. 'A kid puts on a Judas Priest or an Iron Maiden or a Motörhead shirt and it makes a statement,' said Def Leppard and Metallica manager Cliff Burnstein.* 'Hall and Oates don't make a statement.' The kid's statement was the equivalent of painting his room black. The kid's manifesto was 'Fuck you, I won't do what you tell me.'

In the late eighties and nineties, partly as a reaction to the comic-strip excesses of glam metal – now caustically renamed 'hair metal' by its detractors – Slayer, Anthrax, Metallica and Megadeth ditched the movie props, went back to Sabbath's crepuscular roots, pioneered thrash metal, and became the genre's biggest-selling acts; they were treated with great reverence for their darkness, speed and musicianship. 'I could relate to punk lyrics,' said Metallica singer James Hetfield in 1987. 'They were

---

* Motörhead have sold more T-shirts than records.

about me, rather than that "Look at me riding a horse, with a big sword in my hand" typical HM fantasy crap.' Like dance music, the scene developed further splinters (speed, death, doom, black), all the while becoming more and more distanced from mainstream pop. Heaviosity through speed and volume meant that thrash soon found itself, like Oi! before it and gabber to come, chasing its own tail: 'When people first started copying us it was a real compliment, but now we have to get away from the speed metal tag, 'cos all these bands have jumped on the bandwagon,' Hetfield complained. 'The NWOBHM bands each had their own sound and feeling, but you can't tell the difference between most of the new thrash bands. It's fucked. So you're the fastest band in the world . . . so what? Your songs suck.'

Metal embodies modern pop's conservativism. While it has continued to evolve and keep up with technology, it has also rewarded durability and consistency. An excessive lifestyle is prized as much as musical merit, but redemption through rehab gets gold stars too. Aerosmith were handed a lifeline when their 1976 hit 'Walk This Way' (US no. 10) was covered by Run-DMC. They resolved to hit the clinic, cut 'Dude Looks Like a Lady' (US no. 14 '87) and then a monster ballad called 'Angel', which was co-written by soft metal's secret weapon, Desmond Child.* By 1989 Aerosmith were proud to be seen working out on exercise equipment during a promo documentary for their latest album, *Pump*. It sold seven million copies. Mötley Crüe had an even more extreme take on the metal lifestyle: bassist Nikki Sixx was declared legally dead from a heroin overdose in 1987 before he was revived by two adrenalin shots to the heart. A couple of years previously their singer Vince Neil had been drink-driving when he slammed his car into oncoming traffic; his passenger, Hanoi Rocks' drummer Razzle, was pronounced dead on the way to the hospital. Mötley Crüe's 1989 album *Dr Feelgood* was their biggest seller, a US number one whose success the band put down to collective sobriety.

---

* Child helped to add a melodic, commercial sheen to metal in the eighties. After giving Kiss their biggest hit to date with 'I Was Made for Loving You' (US no. 11 '79), he went on to co-write hits for Bon Jovi ('Livin' on a Prayer', 'You Give Love a Bad Name', 'Bad Medicine'), Aerosmith ('Angel', 'Dude Looks Like a Lady', 'Crazy'), Alice Cooper ('Poison') and Ricky Martin ('Livin' la Vida Loca').

Australian group AC/DC ended up as the biggest metal group of all by dint of never changing their look or their sound one iota. They were entirely without ornament, their songs were pure riffing, their drum sound was more basic than the Dave Clark Five and louder than Led Zeppelin and, outside the studio, they made Mötley Crüe look like lightweights. Their singer Bon Scott died in 1980 after a night's drinking at the Camden Palace. Five months later AC/DC, now with Scott-soundalike singer Brian Johnson, released 'Back in Black', dedicated to his memory. It became the second best-selling album of all time. So why stop at a tribute? Three decades later they are still going, still selling hundreds of thousands of albums, still using the exact same musical palette. They haven't written a song in thirty years that anyone could name, but people still wear the T-shirt.

Like country, metal has travelled on a parallel path to modern pop, occasionally scoring a heavy presence on the charts, and occasionally leaving traces of its influence on other genres. Def Leppard's *Hysteria* was produced by Mutt Lange, who, ten years on in 1997, applied a similar, vaporous rock sound to his wife Shania Twain's country album *Come On Over* and was again rewarded with huge crossover sales – both albums were UK number ones. So metal is not as autistically quarantined as indie or punk. It can adapt (after punk with NWOBHM, after new pop with glam metal, after grunge with doom metal) and it's unlikely that anyone in a metal band would suffer guilt pangs from selling out, though – again, like country – people are very serious about the music's history and tradition.

Country, however, is a centuries-old music that has been adopted by and adapted to modern pop's electricity. Metal only came into being around 1970. How has it survived and thrived? What is its continuing allure to new generations?

One key draw – certainly in the NWOBHM era – was metal's respect for tradition. For teenage boys in 1980, the fact that much metal came from a source with a stamp of classic-rock quality – Zep, Purple, Sabbath – gave them confidence to follow the new bands without fear of peer embarrassment. Also, the musicianship – say, Ritchie Blackmore's noodling with Rainbow – was something for them to aspire to. These musicians demanded to have their poster on your wall, their patch on your denim jacket. Radio 1's *Friday Rock Show*, presented by the authoritative Tommy Vance, was a fifty–fifty mix of old and new bands, which was much more comforting than the year-zero approach of punk. It remained gently rebellious, not because it had any real sense of danger or revolution but because it was despised and sneered at by non-believers. Metal's heritage strengthened the fan's resolve. This respect for tradition and camaraderie hasn't gone away – even now, Metallica regularly bring Diamond Head, their favourite NWOBHM act, on stage as guests.

There's humour, too. Metal is rarely knowing or ironic,* and is gloriously unapologetic about its bluster and silliness. Steve 'Dobby' Dawson was the bassist in Saxon, one of NWOBHM's biggest successes with 'Wheels of Steel' (UK no. 20 '80), '747 (Strangers in the Night)' (UK no. 13 '80), 'And the Bands Played On' (UK no. 12 '81) and 'Never Surrender' (UK no. 18 '81). Dawson worked out basslines which enabled him to punch his fist in the air at the same time – he knew it was ludicrous, but not so ludicrous that fans would feel they were being taken for a ride.

Then there's sex. In the eighties metal lyrics and album covers – even band names such as Split Beaver – appealed to pubescent boys not tall enough to reach for the top shelf. Take Whitesnake. Their song titles ('Slide It In', 'Slip of the Tongue', 'Slow and Easy') and the *Liquor and Poker* tour offered teenage boys a fantasy not reflected in real life. This earned them a few UK Top 20 hits in the NWOBHM era, but when singer David Coverdale replaced his hoary bandmates with younger, American, better-looking musicians in the eighties they stepped up to another level. Along with the sequencers that updated their sound on 'Here I Go Again' (US no. 1, UK no. 9 '87) and 'Is This Love' (US no. 2, UK no. 9 '87), there was now poodle-haired eye candy for the girls too, and – just so the boys didn't feel short-changed – Coverdale's

---

* British group the Darkness managed to appeal to an indie crowd with a sound that was pure eighties metal, but given a dusting of knowingness – something in singer Justin Hawkins's voice had an element of ironic distance. Metal fans were equally keen, and this two-pronged approach gave the Darkness a number-one album in the UK with *Permission to Land* in 2003.

wife Tawny Kitaen regularly appeared as a vixen in their Duran Duran-styled, vaguely erotic videos.

Metal is as much a rite of passage as a genre of modern pop. It is about a state of being, of Being Metal. And listening to it confirms your metalness. Almost no other music has this *raison d'être*. This exclusiveness, the total immersion in the genre and its formula, is what gives metal its huge appeal. It spends a lot of time and effort pretending to be less learned than it is. 'It doesn't mean more or less than those old bubblegum acts,' reckoned Jerry Jaffe. 'Except the image is a little more striking.' I love 'Sugar, Sugar', I really do, but I'm not sure I'd want to build my life around it.

POISED OVER THE PAUSE BUTTON: THE SMITHS AND THE BIRTH OF INDIE

English as tuppence, changing yet changeless as canal water,
nestling in green nowhere, armoured and effete.
Vivian Stanshall, *Sir Henry at Rawlinson End*

In 1953 a Florida student called Wade Buff wrote a song called 'It's Almost Tomorrow', and it was very small and very sad. It was about a boy who knows that his girlfriend is going to leave him the next day; he is unable – or unwilling – to go to sleep, watching her lying next to him, not wanting to miss a second of the limited time left in their relationship.

No wonder he sounds so small and sad – the poor sap doesn't want her to wake and see the tears in his eyes. Wade Buff was quite sure he had a hit on his hands, but no one wanted to know – the song was too maudlin, too amateurish, possibly too raw. So he assembled a bunch of college friends, they called themselves the Dreamweavers, and they recorded 'It's Almost Tomorrow' in a shed in Miami. Unstudied, patched together with vinegar and brown paper, it reached the US Top 10 and went all the way to number one in Britain at the start of 1956.*

Not only was its production entirely independent, but its fey sound and defeated yet hopeful stance made 'It's Almost Tomorrow' a good three decades ahead of its time: this was the first indie record.

Indie is short for independent, and indie pop was born out of the British independent-record-label scene in the eighties. The greatest periods in pop tend to coincide with the pre-eminence of independent record labels. This is not exactly a coincidence: a genuine youthquake would be sure to excite the pop-hungry likes of Leiber and Stoller, Phil Spector, Andrew Oldham, Factory's Tony Wilson and Rough Trade's Geoff Travis, talented fans who would always be faster off the mark than the A&R men at unwieldy and lethargic major labels. The difference in the eighties was that the independent labels were frequently seen as being in opposition to the majors – they were opting out of the mainstream quite deliberately.†

---

* I don't want to spoil a good story, but for the sake of honesty . . . Decca in America insisted the Dreamweavers re-record their demo, and this new version was the one that charted. Truthfully, you'd never guess. Buff is no Tony Bennett, no matter who's manning the recording equipment, and at the song's conclusion it sounds like a piano falls on the hapless singer, fulfilling his wish that tomorrow should never arrive.
† The longest run of independent-label success in the modern pop era was in America, between 1956 and 1966, from doo wop to psychedelia via the British Invasion; the majors then got their act together and descended on the San Francisco hippie scene, swallowing it whole. In Britain, from 1977 to '82 – the aftermath of punk – independents became politicised and majors were ostracised for the first time; this time the majors didn't use heavy artillery, but instead created their own boutique labels like Dindisc and Rialto. From 1988 to 1991 house and techno blew Duran Duran's yacht out of the water, and labels like Trax in America, XL in London and R&S in Belgium rewrote the rules again.

In 1983 new pop had started to wobble, and into the void stepped the decidedly pre-punk Rod Stewart (who scored his first UK number one in five years with 'Baby Jane') and Elton John (with the passive-aggressive splurt 'I'm Still Standing', a UK number four and US number twelve); Billy Joel's album *An Innocent Man* was the radio soundtrack of the year. The British scene became dominated by video-driven acts like Eurythmics whose careers would be cemented for the rest of the decade by Band Aid and Live Aid. It was like punk, post-punk and new pop had never happened.

Scattered around Britain in 1983 were a small number of refuseniks who had grown up listening to John Peel and reading a music press so articulate that it was commonplace to buy records on the strength of a review. For this generation, groups like the Fall, Josef K, Orange Juice, Subway Sect, Young Marble Giants and the Television Personalities – none of whom had ever had a sniff of a hit – were of great historical and political significance. They had sold thousands, sometimes tens of thousands of records, and each of them had suggested a different possible future for pop. They *had* scored hits on the independent chart, launched in 1980 by a group of independent labels and distributors,* and printed every week in the *NME*. Geoff Travis's Rough Trade label had provided the first number one (Spizz Energi's 'Where's Captain Kirk') and several other singles in the first Top 30. 'We used to do our own Top 10s in the shop,' he recalled, 'but they were personal taste. The first independent charts were very important. It was significant if the Fall's LP was number one, it gave you a sense of achievement. We were happy in our own world – there was a logic and beauty to it. And the real world's taste is so terrible.' Within weeks, the nascent *Smash Hits* began to publish the chart: to pop kids raised on *Top of the Pops* and the Top 40, this was a parallel universe of music you had never heard of. The song titles and band names conveyed vast mystique: 'Get Up and

---

Turbulence for the industry usually meant the best of times for pop.
* The labels were Rough Trade (London), Factory (Manchester), Y (Bristol), Zoo and Inevitable (Liverpool) and Fast Product (Edinburgh). The distributors listed on the very first chart were Rough Trade and Fresh (London), Pinnacle (Orpington), Red Rhino (York), Graduate (Dudley) and Bullet (Stafford).

Use Me' by Fire Engines; Cabaret Voltaire's 'Seconds Too Late'; 'Simply Thrilled Honey' by the thrillingly named Orange Juice. At number five was the Cramps' 'Drug Train'. There could never be a song called 'Drug Train' in the real chart, whose corresponding number five that week was 'Feels Like I'm in Love' by Kelly Marie.

Three years on came the fallout from the new pop experiment. Some observers were appalled that Kajagoogoo's flimsy, post-new pop 'Too Shy' hit number one in the spring of 1983, while Vic Godard had given up on pop to become a postman. The last survivors of a lost battle, they had nothing to lose and decided to set themselves up in direct opposition. If Radio 1, *Top of the Pops* and even Rough Trade – now concentrating funds on Scritti Politti's soul-meets-critical-theory *Songs to Remember* – were out to reject them, then fuck them, they'd create an alternative pop world.*

'They have their own clothes, language, in-jokes and fanzines,' said Caroline Coon of 1976's punk-rockers. 'There is both healthy camaraderie and competitiveness.' Taking the first spring of punk rock as a base, a British network of geographically isolated groups, gig promoters, labels and fanzine writers coalesced between 1983 and 1985. They made contact via the Royal Mail. There was a high level of collaboration and co-operation. Unlike post-punk, there was no intense urge to

---

* A bunch of other insular mid-eighties movements emerged at the same time who harked back to punk's spirit of '76, tending towards the Clash's set of beliefs and the assumption that there was an inherent true grit in roots music. There was psychobilly (the Meteors, King Kurt), cowpunk (the post-feminist, *Calamity Jane*-inspired Boothill Foot Tappers and Yip Yip Coyote) and a neo-folk scene forged by London's second- and third-generation Irish (the Pogues, the Men They Couldn't Hang). It was an understandable hankering for something of flavour in an era of shiny blandness, but these scenes led nowhere – only the Pogues made any commercial headway thanks to a brace of exceptional singles, 'A Pair of Brown Eyes' (UK no. 72 '85) and 'Fairytale of New York' (UK no. 2 '87). Abandoning post-punk, these ersatz and mannerist movements were heavy on symbols of rebellion and were epitomised by the Pogues' Shane MacGowan, who, with his slurred, gravelly brogue and rotten teeth, made for a bleak Irish caricature. It was a convincing act, and hid well the fact that he had attended the private Westminster School (fees at time of writing: £7,000 per term), whose alumni included Christopher Wren, Henry Purcell, John Gielgud and Tony Benn.

be brand-new, but there was an intense urge to be intense. The model, musically and visually, was one of the best post-punk labels, Postcard Records.

Started by camp, acerbic Glaswegian Alan Horne in 1979, Postcard had packaged everything with considerable style: a great logo (kitten bashing drum), a free postcard (usually of the group, smiling) and a slogan – 'the sound of young Scotland'. Was Horne being arch? Almost certainly, but either way it was true. Postcard's first release had been 'Falling and Laughing' by Orange Juice, so called because the name simultaneously sounded 'fresh' and was the most ridiculous they could think of. Edwyn Collins sang like a drunken calf, but he was a deftly romantic lyricist at a time when romance was in short supply.* Guitarist James Kirk was clearly self-taught. Part of the thrill of Orange Juice records was how close they came to falling apart completely before, always, climaxing with a flourish around two minutes thirty. Postcard had also been first to sign Aztec Camera, basically a front for sixteen-year-old Roddy Frame, who wrote sweet love letters ('Just Like Gold', 'Pillar to Post') that tried to define feelings he was really too young to feel. And Josef K completed the roster, the most clearly contemporary of the three, darker, slightly atonal: they had broken up in 1981, bowing out with 'Chance Meeting', an extraordinarily emotional record that sounded like a brass band playing in a broom cupboard.

Postcard's scratchiness and strength through DIY provided a musical template for the new indie underground.† There was also a lot of politics, about modern pop, and about modern pop consumption. Fanzines were in red and black, the colours of Bauhaus and the Angry Brigade. The price of a fanzine was important, as was the format: vinyl was fetishised; no one released CDs, which were seen as corporate, expensive and

---

* Post-punk had eschewed love songs. The Au Pairs said their songs were 'about politics, personal politics', while Gang of Four's 'Damaged Goods' took the biscuit for anti-love songs: 'Sometimes I'm thinking that I love you, but then I know it's only lust . . . your kiss so sweet, your sweat so sour.'
† The first mention of music being described as 'indie' is in a 1981 *Record Mirror* review by Sunie of a Modern English single. They may have recorded for 4AD but at this point the music produced by independent labels had no specific style, just a shared attitude, not-for-profit values and a sense of spontaneity.

largely a ruse by which the industry could rinse money from unthinking consumers. Similarly, videos were regarded as an enemy of good pop because they were passive – as you sat and watched them, a layer of personal involvement disappeared. Videos also benefited mediocre records – Peter Gabriel's 'Sledgehammer' (US no. 1, UK no. 4 '86) and Paula Abdul's 'Opposites Attract' (US no. 1, UK no. 2 '90) did so well largely because their videos were considerably more exciting than the songs. Indie was hostile to the idea of MTV's technologies as potential platforms in any usable way. Partly through its own puritan choosing, it was entirely disconnected.

Like the American hardcore scene, British indie was also anti-macho to the point of being sexless. Women were suddenly allowed a place in pop that they had been unaccustomed to since the Brill Building era, not only forming groups but promoting gigs and writing fanzines. Though hiding itself from the mainstream, by 1986 the indie aesthetic had at least achieved national recognition in the music press. It had also reached a consensus on how it should sound and look. The musical influences tended towards the melodic Buzzcocks end of punk, the scratchy post-punk guitars of Josef K and the twelve-string chime of the Byrds – freed from year-zero dogma, the musical past now became a library of unexpected detail. The sixties were quickly ransacked for both look (polo necks and bowl cuts for the boys, polka dots and bobs for the girls) and sound: from Scotland came the Pastels, Primal Scream and the Jasmine Minks; Oxford had Razorcuts and Talulah Gosh; Bristol had the Flatmates and the Groove Farm; Newcastle provided Hurrah!; from the East London/Essex border came the Wolfhounds and McCarthy; the Wedding Present and One Thousand Violins were Yorkshire's contribution.

This was impressive and all very brave, worthy of a spot on *Newsnight Review* even, but there was no getting around the fact that it was a self-imposed and self-conscious pop ghetto, too shambolic to have any impact on the eighties mainstream. Worse, the shared likes and dislikes, the closely watched values, meant that almost inevitably the groups began to sound remarkably similar. There was one group who operated outside the ghetto; they had escaped it just before the wall went up.

They also happened to be, by a distance, the most talented indie group of the lot.

Among Orange Juice's biggest fans was Johnny Marr, a guitarist who worked in a Manchester jeans shop. He also had an encyclopedic knowledge of the Brill Building and sixties girl-group 45s. Across town was Steven Morrissey, a loner who spent much of his spare time writing letters to the music papers and listening to Sandie Shaw and Billy Fury. One day Marr knocked on his door and suggested they form a songwriting partnership. They found a bassist and a drummer, called themselves the Smiths and made two rules for themselves: write a new song every week and never make a video.

Morrissey must have felt he'd left it too late, that the boat that had sailed the maladjusted likes of Adam Ant and Kevin Rowland to the heart of the chart was the one he should have boarded. By the time he got the Smiths together in late '82 his home town of Manchester had become Britain's disco capital, with New Order at the fore and the (newly built, usually empty) Haçienda its HQ. The only other local group to use guitars in a way that suggested they'd listened to Orange Juice were fringe Factory acts Stockholm Monsters and James. What Morrissey had on his side, though, was a prolonged incubation period – looking back at the Smiths' single covers, from 1983 to their split in '87, you'd guess that their whole career might have all been in his head all along.

Their writing credit, Morrissey/Marr, had the ring of a lost golden era (Leiber/Stoller, Goffin/King, Lennon/McCartney) and the possibility of a brand-new one. Johnny Marr was also their arranger. Morrissey's voice could have been limited by its distinctiveness, but Marr was always adventurous, finding unlikely homes for it by quoting Chic ('This Night Has Opened My Eyes'), using tape manipulation ('The Queen Is Dead') and darting between hard-rock riffing ('What She Said') and Elton John piano balladry ('Asleep').

The Smiths' touchstones were the Velvet Underground, the Shangri-Las and British kitchen-sink cinema – they wore their bedsit bookishness on their sleeves. Morrissey's conservatism somehow forged a way forward in (differently) conservative times. He quickly became the spokesman for the outsider that Bowie had been in the seventies.

Just as 'This Charming Man' – the Smiths' second single – took them out of the fanzine world and onto *Top of the Pops*, Channel 4 began screening a season of British black-and-white kitchen-sink movies from the late fifties and early sixties: *A Taste of Honey, Saturday Night and Sunday Morning, Room at the Top, A Kind of Loving*. The heroes of these films were all misunderstood young adults, usually with quiffs (Albert Finney's Arthur Seaton) or bobs (Rita Tushingham's Jo). The Smiths appeared not just as heirs to the misunderstood British pop stars of the early sixties – John Leyton, Billy Fury – but to their cinematic equivalents. A new generation latched onto these films, most of which hadn't been screened for years, and the Smiths' emergence couldn't have been better timed.

Timing aside, Morrissey was the best lyricist British pop had ever produced, as fey and distinctive as Marc Bolan, as sensual as Kate Bush, with the super-fandom of Roy Wood and the archness of Noël Coward thrown in for good measure. 'The most impassioned song to a lonely soul is so easily outgrown,' he sang on 1985 B-side 'Rubber Ring', which then segued into 'Asleep' – an impassioned song about suicide written with no one but lonely souls in mind. Such was the acute self-awareness of Morrissey the pop fan, and his awareness of what the Smiths – so soon, just two years after their first single – meant to their fans.

Only a few years earlier it had been commonplace for DIY groups to litter their songs with localised lyrics, but by 1984 new pop, let alone punk, already felt like a lost era. Part of the Smiths' impact was that they found the exotic in the local – as soon as the *Strangeways Here We Come* album came out in 1987, the road sign on the sleeve became a tourist destination. Morrissey's civic pride was instrumental in making Manchester the most popular student city in the country, and that just happened to coincide with a musical renaissance which in turn would render him yesterday's man. So easily outgrown.

Morrissey sang for the underdog, quite specifically, and his lyrics were richly nuanced, designed to appeal to kids who still used the library: if you couldn't relate to 'Belligerent ghouls run Manchester schools . . . jealous of youth, same old suit since 1962', then you were very fortunate. No one in modern pop had ever started a song with the word 'belligerent' before. He captured the collective insecurities of anyone not buying into the wipe-clean eighties dream of a new England: 'The Queen is dead, boys, and it's so lonely on a limb.' Then there were his eccentricities – the flowers, the hearing aid (just like poor old Johnnie Ray), the militant vegetarianism, the celebrated celibacy. At last, we somehow thought, one of us.

Of course, he was nothing of the sort. After an early gig at the Fighting Cocks in Birmingham he asked the group to stop calling him Steve – from now on he was just Morrissey. On the drive back to Manchester, drummer Mike Joyce went to ask 'Steve' the time but checked himself in the nick of time.

'Morrissey, what time is it?'

'It's about a quarter to twelve, Joyce.'

The Smiths' prominence raised the profile of the UK's independent network, and especially the dozens of groups scratching away on cheap guitars every Friday at the George and Dragon in Bedford, or at the Black Horse in Camden Town. The *NME* released a cassette compilation called *C86* in 1986 which pulled twenty-two of them together, and then the scene had a tag. It was largely compiled by *NME* writers Roy Carr and Neil Taylor, who licensed tracks from labels including Subway, Ron Johnson, Pink and Alan McGee's Creation (the Pastels, the Bodines, Primal Scream), the most significant in terms of both reach and jangling solidarity. The number of fanzines on sale increased exponentially, their names echoing a new-found liberty, like a second childhood: *Are You Scared to Get Happy?*, *Trout Fishing in Leytonstone*, *Rumbledethump!*, *Pop Avalanche*, *Big Bad Fire Engine*.

By 1987 indie had started solidifying into a sound rather than a way of living. This was cemented when Channel 4 started a *Top of the Pops* rival show on Friday nights: apart from the standard Top 20 singles, *The Chart Show* featured a rock chart (largely metal), a dance chart (including R&B and hip hop, basically anything black) and an indie chart – effectively, groups that were considered 'indie' were now excised from the story of 'rock'. John Peel started to complain that the Festive Fifty – his end-of-year listeners' poll – was becoming generic. He was particularly upset that, in 1987, MARRS's sample-delic 'Pump Up the Volume', a thrilling harbinger of the nineties, reached number one in the UK singles chart but only just scraped into his listeners' poll; meanwhile, songs from the Smiths' farewell album, *Strangeways Here We Come*, claimed eight spots.

The boom was over as soon as it was recognised. As had happened with Merseybeat and punk, *C86* was quickly subsumed by the major labels, who rushed their new signings into white-walled studios better suited to Duran Duran, and the thrill of the rattling jangle was lost under a battery of gated snare. The industry began to set up boutique labels like Blue Guitar (who signed *C86* acts the Shop Assistants and the Mighty Lemon Drops). Infighting resulted, with micro-indie labels setting up – Sarah Records being both the gentlest musically and the most anti-industry – who were happy to sell five hundred copies of a single in a wraparound, two-colour sleeve to a devoted, tiny audience; groups and labels alike sank within eighteen months. Indie's mid-eighties myopia – its self-regard, its inability to absorb any influence beyond the few flavours endlessly rewritten in almost identical fanzines – was a catastrophe.

The American experience was somewhat different. 'Indie' wasn't a term many people recognised, but 'alternative' boomed. College radio stations had been around since the sixties, but exploded in the eighties. They were non-commercial enterprises run by students and community DJs, and tended to broadcast locally so they also reached listeners off campus. They picked up on music that had a similar parentage to British indie, with the fag-end of new wave thrown into the mix. Soon college rock became a genre all of its own. The name suggested something aspirational and intellectual – music that had the illusion of artiness, with lyrics that were hard to decipher or maybe mentioned Simone de Beauvoir.*

---

* The Bangles' name, though, did not suggest particularly intellectual leanings. They emerged from a west-coast sixties-revival scene called the Paisley Underground and wrote some stunning jangle pop which was perfectly suited to college radio. Then they jumped the fence and became major pop stars with 'Manic Monday' (US no. 2, UK no. 3 '86), 'Walk Like an Egyptian' (US no. 1, UK no. 2 '86) and 'Eternal Flame' (US and UK no. 1 '88), while looking like a

The Smiths were regarded as college rock in the States, as were self-consciously quirky, raised-eyebrow acts like XTC and They Might Be Giants; post-hardcore bands like Hüsker Dü (though only once they put melodies ahead of velocity) and Pixies; introspective electronic acts like the Cure and New Order; and, primarily, jangly guitar bands. So the Smiths, Housemartins, Lloyd Cole and the Commotions and the La's from the UK fitted the college-radio format neatly, as did literate US non-hitmakers like Let's Active, 10,000 Maniacs and Lone Justice. It was like the soundtrack of *Molly Ringwald Goes to Cal Arts*.

The undisputed kings of college rock were REM. They formed in a college town – Athens, Georgia – and, like their UK counterparts the Smiths, they worshipped at the altar of the twelve-string; their sound was like a love-warmed nest of guitars. Singer Michael Stipe and guitarist Peter Buck lived together in a converted church. Stipe was as self-consciously arty as Morrissey, though more naive ('Was Donovan in the Turtles?' he asked an embarrassed Buck during one interview). Though Buck was more voluble than his English counterpart Johnny Marr, he chose to communicate on record in a similar way, harking back to the Searchers and the Byrds' jet-age jangle. But while Morrissey's vocabulary was crucial to the Smiths' reclamation of English pop – quoting Shelagh Delaney, closer to Noël Coward than Jagger/Richards – Michael Stipe's lyrics were mumbled and often unintelligible. On spectral songs like 'Talk about the Passion', his rich voice recalled that of the Byrds' Gene Clark; the meanings of his lyrics were as tangled and spooky as the covering of Spanish moss that adorned the sleeve of their 1983 debut album, *Murmur*.* 'Some grand feeling is being outlined here,' said the *NME*, 'its

---

million dollars in their videos. In this, they fell between every possible alternative stool – hipster boys in specs scorned their chart positions, bowl-cut girls sneered at their big cakey hair – and they had to settle for wealth and fame. They never got their due as one of the best girl groups of the decade, but 'Going Down to Liverpool' should feature in any list of the greatest singles of the eighties.

* If you're looking for a starting point for alt country, the predominant US indie sound of the early 2000s, the sleeve to *Murmur* is as good as any. Attempts to combine punk aesthetics with country had been pioneered by groups like Nashville's Jason and the Scorchers, but REM's artwork and gothic myths and legends added a third layer. Cowboy Junkies, Red House Painters and American

implications telegraphed through a wilful obscurity that blurs meaning
. . . it draws us in, makes us want to play along in its games.' Someone
else called them 'the only band that mutters'.

Stipe had grown up thinking his favourite song, 'Moon River', was
about Huckleberry Hound. He understood a profound pop truth: 'I
doubt very few people in the world can tell you all the words to, say,
"Tumbling Dice" by the Stones. It probably holds a lot more meaning
to be able to make up your own words, and to make up your own meanings about what the words are saying.'

The Smiths split in 1987, when Morrissey's adherence to dusty
antique culture became too suffocating for the restless Marr. The guitarist said leaving or staying was like making a choice between Herman's
Hermits and Sly and the Family Stone, though given his patchy post-
Smiths career this was wishful thinking.* At this point, REM became
the default biggest alternative pop group in the world. Within months,
they had a genuine hit single with 'The One I Love' (US no. 8 '87), and
promptly left their independent label IRS for Warner Brothers. Stipe
took to wearing a dress and make-up on stage and singing through a
megaphone – this, said Jon Savage in '89, 'marked their passing from
cult rock-band status to the blurred, warping world of pop stardom'.
So they left indie behind but, unlike any of their British indie contemporaries, they continued to make better and better records until
they reached the sixteen-million-selling *Automatic for the People* in '92.
Here, Buck ventured into AOR guitar work on 'Ignoreland'; 'Star Me
Kitten' blended the exotica of the early Shadows with a bed of voices
borrowed from 10cc's 'I'm Not in Love'; 'Sweetness Follows' was a
cello-led ballad; 'The Sidewinder Sleeps Tonight' had one of Stipe's

---

Music Club came in REM's wake, doing further acoustic, harmonic and old-west
mythic groundwork, and their music was tagged Americana; Uncle Tupelo's *No
Depression* in 1990 would be retrospectively regarded as the first fully-formed alt-
country album.

* Morrissey's solo career has produced a lot of decent songs ('Hold On to Your
Friends', 'Alma Matters', 'Seasick Yet Still Docked', 'Suedehead') but they could
all have been released at any time between 1987 and the present: they have no
time-specific references, and – in spite of using a variety of producers and musicians – all sound like he is trying to re-create the Smiths.

most indecipherable lyrics and was as vivacious as any Capella or Bizarre Inc. hit of that year. Just for good measure, the album included a rare song by drummer Bill Berry, 'Everybody Hurts' (UK no. 7, US no. 29 '93), which was as corny as 'Octopus's Garden', but you couldn't begrudge him. Settled, content and creative while going six times platinum in the UK alone, few groups have peaked as neatly as REM. Two years later they came back with the raucous, tuneless *Monster*, and the spell was broken. Bill Berry left and – as the Smiths had split when Johnny Marr quit – that should've been the end of REM. But they slogged on until 2011, slowly degrading their legacy year by year, with Michael Stipe edging ever further from Gene Clark shyness, ever closer to Bono, Bob Geldof and a 'world leader pretend' role he had tried to exorcise in 1988.

* * *

By the end of the eighties Morrissey, the British indie poster boy who had seemingly been tied to Manchester's apron strings, would be living in a Hollywood mansion designed by Clark Gable. 'It was never the intention for me to be a flamboyant rock star,' he told Stuart Maconie in 1994. 'I thought that I had spearheaded a new mood for singers. I thought there'd be a rejection of all those old, stereotypical manoeuvres but there hasn't been. Everyone secretly still wants to be photographed with Yoko Ono.'

For the ninety-nine per cent of indie groups who never had a sniff of the Smiths' or REM's commercial success, there would be no Hollywood mansion. Reflected glory came years later in the Manchester boom of 1989, the fanzine-led insurrection of riot grrrl and the brief promise of Britpop.

For those who missed the librarian chic of eighties indie, it would be condensed in the mid-nineties by Glasgow group Belle and Sebastian. They were tailor-made for the disaffected and the wilfully independent, for teenagers who spent 'warm summer days indoors'. Simultaneously updating and reducing the Smiths/*C86* sound, with imagery borrowed from the contemporary American cinema of Hal Hartley, they giggled when they appeared on *Top of the Pops*. In the States, Stephin Merritt's Magnetic Fields fulfilled a similar need. Both were making music that revived the hermetically sealed indie-pop scene of the mid-eighties. It's not hard to imagine either group covering 'It's Almost Tomorrow'. Beyond these cloistered walls, 'indie' became an ever-expanding term, gobbling up sections of the past: by the late nineties Joy Division were regarded as godfathers of indie rather than pioneers of a new kind of rock; George Harrison was the 'indie Beatle'.

By the twenty-first century 'indie' had stretched out to become a meaningless catch-all term that covered almost anything contemporary and guitar-based: Radiohead, the White Stripes, Manic Street Preachers, the Polyphonic Spree, Toploader – anything except metal. It had absolutely nothing do with the physical distribution of vinyl records.

1985: WHAT THE FUCK IS GOING ON?

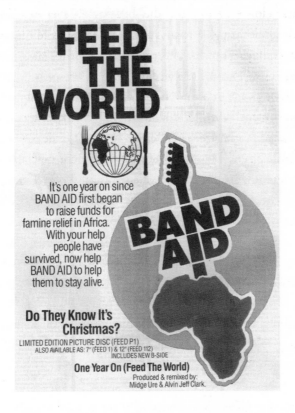

One can have great concern for the people of Ethiopia, but it's another thing to inflict daily torture on the people of England.
Morrissey, 1984

A collective madness took control of Britain between the post-Falklands War general election in '83 and Black Monday in '87. Against a backdrop of the miners' strike, AIDS campaigns, mass unemployment, a steep rise in homelessness and heroin usage, and endless TV montages of trading floors, much of pop was surface noise.

By 1985 new pop seemed to have evaporated through the walls. Despite all the talk about destroying the canon, and making it onto *TOTP* without any rockist baggage, it had proved a very small step from 'soundtracking the eighties' to conspicuous consumption; the ironic sleeve of Heaven 17's *Penthouse and Pavement* – pop group as corporation – was taken by many at face value. New pop had sown the seeds of its own demise.

What had gone wrong? With the commercial failure of bridge-burning, path-finding sequels to major albums (ABC's *Beauty Stab* and Orchestral Manoeuvres in the Dark's *Dazzle Ships* in '83, Dexys Midnight Runners' *Don't Stand Me Down* in '85), it became apparent that the British public had lost its appetite for invention and change. The Conservative government, which had scored all-time-low poll ratings just two years earlier, won a landslide election in the spring of '83; the Republicans did likewise in America a year later. British hits of early '83 – Kajagoogoo's 'Too Shy' (no. 1), the Thompson Twins' 'Love on Your Side' (no. 9), Eurythmics' 'Sweet Dreams' (no. 3) – had the synth leanings and some of the glide of new pop, but were airless and humourless. It hadn't taken long for the industry to right itself, and by 1984 more malleable acts (Howard Jones, Nik Kershaw, King, Paul Young) had superseded the art-school boys (Soft Cell, Human League). Much of new pop's superficial style remained, though; a glume of electro pop, dotted with pre-punk, rockist guitar runs, given gravitas by *du jour*, post-Phil Oakey soulful singing.

One honourable exception to new pop's implosion came from Liverpool, a city Margaret Thatcher had sought to destroy by 'managed decline'. Frankie Goes to Hollywood were a cumbersome mixture of blokey builders and gay macho men. None of them were pin-up material, but somehow they soundtracked 1984, scoring number ones with their first three singles, something that had only been done once before, by fellow Liverpool act Gerry and the Pacemakers in 1963.

In spite of the lack of mid-eighties chart excitement, the British music press had remained alert. Paul Morley reasoned that if musicians weren't learning from the lessons of post-punk and new pop, then the writers would have to take matters into their own hands. Having already written new pop's manifesto, it was no great surprise when Morley set up a label, ZTT, with one of the genre's sonic architects, producer Trevor Horn, and Horn's wife, Jill Sinclair. Off the bat, Morley signed Frankie

Goes to Hollywood: their first single, the sex hymn 'Relax', was banned by the BBC's breakfast show DJ Mike Read and by the end of January '84 it was number one.

By the time their second single, 'Two Tribes',* was released, Frankie were a phenomenon. Singer Holly Johnson, with a face like a cruel mouse, licked his lips every time he appeared on TV to declare, 'We are living in a world where sex and horror are the new gods.' He especially relished the word 'sex'. Soon everybody wore their T-shirts, and 'Two Tribes' spent nine weeks at number one (with a reactivated 'Relax' storming back up to number two). They made the biggest-sounding record of 1984 and it was the biggest hit of the year. But somehow it didn't feel like much of a victory for new pop; it felt more like playing the likes of Phil Collins and Queen (whose first post-Frankie single, in '85, was a raised fist of a thing called 'One Vision') at their own game. It was all *too* big. You yearned for a lightness of touch, the wispiness of a Thereza Bazar vocal, a tender Chic guitar line, and there was none. Even when 'The Power of Love', a ballad, gave them their third number one in three releases, Johnson's sniggering '*make love* your goal' made it seem like a joke. Their first album, *Welcome to the Pleasuredome*, was a double, almost unheard of since the pre-punk era, and it dragged. One too many thunderbolts, their records have not aged well. In retrospect, it feels like Britain got carried away by the enormity of the Frankie event.

By 1984 Britain had the most conservative pop media of any period since the fifties. Specifically, Radio 1 actively encouraged adult-orientated pop. The man in charge was Derek Chinnery. He told John Peel that his programme was only suitable for undesirables, and cut it from four nights a week to three. Off the record,† Chinnery had also told Peel that he wanted Radio 1 to be a soundtrack for 'young professionals in

---

* 'Two Tribes' was one of the few hits of the era to explore the omnipresent threat of nuclear destruction as politics ceased to be part of the post-new-pop agenda. Other notable exceptions were Nena's '99 Red Balloons' (US and UK no. 1), Ultravox's 'Dancing with Tears in My Eyes' (UK no. 3) and the Human League's 'The Lebanon' (UK no. 11). All of them were hits in the first half of 1984, which suggests Orwell-inspired pangs of guilt. None has much ire.
† Peel's tale of humiliation was printed, tellingly, not in a mainstream paper but in the Scottish fanzine *Slow Dazzle* in 1984.

the car on their way home from the theatre, or to the restaurant, who want to listen to something familiar – like Kenny Rogers'. Anything new that had a chance of making it onto Radio 1's playlist was necessarily conservative. So the record companies aimed low. UB40 embarked on their endless retreads of reggae classics with a Bontempi beat. Go West, two men in their early thirties, a little sweaty, clad in fake leather, scored a short string of air-pumped funk-pop hits – the biggest being 'We Close Our Eyes' (UK no. 5, US no. 41 '85) – which defied any kind of logic; people bought these records only because they were used to buying records. The same went for Hue and Cry's 'Labour of Love' (UK no. 6 '87) and 'Living in a Box' by Living in a Box (UK no. 5 '87), singles entirely made up of over-stylised soul tics.

At the apex of this shiny pyramid was Phil Collins. The Genesis drummer had made a break for freedom in early '81 and his first solo single, 'In the Air Tonight' (UK no. 2, US no. 19), was a claustrophobic triumph. Martin Hannett's dub-handed influence could be heard in its sparse fug of misery and impending apocalypse (which occurred with the loudest drums pop had yet conceived, at around three minutes forty). To promote his first solo album, 1981's *Face Value*, Collins appeared on TV with a pot of paint and a brush on his piano – his wife had run off with a decorator from Teesside.* It was painful to watch, but not good painful. When Morrissey sang, 'What do we get for our trouble and pain? A rented room in Whalley Range,' it was leavened by the self-parody of 'Heaven Knows I'm Miserable Now'. *Face Value* contained some impressive blue-eyed soul – the Bee Gees would have been proud of the eerie 'If Leaving Me Is Easy' – but the problem was that Collins wouldn't let go. Three years later he was still banging on, making aesthetic capital from his years-open wound, like a revival of the Plastic Ono Band with Elton John production values. It was the perfect soundtrack for divorced men in wine bars who couldn't find their voice in the Smiths and the impermeability of indie culture but recognised a kindred spirit in bald, angry Phil, standing on his ex-wife's lawn at two

---

* I have a memory of Collins going even further by wearing a Middlesbrough FC football shirt, but can't find any video evidence to back this up.

in the morning, shouting up at her bedroom window: 'Take a look at me now!' ('Against All Odds', US no. 1, UK no. 2 '84).

With this epic self-pity, Phil Collins became one of the biggest-selling artists in the world, and with his drum sound – the one that had stood alone in 1981 – he infected all pop. Collins believed that everything sounded better with gated reverb, which gave the off beat that jackboots-on-rice-krispies sound. Most producers agreed. Studios were rebuilt, stripped bare, all seventies cushioning removed to accommodate this stark, bass-free sound. Collins was a jazz drummer, and his inventiveness could circumvent the brutality of this sound on a 4/4 beat, but most drummers were less talented. Everything got bigger, tinnier, thinner, as the eighties progressed, until it reached some kind of crescendo with T'Pau's UK number one 'China in Your Hand' in 1987. Even Britain's independent sector was no help. They should have been clamouring to change the sonic state of pop, and rising to T'Pau's challenge. Instead, they retreated. Morrissey sang 'Hang the DJ' rather than 'Appoint better DJs and adapt radio to our needs', and pop became a husk.

Lower down the shiny, slippery, mid-eighties pyramid, and desperate to clamber upwards, were groups who had felt the need to move on from the post-punk independents but then failed to realise their commercial potential: Orange Juice enjoyed an isolated hit ('Rip It Up', UK no. 9 '83) but the sound was squelchy, synthetically silly, primped and processed by Polydor until it was hummable and little else.* But it certainly fitted into the new Radio 1 aesthetic – it had a sax break – and even felt slightly daring with its Little Richard-quoting title on the air next to the white soul of Paul Young.†

---

* 'Rip It Up' does have one claim to immortality: it was the first hit single to feature a bassline played on the Roland 303, the root source of acid house.
† Growling Paul Young had been a singer with new-wave act Streetband – who had a novelty hit with 'Toast' (UK no. 18 '78) – then sixties goodtime soul revivalists the Q-Tips before CBS re-marketed him, with a leather tie and a teased-up quiff, as a solo singer of sophisticated soul. In this, Young was the forerunner of brownbread soul, a regular chart feature in the eighties and early nineties, both in Britain (Simply Red, Wet Wet Wet) and America (Michael Bolton, Curtis Stigers). Young's 1983 album No Parlez was – using the terminology of the era

The mid-eighties saw a new wave of pirate radio growing in London, playing new American electro and early hip hop (rap, as it was still known), which Radio 1 and mainstream commercial stations like Capital still avoided entirely. Given the popularity of rap and electro in specialist shops that had no influence on the chart, and on specialist radio stations, the Top 40 – though it pains me to say it – clearly wasn't reflecting what people were listening to, or even buying, in the mid-eighties. It felt like the BPI, the BBC and the major labels were all part of the Thatcherite military–industrial complex.

The peak of this retrenchment into middle-aged, moneyed pop was Band Aid. While I don't doubt Bob Geldof's sincerity, the Band Aid single released at the end of 1984 was, for Britain, an enormous feel-good exercise, and one which has arguably done Africa more harm than good. In a year of event singles ('Two Tribes', 'Careless Whisper', Chaka Khan's electro-soul 'I Feel for You', Stevie Wonder's 'I Just Called to Say I Love You'), 'Do They Know It's Christmas' was the biggest, and it was atrocious.

At the very least, Geldof and Midge Ure should have listened hard and long to local African experts who spoke from informed, critical and realistic perspectives.* Instead, the whole of pop rose up as one with its

---

– a lifestyle accessory, one that signified the owner's good taste (it included a cover of 'Love Will Tear Us Apart'), and a charity-shop regular ten years hence when lifestyles had changed somewhat. And so had Young. In 1994, at the Royal Holloway Freshers' Ball, he performed a set of Jim Reeves cover versions rather than his greatest hits.

* Former Médecins Sans Frontières president Rony Brauman, who was constantly in Ethiopia during 1984/85, has said 'aid could be turned against those toward whom it was directed and those delivering the aid integrated into a system of oppression', and that relief agencies and their funders could be 'part of the problem, not just part of the solution'. Geldof doesn't agree and says that he is happy to 'shake hands with the devil on my left and the devil on my right to get to the people who need help'. David Rieff, author of *A Bed for the Night: Humanitarianism in Crisis*, reckons 'Geldof takes a morally serious dispute, with respectable arguments on both sides . . . and turns it into a pissing match in an alley behind a pub.' Zambian-born economist Dambisa Moyo's book *Dead Aid* is also dismissive of the 'celebrity aid' model and says many aid organisations and NGOs are more interested in perpetuating poverty in order to justify their own existence. She says ten per cent of Africans were living in

own idea of how to feed the world based on ten minutes of BBC news footage. The lyric was comically weak. Just one example: 'There won't be snow in Africa this Christmas time'. Gregory Peck and Ava Gardner could have jogged Ure's memory about *The Snows of Kilimanjaro*. So could the Teardrop Explodes' Julian Cope if he'd been invited along to the party. But he wasn't, and nor was anyone else who could be regarded as a radical or potentially divisive.

Where were the Smiths? Kevin Rowland? Madness?* Band Aid, and the following year's Live Aid concert, saw the final triumph of ageing rockers (Phil Collins), new-wavers (Sting) and the most conservative eighties stars (Dire Straits) over progressive pop forces; they built a castle from Live Aid and pulled up the drawbridge on anything daring or different. It gave all of their careers an extra year or two's grace as the public felt warmly towards their do-gooding. Evidence of this was Midge Ure's 'If I Was', a chest-beating number one in the autumn of '85. Jon Savage declared that 'the Live Aid effect has smeared middle-brow values all over rock music'. The healthy camaraderie and competitiveness on the indie scene, its jostle and crackle, was entirely absent in the Live Aid line-up. Quo, Queen, Clapton, Collins, the taste of a new generation.

Light relief came almost immediately after Band Aid's five weeks at number one, from a production team in South London. Stock, Aitken and Waterman were the jokers in the pack. While Tears for Fears talked in interviews about the weeks they spent agonising over a drum fill, SAW had backing tracks reduced to two or three push buttons. Off-the-shelf hits, largely identical, were their speciality. Stock Aitken Waterman made music for the masses and, beyond the fact that Kylie Minogue and Jason Donovan were soap stars, there was very little difference between

poverty in the seventies, compared to seventy per cent in 2012.
* The Specials' Jerry Dammers, shocked by the complete absence of African influence on 'Do They Know It's Christmas', put together the 2 Tone All Stars. They covered the Pioneers' 'Starvation', and Manu Dibango produced it. Released on Madness's Zarjazz label, it hobbled to number thirty-three in 1985. Geldof was adamant that Live Aid should stay apolitical, hence the inclusion of Quo and Queen, who had both played Sun City, and Eric Clapton, who had notoriously made racist comments on stage in the late seventies, for which he never apologised.

the people singing the records and the people buying them. Mel and Kim clearly bought their clothes at Top Shop. Their very lack of glamour is what made SAW's catalogue both successful and hated. Kylie, Jason, Dead or Alive, Rick Astley, Sonia, Mel and Kim,* Bananarama – they scored a dozen UK number ones between them, and a brace in the States. The SAW sound was everywhere from '84 to '89.

At the beginning of 1984 the homely trio of backroom boys came up with their first production – it was the Cypriot Eurovision entry, and it came seventh. They had to start somewhere. Within months, they were in the UK Top 20 with Hazell Dean's 'Searchin'' (no. 6) and Divine's none-gayer 'You Think You're a Man' (no. 16). By Christmas they had the biggest club hit in the country with Dead or Alive's 'You Spin Me Round', and it became their first number one in February '85, displacing 'Do They Know It's Christmas'. The SAW sound initially came from hi-NRG, the heavy-hitting sound of gay clubs that blew up in the early eighties, but they swiftly adopted house as its pulse beat in '87. It all looked so good on paper, but the records sounded like they had been recorded on keyboards that had come out of a Christmas cracker. No matter. SAW took the underground, married it to light entertainment and became – with their hit rate and production line at least – the closest thing to Motown that Britain has ever produced. Kylie Minogue: 'Stock Aitken and Waterman and the Hit Factory weren't so far removed from my role in *Neighbours*: learn your lines, red light on, perform lines, no time for questions, promote the product, *et voilà*!'

Pete Waterman had cut his teeth as a DJ in the north, starting at the Leeds Locarno with Jimmy Savile in 1965, then working on the Mecca circuit for fifteen years – he knew his Thelma Houston from his Cissy Houston. So once in a while a SAW record like Kylie's 'Hand on Your Heart' (UK no. 1 '89) sounded a little more than cheap and cheerful, had a tug within the tinny tinkling; maybe a chord change sneaked in

---

* After failing to earn even a nomination as Best Producers at the Brits, SAW took out a full page in *Music Week*, saying, 'You can love or hate us, you ain't gonna change us. We ain't ever gonna be respectable.' They then turned the jibe into Mel and Kim's follow-up to their number-three hit 'Showing Out'; 'Respectable' went to number one in 1987.

that caught you on the hop (the move from bridge to chorus on Big Fun's 'Can't Shake the Feeling'). And, occasionally, the whole record worked this well. Brother Beyond's 'The Harder I Try' (no. 2 '88) took a hitless boy band and made them the Temptations for four minutes. Hook was piled upon hook, and the budget even stretched to a real string section. But Waterman – who would have been the foreman of a cotton mill a hundred years earlier – stood by his Woolworths production values, watched the hits roll off the conveyor belt and refused to upgrade. He saw sampling as 'wholesale theft' and, when the underground went entirely overground with the dance-music explosion of the early nineties, the SAW aesthetic swiftly died.*

'Music isn't art,' Waterman said at the team's zenith in 1989, 'it's for enjoyment, and anyone who says it's art is in the wrong business. Music has always been written for a purpose, be it a wedding, a funeral or a birth, and people have always been paid for it. Mozart, Beethoven and Handel all got paid. I've been very poor, I've cleaned toilets for Mecca, I've slept on Euston station, and I never want to be like that again. I don't want to go down in history as a great songwriter because I died penniless. If you can use your talents not to stay poor, you should.'

'We're a dancing nation,' sang Mel and Kim on 'Respectable' – SAW may have been ridiculed but they understood that much, and their sound was as big an influence on the continent as anything from Chicago or Detroit: Whigfield's 'Saturday Night' (no. 1 '94) and Aqua's 'Barbie Girl' (no. 1 '97) were SAW melted down and recast in Danish plastic. Waterman, by this point, had largely retired to the very English hobby of steam trains. Not content with a train set, he bought an entire railway line north of Manchester. So he was no Van Gogh – he had never wanted to be – but he got rich and famous.

Ethiopia aside, there was another major world event unfolding in the

---

* Waterman carried on with the PWL label, signing Dutch act 2 Unlimited, turning Kylie Minogue from TV tomboy into one of pop's sexiest stars (her *Rhythm of Love* album is his crowning glory) and overseeing the career of Steps. He still DJs, can't sit still, wrote an autobiography called *I Wish I Was Me*, and was awarded an MBE in 2005. Personally, I find him one of British pop's most interesting and underused characters; his track record is almost without equal.

mid-eighties, another catastrophe, but AIDS was either ignored, trivialised or – if it was mentioned at all – regarded as the disease of homosexuals and junkies. It was seen as equating sex with death, and although pop had glorified poetic deaths in 'Johnny Remember Me', 'Leader of the Pack' and Terry Jacks's 'Seasons in the Sun' (US and UK no. 1 '74), it didn't deal with the real thing very well at all. Jermaine Stewart's 'We Don't Have to Take Our Clothes Off (to Have a Good Time)' became a major transatlantic hit.* Chastity was worn like a badge of honour. Freddie Mercury wore a housewife's outfit in the video for 'I Want to Break Free' (UK no. 3, US no. 45 '84), and MTV banned it; Mercury, in a canny career move, chose to stay in the closet. David Bowie, who a decade earlier had opened up the door to outsiders and the sexually stigmatised, slammed it shut on his 1983 album *Let's Dance*. He covered an obscure 1976 single by a group called Metro, 'Criminal World', which had originally been banned by the BBC for its bisexual overtones – Bowie changed the line 'I saw you kneeling at my brother's door' to 'You caught me kneeling at your sister's door'. The inference was that Bowie was distancing himself from the adventurousness of the sixties and seventies; in the eighties pop's first bi-guy made the Atlantic crossing that had escalated Rod Stewart's career a few years earlier and – far more than Rod ever did – dumped on his original fans. He successfully courted the mainstream with 'Let's Dance' (UK and US no. 1 '83) and the irresistible Pepsi-pop of 'Modern Love' (UK no. 2, US no. 14 '83), but almost wrecked his reputation for good with *Tonight* (1984) and *Never Let Me Down* (1987). Both albums were weighted with corporate-friendly moves, entirely unlovable, and sold poorly. He luxuriated, foolishly, in high-eighties gloss, embarrassed about his past. In '83 Bowie told *Rolling Stone* that claiming to have been bisexual was 'the biggest mistake I ever made. Christ, I was so young then. I was experimenting.'

You have to wonder how this new straight conservatism affected emerging pop stars. Aside from Frankie, the other act to achieve superstardom in 1984 was Wham!, and they had considerably more staying power. The T-shirts of the year were Wham!'s 'CHOOSE LIFE', designed

---

* Jermaine Stewart later died of AIDS-related liver cancer, aged thirty-nine.

by Katharine Hamnett, and Paul Morley's Hamnett homage, 'Frankie say RELAX'.* Live for now, beamed the face of Wham!'s shiny-skinned singer George Michael. Prioritise fun. They had broken through in 1982 with 'Wham! Rap' (UK no. 8 '82), an *NME* Single of the Week that, like 'Relax', put its politics on a plate. Its rallying cry of 'I'm a soul boy, I'm a dole boy' could have been seen as a libertine cry, with Wham! hailing the leisure time of the individual, but in an era when unemployment nudged three million, this take on dole culture seemed worryingly naive. Wham!'s hedonistic individualism ('Young Guns', 'Bad Boys', 'Club Tropicana', all UK Top 5 in 1983) could also have been read as an excuse for consumerism, encouraging people to define themselves by their own desires. Their hearts were clearly in the right place – they played a miners' benefit at the Festival Hall in 1984 with the Style Council, and split with management company Nomis when they discovered a dubious South African connection – but the music Wham! produced ended up as the ultimate reflection of eighties selfishness.

The sleepy-eyed Andrew Ridgeley and square-jawed George Michael were from Bushey in Hertfordshire, not far from the birthplace of George's hero, Elton John. They were managed by a dapper rogue called Simon Napier-Bell, who had once been in charge of Marc Bolan-connected psychedelic mods John's Children, and had co-written the lyrics to Dusty Springfield's 'You Don't Have to Say You Love Me'. 'I saw something in Wham! that no one else seemed to see,' he crowed to the *NME*'s Barney Hoskyns, 'which is the Hollywood thing of the two buddies, the two cowboys. You know, during the film one falls in love, the other goes to a brothel, but at the end they always ride off together. It's never sexual, but it's definitely homoerotic, and it's never really been done in rock before.'

George Michael turned out not to be quite the happy cowboy Napier-Bell presented him as, or as high on life as he seemed in 'Wake Me Up Before You Go Go' (UK and US no. 1 '84), 'I'm Your Man' (UK no. 1, US no. 3 '85) or the gaudy Wham! videos. 'The world is so fucked,' he

* Queen's Roger Taylor wore another Hamnett slogan shirt that read 'WORLD-WIDE NUCLEAR BAN NOW' at the 1985 Rock in Rio festival, but sadly it didn't catch on.

said in an *NME* interview shortly after Wham! split in '86. 'You look at the acceleration of all the negatives compared to the positives, and you just have to say it's all going to finish. We have to be drawing ourselves to the end of our natural lifespan because we're fucking everything up.' Closeted during the AIDS era, he wrote the racked 'A Different Corner' (UK no. 1, US no. 7 '85) as his first post-Wham! single, and it was an impressive *cri de cœur* – 'I'm so scared,' ran the chorus, and it wasn't a stretch to imagine it as a track on *Scott 3*. George said that Joy Division's *Closer* was his favourite album, and he became very sensitive to bad press. He wasn't untalented, but his creamy voice – not unlike Cliff Richard's – conveyed little soul. This, perversely, meant it was perfectly suited to the times, and his 1987 album *Faith* was huge with both black and white audiences in the States, selling twenty million copies and reaching number one on the R&B album chart. George Michael was the first white act to achieve this feat.*

Nelson George wrote a book called *The Death of Rhythm & Blues* shortly after this. He stated that the mainstream had become a blur of black and white influences, pop, rock and soul, with no obvious underground, and this made him sad. He couldn't see any future for rootsy black music. Quite possibly, he was thinking of Tina Turner as the summation of this grim period. A screamer from way back who had scored major UK hits in the sixties (Spector's 'River Deep – Mountain High', no. 3 '66) and seventies (husband Ike's itchy Moog-funk 'Nutbush City Limits', no. 4 '73), while regularly tearing chunks out of rock classics like 'Proud Mary' (US no. 4 '71) and 'Whole Lotta Love' on stage, she re-emerged in the eighties as a kind of rock-soul mutant, all lungs, legs and leathered skin – it was no coincidence that she was asked to sing the theme for *Mad Max III*. In 1987 Turner released an album called *Break*

---

* He followed it with *Listen without Prejudice Vol. 1* – possibly the worst album title in pop – and spent a good few years badly overplaying his hand as a serious artist. Then, with the mature years out of his system, he partied hard and made headlines by repeatedly crashing his car and being arrested in toilets. As a career arc it was all back-to-front; the previously prematurely middle-aged George now started to act like an errant teenager with an unhealthy love of weed. It's hard to believe he was born in the same year as Jarvis Cocker and Ian Brown.

Every Rule. It was not an appropriate title. Turner's mega-selling album featured star turns from Steve Winwood, Eric Clapton, Mark Knopfler, Bryan Adams and king of the rock/pop/soul blancmange Phil Collins. It went Top 5 everywhere, spent twelve weeks at the top of the German album chart, and was so shiny and hollow that no one could recall a thing about it by the start of the next decade.*

Not everyone was happy with this state of affairs, with success measured in terms of cold, hard cash. Pop's initiative was entirely geared towards sales figures, accreting catalogue, amassing a portfolio. It was no longer as eloquent, informed or demanding; post-punk and new pop had created an audience which was then denied what it felt had been promised. As fanzines went into overdrive, as hip hop regrouped underground, as geeks built new electronic sounds in Detroit bedrooms and independent labels started to become more politicised, a new group reached number one in 1985 who calmly suggested a better future while cocking a snook at high-eighties orthodoxy.

'When they had that Freddie Mercury tribute concert we were going to offer our services to do "We Will Rock You". We were going to come onstage with one of those old drum boxes with a little pitter-patter beat and make "We Will Rock You" into this tiny little fey statement. It would have been great if we'd done it wearing dunces' hats, waving our heads from side to side.'

Neil Tennant became a pop star in 1985 and, gradually, the charts started to become more bearable.

---

* *Break Every Rule* sold largely on digital compact disc. A product of Philips's and Sony's laboratories in the seventies, the 4.7-inch, crackle-free compact disc had been launched in 1982 and was vigorously promoted in the mid-eighties: by 1986, there were some 10,000 titles available on the new format. Sony's Norio Ohga claimed the CD 'removed a heavy winter coat from the sound'. The perfect vehicle for high-eighties pop, it was seen to have no frailties, no weaknesses. Yet without that 'winter coat' the sound, especially on early, poorly mastered CDs, was noticeably too bright, as if you were listening to music with all the lights on. There were prominent objections to their perceived sterility: Morrissey compared the CD to Shake 'n' Vac; Neil Young claimed, 'All you have left is the semblance of sound.' Sales of CDs would surpass vinyl in 1989, and the cassette in '92. Many people replaced their entire vinyl collections with CDs, to the music industry's delight.

WE WERE NEVER BEING BORING: PET SHOP BOYS AND NEW ORDER

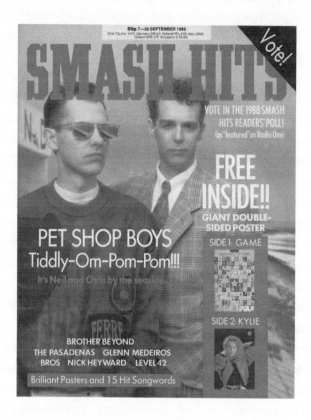

On 'West End Girls', the Pet Shop Boys' transatlantic 1985 number one, Neil Tennant spoke in deadpan RP of the dead-end world that pop had become. It was a set of verbal snapshots, a photofit of entertainment in the high eighties: 'How much have you got? Do you get it? If so, how often? And which do you choose, a hard or soft option?'

The Pet Shop Boys and their Mancunian counterparts in arch, lyrical electronica New Order were chart-friendly radicals – harbingers of another world that would irrevocably change the stasis of British pop, one which was kept cocooned in the mid-eighties. In a way, they were a mirror image to the Velvet Underground and the Stooges, groups who had hidden in the shadows before becoming a huge influence on pop. What's more, New Order and the Pet Shop Boys were how new pop actually triumphed in the end, not by building on the bangs and crashes of Frankie Goes to Hollywood but by setting Che Guevara and Debussy to a disco beat. New pop hadn't died, after all. It had bided its time, shed its unhelpful genre name and, by the late eighties, opened up modern pop to thrillingly anti-muso forms and possibilities.

New Order and the Pet Shop Boys would be the only British pop acts to link two worlds that, in retrospect, seem light years apart: the early-eighties post-disco explosion in electronic dance music (electro, hi-NRG, freestyle), and the house and techno scene at the far end of the decade which would have such social significance that the British legal system had to be amended. Both groups had elegance, an English mix of restraint and hedonism, and a deep understanding of the importance of Donna Summer's 'I Feel Love'. Both groups shunned pop's burgeoning obsession with celebrity, helmed by Madonna and, in his role as sage and insightful commentator, Morrissey. New Order, especially, refused to do interviews for years, and didn't appear on their sleeves, claiming (quite rightly) that there were far more appropriate and attractive images to reflect their music.

It's one of pop's most unlikely stories that 'West End Girls', the Pet Shop Boys' breakthrough hit, was meant to be an English take on Grandmaster Flash's 'The Message'. In reality it was closer to John Betjeman backed by Orchestral Manoeuvres in the Dark's melancholy Mellotrons.

Their album titles were the marrow of Englishness: *Please*, *Actually*, *Behaviour*, *Very*. Their electropop-duo look was a few years past its best; unlike Blancmange or Erasure, though, front man Tennant was as motionless as keyboard player Chris Lowe. Straight man and straight man. They were as personality-free as Pink Floyd. Tennant did what little talking there was, standing stock still, like Roy Orbison in eyeliner, while Lowe hid beneath a peaked cap and pretended to play a synth. 'Chris likes to eat during interviews,' Tennant told the *NME*. 'Normally, there's a request for a fried egg sandwich. If he doesn't get what he wants he'll suddenly snap.'

What they had, what was so sorely lacking in 1985, was a sense of humour and a sense of proportion. 'Most dance music is terribly banal,' sighed Tennant, 'which isn't necessarily a bad thing.' In the by now musically segregated States, they confused everyone but sold a ton of records anyway. Were they pop? Urban? Po-mo? Was there any category they didn't slip into?

'Well,' sniffed Tennant in the *NME*, 'we certainly don't slip into rock.'

Pet Shop Boys records had the clarity of line and the cleanliness of freshly laundered and folded linen. New Order's output – though their artwork was never less than draughtsman-perfect – came over like their slightly cumbersome sibling. For a start, New Order definitely did come out of rock. Joy Division had been leftfield, and – in the hands of Martin Hannett – avant to an awesome degree, but the influence that echoes through a song like 'Novelty' isn't Giorgio Moroder's 'From Here to Eternity', it's 'Badge' by Cream. So when Ian Curtis took his life, leaving two unrecorded songs, the three remaining members used them as a full stop and a new beginning. Their second career began with a single that topped anything Joy Division had recorded. 'Ceremony' (UK no. 34 '81) was a restless ghost, a fierce and piercing piece of guitar music that Curtis must have written with posterity in mind: 'Avenues all lined with trees, picture me and then you start watching, watching forever.' The bass surges, rolling and wrestling with the half-dozen different guitar lines. The twelve-inch sleeve was a rich, racing green, which was somehow perfect. And so, with their youth laid to rest, New Order moved on.*

Bernard Sumner (né Albrecht) became *de facto* singer, and Stephen Morris's friend Gillian Gilbert joined on keyboards. She was well attuned to their aesthetic – you only need to know three notes but you

---

* I'm politely ignoring all of their gloomed-out first album, *Movement*. Like the Cure's 1982 album *Pornography*, *Movement* was harrowing to the point of tedium. Both albums appeared just as the raincoat-wearing post-punk scene was splintering: some (New Order, Echo and the Bunnymen, the Cure) moved out of the shadows and into primary-coloured pop; the likes of Bauhaus, the Sisters of Mercy and Southern Death Cult kept their heads down and fostered the goth movement.

need to make them sound bigger than 'Shine on You Crazy Diamond'. Second single 'Everything's Gone Green' was a dizzying electronic mesh of Moroder and, well, Joy Division; anyone could dance to 'Everything's Gone Green'. While the British club scene was besotted with jazz funk in 1981,* New Order were looking to the new electric pulse of New York. Post-punk had scratched around in the dirt, awkwardly adapting funk to suit its anti-rock needs, but 'Everything's Gone Green' was silvery, clean, and unlike anything previously attempted by a British guitar band. Right on the fade, you can hear Sumner go *whoo!* He may as well have broken into a chorus of 'Highway to Hell' for the culture shock that caused. These post-punk pioneers had twenty–twenty vision, were primed for the future, and when they heard 'Planet Rock' they were on the next flight to Newark. Dope, acid and NYC clubbing were how they got over their friend's death; they shed their raincoats for terrace-casual clothes, Fred Perry shirts and soft leather slip-on shoes. They slept through the day and set their alarms for eleven thirty at night. Martin Hannett's days as their house producer were over.

1983's 'Blue Monday', New Order's fourth single, had beats as crisp as apples. It physically bridged the gap between rock and dance culture in that it was only available as a twelve-inch single, the chosen format of DJs. The mood was electric blue, and the gauntlet was thrown down to every guitar-based post-punk outfit – follow us! It was a massive seller, an international hit that stayed in the British charts longer than any other single in the eighties, becoming the best-selling twelve-inch of all time, eventually peaking at number three in the UK five years after it first came out. Just to show they didn't need Hannett and could master

---

* Though the clipped, freeze-dried funk of records like Beggar and Co's '(Somebody) Help Me Out' (UK no. 15 '81) seemed to have little to do with Sam Cooke or Marvin Gaye, pirate stations like Invicta and Kiss held them in high esteem. Clubs like the Goldmine in Canvey Island, and the Lacy Lady in Ilford played Philly soul, jazz funk, Salsoul and new records from New York and Miami that kept the slap-bass, late-disco boogie sound alive. For advocates of this continuity disco it was simply called 'soul', and was celebrated at the annual Caister Soul Weekender, which started in 1979. What you would never, ever hear on these stations or at these clubs or weekenders was electronically derived dance music.

the space their former producer seemed to carve out of thin air, they covered Keith Hudson's heavy dub 'Turn the Heater On' for a Peel session. Sumner's spectral melodica glided over icy Korg chords with the same romantic distance as Peter Green's guitar on the middle eight of 'Albatross'.

In reality, New Order were hardly distant or furrowed at all. They refused to appear on British TV unless they could play live; when they finally did – playing Blue Monday on *Top of the Pops* – it was less like Kraftwerk's icy precision, more like *Lancelot Link and the Evolution Revolution*. Gillian's keyboard ability was akin to a schoolgirl's first attempts at typing, and Bernard delighted in looking gormless, mouth agape, screwing with his own lyrics: '. . . and I thought I heard you squeak'.

Finally giving the *NME* an interview in 1985, Sumner didn't come across as a noble artiste, or even a pop star: 'War's wrong, fighting's wrong, but defending yourself isn't wrong,' he said, cheeks turning purple, breath turning beery. 'If someone hit me I'd hit them back. I did think of joining up when the Falklands conflict was on. I'm a patriot, mate.' Shortly afterwards, New Order released a live video called 'Pumped Full of Drugs'.

They had fallen in love with the sounds at New York's Danceteria, and after a muddled Arthur Baker-produced single called 'Confusion' (UK no. 18 '83) that was as clothy as 'Blue Monday' was shiny, they cut the tick-tock clinical 'Shellshock' for John Hughes's *Pretty in Pink* soundtrack and became fully assimilated into eighties pop culture: 'Thieves Like Us', 'Perfect Kiss', 'Bizarre Love Triangle', 'Fine Time', a peerless run of twelve-inch singles, all packaged in Peter Saville's economically beautiful sleeves – New Order records were very wantable.

The Pet Shop Boys, meanwhile, were in awe of another electro-disco underground – the proto-hi-NRG of Bobby O. Before even writing a song, they travelled to New York to track him down.

Though the sound he spawned was almost entirely confined to gay clubs, Bobby O was a straight Puerto Rican, and obsessed with boxing. His aim was to make the beats sound as tough and pummelling as punches – 'Native Love' and 'Shoot Your Shot' shared the synthesised bass pulse of 'Blue Monday' and (by now five years old) 'I Feel Love'.

The sound was taken up by the London club scene, which needed a new speed-fuelled soundtrack now that disco had run its course.

Bobby O's subtlety-free productions also appealed to a segment of the northern-soul scene. While the Wigan Casino had been loyal to sixties soul, rival club the Blackpool Mecca had often played brand-new sounds that fitted the talcum-coated dancefloor. Mecca DJ Ian Levine was so taken with the Bobby O sound that he began creating similar-sounding records on his own Record Shack label – with more than a whiff of show tune, Miquel Brown's 'So Many Men, So Little Time' typified a camp but bludgeoning sound, jackbooted cowboys with whipcracking snares, bashing their cowbells with a hammer. It was ugly but effective. Record Shack's follow-up was Evelyn Thomas's 'High Energy' (UK no. 5 '84), which crystallised the sound and gave it a name.

The title of Miquel Brown's hit became a bad joke once AIDS started to decimate the gay community;* the politics of dancing dictated that by 1985 hi-NRG's time was up. This was the greyer, homophobic world that 'West End Girls' was born into. The Pet Shop Boys, however, had reshaped the Bobby O sound to their own ends, rechannelled it with the unlikely inputs of Grandmaster Flash and Alan Bennett, and scored a global number one.

Neil Tennant had begun 1985 as the assistant editor of fortnightly pop mag *Smash Hits*, performing such humdrum tasks as interviewing the poorly dressed keyboard player Paul Hardcastle, dining with the dour Eurythmics, going on the road with Scottish heartland rockers Big Country; he ended the year on the cover of *Smash Hits* and with a number-one single. He wasn't about to go telling the press how he was a fighting pit prop, ready to defend the Falklands with a Roland 808 in his hand. But he still sounded as far away from Phil Collins† as

* Until September 1982, when the name AIDS was first coined for the disease, it was more commonly called GRID – Gay Related Immune Deficiency. This was a boost for homophobia, and early victims like Patrick Cowley received little sympathy outside the gay community.
† 'A song like "Why Can't It Wait until Tomorrow" is a pretty cosy song, but it's got a nice feeling to it, and I get the required reaction from people.' Phil Collins, *NME*, 1982.

Bernard Sumner's pub talk. 'We were always anxious to come over as not really like proper pop groups,' Tennant told *Q*. 'We didn't want to be the biggest group in the world. We didn't want to be seen as a world-ambitious band who wanted to have an amazing live act with a tragic band of musos behind us. We didn't want to appear to be like Go West or someone.'

The Pet Shop Boys and New Order had come from quite different routes but their paths converged sonically in 1987 – the same year the KLF formed in defiance of pop's descent into mediocrity, and Steve 'Silk' Hurley's 'Jack Your Body' ushered in the house-music era – when Stephen Hague produced New Order's 'True Faith' (UK no. 4, US no. 32), as well as the Pet Shop Boys' 'What Have I Done to Deserve This' (UK and US no. 2) and 'It's a Sin' (UK no. 1, US no. 9). The *NME* said 'True Faith' plumbed 'the depths of disco, and approximates the sound of Pet Shop Boys . . . compromised in a forelock-tug towards commercialism', while finally admitting it was 'soul-stirring'. The Pet Shop Boys brought their heroine Dusty Springfield out of the shadows to sing on 'What Have I Done to Deserve This', then produced a whole album for her (*Reputation*) which included the weightless, exquisite 'Nothing Has Been Proved' (UK no. 16 '87), her first solo Top 20 hit in over twenty years. It couldn't have got any better.

These records were also a commercial high-water mark for both groups. From here on, their paths diverged again. New Order dived headfirst into acid-house culture – the *TOTP* performance of 'Fine Time' (UK no. 11 '89) could be used as an anti-advert for Ecstasy – before crumbling slowly in a most undignified manner. The Pet Shop Boys, after covering Sterling Void's contemporary house hit 'It's Alright' (UK no. 5 '89), released the beautifully reflective *Behaviour* album in 1990 (sample song title: 'My October Symphony'), before a slight lapse into self-parody on '93's *Very* called time on their imperial phase. It's unlikely they'll ever split – they are the Gilbert and George of pop. By the turn of the nineties both groups had done their work. Margaret Thatcher and Go West were gone. The world turned, and the KLF sensed their chance.

PART FIVE

THE gallup chart

THE OFFICIAL NATIONAL TOP 100 SINGLES, TOP 75 ALBUMS AND TOP 20
COMPILATION ALBUMS, AS USED BY RADIO 1 AND 'TOP OF THE POPS'

TOP THE POPS

March 31 — April 6 1991

U K   S I N G L E S

TW	LW	W/C		
1	1	8	THE ONE AND ONLY Chesney Hawkes	Chrysalis
2	7	2	SIT DOWN James	Fontana
3	3	4	RHYTHM OF MY HEART Rod Stewart	Warner Brothers
4	5	5	JOYRIDE Roxette	EMI
5	10	6	SECRET LOVE Bee Gees	Warner Brothers
6	4	3	WHERE THE STREETS. . ./. . .SERIOUSLY? Pet Shop Boys	Parlophone
7	6	3	LET THERE BE LOVE Simple Minds	Virgin
8	8	10	IT'S TOO LATE Quartz introducing Dina Carroll	Mercury
9	2	5	THE STONK Hale & Pace And The Stonkers	London
10	13	2	SNAP! MEGA MIX Snap!	Arista
11	—	1	THE WHOLE OF THE MOON The Waterboys	Ensign
12	14	5	I'VE GOT NEWS FOR YOU Feargal Sharkey	Virgin
13	9	6	SHOULD I STAY OR SHOULD I GO The Clash	Columbia
14	25	2	HUMAN NATURE Gary Clail On—U Sound System	Perfecto
15	31	2	LOVE & KISSES Dannii Minogue	MCA
16	16	7	THIS IS YOUR LIFE Banderas	London
17	22	5	WEAR YOUR LOVE LIKE HEAVEN Definition Of Sound	Circa
18	11	7	BECAUSE I LOVE YOU (THE POSTMAN SONG) Stevie B	Polydor
19	—	1	ANTHEM N—Joi	deConstruction
20	24	4	SHE'S A WOMAN Scritti Politti (feat Shabba Ranks)	Virgin
21	33	2	HERE WE GO C & C Music Factory feat Freedom Williams	Columbia
22	—	1	DEEP, DEEP TROUBLE The Simpsons	Geffen
23	12	10	YOU GOT THE LOVE The Source feat Candi Staton	Truelove
24	19	5	LOSING MY RELIGION R.E.M.	Warner Brothers
25	18	11	DO THE BARTMAN The Simpsons	Geffen
26	—	1	STRIKE IT UP Black Box	deConstruction
27	15	12	MOVE YOUR BODY (ELEVATION) Xpansions	Arista
28	32	3	OVER TO YOU JOHN (HERE WE GO AGAIN) Jive Bunny & The Mastermixers	Music Factory
29	29	2	HIGH WIRE Rolling Stones	Rolling Stones
30	36	2	CARAVAN Inspiral Carpets	Cow
31	20	7	UNFINISHED SYMPATHY Massive	Wild Bunch
32	17	10	LOVE REARS ITS UGLY HEAD Living Colour	Epic
33	35	5	CAN YOU DIG IT? The Mock Turtles	Siren
34	23	6	CRAZY FOR YOU (REMIX) Madonna	Sire
35	39	4	WORD OF MOUTH Mike & The Mechanics	Virgin
36	—	1	RING MY BELL Monie Love vs Adeva	Cooltempo
37	21	5	LOOSE FIT Happy Mondays	Factory
38	—	1	HYPERREAL The Shamen	One Little Indian
39	44	2	WHERE LOVE LIVES (COME ON IN) Alison Limerick	Arista
40	26	6	WHO? WHERE! WHY? Jesus Jones	Food

L a t e   n e w s

Donnie Wahlberg of **New Kids On The Block** has been freed on £30,000 bail after pleading not guilty in a Kentucky court to setting fire to a hotel carpet.

Donnie was arrested and charged with arson after the fire caused slight damage on the ninth floor of a hotel in Louisville where the band were staying. It's alleged he set fire to the carpet outside his hotel room after an argument with a girl and if he's found guilty he could face 20 years in the clink. A date for Donnie's trial will be set later.

*STOP PRESS: We have just discovered that *Record Mirror* is closing and will not be publishing any more issues. Thank you for your support in the past.

CHICAGO AND DETROIT: HOUSE AND TECHNO

I lost control, I saw my soul.
Adonis, 'No Way Back'

In January 1987 a record by Steve 'Silk' Hurley made number one on the UK singles chart. There was no video, there wasn't even a biog on Hurley for DJs to claim, brow furrowed, as their own research. Heck, there was only one black-and-white photo of him, which Channel 4's *Chart Show* held on screen for a full two and a half minutes to accompany the dark, relentless clatter of 'Jack Your Body'. People were appalled, they genuinely didn't know what the hell to make of this record. 'Jack Your Body' was monotonous, little more than a bassline and a dustbin-lid rhythm, with Hurley's odd, disembodied, processed voice repeating the title. It was also intensely physical, unnerving, robotic, a future shock.

Within days, Radio 1's Peter Powell took the brave step of retiring, explaining that if 'Jack Your Body' could get to number one, he just didn't understand modern pop music any more. A fortnight later George Michael and Aretha Franklin stemmed the tide and soothed conservatives by knocking 'Jack Your Body' from its perch with the clean, airless soul of 'I Knew You Were Waiting for Me',* but it was too late. The cat was out of the bag, and 1987 joined the shortlist of years credited with a sea change in pop.

As hip hop had developed unheard outside of the South Bronx, so house grew in an isolated, post-disco pocket. Chicago's Warehouse, with Frankie Knuckles as the club's main DJ, had existed since '77 and, like New York's Paradise Garage, it started to redefine disco when the barbarians were at the gate, stripping things back to the primary colours of rhythm and soulful, almost gospel vocals. Both clubs had a largely gay, black clientele.

The Warehouse had been the more radical of the two clubs, and at the turn of the eighties began to gently shift away from a Philly sound into something more clinical, still song-based but with the pulse of the drum machine at its heart. New York-based disco labels Prelude, West End and Salsoul had merged the sweeping strings of Philadelphia with the tortured gospel heat of soul singers like Loleatta Holloway, and this was the sound Knuckles's spiritual crowd craved. An evangelical DJ, he had mixed Martin Luther King speeches into the Salsoul sound, and one of his most-played records, Holloway's piano-driven 'Love Sensation', would become a working model for house.

As disco died out completely and R&B slowed down, Frankie Knuckles started to play reel-to-reel re-edits of old disco records,† extending them with the help of a Rhythm Master (the box built into most electric organs to help the suburban Reginald Dixon keep time).

---

* 'Rock around the Clock' had been dislodged by Dickie Valentine's 'Christmas Alphabet'; the Rolling Stones' 'Get Off of My Cloud' by the Seekers' 'The Carnival Is Over'; the Beach Boys' 'Good Vibrations' by Tom Jones's 'Green, Green Grass of Home'; Donna Summer's 'I Feel Love' by Brotherhood of Man's 'Angelo'. George and Aretha, meet your new neighbours.
† Knuckles is known as the Godfather of House, which seems appropriate as he oversaw the scene, attaching his name to various projects without getting his hands too dirty. The Warehouse, by dint of timing, never played any Chicago-made house music.

A local record store called Imports Etc started to label records with an
'as played at the Warehouse' sticker, which was soon pared back to 'the
'House', and a new genre had been tagged.

In the early eighties house was in a half-frog, half-tadpole state.
American disco was gone, but Italo disco records – Doctor's Cat's
'Andromeda', Klein and MBO's 'Dirty Talk' – kept the flame burning,
building on disco's electronic side. Sparse and highly synthetic, they
were easy for Chicago DJs to beat-match. On the extreme edge was an
Italian compilation of pure rhythm tracks called *Mix Your Own Stars*.
The most popular track was called '119' – it was nothing more than a
Roland drum machine's bass drum, snare, tom-toms and a handclap.
And it played at 119 beats per minute. It was an achievable sound for
Chicago's budding producers to mimic.

After the Warehouse closed in '83, Knuckles moved on to the more
upmarket, soulful Power Plant, but it was the Music Box across town,
on a Saturday night with DJ Ron Hardy, that took the Warehouse
sound into deeper waters. The crowd got younger. The look was paisley
shirts, solid-colour baggy slacks and slippy, shiny shoes; the haircut was
a high-rise flat top called a pump. Because Frankie Knuckles's re-edits
weren't available in the shops, kids started to make their own approximations. One of the most inspired was a Prince fanatic called Jamie
Principle, who stayed home, never going out to clubs, and worked on
his own brand of house. His tracks would get played out by Knuckles
at the Power Plant off reel-to-reel tapes: his 1985 recording 'Your Love'
– later to become a huge hit with Candi Staton's a cappella 'You've Got
the Love' grafted onto it – was played off a tape for a whole year before
it was released on vinyl. Rich, dark chords worked like a ghost echoing
the spirituality of Knuckles's Warehouse sets, and the sense of space was
enormous. By the time the *NME*'s Stuart Cosgrove wrote a piece in
1986 entitled – with reference to the ongoing battle between indie- and
black-music-supporting writers on the paper – 'The DJs They Couldn't
Hang',* Chicago was dancing to a beat entirely of its own making.

* The role of the UK as curator/creators in the eighties shouldn't be under-
estimated. Hungry for new sounds and scenes, Britons collated exotic American
dance music on compilations: Morgan Khan's Street Sounds label released a series

So how did house fundamentally differ from disco? Like hip hop, it was built on new technology. Cosgrove found Chicago's record shops to be crammed with European electronic import singles. Like Knuckles, Ron Hardy had disciples who used cheap new technology to make tapes or cassettes of new music for him to play at the Music Box. The Kurzweil and Fairlight keyboards used by Trevor Horn cost thousands, but for less than $2,000 there was the Ensoniq Mirage, a polyphonic sampling keyboard. Jesse Saunders was first with the primitive 'On and On', which came out on Vince Lawrence's Mitchbal label;* Chip E. used a Boss guitar sampling pedal (retailing at just $200) to make the ESG-sampling 'Like This'. Unlike disco, this wasn't music made by musicians, it was made by clubbers for clubbers. The distance between self-starter impulse and execution was, as it had been with punk, rapidly diminished.

Secondly, the sexuality was blunt. It may have been expelled altogether from early hip hop, but in house it was blatant – that rush to orgasm was clear in its ebbs, flows and jump cuts between dark chords and uplifting piano breaks. Then there were the titles of house records: with 'jack' short for ejaculate, records like 'Jack Your Body' and Hercules' 'Seven Ways to Jack' lacked Chic's sensuality. So they made up for it with deep, often melancholy basslines and sparse minor-chord keyboard lines (Fingers Inc.'s 'Mystery of Love'). In this hi-tech, low-drama paring down, ethnicity, roots and sexual orientation were slowly rendered insignificant.

Stuart Cosgrove's *NME* article had been about a very local scene. The beauty of 'Jack Your Body' is that its UK success is still largely inexplicable – why not Kenny 'Jammin'' Jason's '87 club classic 'Can

---

of electro compilations between 1983 and 1985, Brummie Neil Rushton put out *Techno! The New Sound of Detroit* in '88, and even the Washington go-go scene (funk with brass riffs played endlessly) was briefly lionised by the *NME* in 1985, earning its own compilation. There was no American equivalent to these albums.
* House pioneer Marshall Jefferson later told Frank Broughton: 'It was Jesse who made everyone want to go and get a drum machine and start making records, because . . . Jesse's shit wasn't that good. It made it more accessible. It gave us hope, man . . . Jamie [Principle]'s stuff was too good. Nobody thought they could duplicate it. Everybody thought that Jamie was somebody from Europe.'

U Dance', with its infectious, distorted ice-cream-van hook? Or Raze's similar but superior, more atmospheric, more definitively *house* single, 'Jack the Groove'? The sense of confusion it caused among the rockist media was fabulous – where was the ideology? Call this a revolution? It's just ear candy. It was, instead, raw electricity.

When the *House Sound of Chicago* albums appeared in the UK,* the monochrome pictures of Marshall Jefferson and Steve 'Silk' Hurley were reminiscent of Delta blues singers, or the deep-soul singers simultaneously anthologised on the Charly label: grainy, lost, a parallel and exciting America, nothing to do with *Flashdance* or *Baywatch* or *ALF*. Where did they come from? How could this have been going on while Steve Wright in the afternoon was playing Johnny Hates Jazz? They were unknowable. Such mystique.

It turned out that Marshall Jefferson had been a postman and a Led Zeppelin fan, firmly in the 'disco sucks' camp. But there was a cute girl who sat next to him at the post office, and she went to the Music Box. He tagged along one night, just to see her body in action, and had the closest thing he'd ever experienced to a religious visitation. Two days later he spent $9,000 (post-office workers in the US got easy credit as they were virtually unsackable) on keyboards and studio equipment; within a few weeks he made the terrifying 'I've Lost Control' (credited to his sleazy cohort, Sleezy D); within a year he had cut the ultimate house anthem, 'Move Your Body'.

Growing in tandem, across the Great Lakes, the underground nature of Detroit's techno scene made house seem like a *Smash Hits* Christmas party. Photos were pretty much unheard of. In a way it was the exact opposite of house; techno was developed in bedrooms by loners, whereas house was inspired directly by reactions on the dancefloor. Techno was more austere, more glacial and totally tonal – it sounded exactly like

---

* These essential primers were released on the London label, which – as an offshoot of Decca – had done so much to get American rock 'n' roll to the grey streets of fifties Britain. Now part of the Polygram group which had swallowed up Decca in the early eighties, it became, along with its FFRR offshoot run by Kiss FM DJ Pete Tong, a reliable sign of quality US and UK dance music from 1987 to 1991.

a science experiment that had escaped from the lab. People talk about electronic music as 'cold', but certain Detroit techno records do seem to cause a perceptible drop in the room temperature.

The three shy boys who birthed this new sound – Derrick May, Juan Atkins and Kevin Saunderson – were wealthy black kids from the Detroit suburb of Belleville, and they only ventured out of their homes to DJ at debutante parties. Atkins and May got acquainted by playing chess; May's masterpiece, 'Strings of Life', was written and recorded after he spent a year hibernating in his room, living on breakfast cereal, barely bothering to dress. Neither was exactly cut from Marvin Gaye's cloth.

'The thing is,' said Atkins, 'being in Belleville the next person I could play with was ten miles away. It was hard for me to get together with other musicians.' Young Juan would walk around the house with a bass guitar round his neck at all times, until one day in 1980, when he was fifteen, his gran took him into a local music shop to buy spare parts for her Hammond B3 home organ. Sat in a room at the back of the shop was a Minimoog and a Korg MS10, the future sounds of pop. Juan begged and pleaded until the MS10 was his, and in no time he was making home demos. At college a few weeks later, Atkins played his home recordings in a show and tell, and freaked out a classmate and Vietnam vet called Rik Davis – the two soon formed a duo called Cybotron.

Davis was an out-there fan of Jimi Hendrix and sci-fi, and had changed his name to 3070 by the time the duo released 'Alleys of Your Mind' and 'Cosmic Cars' on Atkins's own Deep Space label. They were local hits, pummelled by local radio jock Electrifying Mojo,* the John Peel of Detroit, but – as with early hip hop in New York – this music meant nothing outside the city limits. Chicago DJs began to pick up on them, and by '83 Cybotron's third single, 'Clear', which sounded like Darth Vader guesting with Kraftwerk, placed on *Billboard*'s black-music

---

* Like Rik Davis, Electrifying Mojo was also a Vietnam vet and a DJ out there during the war; back home in eighties Detroit his radio show went against the grain of hits-of-the-day black radio and got huge ratings. A typical show started with the *Close Encounters* theme followed by plenty of Prince, James Brown and Jimi Hendrix, with the occasional unlikely head-turner, like America's 'Horse with No Name'.

chart. They followed it with their best record, the hugely atmospheric 'Techno City', which would soon lend its name to a whole genre. By 2010 Cybotron were featured on *Grand Theft Auto* – that's a long trickle down, but then they had been ridiculously ahead of their time.*

Cybotron split in 1985, when Atkins decided to drop the few rock references they had and pursue something purely electronic. He reconnected with his old school pals. Juan Atkins was a spiritual benefactor, techno's Curtis Mayfield. He was very shy, but he gave May and Saunderson confidence: if he was techno's originator, then Derrick May became the innovator and Kevin Saunderson the elevator. There had been playground scraps – Kevin beat Derrick up after he reneged on a bet on the Superbowl, aged fourteen – but they were pretty tight. They would drive together through the streets of Detroit; they didn't see ruins in its abandoned industrial zone, they saw pyramids. Robots had taken over in the automotive industry; for the Belleville Three, it was a natural transition for music in the city to do the same. After weeks, months, in his room May emerged with one cassette, a piece of music which would come to be called 'Strings of Life'.† 'I didn't know what I had done,' he said later. 'It scared me.' It was quite beautiful, with near-atonal chords brushing up against jazz-piano runs that May rendered stunted and mechanical. Saunderson, not to be outdone, created the soulful 'Big Fun' (UK no. 8 '88) and 'Good Life' (UK no. 4 '88) and, under the name Inner City, took techno‡ to the masses.

'Jack Your Body' had nudged the door ajar, but the biggest breakthrough for house and techno didn't come from a track that anyone had sweated blood over. It came from an accident, a piece of malfunctioning, defunct technology.

* The name Cybotron came from Atkins, a blend of 'cyborg' and 'cyclotron'. A true bedroom kid, he loved to invent his own futuristic language, and followed through with his Metroplex and Transmat labels.
† Apparently Frankie Knuckles came up with the title 'Strings of Life' after Juan Atkins took it to him.
‡ When Atkins and May heard that the *NME*'s Stuart Cosgrove was set to fly over and write a feature on the new Detroit sound, they realised they only had a few days to think of a name for the sounds they were creating. May wanted to call it hi-tech soul. Luckily Atkins won the fight.

DJ Pierre was a clarinet player from the Chicago suburbs. He was involved in local DJ battles, too shy to make many inroads into the Music Box crowd until his friend Spanky bought a cheap piece of gear called a Roland TB-303. It had been designed in 1982 to play basslines for buskers, but was fiddly, had failed commercially and had been pulled from the market in 1984. Spanky and Pierre discovered that no matter how much they turned the knobs and tweaked the controls, it sounded less like a bassline than an approximation of a melting brain. The batteries died, they put new ones in, but the brain-melting sound was still there – it just wouldn't die. So they recorded it, over a beat that was already in the 303, called it 'In Your Mind', and gave a cassette of it to Ron Hardy. The first time he played it, 'In Your Mind' cleared the floor. A few spins later, at four in the morning, it caused a riot. People were screaming, on their backs kicking their legs in the air, slam-dancing into each other. Someone taped the mayhem and it got passed around Chicago on a bootleg cassette labelled *Ron Hardy's Acid Tracks*.

House had been minimal, two steps away from conventional song structure, but acid house sounded like nothing on earth – atonal, disorientating, genuinely frightening. Spanky and Pierre released the freshly rechristened *Acid Tracks* under the name Phuture and invented a whole new subgenre which was as far removed from *Trans-Europe Express* as it was from James Brown. Just as Britain was deluged with first-generation house, Chicago started creating opportunistic skirmishes, all utilising the Roland 303, this weird contraption, a piece of junk neither Shep Pettibone nor Trevor Horn would give the time of day to. Phuture released the even heavier 'Slam'; Bam Bam's 'Give It to Me' repeated the title, deadpan, over a woman's cry. All shared the random squelched melody generated by the 303. Charismatic and modern, these records were exported to the UK, snapped up by DJs eager to be seen with a new square foot of Chicago real estate, and it was chaos.

Partly because so much of it was instrumental, free of boundary-drawing linguistics, house and techno were the first truly international sounds of modern pop; they could be easily mimicked, exploited, expanded by musicians in any country. They transcended language and culture. Within ten years of making his first recording, fuelled by cornflakes, Derrick May had DJ'd in Bosnia, Jerusalem and at the foot of the Andes. Frankie Knuckles, interviewed on the BBC's *Dancing in the Streets* documentary in the mid-nineties, remembered that Madonna's 'Vogue' – a worldwide number one in 1990 – was, for him, the moment when house music was validated, when it became the people's music that had been trumpeted on Mr Fingers' 1986 single 'Can You Feel It':

'I am the creator, and this is my house! And, in my house there is only house music. But, I am not so selfish because once you enter my house it then becomes *our* house and *our* house music! And, you see, no one can own house because house music is a universal language, spoken and understood by all. You may be black, you may be white; you may be Jew or Gentile. It don't make a difference in our house.'

SMILEY CULTURE: ACID HOUSE AND MANCHESTER

Roll on the future when the new wave of British club-goers start turning out their own music. Having experienced for themselves what actually makes people dance . . . The new music is coming sooner than you think.
Mark Moore, *Virgin Rock Year Book*, 1987

Different drugs soundtrack different eras. Rarely have music and nar-cotics been so intertwined as they were in the late eighties. MDMA, or Ecstasy, transformed the pop scene.

Amongst the UK's earliest converts to E were Soft Cell, who had gone to New York in 1981 to record their first album, *Non-Stop Erotic Cabaret*. A Brooklyn drug dealer called Cindy Ecstasy (whose flat vocals can be heard on 'Torch', a number-two UK hit in '82) gave a white capsule of MDMA to Marc Almond as he listened to the Cure's third album, the rainy-sounding *Faith*. He came up while listening to 'All Cats Are Grey', a sleepy, percussive, decidedly grey lament: 'I remember thinking that it was the best song I'd heard in my entire life.'

The drug also flourished in Spain's holiday resorts: with Franco's despotic grip loosened to keep the tourists flooding in during the seventies, native outsiders – gays, hippies, artists – had made new homes for themselves in Torremolinos and on the island of Ibiza. By the early eighties the latter had become a thriving club scene for the rich and famous, Studio 54-on-Sea, and young working-class Britons went there for a cheap beach holiday, pressed their faces up against the window and wanted in. They took a pill at an after-hours bar called Amnesia* which played new releases from Chicago, but blended them in with such unlikely records as Sting's 'Englishman in New York' and Cyndi Lauper's cover of 'What's Going On'; suddenly a record that would have seemed naff, too pop, at a suburban London soul night draped itself around them like a magical suit. The drug didn't make the music any better or worse, it just annihilated snobbishness. Barriers that had been put up in the late sixties (by Brian Jones, Bob Dylan and Eric Clapton) and stayed in place pretty much ever since (thanks to the likes of soul DJ Chris Hill) suddenly became permeable.

Danny Rampling was a funk and soul DJ who discovered Ecstasy on holiday in 1987. Returning from Ibiza, he got to hear the occasional house record in West End gay clubs, where the look was still black flying jackets and Levi's 501s, the look of Thatcherite consumerism. Rampling and a few dozen other Ibiza veterans found brief solace at Paul Oakenfold and Trevor Fung's Project club on Streatham High Road, playing Ibiza-style sets from two till six. But Rampling realised he

* Amnesia had been run by an Argentinian DJ called Alfredo since 1984. He became obsessed with Chicago's DJ International and Trax labels – Adonis's 'No Way Back' was his all-time favourite – but he always played an adventurous mixture. His summer 1987 mix included the Woodentops' rattling indie single 'Well Well Well' and Art of Noise's dreamy, dead slow, and virtually undanceable 'Moments in Love'.

needed his own night and started Shoom in late '87. Its flyer read 'the happy happy happy happy happy Shoom club' and was decorated with a yellow smiley face that hadn't been seen since the Nixon era. Shoom was based in a fitness centre in Southwark, and Lucozade – the only drink available at the centre – became the only drink anybody wanted. People were so obsessed with the music they tried to climb inside the speakers to get closer.

'You're so anti-fashion, so wear flares,' Kevin Rowland had said at the beginning of a decade which would be dominated by style over substance. The Ibiza ravers wore flares. Flares, Lucozade, smileys, bandanas – it was a revolt against everything restrictive. Other Shoom DJs included Ibiza regulars Lisa Loud and Nancy Noise, their nicknames indicative of a general lack of studied cool. The February 1988 issue of *The Face* included a feature by Jon Savage about the seventies: 'The Decade that Taste Forgot'. The end of taste, suddenly, seemed a good thing. Taste and style had disfigured the eighties, and they now gave way to utility. The eighties were being sent packing.*

Shoom's major step forward – along with the functional dancewear, the flavoured smoke machines, the strobes, the darkness, the free ice pops, the hundred-per-cent humidity – was that people stumbled out into the morning light having made new friends. Since the sixties clubs had been about attitude, posing, territory and one-upmanship. Shoom didn't set out to change the world, but it defined a new way of life; people who had previously stayed home, intimidated by style-mag decrees and post-Studio 54 door policies, and people who had been putting up with mediocre mid-decade indie jumped ship and found they were suddenly in (very) close proximity to many like-minded souls.

* The post-house pop revolution would bring to the fore dozens of people who had been around in the post-punk era but seemed to have sat out the eighties, either through lack of opportunity or boredom, or both: Cabaret Voltaire's Richard H. Kirk recorded as Sweet Exorcist for Warp; new-wave pranksters Freur re-emerged as Underworld; Soft Cell's Dave Ball was half of the Grid; If?, who had a major club hit with 'Saturday's Angels', were ex-members of Subway Sect; the Guerilla label was formed by former anarchist squatter William Orbit and Dick O'Dell, former manager of the Pop Group; Kiss FM and Rage DJ Colin Faver had worked for Small Wonder in Walthamstow.

Unsurprisingly, Shoom quickly outgrew its tiny venue. The next step was Paul Oakenfold's Spectrum, which held fifteen hundred people, used a garish dayglo eyeball for a logo and played every available acid-house record; Chicago began to feed the demand with purpose-built records like Mr Lee's 'Pump Up London', saluting the mania of 'Notting-ham' and 'L-L-Leeds'. The scene grew exponentially.

Who was filling these clubs? Terry Farley was an ex-football hooligan, a soul boy with a taste for eighties West End club culture. At a club called Raid in late '87 he saw 'guys I knew from Millwall coming up in really dusty old shoes, Chevignon jackets and fucked-up trainers. Obviously they'd all come back from a mad Ibiza summer and they had the start of pony tails, with little top knots.' By the summer of '88 the pony tails were fully formed, and formerly violent, disenfranchised youth was united in a group hug.

Moral panic broke out in October 1988. Only two weeks after running a story about the giddy delights of acid house, the *Sun* linked the scene with rumours of new horror drug Ecstasy, bearing the headline 'Evil of Ecstasy' on October 19th. Other newspapers ran similar stories, many on their front pages, with photographs of writhing masses of sweaty teenagers. Short-lived tabloid *Today*'s headline squawked 'The New Sex and Drugs Cult Exposed!' alongside a picture of S'Express's Mark Moore. One *Sun* photo caption read: 'Night of ecstasy . . . thrill-seeking youngsters in a dance frenzy at the secret party attended by more than 11,000.' The ravers in the photo look hot, crazed and quite demented.

Acid house clearly wasn't long for this world, but it had a few weeks of vital chart infiltration. As soon as *Top of the Pops* banned the word 'acid', D Mob's half-cocked anthem 'We Call It Acieed' went as high as number two, and Jolly Roger's 'Acid Man' made the Top 20 after languishing for weeks in the lower reaches of the Top 75. Acid remixes were everywhere: the Wee Papa Girl Rappers and Samantha Fox found Kevin Saunderson happy to twiddle his 303 for them, and even boy band Bros's 'I Quit' was given an acid bath. House purists quickly swapped their copies of 'Pump Up London' for the less tainted, fresh new techno sound of Detroit and acid was off the charts by the autumn, strangled by the sweaty hands of the Goss brothers. But ravers weren't going away – if the sounds were now in short supply, then people would just have to create new material themselves.

The next wave would come from Manchester.

The Haçienda – otherwise known as FAC51 (like all Factory Records projects, it had its own catalogue number) – had opened in 1982, when Factory looked to build a post-Martin Hannett future based on the dance music that New Order were now creating. The problem was that, aside from New Order, Factory's dance singles had been flat and forgettable: A Certain Ratio abandoned their impressively frosty post-punk ('All Night Party', 'Flight', 'Forced Laugh') for stone-cold jazz funk; 52nd Street, Biting Tongues and Quando Quango left no impression whatsoever.* The club had survived, barely, as a regular gig venue: the Smiths had played there three times in 1983; Madonna had made her first UK appearance there on January 27th 1984, captured by Channel 4's *The Tube*. But it wasn't until 1986 that the club started to fulfil its ambitions with the Nude night on Friday, where DJ Mike Pickering (of Quando Quango, and later M People) played early house. Within a year it was full every night of the week, and – as had happened in Chicago – its denizens were inspired to go home and create more of the music they wanted to hear. 808 State were formed by Graham Massey, formerly of DIY act Danny and the Dressmakers, and contemporary-dance student Gerald Simpson: they broke through with the Balearic dreaminess of 'Pacific State' (no. 10 '89), but not before Simpson had left and, as A Guy Called Gerald, released his own single, 'Voodoo Ray', in late '88. Over a deep, echoed backing track, with keyboard whooshes like cars on wet streets, Gerald added cooing, wordless female vocals and a smidgin of house piano. It was midnight blue, rainy and mysterious (what, or who, was a Voodoo Ray?); it was the exact sound of the Haçienda. Almost on its own, 'Voodoo Ray' changed Manchester's musical landscape. By the time it reached number twelve nationally in

---

* The exception was Blackpool group Section 25, who, with two drummers and melodic, upfront basslines, took a singular route between PiL, Manchester miserabilism and emergent electronica: 'The Beast', 'Looking from a Hilltop' and 'Friendly Fires' straddle Factory's two peak periods.

the summer of 1989, the city was Britain's musical capital.

Happy Mondays had signed to Factory in 1985. They looked like drug dealers from a run-down Manchester estate because that's exactly what they were. Their music always seemed to be on the point of collapse, drums galloped ahead of their strange cowboy-funk guitar sound, and singer Shaun Ryder's barked lyrics were often incomprehensible: 'You don't like that face because the bones stick out'. Interviewed, Ryder confessed that they were trying to sound like the Rolling Stones, but their lack of musical ability meant they ended up sounding very much their own invention. 'Freaky Dancin'', their first truly inspired record, came out in 1987 as Ryder and his hooded cohorts, now in flares, discovered E and loosened up. 'When we first had E,' said Ryder, 'there couldn't have been more than a dozen of us in our corner of the Haçienda. No one had a clue. We had the end of '87 to ourselves.' Martin Hannett was brought in to produce their second album, 1988's *Bummed*, which featured a garish acid-dream painting of Ryder's face on its sleeve. Hannett gave them space and density, made sense of their loping groove and basic tunelessness. The album crossed the great divide between guitars and electronic pulse beats and, with a club-friendly mix of 'Wrote for Luck' by Paul Oakenfold in '88, Happy Mondays became the first group to unite indie students and house-loving clubbers.

Happy Mondays' biggest fans were a former goth rock band called the Stone Roses, who were mainly known in Manchester for spray-painting their name across some of the city's most beloved buildings and monuments in 1985. Melodically, they were *C86*-inspired, but John Squire was far better than the stereotypical indie guitarist. Initially, the Stone Roses had little to do with the dance scene at all, save for playing in warehouses around Manchester; still, when their first album was released in May '89 it was the hallucinogenic ending to 'This Is the One', the rush of backwards noise on 'Don't Stop' and the extended rave-up 'I Am the Resurrection' – which built, dropped and surged over nine minutes exactly like a house record – that drew people in. In February '89 they had played to thirty-odd people at the Seven Sisters campus of Middlesex Polytechnic; by the time the loping 'Fools Gold' (UK no. 8 '89), based on a loop from James Brown's 'Funky Drummer', came out in November they were the biggest group in Britain and drew eight thousand people to Alexandra Palace, a far bigger crowd than the Smiths had ever played to.

People had been pining for the Smiths since they split in '87 and trying to find enjoyment in Morrissey's Smith-lite solo records. Between them, the Roses and the Mondays made the Smiths obsolete. The exact point at which this happened was at 7.30 p.m. on November 23rd 1989, when they both appeared on *Top of the Pops*, playing 'Hallelujah' and 'Fools Gold'. A week earlier, 808 State had played 'Pacific State' on the show. Happy Mondays came up with the phrase 'Madchester'* to sum up the unlikely annexation of British TV by these bowl-cutted northerners in shapeless rave-wear; the British music press tagged the scene 'baggy', and it stuck.

By the end of '89, with the Stone Roses, Happy Mondays and 808 State sharing Top 40 space with Chicago house and Detroit techno, there were queues around the block to get into the Haçienda three hours before it opened. The crowd was largely made up of white students.† Some, including future Chemical Brothers Tom Rowlands and Ed Simons, brought sandwiches and made an event of the long wait. Eventually a fanzine called *Freaky Dancing* was made by the queue and for the queue, in an attempt to share and explain the excitement. When the Haçienda closed, after-hours clubs proliferated in the brutalist crescents of the nearby Hulme housing estate. If you wanted a seven-day weekend, here it was.

Also in the charts of 1989 were a Sheffield father-and-son team called Jive Bunny who, cloth-eared and glassy-eyed, were fighting a desperate

---

* T-shirts emblazoned with the name trailed Happy Mondays' *Madchester Rave On* EP by a few weeks, presumably manufactured by the group's mates. Shaun Ryder's self-contradictory memory is that 'It was our video directors, the Bailey Brothers, who came up with the term "Madchester", but we said, "Great, yeah, go with it," because Manchester was mad at the time. But no one used the term in Manchester, unless they were a prick.'

† The previous Christmas, John Peel's Festive Fifty, a reasonable measure of student tastes, had included nothing close to house or techno, but multiple entries for the House of Love (whose 'Destroy the Heart' was number one), the Wedding Present, Pixies, My Bloody Valentine and the Fall.

rearguard action against the new music, hanging onto the past just as David Whitfield and Dickie Valentine had done in the face of the mid-fifties rock 'n' roll boom. Jive Bunny scored three straight number ones – 'Swing the Mood', 'That's What I Like', 'Let's Party' – with cloddish cut-and-paste medleys of Bill Haley, Chubby Checker and the *Hawaii Five-0* theme. A sickly cartoon rabbit, one that you wouldn't allow near your kids, was the music's physical representation.

Meanwhile, bursting out of cellars and into warehouses across the country was an Italian record called 'Grand Piano' by the Mixmaster, which cut up Ralph Rosario's 'You Used to Hold Me', Coldcut and Lisa Stansfield's 'People Hold On', Kaos's 'Definition of Love' and Tyree's 'Turn Up the Bass'. 'Grand Piano' used the same principle as Jive Bunny but headed in the exact opposite direction: the sampled songs were largely unfamiliar, they were used creatively – they were set to sound-track your tomorrow. Italian house provided several of 1989's most jubilant singles: Starlight's 'Numero Uno' (UK no. 8), Gino Latino's 'Welcome' (UK no. 17) and FPI Project's 'Going Back to My Roots' (UK no. 5), essentially a monotonous backing track of the old Odyssey/Lamont/Dozier hit, but with irresistible house-piano chords that gave it an extraordinary warmth. A further cut-and-paste Italian job, Black Box's 'Ride on Time'* was everywhere in the summer of '89, a phenomenon, number one for six weeks. Jive Bunny could be easily ignored. As the door to the nineties opened, here was a modern pop revolution which could be traced back to a malfunctioning machine rather than a musician – the accidental, idiot joy of the Roland 303.

Three unexpected things happened in the wake of acid house. Firstly, it invigorated indie. In the wake of the Stone Roses and Happy Mondays, other groups adapted to a more groove-led production. There was a second wave of Manchester acts – neither Inspiral Carpets nor the Charlatans had to reconfigure their sixties, organ-based sound too

---

* An Italian DJ called Daniele Davoli was behind 'Ride on Time', which was basically a remix of Loleatta Holloway's 1980 single 'Love Sensation'. Davoli was also behind the Mixmaster's 'Grand Piano' and Starlight's 'Numero Uno', as well as 'Airport '89' under the pseudonym Wood Allen. 'I like Woody Allen,' explained Davoli.

much to fit in perfectly, and the latter's 'The Only One I Know' (UK no. 9 '90) has been an indie disco staple ever since. The Soup Dragons and Primal Scream, two Glasgow groups who had both featured on the *C86* compilation, were more radically reinvented – the former with a desperate baggy cover of the Rolling Stones' 'I'm Free' (no. 5 '90) featuring an ill-advised ragga break, the latter with the rather more cosmic *Screamadelica*. In the long term, groups began to take their own DJs on tour to warm up the crowd, rather than relying on the sound man's CD collection.*

Secondly, it opened Britain up to European dance music, because lyrics didn't really matter. Italian house was just the beginning. The introduction of £1 ferry deals at the end of the eighties meant that people could now afford to go from Hull to Amsterdam and sample European clubbing. Some returned with a taste for the Lowlands' harder, darker techno variant which quickly became part of the outdoor rave scene – Joey Beltram's 'Energy Flash', T 99's 'Anasthasia' (no. 14 '91) – while the new brand of European post-techno pop made regular incursions into the chart: 2 Unlimited ('Get Ready for This', 'Twilight Zone', 'No Limit'), Haddaway ('What Is Love', 'Life', 'Rock My Heart') and Capella ('U Got 2 Know', 'U Got 2 Let the Music', 'Move On Baby') became Top 10 fixtures. Livin' Joy's 'Dreamer', an Italian-made house record that reached number one when it was reissued in '96, had a lyric that defied analysis: 'Here we lie all alone, am I dreaming? Your heart's smooth, my soul is unbelieving. Now you see the me and I'm a-feeling, I'm a-feeling.' When Baccara's 'Yes Sir, I Can Boogie' had been number one in 1977 the lyrics and Spanish accents were a national event, fodder for stand-up comedians for the next five years. I don't recall a single note of dissent about Livin' Joy's violation of the English language; the atmosphere of the record, the intensity of the vocal and its minor-chord uplift meant no one really cared. It just felt right.

Acid house also woke up the British soul scene, partly as a backlash to

---

* Working for Inspiral Carpets became an unlikely nineties nursery: they took the future 'superstar DJ' Paul van Dyk on tour with them in '91, and gave a young Noel Gallagher his first break as a roadie.

dayglo bagginess. Haçienda DJ Mike Pickering started a group called M People with Muppet-voiced singer Heather Small and captured – presumably unintentionally – a post-rave wine-bar crowd, the same contingent who would have bought Paul Young records a decade earlier. M People had scored ten flavourless Top 10 hits by the late nineties. More intriguing were a pair of labels – Acid Jazz and DJ Norman Jay's Talkin' Loud – which were similarly touched by acid's liberation yet, clearly of the belief that there had been worthwhile records made in the olden days, were rooted in seventies funk and soul. Even with a single as loose and memorable as the Young Disciples' 'Apparently Nothin'' (UK no. 13 '91) it felt a little like you were partying in a library.*

It wasn't just the older soul fraternity who felt the need to slow things down. For many early adopters, the intensity of Ibiza and acid house had begun to give way to a desire for something more mellow by 1989. This coincided with the overground emergence of a North London DJ/club/shop/sound-system hire collective called Soul II Soul who had released the midtempo beauty 'Keep On Movin'' (UK no. 5 '89) in the spring. Mixing soul and lovers' rock, its soft, tactile vocal from Caron Wheeler was backed by house-piano riffs played at quarter speed, Jazzie B's daydreaming lyric – which had an obsession with the weather that recalled Noël Coward or Ray Davies – and, most importantly, a distinctive, rolling, 98 bpm loop taken from Graham Central Station's funk track 'The Jam'; with 'Keep On Movin'', it felt as if Soul II Soul had tapped into the exact velocity of MDMA.† They revisited the loop for 'Back to Life' in the summer of '89 and this time scored a UK number one. By the year's end the 98 bpm Soul II Soul rhythm was all over a bunch of midtempo records that found a ready audience in post-acid Ibiza, where people wanted something that felt and sounded like the sun rising: One World's 'Down on Love' and the Family Stand's 'Ghetto Heaven' (UK no. 10 '90) were built on Soul II Soul's spiritual feel; from Italy came J. T. and the Big Family's 'Moments in Soul' (UK no. 7 '90);

---

* Has there ever been a more symbolic group name than the Young Disciples? We are young, we know our place, but we understand our heritage.
† The tempo of 'Keep On Movin'' is close to that of the Cure's 'All Cats Are Grey', which may help to explain Marc Almond's epiphany.

from St Albans came the Grid's 'Floatation', which celebrated the raver's favoured non-chemical method of relaxation. A bootleg of US folkie Edie Brickell's 'What I Am' emerged with the Soul II Soul beat planted underneath it,* and – with all snob barriers down – DJs even found room for such unlikely, but rhythmically perfect, dancefloor material as Chris Rea's 'Josephine' and Mr Mister's AOR ballad 'Broken Wings'. Summing up the whole scene was 'Joy and Heartbreak' by Movement 98, a pseudonym for one of the Ibiza pioneers, Paul Oakenfold. 'We'd come through E, and what we were into was smoking joints and chilling. For me, at the raves it was all sheep. Everyone would look the same, dress the same . . . it was full of younger people.'

By 1990 Oakenfold and his erstwhile Ibiza revolutionaries were bemoaning the influx of youngsters with their white gloves, white tracksuits and glow sticks. They came across exactly like '76 punks, moaning about how the scene had been wrecked by 'acid teds . . . groping E-heads who don't know how to handle drugs properly'. But unlike the '76 punks, they also realised the various futures this fervent scene was opening up. In the summer of 1991 DJ Andy Weatherall and Primal Scream created 'Higher than the Sun', which somehow blended Bobby Gillespie's vaporous vocal, dub thunderclaps and distorted harpsichord to create a modern psychedelia. *Melody Maker*'s Simon Reynolds acted as rave's own Leonard Bernstein, an observer from the beached and increasingly irrelevant indie scene who was seized by enthusiasm for the new music and accordingly wanted to share his love with more cynical contemporaries. Reviewing 'Higher than the Sun', he called it 'ahead of the times, at once new and timeless . . . octopoid tentacles of gooey bliss, freak-out guitar, adding up to an inspired, inspirational mess. Space rock/acid dub/cosmic house – all of these and none of them apply.'

Things had evolved dramatically since 'Acid Tracks', just two years earlier. You could understand why first-wave, knackered ravers were retiring to Ibiza, opening bars where they could chill out and listen to

* This predated the bootleg/mash-up trend of ten years later, which culminated in the Sugababes' number one 'Freak Like Me', a mix of an Adina Howard vocal line with the backing track from Tubeway Army's 'Are "Friends" Electric'.

'Higher than the Sun' on a loop, a 98 bpm mix all day long, leaving London to the groping, hapless acid Teds. You *could* understand, but they really missed a treat.

As for the conservatives at Radio 1 and their stated desire to appeal to executives and theatregoers, the tide had turned against them in the first week of October 1989, when the Top 3 was made up of Black Box's 'Ride on Time' (which ended up as the biggest-selling single of the year), Belgian act Technotronic's bouncy but stripped-back 'Pump Up the Jam' (or 'pormp orp the jam') and Sydney Youngblood's 'If Only I Could', R&B with a tough but tender vocal that recalled early-sixties strongmen like Jerry Butler and Chuck Jackson. Bros, Billy Joel, Aerosmith and Deacon Blue were all hovering lower down the Top 40, but who cared about the rest of the chart? The nineties couldn't wait to begin.

1991: TIME FOR THE MU MU

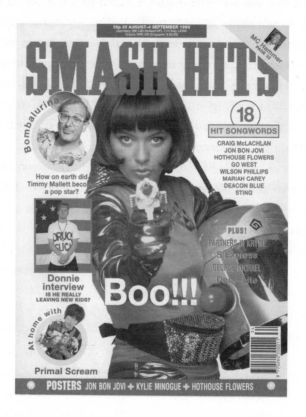

In August 1990 Factory Records' Tony Wilson was asked to host a talk at CMJ, an annual industry get-together in New York. His panel was called 'Wake Up America, You're Dead!' and on it were Happy Mondays' manager Nathan McGough and comedian Keith Allen, plus Chicago's Marshall Jefferson and Detroit's Derrick May. Wilson reckoned that the major labels had been 'shitting themselves for the last twelve months because they've invested hundreds of thousands of pounds in groups which they could no longer sell . . . the point is, kids in Britain for the last few years and still today and tomorrow are having the times of their lives, in the words of the *Dirty Dancing* movie. I don't see any kids in America having the time of their lives.'

This wasn't quite true, but British and American pop culture seemed a long, long way apart. Rock and hip hop were still dominant in the States. Hard rock was going through a metamorphosis as the Sunset Strip glam-metal bands began to seem tired, and too prone to soppy ballads for Led Zep lovers: 1988 had seen the release of two albums that toughened up rock and made it seem dangerous and viable again, Metallica's . . . *And Justice for All* and Guns n' Roses' *Appetite for Destruction*.* Both groups referenced punk as an influence, both helped to create an audience for the alternative stadium rock of the Red Hot Chili Peppers, Faith No More and Jane's Addiction.

Guns n' Roses were led by Axl Rose, a Los Angeles showman in the Jim Morrison tradition. His lyrics could romanticise his LA woman ('Sweet Child o' Mine', US no. 1 '88, UK no. 6 '89) or the city at night ('Paradise City', US no. 5, UK no. 6 '89), or they could just be flippantly offensive ('One in a Million': 'Immigrants and faggots, they make no sense to me. They come to our country and think they'll do as they please'). His penchant for wearing T-shirts of Hollywood's least favourite, Charles Manson, also rubbed the locals up the wrong way, but *Appetite for Destruction* still became the biggest-selling debut album in US history, at twenty-eight million copies. A different slant on American rock came from the documentary *1991: The Year Punk Broke*. Director David Markey said the title had come to him as he watched MTV Europe, while he was jet-lagged in a Cork hotel with Sonic Youth, whose European tour he was set to film. Footage of Mötley Crüe singing 'Anarchy in the UK' to thousands of people in an American stadium came onto the screen, and the phrase spilled out of Markey's mouth. British viewers may have thought the title had some irony, but interviews with Markey suggested not: 'For many years punk rock only existed on this underground level . . . finally it is being digested and embraced by pop culture at large.' His understanding of punk's influence may

---

* In 1989 Guns n' Roses were called 'the most dangerous band in the world' by the *LA Times*, who, in the same article, called the 1989 Rolling Stones 'the greatest rock 'n' roll band in the world'.

have seemed underdeveloped but Markey was very fortunate that Sonic Youth's support act on the tour was Nirvana, just two months before they released *Nevermind*, an album that shifted rock's focus away from Axl Rose's snotty antics and singlehandedly resumed Anglo-American pop-cultural relations.

Elsewhere in the old new world in 1991, New Kids on the Block's Donnie Wahlberg was getting himself arrested for setting fire to his hotel room;* on the west coast, Ice-T made his first record with Body Count, allying metal and gangsta rap, while another unholy musical alliance – funk metal – peaked with the Red Hot Chili Peppers' album *Blood Sugar Sex Magik*. The similarly smack-heavy Jane's Addiction were on a farewell tour called *Lollapalooza*,† which seemed more like a travelling festival as it featured high-profile guests such as Siouxsie and the Banshees, Ice-T, Nine Inch Nails and some Shaolin monks. The group's singer Perry Farrell coined the term 'Alternative Nation' to describe the tour; it has run as a festival ever since. The title of Douglas Coupland's novel *Generation X* was used to describe 1991's disaffected youth, slacker culture and the alternative American nation, which hit a commercial and cultural peak when *Nevermind* was released on the same day as *Blood Sugar Sex Magik*. Meanwhile, Britain remained oblivious to the biggest American name of '91, Garth Brooks, who became the first country star to incorporate elements of rock into his music, rather than vice versa. His third album, *Ropin' the Wind*, had advance sales of four million, went straight in at number one and dragged his first two albums into the US Top 20 with it; as only Elvis and the Beatles have sold more albums in America than Brooks, it seems churlish not to mention him. You can see Tony Wilson's point, though – not much of this looked like 'fun'.

Let's look at some British chart stats for 1991.

---

* NKOTB scored seven Top 10 hits in Britain in 1990, but had managed only one in '91 as they faded fast, which may explain Wahlberg's behaviour.
† 'Lollapalooza' was an antiquated term beloved of P. G. Wodehouse that meant 'something rather extraordinary'. Perry Farrell picked the term up from a Three Stooges film.

BREAKDOWN OF UK TOP 40 HITS IN 1991

Rock	56 (14%)
Indie	59 (14.5%)
R&B/Hip hop	55 (13.5%)
Dance	92 (23%)
Other	142 (35%)

A few of the indie hits were late-period baggy – from the Charlatans ('Over Rising', no. 15), Happy Mondays ('Loose Fit', no. 17 – their last Top 20 hit) and a few groups who rode the indie-dance bandwagon around the yard for a few months: Blur ('There's No Other Way', no. 8), Jesus Jones ('International Bright Young Things', no. 7), the Farm (whose *Spartacus* album was a number one in March), the Mock Turtles (with the incredibly accurate Stone Roses-alike 'Can You Dig It', no. 18) and James ('Sit Down', no. 2). The last mentioned were a group from Manchester who had initially emerged on Factory in 1983; their rattling *Jimone* EP had been a bridge between post-punk and *C86* indie, and a joint *NME* Single of the Week alongside the Smiths' 'This Charming Man'. By '91 James were reborn as indie dance and, with the karmic hippie message of 'Sit Down', came across like a bunch of creepy yoga teachers; their 1993 single 'Laid' was possibly the least attractive song about sex ever written. Primal Scream's 'Higher than the Sun' only reached number forty, but their *Screamadelica* album was a Top 10 hit – it stayed in the chart for over six months, and won the inaugural Mercury Music Prize the following year.* 1991 was also a boom time for a lank-haired, post-acid, largely post-political brand of indie: Midlanders the Wonder Stuff ('Size of a Cow', no. 5) and Pop Will Eat Itself ('X Y and

---

* Primal Scream therefore became the first group to develop feet of clay after winning the prize. The curse of the Mercury follow-up also struck Pulp (the low-selling *This Is Hardcore*), Suede (who split during the making of *Dog Man Star*), Roni Size, Speech Debelle and Gomez (whose careers sank without trace). The follow-up to *Screamadelica* – *Give Out but Don't Give Up* – was panned by critics. 'Don't expect any expansionist moves towards a gleaming polycultural future *à la Screamadelica* here,' warned *Melody Maker*'s Paul Lester. '*Give Out but Don't Give Up* is authentic, all right – an authentic Rolling Stones record. What is the point? What is the fucking point?'

Zee', no. 15) briefly ruled student discos, as well as leftie squat rockers Carter the Unstoppable Sex Machine, who had a brace of '91 hits with 'Sheriff Fatman' (no. 23) and 'After the Watershed' (no. 11).

A 1991 'Indie Disco' incorporated pretty much anything with fuzzy guitars that wasn't metal. In Glasgow, Teenage Fanclub conflated Neil Young and Big Star to create the spangly chug of the *Bandwagonesque* album, akin to power pop with the handbrake on; in their wake came soundalikes Eugenius and Velvet Crush. At the other end of the spectrum were vinegary Welsh group the Manic Street Preachers, who showed a complete disinterest in dance and baggy – they were all adrenalin and nihilist slogans, the antithesis of Teenage Fanclub's Brit slackerisms: 'Skin up . . . you're already dead!' teased bassist Nicky Wire.

Wire and guitarist Richey Edwards were both pretty and fiercely intelligent. If 1991's dance music was short on lyrical bite, then the Manics made up for it all by themselves. They quoted Rimbaud and Debord in interviews, and said they would go on *Top of the Pops* and commit suicide. 'England needs revolution NOW' read Wire's détourned school shirt. They believed in a musical scorched-earth policy, looked for kindred spirits and found none. Outsiders in the Dexys mould, singles like 'Stay Beautiful' (no. 40 '91) and 'You Love Us' (no. 16 '92) gained them a devoted following which grew exponentially when Edwards disappeared in 1994.

Bubbling under were a few groups who dressed up and weren't afraid to reference the past, specifically a British past. Most notable were Manchester's World of Twist, who were initially lumped in with the baggy groups but referenced northern soul and Peter Gabriel-era Genesis, and included a band member who made 'sea noises'. On stage, they looked like a glamorous circus act and in 1991 they made very little sense but, if 'Sons of the Stage' (UK no. 47 '91) had got radio play, things might have been different. They had to settle for being harbingers.

The biggest rock hits were largely metal and all by American acts, the most sizeable coming from Metallica ('Enter Sandman', no. 5) and Guns n' Roses, who had a trio of hits: 'You Could Be Mine' (no. 3), 'Don't Cry' (no. 8) and 'Live and Let Die' (no. 5), all of which did better in the UK than America. In the R&B department, Color Me Badd took harmonic swingbeat to number one ('I Wanna Sex You Up'), while hip hop was almost entirely represented by soft, east-coast material: Jazzy Jeff and the Fresh Prince's mellow 'Summertime' (US no. 4, UK no. 8) predicted mid-nineties G-funk, while PM Dawn's 'Set Adrift on Memory Bliss' (US no. 1, UK no. 3), with vocals that sounded like the Association had re-formed with a whispering rapper as a front man, wove layered harmonies around a Spandau Ballet sample. It proved to be a gentle kiss goodbye to hip hop's golden age – the genre would go on to embrace Ice-T's 'Cop Killer', Dr Dre's *The Chronic* and the rise of Death Row Records in '92.

As for 'other'? Bryan Adams's *Robin Hood* love song 'Everything I Do (I Do It for You)' overshadowed the year: the single that wouldn't die hogged the number-one spot for a record-breaking sixteen weeks; this was the longest stretch at number one by any single since Slim Whitman's 'Rose Marie' (a mere eleven weeks) in 1955, and it came from the same stock as the first number one, Al Martino's 'Here in My Heart' in '52. 'Everything I Do' was part of a pop-ballad tradition that went back even further than Martino, all the way back to John McCormack, Enrico Caruso, Jenny Lind, and – often with a country or continental twist – had carried on through the sixties, providing some of the biggest hits of the modern pop era. Pure schmaltz, these singles had served their purpose for a short while before being replaced a year or so later by the latest mega-ballad. Few of them, despite all being UK number ones at the time, get radio play any more: 'Tears' (Ken Dodd, '65), 'Green, Green Grass of Home' (Tom Jones, '66), 'Release Me' (Engelbert Humperdinck, '67), 'The Last Waltz' (Engelbert again, '67), 'I Pretend' (Des O'Connor, '68). A modern variant, the 'power ballad', was born with Harry Nilsson's 'Without You' (no. 1 '72): the ingredients were a slow rock beat, quiet verse and surging chorus; like the ballads of old, the power ballad would always include degrees of mawkishness, manipulation, self-pity and emotional blackmail. From the opening line – 'Look into my eyes' – Bryan Adams sounds like he's covering up for a dirty deed on 'Everything I Do': 'You *know* it's true,' he whimpers – methinks he doth protest *way* too much. But 'schmaltz' comes from the German '*schmelzen*', 'to melt', and 'Everything I Do' made plenty of record buyers feel gooey enough to buy it in '91. Adams must have thought he'd won the all-time power-ballad gold medal, but he wasn't accounting for a new kid who appeared on the block in '92, the French-Canadian Celine Dion, who proceeded to knock out soggily aggressive monsters on a bi-monthly basis.

1991 was a big year for novelty records in the UK: Hale and Pace's 'The Stonk' and the Simpsons' 'Do the Bartman' were both number ones; Right Said Fred's 'I'm Too Sexy' was stuck behind Bryan Adams at number two for six weeks. Rod Stewart had his last two Top 10 hits ('Rhythm of My Heart', 'Motown Song'), and a swathe of the eighties' bigger names – Erasure, Chris Rea, Level 42, Phil Collins – weren't off the chart just yet. But 1988's acid-fuelled 'second summer of love' had planted seeds in chart pop that bloomed beautifully in the early nineties.

Deee-Lite were brand new, from New York, and they released a single in the summer of 1990 called 'Groove Is in the Heart' that inhabited a cartoon world all of its own. There were swanee whistles, rattling cowbells, lines about 'succotash' and probably the catchiest bassline in history. It was insanely joyous and reached number two in the UK, number four in the States. Their singer, Lady Miss Kier, was straight out of *Alice in Wonderland*, loved by men and women alike, and could have been a Debbie Harry for the nineties. The problem was that Deee-Lite forgot to write another good song. People were willing them to release something even a fifth as good as 'Groove Is in the Heart', but it wasn't forthcoming. It was a real pity.

Betty Boo partly made up for this disappointment. She looked like a panther and had a squeaky voice. Originally she was Alison Clarkson; she had learnt to rap along to 'Rapper's Delight' when she was ten, and then got into graffiti (her tag 'Ali*Cat' appeared all over White City and Shepherd's Bush in the eighties). Like Lady Miss Kier, she looked as if she'd been rustling through Emma Peel's *Avengers* wardrobe, and her hits had a grab bag of sixties samples to match: 'Doin' the Do' (no. 7 '90), 'Where Are You Baby' (no. 3 '90) and 'Let Me Take You There' (no. 12 '92) fizzed like Tizer with a playful dollop of attitude – 'I've used up all my tissues on more seriouser issues,' she said, screwing up her face and wiggling her tail. 'A lot of people use clichés in their lyrics,' she haughtily told Q magazine, 'like Gloria Estefan – love this, love that. But listen to "Let Me Take You There": I say, "cashews and champers". Nobody says "cashews and champers".'

Betty briefly threatened to take over from Kylie Minogue as Britain's pet pop star. But Kylie was going through a golden period herself. When she had first emerged as tomboy Charlene from *Neighbours*, with her Stock Aitken Waterman-produced breakthrough hits, *Smash Hits* had dubbed her Corky O'Reilly. Later, re-emerging in 1994 after a two-year hiatus, she was Indie Kylie, keen to distance herself from anything that appeared manufactured; overthinking the direction of her career, the Top 10 hits soon dried up. Later still, she was Disco Kylie, more concerned with her hot pants and pert bottom than notions of *NME* credibility, and the public loved her all over again. But her imperial phase, even allowing for the classical perfection of 2001 hit 'Can't Get You out of My Head', had been at the turn of the nineties, when she changed from PWL poppet into SexKylie. 'I guess you can pretend to be something you're not but only for so long,' she told the *NME*'s David Quantick, who coined the name SexKylie in '91. 'When I decided I wanted to make some changes, the suits at the record company just about had a heart attack. "Kylie? What are you doing?! You're going to ruin us!"' To match Kylie's new-found libido, and to compete with newbies like Betty Boo as well as the house and techno DJs taking control of the chart, Stock Aitken Waterman's writing and production went into fourth gear. The quartet of singles from her *Rhythm of Love* album – 'Better the Devil You Know' (no. 2 '90), 'Step Back in Time' (no. 4 '90), 'What Do I Have to Do' (no. 6 '91) and 'Shocked' (no. 6 '91) – were super-modern, super-melodic and as well tuned as Motown records of old.

While Kylie and Betty represented 1991's spirit of abandon, the real story of the year was hidden in a breakdown of the Top 10 hits. The Top 40 may have suggested dance music held sway but, if we look at the statistics for the sharp end, the results are even more extreme:

TOP 10 HITS

Rock	12 (8.5%)
Indie	12 (8.5%)
R&B/Hip hop	13 (9%)
Dance	44 (31%)
Other	62 (43%)

Almost one in three Top 10 hits was a dance record,* and I'm not including anything in this category – like Kenny Thomas's smooth eighties-revivalist soul, or even PM Dawn's Balearic hip hop – that could have conceivably been made pre-house. Consider also that even Kylie's 'Shocked' (filed under 'other') and Happy Mondays' 'Loose Fit' (filed under 'indie') aren't included in that slice of the pie. The Top 10 was all about rave – the takeover was that complete. 'I've always hated commercial pop music,' said Happy Mondays' manager Nathan McGough, speaking for generations raised on the Stones, or prog, or punk, with their collective mistrust of Top 40 pop, 'and now if you asked me to list my ten favourite records I'd guess eight of them would be in the British Top 40.'

As had happened with 'indie' in the eighties, 'dance' became a genre rather than just a descriptive word in the early nineties. Dance music was all about rhythms and textures. It was post-house and, for the most part, post-melody. In 1990 the only terms used for dance music were still 'house' and 'techno', the former used to signify a more vocal-based

---

* Though people had never left the dancefloor, the blanket term 'dance' had first been used to indicate a vaguely 'other' subset of pop in the late eighties. The compilation series *Now That's What I Call Music* began releasing twelve-inch albums called *Now Dance* in 1985, while *The Chart Show* included a weekly Top 10 'dance chart' from its launch in 1986 (initially it also featured a reggae Top 10, which suggests that either the programme's producers didn't dance to reggae, or the term 'dance' already meant something different from Jamaican rhythms). These were big, broad definitions of dance, though, suggesting little more than a twelve-inch mix that wouldn't get airplay but might get played by a DJ in a club. By 1989 'dance' was a ubiquitous enough term for the likes of the Stone Roses to be tagged 'indie-dance crossover'. As an umbrella term, in the nineties 'dance' seemed to elbow out previous names – like 'nightclub', 'disco', 'hi-NRG' and 'Eurobeat' – some of which had been narrow, but useful. Many are now used retrospectively.

sound, a little closer to R&B, and the latter suggesting something more purely electronic; 1991 was the year in which 'rave' became more commonly used shorthand for the gleeful airhorn-and-breakbeat noise dominating the chart. By the middle of the decade dance music had become a nightmare of semantics. It would evolve so fast and frequently that it was almost impossible to keep up; even with two decades' distance there are plenty of barely remembered experiments, worked at for a few weeks then abandoned in favour of some grand new futuristic design. Others were swept aside not only by the pace of change, but by the law. Beyond this, the music press ignored whole swathes of it. The era remains ripe for deeper exploration.

Novelty and fun were what people wanted in 1991 – supposedly serious music like Enya's new-age number one 'Orinoco Flow' could be gleefully chewed up and spat out as RAF's 'We've Got to Live Together'. A recurring theme on early rave records was the plea for everyone to get together – Sabrina Johnston's 'Peace' and Rozalla's 'Everybody's Free (to Feel Good)' were among '91's bigger hits; both did their best to promote the cause. There was no hierarchy. Rave thrived on mass unity and, for this reason, it didn't need pin-ups; the mere act of going on *Top of the Pops* was enough.* So Xpansions ('Move Your Body', no. 7) would hold the conch one week, before passing it on to the Bassheads ('Is There Anybody Out There', no. 5), or K-Klass ('Rhythm Is a Mystery', no. 3), or whoever happened to be on *TOTP* the following week. The only message to get across was 'raving is fun' – it was a totally unified scene.

The indie music press, *Top of the Pops* and Radio 1 tended to describe rave, and dance music generally, as 'faceless'. In fact, there hadn't been as much dressing up since the turn of the eighties. At the sillier end of the fancy-dress spectrum there was Guru Josh ('Infinity', no. 5 '90),

---

* Adamski, whose 'Killer' (with a little help from Seal) reached number one in 1990, wasn't much of a looker but he was young, blond and had an ego. He was no interloper, having played live at the opening party of Amnesia nightclub in Ibiza in 1989, with future KLF MC Ricardo Da Force. As soon as he started acting like a star, like he might engage in Donnie Wahlberg-like hotel-room behaviour, he was dropped by the scene like a hot potato. After one more hit, the appalling 'Space Jungle' (no. 7 '90), he disappeared from sight.

who waved his arms and wore clothes like a TV magician, but when
you looked closely you could tell he was actually a dentist. Altern-8
were much more exciting, a duo from Stafford who wore boiler suits
and face masks – in this respect they were faceless, but it was a pretty
distinctive faceless look. 'Infiltrate 202' (no. 28 '91), 'Activ 8' (no. 3 '91)
and 'E-Vapor-8' (no. 6 '92) epitomised rave with airhorns, gargantuan
keyboard riffs, galloping breakbeats and wailing female vocal samples.
Altern-8's sole album had the glorious title *Full on . . . Mask Hysteria*. In
the 1992 general election, the duo's Chris Peat stood as a candidate for
the Stafford constituency, representing the Hardcore Altern8-ive Party;
he received 158 votes and came fourth.*

European dance music began to realise it was no longer reliant on
imports from Detroit and Chicago at the turn of the nineties. By 1991
Britain had become remarkably self-sufficient. DJs cut records at home
(The Prodigy's 'Charly', no. 3 '91) or in small, local studios (Cola Boy's
'7 Ways 2 Love', no. 8 '91). They pressed white-label twelves and took
them to nearby specialist dance shops. The shops then often started their
own record label to distribute the music more widely – these included
Flying (Soho), Suburban Base (run from the Boogie Times shop in
Romford) and Warp (Sheffield). Sometimes the DJs worked in the shop
and played the records out; you could see this as rather incestuous, or as
a rather successful cottage industry. Either way, it kept everything fast-
moving, and largely bypassed the music industry. Warp was the most
successful shop-cum-label, scoring hits with a brace of 'bleep' singles,
'LFO' by LFO (no. 12) and 'Tricky Disco' by Tricky Disco (no. 14),
as well as Nightmares on Wax's pulverising 'Aftermath' (no. 38), in the
summer of 1990. This Sheffield-specific sound was based around a sampler's sine-wave test tones: they weren't on the sampler for making music
but, as acid house had been born from abusing the Roland 303, Warp's
acts created 'bleep' techno by emphasising the high end and, more significantly, extreme sub-bass notes, so low that you felt them rather than
heard them. Warp's new techno strain found favour at the Labyrinth

---

* Their manifesto included adapting police uniforms to include smiley faces and
bandanas; changing the BBC's classical Radio 3 into a rave station called Radio
303; and free raves funded by the despised poll tax.

club in Dalston and with London DJs Fabio and Grooverider, who were soon to take over at Rage, a weekly night at the Heaven nightclub next to Charing Cross station.

As with disco, different European countries developed their own strains of Dionysian dance music: the R&S label in Belgium, Harthouse in Germany and Djax-Up-Beats in the Netherlands were all reliable signs of quality control. Local scenes mutated: in the Netherlands there was a demand for ever harder, faster beats, until gabber appeared,* the Oi! of dance music, while the Germans – led by Sven Väth – pioneered trance. Sometimes you couldn't dance to dance music at all. The KLF's 1990 *Chill Out* album had pioneered the tautological 'ambient house', mixing train noises, post-punk dub and pre-punk Floyd; DJ and KLF associate Alex Paterson took this gag to another level with the Orb, who had tracks with giveaway titles like 'Back Side of the Moon'. Sniggering stoners, they were silly at best, but proved hugely popular with students and worn-out ravers – *U.F.Orb* was a number-one album and 'The Blue Room' a number-eight single in '92, the longest hit single ever at just under forty minutes. They appeared on *TOTP* playing 3D chess rather than miming on unplugged keyboards, which may have seemed like a bit of a jolly at the time, but caused a complete rethink of the show's policy.†

---

* Gabber sounded more like war than music. It was gleefully unpleasant, with a thudding, distorted 909 kick drum always to the fore. Melody was entirely absent. Rotterdam had been razed to the ground by German bombers and here was its soundtrack, on the dancefloor, forty years later (the more cultured techno-producing cities of Amsterdam and Eindhoven, home of Djax-Up-Beats, were roundly ridiculed on records like Euromasters' 'Where the Fuck Is Amsterdam'). 'Poing' by Rotterdam Termination Source is maybe the single most belligerent and uncomplicated record to ever reach the UK Top 40 (no. 27 '92). When the tempo of gabber reached 300 bpm in 1994, it was time to call a halt to the bombardment. DJ and gabber overlord Paul Elstak started creating happy gabber at much the same time as the UK's hardcore scene, descending into drug paranoia, developed its happy-hardcore splinter.
† The BBC felt foolish, and declared that dance acts would be forced to sing live, no matter if the front person for Capella would have to sing a cut-and-shut Loleatta Holloway sample. Radio 1 was similarly averse to dance music. As 1991 bled into 1992, 2 Unlimited's 'Twilight Zone', the KLF's 'Justified and Ancient' and the Prodigy's incendiary 'Everybody in the Place' all peaked at number two, but Radio 1 was spiritually closer to the singles keeping them from the top: Wet

* * *

Who are your favourite pop group? It's not easy, is it? I could plump for the Beach Boys, but there's always the difficulty of loving Mike Love. The Who? Far too patchy. The Pet Shop Boys? They didn't know when to quit. The Bee Gees? Oh, too much to explain.

If you were forced to name your favourite group of all time, then the Beatles would be a hard one to argue with, but so would the KLF. Their catalogue is patchy, deeply flawed, and they never made a consistently strong album. But they showered the crowd at an Oxfordshire rave with £1,000-worth of Scottish pound notes bearing the legend 'Children we love you'. They played at the 1992 Brit Awards with vegan punks Extreme Noise Terror, before picking up guns and firing blanks at the audience. They were independent, euphoric, iconoclastic, and they were enormously successful in 1991.

The KLF – Bill Drummond and Jimmy Cauty – epitomised everything that had changed in pop since acid house. They weren't young, or pretty, but they had ideas, a lot of good ones, a lot of stupid ones, and they were smart enough to put them all into practice. They weren't afraid to be held up as fakes, or derided as insincere. They welcomed it all.

Originally, Bill Drummond was an art student in Liverpool, where he had joined a band called Big in Japan. Staying in the city, he had run the Zoo label and handled the affairs of Echo and the Bunnymen and the Teardrop Explodes. Primarily, he was a music fan. One day in the late seventies he had written to Seymour Stein, head of Sire Records, explaining how albums were bringing about the destruction of pop music, and that pop was always about singles. He told Stein that Sire had released two of the greatest records of the decade – 'Shake Some Action' by the Flamin' Groovies and 'Love Goes to Building on Fire' by Talking Heads – and that, having created such perfection, neither group should have been allowed into a studio again. 'Both bands', he wrote, 'should have been forced to disband instantly.'

Wet Wet's 'Goodnight Girl', Shakespear's Sister's 'Stay' and 'Bohemian Rhapsody' by (the recently deceased) Freddie Mercury and Queen.

Drummond was in his mid-thirties when the KLF broke through, and he had a talent to annoy that a younger, more obviously attractive pop star might have used in a misguided way. Shortly after the KLF – under the name the Timelords – had scored a 1988 UK number one with 'Doctorin' the Tardis', Drummond wrote *The Manual.* It purported to be a guide on how to create a number-one hit. Its rules included using the latest dance beat, a direct title and universal lyrics. That 'Doctorin' the Tardis' broke all these rules was irrelevant. You willed them on, and when a Swiss group called Edelweiss did score a pan-European hit called 'Bring Me Edelweiss' (UK no. 5 '89) by following *The Manual* to the letter, it perversely restored your faith in pop's sweet little mystery. It was rare enough for journalists to jump from one side of the fence to the other – the Pretenders' Chrissie Hynde and Pet Shop Boys' Neil Tennant had been by far the most successful – but for a manager to do it? Only Malcolm McLaren had made it before. The KLF were the return of McLarenite new pop pranksterism – justified mischief. While detractors saw rave as faceless, tuneless, mindless, the KLF showed how calculus and intellect could operate in the brave new world.

In the beginning, Drummond and Cauty's efforts had seemed like little more than novelty records. 'Whitney Joins the JAMs' from 1987 had sampled Whitney Houston's 'I Wanna Dance with Somebody' and may have sounded pretty rum in a student disco, but no better or worse than Sonic Youth's wry noisenik cover (as Ciccone Youth) of Madonna's 'Into the Groove' – nothing to trouble Radio 1's playlist meetings. Drummond, though, was clearly as excited as a twelve-year-old by the endless possibilities of sampling, and they followed 'Whitney Joins the JAMs' with an album called *1987: What the Fuck Is Going On?* If you caught them on a good day, as the *NME* did in 1990 at their commercial peak, you could even get straight answers out of them. 'At the time I was getting really pissed off with the way the whole history of music, from Marvin Gaye and James Brown to the present day, was treated so reverentially. Hip hop seemed to tear right through that.' *1987* was an incredibly crude album. 'Neither of us were DJs. We didn't know what the hell we were doing so it came out in a very British punk, white, ungroovy kind of way.'

But they learnt quickly, helped out by the addition of rapper Ricardo

Da Force and Nick Coler, an engineer who'd had a stint in the Rubettes and knew how to make records that sounded as ebullient as the inside of Bill Drummond's mind. After spending all the money they had made from 'Doctorin' the Tardis' on an aborted film called *The White Room*, Jimmy Cauty wrote and recorded a song called 'What Time Is Love' on an outmoded Oberheim OB-8 in his Stockwell basement – the song had what Nick Coler described as an 'all-encompassing drug thing', an unforgettable three-note hook, and it became one of the biggest club tracks of 1989. Suddenly, Cauty and Drummond became in-demand DJs at raves all over the country. *The Face* wrote that 'with their pervy mail-order black-hooded packamacks, their propaganda and their perfect assimilation of rave culture, they are corrupting a generation of pop kids brought up on Lucozade and Technotronic'. It all happened very quickly. With 'What Time Is Love' they invented stadium house; with a fresh mix from Coler it became a number-five hit at the end of 1990, and now the KLF became stars: '3 A.M. Eternal' (no. 1), 'Last Train to Trancentral' (no. 2) and 'Justified and Ancient' (no. 2, with a guest vocal from Tammy Wynette) followed in 1991, a year in which they sold more singles than anyone else in Europe.

The KLF took people by the hand, they said mischief is fine, mischief is good. They dumped a dead sheep at the 1992 British Phonographic Industry awards aftershow party; everyone present pretended to be ignorant of its meaning. And with this they bailed out, deleting their catalogue with immediate effect just as the record industry started to go into irreversible decline. In this way they were truly heroic. They could have claimed magic powers.* Very few had been this smart, subversive and successful.

The KLF could have turned Britain into a nation of art terrorists. Theirs was the kind of misbehaviour that had made up the spine of twentieth-century art, but the KLF weren't underground pranksters,

* 'The urge to make recorded music is redundant and a creative dead end,' said Drummond when they split. The KLF's records haven't been in print since. Their intention to leave a KLF-shaped hole in pop history, a moment that could never be revisited, has since been undone by their presence on Spotify and YouTube, but you've got to admire their effort.

they were on *Top of the Pops*! They were *number one*! They had five-year-old fans who would send them crayon drawings of the band. The Pet Shop Boys' Chris Lowe said they were the only other worthwhile group in the UK. And when they called it a day at their peak in early '92, they must have been shocked that nobody picked up the baton. Beyond a rough musical template, their influence would be almost non-existent. The only group who cited them regularly were Scooter, a European techno-pop act who eventually sold even more records than the KLF. Scooter may have borrowed the air horns and the trappings of stadium house, but they left the dead sheep and the situationist pranks at home.

Drummond and Cauty called it a day at precisely the right moment. The Shamen's 'Ebeneezer Goode', a 1992 number one, would encroach on their territory and show how bad their brand of pop could sound without the necessary brio: like a cross between Teutonic trance and Blur at their most gauche. With the KLF's split, though, the unitary forward motion of rave began to falter. It was inevitable. It could not self-sustain as so much of its charm had been about an interruption of the status quo. How could you extend and regularise the project? No one was in agreement on where it should head next. This uncertainty coincided with a surprise Tory victory in the May '92 election; the mood of the country began to darken, and the fragmentation of house, techno, rave and hardcore soon followed.

By late 1992 house appeared to have run its course entirely, as it mutated into the joyless, functional grooves of progressive house.* Without the KLF as a guiding light, rave's consciousness began to wander aimlessly over the pop-cultural landscape. Candy Flip's baggy makeover of 'Strawberry Fields Forever' (no. 3 '90) had had a canon-trashing point to make; now rave was chewing up odd bits of history – public-information films, Dickensian characters, children's TV

---

* Progressive house lost the peaks and troughs – the rave gaps – and the wailing diva vocals that were central to the music's excitement. Gat Decor's 'Passion' (no. 28 '92) was one of the few hits in the genre, and it did much better (no. 6 '96) with a remix when house had its first rebirth – as handbag house – in the mid-nineties.

themes – and spitting them back as Smart E's' 'Sesame's Treat', Shaft's 'Roobarb & Custard', the Prodigy's 'Charly', the Shamen's 'Ebeneezer Goode'. Climactically, Slipstreem's 'We Are Raving' – to the tune of Rod Stewart's 'Sailing' – breached the Top 20 over Christmas '92. If Scooby Doo had turned up on *Top of the Pops* with a dummy round his neck, nobody would have been surprised.*

* The raver's habit of sucking on a dummy led to them being banned at some schools in Britain – it's quite likely that kids hadn't associated dummies with drugs before this. Vicks inhalers, which ravers stuck up their noses to intensify their rush, led to the company publicly stating they had nothing to do with illegal drugs.

ALL EYEZ ON ME: HIP HOP

PUBLIC ENEMY

Tracy Marrow parked his sleek black Porsche turbo next to his customised vintage Ford Model T and walked through the front door of his home, halfway up a hill above the Sunset Strip. Sitting on the enormous black leather sofa in his LA moderne sitting room, he contemplated a pair of large California abstracts on the wall, which sat either side of a poster for his movie, *New Jack City.* He got up and walked onto the sun deck, taking in a view of the city below him: Hollywood, Downtown, Westwood, beyond that LAX and the suburbs; Hawthorne, home of the Beach Boys; Downey, where Richard and Karen Carpenter grew up; closer to home there was Crenshaw, where Tracy had spent his scuffling days.

One clue as to how Tracy could have come to live in a home with an 'Armed Response' sign in the garden could have been gleaned from his clothes – jogging sweat pants, Air Jordans and a baseball cap. Then

there was Tracy's pet pit bull, Felony, pacing around the house's internal courtyard. If that didn't give you any clues, there were the CDs on
his Noguchi coffee table. One was called *Power*, and the cover featured
Tracy, his shapely, near-naked girlfriend Darlene and DJ Evil E holding
Uzis and pump shotguns; another was called *Rhyme Pays*. Tracy had
changed his name to Ice-T some years back and made his millions from
hip hop – more specifically, from a subgenre he had invented called
gangsta rap.

Grandmaster Flash and Melle Mel's 'The Message' ('It's like a jungle
sometimes, it makes me wonder how I keep from going under') was ten
years old when Ice-T released *OG: Original Gangster* in 1992. As Ice
was taking in the panoramic view from his LA home, Melle Mel was
sparring in a run-down boxing gym, reduced to humiliating defeats in
amateur bouts, out of the rap game, broke and desperate. 'The Message'
counted for nothing in 1992 – Ice-T romanticised street crime rather
than bemoaning it. He dealt in instant gratification, not analysing the
ghetto's social infrastructure (unless you counted 'Cop Killer' as a viable
solution). This was Ice-T's LA. Hollywood, another world of desires,
was just next door.

The millions to be made in hip hop, the gold discs, the LA vistas and
Porsches, none of these would have seemed remotely plausible a few
years earlier. At the beginning of 1984 rap music had the air of a modern pop trend in its terminal phase; after all, it had been five years since
'Rapper's Delight', and five years was a genre's standard life cycle. Recent
hits had included the Rock Steady Crew's electrifying Jackson 5 update
'Hey You (The Rock Steady Crew)' (UK no. 6 '83) and Grandmaster
and Melle Mel's anti-coke 'White Lines' (UK no. 7 '84), but there were
also the telltale novelty hits – Roland Rat Superstar's 'Rat Rapping' (no.
14 '83) and Mel Brooks's 'To Be or Not to Be (The Hitler Rap)' (no.
12 '84). When Mel Brooks has caught up with you, you know your
number's up.

Rap's pop-culture rise had climaxed in the summer of '84 with a brace
of movies, *Beat Street* and *Breakdance*, that cemented rap and break-
dancing as pre-teen novelties to be tolerated by adults until, like skate-
boarding, they impinged on their fiercely guarded public spaces. The

two biggest spin-off hits – Break Machine's 'Street Dance' (UK no. 3 in the spring of '84) and Ollie and Jerry's 'There's No Stopping Us' (US no. 9, UK no. 5 in the summer) – dispensed with rapping altogether; they were sweet enough electro-fied pop-soul records, but could just as easily have been straightforward love songs if they hadn't included the odd reference to 'city kids spinnin' on our backs'.

And yet 1984 was also the year the Def Jam label put out its first records,* LL Cool J's 'I Need a Beat' and the Beastie Boys' 'Rock Hard': rap was about to be reborn as hip hop. Def Jam gave rap muscle, stealing it with intent from their kid brother's bedroom, and they weren't subtle about it. Graceful electro backing tracks were binned in favour of pared-down beatbox crunch and samples as heavy as AC/DC's 'Back in Black' or John Bonham's drums on 'Kashmir'. Suddenly rap wasn't a played-out novelty at all. Within three years, Def Jam made it the biggest commercial force in pop, a position that it has yet to relinquish.

Def Jam also signed Run-DMC, from Hollis in Queens, who had started out as a three-piece version of the Furious Five but stripped the disco samples and ditched the colourful suits as they gained confidence. In 1984 they released 'It's Like That' backed with 'Sucker MCs', a single that consisted of nothing more than hard rap and harder beatbox – no disco, no bassline, no melody at all – and to match the new minimal sound the boys eschewed visual excess by dressing in black. Without troubling the US charts, Run-DMC's debut sold a quarter of a million copies. Def Jam's founders, Russell Simmons and Rick Rubin, managed to convince Columbia of the label's, and hip hop's, crossover potential. Simmons was black and Rubin was a Jewish NYU student; Columbia bit and gave them a million-dollar deal.

What Simmons used to convince Columbia, and what he introduced to hip hop, was entrepreneurial flash. Two years on, Run-DMC were covering 'Walk This Way', which had been a US Top 10 hit for heavy-rockers Aerosmith in 1976. If this wasn't crossover enough, they got

---

* Technically, the very first Def Jam single was released in '82 by Rick Rubin's band Hose – it came in a brown paper bag, had no label and was a dead slow, super-fuzzed hardcore track called 'Mobo'.

members of Aerosmith to guest on it and play the original's guitar-boogie riff. And, in case you *still* didn't get Simmons and Rubin's cross-cultural message, the video had the two acts in neighbouring studios, initially winding each other up before literally kicking down the wall between them and doing a crazy little show together with their arms around each other. This racial blending was something that had occurred, unforced, in modern pop forever, from Bill Haley through to Jimi Hendrix, Sly Stone, Thom Bell, Todd Rundgren and Blondie. What 'Walk This Way' did was to make it seem like a breakthrough, physically so. The song was a crossbreed all right, like a pit bull; with rare MTV approval for a rap record, 'Walk This Way' went Top 10 in Britain and America.

With one foot in the door, Def Jam then kicked it open with the Beastie Boys. By 1986 pop was aware enough of its history to anticipate hip hop's Elvis moment, white kids borrowing black kids' culture and scoring Pat Boone-like sales figures. The Beastie Boys' breakthrough hit 'Fight for Your Right (to Party)' (UK no. 11 '87) was barely hip hop at all, though, a frat-metal burn-up that may or may not have been a parody; the only real difference between 'Fight for Your Right' and *This Is Spinal Tap* was the dress sense – baseball caps and VW medallions – and the rhythmic vocal delivery. Self-fulfilling prophecies, Run-DMC's *Raising Hell* sold three million in '86, while the Beastie Boys' *Licensed to Ill* sold four million in '87 and became the first number-one hip-hop album in America.

So, Russell Simmons and Rick Rubin's commercial senses were acute. Fortunately they were fans, too. Def Jam also had LL Cool J (whose 'I Need Love' – US no. 14, UK no. 8 '87 – was the first hip-hop ballad hit, a far cuter innovation than 'Walk This Way') and, soon enough, Public Enemy. Nevertheless, Def Jam cashed cheques that were many times larger than any that had been paid out to Grandmaster Flash or Afrika Bambaataa. In part, this was down to the less prominent role of the DJ. In 1979 the DJ had been the fount of hip hop, but beatboxes and record producers meant the art of scratching and mixing was suddenly 'old school' – a term of endearment that also rendered it passé. The MC was now the central character, and rapping veered away from 'throw your hands in the air' gaiety. As Reaganomics bit hard, and Louis Farrakhan's Nation of

Islam wowed black youth the way Malcolm X once had, hip hop began to investigate the textures and persuasive powers of dialogue and flow.

Between 1983 and 1989 the top one per cent of American households saw their wealth increase by sixty-six per cent; in 1983 the average white American family was eleven times wealthier than its black counterpart, and twenty-two times wealthier in 1989. Racial equality was only real on MTV. Crack cocaine was riddling and wrecking black communities by the mid-eighties: high-profile casualties included the Furious Five's Cowboy and Rock Steady Crew's Buck 4 and Kuriaki; everywhere was murder, crime, and the dream of Bambaataa's Zulu Nation was in tatters.

Public Enemy weren't as MTV-friendly as Run-DMC or the Beastie Boys. They looked like Stokely Carmichael and his buddies twenty years on, had their own 'minister of information' – Professor Griff – and were not about to be gently ribbed on a Mel Brooks record. Carlton 'Chuck D' Ridenhour, Hank 'Shocklee' Boxley and Richard 'Professor Griff' Griffin grew up in relatively affluent and culturally rich Long Island. Chuck's mum formed and ran the Roosevelt Community Theater. When they were barely in their teens, along with Chuck's childhood pal Eddie Murphy, they attended a course called the Afro American Experience led by Black Panthers, black Muslims and students at Adelphi and Hofstra universities; Chuck and Hank were impressed enough to attend these largely white universities a few years later.

Def Jam's publicist Bill Adler pitched Chuck D to the music press as 'the new Bob Dylan', the first time in a generation that that old chestnut had been reheated. Like Dylan and Dexys Midnight Runners before, and the Manic Street Preachers a few years later, Public Enemy's interviews were at least as challenging and entertaining as their music. The *NME* made their middling debut *Yo! Bum Rush the Show* album of the year in 1987; it sounded exciting but, alongside Eric B. and Rakim's inner revolution on 'I Know You Got Soul' or producer Marley Marl's high-tech crunch,* it was a little clunky, dated even. They knew it, and

---

* Marley Marl was the first producer to sample James Brown loops, cut them up and mix them with programmed drum-machine beats. The results were harder than anything else around: MC Shan's 'The Bridge', Roxanne Shante's 'Bite This', Biz Markie's 'Make the Music with Your Mouth Biz'. He later produced LL Cool

raised their game for the next single: a sample from the JBs' 'The Grunt' provided their production team, the Bomb Squad, with a relentless boiling-kettle sax squeal which made 'Rebel without a Pause' as relentless and thrilling and scary as any record since 'Anarchy in the UK'. 'Man, you gotta slow down!' yelled Flavor Flav on the record's brief moments of release. 'Man, you're *losing* them!' But Chuck D would not slow down. By the time of their second album, 1988's *It Takes a Nation of Millions to Hold Us Back*, they had the music to match the message: their sound was astonishingly dense and confident, overloaded with party noise, sirens, pressure-drop bass notes, atonal brass bursts, and the raps were direct – 'Get down for the prophets of rage.'

With astonishing cheek, Public Enemy had taken the entire history of hip hop up to this point and turned it into a forty-minute manifesto; there was no dead space between the tracks. They may not have been seen sharing a stage with Steven Tyler but they were smart enough to appreciate Def Jam's elevated profile and Run-DMC's groundbreaking step of turning a crew into a pop group ('There's three of us but we ain't the Beatles,' as they'd said – four years after John Lennon had been shot). They had a DJ, Terminator X, and the Bomb Squad: too black, too strong, almost too powerful to deal with. It was such an overloaded sound, such a lot to take in, and it was giving so much simultaneously (message, noise, inspiration) that it was hard to listen to in one sitting.

By October '88 they graced the cover of the *NME* with a tagline of 'Public Enemy. The greatest rock 'n' roll band in the world?!' Chuck D told Danny Kelly, 'Rock 'n' roll is there to be studied and learned about. Rap has closer links to rock 'n' roll than to any other music. What is rock 'n' roll? It's the projection of attitude, not the deliverance of sound. Attitude! Rap's acts have that attitude, that character, that rock bands have used to get across to the public. They just haven't learned to project it.'

Run-DMC had boiled the sound down, but almost no one had

J's 'Mama Said Knock You Out' and TLC's debut album. Marley Marl's Queens-based Juice Crew (Shan, Shante, Biz Markie and Big Daddy Kane) also got into the first hip-hop feud, with KRS-One and DJ Scott La Rock of the South Bronx's Boogie Down Productions.

delivered a message since, well, 'The Message', apart from the Furious Five (on 'White Lines' and 'Message II'). With Public Enemy, out went the bragging. They wanted to cause a stink. 'Never be average or mediocre,' said Chuck D. 'I remember our first tour, the Richmond show, we played the Public Enemy tone throughout the whole show. Kids were tugging at their moms, people were running for the exit, someone called the fire department – they thought it was an air raid! They hated it, but they remembered us.' Their music was incendiary. Rappers, and Public Enemy especially, had the potential to affect racial affairs in the US like no one since the Black Panthers: 'In five years, we intend to have cultivated five thousand black leaders.'

Elsewhere, hip hop had become big enough that it had to defend itself against more than just trad-rock critics. R&B songwriter Mtume (Stephanie Mills's 'Never Knew Love Like This Before', Roberta Flack's 'The Closer I Get to You', his own 'Juicy Fruit') posited on a New York radio station that hip hop's sampling culture was 'nothing but Memorex music'. Tuning in were Stetsasonic, who wrote 'Talkin' All That Jazz' as hip hop's own 'It Will Stand', as history lesson and defence of the music's past, present and future: 'Rap brings back old R&B . . . we wanna make this perfectly clear, we're talented and strong and have no fear.'

Mtume's charge that hip hop added nothing new to the black musical vocabulary seemed nuts in 1988. Eric B. and Rakim's 'Follow the Leader' introduced chilled, understated beats and Rakim's beyond laid-back, almost whispered style; Mitcham-born storyteller Slick Rick released his first album, sounding like a hip-hop Paddy Roberts with his long narratives and shaggy-dog tales; Salt-n-Pepa and their DJ Spinderella (who *Smash Hits*' Tom Hibbert coyly described as 'rather handsome') became the first female hip-hop act to become pop stars with 'Push It' (UK no. 2, US no. 19), the first in a string of fifteen UK Top 40 hits, almost all of which had a forceful sexuality and a sense of humour to match Mae West; Ultramagnetic MCs, with producer Ced-Gee, were the first act to chop samples up, tweak them and use them out of context on 'Critical Beatdown'. Everywhere you looked, there was innovation.

More significantly, though, NWA's *Straight outta Compton* appeared in 1988. There was no Nation of Islam revolution in their words – this was a world of dope deals, ho's and violence, tagged 'reality rap' by main lyricist Ice Cube. It was brutal. If dissenters had seen violence implicit in pop from Elvis to the Rolling Stones, even the Beastie Boys, it had never been as blatant as west-coast rap made it. At this point something was lost, a spell was broken.

Ultramagnetic MCs' Tim Dog released a single called 'Fuck Compton' in 1991, which made its point without anyone having to hear it. Crews in the Bronx projects had long been suspicious of LA rappers bragging and beefing about how tough their lives were. Who were they kidding? thought Tim. Look at their houses – they live in bungalows! They've probably got net curtains and gnomes in their gardens.

Public Enemy's intensity was struggling to sustain itself by '91. 'Once you getting into tit-for-tat rhetoric,' said Chuck D in his autobiography, 'then you fall into a sea full of contradiction.' The righteous anger they'd brought out in the open was mixed up with a fondness for seventies blaxploitation movies and taken down another route by west-coast acts like NWA and Ice-T – gangsta rap was the outcome.*

* * *

> I remember Afrika [Bambaataa] called me that night, like, two in the morning. 'Yo these kids, De La Soul, you gotta meet 'em! I swear we're just alike!' I went there, met them, and it was just fuckin' love at first sight. It was disgusting! Hip hop, it praises individualism. I think that's the main achievement of the Native Tongues – it just showed people could come together.
>   Q-Tip

* The source of gangsta rap can be found in a 1985 DIY twelve-inch by Philadelphia's Schoolly D. The label was written with a Berol pen, the rap was slurred, addled, drowned in reverb, and the title was 'PSK', short for 'Park Side Killers'. Schoolly D was bred on Run-DMC's primitive first records, and the backing was all beatbox and scratching, but his lyrics were unsettlingly immoral tales of shootings, beatings and God knows what else. Urban realism, if you like. He was representing his gang, the Park Side Killers, and that was the be-all and end-all of 'PSK'. No call to arms, or Islam, or love peace and unity. No wit, either. Nothing but cold fear.

While Ice-T was taking hip hop in a direction that Spike Lee found analogous to a minstrel show, there was a simultaneous movement on the east coast based around the Native Tongues collective. Groups like the Jungle Brothers, Beatnuts and A Tribe Called Quest used Steely Dan samples, preached togetherness and wore baggy, bright-coloured clothes. This certainly chimed with a British audience ready to bliss out after three years of relentlessly increasing dancefloor beats. De La Soul, from Amityville, Long Island, turned out to be the Monkees of hip hop.

They were a hit with students, stoners, teenagers coming home from illegal raves and kids looking for an easy way into hip hop; the *Sesame Street* cartoon imagery of their artwork chimed with late-sixties British psychedelia and in short order they had four UK hit singles: 'Me, Myself and I', 'Say No Go' (which sampled Hall and Oates), 'Eye Know' (ditto with Steely Dan) and 'The Magic Number', each scoring a progressively higher chart position. Helmed by producer Prince Paul, they were hip, nimble-witted, used previously untapped and unimagined source material (one track on their 1989 debut *Three Feet High and Rising* album sampled a French-language course over the intro of Wilson Pickett's 'Hey Jude'), and looked like the Banana Splits.

A Tribe Called Quest's 1990 album *People's Instinctive Travels and the Paths of Rhythm* showed the airiness of *Three Feet High and Rising* was no one-off, and this nascent movement was tagged 'daisy age'. They sampled Lou Reed's 'Walk on the Wild Side' on their sweet, summer-soundtracking 'Can I Kick It' (UK no. 15 '91) and wooed a girl from their high school on 'Bonita Applebum':* 'Satisfaction? I have the right tactics. And if you need them I've got crazy prophylactics.' MC Q-Tip got to act alongside Janet Jackson in *Poetic Justice* in '93, romance blossomed, and they recorded 'Got Till It's Gone' (UK no. 6 '97). Later on he'd work with the Beastie Boys, Cypress Hill, Mobb Deep, J Dilla, Raekwon, Common – 'I'm just a people's person,' he said modestly, 'and that's it.' A Tribe Called Quest were proof

---

* PM Dawn would shortly nod to 'Bonita Applebum' as part of an extended chat-up line to *Married with Children* actress Christina Applegate, in 'Set Adrift on Memory Bliss'.

you could be all-round nice guys in hip hop and still get respected.

Parallel to the daisy-age movement, conscious rap had its moment in the sun headed by Atlanta's Arrested Development, who were briefly enormous. They aimed to create a rural, Afrocentric alternative to gangsta rap's urban malaise and pulled it off with three hits that made the British and American Top 20 in 1992: 'Tennessee' saluted their roots, 'Mr Wendal' turned the spotlight on the homeless, and 'People Everyday' (US no. 8, UK no. 2) sampled Sly Stone, the original gangsta (whatever Ice-T might have been claiming). They could have been a Georgian counterpart to New York's Native Tongues, but the trouble was they took themselves frightfully seriously; they even had an official 'spiritual elder' in the group, a bearded, shoeless man called Baba Oje. 'We try to make sure our minds are clear so that we can address the issues as opposed to let them totally engulf us,' their front man Speech told *Vogue* magazine. He wanted to 'take this rap thing beyond entertainment, to turn it into a soul-searching experience'. Arrested Development were full of such well-meaning platitudes, and everyone was heartily tired of them by the time of their second album, the unwelcomingly titled *Zingalamaduni*, in '94. Still, they laid the groundwork for the hugely successful Fugees – who would score two UK number ones in '96 with 'Ready or Not' and 'Killing Me Softly' – as well as the conscious soul of Erykah Badu and Jill Scott, none of whom felt the need to have a spiritual elder on bongos.

A lone exception to the west coast's gangsta fixation was Oakland outfit Digital Underground, who practised what they called 'ancestor worship',* heavily influenced by P-Funk's grooves and humour. Their loping 'Doowutchyalike' and 'Humpty Dance' (US no. 11 '89) singles came from an album called *Sex Packets*, a concept album about a pharmaceutical substance called GSRA (Genetic Suppression Relief Antidotes): 'Now I can still be getting busy with any girl I like. No more will I ever have to jack it, 'cos instead I can just take a packet.'

---

* In 1998, eight years after their first record, Digital Underground released *Who Got the Gravy?*, which featured several west-coast rappers, as well as old hands like Biz Markie and KRS-One at a time when the east coast–west coast rivalry was at its height – their intention was to both ignore and ridicule it.

They were quite preposterous. Founder member Shock G, aka Humpty Hump, dressed like Groucho Marx and had a Hair Bear Bunch voice to suit their cartoon imagery. The young Tupac Shakur was part of the group, dressing up as an African king in the video for 'Same Song', and quitting after he contributed a verse to their unusually serious cultural awareness-raiser 'Wussup wit the Luv'. Soon afterwards he lost his sense of humour, which was really too bad.

De La Soul loved Steely Dan and Hall and Oates, and this left them open to sniping – like the soft-rockers of the sixties – from the more credibility-hungry rappers. Arsenio Hall, in an unlikely dig, introduced them on his show as 'the hippies of hip-hop'. Jeff Chang's lauded *Can't Stop Won't Stop: A History of the Hip-Hop Generation* mentions them twice in passing. You can understand their hankering for acceptance.

Their second album featured a broken flower pot on the cover to bluntly signify the end of the daisy age. *De La Soul Is Dead* was unsurprisingly low on laughs but did include one joyous cut, maybe their best single of all, 'A Roller Skating Jam Named "Saturdays"' (UK no. 22 '91). At the same time as they distanced themselves from their daisy-age creation, they had a pop at gangsta rap on 'Afro Connections at a Hi 5 (in the Eyes of the Hoodlum)'. Who did they end up pleasing? Well, *The Source* – by now America's most important hip-hop magazine – gave it a 5-mic review, but white kids snubbed the dourness of tracks like 'Millie Pulled a Pistol on Santa', and the west-coast hard core just shrugged. By 1993 Trugoy the Dove declared 'that Native shit is dead', and the Native Tongues collective disintegrated.*

Being slagged off by Arsenio Hall wasn't the only reason for De La Soul and the Native Tongues' demise. Neither conscious-rap nor daisy-age videos featured girls in bikinis and, consequently, they received less exposure

---

* There was a lot of international potential in this pacific, anti-macho, non-partisan hip hop. It blended with jazz (Gang Starr, Stetsasonic) and crossed borders, to Canada with bright colours 'n' beads duo the Dream Warriors ('Wash Your Face in My Sink', UK no. 16 '90; 'My Definition of a Boombastic Jazz Style', no. 13 '90), and to Britain with Definition of Sound ('Wear Your Love Like Heaven', UK no. 17 '91), who effectively blended house, dub and hip hop. They were fun, and it's probably not a coincidence that they shared a producer – John Coxon – with Betty Boo.

and fewer requests from excitable teenage boys. Snoop Doggy Dogg and Dr Dre, with their ladies draped across them on MTV heavy rotation, defined mid-nineties hip hop. Their G-funk, with its Michael McDonald samples and pat gang-culture raps, was the sound of '93 and '94.

The lead single from Dr Dre's 1992 album *The Chronic*, 'Nuthin' but a "G" Thang' (US no. 2 '92), became an anthem for frustrated American youth. It wasn't exactly a cry of liberation in the style of the Prodigy's contemporaneous 'Everybody in the Place' (UK no. 2 '92) or SL2's 'On a Ragga Tip' (UK no. 2 '92) – it was simply a numbed, Generation X shoulder shrug: don't know, don't care, get trashed, pass out. 'Music is an art,' said Dre's sidekick Snoop Dogg by way of explanation. 'It ain't made to preach – that's literature.' Still, the reformed drug dealer was happy to blur the distinctions between the images of the lyrics and his real life if it helped to pay the rent. By the time of his own *Doggystyle* album a year later he was on bail awaiting trial in a gang-related murder trial. As he began a UK tour in February '94, the *Daily Star* headline ran 'Kick this evil bastard out'. In the meantime, the spat between Suge Knight's Death Row label on the west coast and Sean 'Puffy' Combs's Bad Boy Records in New York was getting out of hand. Knight's buddy Tupac Shakur forged a rivalry with Combs protégé Biggie Smalls; in a recording studio in 1994 he was shot five times but survived, and publicly accused Smalls and Combs. The profile and sales figures of everyone involved proceeded to spiral upwards. After a while, MCs and fans alike became battle-hardened, inured to the cruelty, the violence, the casual acceptance of death. Ice-T had his private security, the 'Armed Response' sign on his lawn – from the sound of his records, you'd think that was his idea of fun.

While Melle Mel was flat on the canvas, and Public Enemy were floundering in internal political issues, the team of young hip-hop rebels who would step in and save the day – creatively, morally, politically – were plotting their rise in unlikely and unfashionable Staten Island, the Essex of New York boroughs. Robert Diggs, aka the RZA, aka Bobby Digital, assembled eight like-minded souls in a basement studio in the winter of 1992. He was bored with the way hip hop had smoothed out, lost energy, become a cliché. In the charts it was represented by MC

Hammer's child-friendly run of hits* or Ice-T and Dr Dre's gang lore; it was resting on the laurels of its easy alternative culture. Diggs played his cohorts a bunch of loops which contained the dirt, grime and history of the original vinyl; the chords were almost all minor. Then he explained how he had spent the summer walking the streets of Staten Island, reimagining it as Shaolin; for Diggs, this fantasy grew from a lifetime's obsession with kung fu movies. He wanted to christen the nine rappers the Wu-Tang Clan, after a gang of sword-wielding renegade monks. Wu-Tang Clan, he explained, would use their vocal dexterity as the monks had used their swords. 'Let me drive the bus,' he told them.

At a stroke, the Wu-Tang Clan reconnected hip hop with its Bronx roots, its crate-digging days, and at the same time became its most formidable crew. With a thunderstorm behind them, over dark chords and a Gladys Knight vocal sample, 'Can It All Be So Simple' found them on a street corner, reminiscing, while also knowing they had the future mapped out: '1993 exoticness!' Within a year of releasing their first album, *Enter the Wu-Tang (36 Chambers)*, six members of the Clan had released solo albums; they all went Top 10 in the US. Each of the Clan was distinctive enough to operate alone: Ol' Dirty Bastard could growl and slur, like a demented *South Park* character – 'Stop annoying me! Play my music loud!'; Method Man smoked industrial-strength weed, turned in the most laid-back, spontaneous-sounding solo album with *Tical*, and also scored Wu-Tang's biggest single, 'All I Need' (UK no. 10 '95), a duet with Mary J. Blige. Even better solo albums came from Chef Raekwon

---

* MC Hammer's second album, 1990's beautifully titled *Please Hammer, Don't Hurt 'Em*, was the first hip-hop album to sell ten million copies. Pop culture remembers his baggy 'Hammer pants' more than his hits, with the possible exception of 'U Can't Touch This' (US no. 8, UK no. 5 '90). Originally he had been in a Christian rap group called Holy Ghost Boys and later starred in his own movie (also called *Please Hammer, Don't Hurt 'Em*) about a rapper, Reverend Pressure, who returns to his home town and defeats a criminal mastermind who has been using children to traffic drugs. His music was weedy and his rhymes rather comical (take 'Addams Groove': 'They do what they wanna do, say what they wanna say, live how they wanna live, play how they wanna play, dance how they wanna dance, kick and they slap a friend'), but Hammer was an effective pre-teen hip-hop entry point.

– *Only Built 4 Cuban Linx* was put together like a Mafia movie, with Raekwon as the star and the RZA as director – and GZA with *Liquid Swords*, loaded with odd echoes and clipped, minimal samples.

They loved maths almost as much as they loved self-mythology – *Enter the Wu-Tang (36 Chambers)* cost $36,000 to make. Their solidarity was crucial; together Wu-Tang had nobility, sorrow and heroism. On many levels they failed – they pretty much disintegrated straight after the release of their second album, the transatlantic number one *Wu-Tang Forever* in '97 – but their fallibility is a large part of their appeal.

They had as many aliases as the KLF; in some ways they're the American counterpart, even producing their own *Wu-Tang Manual*. In it, the RZA talks about his superhero alter ego Bobby Digital and how, when the group imploded in '97, he decided to 'become Bobby Digital for real. I had the car and I had the suit. I had this suit built for me that's literally invulnerable to AK fire. The car was bomb-proof, up to government security standards. I even had a good butler almost ready to go. I was really on a mission, I really felt compelled. I spent hundreds of thousands of dollars.'

The Wu-Tang Clan reintroduced a cartoon element and playfulness to hip hop that had been missing since the turn of the nineties. The inevitable conclusion to the west coast–east coast wars came when Tupac Shakur was shot dead in 1996, and Biggie Smalls a few months later. Though gangsta rap's resentment and intolerance still dominated the nineties and the early part of the next decade – through essentially filler acts like Ja Rule, the Game and 50 Cent – the biggest names to emerge in the wake of the Wu-Tang's realignment were Jay-Z and Kanye West, both of whom have acknowledged them as a major inspiration. Ol' Dirty Bastard was in the studio recording an album for Jay-Z's Roc-A-Fella label when he collapsed and died in 2004.

By the end of the nineties hip hop had become part of the furniture, albeit with a continued, daft adherence to arrogance and machismo. Take tattooed lover boy Ja Rule, who released an album that sampled the ultra-mainstream Coldplay and the Script; it came out while he was serving a two-year jail sentence for gun possession. Like pro wrestling, it was superficially violent and deadly serious, while refusing to accept that part of its appeal lies in its ludicrousness.* Eminem and Mariah Carey took to musical sparring (he claims they had a fling, she denies it), which at least proved a lot more fun than the east coast–west coast battles.

Prince Paul, the daisy-age innovator and De La Soul producer, has said that he finds hip hop in the new century 'uninspiring . . . everything is so recycled and repetitive and nothing makes you want to freak out and do something new. I have to go back and listen to stuff like the Beatles or someone to get amped on. I can't find anyone new I really want to hear, I have to listen to the Beach Boys or something.' Still, hip hop continues to make money, whether it's inspiring or not: Busta Rhymes can demand $70,000 for writing a single guest verse on someone else's record; the Neptunes can still get $100,000 for a mix. Kanye West at least recognises the tensions and ironies of being a socially aware, business-conscious hip-hop superstar in the twenty-first century: in 2011 he showed solidarity by turning up at an Occupy demo in New York, albeit wearing a plaid Givenchy shirt.

---

* Tupac Shakur had 'THUG LIFE' tattooed across his belly. Rather unconvincingly, he claimed it was an acronym for 'the hurt u give little infants fucks everything'.

BASSLINE CHANGED MY LIFE: DANCE MUSIC

The whole thing was offensive and obscene in many ways. You would have been surprised at some of the people there. There had been university people from America, Oxford and Cambridge, and ordinary decent people. They just wanted to do what they wanted to do and they did it. I just cannot understand it.

Mr E. T. Oates, public health inspector, Phun City festival, 1971

Hardcore has once again astounded the house nation with its diversity. No longer is a rave track a selection of obscure noises from an ancient analog keyboard, the modern era rave tune is now more likely to contain a multiplicity of elements such as soul, techno and rap from diverse musical cultures. All the tracks on this album have some of the elements; ruff cut up beats, severe bass lines, uplifting vocals, piano breaks, dark sounds (sometimes samples from horror films). The end result is music that has a power and intensity that elevates the mind.

Sleevenotes to *The Dark Side: Hardcore Drum & Bass*, 1993

The most significant event for modern pop in 1991 hadn't been Bryan Adams's record-breaking run at number one, or the Prodigy sampling a cartoon cat from a public-information film. It had taken place in an American court, where Gilbert O'Sullivan was up against rapper Biz Markie, who had sampled his 'Alone Again (Naturally)' without getting clearance first. Judge Duffy concluded 'the defendants . . . would have this court believe that stealing is rampant in the music business and, for that reason, their conduct here should be excused'. His written opinion began with the line 'Thou shalt not steal'. Gilbert was awarded one hundred per cent of the royalties on Biz's track, 'Alone Again'.

The sound of hip hop was radically altered by the case. The Bomb Squad's late-eighties productions for Public Enemy had been entirely reliant on dozens of samples – it was simply no longer possible to make records like this, unless you cleared each and every sample, and that could prove prohibitively expensive.* One way of avoiding a legal quagmire was to sample acts who were amenable to hip hop, like Parliament/Funkadelic, who let you sample their catalogue rather than sending a writ. Another way forward was 'interpolation', meaning you replayed the sample rather than use the original recording – this was Dr Dre's solution, and explains the prevalence of G-funk's stripped-back, sample-light sound.

At first, this was largely seen as an American problem. Britain was a far less litigious place in the nineties. Besides, it had a growing remix

---

* Some holders of the mechanical rights to recordings demanded up to a hundred per cent of any royalties generated by the new song. The Verve came unstuck by releasing 'Bitter Sweet Symphony' (UK no. 2 '97) without first clearing its string-sample hook, taken from David Whitaker's arrangement for the Andrew Oldham Orchestra's 'The Last Time'. Mick Jagger and Keith Richards copped all the publishing.

culture largely based on co-operation and kinship. While the likes of New York garage-house team Masters at Work could charge $30,000 for a remix, acts in Britain would ask for a fraction of that, or do swap mixes for nothing. Expression through reinterpretation; producers sometimes delivered their finest works for other people's intellectual property (Andrew Weatherall's 'Loaded' for Primal Scream, UK no. 16 '90; Todd Terry's 'Missing' for Everything but the Girl, UK no. 3 '94; K-Klass's 'Two Can Play That Game' for Bobby Brown, UK no. 3 '95). Remix culture highlighted the innocence that informed the dance scene of the decade.

On top of this, the legal system in Britain – and the music industry – simply struggled to keep up; dance music in the early nineties was as constantly shapeshifting as beat music had been in the mid-sixties. To make your skin tingle, to match the rush of whatever you were dancing to two weeks earlier, producers and DJs had to be reactive. For a good five or six years they did their best, and genres within genres sprouted on a monthly basis. Their functionalism matched Cameo Parkway's keenness to keep the kids of Philadelphia on their feet in the early sixties, practising new moves on a weekly basis.

Of the new cottage-industry dance labels, London's most successful was Shut Up and Dance, which was based on the border of Stoke Newington and Dalston, an area once known for its tailors and furniture makers but by 1991 renowned for its itchy beats and pirate stations. Red Bird had self-destructed through George Goldner's racetrack habit; Philles had the plugs pulled by Phil Spector in a fit of pique when 'River Deep – Mountain High' flopped, but the rise and fall of Shut Up and Dance was entirely down to dance music's rapid motion and the American legal system.

Childhood friends Philip 'PJ' Johnson and Carl 'Smiley' Hyman were Hackney-born DJs who had started off in a mid-eighties sound system called Heatwave. They loved hip hop, the whole lifestyle, entering dance battles and making their own tapes. Inspired by sound system-turned-record producers Soul II Soul, they had made their first records as Shut Up and Dance in 1989 with '5678' and '£10 to Get In' – these had raw, pitched-up hip-hop beats, fast enough to body-pop to, fed through a reggae sound-system sensibility that, like Sheffield's bleep crowd, gave them gut-churning, half-speed, subsonic basslines. This was entirely new and pretty soon became the most influential sound in East London. Originally it was called breakbeat house* but then, like the extreme end of American punk before it, the new sound was tagged 'hardcore'.

PJ and Smiley's productions were DIY, incredibly basic (a loop, a sample, a bassline and a vocal – that'll do), paid no heed to copyright and had blatant samples from deeply uncool mainstream acts like Annie Lennox and Terence Trent D'Arby floating over tracks like 'Derek Went Mad';† unsurprisingly, it served SUAD's purpose to stay underground and sell their product from the back of a car. They were also irresistible, playful, dark and hilarious: Rum and Black's 'Fuck the Legal Stations' – with its intentionally erased mid-section – was a pirate-radio pinnacle; Nicolette's coy 'Waking Up' was the sexiest record of 1990; the Ragga Twins' 'Spliffhead' as clean and urban as freshly laid cement. All came out on the Shut Up and Dance label, which had basic black-and-white artwork that would embarrass a nine-year-old, and sold tens of thousands of copies in the myriad dance shops booming across London at the turn of the nineties. Few were stocked by chart-return shops; none troubled the Top 40. With 1992's 'Raving I'm Raving', though, they finally scored a massive hit, a UK number two, and the label imploded. The song took liberties with Marc Cohn's weighty 1991 MOR hit 'Walking in Memphis' (US no. 13, UK no. 22). 'Put on my blue suede shoes,' crooned Cohn, about to embark on a dues-paying trip to the home of the blues – 'W. C. Handy, won't you look down over me?'

---

* The differences between hardcore, jungle and drum and bass would be fluid and negotiable. In 1993 and '94, after Rage closed, all three co-existed separately, with jungle largely an East London phenomenon (girls dressed in short skirts, boys in heavy jewellery), drum and bass at LTJ Bukem's Speed night in the West End, and hardcore still ruling most mainstream clubs.
† This was recorded after Derrick May sulked in *Muzik* magazine that 'Guys in England had started making their own music . . . it seemed like we weren't invited to the party any more.' Shut Up and Dance ribbed the innovator with a hardcore track that sampled May's protégé Carl Cox ('And I'll return a stronger man') over the classic breakbeat from the Winstons' 'Amen, Brother'.

Shut Up and Dance employed a soulful Hackney boy called Peter Bouncer to sing their cheeky rewrite. Cohn's blue suede shoes became 'raving shoes'; the plea to W. C. Handy became 'Everybody was happy, ecstasy shining down on me.' Finally, the chorus laughed in the face of Cohn's guilt-ridden cultural tourist taking a holiday in the city of his heroes: 'I'm raving till the sweat just pours down off me . . . but do I really feel the way I feel?'

Cohn's version was all about fear of inauthenticity, and how he felt that real life, real music, and maybe even real fun, could only happen in Memphis – everything else felt phoney to him. Shut Up and Dance, true to their name, turned 'Walking in Memphis' into a hedonistic anthem. Their footwear was functional, their plane ticket – as it should be – was a passport to pleasure. And where Cohn went into NYC therapy-speak with the tautological pay-off 'do I really feel the way I feel?', SUAD spun it as an E reference and used the line as jump-off point – straight away there was a key change, dark chords, then a disembodied androgynous wail and finally the rave riff, a familiar plastic keyboard sound that dominated the charts in the early nineties.

Marc Cohn was not amused when he heard 'Raving I'm Raving'. Admitting, hands in the air, that they'd raided his song, SUAD offered to give the proceeds to charity, but Cohn wouldn't budge. The record was instantly deleted.* Shut Up and Dance, mercurial heroes responsible for the birth of jungle, drum and bass and, in turn, UK garage and dubstep, were hit by a bunch of other claims by the copyright-protecting

---

* Shut Up and Dance hurriedly recorded a new 'Raving I'm Raving' without the samples and with altered lyrics. It bears almost no resemblance to the hit, but it remains the only commercially available version. 'Raving I'm Raving' had been number one on the Thursday midweek chart, which is when stocks ran out. The label had pressed two hundred thousand copies. On the Sunday, KWS's cover of KC and the Sunshine Band's 'Please Don't Go' enjoyed its fifth and final week at number one; it's unlikely that its sales that week would have topped two hundred thousand. Conspiracy theorists who suspect another 'God Save the Queen'-type situation would ask how the BPI and BBC could allow a record to be number one that you couldn't go out and buy? 'It was scary to be honest,' said Smiley. 'We were novices in the business, we weren't businessmen, never wanted to be. And we were in the middle of the biggest hype, as if it was a Hollywood blockbuster, like *Spider-Man*, not just a rave tune! It outsold everything that week.'

MCPS for more uncleared samples. The phone never stopped ringing. The news was never good. The brown envelopes piled up. The label simply folded.

Smiley later recalled how in 1992 the major labels 'didn't even know what a sample was, they were like "Who? What?" Even trying to speak with the publishers, no one knew what anything was. Now you've got whole departments set up just to sit down and deal with it – whether it's a sample or you've re-played it or whatever. Back then they didn't know what the hell you were on about. So we were just sort of ten years too early.'

* * *

Once the term 'acid house' had entered the public domain, it became inevitable that it would prick up the ears of the enduring hippie subculture. This had lived on since the early seventies in West London squats, and in semi-rural Britain where people could smoke dope in peace. By the late eighties a loose agglomeration of hippies, anarcho-punks, new-age travellers who favoured crusty rock groups like the Levellers, and urban squatters started to band together at places like Club Dog* in Finsbury Park. After punk and before acid house, 'hippie' had been a term of abuse, yet now it was being used in band names (A Homeboy, A Hippie and A Funki Dredd scored two minor hits in 1990), and groups like the Shamen – psychedelic revivalists with a political slant in the late eighties – could safely grow their hair and come out into the open. What all these factions agreed on was that free festivals, and the drugs you took to get you through the inevitable mud and the rain, were good things: hippie travellers had the network; ravers had the music and the drugs. The two came together in a crew called Spiral Tribe. In 1991, with shaved heads, combat gear and a decent sound system, Spiral Tribe permanently travelled around the country, pitching up at camp sites, in gypsy caravan sites, at a disused dog-food factory in Greenwich, or in the

* The name was apt as many of the clubbers took their own dogs, on home-made leads; 'dog on a string' soon became shorthand for the whole movement.

car park of the Camelford festival, where Hawkwind were headlining.

In the summer of 1992 they arrived at Castlemorton Common near Malvern, where, along with other travelling sound systems and twenty-five thousand hippies and ravers, they staged a five-day impromptu free festival that wound up not only local residents and the police but also old-school hippies who just wanted to get a bit of peace and quiet. Spiral Tribe were unrepentant, the first sound system onto the site, the last to leave: 'There are some people who moan and they do moan very loudly,' Spiral Tribe founder Mark Harrison told *i-D* magazine, 'but as far as we know free festivals are about playing music non-stop. Techno is folk music. We play the people's music. Anyone who comes down and asks us to turn it down, I'm sorry, we're not going to. Turn it up if anything. If you've got a voice, shout. Our attitude is "Make some fucking noise".'

With the introduction of the Criminal Justice Act in December 1993, designed to ensure another Castlemorton couldn't happen, house took over in the nightclubs (which prospered, leading to superclubs), while rave, refusing to become so restricted, reluctantly moved into a number of exclusive legal venues (such as the Blue Note in Hoxton Square, where jungle morphed into drum and bass and became rhythmically tricksier) and smaller-scale illegal parties. Dance now had a separate rave culture (served by magazines like *Eternity* and *Ravescene*, bought and sold at raves) and a club culture (covered by *Mixmag*, *Muzik* and *Jockey Slut*, which you could buy in W. H. Smith), with the two areas attracting quite different crowds, and little overlap. The government's plan to eradicate 'repetitive beats' didn't work but did split the scene and – at least temporarily – weaken the camaraderie.

Another splinter of dance music, one which suited people who didn't really like clubbing, was electronica. Sheffield's bleep label Warp became the major purveyor of undanceable but studiously cool music. In '92 they signed Cornishman Richard James, aka Aphex Twin. While the ambient Orb were grinning loons, smirking through their *Top of the Pops* appearances, Aphex Twin was much stranger and genuinely intriguing. He had a smile that was familiar to loved-up clubbers but would also have suited a police photofit for a Dartmoor escapee. He played on his otherness – the Kernow upbringing (even though he lived in Islington), his home-made keyboards (even though no one ever saw them), the endless pseudonyms (Caustic Window, Polygon Window, AFX, Blue Calx, Martin Tressider). He told *Melody Maker* that he had roughly a thousand unreleased recordings: 'Every time I go back to Cornwall my friends play me tapes of tunes I gave them, stuff I haven't heard in years. In their cars I'll find cassettes of material that I haven't even got copies of.' No one doubted any of this, possibly because they wanted a genuine auteur, a techno Mike Oldfield to emerge from the anonymous pack. The highlights of his alleged pre-fame career made up *Selected Ambient Works 85–92*. He claimed to sleep for only two or three hours a night – sleep, he said, was 'a bit of a con'. On stage, he hid behind a curtain, prodding a laptop, the dullest thing you'd ever seen, but he was wise enough to know his fans would love him all the more for it. ('Was that even him behind the curtain?' 'I thought he was taller.') He was pop's own Chris Morris, a prankster and something of a genius.

Aphex Twin never had a major hit ('On', no. 32 '93; 'Come to Daddy', no. 36 '97; 'Windowlicker', no. 16 '99) but he was an MTV regular, he sold a ton of albums and his debut single was extremely influential: Aphex recorded 1992's post-acid 'Didgeridoo' at a breakneck speed, 160 bpm, crazily fast, deliberately creating something you could never dance to. But clubs like Rage caught up with it immediately, and within weeks records sped up to match his gag. Using Shut Up and Dance's template – subsonic dub basslines, reggae samples, ever faster beats – the music was now being created to match the speedier drugs people were taking. The battle cry nationwide was 'Hardcore! You know the score!'; the cry at Rage was 'Jungle!' At Rage, Fabio and Grooverider would play 33 rpm singles at 45, mix Belgian rave tracks like Joey Beltram's 'Mentasm' in with East London hardcore dubplates, Kevin Saunderson's breakbeat-based Tronik House singles and Underground Resistance's hard-edged, second-wave Detroit techno; often they played two records at the same time to create a mind-melting hybrid. The crowd were hands in the air, gloves off, tops off, no stilettos. Once time-stretching – where a sample could be sped up or slowed down without altering the pitch – was used on records like Rufige Kru's 'Terminator', it created a distorted, grainy, snaking and disturbing sound. Darkcore was the sound of British rave in late '93 and a lot of people, girls especially, were turned off. The bpm had reached 180, the time-stretching made everything sound like a horror movie. Rage closed down as so many of its regulars were repelled by this punishing experimentation.

People yearned once again to hear something as simple and joyous as Bizarre Inc's 'Playing with Knives' (no. 4 '91), and happy hardcore's moment had arrived. It reignited the greatest record of the breakbeat era, Baby D's 'Let Me Be Your Fantasy', and sent it all the way to number one at the end of 1994. Originally recorded in 1992, it was a love song to rave itself, floating on chords that were John Barry via Aphex Twin: 'I'll take you up to the highest high,' it went, and it was somehow incredibly sad. Hot on its heels, peaking at number two in early '95 was N-Trance's similarly celebratory but much more visceral 'Set You Free'. Not shy, it opens with the sound of falling rain, massed airhorns and a silky three-note piano motif before the breakbeat kicks in and pushes Oldham-born teenager Kelly Llorenna to even higher heights of passion than Baby D: 'When I hold you baaaay-beeeeeehh, feel your heartbeat close to meeee, wanna stay in your arms forever,' she roars as if this was the only three minutes she'd ever get to be with her man. She has to get it all out, has to let the world know. And then she really lets rip. 'OOOOOOONLY LOVE can SET you FRRREEEEEE!!!' What a beautiful, daft, emotional, exciting record. Kelly Llorenna sounded twenty storeys high.*

Apart from happy hardcore, the mid-nineties dance scene was the era of handbag house (initially a derogatory term – as in music for girls, therefore it can't have much substance). This revived house piano and diva vocals: the look was fluffy bra tops and short skirts, the crowd

---

* It's such a guileless performance you'd hope Llorenna either became a superstar or never made another record – sadly she fell into a hole, cut a series of dispiriting pop-dance covers ('Do Ya Think I'm Sexy', 'Dress You Up') and was last heard of hanging out with exiled New Order bassist Peter Hook. The career of 'Set You Free' has been more thrilling – it has resurfaced as a hit a few times since, and echoes of its enormity and ebullience could still be heard in 2011 'stadium dubstep' hits like Nero's 'Guilt' and Chase and Status's 'Blind Faith'.

was girls and gays. It was just like disco – the good times were back. The natural home of handbag house was the superclub* – urban, legal and huge – which rose in direct response to the Criminal Justice Act. Superclubs didn't just offer a good night out but clothing, merchandise, CDs. Ministry of Sound in Southwark had been opened by city boy James Palumbo in September '91. It had the first twenty-four-hour licence in London, largely because it was in the middle of nowhere, a dead zone between London Bridge and Elephant and Castle. Palumbo's record collection was entirely classical, but he had the funds to bring in every legendary DJ he wanted to the new venue: DJ Pierre, Frankie Knuckles, Larry Levan. By 1998 Ministry of Sound had a turnover of £20 million.

Before Ministry changed the rules, mixtapes from Camden market were the way to take your DJ kicks home. Quite often the sound quality was grisly but, like copies of *Ravescene*, they had a DIY charm and bypassed any industry watchdog. Ministry of Sound compilations looked smart, like portfolios, and sold tens of thousands – you wondered why no one had had the idea before. Other superclubs soon followed: Leeds had Back to Basics; Sheffield had Gatecrasher; there was Renaissance in Mansfield and Cream in Liverpool. Unlike most of their house-era predecessors, the superclubs all negotiated with local police to ensure they could build a reputation, like a regular business, and not get shut down overnight. On Cream's behalf, former Big in Japan singer Jayne Casey argued to the council that clubbers were filling hotel beds and bringing economic regeneration to a city still recovering from severe industrial decline. Like the Haçienda in 1989, Cream became a magnet for students: in a 1996 survey, seventy per cent of students at Liverpool's John Moores University said they chose to go there because Cream was around the corner.

When 'Let Me Be Your Fantasy' reached number one in November '94 (keeping the Stone Roses' comeback single 'Love Spreads' at number two), it provided much-needed oxygen for dance music in the chart. Along with house, Eurodance had waned, with 2 Unlimited, Capella,

* The term was first coined in *Mixmag*, in March '95.

Haddaway, Snap and Culture Beat all scoring their last Top 10 hits in the spring of '94. The only new Euro name on the scene was Danish girl Whigfield, whose 'Saturday Night' (UK no. 1 '94) straddled a line between playground chant and Eurovision. As rave had waned, 1994's Top 40 had been dominated by soft reggae (Ace of Bass, China Black), soul ballads (All-4-One, Boyz II Men) and rock ballads (Aerosmith, Wet Wet Wet – whose 'Love Is All Around' clocked up fifteen weeks at number one over the summer), but by April '95 the Top 10 was ringing once again with the house-piano hooks of Grace's 'Not Over Yet', Strike's 'U Sure Do' and the Nightcrawlers' 'Push the Feeling On'. The Bucketheads' 'The Bomb! (These Sounds Fall into My Mind)' recalled the giddy joy of Deee-Lite, and there was even room for an acid revival: Josh Wink's 'Higher State of Consciousness' (UK no. 8 '95) was based around a familiar Roland 303 sound which started at a low pitch then moved up, higher, higher still, to a place no one had gone to back in '88. It was regressive but it was enjoyably exhausting, and felt like it was carrying on unfinished business.

It seemed that every time the dance scene started to calcify (as with the great misnomer of 'progressive house', circa '91), or drift too close to aimless noodling (the Orb and their ambient brethren), or decide it was time for a Grand Statement (Goldie's extraordinary but overly tasteful seventy-two-minute drum-and-bass symphony *Mother*, from 1998), then the breakbeat would return, the basslines would once more jump to the fore and the essence of Shut Up and Dance's floor-filling noise would reinvigorate dance music. By the mid-nineties, away from happy hardcore's strongholds in Scotland and the north of England, the breakbeat was also being reborn, twisting into something new in the Home Counties.

Hip-hop fans Tom Rowlands and Ed Simons had met at Manchester University and were regulars at the Haçienda. Originally they called themselves the Dust Brothers in a spectacularly direct tribute to the Beastie Boys' production team; when their American namesakes objected, they became the Chemical Brothers. Rowlands was a dead ringer for *The Magic Roundabout*'s Dougal, and was as musically unschooled as the canine puppet. This didn't matter at all, as they opened up a new, cavernous, rock-friendly side to breakbeat. Making their name as DJs at London's Sunday Social, a basement club beneath the Lord Albany pub on Great Portland Street, the Chemical Brothers mixed the Beatles' 'Tomorrow Never Knows' in with hip hop and Philly soul (Love Unlimited's ecstatic 'Under the Influence of Love' was their classic ender), creating a psychedelic stew. Soon they added DIY record-ings of their own, primitively recorded on a Hitachi midi system. One track, 'Chemical Beats', used one of the ultimate legal no-nos: it sam-pled the Beatles, taking the off-rhythm of 'Tomorrow Never Knows' and underlining it with hip-hop beats. Crunching, elastic and hypnotic all at once, released in January '94 it was thrilling enough to become the blueprint for a whole new genre – 'Chemical Beats' was the birth of big beat.

In the meantime, without jungle's media-unfriendly handle, drum and bass finally began to gain press attention. Soon you had 'intelligent drum and bass', which shoehorned in jazz moves and, as jazz moves are wont to do, sucked all the fun out of it. Roni Size and Reprazent won the Mercury Music Prize in 1997, the equivalent of the hardest kid in school receiving a handshake and a book voucher from the head-master. The whole scene wilted with grief, died overnight, killed by well-meaning liberals. In its place, back in the clubs of Clapton, Stoke Newington, Dalston and Hackney, the beats had been simplified, pared and sweetened; vocals were back and UK garage was born. The whole process was repeated (too much champagne, not enough street feel and the emergence of Craig David being the steps too far in 2000), and grime appeared. And so on, and so forth. SUAD's ragga/hip-hop amal-gam was still the source – the music adapted, moved on.

* * *

In 1993 Matthew Bannister was chosen as the new Radio 1 control-ler, replacing Johnny Beerling, who, rather shockingly, had worked at the station since its birth in 1967. The old guard who refused to play the Prodigy's 'Everybody in the Place' were swept away and in came *NME* writer and indie geek Steve Lamacq and R&B aficionado

Trevor Nelson from Kiss, while Pete Tong (who had broken records like Orbital's 'Chime' on his Friday early-evening show) and hip-hop DJ Tim Westwood would be poached from London's Capital Radio. Slowly, for the first time in years, the industry started to listen to what pop fans actually wanted.

In March '97 the Chemical Brothers had a UK number one with 'Block Rockin' Beats'. It sampled a Schoolly D line and the bassline from 23 Skidoo's 'Coup'; the Sunday Social underground was now entirely overground, and big beat was all over the charts – Fatboy Slim ('Praise You') and the Prodigy ('Firestarter', 'Breathe') scored further number-one hits. And, significantly, as these acts crossed over into traditional rock and pop fields, the major labels finally got a handle on how to sell and promote dance music. Crucially, they sold albums. They made money for the industry.

By 1997 Shut Up and Dance, having kept their heads down for a few years, were once again selling twelve-inch singles from the back of a car, on their new Red Light label. A single called 'The Burial' sampled Tracy Chapman. But this time they wouldn't get shut down – now there were entire legal teams to deal with samples. The industry had caught up and, if they hadn't tamed dance music, they'd still turned it into a manageable, album-format genre. PJ and Smiley weren't bitter. They were aware of their place in the scheme of things. 'It's how you do things,' said PJ. 'You just have to be clever with things, and obviously be careful . . . but, y'know, you must express yourself.'

THIS IS HOW YOU DISAPPEAR: BRISTOL, SHOEGAZING AND A NEW PSYCHEDELIA

While jungle and rave were the definitive East London/Essex pop sounds, there was a railway line that ran from Paddington station in West London – Notting Hill, Portobello, Ladbroke Grove – to the ancient port of Bristol, and this axis threw up something quite different, a mixture of narcotically influenced escape and a quest for a modern, multiracial British sound. Compared to the intensity of Hackney and Dalston, the pace of the west was sloth-like.

In the late sixties and early seventies Notting Hill's cheap housing had not only provided sanctuary for Jamaican immigrants but a haven for freaks, hippies, stoners and political agitators. There were Legalise Cannabis benefits at the All Saints Hall; Richard Branson had set up his Virgin Records label on Portobello Road in '73; Chris Blackwell had founded Island Records on Basing Street just off Ladbroke Grove in the mid-sixties to promote the sounds of Jamaica, recording Bob Marley there but also signing white British counterculture acts like Traffic and Ladbroke Grove spiritual seekers Quintessence. Other Grove residents the Pink Fairies, Hawkwind and the Deviants – psychotropic adventurers all – were free-festival regulars, venturing west from Paddington to Shepton Mallet, Trentishoe in Devon and the first Glastonbury Fayre in '71. Most successful, musically and commercially, were space rockers Hawkwind,* who played a free festival on Wormwood Scrubs the weekend before the 1970 Notting Hill Carnival. By the late seventies the Clash were making a blunter attempt at uniting the white squat scene and the embattled black community with their debut 'White Riot' (UK no. 38 '77) and a cover of Junior Murvin and Lee Perry's Jamaican hit 'Police and Thieves' – noble and excitable, but less than essential once you'd heard the gossamer aggression of the original.

Bristol, once a slave port, was one of England's first multicultural cities. In the early nineties Massive Attack made the transcontinental blend of dub reggae, sampled ephemera, politics, dope philosophy, rap and post-punk seem incredibly simple. They took everything at the slowest pace imaginable and, by stealth and with deceptive ease, they became one of the most influential British groups of the nineties.

Prior to the arrival of hip hop, progress in the search for a black British pop had been rather random: the Equals – from Tufnell Park via Guyana – and Notting Hill's Foundations had been mixed-race goodtime acts in the late sixties.† Hot Chocolate had created a kind of British soul in the

* Resolutely unfashionable, Hawkwind's blend of drone rock, synths, drug intake and onstage nudity has remained an unspoken influence. Their single 'Silver Machine' (UK no. 3 '72) continues to give them an unlikely oldies-radio presence.
† The London club scene of the sixties threw up a bunch of British-based American singers like Geno Washington and Herbie Goins, who became major

seventies, mixing the dark Fender Rhodes of Isaac Hayes with high, eerie strings and Denmark Street funk to create some extraordinarily gloomy and effective hits: 'Rumours', 'Cheri Babe' and the space-age 'Put Your Love in Me' (UK no. 10 '77) being leavened by party pieces like 'Every 1's a Winner' and 'You Sexy Thing'.* In the eighties came Jazzie B's Soul II Soul sound system in North London, mixing smooth soul, jazz funk and a little lovers' rock; South and East London were more ragga-leaning. Quietly, Bristol produced an unforced synthesis of all these elements.

Massive Attack's roots were in the contemporaneous Wild Bunch, an almost mythical Bristol group who included Nellee Hooper – producer of Soul II Soul's hits, Sinead O'Connor's 'Nothing Compares 2 U' and Björk's *Debut* – and Tricky. They put out a single of Burt Bacharach's 'The Look of Love' in 1986, basically no more than a 98 bpm drum-machine track with a soulful-femme vocal, and were instantly seers: two years later Bomb the Bass's 'I Say a Little Prayer' (UK no. 10) nabbed the idea; a year later Soul II Soul had their breakthrough with the sublime 'Keep On Movin'' and 'Back to Life'. By 1990 you couldn't move for 98 bpm remakes of oldies, and Beats International took their SOS Band remake 'Dub Be Good to Me' all the way to number one. 'Three days' work in seven years' was how Massive Attack described the Wild Bunch; they weren't proud of their church-of-the-tortoise work ethic, but they must have known that if they went any faster the spell might be broken.

---

live attractions without troubling the chart. The Foundations used Brit Building writers Tony Macaulay and John MacLeod's 'Baby, Now That I've Found You' to break through, scoring a number one in the autumn of '67. It presaged a return to a simpler pop, exemplified by the Equals' relentless riff-based 'Baby Come Back', a number one the following summer. Led by Eddie Grant, a solo star of the early eighties, the Equals were an odd group, capable of both whimsical bubblegum ('Michael and the Slipper Tree', no. 24 '69) and flat-out funk rock ('Black Skin Blue Eyed Boys', no. 9 '71).

* Most extraordinary of their thirty UK hits between 1970 and 1983 was 'Emma' (no. 3 '73). From its swampy rhythm track to the pitch-black string arrange-ment, it's clearly informed by US soul, specifically Allen Toussaint and Isaac Hayes, yet Errol Brown sings of a ghetto straight out of a Peter Ackroyd novel. The broken hopes, the girl's lonely death, the shriek that echoes Levi Stubbs's cry on 'Bernadette', this is Dickensian soul and – unlike other UK seventies soul acts Cymande and the Real Thing – its sound is quite, quite British.

Their unhurried, non-purist attitude allowed everything to stew nicely. John McCready of *The Face* met Massive Attack in early '91, just before their first album, *Blue Lines*: 'One minute they'll be worrying about the environment or slagging off Thatcher, the next they'll be talking about Studio One, Subbuteo, old Paper Lace records and the Beatles. 3D has no explanations ready when I make it clear that all this amuses and impresses me. "In a way I was just fired by the originality of the old school rappers. The accent comes easy. I have to check myself sometimes before it gets too Bristolian and we end up sounding like the Wurzels. It's really just a bit of everything and a bit of nothing. I hope nobody's looking for guidance in there because there isn't any. They're just thoughts about good things, about nature and stuff."'

Nature and stuff was configured with help from guests, like reggae singer Horace Andy (backed by a didgeridoo on 'Hymn of the Big Wheel') and Irish cellist Caroline Lavelle, who sang the folk melody of 'Home of the Whale'; they may have moved slowly, slowly, ever more slowly, but they were bloody hard to pin down. Shara Nelson was the singer on two Massive Attack songs that defined 1991: she was the tough, sexy mama on 'Safe from Harm' (UK no. 25 '91) – 'but if you hurt what's mine, I'll sure as hell retaliate' – and then there was 'Unfinished Sympathy' (UK no. 13 '91). The strings (by Wil Malone, late of pop-psych group Orange Bicycle) recalled the warm, wooded sound of Robert Kirby's seventies arrangements. The cowbell pushed it along but the strings dragged it back, and you were caught in the slipstream. Shara Nelson was permanently on the edge of dissolving into tears; you can picture her setting the table for two, sitting down, realising that the front door will not open at six, never again, and sobbing. The sound was a dark Utopia, newness and freedom coursed through it. But it was hardly music for candlelit dinners.

* * *

Were there precedents for this stark, slo-mo sound that opted out of modern pop's natural speed? There were some, and not often in the most obvious places.

Back in 1983 New York graffiti artist Rammellzee had created 'Beat Bop', a freaky, ten-minute, dub-handed hip-hop track that reached a wide audience in the UK on Street Sounds' *Electro 2* compilation. The early seventies had seen British folk rock disappear into guitar-pedal ambience that mixed bliss and stoner paranoia (Roy Harper, John Martyn), while others opted out of time, making music that could have either been recorded centuries ago or last week ('Horn' by Nick Drake, almost anything on the *Wicker Man* soundtrack). The sense of wandering into the ether had also been strong on records by the Cocteau Twins, a Scottish three-piece who had first appeared as a Siouxsie and the Banshees soundalike in 1981, but became more and more focused on their numerous effects pedals and echo boxes, as well as singer Elizabeth Fraser's tremulous voice, something like a narcotic yodel, as the eighties progressed. Fraser's lyrics and titles – 'Pearly Dewdrops' Drops' (UK no. 29 '84), 'Persephone', 'Sugar Hiccup', 'How to Bring a Blush to the Snow' – freed themselves from language; they melded, waxed, waned, with a backdrop of filmic chords and Roland Chorus Echo. The result was like a post-Impressionist Martin Hannett producing Kate Bush.

New York's no-wave scene hadn't been filmic or pretty in the slightest but was still about opting out, a screeching reaction to the commercial outreach of new wave after punk burnt up. The phrase was concocted by one of its main players, Lydia Lunch, and its participants were captured by producer Brian Eno on a compilation called *No New York* in '79. *Creem* described it as 'a solid statement of no-ness which shakes the listener's complacency and (this is important) gives you something new to think about. Still . . . what do they do for an encore?' One answer was Sonic Youth, who used peculiar tunings to make their cheap pawn-shop guitars sound like bells. 'When you're playing in standard tuning all the time,' explained guitarist Thurston Moore, 'things sound pretty standard.' When their career took off in the late eighties, they could afford to get custom-made guitars, amps and effects boxes, including one which they called the Sound Destruction Device. Another suggestion on how to move on from no wave came from a group called Swans, who wanted to finish music completely. Their records were a slow, mean, physically overwhelming grind, with titles like 'Time Is Money (Bastard)'. Of course, they didn't succeed. They'd end up getting back together for a thirtieth anniversary of the end of music.

British ambitions were a little more restrained, as ever, but rather more fully realised. There was an urgent desire, as with no wave, to escape from the horrors of the present. As the eighties became progressively more conservative and unwelcoming to outsiders, some looked to escape in time – the *C86* crowd's Byrds jangle and '76 manifestos; the Smiths, immersed in their late-fifties Manchester reverie – while others looked to escape in time *and* space. The Jesus and Mary Chain were Creation Records boss Alan McGee's first commercial discovery. They wore their hair like the Cure's Robert Smith, looked surly, and incited riots at their early shows, but their songs revealed a keen love of sixties pop. You can imagine Beach Boys harmonies on 'Never Understand' (UK no. 47 '85), and Mary Weiss would have been the perfect singer for 'Just Like Honey' (no. 45 '85). The reason they didn't sound like sixties revivalists is because they covered their songs with deafening layers of squalling feedback – not just from one guitar, but a whole orchestra of them. It was unsettling and uplifting. It wasn't quite like anything else pop had experienced. Afraid of being tagged as one-trick ponies, they ditched the feedback on their second album, *Darklands*. Now you could hear the tunes and the lyrics, clear as a bell, on 'Some Candy Talking' (no. 13 '86) and 'April Skies' (no. 8 '87), and they weren't bad – they even got played on Radio 1. But the point of the group was entirely lost.

It was hard to imagine Rugby group Spacemen 3 getting it together to go to the post office, let alone getting played on the Radio 1 breakfast show. If the Jesus and Mary Chain used sheer noise to lift you physically out of the eighties, then Pete 'Sonic Boom' Kember and Jason 'Spaceman' Pierce's group plumped for the chemical as well as the spiritual escape route on songs like 'Walking with Jesus'. Recording an album in '87, the smoke from their roll-ups and spliffs got so thick that, prior to each session, the engineer decided to disconnect the studio's smoke alarm. They weren't shy in admitting their influences with titles like 'Ode to Street Hassle' and 'Come Down Easy'. 1989's 'How Does It Feel' was seven minutes of minimal electro blips, lightly phased, over a three-note guitar dronescape, with Kember asking repeatedly, 'So tell me, how does it feel?' For unbelievers, they seemed staggeringly obvious, but if you wanted a soundtrack to narcotic oblivion – one which had been created in a state of narcotic oblivion – they were the perfect prescription.

'We felt there would be other people who felt like us out there,' Kember said in 1989, 'people who lived their lives like us. The antithesis of the yuppie. Certainly we hoped the renaissance that was washing in on a wave of ecstasy would be fertile ground for us.'

Conceivably, there was no one else in Britain who consumed as many drugs as Pete Kember in the eighties, but there were musical kindred spirits. My Bloody Valentine took the *C86* indie template, first adding the Jesus and Mary Chain's fiercely overloaded guitar sound ('Sunny Sundae Smile', '86), then minor chords and a woozy elixir of vocal harmonies ('Strawberry Wine', '87), before ditching the original brief and just keeping the disorientating noise and the washed-out, loved-up vocals. The results – on 1988 album *Isn't Anything* – were incredibly sensual. 'You Made Me Realise' and 'Feed Me with Your Kiss', singles in '88, gave the impression of seeking escape through intense sex and intense volume, with Kevin Shields's treated guitars sounding alternately like harpsichords, elephants, Chinese orchestras and fire alarms. On stage, they married their romantic sense of linguistic abandon to ear-splitting feedback and guitars louder than anything even Motörhead could muster. My hearing, I'll vouch, never recovered. 'I think there are a lot of out-of-focus qualities in our songs,' drummer Colm Ó'Cíosóig told the *NME*. 'A lot of sounds swirl about in them and it's easy to imagine things in them that aren't actually there.' Did he think My Bloody Valentine had a problem with reality, then? 'Probably.'

Sexy and dangerous, it wasn't surprising that My Bloody Valentine's sweet narcosis quickly drew escapist followers and imitators. By 1989 a slew of acts from the Thames Valley – notably Ride, Chapterhouse and Slowdive – were following a similar route, lost in music. They were tagged 'shoegazing' by *Melody Maker* but, as a whole generation jumped headfirst into the emergent dance-music scenes, fashion swiftly brushed them aside. Ride were pretty enough to become *Smash Hits* material, scoring hits with 'Today Forever' (UK no. 14 '91) and 'Leave Them

All Behind' (UK no. 9 '93), though Slowdive became something of a punchline, which seemed very unfair. Their sales trailed off into the blue distance, as did their music: third album *Pygmalion* (1992) sat sonically between the KLF's *Chill Out* and Portishead's *Dummy*, an album of somnambulant escape. Slowdive didn't fit in 1992, though, and they would have to wait more than a decade to get their due from the critics. The Cocteau Twins' Elizabeth Fraser, there at the beginning of this effects-pedalled escapism, had in the meantime moved to Bristol and ended up guesting on Massive Attack's deeply atmospheric 'Teardrop', a UK number ten in 1998.

As G-funk bossed America in 1994, Massive Attack – like hip-hop snails leaving silver traces – saw their sound adopted by sometime colleagues and lesser chancers. The only surprise was that it had taken so long. Their sidekick Tricky Kid, as Tricky, took things further into the mist on the entirely undanceable dreamscape 'Aftermath', with its dub bassline, woodwind and occasional atonal, echoed quacks. Then he really opened up a bag of nails with a cover of Public Enemy's 'Black Steel in the Hour of Chaos'; it sounded like the early Who playing 'Public Image' underneath his girlfriend Martina Topley-Bird's soft, unbothered vocal. Tricky's album *Maxinquaye* (named after his mum) was hit-and-miss, but nothing later in his career came close. By the twenty-first century Tricky was fronting a punishing grind-rock band and getting lairy at festivals in Suffolk, chatting up girls by saying he had 'a semi hard-on'. He was a disappointment.

Then there were fellow Bristolians Portishead.

The main sound on Portishead's *Dummy*, like an electric fan slowly turning in an airless, fuggy room, was a Wurlitzer electric piano. This threw up echoes of a bygone era as surely as the strings on 'Unfinished Sympathy'; in this case it was 1971's *Get Carter*, the bleakest of British crime movies. The cimbalom recalled John Barry's silver-blue score for the equally dour 1965 spy film *The Ipcress File*. Vocals were recorded on a hand-held tape recorder, the most impressive use of deliberately lo-fi techniques since the Fall's *Dragnet*. Someone opened a window – and suddenly there was snow falling outside, courtesy of a festive sample on 'Strangers'. Just as quickly, the window shut. Throughout, Beth

Gibbons's voice was cracked and full of regret: 'Dreams have passed me by – salvation and desire keep getting me down.' Like Del Shannon, Portishead couldn't help but keep dragging up their memories. Over and over, *Dummy* relived lost love, gradually blurring the reality and the memory in a half-speed wagonload of samples. Like Johnnie Ray – whose 'I'll Never Fall in Love Again' they sampled on 'Biscuit' – this sad music could only end in tears.

My Bloody Valentine reached stasis after 1991's *Loveless* album. Kevin Shields and Colm Ó'Cíosóig were tuning into South London pirate-radio stations in early 1993 and getting their minds blown. 'When I first listened to jungle,' said Ó'Cíosóig, 'it seemed full of possibilities in a way I hadn't encountered since hip hop. Jungle was like hearing that very early, very stark hip hop like LL Cool J – really raw and unpretentious, yet as out there as you can get.' Their foray into jungle never happened, though lost recordings may be out there somewhere, amongst the hours and hours of abandoned My Bloody Valentine tapes that furnish their mystique.

With jungle and ambient hip hop, Britain had developed new forms from rap, mutations barely recognisable as foreign relatives to an American hip-hop audience. Mo' Wax added an aesthetic aloofness. This reflected owner James Lavelle's love of weed, skateboard and graffiti culture, as well as his taste for mashing together all manner of eclectic found sounds, be they from hip hop, jazz or a 1968 easy-listening album on A&M. Its output was knowingly obscure, sometimes haunting, but often one step away from the purely academic; a Major Force twelve-inch on Mo' Wax described itself as 'a jigsaw puzzle for the intellect . . . a mental mystery movie'.

Mostly Mo' Wax's output was instrumental, eliminating the MC from hip hop entirely. Lavelle's major discovery was Californian Josh Davis, who worked under the name DJ Shadow. Davis said he found lyrics to be 'confining, too specific', and his debut album would be made up entirely of samples from his vast record collection; the *Guardian* described *Endtroducing* as having 'chords of such limpid dignity they could have come from Handel'. It finished up in the top ten of almost every 1996 end-of-year poll.

By this point the Bristol sound was everywhere, and had become depressingly formulaic. 'A lot of people took that record [*Blue Lines*] and created something of their own,' reckoned Massive Attack's Grant 'Daddy G' Marshall. 'And some of them took it and created something of ours.' A 1994 DJ Shadow review in *Mixmag* had tagged his music as 'trip hop', which quickly became a term that attracted chancers and the less adventurous.* The delicacy and refinement of *Endtroducing* – with its rediscovery of late-sixties orchestral arranger David Axelrod – and Massive Attack's second album, *Protection*, much more of a bedroom soundtrack than *Blue Lines*, were widely, and poorly, imitated. Soon the sound – slo-mo beats, sampled string sections, maybe a harp – was in every bar and restaurant with pretensions, courtesy of Groove Armada, Lemon Jelly, Morcheeba† and Zero 7. By heavily sampling easy listening, trip hop became a modern muzak, built for the soundtrack of *Sex and the City* or *Top Gear*, and compilations with titles like *The Chillout Project: A Soundtrack to Modern City Life*; this was, effectively, easy listening fifty years on from Mantovani's 'Moulin Rouge' and Les Baxter's 'Unchained Melody'. The uneasy chords of *Dummy*, the unsettling squeaks of 'Aftermath' and the sound-system connection were absent. On top of this indignity, the thunderclouds of *Blue Lines* and *Dummy* had been blown away as the media's short attention span switched to a nationalistic, retrograde pop wave. By 1995 Bristol's brave new sound had been relegated to little more than a post-clubbing soundtrack.

* The term 'trip hop' was so disliked that the first compilation of the genre was called *This Ain't Trip Hop*.
† Morcheeba's name: 'mor' as in MOR, middle of the road, and 'cheeba', slang for cannabis.

AS A DEFENCE, I'M NEUTERED
AND SPAYED: GRUNGE

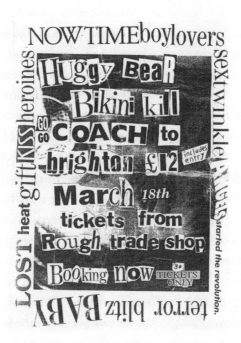

I have a request for our fans. If any of you in any way hate homosexuals, people of different color or women, please do this one favor for us – leave us the fuck alone! Don't come to our shows and don't buy our records.

Nirvana, sleevenote to *Incesticide*

Motörhead, then Metallica, had introduced the concept of nobility to the comic-book world of metal. Both bands had the speed and volume of punk, but nevertheless remained almost unmentioned in the closeted circles of the British music press and American college radio. They were not deemed alternative. When grunge became an international sensation, a teen wave with its own wardrobe, its own language, it felt to many as if it was the first music to breach classic rock with the ethics and attitude of 1977, as if it could be a new future for rock. In reality, it was an endgame.

Though punk's anger and entry-level energy and metal's theatrical thunder and lightning had rarely crossed paths before, they had first melded as far back as 1980, on early singles by a Stoke-on-Trent band called Discharge. Theirs was the first name to ever be written in Tippex on the back of a punk's studded leather jacket;* guitars dive-bombed, lungs were roared raw, the pace was ferocious, and their titles ('Realities of War', 'Society's Victim', 'Two Monstrous Nuclear Stockpiles') gave away the fact that their uniform was spiked hair and safety pins, their audience gobbers rather than headbangers. Even though it now seems inconceivable that Discharge hadn't been listening to Motörhead's *Overkill* as much as they had to *Never Mind the Bollocks*, the music papers missed the connection completely: 'They conform to the ancient idea that punk music must be a boring unvariable screech,' reckoned *Sounds*. In 1980 the concept of punk and metal blending was almost inconceivable.

Though they were innovators, Discharge seemed callow, belligerent, comically dim. Bassist Rainy's party trick was shitting in people's beds. 'I hate the CND, the Anti Nazi League, the NF, religion . . . all of them,' sneered singer Cal. 'All they're after is your money.' In 1981, the year they peaked as they topped the UK independent chart with 'Why', Discharge supported goth-punk baddies Killing Joke at the Lyceum in London and Cal threw up on stage; the unimpressed and genuinely intimidating Killing Joke made him mop it up before they went on. And yet their intensity, the way their music sounded so compressed and claustrophobic, was hairs-on-neck effective. Fans seemed to have missed their metal influences, too. In 1983, in an attempt to make some

---

* The sleeve of Discharge's first single, 'Realities of War' (no. 5, and forty-four weeks on the independent chart), features a jacket exactly like this. It sold fifty thousand copies, and a large proportion of the fans who bought the record seem to have aped the sleeve. In fact, Discharge were as aesthetically inspiring as they were musically: in the 2010 video for 'Telephone' by Lady Gaga, she sported a spiked leather jacket with the painted-on logo of late-eighties anarcho-punk/ thrash-metal band Doom, disciples of Discharge.

musical advances, Discharge 'came out' as a metal act at the Clarendon in Hammersmith. Cal wound himself up to sing in a Robert Plant falsetto and was duly bottled off.*

Just as Discharge and their 'punk's not dead' spike-haired allies had found their sound was a cul-de-sac, American hardcore groups were coming to terms with the notion that harder/louder/faster had severe limitations. At least as important as the music had been the setting up of local hardcore scenes, connecting the country like a series of underground tunnels. Each town had its own alternative club, which meant that bands from other locales could put a tour together. In the absence of a national paper like the *NME*, the newsletter of this underground network was a fanzine called *Maximum Rock & Roll*; local writers documented each scene, not especially well, but that wasn't really the point either (sample line: 'San Jose has long had a very active and dedicated, but a very elusive punk scene').

Coming out of the Minneapolis punk scene were the Replacements. Paul Westerberg's gravelly intensity came over like Springsteen with a runny nose. The band were ragged, but tough and melodic, and could have been genuine chart contenders if they hadn't felt the 'punk rock' urge to sabotage every single attempt by Warner Brothers to get their name out there: they remain the textbook example of a post-punk American band tying itself in existential knots – which for many people is their appeal. Also from Minneapolis, Hüsker Dü had released a couple of breakneck, tuneless 45s before their first album, which had the giveaway title *Land Speed Record*. Still, a group named after a Danish board game that translates as 'Do you remember?' were always likely to be rather more intriguing than contemporaries with names like Roach Motel.

Hüsker Dü were a blueprint for a new American rock: they were a

---

* By this point they had been the single biggest influence on Scandinavian punk, where acts copying the Discharge sound had become a genre of their own, tagged D-beat: there were Rattus, Bastards and Tampere SS in Finland, closely followed by Swedish bands such as Mob 47, Asocial and, ultimately, Anti Cimex, whose extraordinarily intense 'Raped Ass' took D-beat about as far as it could go – which didn't involve the shelves of Woolworths.

power trio, they were fuzzed-out, they used splintering feedback and – while not exactly pin-ups – they were sexually challenging. Though they came from a metropolis, Hüsker Dü's songs positioned themselves in Anytown, USA, on the endless plain of misfortune. Reviewing them in 1984, the *NME* reckoned they were forsaking 'the easy route of retreading Grandmaster Flash's glitzy inner city glam grime, instead getting to grips with a far more pervasive greyness'.

'We're going to try to do something bigger than anything like rock 'n' roll and the whole puny touring band idea,' their singer Bob Mould told Big Black's Steve Albini. 'I don't know what it's going to be, we have to work that out, but it's going to go beyond the whole idea of "punk rock" or whatever.' It turned out to be a double album, and a concept album at that, called *Zen Arcade* in 1984: 'the closest hardcore will ever get to an opera,' said *Rolling Stone*, 'a kind of thrash *Quadrophenia*.' Hüsker Dü rarely turned down the volume, but the velocity was gradually harnessed, they added harmonies and, crucially, they even wrote love songs. 'Pink Turns to Blue' was an astonishing death ballad; 'Celebrated Summer' compacted the Moody Blues' multi-part 'Question' and the Beach Boys' mythology. They signed to Warner Brothers. They appeared on *The Joan Rivers Show*. And, just as they were on the verge of a commercial breakthrough, they split in 1987.

Hüsker Dü's dynamic was heavily informed by the platonic relationship between drummer Grant Hart (who was out) and singer Bob Mould (who wasn't). In the mid-eighties it was still highly unusual to be a gay rock star – even Freddie Mercury was officially in the closet until he died. For Mould and Hart, in the most viscerally macho of all genres, their situation was unique.* Hardcore had its own ritual dance, with the moshpit and the severe, neo-military self-image; Mould wore the fatigues, Hart grew his hair long. If only they'd got on, they could have been Grammy contenders. Hart later mused, 'You hear some live bootlegs, and Bob and I are working so hard to outshine each other that it just lifts the whole thing off the ground with peace and wonderfulness.'

---

* It's almost too good to be true that bassist Greg Norton, with his outrageous Mercuryesque moustache, was the only straight member of the band.

Dinosaur Jr were also a trio, but let their adherence to hardcore drift even more dramatically. Singer and guitarist J Mascis looked like a long-haired kid who'd sit on the toilet for forty-five minutes at a time reading Marvel comics, because that's exactly what he was. He was also greatly fond of Neil Young. If Grant Hart's long hair was enough to cause a stir in US punk circles, then the extended squalling guitar solos on Dinosaur's 'You're Living All over Me' (1987) were a total revolution. As Discharge had done in Britain, they blurred hard rock with what had been broadly called 'alternative', and introduced a new generation to Neil Young's clangorous catalogue and simple over-driven guitar style. It harked back to seventies rock, a tradition punk and hardcore were meant to have obliterated, but suddenly, by 1987, it was OK. Hardcore's obsession with rules and regulations was slowly being relaxed. Boston band Pixies introduced another element to the new rock stew, edging from quiet, almost acoustic verse to punishing power chords on their choruses. It was as if they had taken their cue from the Isley Brothers' 'Shout' – 'a little bit softer now, a little bit softer now, a little bit louder now, a little bit *louder now*' – but dispensed with the caution. In America they were largely ignored but, signing to 4AD in Britain, they scored a string of independent-chart hits (number ones with 'Gigantic' and 'Monkey Gone to Heaven') and – like Hüsker Dü before them – splintered just as the going got good.

Pixies had the style, but – Kim Deal aside – they looked like plumbers. Dinosaur had the tunes, but with the slovenly, moth-eaten Mascis at the helm, they were destined to peak at only number twenty in the UK with their best single, 'Start Choppin''. American slacker punk wasn't destined to be *Smash Hits* material, at least not until another three-piece emerged and briefly made Seattle, birthplace of Jimi Hendrix, the epicentre of pop.

There is a great pop strain of big men on the brink, tough guys choking back the tears, brought to their knees and reduced to falsetto shrieks. It stretches back to Frankie Laine, and was turned into an art form by Del Shannon. This didn't happen as much in the eighties in spite of (or because of) the heightened sexual temperature. Kurt Cobain's best songs erased the blue-collar romanticism beloved of Bruce Springsteen to reveal small-town suffocation and male confusion; Cobain was a different kind of romantic outsider, and he bellowed out his own insecurities. The Mascis whine, the Mould holler, neither could stand up to the sheer volume of Kurt Cobain and Nirvana. Summoning up the hard-rock noise of Led Zeppelin, Black Sabbath and Motörhead as a backdrop for their underclass concerns, Nirvana became the biggest alternative group in the world.

> My body is damaged from music in two ways. I have a red irritation in my stomach. It's psychosomatic, caused by all the anger and the screaming. I have scoliosis, where the curvature of your spine is bent, and the weight of my guitar has made it worse. I'm always in pain, and that adds to the anger in our music. I'm grateful to it, in a way.
> Kurt Cobain

Coming from Aberdeen, 180 miles away from Seattle in the Pacific North West, at first Nirvana were just another local scene band on a local label, the shruggingly named Sub Pop. If anything, they seemed late to the party when they released their first album, *Bleach*, in June '89. 'The early songs were really angry,' Cobain told John Robb of *Sounds*. 'But as time goes on the songs are getting poppier and poppier as I get happier and happier. The songs are now about conflicts in relationships, emotional things with other human beings.'

The first gig Cobain ever attended had been a Black Flag show, primal hardcore punk, and it changed his life. From this point on he started to listen to British indie (he was the world's biggest fan of Scottish duo the Vaselines), as well as Hüsker Dü and Pixies. He formed a band, they covered songs by the Meat Puppets and the Vaselines and, eventually, he made a lot of money for his heroes. Generous to a fault, he talked of his admiration for REM's integrity as he followed Michael Stipe into beatified rock-star territory. Soon they appeared in the tour documentary *1991: The Year Punk Broke*; more truthfully it should have been called *The Year Grunge Broke*, because this was the tag given to Nirvana and a crop of Seattle bands (Mudhoney, Tad, Soundgarden), with their mix of punk ideology and an ever increasing dose of pre-punk hard rock, by Sub Pop's sloganeering owners, Bruce Pavitt and Jonathan Poneman.

1991 was also the year riot grrrl broke. At Olympia, Washington's International Pop Underground convention, there was an all-female event billed 'Love Rock Revolution Girl Style Now' that included Bratmobile, Heavens to Betsy and Bikini Kill's Kathleen Hanna. Formed in 1990, Bikini Kill were the firestarters and, while they played with Nirvana and ex-Runaway Joan Jett, they resolutely refused to toy with the mainstream. Musically riot grrrl was light on melody, heavy on aggression – its real impact was lyrical. Riot grrrl brought the issue of 'women in pop' – an unspoken undercurrent since Lesley Gore's 'You Don't Own Me' (US no. 2 '64) – into the open.

There were other girl-led alternative-rock bands around. The Lunachicks, L7, Babes in Toyland and Hole all had a sexually conscious aesthetic which didn't necessarily tickle male fantasy or follow a feminist doctrine; these women hoped to create music and assume an image without being categorised only as 'women'. Unfortunately, their pursuit of equality also extended to their adopting hoary male rock clichés – the riffs, the drugs, the sulks, the falling out with the major label. The Lunachicks may have sung about non-obvious subject matter like TV's favourite middle sister Jan Brady, but their music was warmed-over hard rock, largely uninteresting.

Of the girl bands, Hole took the lion's share of media interest, mainly because singer Courtney Love began dating Kurt Cobain, and also because of her tendency to hang out with Madonna, her urge to spill her guts in public and her desire to be a perennial prom queen. Just as Hole's debut album, *Pretty on the Inside*, was released, Kurt and Courtney were spotted by the *Village Voice* shopping for a wedding ring in Tiffany's. 'Perhaps she'll find infinite and ever more subtle ways to torture herself,' they wrote. 'Long may she bleed.' American indie's screeching, insides-out nature seemed to encourage such baffling comments.

Bikini Kill were much more interesting. While Hole ('Teenage Whore') wrote self-centred therapy blow-outs, and Babes in Toyland penned bitchy responses to them ('Bruise Violet'), Bikini Kill built a creative support network. Their best song, the Joan Jett-produced 'Rebel Girl', was like a girl-positive rewrite of Blondie's 'Rip Her to Shreds'; they were about unapologetic activism.

Bikini Kill wrote manifestos and slogans: 'Stop the j-word jealousy from killing girl love'; 'encourage in the face of insecurity'. Kathleen Hanna had originally been a feminist poet but took encouragement to form a band from Courtney Love, and from Babes in Toyland, who helped Bikini Kill to get their earliest gigs: 'I just started thinking, like, if fucking Coca Cola has advertisements then feminism should too . . . Part of my mission was to advertise that feminism didn't have to look a certain way or be a certain thing.' Hanna's best, most succinct slogan was 'Revolution Girl Style Now!' It worked. Hundreds of fanzines were photocopied,* and fliers and cassettes were distributed, often by hand, and often purely within riot-grrrl circles. A British wing developed: Huggy Bear, Blood Sausage, Batfink. There was a two-page spread in *Smash Hits*. In the States, having been badly misrepresented in the press,† Hanna and her tight riot-grrrl cohort imposed a media blackout. The scene was incendiary but intentionally underground; no one was about to sign a record deal – why bother when you could do everything yourself? Unsurprisingly, riot grrrl had no chart presence whatsoever.

Nirvana left Sub Pop in '91 and signed to Geffen; the cover of their major-label debut, *Nevermind*, showed an innocent just about to grasp a dollar bill. Produced by Butch Vig,‡ it had a radio-friendly sheen and was purpose-built to take the underground overground. The Replacements

---

* Bikini Kill drummer Tobi Vail had been publishing her *Jigsaw* fanzine since 1988, which read like an advance riot-grrrl manifesto: 'First of all, I would like to inform you that the Go-Go's don't suck so stop putting them down. YES that means you mr/ms rock journalist . . . they were five women who wrote some cool pop songs and got famous on a fluke . . . and they rock. Check out the first LP if you don't believe me . . . Girls + guitars is equal to sex + power . . . which is something that is not supposed to be associated with women in our culture . . . Young Marble Giants, Kleenex, Delta 5, Raincoats, Slits. And then there's the Marine Girls and Pylon. And Poly Styrene from X Ray Spex was so fucking cool. All that stuff was so punk rock and revolutionary. It doesn't deserve to be obscure. So what if it was ten years ago? It's amazing. Girls rock. Do you wanna trade tapes?'
† The *Washington Post* claimed that 'Kathleen Hanna accused her father of abusing her when she was young', which she denied.
‡ Smashing Pumpkins producer Butch Vig's status was elevated hugely by his work on *Nevermind*. He later formed his own band, Garbage, who had five Top 10 hits in the UK between 1996 and 1999.

had ended up as drunken embarrassments, singing about selling out over a hi-gloss production, but Nirvana's rise to the top was so rapid they didn't have time to lose themselves in semantics.

'With its oscillation between rage and resignation, its lust for revolution that's immediately crippled by bitter irony, "Smells Like Teen Spirit" is an "Anarchy in the UK" for the twenty-something generation,' said *Melody Maker*. The major difference was that 'Anarchy in the UK' stalled at number thirty-eight in the UK chart and wasn't even released in most countries. At the end of 1991 'Smells Like Teen Spirit' went to number seven in the UK, number six in the US, number one in New Zealand, number one in France. Eighteen months earlier Cobain had said, 'If we hadn't done this band thing, we would have been doing what everyone else does back home, which is chopping down trees, drinking, having sex and drinking, talking about sex and drinking some more . . .' Now they were in a whole other world, winning two best-video awards from MTV and being touted as the spokesmen for Generation X.

'Smells Like Teen Spirit' took the Pixies' quiet/loud aesthetic and nailed it to something that sounded like Hüsker Dü covering 'More than a Feeling'; it was, in the space of three minutes, the climax (and downfall) of an eighties outsider music and the beginning of a new, nineties corporate rock.

Kurt Cobain was both a role model for disaffected boys and the kind of shy kid that girls wanted to mother as well as sleep with – as fragile as Billy Fury. It only took one look at Nirvana on MTV, one listen to 'Smells Like Teen Spirit', and you knew he was a real star. Simon Reynolds saw them at the Kilburn National and 'got the sense that Nirvana, wary of their sudden enormity, feel perversely driven to deflate their own importance. At the moment they're uncomfortably poised between their Sub Pop slob-rock past and their future rock godhood. They seem embarrassed and bemused, it's like their boots are too big for them. Did they seize the time with "Smells Like Teen Spirit" or did the time seize them?'

He couldn't have been more right. Cobain was heard to talk about the 'B' word – Beatles, Beach Boys, Byrds, Big Star – and he wondered out loud, hadn't it all been done? Who the hell did Nirvana think they were? What they were was a gateway for the full re-emergence of guitar-based hard rock after the fripperies of the hi-tech eighties. A former Nirvana member called Jason Everman was the first to benefit from Seattle's grunge windfall when he pitched up as bassist in Soundgarden, a heavy gothic act who went on to score a US number nine with the remorselessly grim stoner-rock 'Black Hole Sun' in '94. Then there was Pearl Jam, born from Washington-state bands Green River and Mother Love Bone. Their sound veered even closer to American rock's riffs and roots than their Seattle forebears, all post-punk ideals abandoned, and singer Eddie Vedder's voice was reminiscent of Blood, Sweat and Tears' David Clayton-Thomas with its actorly, stentorian tones (more likely he was going for Jim Morrison, but you can't win them all). Pearl Jam were seen as a commercial-rock behemoth by the fanzine writers, a rockist sell-out by Cobain, though – constantly trying to prove otherwise – they spent the next ten years fighting Ticketmaster to keep concert prices down, refusing to do videos for MTV, and releasing records for Kosovan refugees. Very good boys they turned out to be, then, but entirely joyless nonetheless.

Neither Soundgarden nor Pearl Jam could be called Nirvana copyists, but soon a caravan of lank-haired whiners pitched up on the doorsteps of Geffen, Warner and EMI. The band that summed up the real horrors of grunge turned out to be British. Bush were from Shepherd's Bush, and could barely get third billing in a local pub at home. They started off sounding like INXS, then heard a Pixies album and changed their tune. 'Three million albums, five hit singles, why won't anyone take Bush seriously?' read the words on the cover of *Rolling Stone* in 1996; these were placed, possibly not by chance, alongside a topless picture of singer Gavin Rossdale, exactly as the magazine had shot weightless teen dream David Cassidy in 1972. Inside, the magazine declared Bush 'genetically-engineered bubble-grungers . . . REM, Sonic Youth and the Pixies did not slog around the eighties college circuit in unheated vans to make the world safe for a bunch of MTV confections like Bush.' You wanted to warm to them simply because they were so despised as also-rans at best, grave-robbing chancers at worst. Rossdale defended himself like a kid caught by the teacher with fags in his pockets: 'In some of the songs I complain a bit, but I'd do that anyway – I'm from England.' Their breakthrough single was 'Everything Zen', a composite of Nirvana's volume levels and some of the worst lyrics – 'Mickey Mouse has grown up a cow, Dave's on sale again. We kissy kiss in the rear view, we're so bored, you're to blame' – to ever grace a million-seller. But with a six-times platinum album on his wall, Rossdale felt able to defend himself. 'We're a real fucking band,' he railed at *Rolling Stone*. 'We live a crazy, crazy life.'

At a New York industry showcase gig in August '93, Nirvana refused to conform to the crazy, crazy rock 'n' roll stereotype. They stood stock still, played acoustic numbers, mumbled, and brought on a female cellist for the rape-themed 'Polly'. Right at the end, they played the song everybody wanted to hear, 'Smells Like Teen Spirit', and then Cobain sat crouched, alone, producing a wail of feedback for ten solid minutes.

In Britain such contrary behaviour would have still caused an outrage, but we might have taken their gender-bending more lightly. Machismo isn't central to British culture. In America, though, trashing male gender codes was unheard of. Nirvana played pro-gay benefit shows, kissed each other on the networked *Saturday Night Live* and wore dresses in the video for 'In Bloom'. At the MTV awards, they smashed up their equipment and mocked Guns n' Roses.

Yet Cobain knew he had unleashed a monster by the time of their third album, *In Utero*, in '93. He felt part of the corporate sausage machine, just as compromised as the Replacements before him, but with the added pressure of being the flannel-shirted spokesman for a generation, and with a multi-million-selling album to follow up. He struggled to see a way forward.

Staying true to punk's school while moving into fresh fields was a recurring problem. The Clash sounded silly making white rap. Discharge had found no salvation in switching to pure metal. The Replacements had gone round in circles trying to prove they were '4 Real'. One of the sad ironies of Nirvana's short existence is that their *Unplugged in New York* album, released posthumously in 1994, was not only their best and most influential record but showed how easy it would have been for Kurt Cobain to continue, as John Lydon had done after the Sex Pistols imploded, as Elvis had done once his Hollywood contract was up. He sings Leadbelly's 'In the Pines (Where Did You Sleep Last Night)' and here is as distinct an American voice as Brian Wilson's or Bob Dylan's, one that needs none of Butch Vig's production gloss or Nirvana's quiet/loud constructs. It is quite intense enough already.

After Kurt Cobain committed suicide in April '94, Pearl Jam's Eddie Vedder was inconsolable – he said that he'd always thought he'd be the first to go. Even in death, it seemed, grunge one-upmanship was rife, and Nirvana's anti-macho, anti-corporate stance had counted for little. A grunge song and a grunge band purpose-built for a Levi's ad – 'Inside' by Stiltskin – was a UK number one just weeks after Cobain's death. Grunge soon fed into new crossbreeds – rap metal, nu metal – and led indirectly to the Red Hot Chili Peppers, with their ultra-masculine mix of funk, hip hop and metal, becoming the biggest-selling rock group in the world. Meanwhile, Kurt Cobain's love of punk – once filtered down to their millions of fans, and watered down by an industry sensing a gold rush – opened the door for stereotypical old-school punk revivalists like Green Day and Blink 182. A few years later came another sub-level of pre-teen punk: Busted and McFly owed plenty to Nirvana.

Like Public Enemy, Bikini Kill – and the forward thrust of riot grrrl – would splinter in a confusion of minutiae, qualifications and recriminations. Wasn't race an issue? Wasn't it all too middle class? Kathleen Hanna eventually formed Le Tigre in 1998, who channelled the Go Go's, the Red Bird sound and lo-fidelity electro leanings on 'Deceptacon'. They wrote zippy, catchy songs about feminist icons like Shulamith Firestone and fellow riot-grrrl act Sleater-Kinney. Their songs got played at Boston Red Sox games. By 2013 you could buy a not-for-profit, fundraising Bikini Kill chapstick.

Hole's profile soared in the wake of Kurt Cobain's death. Courtney Love eventually channelled her attention away from media-baiting, until 1998's *Celebrity Skin* felt like a proper record rather than just a vehicle for her problems: 'Boys on the Radio' was a song about falling in love with pop; 'Heaven Tonight' was closer to the Bangles than the Pixies; the title track (UK no. 19 '98) and 'Malibu' (UK no. 22 '99) were genuine, radio-friendly hit singles. You had to admire her powers of recovery.

While grunge had turned out to be a cul-de-sac, musically and philosophically (an astonishing number of its practitioners were left dead or incapacitated by drug habits), NYU's Fales Library steadily amassed a riot-grrrl archive. It had little impact on the chart but, like first-wave punk rock, its influence stretched well beyond alternative rock; without it Shampoo, the Spice Girls and the Gossip wouldn't have existed, groups where nobody wondered or cared whether men were holding the strings. 'The future of rock belongs to women,' Kurt Cobain had said, and, looking at the state of guitar bands in the early 2010s, you hope he was right.

Nirvana's *Unplugged in New York* reached number one in the US album chart and sold five million copies. It effectively brought out into the open another new American music: alt country, which would become the dominant sound of the indie world over the next decade. The marriage of hardcore ideals to what Greil Marcus called 'old, weird America', combined with the kind of middling success enjoyed by Bonnie 'Prince' Billy, Smog or Lambchop, would have suited Cobain's temperament to a tee. If he'd lived, he would have been curating festivals like All Tomorrow's Parties, and the Vaselines' reunion – largely a result of his patronage – would have been his proudest moment. Though Kurt Cobain's talent had created his own prison, it had also provided him with a means to escape, and it really is a shame that he didn't stay around to work that out.

EVER DECREASING CIRCLES: BLUR, SUEDE AND BRITPOP

You interview a band now and the big cliché is that they can't think of more than a handful of current bands that they dig, everyone is going into the past to dig out reference points . . . the semi-fossilised moments of magic from the past that seem more contemporary in today's mishmash of pop culture than at any other time.

John Robb, 1992

The government had fought to contain the energy and collective will surrounding dance music in 1992, when it seemed clear that the future of modern pop was electronic. Within three years, though, guitar music – and an explicitly nostalgic version – would be back on magazine covers.

Bootcut Levi's were in the shops, and the Union Jack would become an acceptable fashion accessory for the first time since the sixties. When Labour finally won the election in '97, Noel Gallagher of Oasis and Blur's Damon Albarn would be invited to meet new prime minister Tony Blair. It felt a very long way from the vilification of rave: Britpop would prove to be the last time there was a British consensus on pop music.

It rose as Britain attempted to redefine itself after more than a decade of Tory rule. Tony Blair became Labour leader in the summer of 1994, as *Four Weddings and a Funeral* became the cinema hit of the year – the most successful British-made film in years – and Oasis's first album *Definitely Maybe* was released: until the '97 election Blair was regarded as a leader in waiting, and this pre-honeymoon period imbued the country with a new confidence. Almost in tandem with the rise of Britpop came the Britart movement, and there were several parallels.

Colonising parts of East London, the YBAs – Young British Artists – shunned, like post-indie Britpop, the traditional artistic stance of self-sacrifice, opposition and exclusion. They were loud and trashy; their exhibitions had names like *Minky Manky*, *Zombie Golf*, *Cocaine Orgasm* and *Sick*; they wanted to be rich and famous, like pop stars. A decade earlier, *C86* indie had defined itself in opposition to the major labels and had a hair-trigger reaction to anything that suggested 'selling out'. By 1995 Blur and Oasis were in competition with each other for the number-one position in the singles chart, and the tabloid press was courted and accepted as a promotional tool. Art and commerce had never mixed quite like this before. Another common denominator of Britpop and Britart was their revelling in the pleasures of popular culture – specifically drug consumption, pornography and cheap TV. Britart would reach a peak with the *Sensation* exhibition at the Royal Academy in 1997, the same year Noel Gallagher was welcomed into 10 Downing Street. The video for Blur's 'Country House' featured cameos from page 3 pin-up Jo Guest and comedian Matt Lucas. It was directed by Britart's most famous son, Damien Hirst, who, according to the *Sensation* catalogue, 'was as good and skilful a publicist for his art and his contemporaries as he was a maker of art himself'.

Initially, no one seemed embarrassed to be given the Britpop tag

– there was even a BBC show in 1995 called *Britpop Now*, presented by
the scene's self-appointed leader, Damon Albarn. It started as a collective will to power, from the music press as well as the bands involved.
In the wake of baggy in 1989, the rock-based music press had been
desperately casting around for new movements, launching their own
half-baked tags – shoegazing, fraggle, new wave of new wave* – to see if
anything would stick, and to be seen to be ahead of the game. Nothing
stuck. Then along came Suede – an unassuming, skinny, not unattractive group from London who played melodic indie with slightly saucy
lyrics – and suddenly there was a frisson. The *Independent*'s William
Leith described Suede's press reviews as 'florid, poetic, half-crazed; they
express the almost lascivious delight of journalists hungry for something
to pin their hopes on'. With the bit between their teeth, journalists
wouldn't be stopping at Suede; the music press didn't create Britpop,
but they certainly wanted it to happen.†

It would end up as an extraordinarily tribal affair: Blur versus
Suede, Blur versus Oasis, north versus south, grammar versus sec-
ondary. Enmity in the sixties had been reserved for non-rock acts
like Ken Dodd. Mostly groups got on fine – everyone from Cream
to Herman's Hermits politely sang the praises of the Beatles. In the
seventies Patti Smith gave Debbie Harry a hard stare, but no more; in
the eighties Liverpool acts Echo and the Bunnymen, Wah! Heat and
the Teardrop Explodes bitched about each other, but they were basically family, so that was OK too. In Britpop, everything seemed to

---

* In 1993 the *NME* coined 'the new wave of new wave' for a rash of acts who
made a concerted attempt to get sharpness and angularity back on the agenda.
Championed by the *NME*'s Paul Moody, S*M*A*S*H, from Welwyn Garden
City, had a punk/mod hardline ethic, as well as an endearingly awkward take on
feminism (their second single was called 'Lady Love Your Cunt'). They toured
heavily, and opened up a gig circuit for other, younger bands coming through:
acts who supported S*M*A*S*H included Echobelly, Catatonia and Sleeper.
Brighton's These Animal Men were similarly rough and ready. Both groups
anticipated what was around the corner but, unlike Suede, they lacked any good
tunes.

† John Robb of *Sounds* and *Melody Maker*'s Paul Lester both claim to have
coined the term first, though Robb used it in the eighties, which is a little like
Crawdaddy's Paul Williams claiming to have christened punk rock.

be about one-upmanship: Blur got Stereolab's Laetitia Sadier to sing on one of their singles, so Suede tried to trump them with the sexier, more famous Jane Birkin; Blur spitefully released a single, 'Country House', on the same day as Oasis's 'Roll with It', just to beat them to the number-one spot.

In 1990 Brett Anderson was a humble town-planning student from the Sussex town of Haywards Heath who sang in a group called Suede. His girlfriend was Suede's bassist, Justine Frischmann, who made him packed lunches for his college field trips to Milton Keynes. This cosy domesticity was shattered when Frischmann left Anderson for a handsome lad who had been hassling her for months, Blur's Damon Albarn. When Frischmann started turning up late for Suede rehearsals, Anderson kicked her out – he was convinced she was only dating Albarn because he was famous. He was consumed with jealousy and spite – suddenly he had real motivation. Brett Anderson and Bernard Butler, Suede's quietly spoken teenage guitarist, set their hearts on becoming not just bigger than Blur, but the most acclaimed songwriting team in the country, the new Morrissey/Marr.

Suede's breakthrough in 1992 was the first major indicator that, beyond thrill-seeking journalists, there was an appetite for a new patriotism. They hit national consciousness when they appeared on the cover of the April 21st issue of *Melody Maker*, under the headline 'Suede: The Best New Band in Britain': in 1992 the music press – even second-stringer *Melody Maker* – held such sway that this virtually guaranteed success. Their first three singles – 'The Drowners', 'Metal Mickey', 'Animal Nitrate' – were louche and lithe, clean and classy where post-dance pop had been distinctly unstylish. There were no cyber-dayglo graphics, no handwritten titles, no pirate flags or smiley faces or dreadlocks in sight. Suede's artwork and aesthetic was simple, and that suddenly seemed very sexy. Brett Anderson's vocal inspiration appeared to come from one record – Elton John's version of 'Lucy in the Sky with Diamonds'. Their musical and lyrical influences were equally straightforward and pure: Bowie and the Smiths. That was it. Anderson came out with a line that could have been a composite of Morrissey and Bowie quotes – that he was 'a bisexual who has never had a homosexual experience'* – and by now they were set for stardom.

How could this have happened? How did Suede get everyone, even Mark E. Smith, who had never sung the praises of anyone apart from M. R. James, to talk about them as the 'best new band in Britain'? One reason is that the competition was so poor. The early nineties had been an embarrassment for British guitar bands, a lull in proceedings after Madchester had allowed a bunch of scrappy indie groups (Carter the Unstoppable Sex Machine, Pop Will Eat Itself, the Senseless Things and the Wonder Stuff) to become Top 40 fixtures. They shared an unwashed look and a sneering mix of contempt for pop culture and 'disco'.† The Wonder Stuff's Miles Hunt told riot-grrrl-inspired sulk queens Shampoo that 'girls don't belong in studios', while Carter's Fruitbat rugby-tackled children's TV presenter Phillip Schofield at the 1991 *Smash Hits* awards. These acts were small-time, mean-spirited and distinctly lacking in glamour.

Secondly, the music press suddenly had a need for a consensus group like Suede to justify their existence. According to sales reports from the high streets, computer games were fast gaining ground on music as the new dominant pop culture. Comics (especially *Deadline*, featuring Jamie Hewlett's Tank Girl) and even piercings and tattoos seemed to be generating more interest and press coverage than pop music. As British indie had begun to congeal, there had been a simultaneous boom in stand-up comedians: Rob Newman and David Baddiel became bigger on the student circuit than almost any pop group; the Wonder Stuff scored a number one covering Tommy Roe's 'Dizzy', but only with

* Apparently this didn't go down well with Suede's drummer Simon Gilbert, who was gay.
† 'Disco' was used as a catch-all insult for house and techno by indie purists – the Wonder Stuff's 'Who Wants to Be the Disco King' was a dig at guitar groups attempting to expand their horizons by getting remixes. I always found it sad that no late-eighties or -nineties guitar bands tried to adapt their classic four-piece beat-group set-up to tackle house, techno and garage singles, as beat groups of the sixties had assimilated soul and punk groups had adopted reggae. Hats off to the Style Council (Joe Smooth's 'Promised Land') and the Pet Shop Boys (Sterling Void's 'It's Alright') for giving it a go, but it seems like a missed opportunity for a younger generation.

assistance from comedian Vic Reeves. 'Comedy is the new rock 'n' roll' quickly became a cliché.

Thirdly, despite winning the 1992 election, John Major's Conservative government was now in its death throes. The new optimism abroad in Britain related to neither the grunge acts nor the Wonder Stuff's grubby ilk. Damien Hirst's shark, the tart Scottish movie *Trainspotting* and Brett Anderson's half-unbuttoned acrylic blouse all seemed peculiarly British and irreverent. Once the war was won, once Britpop ruled the charts and Blair was in power, this would curdle and become jingoistic arrogance. But not just yet.

In the summer of 1992, while Morrissey was being derided by the *NME* for playing in Finsbury Park draped in a Union Jack, Brett Anderson was telling the same paper that 'all great British pop artists from the Beatles to the Fall have celebrated Britain in some way. I'm not remotely attracted by New York. I mean, all the streets are laid out in a grid. Doesn't that say everything? In Britain it takes this convoluted arcane knowledge to get from one bus stop to the next.' Here was an effete group, unashamedly borrowing from past pop heroes, prepared to turn their back on the States. By February '93, at the height of grunge, their third single, 'Animal Nitrate', went Top 10. They were invited to play at the Brits, alongside George Michael, Genesis and Annie Lennox, intruders at the corporate-rock ball.

Anderson's muses may have been oblivious* but in the spring of '93 came the first acknowledgement that this nameless nascent scene was going overground. *Select* published a 'Yanks go home' issue, with Suede on the cover alongside other ur-Britpop acts Denim, Saint Etienne, Pulp and the Auteurs. Suede's debut became the fastest-selling album in almost ten years.

Blur were similarly in thrall to Bowie but also referenced Syd Barrett-era Pink Floyd, Canterbury hippie loon Kevin Ayers and American

---

* Bowie, having overcome the baying critics with his *Sound and Vision* 'greatest hits' tour in 1990, then gave the world exactly what it wasn't asking for – *Tin Machine II* – in 1991. Morrissey called on Mick Ronson to produce his musically feisty though lyrically out of sorts '92 album *Your Arsenal*: 'We look to Los Angeles for the language we use,' ran 'Glamorous Glue': 'London is dead.'

eighties slacker indie. Tying this up and underpinning it with a baggy beat, they had scored a Top 10 hit with their second single, 'There's No Other Way', in '91. Three of them were foppish lookers and they quickly found their way into *Smash Hits* as indie pin-ups. At the tail end of '93, though, on returning from an arduous and thankless tour of the US, they were horrified to find Suede – 'these little pricks from UCL', as bassist Alex James called them – all over Britain's magazine covers.

If Suede's naked influences implicitly suggested they thought things were better in the past, Blur came right out and screamed it. They had faded badly after 'There's No Other Way' and spent 1992 reinventing themselves with a Suede-like sound for their second album, *Modern Life Is Rubbish*. It was loaded with social observations on a Britain that barely existed any more. Lead single 'For Tomorrow' ransacked Bowie's back catalogue – specifically 'Starman' and 'The Bewlay Brothers' – while the Kinks-like chorus showed that they knew how to write anthemic singalongs. It stalled at number twenty-eight in May '93 but left a stronger impression, and the music press detected more new heroes. Damon Albarn may have won Brett Anderson's girlfriend, but he wasn't about to let him have the cover of the *NME* all to himself. Blur chucked out the baggy gear and reacquainted themselves with the wardrobe of their early teens: the moptops remained but they now sported suit jackets and Fred Perry polo shirts, and looked every bit the 1980 suburban mod.

If Blur had intentionally avoided mentioning clubbing, raving, glow sticks or the declining quality of MDMA on *Modern Life Is Rubbish*, they would make up for it with 'Girls and Boys' in '94. Feeling the weight of indie fans straying back from the pulse of house to the scratchy guitars of indie, Blur felt they were on safe ground mocking young clubbers and sun-seekers; it wasn't too much of a stretch to see it as an attack on the working classes, who by now made up the majority of any rave crowd. The catty lyric was outweighed by a tremendous, club-friendly production that recalled early Duran Duran – it entered the chart at number five and officially announced their re-emergence. The parent album to 'Girls and Boys', *Parklife*, combined *du jour* French wispiness ('To the End', no. 16 '94) and the breezy thuggishness of the title track (no. 10 '94), which featured a guest vocal from Phil Daniels, a star of *Quadrophenia* and a hero to 1979's mod revivalists. *Parklife* was as unavoidable in 1994 Britain as *Thriller* had been ten years earlier; in the States, though, it meant as little as Slade had done in 1973. It was a very localised thrill.*

The intensity of Britpop spiked in 1994 with the arrival of Elastica, formed by Justine Frischmann after she was booted out of Suede. They were smart, and very calculated, to the point where they were rather hard to love. Not content to just have a famous boyfriend, singer Frischmann had now teamed up with the perfect Britpop face, a blonde moppet called Donna Matthews, and their appropriation of post-punk spikiness was several years ahead of the pack. Brevity and archness were their stock in trade; folly and sweetness were not for Elastica. Drummer Justin Welch's belched percussion throughout 'Line Up' on their *Top of the Pops* debut in February '94 predicted the art-school sniggering of the late-nineties Hoxton scene, and took Blur's sneers to a colder level. All of their songs seemed heavily indebted to the late seventies, and debut single 'Line Up' was so close to Wire's 'I Am the Fly' that they were forced to settle out of court. 'Waking Up' bore a strong resemblance to the Stranglers' 'No More Heroes'. No one's enthusiasm was dampened. 'This is happening *with* our permission,' wrote Paul Lester, reviewing Suede in '94. 'We wanted it to happen. We virtually *willed* it to happen. But are Suede really the *only* thing happening in pop right now? Of course they're bloody not, but it feels good to pretend we're all united by a single cause.' He wasn't alone in feeling this enthusiastic. Elastica's album went straight in at number one and became the fastest-selling British debut of all time.

* Britpop's nerve centre was Smashing, a London club hosted by close-cropped DJ Martin Green and his louder sidekick Adrian Webb. Starting in 1991, with a musical policy that ran from X-Ray Spex to Burt Bacharach to Bowie and Blur, it typified the mid-nineties with its reappropriation of twentieth-century high points, effectively creating the *fin de siècle* in exactly the same way that film-makers and fashion designers of the fifties and sixties had imagined it would be. By 1993 Smashing was based in the unreconstructed sixties cellar club Eve's on Regent Street; superstars in waiting Damon Albarn and Jarvis Cocker would be sat next to Leigh Bowery and Damien Hirst.

They are quarrelsome, clannishly protective and socially rumbustious . . .
All have fuelled, usually in very direct ways, the articulation and transformation of imagery drawn from daily, urban life – a bed, a room, a hospital
door, sport, poverty, rural dreams, television, food and death.
    Richard Shone, *Sensation* catalogue

Pulp, who had been around since the early eighties, became the defining
Britpop group and Jarvis Cocker its enduring star. After attending Saint
Martins art school at the turn of the nineties, he had begun to write
acute working-class observational pieces; unlike Blur, these all seemed
to be based on first-hand experience. Sex and class were Cocker's spe-
cialities. 'Common People' – a number-two hit in June '95 – aimed its
sights on both and became an anthem for the dispossessed, the outsiders; a poor boy/rich girl yarn, it sounded strikingly reminiscent of the
first meeting of Justine Frischmann and Brett Anderson.

    Intriguingly, Pulp were the only successful Britpop group to incor-
porate electronics, channelling early Roxy Music and getting Motiv 8
to remix 'Common People'. They didn't give the impression that they
thought modern life – the world outside Britpop – was rubbish at all.
'Common People' soared and dipped like a rave tune, and 'Sorted for
E's and Wizz' (also no. 2 '95) addressed an issue familiar to a large section of nineties British youth – that of being in a field, somewhere off
the M25, with thousands of other people. Alone among their peers,
they wrote about rave culture: 'At four o'clock the normal world seems
very, very, very far away.'

    Where had this sudden appetite for new British guitar bands come
from? Matthew Bannister's appointment as head of Radio 1 in late '93
was the point at which Britpop was allowed to become part of the mainstream. Out went DJs like the self-named 'Hairy Cornflake', Dave Lee
Travis, who had been there since the sixties; out went Simon Bates's
gloopy mid-morning slot 'Our Tune'; in came the *NME*'s most hardline
indie fan, Steve Lamacq, and Jo Whiley's *Evening Session*. In the late
eighties the Smiths had been Britain's most successful indie act, Top
20 regulars, but found themselves sidelined as 'specialist' by Radio 1.
In 1993 the likes of Elastica and Oasis – before they had even officially
released a single – were suddenly on the playlist.

Suede, Blur and Elastica had pillaged the past, turned forty years of British pop culture into a theme park. In itself, this was no bad thing. This essentially retrogressive stance had other, rather unforeseeable consequences, in that it allowed for some overdue reassessments of pop's past: Dusty Springfield was hailed as the greatest female British singer, bar none; the Beatles' *Revolver* was deemed a better album than *Sgt Pepper*; the Kinks were elevated to the same level of critical respect as the Beatles, the Stones and the Who; even British folk rock was allowed to creep out from under its mossy stone, as Sandy Denny and Nick Drake were beatified. Blur and Oasis played at a Beatles/Stones rivalry and successfully divided the country. *Top of the Pops* was reborn under the directorship of Ric Blaxill, who attempted to take it back to its seventies glam peak by including new acts who hadn't yet charted; in one case – 'Kandy Pop' by minor Scottish indie cutesters Bis – a self-released single which wasn't yet in the shops made it onto the show. This was a peculiarly subjective take on *Top of the Pops*, but it all seemed for the best. Pop was front-page news; even at the height of Beatlemania it hadn't reached such levels of media excitement.

The problem with the past as a theme park was that the biggest attraction, clearly, were the Beatles. There had been an unspoken agreement, even in the ungentlemanly world of Britpop, that the Beatles were out of bounds. To use them as a direct influence was tantamount to cheating. Oasis appeared with 'Columbia', a promo twelve-inch that made it onto the Radio 1 playlist in late '93; a few months later came the blisteringly loud 'Supersonic' (UK no. 31 '94); by Christmas '94 they were number three with 'Whatever', a festive rewrite of 'All You Need Is Love' with a touch of 'I Am the Walrus'. With the genie out of the bottle, Britpop's momentum began to slow.

Damon Albarn had come from an art-school background. His dad had set up a design consultancy and a gallery at 26 Kingly Street in the sixties. He had grown up with African field recordings. Liam and Noel Gallagher were from the working-class Manchester suburb of Burnage; the only cultural reference point for the Gallaghers was Sifters record shop. They had no airs and graces, and no schooling in cool. Noel Gallagher claimed that the three most important albums ever made were the Beatles' red and blue albums and Pink Floyd's *The Wall* – no one from Suede or Blur would have made the gauche mistake of citing two compilations and an album from the least hip end of Floyd's career.

This unfettered everyday blokeishness helped Oasis become the biggest-selling Britpop act of all. 'Never mind the bollocks, here's the Sex Beatles,' said *The Face* in 1993. Will Self described their sound as the 'wall of lager'. There was no Bowie, Smiths or Syd Barrett in the sound of Oasis; the group they were most reminiscent of was Slade – loud, raucous, goodtime music. Liam Gallagher had far and away the strongest voice in Britpop, as rough and raging as John Lennon on 'Twist and Shout', with rounded yowling Mancunian vowels that turned 'sunshine' into 'soon-shee-yine'. Noel Gallagher, like Marc Bolan before him, had the knack of rewriting his favourite riffs and creating something new and irresistible: 'Don't Look Back in Anger', 'Wonderwall', 'Cigarettes and Alcohol'. And, like Bolan, his ego quickly got the better of him.

In 1996 they played to two hundred and fifty thousand people at Knebworth – over ten times that number had applied for tickets. Backstage, Noel said, 'Yeah, we are bigger than the Beatles. We are the biggest band in Britain of all time.' With this mind state he wrote the songs for third album *Be Here Now*, an unlistenable collection – too long, too loud, too few decent tunes – that came out in 1997. Its failings were left unchallenged by the press, who hugely overcompensated for backing Blur in the 1995 chart war and giving Oasis's second album, the fine *(What's the Story) Morning Glory*, mediocre reviews.

Oasis had stratospheric fame, eight number-one singles (two more than Slade, six more than Blur) – and they blew it. It was a classic working-class tale, rags to riches and back again, previously told by pools winner Viv Nicholson in *Spend, Spend, Spend* and by the Bay City Rollers in the seventies. The Gallaghers were luckier than the Bay City Rollers – they didn't end up broke and bitter – but their legacy was discoloured after *Morning Glory* (which included 'Some Might Say', 'Wonderwall', 'Champagne Supernova' and 'Don't Look Back in Anger') by a series of records that trod the same ground to ever-dwindling effect. By the time of their final album, *Dig Out Your Soul*, there was no phrase – lyrically or musically – that wasn't directly taken from the Beatles; it was as if they had become an obsessive, miniaturist art project.

Oasis represented Britpop's limitations and its folly. Noel revealed in a *Mojo* interview how a fan had given him a CD of sixties baroque pop group the Left Banke, and that – to his surprise – he loved it. Would it be an influence on the next Oasis album, asked the journalist? 'Nah. The idea of [rhythm guitarist] Bonehead dressed in a cravat and a frilly shirt playing a harpsichord doesn't do it for me.' He talked about his love of the Bee Gees: 'In my book they're right up there with the Beatles in terms of how I learned to like music. But only the first few albums. Once they get into disco and all that fucking nonsense, it's music for women.' In 1995 Noel had moved into a house in Belsize Park and renamed it Supernova Heights. He had a Union Jack hot tub fitted; it was so large that by the time the tub was full, the water had gone tepid.

At the start of the decade the Manic Street Preachers had been the only credible post-grunge UK rock group, peaking first with the anti-capitalist AOR of 'Motorcycle Emptiness' (UK no. 17 '92), based on the chords to Abba's 'Dancing Queen', and again with their third album, *The Holy Bible* in '94. Released in the same month as Portishead's *Dummy*, it was equally claustrophobic – Richey Edwards's lyrics mixed references to the Balkan wars ('I am an architect, they call me a butcher'), self-harming and anorexia. He disappeared soon after it was released and was never seen again.

Understandably there was a lot of goodwill behind their next single, the orchestrated rock ballad 'A Design for Life' (UK no. 2 '96). It turned out to be an early sign that things had gone awry. The most influential singles of 1997 weren't by Blur ('Beetlebum', 'Song 2') or Oasis ('D'You Know What I Mean', 'Stand by Me') but by Wigan band the Verve: 'Bitter Sweet Symphony' (UK no. 2 '97) and 'The Drugs Don't Work' (UK no. 1 '97) were grandiose and sluggish, as if the plug had been pulled on the scene's vim and vigour. For the rest of the nineties, 'A Design for Life' and the Verve's anguished rock ballads provided British rock's rough template, and drear quickly took hold. 'Dad rock' was coined as a new genre name – youthful playfulness was jettisoned. The arrival of the surly Welsh act Stereophonics in '97 and the blues-based Gomez in '98 only confirmed this fear. The Manic Street Preachers' 'If

You Tolerate This Your Children Will Be Next' (UK no. 1 '98) was their commercial high and creative low, so slow and big and dull, seemingly drained of any enthusiasm for the actual making of music. The legacy of dad rock was a new bedsit music, the doyens of which were Radiohead, whose singer, Thom Yorke, sang as if he was in the foetal position. In turn they led to Travis (key song title: 'Why Does It Always Rain on Me') and the world-swallowing success of Coldplay.

The swinging London of 1996 was quite different from the London of 1966, where newness had been at every turn. Ultimately, Britpop was a reaction *against* new ideas; it was against rave, hip hop and R&B, wrapped in a Beatles/Stones comfort blanket. So wrapped up in an ultra-specific past – the 1966 World Cup and the Second World War; *The Italian Job* and, always, the Beatles – it had no distance left to run. Why did it become such a dead end? One explanation is that Radio 1 and *Top of the Pops* had always previously been at odds with the music press, and this tension had been healthy; it may have seemed like a triumph when Matthew Bannister and Ric Blaxill embraced the underground but it turned out to be a disaster. It led to a narrowing of influence and, with no opposition left, bands turned on each other. Worse, without a big enough pool of high-quality British guitar bands, the charts became filled with third-rate acts: Sleeper, Echobelly, the Longpigs, the Bluetones, and York four-piece Shed Seven, who had fifteen Top 40 hits, not one of which has remained in the collective consciousness. Ultimately, there was Menswear.*

---

* Menswear – managed by Smashing DJ Adrian Webb – were, in their way, Britpop's defining band. Caitlin Moran nailed their meteoric rise in a *Melody Maker* piece called 'You too could be famous the Menswear Way':

1. Go up to members of famous bands in pubs and start chatting to them. Flatter them endlessly. Say that you're in a band too, and ask for advice. Hang around with said famous person until closing time, whereupon famous person will announce his intention to go on to a club, say Blow Up or Smashing. Say, 'Oh, I'm meeting my friends there – the trouble is, I appear to have eaten all my money. Could you get me in on the guest list?' Famous person gets you in on the guest list. Famous person gets exceedingly shitfaced. You bond. Repeat every night for three months.
2. With famous person now your 'mate', you can approach other famous

Post-post-modern Britart had bridged the great divide between popular culture and high culture – by the late nineties the split was formally a dead issue. In Britpop, to the contrary, it was revived. By the time Blur had kissed Jo Guest goodbye, pulled their pants up and started toying with gospel on 'Tender' (UK no. 2 '99), neither they nor Oasis were calling the shots. A group called the Spice Girls had set a new tabloid-friendly agenda with 'Wannabe', which went to number one in the summer of '96. It was clumsy, almost DIY, and had a lyrical gimmick ('zig-a-zig-ah!') that meant once heard it could never be forgotten. Their loose connection to Britpop was that the girls echoed the big British stars of the sixties – Dusty, Sandie, Cilla, Lulu, Marianne – only this time all in one package. None was spectacularly good-looking, none was ugly. Their songs were catchy, none was a masterpiece, but almost no one hated them and they had the hottest hit run in UK chart history – nine singles were released over the next two and a half years and all of them got to number one, except the Motown-esque 'Stop', a relative failure that reached number two.

In the wake of the Spice Girls, 1998 saw a bubblegum breakthrough with Billie Piper ('Because We Want To') and B*witched ('C'est la vie') topping the chart, modern pop that celebrated a new youthful optimism with a new Labour government and a buoyant economy. S Club 7 and Steps were just behind; All Saints provided a West London, R&B-influenced alternative to the Spice Girls; in the US, Britney Spears and

---

people and say 'I'm a friend of Graham Sparkly Trousers, gizza drink.' Famous people buy you drinks. You get shitfaced together. You bond.

3. Form a band.

4. Use your famous mates to get you into after-shows, backstage at festivals and record label Christmas parties. Wander drunkenly up to record label managers and say 'I'm Chris from Menswear, we're ace.'

5. Get the owner of Club Smashing – celeb hangout – to be your manager.

6. Observe with glee the way you're using the music industry's machinations to your own advantage; witness the Chinese Whispers at parties along the lines of, 'How you heard of this band Menswear?' 'Menswear? They sound familiar.' Gloat that this is because of successful employment of 4.

7. Get pop-star girlfriend using Step 2.

8. Get top press officer using Step 2.

9. Get on people's tits everywhere you go using Step 2.

10. Get front cover of *Melody Maker*. It's so easy!

Christina Aguilera raised the stakes. Set against this unabashed glee, the curtain fell on Britpop with Pulp's 1998 album *This Is Hardcore*. Detailing a band's virtual (and artistic) disintegration in the spotlight, it was in stark contrast to the high gloss and chipperness of *Spiceworld: The Movie*. Did the British public want to listen to a singer moaning about how many bukkake videos he'd watched while bored in an Amsterdam hotel room? No, it did not. It wanted to see sixteen-year-old Billie Piper's unfeasible, United Kingdom-sized smile.

A VISION OF LOVE: R&B

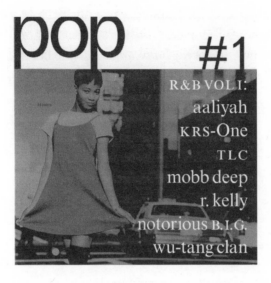

As the nineties spluttered to a close, one pop genre sped up and overtook all comers, one that had barely been breathing a few years earlier. Kicked and punched and beaten down first by disco, then by hip hop, then by house and techno, soul – reborn under its older, Jerry Wexler-invented name R&B – had an unlikely and glorious golden age that ran from the mid-nineties into the middle of the following decade. Some of the most experimental, thrilling and just plain weird music of the whole modern pop era emerged just as pretty much every other genre – hip hop, rock, techno – was running out of creative juice. A swathe of auteur producers emerged, happy to take the most oblique rhythm, the most exotic instrumentation, and deliver the most outré chart hit. 'Milkshake' by Kelis placed a lyric about her sex appeal, delivered with deadpan cool, over what sounded like a Radiophonic Workshop soundtrack to a film on dairy-farm automation. It reached number three in the US and number two in the UK. How did this happen? By blending R&B with other genres, a habit R&B had lost once disco imploded, and one it didn't regain for almost two decades. In effect, it had been held back, allowing its final creative burst to happen just as everyone else had filled in all the white space on their canvas.

The complex evolution of R&B, and its place in pop, is distilled in the changing names of *Billboard*'s relevant singles chart. In Britain, soul had been a catch-all term from the mid-sixties until the nineties, but America was more nuanced; *Billboard* had divided up the different eras like this:

1942–45	The Harlem Hit Parade
1945–49	Race
1949–69	Rhythm & Blues (abbreviated to R&B 1958–63)
1969–82	Soul
1982–90	Black
1990–99	R&B
1999–	R&B/Hip Hop

We can see that when disco was finally buried in 1982, R&B reverted to being purely 'black music', something that hadn't happened before in the progressive modern pop era. Disco had allowed everybody in, but in the eighties it seemed that either racial stereotyping was back or the tastemakers had a guest list.

Though the Hot Hundred may have suggested it was in decline, disco hadn't killed off soul. There were plenty of soul acts who became UK chart regulars at the tail end of the seventies: among the biggest were Odyssey, who could switch from Latino rave-ups ('Use It Up and Wear It Out', UK no. 1 '80) to Thom Bell-like woozy balladry ('If You're Looking for a Way Out', UK no. 8 '80), and Kool and the Gang, a JBs-styled funk act of the early seventies who hit a winning formula with brassy party anthem 'Ladies' Night' (US no. 8, UK no. 9 '79) and stuck with it. With the novelty elements of disco off the menu as the decade turned, and with the fizzing hi-hat replaced by electronic handclaps, the early eighties – rather than being devoid of floor-friendly pop – became something of a golden age. Quincy Jones killed time waiting for Michael Jackson to write a new album by producing the Brothers Johnson's towering 'Stomp!' (US no. 7, UK no. 6 '80). Fine singles that failed to register at all in the American chart but fed Britain's pop soundtrack include Quincy's own 'Razzamatazz' (UK no. 11 '81), the chilled desperation of Odyssey's 'Inside Out' (UK no. 3 '82) and Stacy Lattisaw's 'Jump to the Beat' (UK no. 3 '80), which anticipated Madonna's style by four years.

The clearest evidence that the discotheque wasn't dead came from Solar (Sound Of Los Angeles) Records, which had been set up in 1978 and began to pour out crisp R&B hits in 1980 – the *New York Times* even claimed it 'could be the Motown of the eighties'. In-house producer Leon Sylvers had previously been part of a post-Jacksons family act called the Sylvers; he was in love with Chic's clipped, rhythmic guitar lines, handclaps on the beat and the same synths that would soon inform new pop in Britain: Sylvers and Solar's squiggly, melodic electro-funk productions provided hits for Shalamar ('I Owe You One', 'The Second Time Around', the magnificent *Friends* album in '82), Dynasty, Midnight Star and, a holdover from the last days of doo wop, veteran Philly vocal act the Whispers ('And the Beat Goes On', UK no. 2 '80; 'It's a Love Thing', UK no. 9 '81).

In 1980 British soul fans also looked to the untainted, though disco-related, world of jazz funk for salvation: Tom Browne's 'Funkin' for Jamaica' (a chattering block-party update of Gary U. S. Bonds's 'Quarter to Three') and Rodney Franklin's 'The Groove' (a piano instrumental just a few steps away from the cocktail lounge) became unlikely UK Top 10 hits in 1980; stranger yet were Top 20 jazz-instrumental hits for Spyro Gyra ('Morning Dance') and Mezzoforte ('Garden Party') which sounded like the incidental music from *Moonlighting*. Kool and the Gang's run of seventeen Top 40 hits came to an abrupt end with 'Cherish' (UK no. 4 '85), by which point Shalamar and Odyssey had been off the chart for over a year.

Part of the reason for post-disco soul's rapid demise was the rise of hip hop, which was happy to ransack Solar's back catalogue for samples. The influence and inspiration was all one way – borrowing, even in part, from hip hop's backpack was still almost entirely frowned upon in eighties R&B circles. Hip hop and electro were seen as kids' stuff by British DJs like Chris Hill and American writers like Nelson George

– they had no 'soul'. The trouble was that 'soul', by the mid-eighties, had become extremely watery, little more than shorthand for bedtime; Luther Vandross ('Never Too Much', US no. 33, UK no. 13 '81) and Alexander O'Neal ('Criticize', US no. 70, UK no. 4 '87) were singers in the Teddy Pendergrass mould, but the likes of Eugene Wilde ('Gotta Get You Home Tonight', UK no. 18 '84) and Atlantic Starr ('Secret Lovers', US no. 3, UK no. 10 '86) represented a quick spin around a pink satin bedroom with fur trim, as the ubiquitous Yamaha DX7 tinkled away in the background like a cheap greetings card. It seems extraordinary that, at a time when Run-DMC and the Beastie Boys were crossing hip hop and the bluntest of white heavy rock – not obvious bedfellows – so few people attempted to integrate soul and hip hop.

Why was this? Possibly because kids were fully absorbed in hip hop – now entering its golden age with an almost monthly innovation in rhymes, beats and samples – while the older black fans were quite happy with the smooth, lifestyle sound of Atlantic Starr. The route to R&B's glittering future would be slow and complex, mostly B roads and back streets, yet by the end of the century it would be the only strand of modern pop which seemed forward-looking.

Unsurprisingly, Prince had a lot to do with the initial turnaround.

Jimmy Jam and Terry Lewis were Paisley Park protégés, initially pretty-boy hoodlum types in cartoon-funk pop act the Time.* They emerged, with a bang, as producers of the SOS Band's 'Just Be Good to Me', an electronic waterfall of sound, intense and incredibly refreshing. Recorded on a day off from the Time's support slot on Prince's *1999* tour, it had the hardest electro pulse to chart in 1984 (UK no. 13, US no. 55), with an almost tearful vocal from Mary Davis. When Prince discovered Jam and Lewis's infidelity, he sacked them, but they kept hitting that 808 cowbell on a string of SOS Band hits over the next couple of years – 'Just the Way You Like It', 'The Finest', 'Tell Me If You Still Care'.

---

* Early line-ups of the Time also included Madonna producer Jellybean and (when they were still called Flyte Tyme) soul singer Alexander O'Neal. They were the Byrds of eighties pop/soul.

Highlights of their hard, shiny, beatbox-led productions included Cherrelle's 'I Didn't Mean to Turn You On', which was denied a chart placing by Robert Palmer's well-timed cover (US no. 2, UK no. 9 '86). Their greatest success came with Janet Jackson's 1986 album *Control*, on which she made her big brother Michael sound wheezy and arthritic: 'What Have You Done for Me Lately' (US no. 1, UK no. 3 '86) showed that Jam and Lewis could not only compete with Prince and Michael Jackson, but sound one step ahead. Even now, the perfectly named *Control* has precision and poise; in 1986 it sounded like a sunshower, so light on its feet. Also in '86, Jam and Lewis breathed new life into new pop by recording and co-writing an album with the Human League; the first single off it was a gently ticking ballad called 'Human'. 'On the first Human League LP we did "You've Lost That Loving Feeling",' Phil Oakey told *Q*'s Tom Hibbert, 'and we sort of said, "Why can't we write a great ballad like that?"' The answer was because they had been too busy bickering. But Jam and Lewis hadn't, and 'Human' gave the League a US number one in '86.

Teddy Riley had been pronounced a musical prodigy aged five, a new Thom Bell in the making, and he was given the run of his uncle's Harlem studio. In 1985 he had scored a UK Top 10 hit with human beatbox Doug E. Fresh's 'The Show', which sampled the *Inspector Gadget* theme; a year later, aged seventeen, he was sole producer on Kool Moe Dee's hip-hop novelty 'Go See the Doctor' – a sniggering teenage confection in the age of AIDS – and scored himself a minor Hot Hundred hit. At eighteen he had his own group called Guy, and quickly got to work piling Philly soul harmonies onto hip-hop beats and Jam and Lewis's electro sharpness. Their biggest hit, 'Groove Me', sampled the Mohawks' 'The Champ', previously used by Eric B. and Rakim. Before Guy broke down the wall, explained Riley, 'rappers and singers didn't want anything to do with one another . . . singers were soft, rappers were street'. Riley created a boom: Guy's 'Groove Me' was the blueprint for Keith Sweat's 'I Want Her' (US no. 5 '88), Al B. Sure!'s 'Nite and Day' (US no. 7 '88) and Babyface's 'It's No Crime' (US no. 7 '89). In 1989 Riley produced a Wrecks-n-Effect single called 'New Jack Swing', and his blend of street hip hop and sweet R&B had a name of its own.

'I define the term as a new kid on the block who's swinging it,' said Riley. But much of new jack swing, also known as swingbeat, didn't really swing – hits like Bobby Brown's 'My Prerogative' (US no. 1, UK no. 6 '89) and Color Me Badd's 'I Wanna Sex You Up' (US and UK no. 1 '91) incorporated the hard, hammered precision of the beatbox but lacked litheness. A batch of girl groups, quickly tagged 'new jill swing', appeared in the wake of this new breed, of which Atlanta's TLC were easily the best.

Growing up, Tionne 'T-Boz' Watkins had been a tomboy who hung out at the same roller disco as producer Dallas Austin on Saturday and sang in her Atlanta church choir on Sunday. She was neighbours with producer Rico Wade – who ended up producing TLC's multi-million-selling *CrazySexyCool* in '95 – and copied his baggy dress sense so closely he called her his 'little brother in lipstick'. Lisa 'Left Eye' Lopes had arrived in Atlanta having followed a boyfriend–manager down from Philly on a promise that he knew a group looking for a female rapper. 'I didn't trust him, but I trusted myself,' she told *Rolling Stone*. 'I knew I could take care of myself because I'd already been out on my own all this time without a stable place to live.' She was possibly the fiercest-looking girl in all pop. Rico Wade got T-Boz and Left Eye to audition for a girl group; the quite beautiful half-black, half-Indian Rozonda 'Chilli' Thomas was a dancer who rounded out the group vocally and visually. Crazy, sexy, cool. They harked back to the bitchier end of the girl-group sound – Little Eva's 'Keep Your Hands off My Baby', the Cookies' 'Girls Grow Up Faster than Boys' – but broke new ground by picking on boys rather than other girls. What's more, they were far from an anonymous harmony act: musically, each had a distinct vocal style, so TLC blended funk (Watkins), hip hop (Lopes) and R&B (Thomas). On their '92 debut album *Oooooooohhh . . . On the TLC Tip* they looked like Salt-n-Pepa's kid sisters and wore condoms as jewellery. By '94 Lopes was in and out of rehab, and the mood was a lot more subdued: still, all four singles from that year's *CrazySexyCool* reached the Top 5 in the US, with 'Creep' and 'Waterfalls' peaking at number one. 'I seen a rainbow yesterday but too many storms have come, leaving a trace of not one God-given ray. Is it because my life is ten shades of grey? I pray all ten fade away': 'Waterfalls' was the best anti-drug song since Curtis Mayfield's 'Freddie's Dead'.

TLC's story felt like nothing much had changed since the days of Frankie Lymon and the Teenagers. They were mismanaged horribly, and somehow went bankrupt after selling twenty-five million albums. The feisty Left Eye turned out to be quite the Tasmanian devil, burning down her boyfriend's house in '94 and being very rude about the other girls, their producer and their record company. In 1999 she threw down the gauntlet in *Entertainment Weekly*. 'I challenge Tionne "Player" Watkins [T-Boz] and Rozonda "Hater" Thomas [Chilli] to an album entitled "The Challenge" . . . a 3-CD set that contains three solo albums. Each [album] will be due to the record label by October 1, 2000. I also challenge Dallas "The Manipulator" Austin to produce all of the material and do it at a fraction of his normal rate. As I think about it, I'm sure LaFace [TLC's label] would not mind throwing in a $1.5 million prize for the winner.'

On her own, Left Eye quickly scored a UK number one ('Never Be the Same Again' with Melanie C in 2000). She hosted MTV's *The Cut*,* the precursor to *X Factor* and *American Idol*, and was talking to David Bowie about working on a fourth TLC album when the jeep she was driving came off the road in Honduras and she was killed. Lisa 'Left Eye' Lopes was thirty-one.

Swingbeat was still small change compared to mainstream R&B. En Vogue were a full decade ahead of their time. They were put together by Oakland, CA, producers Denzel Foster and Thomas McElroy, soul fans who were equally fond of Prince, Funkadelic and Digital Underground. Foster and McElroy had previously grafted contemporary urban productions onto vintage soul structures for the oddly named trio Tony! Toni! Toné! (Feels Good, US no. 9 '90). With En Vogue, they wanted to create a latter-day Supremes, but from the start Terry Ellis, Cindy Herron, Maxine Jones and Dawn Robinson looked more like forties Hollywood vamps, straight out of the cast of *The Women*, than Brewster-project

---

* Though it only ran for one series, *The Cut* managed to unearth Anastasia, arguably a bigger star than any talent-show discovery since.

urchins; their hits ('Hold On', US no. 2, UK no. 5 '90; 'My Lovin'', US no. 2, UK no. 4 '92; 'Don't Let Go', US no. 2, UK no. 5 '96) were similarly lush, leggy and glamorous, and MTV fell at their feet. It was too bad that Robinson quit in '98 and the group quickly fell off the map, just as their influence was being felt with the rise of Destiny's Child. They deserve to be remembered most favourably.

Bigger – much bigger – than either TLC or En Vogue were a pair of singers with maximum lung power and backings smooth and shiny enough to skate on, and they ruled the nineties like no one else in pop. Whitney Houston had it in her blood – mum was soul singer Cissy, and Dionne Warwick was an aunt – and from childhood she was regarded as a special talent, caged and protected like Kate Bush until she was fully feathered, at which point she was released, flew – 'Saving All My Love for You', her debut single, was a transatlantic number one – and never came down. All that cosseting and pampering, though, left Whitney without a sense of judgement, and mostly she was foisted mush. Once in a while, though, she really clicked: 'I Wanna Dance with Somebody' (US and UK no. 1 '87) had a natural electro glide and her whoops were as ecstatic and infectious as anything Motown or Stax had ever come up with. 'How Will I Know' (US no. 1, UK no. 5 '86) was a comic-strip romance – you can picture Whitney's quizzical face as she sings, cartoon thought bubbles appearing from it. Whitney's success – she scored seven consecutive US number-one singles – meant she was a phenomenon, and the hunt was on for singers to follow in her slipstream. Melisma, multiple notes on a single syllable, became the new guitar solo, gauche in all but the most capable hands – though even those hands were no guarantee of quality.*

---

* The melismatic style had spun out of gospel, which had first impacted on the charts in the Jesus Freak era – in 1969 and 1970 – when every other record seemed to have a religious calm, as if to provide a reliable old crutch at the end of a turbulent decade. Specifically it can be traced to the Edwin Hawkins Singers' extraordinary 'Oh Happy Day', a record the choir leader sold out of the back of his car until a DJ in Oakland picked up on it, a snowball was created, and it ended up a number-two hit in Britain. Whitney sang in church, almost certainly sang 'Oh Happy Day', and would have been familiar with its ebbs and flows, its dam-busting chorus (try working out any of the lyric on that section), its rivulets

By the end of the eighties the *NME* had firmly tied its colours to hip hop. Mariah Carey's emergence in 1990 presented it with a problem: how would rock fans and indie kids – freshly sold on hip hop as the authentic sound, the *future* sound of black America – relate to this new black consumer pop? Things seemed to have gone into reverse. What the hell was going on with 'Vision of Love' (US no. 1, UK no. 9 '90)? It was finger-clicking smooth, a waltz-time canvas for Carey to paint with canary-coloured vocal trickery.

In the way that blue-collar American rock fans gravitate towards the gritty and workmanlike, the sweaty hard-grafting lumberjacks Nickelback and cowhands Lynyrd Skynyrd, so people admired Houston and Carey for their acrobatic skill. You got your money's worth. Did Harry Nilsson's version of 'Without You' reach quite as high as Mariah's? Could it shatter glass like the lady in the Memorex ad? No, sir, it could not, and all other considerations (subtlety, mostly) were marginalised. When either singer aimed for the dancefloor, the results were spectacular, notably Mariah's 'Fantasy' (US no. 1, UK no. 4 in '95), and Whitney's 'I Wanna Dance with Somebody' and 'It's Not Right but It's OK' (US no. 4 and UK no. 3 in '99). Unfortunately they both majored in gloopy ballads with chocolate-box keyboard sounds and swimmy reverb tracks, as blank as possible (save for a carefully placed thundercrack snare) to leave maximum room for the ornate, excessive and self-admiring vocals. When Whitney Houston sang the Atlanta Olympics anthem 'One Moment in Time' (US no. 5, UK no. 1 '88), it was the closest pop music and sport had ever got.* Naturally, she got a 10 for technique.

* * *

of headshaking emotion ('Oh Lord, ohhhhh good God'). It had undeniable – even to a confirmed atheist – raw power.

* There had been numerous hits from English football clubs before – the 1970 World Cup Squad even had a number one with 'Back Home' – but their musicality was a little basic. 'One Moment in Time' was the first record to mix patriotic balladry with the pomp and unnecessarily expensive feel of an opening ceremony. Two years later, New Order's 'World in Motion' captured the vim of sport and added a singalong chorus for a far more satisfying result.

That's the problem with most R&B today; it doesn't reflect the masses. When I started to write I tried to combine that Motown way of putting feeling into people with the way that some rap people, say Melle Mel or Run-DMC, were able to get across an idea. It's a science.
    Chuck D, 1988

If R&B was too proud to make a move on hip hop, that didn't stop the situation working in reverse. The same year TLC released their first album, Mary J. Blige emerged from the new-jill-swing mass as a protégée of emerging east-coast hip-hop producer Sean 'Puffy' Combs, who, at the time, was just nineteen and doubling up as an A&R man for Uptown Records. She had a husky voice reminiscent of early-seventies strongwomen like Millie Jackson – you wouldn't pick a fight. Combs was smart enough to see her as Mick Jagger to Mariah's Paul McCartney. Mary J. was always seen with a baseball cap, combat boots and baggy clothes – no tiara. She had both class and lack of class. Uptown Records proclaimed her to be the 'Queen of Hip Hop Soul', and – as there was no competition – it was hard to argue. The opening track on her '92 debut *What's the 411?* was no more than a succession of answering-machine messages over a drum-machine groove, which then ran into the intense minor-chord balladry of 'Reminisce'; there was scat and there was melisma, but it was immediately obvious that Blige was not shiny or chic, and you could detect her miserable upbringing in a South Yonkers housing project – you were meant to. 'They think this is entertainment,' Blige told *Ebony* magazine. 'This Mary J. Blige thing is not entertainment. This is my life and I put it out there on the line for everybody.'

What's the 411? went three times platinum and, once the 'hip hop soul' idea was proven to be a winner, new-jill-swingers ditched the crashing drum machines and shrill eighties synths, taking Mary J.'s more emotive, more sample-heavy route: a more soulful girl-group R&B – SWV's 'Right Here' (UK no. 3, US no. 2 '93), with its sweetly placed sample from Michael Jackson's 'Human Nature', and Jade's 'Don't Walk Away' (UK no. 7, US no. 4 '93) – came in its wake, as did a rollicking collaboration between Salt-n-Pepa and En Vogue ('Whatta Man', US no. 3, UK no. 7 '94) and TLC's switch from bubblegum rap to the dark beauty of 'Waterfalls'. Mary J. was also year zero for a crop of new, more glamorous singers waiting in the wings – Aaliyah, Beyoncé and, beyond them, Ashanti and Amerie – all of whom might have plumped for the Whitney/Mariah career model without Mary J.'s breakthrough.

On the west coast, as Puffy and Mary J. were working on her 'broken street kid' soul, Dr Dre's *The Chronic* had brought real instrumentation into hip hop. He still used samples but was under the influence of smooth late-seventies and early-eighties soul, which led Dre to drafting R&B and funk session musicians into the Solar Records studio in LA, and ushering in a microgenre all of its own called G-funk. The pinnacle of the G-funk sound was Warren G's *Regulate . . . G Funk Era* album in '94, which fused Kool and the Gang-style synth lines, R&B vocal harmonies care of the Dove Shack, buttery Fender Rhodes electric piano and the bear-with-a-sore-head mumbled stylings of singer Nate Dogg. All of this would have won the approval of Luther Vandross and Whitney Houston fans – if only it wasn't for those pesky lyrics. By '96 Dre was working with Teddy Riley's post-new-jack-swing R&B boy band Blackstreet on the insistent piano groove of 'No Diggity' (US no. 1, UK no. 9), and the blend was complete. Now hip hop and R&B had realised they were kissing cousins, it was finally possible for the latter to move on.

'It's Not Right but It's OK' was Whitney Houston's last great record. For once it didn't have a beige backing, but instead something entirely different: it stuttered, drily, eerily, with Whitney calm and collected as she lists her man's indiscretions over a burbling xylophone hook. It didn't swing but it wasn't meant to – this combination of tinderbox percussion, algebraic rhythm and soulful vocal was the product of another auteur, a Teddy Riley-schooled prodigy called Rodney Jerkins.

Reality, whether in *Nevermind, Different Class* or *The Chronic*, had been the rule of the day for most of the nineties, but people missed Prince and Michael Jackson; they wanted a little optimism and eccentricity. Rodney 'Darkchild' Jerkins was just nineteen when he produced Brandy and Monica's R&B landmark 'The Boy Is Mine' (US no. 1, UK no. 2 '97); the herky-jerky beat of 'No Diggity' was gone, there was no semblance of hip hop's familiar 4/4. Jerkins pulled the rhythmic rug and it became apparent that the work of Jam and Lewis, Teddy Riley, and Babyface and L. A. Reid had all been a slow build to something as new and thrilling as jungle had been in Britain. And, being American, this new R&B had the glamour to score very heavily.

Since disco's demise, most of R&B's voices had been coastal, but its future was decidedly Southern. From Virginia, up stepped Tim 'Timbaland' Mosley, Missy Elliott and the Neptunes. The latter's Pharrell Williams and Chad Hugo had been discovered by the omnipresent Teddy Riley at a 1991 high-school talent contest, when Pharrell and Timbaland were playing together in a school band called Surrounded by Idiots. Pharrell's grounding was not in the industry (like Puff Daddy) or in classic soul (like Whitney Houston). All of the Virginians had grown up with hip hop and rock and Motown on the radio, and they were bold enough to step out of their peer group and admit to listening to a group with a *C86* heritage and a love of outmoded synthesizers – Pharrell's favourite band was Anglo-French pop experimentalists Stereolab.

In the turnaround year of 1997 Timbaland produced Missy Elliott's debut album *Supa Dupa Fly*. Like 'The Boy Is Mine', it performed rhythmic gymnastics, possibly drawing on drum and bass but adding a relaxed swagger and lyrical non sequiturs. Unlike the glamorous golden girls Brandy and Monica, Missy was definitely a woman – all of twenty-five, no need for hair extensions, and capable of taking on any men in the field. Sean 'Puffy' Combs, now calling himself Puff Daddy, had a UK and US number one in 1997 with a dismal eulogy to Tupac Shakur, 'I'll Be Missing You', that sampled the Police's stalker anthem 'Every Breath You Take'; it couldn't have thrown the lightness of touch on the Jerkins and Timbaland productions into sharper relief.* The game was on, and auteur producers dared each other with outlandish hybrids, dry, salty beats and outré instrumentation. There was plenty of new talent to work with: Aaliyah had the sweetest voice; R. Kelly cribbed from doo wop and Sam Cooke, adding priapic self-belief; the chivalrous, much

---

* 'I'll Be Missing You' was just one dirge at the top of the charts in September '97. The Verve's 'The Drugs Don't Work' called time on Britpop, while Elton John's 'Candle in the Wind 1997' seemed to presage the end of the royal family.

screamed-at Usher wore a diamond-encrusted wrist shackle because he was 'a slave to the rhythm';* Outkast were a crackpot dandy duo, one of whom was a teetotal vegetarian who read Pushkin, while the other bred pit bulls in his spare time – you could pretty much tell this was the case when you heard their baby-mama saga 'Miss Jackson' (US no. 1, UK no. 2 '00).

1999 belonged to Kevin 'She'kspere' Briggs, with TLC's 'No Scrubs' (US no. 1, UK no. 3) and Destiny's Child's 'Bills Bills Bills' (US no. 1, UK no. 6), on which the chorus rhythm sounded like a cartoon cat burglar tiptoeing downstairs. 2000 brought champion pouter Kelis, with her multicoloured fright wig and 'I hate you so much right now! *Grrrrrrr!*' roar on the Neptunes-produced 'Caught Out There' (UK no. 4, US no. 54). A year later Missy Elliott took things to a cosmically minimal level with 'Get Ur Freak On' (US no. 7, UK no. 4), a six-note riff on an Indian tumbi, with a hand drum not heard since the Shadows' 'Apache'; that was pretty much the only instrumentation. And in 2003 came former Destiny's Child singer Beyoncé's first solo megahit, 'Crazy in Love' (US and UK no. 1), a phenomenal party record, driven by continuous build-up and release via a Chi-Lites horn sample and a cheeky 'uh oh uh oh' hook. 'Crazy in Love' marked the point at which this super-modern R&B started to take on more straightforward pop traits – there's that driving bassline on the chorus, straight out of northern soul, and a hint of Blondie in its glossy, retro-futurist structure. Six years on from 'The Boy Is Mine', R&B's experimental bent needed a rest and, for once, a golden era went out with a bang rather than a descent into novelty. '"Crazy in Love" was one of those classic moments in pop culture that none of us expected,' Beyoncé told

---

* Usher was taken from Atlanta to New York at the age of fourteen by his mentor Puff Daddy. 'I'd be thinking, "Here I am, fifteen years old, out at the club on the dancefloor, wild and crazy at three o'clock in the morning, with everyone popping bottles of Moët and smoking weed, and women throwing themselves at me" . . . the next day my tutor would say "You've got rings round your eyes, you've been out with Puffy again".' His debut album flopped, though, and Puffy dumped him back in Atlanta, still not yet sixteen. His voice broke, he worked out, and he returned with the transatlantic number one 'You Make Me Wanna' in '97.

Billboard. False modesty would have been entirely inappropriate.

Together these singers and producers recalled an older language: R&B before it became codified as soul. Bo Diddley's rhythmic daring, Leiber and Stoller's use of arcane instruments, Dee Clark's falsetto. Of course, this blew any smart-arsed critic's cosy theories about a millennial pop doomsday out of the water, but who cared? R&B's sloth-like progress since disco had been continually hampered by conservatism and division. Belatedly, happily, it remembered that the interdependence of living musical forms is essential for great pop.

EPILOGUE

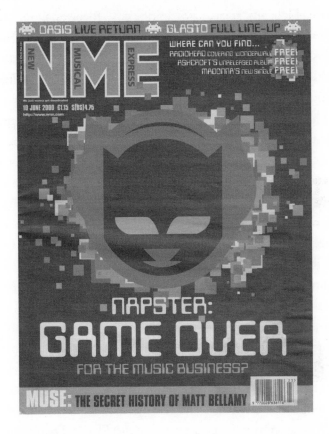

In the future, the artist will be not so much creator as curator: someone who takes historical resources from the archives and arranges them, finding provocative juxtapositions and unexpected affinities.

Simon Reynolds, 1992

When I first walked into the music business in '67 it was linoleum on the floor, in about '69 they got carpets. From 1970 the pile of the carpet began to rise, and in some offices, particularly the head of A&R's and the managing director's, it rose

to about four inches. You could shag in there. Then from 1974
it started to come down again. It reached carpet tiles and now
we're down to even cheaper carpet tiles.
    Roy Harper, *NME*, 1990

Modern pop had started with the introduction of vinyl, the charts and
the modern music press in 1952, and each of these components had
grown in significance through rock 'n' roll, the Beatles era, the album era,
punk and the eighties, before fracturing in the rave era and dissolving in
the late nineties as the digital era began in earnest. Since peaking in 1999,
physical sales have steadily and rapidly slipped, magazines like *Smash Hits*
have gone, and so have TV outlets like *Top of the Pops*. The pop media of
1992 was remarkably similar to the pop media of 1952, but pop music is
now consumed and absorbed in a completely different way.

    What brought the modern pop era to an end? Greed, ignorance and
the compact disc, the Trojan horse of digital technology. While it had
fattened the industry in the eighties, the new format's own sales began
to fall annually from the year 2000 once the blank CD became available in supermarkets, chemists and corner shops for pennies, and the
public realised just how much they'd been fleeced; it still seems shocking to find a nineties CD in a charity shop with its original £16 price
sticker. Pig-headed and arrogant, the major labels cried foul when
Napster and Limewire became a means by which you could hear music
free of charge at the dawn of the twenty-first century. Public Enemy's
Chuck D, a supporter, and Napster founder Shawn Fanning hosted a
ninety-minute open forum in Washington in April 2001, just ahead of a
Senate Judiciary Committee's hearing about the growing phenomenon
of swapping music via the internet. In a June 2000 issue of the *NME*,
editor Steve Sutherland reckoned it was 'game over' for the music industry. KLF accomplice Nick Coler predicted the industry wouldn't stand
for it and civil war would break out.

    While all of this was going on, the major labels had happily allowed
Apple's iTunes to legally acquire pretty much all of their catalogue for
downloads. They were fighting the wrong battle; there was an enemy
within.

A pair of former employees of the Apple technology company, Jeff Robbin and Bill Kincaid, developed SoundJam MP in California in 1999. Kincaid remembers 'listening to NPR on the radio and somebody was talking about the latest geek toy, a little device called a Rio that was like a solid-state Walkman that played something called MP3 files – first I'd ever heard of them. It all sounded really interesting. And when, at the end of the spiel, the fellow said something about "Don't get excited, Mac users, 'cos it won't work with Macs," I thought, "Ha! I can fix *that*!"' SoundJam MP was bought by Apple and renamed iTunes in 2000. A year later Apple brought out the iPod – a digital music player and a data-storage device – rendering the need for physical copies of music redundant. Civil war was avoided, but the *NME* had been spot on – the CD soon felt like dead technology, though vinyl still kept its allure.

What the *NME* didn't read as clearly in the tea leaves was the almost simultaneous demise of the music paper. The *NME* lives on as a source of information for the rump of the industry, but on sales of fewer than twenty-five thousand a week (it was selling a hundred and twenty thousand copies at the turn of the century). Of the other British weekly papers, *Sounds* (the go-to weekly for rock fans since 1970) and *Record Mirror* (the chart obsessive's paper of choice, and the only one to feature the official BBC charts) had already fallen on the same day in April 1991; the oldest weekly, *Melody Maker*, which was first published in 1926, lasted until the year 2000. *Smash Hits*, such a breath of fresh pop air when it was launched in 1978, went in 2005, a year before *Top of the Pops*.

Top of the Pops could not survive the digital era. If MTV had wounded it, and *The Chart Show* made it look grandfatherly, then the dozens of music channels (on TV and radio) available by 2006 meant that a weekly digest of hit singles was only relevant to an ageing, working audience who watched it partly out of a sense of duty. The charts had become a minority interest. The kids weren't united; there was no pop consensus.

Though it was compounded by the loss of *Top of the Pops*, the chart's significance had started to shrink around 1994, when singles regularly began to debut at their peak position and fall off the chart completely just three or four weeks later. One industry strategy that led to this was getting radio play for a single weeks before it was in the shops, thus building up demand and ensuring a high first-week chart position. Between 1952 and the mid-nineties pop fans and DJs had kept a keen eye on highest new entries, biggest climbers and bizarre drops (I remember the Four Seasons' 'Silver Star' falling from three to twenty-one on one memorable 1976 chart). Entering the chart at number one had been an extraordinarily rare feat, the province of superstars like Elvis, the Beatles, Slade, the Jam and Adam and the Ants. By the late nineties it was the norm, whether you were Madonna or Wamdue Project. When the UK's number-one single became more a triumph of marketing than popular consensus, the public began to feel disenfranchised. As Westlife came within an ace of equalling Elvis and the Beatles' record tally of number ones (seventeen each if you don't count reissues), there was a general sense of panic.

This has been partially corrected in the age of the download, when records can build in popularity as they did before the industry almost killed the chart, and now singles are more likely to sit around for months on end than fly in and out in a fortnight. To the artists and the industry, at least, the UK singles chart is still number one. A major reason for its continued authority is that it has always been entirely sales-based. Since the forties America had used its complex and potentially corruptible mix of sales, radio play and jukebox plays; when the more accurate and sales-orientated Nielsen SoundScan chart was introduced by *Billboard* in 1991, alternative and country records suddenly leapt up the charts at the expense of middle-of-the-road, major-label-promoted fare like Paula Abdul's 'Promise of a New Day' and Roxette's 'Fading Like a Flower'. For this reason, the Official Charts Company in Britain remains hesitant to introduce streaming to the singles chart.

On the airwaves Radio 1 survives in Britain, for now, but the 2002 introduction of Radio 1Xtra (urban) and 6 Music (indie) marked the first time the BBC decided that pop was too fragmented to be contained by one station. As an unlikely glue for this endless splintering, YouTube has made the past part of a permanent present, and old *TOTP* clips – not to mention other more esoteric TV performances – are as readily available as the new Kylie video. If something new deserves attention, then word spreads overnight.

How did the music itself change? It had become apparent by the turn of the century that rock, the vocals/guitar/bass/drums set-up pioneered by the Crickets, Shadows, Beatles and Led Zeppelin, had become as fossilised and ancient as Dixieland jazz was in 1952. It had run its course. While post-grunge blue-collar rock by the likes of Live, Nickelback and Creed continued to be hugely popular in the States, and the Strokes and the Libertines reminded British schoolkids and students that electric guitars could be fun, rock had lost its sense of progress; it existed like Wal-Mart or Wilkinson existed, to serve a need, to fulfil a consumer demand.

In the nineties Nik Cohn likened rock to a boulder dropped in the middle of a lake; there had been several ripples since the first wave in 1955, he reckoned, with each progressively smaller and less impressive. Simon Reynolds compared rock to a blank sheet of paper that had been gradually coloured in since the fifties until, by the early nineties, there were virtually no white spaces left.

The late nineties saw a widespread embrace – from the music critics as well as the public – of teen-orientated pop, the kind that was written by professional songwriters and sung by professional singers. Hanson's giddy, Jackson 5-channelling 'MMMBop' ended up as *Village Voice*'s single of the year in 1997. The Spice Girls had led the way in Britain with 'Wannabe' in 1996, a song as uncomplicated and pleasurable as squeezing bubble wrap.

In the US, the Backstreet Boys became stars in 1996 thanks to a shy Swedish hit machine called Max Martin; his style was rhythmically martial and lyrically awkward (Backstreet hits were catchy enough to get around clunky titles like 'I Want It That Way' and the almost surgical 'Shape of My Heart') but also a return to simple, modern, pop songwriting. Louisiana teenager Britney Spears was the foil Martin needed to cause a real stir. Her first single, 'Baby One More Time', had an astonishing, ever-climbing chorus with a moist-eyed, killer lyric ('my loneliness is killing me'). Unlike Kylie, say, or the equally mute Backstreet Boys, Britney was unguarded, and the video for 'Baby One More Time'

– with Britney as hard but vulnerable schoolgirl – was startling enough to make her an instant superstar.

So none of the changes in hardware or consumption meant that pop itself died, or that the Smiths, White Stripes, Arctic Monkeys or Radiohead were 'the last great band', or that, in the future, no one will ever take Madonna's crown as pop queen (Lady Gaga gave that an almighty try, and the tribulations of Britney Spears – documented in the style of a hospitalised robot on 2007's *Blackout* – might even make her a more interesting long-term case study). What they have meant is that we have entered a different era, the digital age, in which great records will continue to be made but, with such a choice of influences a click away, it will be much harder to create a brand-new form of music. All that a musician needs to do is to rearrange the constituent parts of the modern pop era in a way that no one has done before, and I hope that some fifteen-year-old in Newark, New Jersey, or Newark, Notts, is working on it right now.

The first flush of the pick 'n' mix digital era has led to many of pop's biggest names appearing on each other's records: Rihanna and Coldplay; JLS and Tinie Tempah; Katy Perry and Kanye West; David Guetta and Flo Rida *and* Nicki Minaj. While the possibilities of merging R&B, hip hop, Eurobeat and rave had seemed thrilling, the results have largely been a generic blur of unchallenging rhythms and predictable song structures – the Top 40 had never sounded more samey than it did in 2011 and (to a lesser extent) 2012. People who miss certain aspects of the modern pop era could find solace in twenty-first-century country, which – for now at least – remains a singles-based format, still driven by radio. Anyone bemoaning the lack of teen traumas, witty love songs or just verse/chorus-based pop on Radio 1 will find something of what they need in the work of Taylor Swift and Toby Keith; these acts still adhere to classic pop structures, just with a Southern twang in the accent and maybe a Southern frame of reference.

Do I mourn the passing of the modern pop era? I don't miss the delusions of authenticity and tribal pride that killed Kurt Cobain, Richey Edwards, Biggie Smalls and Tupac Shakur in the nineties; almost no one thinks in terms of 'selling out' any more, and it's getting ever harder to understand why somebody would have carved '4 real' into their arm to prove a point to an *NME* journalist. I do miss being able to go into a local record shop and buy a single of, say, Beyoncé's 'Crazy in Love', take it home and go through the ritual of putting the needle on the record. I miss the fact that, with downloads replacing physical artefacts, no one really knows what a single even is any more – Rihanna's 'Man Down' and Nicki Minaj's 'Stupid Ho' were stand-out album tracks, with pricey videos, but neither was officially a single.

Without the detail, pop music doesn't have the desirability it once had; it's not as wantable. Instant downloads require no effort, and so demand less of an emotional connection – it's less likely that you will devote time and effort to getting inside a new record, trying to understand it, if you haven't made a physical journey to track it down in the first place. Still, the modern pop era was as long as the jazz era; there's enough in those five decades to spend a lifetime digging through, and even then you'll never hear all of it. Things changed fast – almost weekly in particularly fertile periods. There was no time for boredom.

Music, as it was in the pre-Edison nineteenth century, is in the air. The modern pop era is all there to be enjoyed and pilfered, curated, compiled and recompiled, an endless, interchangeable jigsaw puzzle for future generations. I feel incredibly lucky to have been conscious of so much of it while it was happening.

ACKNOWLEDGEMENTS

Very special thanks to Cassandra Gracey and Alex O'Connell who encouraged me to start writing a book in the first place; Daniel Scott and my agent David Godwin, who both read a piece I wrote for the *Guardian* about the folly of condensing the story of pop, then convinced me that I was the kind of fool who should try and take it on; Martin Green for coming up with the perfect title; my editor Lee Brackstone for his enthusiasm, patience and good humour; Dave Watkins and Becky Fincham at Faber; my copy-editor Eleanor Rees; proofreader Ian Bahrami; and especially to Mark Sinker, who put in an extraordinary amount of work dissecting my first draft, offering many insights and enriching suggestions, happy to talk things through at a moment's notice – his invaluable contribution helped me to make sense of my often conflicting thoughts.

I received considerable help on some chapters from Tom Ewing, Kevin Pearce, Jane Bussman, Tim Hopkins, Daniel Scott, Martin Green and Cecily Nowell-Smith – I am very grateful to all of you. Alex Conway, Travis Elborough, Paul Kelly, Matthew Lees, Adrian Lobb and Pete Paphides all ploughed through early drafts of the book out of sheer kindness, which kept my spirits up during tough times.

For support and inspiration, direct and indirect, I am indebted to Mike Alway, Danny Baker, Rob Baker, Jeff Barrett, Malcolm Baumgart, Jane Beese, James Brown, Sheila Burgel, Ian Catt, Emma Chambers, Lucienne Cole, Nick Coler, Elaine Constantine, Paloma Cordon, Fabrice Couillerot, Paul Coyte, Scot Crane, Ossie Dales, Matt Dixon, Anna Doyle, Julian Fernandez, Lora Findlay, Jo Forshaw, Tariq Goddard, Steve Hammonds, Elain Harwood, Brian Henson, Emma Jackson, Jerry Jaffe, Gerard Johnson, Shoichi Kajino, Johan Kugelberg, Lawrence, Keith Lee, Andres Lokko, Niamh Lynch, Dorian Lynskey, Lucy Madison, Robert McTaggart, Anneliese Midgley, Leanne Mison,

Caitlin Moran, Gail O'Hara, Ben Olins, Bryn Ormrod, Carolyn Parmeter, Mick Patrick, Sian Pattenden, Tris Penna, Alexis Petridis, Emma Pettit, Alison Poltock, Simon Price, Paddy Pulzer, Robert Rider, Michael Robson, Jude Rogers, Andy Rossiter, Andrew Sandoval, Jon Savage, Neil Scaplehorn, Andrew Sclanders, Dale Shaw, Caroline Sullivan, Gareth Sweeney, Jonny Trunk, Robin Turner, Kieron Tyler, Adam Velasco, Audun Vinger, Isabel Waidner, Quentin Walshe, Emma Watkins, Liam Watson, Andrew Wickham and Harvey Williams. For eleventh-hour help on fine details, thanks to Emily Bick, Sonny Marr and Joni Tyler. Special thanks to my bandmates, who had to put up with my furrowed brow and scattered piles of half-finished manuscripts for five years – much love to Pete Wiggs, Sarah Cracknell, Debsey Wykes, our liaisons officer Andrew 'Pep' Peppiatt, and the hardest-working person I know, our manager Martin Kelly.

For keeping me supplied with new records and new sources of inspiration over many years I am deeply grateful to my dear and generous friends Geoffrey Weiss and Ian 'Hector' Black. I am also lucky enough to be within a bus ride of four record shops run by some of the most friendly, knowledgeable and helpful people I know: hats off to Alan Dobrin (Alan's Records), Derek Burbage (Record Detective Agency), Darren Reed (Vinyl Frontier) and Roger Spiers (Oxfam Crouch End).

To my mum and dad, thanks for giving me that stack of old 45s – 'Red River Rock', 'Teen Beat', 'FBI' – when I could barely toddle. Look where it got me! It's all your fault! And to my sister Jules, lots and lots of love.

Finally, I could never have finished this book without the constant love, belief and tenderness of my wonderful girlfriend Tessa Norton, who never flinched from reading and re-reading drafts, then added all the best jokes. I love you very much.

SOURCES

One of the challenges of this book was to find contemporary quotes wherever possible. Quotes which aren't acknowledged in the text are courtesy of David Dalton (Little Richard), Andrew Sandoval (Everly Brothers), Jon Savage (Larry Parnes, Nirvana), Marvin Bronstein (Bob Dylan), Barney Hoskyns (the Monterey Pop Festival), Jay S. Jacobs (Tony Burrows), Paul Lester (Kid Creole), David Menconi (Chip Shearin, Sugarhill Gang), Angus Batey (Wu-Tang Clan) and Everett True (Nirvana).

Though this book gave me an opportunity to make use of my yellowing stacks of old music papers, many of the contemporary quotes I did find were thanks to the work of Barney Hoskyns and rocksbackpages.com – which I urge you to support. Finding Keith Altham's Black Sabbath feature online was infinitely preferable to locating it on microfilm.

The digital age has also given us some of the most insightful, intense and adventurous new writing on pop music. I am hugely grateful to Tom Ewing's *Popular* blog and its family of contributors, especially Pete Baran, Rob Brennan, Lee Caulfield, Lena Friesen, A. J. Hall, Steve 'Carsmile' Hewitt, Steve Mannion, Hazel Robinson, Billy Smart, John Martin Somers and Kat Stevens. Not only does *Popular* have great wit, depth of knowledge and good humour, but it has also led me to discover other exceptional writers and blogs: Marcello Carlin's *Then Play Long*, which made me listen to Slim Whitman, Jim Reeves, Fleetwood Mac's *Rumours* and many other records in a totally new way; Sally O'Rourke's crisp essays about US number-one hits on *No Hard Chords*; and Chris O'Leary's *Pushing Ahead of the Dame*, which contains the best writing on David Bowie bar none.

The American chart positions I have used are from *Billboard*, while the British ones are those recognised by the Official Charts Company. I have spent many hours thumbing through Joel Whitburn's *Record*

Research books – he is a giant among music historians. The first edition of *The Guinness Book of Hit Singles*, published in 1977, was my bible; it helped define my idea of pop history, the one that shapes this book, and I owe a great debt of gratitude to its authors, Jo Rice, Tim Rice, Paul Gambaccini and Mike Read.

The December 18th 1954 chart at the front of the book is from the *NME* archive: many thanks to Marc Walker, Karen Walter and Alan Woodhouse.

All other images are from the author's collection, with the exception of Chapters 8, 18 and 60 (courtesy of Geoffrey Weiss), 23 (courtesy of Ace Records), 63 (courtesy of Dale Shaw) and 65 (courtesy of Pietro Maglio).

Finally, I would like to pay tribute to the many great writers at the *New Musical Express, Fabulous, Record Mirror, Crawdaddy, Creem, Who Put the Bomp, Sounds, Smash Hits, Melody Maker* and *Select*, all of whom have played a major part in developing my understanding and love of music over the years. It was a joy to have an excuse to re-read their work and dig out these publications again. I hope I have fully acknowledged their contribution to the era throughout the book. Special thanks to James Brown for giving me a start at the *NME* back in 1987, and to the late Tom Hibbert, my first pop-writer hero.

SELECTED BIBLIOGRAPHY

Jonathan Aitken, *The Young Meteors*, Secker & Warburg 1967

John Aizlewood, *Love Is the Drug*, Penguin 1994

Peter Alex, *Who's Who in Pop Radio*, New English Library 1966

Adam Ant, *Stand and Deliver*, Sidgwick & Jackson 2006

Hugh Barker and Yuval Taylor, *Faking It*, Faber and Faber 2007

Bill Brewster and Frank Broughton, *Last Night a DJ Saved My Life*, Headline 1999

Bill Brewster and Frank Broughton, *The Record Players: DJ Revolutionaries*, DJ History 2010

Marcello Carlin, *The Blue in the Air*, Zero 2011

David Cassidy, *Could It Be Forever*, Headline 2007

Frank Clews, *Teenage Idols*, Digit 1962

Nik Cohn, *Pop from the Beginning*, Paladin 1970

Nik Cohn, *Ball the Wall*, Picador 1989

Julian Cope, *Head On*, Magog 1994

Dave Davies, *Kink: An Autobiography*, Boxtree 1996

Jim Dawson and Steve Propes, *What Was the First Rock 'n' Roll Record?*, Faber and Faber 1992

Pat Doncaster, *Tops of the Pops*, Daily Mirror 1961

Bill Drummond, *45*, Little, Brown 2000

Chuck Eddy, *Rock and Roll Always Forgets*, Duke University Press 2012

Travis Elborough, *The Long Player Goodbye*, Sceptre 2008

Ken Emerson, *Always Magic in the Air*, Viking 2005

Mark Fisher, *The Resistible Demise of Michael Jackson*, Zero 2009

Pete Frame, *The Restless Generation*, Rogan House, 2007

Simon Frith and Andrew Goodwin, *On Record*, Routledge 1990

Phyl Garland, *The Sound of Soul*, Regnery 1969

Sheryl Garratt, *Adventures in Wonderland*, Headline 1998

Nelson George, *The Death of Rhythm & Blues*, Pantheon 1988

Nelson George, *Hip Hop America*, Penguin 1998

Peter Guralnick, *Careless Love*, Little, Brown 1999

Peter Guralnick, *Dream Boogie: The Triumph of Sam Cooke*, Little, Brown 2005

Alex Halberstady, *Lonely Avenue: The Life and Times of Doc Pomus*, Jonathan Cape 2007

Colin Harper, *Dazzling Stranger: Bert Jansch and the British Folk and Blues Revival*, Bloomsbury 2000

John Harris, *The Last Party*, Fourth Estate 2003

Chris Heath, *Pet Shop Boys, Literally*, Viking 1990

Dave Hill, *Prince*, Faber and Faber 1989

The Hollies, *How to Run a Beat Group*, Daily Mirror 1964

Ian Hunter, *Diary of a Rock 'n' Roll Star*, Panther 1974

Frank Kogan, *Real Punks Don't Wear Black*, University of Georgia Press 2006

Al Kooper, *Backstage Passes*, Stein and Day 1977

Jerry Leiber and Mike Stoller, *Hound Dog*, Simon & Schuster 2009

Richard Mabey, *The Pop Process*, Hutchinson 1969

Ian MacDonald, *Revolution in the Head*, Fourth Estate 1994

Greil Marcus, *Like a Rolling Stone*, Faber and Faber 2005

Dave Marsh, *The Heart of Rock and Soul*, Plume 1989

George Melly, *Revolt into Style*, Penguin 1970

Greg Milner, *Perfecting Sound Forever*, Granta 2009

Paul Morley, *Ask*, Faber and Faber 1986

Jeff Nuttall, *Bomb Culture*, MacGibbon & Kee 1968

Andrew Loog Oldham, *Stoned*, Secker & Warburg 2000

Richard Osborne, *Vinyl: A History of the Analogue Record*, Ashgate 2012

Kevin Pearce, *Something Beginning with O*, Heavenly 1993

Ulf Poschardt, *DJ Culture*, Quartet 1998

Dave Rimmer, *Like Punk Never Happened*, Faber and Faber 1985

David Ritz, *Divided Soul: The Life of Marvin Gaye*, Da Capo 1985

The RZA, *The Wu-Tang Manual*, Penguin 2005

Andrew Sandoval, *The Monkees*, Backbeat 2005

Jon Savage, *England's Dreaming*, Faber and Faber 1991

The Shadows, *The Shadows by Themselves*, Consul 1961

Peter Shapiro, *Turn the Beat Around*, Faber and Faber 2005

Joe Smith, *Off the Record*, Warner 1988

Ronnie Spector, *Be My Baby*, Harmony 1990

J. Randy Taraborrelli, *Madonna*, Sidgwick & Jackson 2001

Derek Taylor, *As Time Goes By*, Straight Arrow 1973

Stewart Tendler and David May, *The Brotherhood of Eternal Love*, Cyan 2007

Ben Thompson, *Seven Years of Plenty*, Victor Gollancz 1998

Nick Tosches, *Hellfire: The Jerry Lee Lewis Story*, Delacorte Press 1982

Fred Vermorel and Judy Vermorel, *Starlust*, Comet 1985

Elisabeth Vincentelli, *Abba Gold*, Continuum 2004

Elijah Wald, *How the Beatles Destroyed Rock 'n' Roll*, Oxford University Press
   2009

Michael Wale, *Voxpop*, Harrap 1972

Pete Waterman, *I Wish I Was Me*, Virgin 2000

Judith Wells, *Keith Moon Stole My Lipstick*, UKA Press 2008

Ian Whitcomb, *Rock Odyssey*, Hutchinson 1983

Timothy White, *The Nearest Faraway Place*, Henry Holt 1994

Richard Williams, *Out of His Head: The Sound of Phil Spector*, Sphere 1972

Carl Wilson, *Let's Talk About Love*, Continuum 2007

Rob Young, *Electric Eden*, Faber and Faber 2009

INDEX